SECURITIES ANALYSIS AND PORTFOLIO MANAGEMENT

V.A. AVADHANI

M.A., Ph.D. (U.S.A.), M.A., LL.B., C.A.I.I.B.

* Retired Adviser in the Reserve Bank of India
* Former Director of Research and Training in Bombay Stock Exchange
* Former Adviser in Hyderabad Stock Exchange

ISO 9001:2015 CERTIFIED

First Edition	**: 1997**	**Ninth Revised Edition**	**: 2008**
Second Revised Edition	**: 1999**	**Reprint**	**: 2009**
Third Revised Edition	**: 2000**	**Tenth Revised Edition**	**: 2010**
Fourth Revised Edition	**: 2001**	**Edition**	**: 2011**
Fifth Revised Edition	**: 2002**	**Eleventh Revised Edition.**	**: 2014**
Sixth Revised Edition	**: 2003**	**Twelfth Revised Edition**	**: 2016**
Seventh Revised Edition	**: 2004**	**Reprint**	**: 2017, 2019,**
Reprint	**: 2005**	**Reprint**	**: 2021, 2023**
Eighth Revised Edition	**: 2006**	**Reprint**	**: 2024, 2025**
Reprint	**: 2007**	**Reprint**	**: 2026**

Published by : Mrs. Meena Pandey
for **HIMALAYA PUBLISHING HOUSE PVT. LTD.,**
Vishal Industrial Estate, 1st Floor, Office No. 63/64,
Bhandup Village Road, Subhash Nagar (Opp. CEAT Tyres),
Nahur (W), Mumbai - 400 078. **Phone:** 022-35131464/65/66/67
E-mail: himpub@bharatmail.co.in; **Website:** www.himpub.com

Branch Offices :

New Delhi : Pooja Apartments, 4-B, Murari Lal Street, Ansari Road, Darya Ganj,
New Delhi - 110 002. Phone: 011-23270392, 23278631; Fax: 011-23256286

Nagpur : Kundanlal Chandak Industrial Estate, Ghat Road, Nagpur - 440 018.
Mobile: 09325409992, 09325908881

Bengaluru : Plot No. 91-33, 2nd Main Road, Seshadripuram, Behind Nataraja Theatre,
Bengaluru - 560 020. Phone: 080-41138821;
Mobile: 09379847017, 09379847005

Hyderabad : No. 3-4-184, Lingampally, Besides Raghavendra Swamy Matham, Kachiguda,
Hyderabad - 500 027. Phone: 040-27560041, 27550139

Chennai : No. 34/44, Motilal Street, T. Nagar, Chennai - 600 017. Mobile: 09380460419

Pune : First Floor, Laksha Apartment, No. 527, Mehunpura, Shaniwarpeth
(Near Prabhat Theatre), Pune - 411 030. Phone: 020-24496323, 24496333;
Mobile: 09370579333

Cuttack : Plot No 5F-755/4, Sector-9, CDA Markat Nagar, Cuttack - 753 014,
Odisha. Mobile: 09338746007

Kolkata : 3, S.M. Bose Road, Near Gate No. 5, Agarpara Railway Station,
North 24 Parganas, West Bengal - 700109. Mobile: 09674536325

DTP by : Priyanka M.

Printed at : Geetanjali Press Pvt. Ltd., Nagpur. On behalf of HPH (P).

PREFACE TO TWELFTH REVISED EDITION

It is gratifying to note that this book has come for the twelfth revision, for which the credit should be given to the faculty and students alike interested in this subject. This is particularly tuned to the Indian students and to the Indian environment or to the similarity of this. The theoretical part is kept simple and lucid for the average student to understand easily. The tenor of the treatment is that the subject is practical oriented and useful for self study and the student's own analysis and research, on many topics of this subject.

Every edition has included some new changes such as new case studies or examples in addition of the updating of the material. Many errors which crept into it at various stages have also been rectified. The effort of each edition is at improving the subject and further simplification of the material. In a subject as this, there are bound to be some repetitions and they are purposely kept intact for the benefit of the students. Each chapter is made self-sufficient, so that the reader can concentrate only on those topics without going back and forth. As such, some concepts and material have to be repeated quite often such as the return and risk, types of return and risk, etc.

The revision has to bear in mind that although the conceptual part of portfolio management or security analysis may remain unchanged, the environment in which practical operations take place change from time to time depending on a host of factors. For this reason, the material needs to be updated from time to time. The portfolio management depends on the securities pricing, their risk-return characteristics and the corporate state of affairs, which depends on the economy, industry, and savings and investment trends in any sector and the economy. In fact, the stock market being a window of the economy, has to reflect all facts and figures of the economy — internal and external.

The GDP growth rate was robust up to 2007-08 but declined to around 6.8%, in 2008-09 and hopes are that it will continue to grow at around 8% in 2009-10 and 8.5% in 2010-11 but fell to 5% in 2013-14 and expected to be up to 8% in 2015-16. Despite such hope, the IIP growth rate was only 8% and in particular the infrastructure industrial growth rate was lower at 3.6% in 2013-14 as against 5% in 2011-12. Even then, the continued growth rate of GDP in the economy of India was maintained by the growth of around 9% to 10% in services sector. This was also adversely affected by the global slowdown and recession in the economies of the USA and other developed countries and slowdown in agricultural sector. In this context, there was a slowdown in FII inflows for portfolio management during the years 2008-10 although the FDI inflows continued in a positive direction. The financial markets were sustained by the growth of money supply at a rate of around 20% and large inflows of FFI and FIIs during the recent years. It was in this context, that sensex of BSE reached 52 week high of 17,790 on January 6, 2010 from a low of 8,047 on March 6, 2009. The all-time high of 21,207 was noted on January 10, 2008 and all-time low of 7,697 on October 2008 and at end January 2010 the market Sensex was hovering around 27,500 at end 2014. The market P/E multiple was at a high of 21.6 times in India as against 18 in China and 13 in Brazil, etc., the market expectations are such as to reflect sound fundamentals of the corporate sector and of the economy. The market capitalisation was 58% of the GDP in 2008-09 as against 27% in 2000-01. The market performance was at a peak in 2007-08, when its capitalisation was at 109% of the GDP. But the symptoms of downslide were noticed since October 2008 and continued to affect the economy in 2009 and 2010. The Government was however faced with a fall in exports and rising current account deficit in addition to the higher fiscal deficit than anticipated due to government measures for boosting the economy, sliding into recession accompanied by the rising inflation at around 8% on average in 2008-09 and 20% of food price inflation in 2010. By March 2014, inflation came down to 6% and expected to be around 5.5% in 2016-17.

The market (BSE) witnessed high turnovers of ₹ 15.78 lakh crores in 2007-08 and ₹ 11.03 lakh crores in 2010-11, and went up again in 2010 to about ₹ eleven lakh crore. The year 2009-10 witnessed huge fluctuations and high volatility due to uncertain trends in the economy, such as the expected fiscal policy changes, and monetary policy measures like hike in CRR and tightening of the interest rates to curb the rising inflationary trends. Thus, it, becomes difficult for operators to be happy about the global trends or internal economic factors. Portfolio management has, thus, to face a tense situation in their operations both in the cash and futures and options markets. It is in this background that the subject has to be read and understood.

The government has initiated steps for insurance coverage in 2014-15 and urban housing for the poor. The RBI has allowed banks to borrow abroad without its prior permission which would lead to large inflow of FII and FFI funds into the markets and for portfolio investment as well.

V.A. AVADHANI

CONTENTS

1 INTRODUCTION TO SECURITIES

This book is on investment and securities. Security analysis is a pre-requisite for making investments. In the present day financial markets, investment has become complicated and is both an art and a science. One makes investments for a return higher than what he can get by keeping the money in a commercial or co-operative bank or even in an investment Bank. In the finance field, it is a common knowledge that money or finance is scarce and that investors try to maximise their return. But the return is higher, if the risk is also higher. Return and Risk go together and they have a trade off. All investments are risky to some degree or other. The art of investment is to see that the return is maximised with the minimum of risk, which is inherent in investments.

If the investor keeps his money in a bank in savings account, he takes the least risk, as the money is safe and he will get back when he wants it but he runs the risk that the return in real terms, adjusted for inflation is negative or small and even if positive, it may not come upto his expectations or needs.

In this above discussion, we concentrate on the word "Investment" and for making investment, we need to make security analysis. It then becomes necessary to define investment and security analysis at the outset.

WHAT IS INVESTMENT?

Investment is parting with one's fund, to be used by another party, user of fund, for productive activity. It can mean giving an advance or loan or contributing to the equity (ownership capital) or debt capital of a corporate or non-corporate business unit. Generalised, investment means conversion of cash or money into a monetary asset or a claim on future money for a return. This return is for saving (as abstaining from present consumption), parting with saving or liquidity (to be rewarded for waiting for a future consumption) and lastly for taking a risk involving the uncertainty about the actual return, time of waiting and cost of getting back funds, safety of funds, and risk of the variability of the return.

Definition of Security Analysis

For making proper investment involving both risk and return, the investor has to make a study of the alternative avenues of investment — their risk and return characteristics and make proper projection or expectation of the risk and return of the alternative investments under consideration. He has to tune the expectations to his preferences of the risk and return for making a proper investment choice. The process of analysing the individual securities and the market as a whole and estimating the risk and return expected from each of the investments with a view to identifying undervalued securities for buying and overvalued securities for selling is both an art and a science and this is what is called security analysis.

WHAT IS SECURITY?

Investment in capital market is in various financial instruments, which are all claims on money. These instruments may be of various categories with different characteristics. These are all called securities in the market parlance. In a legal sense also, the Securities Contracts Regulation Act, (1956) has defined the security as inclusive of shares, scrips, stocks, bonds, debenture stock or any other marketable instruments of a like nature or of any debentures of a company or body corporate, the Government and semi-Government body etc. It includes all rights and interests in them including warrants, and loyalty coupons etc., issued by any of the bodies, organisations or the Government. The derivatives of securities and Security Index are also included as securities in the above definition in 1998. The word "inclusive" is used deliberately in law so as to give authority to the government to add or subtract any instrument.

In the strict sense of the word, a security is an instrument of promissory note or a method of borrowing or lending or a source of contributing to the funds needed by a corporate body or non-corporate body. Private security for example is also a security as it is a promissory note of an individual or firm and gives rise to a claim on money. But such private securities or even securities of private companies or promissory notes of individuals, partnerships or firms to the extent that their marketability is poor or nil, are not part of the capital market and do not constitute part of the security analysis.

If the capital market is efficient and security prices reflect perfectly all the market information, then all the investors get the same average returns and no one can get exceptional returns. But in India the markets are not efficient, information is not free and not easily accessible and the market does not fully absorb immediately all the information. In this scenario, exceptional returns or superior returns are possible due to varying degrees of information available with investors.

In an efficient capital market, superior returns are possible by proper security analysis and investment through the insider information on the company or security and through better forecasting ability of the investor and superior expertise in security analysis.

WHAT IS PORTFOLIO?

A combination of such securities with different risk-return characteristics will constitute the portfolio of the investor. Thus, a portfolio is a combination of various assets and/or instruments of investments. The combination may have different features of risk and return, separate from those of the components. The portfolio is also built up out of the wealth or income of the investor over a period of time, with a view to suit his risk or return preferences to that of the portfolio that he holds. The portfolio analysis is thus an analysis of the risk-return characteristics of individual securities in the portfolio and changes that may take place in combination with other securities due to interaction among themselves and impact of each one of them on others.

INVESTMENT AND SPECULATION

Having seen what is investment it is necessary to know what is speculation, as investment and speculation are next door neighbours. Speculation involves the investment and *vice versa.* Both are leading to claims on money, aim at maximisation of return consistent with the risk taken. Motive is the determining factor, distinguishing between investment and speculation. In investment, the investor has long-term and medium-term objective, takes delivery of securities and books profits as and when the returns are higher than his target expectations. The speculation has a short-term perspective and maximises the returns through buying and selling and delivery of securities is least important in trade. Stakes of risk are higher and returns are higher in speculation than in investment. Both aim at capital gains or appreciation in share prices and maximisation of returns. The difference is only in degree as between investment and speculation.

In the Indian stock markets, nearly, 80% of trade is speculative in nature and do not involve deliveries of shares. Values of trade increase with increase in speculation, but the genuine investor takes the delivery and gets the securities transferred into his name in the company's registers, whether, it is an ownership (equity) or debt category. Speculation is increasing ingredient of the stock markets all over the world to impart liquidity and continuing trade and quotation.

WHAT IS SECURITY ANALYSIS?

Security Analysis in both traditional sense and modern sense involves the projection of future dividend, or earnings flows, forecast of the share price in the future and estimating the intrinsic value of a security based on the forecast of earnings or dividends. Thus, security analysis in traditional sense is essentially an analysis of the fundamental value of a share and its forecast for the future through the calculation of its intrinsic worth of the share. Any investor is interested in the future returns and the present price he pays, should reflect the potential future returns.

Modern security analysis relies on the fundamental analysis of the security, leading to its intrinsic worth and also risk-return analysis depending on the variability of the returns, covariance, safety of funds and the projections of the future returns. If the security analysis is based on fundamental factors of the company, then the forecast of the share price has to take into account inevitably the trends and the scenario in the economy, in the industry to which the company belongs and finally the strengths and weaknesses of the company itself — its management, promoters' track record, financial results, projections of expansion, diversification, tax planning etc. All these studies are only a part of the total security analysis that the investor should aim at.

Portfolio Management

As this book is on Portfolio Management, security analysis is only a tool for efficient portfolio management; both of them go together and cannot be dissociated. This book should contain all the elements necessary for portfolio management in the Indian context.

As referred to earlier, portfolios are combinations of assets held by the investors. These combinations may be of various asset classes like equity and debt and of different issuers like Government bonds and corporate debt or of various instruments like discount bonds, warrants, debentures and Blue chip equity or scrips of emerging blue chip companies.

The traditional Portfolio Theory aims at the selection of such securities that would fit in well with the asset preferences, needs and choices of the investor. Thus, a retired executive invests in fixed income securities for a regular and fixed return. A business executive or a young aggressive investor on the other hand invests in new and growing companies and in risky ventures. Modern Portfolio Theory postulates that maximisation of return and or minimisation of risk will yield optimal returns and the choice and attitudes of investors are only a starting point for investment decision and that vigrous risk return analysis is necessary for optimisation of returns.

In risk-return analysis, the attitudes and preferences of investors are taken into account as also their risk-return trade off stemming from the analysis of individual securities. The return on portfolio is a weighted average of returns of the individual stocks; and the weights are proportional to each stock's percentage in the total portfolio. Besides the stocks when put together in a basket may not give a total risk which is the mathematical equivalent of total of risks of all the individual stocks, due to the simple reason that the risks of some stocks may be offset by the risks of other stocks or *vice versa.* The risks of some stocks can also be accentuated by those of others in the portfolio. The modern portfolio theory states that the combined risk of a portfolio may be greater or lesser than the sum of the risks of the components of individual securities.

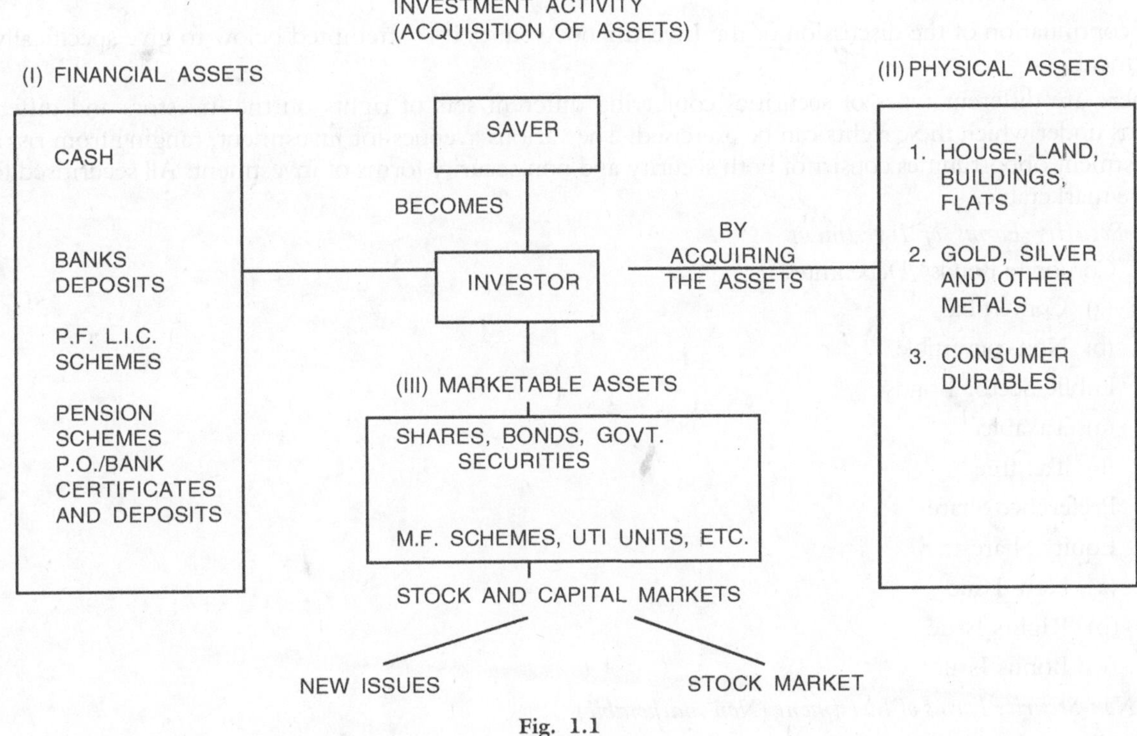

Fig. 1.1

Portfolio analysis includes portfolio construction, selection of securities, revision of portfolio, evaluation and monitoring of the performance of the portfolio. All these are part of the subject of Portfolio Management which is a dynamic concept, subject to daily and hourly changes based on the information flows, money flows and a host of economic, and non-economic forces operating in the country on the markets and securities.

INVESTMENT ACTIVITY

Investment Activity involves the use of funds or savings for further creation of assets or acquisition of existing assets. Investment is explained by Fig. 1.1, in terms of Financial and Physical assets and Marketable assets.

Macro-Household Savings and Investment

As per the RBI data, published from time to time total financial savings and physical assets held by households are available for discussion. During recent years, the data shows that the net investments in financial assets and net physical assets are in the ratio of about 40% and 60%, respectively. A sample study made by Business Line shows the following pattern of portfolio assets held by household in Metro, Urban and Rural centres.

Current Portfolio

By Socio-economic Classification

Investment Type	*Total*	*A*	*B*	*C/D*
		% of Portfolio		
Primary market investment	5	9	5	2
Shares in security market	5	9	5	1
Fixed deposits	31	27	31	38
MFs other than UTI	1	2	1	1
UTI units	8	9	7	6
Chit funds	6	4	6	10
Gold	3	4	4	3
Jewellery	6	8	6	4
LIC/NSS/P.O. Savings	32	28	33	35
Teak plantations/orchards	1	1	1	1

Source: Business Line. A, B and C/D refer to Metro, Urban and Rural Centres, respectively.

Modes of Investment

In continuation of the discussion of the Investment Avenues it is attempted below to give specifically all modes of investment.

There are different types of securities conferring different sets of rights on the investors and different sets of conditions under which these rights can be exercised. The various avenues for investment, ranging from riskless to high risk investment opportunities consist of both security and non-security forms of investment. All securitised forms given below are marketable.

A. Security Forms of Investment

1. Corporate Bonds*/Debentures
   (a) Convertible
   (b) Non-convertible
2. Public Sector Bonds
   (a) Taxable
   (b) Tax free
3. Preference Shares
4. Equity Shares
   (a) New Issue
   (b) Rights Issue
   (c) Bonus Issue

B. Non-Security Forms of Investment (Non-marketable)

1. National Savings Schemes
2. National Savings Certificates
3. Provident Funds
   (a) Statutory Provident Fund
   (b) Recognised Provident Fund

* Innovations in the traditional instruments include, among others
(a) Zero Coupon Bonds (ZCBs)
(b) ZCBs with option to convert interest earned to equity on maturity
(c) Bonds with detachable warrants
(d) Deep Discount Bonds
(e) Flexibonds or Floating Rate Bonds, etc.

(c) Unrecognised Provident Fund
(d) Public Provident Fund

4. Corporate Fixed Deposits
   (a) Public Sector
   (b) Private Sector
5. Life Insurance Policies
   (a) Whole Life Policies
   (b) Limited Payment Life Policy
   (c) Convertible Whole Life Assurance Policy
   (d) Endowment Assurance Policy with Profits
   (e) Jeevan Mitra, Jeevan Anand
   (f) The Special Endowment Plan with Profits
   (g) Jeevan Saathi, Jeevan Rekha
   (h) The Money Back Plan and New Money Back Plan
   (i) Marriage Endowment/Educational Annuity Plan with Profits
   (j) Bima Sandesh Premium Back Term Insurance Plan
   (k) New Children's Deferred Assurance Plan
   (l) Jeevan Dhara, Jeevan Suraksha
   (m) New Jana Raksha Plan with Profits
   (n) Jeevan Akshay Plan, Jeevan Samruddhi
   (o) Jeevan Balya Plan, Jeevan Vishwas
   (p) Jeevan Kishore, Jeevan Surabhi
   (q) Jeevan Griha, Jeevan Sukanya, Jeevan Akshay
   (r) Jeevan Sarita, Jeevan Shree, Jeevan Chaya
   (s) Bhavishya Jeevan and Asha Deep
   (t) New Bima Kiran
   (u) Komal Jeevan
   (v) Anmol Jeevan
6. Unit Schemes of Unit Trust of India (Some are marketable among these)
   (a) Unit Schemes of UTIMF (UTI – II)
   (b) Unit Schemes of UTI – I
   (c) Unit Linked Insurance Plan, 1971
   (d) Capital Gains Unit Scheme, 1983
   (e) Children's Gift Growth Funds, 1986
   (f) Parents' Gift Growth Funds, 1987
   (g) Monthly Income Unit Scheme with extra bonus plus growth
   (h) Equity Linked Savings Scheme
   (i) Growing Monthly Income Unit Scheme

   There are many other UTI schemes on similar lines numbering about 60 and a number of commercial banks and financial institutions have set up Mutual Funds. Various schemes including the Personal Equity Plan and Tax Saving Schemes, have been launched by many public sector and private sector Mutual Funds; some of which are marketable and listed on the stock exchanges.
7. Post Office Savings Bank Account
   (a) Recurring Deposits
   (b) Time Deposits

(c) Monthly Income Scheme

(d) Senior Citizens' Saving Scheme

8. Others

(a) RBI Relief Bonds Phased out

(b) Kisan Vikas Patra

(c) Deposits in Co-operative Banks

(i) Recurring Deposits

(ii) Time Deposits, etc.

(d) Chit funds, Nidhis, etc.

FEATURES OF INVESTMENT AVENUES

The investor has various alternative avenues of investment for his savings to flow in accordance with his preferences. Savings flow into investment for a return, but savings kept as cash are barren and do not earn anything. Savings are invested in assets depending on their risk and return characteristics. But a minimum amount of cash is always kept in hand for transactions and contingencies. Any rational investor knows that money is losing its value by the extent of the rise in prices. If money lent cannot earn as much as rise in prices or inflation, the real rate of return is negative. Thus, if inflation is at an average annual rate of 5%, then the return should be 5% or above to induce savings to flow into investment. Thus, if an investment is made in short-term deposits with banks or in securities of Government, then the rate of interest is around 4% to 10%. As the risk of loss of money is almost negligible in such cases, this rate can be called a risk-free return. All investments involve some risk or uncertainty. The objective of the investor is to minimise the risk involved in investment and maximise the return.

Characteristics of Investment

1. ***Risk:*** The risk depends on the following factors:

(1) The longer the maturity period, the larger is the risk. Thus, deposits of two years carry a higher rate than one-year deposits.

(2) The more the creditworthiness of the borrower or agency issuing securities, the less is the risk. Thus, the risk of loss of interest and principal is less with the Government or semi-Government bodies than with the private corporate units.

(3) The nature of instrument, namely, the debt instrument or fixed deposit or ownership instrument like equity or preference share, also determines risk. The risk of loss of money is less in the case of debt instruments like debentures, as these are secured and fixed interest is payable on them. In the case of ownership instruments, the risk of loss is more due to their unsecured nature and variability of their return and ownership character which burdens them with all the risks connected with the enterprise.

(4) The risk of variability of returns is more in the case of ownership capital as the return varies with the net profits after all commitments are met. As such, equity and preference shares of companies are more risky than debentures or bonds. Among the ownership instruments, equity is more risky than preference shares or other forms of ownership instruments such as partly or fully convertible debentures, convertible and cumulative preference shares, as equity holders are residual owners of the firm.

(5) The nature of tax liability on the instruments — the tax provisions would influence the return as the net effective return for a tax-payer would be higher for tax-free instruments as in the case of NSS, NSC, (VIII Series) or those whose interest income is tax-free up to a limit as in the case of UTI dividends or interest on P.O Savings deposits. The net return on instruments is higher by different degrees to the tax-payers, depending upon the income tax brackets into which they fall.[1] Thus, tax implications of investment are an important factor in considering the retun on investment. Besides risk, investment decisions are based upon return, safety, liquidity, marketability, etc., which are examined below.

---

1. Another factor influencing the average investor is whether interest/dividend on the investment is paid without any tax deduction at source. Thus in the case of P.O. deposits and certificates, etc., there was no tax deduction at source except for NSS of 1987. The investor is interested in the return net of his tax liability and tax deduction. Income from mutual funds and interest on bank deposits is also subject to TDS from 1995-96. For three years from 1999-2000, income from UTI and Mutual Funds have become non-taxable in the hands of investors.

2. Return: A major factor influencing the pattern of investment is its return, which is the dividend or coupon rate plus capital appreciation, if any. The difference between the purchase price and the sale price is capital appreciation and the yield is the interest or dividend divided by its purchase price. Thus, if ₹ 25 is the dividend on a share of the face value of ₹ 100 but purchased at ₹ 150, then the return is 25/150 = 16.6%. Suppose, there is capital appreciation also in a year, say, ₹ 10 on the purchase price of ₹ 150, then the total return is (25+10)/150, which is 23.3% per annum.

3. Safety: The safety of capital is the certainty of return on capital without loss of money or time involved. In all cases of money lent, some transaction costs and time are involved in getting the funds back. But leaving aside such general costs like stamp duty, postal charges, etc., the time involved is also an important factor. If money is returnable not on the same day but after a lapse of time, then the loss of liquidity is involved and if the time of return of funds is not certain and if costs of selling or realisation of proceeds are involved, then the safety of funds is also not perfect. Thus, if safety of capital is to be assured, then riskless return as in the case of Government bonds is to be chosen. If the return is higher, as in the case of private securities, then the degree of safety is less.

4. Liquidity: If a capital asset is easily realisable, saleable or marketable, then it is said to be liquid. If an investment can be encashed with a time lag as in the case of equity shares or with loss of money as in the case of u/s 64 of UTI then they are less liquid. If, on the other hand, there is a good market for the capital asset and no risk of loss of money or capital and no uncertainty of time involved, then the liquidity of the asset is good. If liquidity is high, then the return may be low as in the case of bank saving deposits.

An investor generally prefers liquidity for his investments, safety of his funds, a good return with a minimum risk or minimisation of risk and maximisation of return (dividend plus capital appreciation).

5. Marketability: This means easy and quick means of transferability of an asset. Thus, assets of listed companies and shares of public limited companies are more easily transferable than those of non-listed companies and private limited companies.

RISK-RETURN RELATIONSHIPS

1. Risk: Risk is inherent in any investment. This risk may relate to loss or delay in repayment of the principal capital or loss or non-payment of interest or variability of returns. While some investments are almost riskless like Government securities or bank deposits, others are more risky. There are differences in risk as between instruments, which can be represented as a spectrum of risk, as in Fig. 1.2. This also shows the risk-return relationship.

2. Return: Yield or return differs from the nature of the instruments, maturity period and the creditor or debtor nature of the instrument and a host of other factors. The most important factor influencing return is risk. Normally, the higher the risk, the higher is the return. The return is the income plus capital appreciation in the case of ownership instruments and only yield or interest in the case of debt instruments like debentures or bonds.

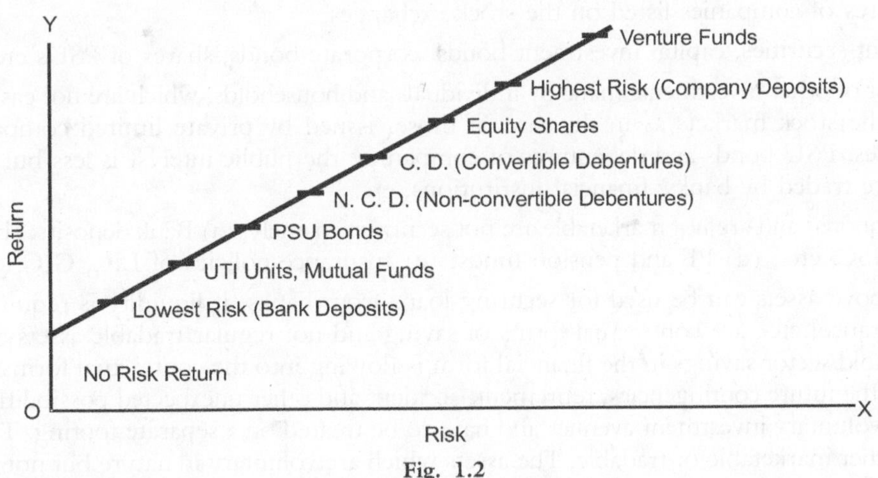

Fig. 1.2

Tax Benefits

Some instruments floated by the Government and semi-Government bodies enjoy tax benefits and hence their net return is higher. Thus in India, P.O. deposits, bank deposits, Government securities, etc., are exempt from income tax either in part or in full. Under Section 80L of IT Act, the income emanating from certain investments like bank deposits, NSC, P.O. deposits, etc., and in respect of income from UTI units and mutual funds is exempt upto ₹ 12,000 p.a.

The other forms of tax benefits are the exemption or rebate with respect to wealth tax or capital gains tax. The investments made in specified instruments of Government and Semi-Government securities, NSS, PPF, etc., are fully exempt from income tax. Exemption of original investment as also the income from it is granted in the case of PPF and some selected instruments, subject to certain conditions. Since 2005-06, all these rebates under Section 80L and Section 88 were deleted and replaced by one Section 80C, which gives exemption for specified categories of investment upto ₹ one lakh only.

Marketability and Liquidity

Some Instruments are not marketable like company and bank deposits, P.O. deposits, NSC, NSS, etc. Only advances can be secured against bank deposits and NSC subject to margins from banks. Some instruments like preference shares and debentures are marketable but there are no buyers in many cases and hence liquidity is negligible in respect of these instruments. Liquidity arises from the availability of marketing and trading facilities as also buyers and sellers.

Safety vs. Riskiness

Safety is another feature which the investor desires for investments. Normally, savers invest only in safe or risk-free investments. Only a few opt for risky investments for which the returns would also be higher. Thus, a higher return of 14% or more is available for three-year deposits of companies which are most risky. Besides, there are debentures of companies whose yield may be more than 11%, if they are purchased at a discount in the market. But debentures and bonds carry a coupon rate of 10%-12%. Some of the equity shares might give a better return but the general average yield rate on equities is lower than on other types of securities available for investment. But equities are chosen more for their capital appreciation rather than dividend yield.

The maturity period of the instrument, the creditworthiness of the issuer and the nature of the instrument, whether debt or ownership instrument would all influence the risk, return and other features of the instrument. The Government policy or tax treatment of the instrument, etc., would also determine the yield on the instruments.

NEED FOR TRADABILITY

The marketability and liquidity of funds depend on the tradability of the instruments of investment. In India, although there is a wide variety of instruments, the marketability is limited to a few assets only. Thus, the assets tradable in the money and capital markets in which individuals do invest may be set out as follows:

(a) UTI units, some schemes of Mutual Funds, etc.

(b) Units/shares of mutual funds, if they are quoted on the stock markets.

(c) Debentures of companies and bonds of public sector units, in which there is a limited market.

(d) Equity shares of companies listed on the stock exchanges.

(e) Government securities, capital investment bonds, corporate bonds, shares of PSUs etc.

There are a host of other investments made by individuals and households, which are not easily marketable. These are not quoted on the stock markets as in the case of those, issued by private limited companies. In the case of Government securities, PSU bonds and debentures of companies, the public interest is less but quoted on the stock markets, and they are traded by banks, financial institutions, etc.

The assets not quoted and are not marketable are not securities, namely, (a) Bank deposits; (b) Company deposits; (c) P.O. deposits, NSC, etc.; (d) PF and pension funds; (e) Insurance policies of LIC, GIC, etc.

Some of the above assets can be used for securing loans from banks, if liquidity is required. The investments in PF, pension, insurance, etc., are contractual forms of saving and not regular tradable assets as such. Thus, nearly a third of the household sector savings in the financial form is flowing into the contractual forms of investment. They are meant to protect the future contingencies, retirement, accident and other unexpected possibilities. These contractual savings are thus not voluntary investment avenues and have to be treated on a separate footing. They are not the usual investment assets, either marketable or tradable. The assets which are voluntary in nature but not tradable are deposits with banks, PO, NSCs and instruments of savings with banks and POs and investments in chit funds, investment/ finance companies, etc.

CLASSES OF INSTRUMENTS

Instruments traded can be classified on the following criteria:

1. By ownership or debt nature of instruments.
2. By term period to maturity — short-term, medium-term and long-term.
3. By the issuer's creditworthiness, say, Government securities or private securities or PO certificates, etc.

Ownership category instruments are equity, preference shares, deferred shares, non-cumulative preferred shares, cumulative preferred shares, etc. Debt category assets are debentures, bonds, deposits with banks and companies, etc.

The term period of a security or the maturity period also varies from security to security and with the time of purchase. Barring the equity shares, other securities have some maturity period and redemption. Thus, the debentures may be up to 7 years and preference shares up to 12 years. Fixed deposits may vary from 1 to 5 years. Almost all the debt instruments must have a maturity period, as per law.

The creditworthiness of the issuer of securities will determine the risk involved in the payment of interest and repayment of principal. If the issuer is the Government, the risk is the least as the Government does not default. There is no uncertainty in respect of these instruments.

The data in Table 1.1 presented below show that the various instruments can be classified by risk-return characteristics and that the returns are variable on these instruments as also the tax treatment given by the government in respect of these instruments. The interest rates have gone down due to flexible rate policy adopted from 2001 onwards and tax changes are taking place every year and they are subject to frequent updating by the reader. After 2005, many lending rates and deposit rates have gone up again.

Table 1.1
Investment Avenues

Name of Security (1)	*Rate of Interest Per Annum* (2)	*Income Tax Concession* (3)
1. Post Office Saving Bank accounts	4%	Exempt under Sec. 10(15)(ii)
2. Saving Deposits of Banks	4%	— do —
3. Public Provident Fund Accounts (15 years)	8.8%	Exempt under Sec. 80C
4. Post Office Time Deposit Accounts	8.2 to 8.5%	Exempt under Section 80L
5. Bank Fixed Deposits	8.75 to 9.6%	— NA —
6. RBI Bank Rate	6%	— do —
7. Post Office Recurring Deposit Accounts (period 5 years)	8.4%	— do —
8. Bank's Lending Rate	10 to 10.25%	— do —
9. 5-year Post Office Monthly Income Scheme	8.5% (Payable monthly)	Qualifying for deduction under Sec. 80L within limit of ₹ 12,000.
10. Kisan Vikas Patra (8 years and 7 months)	8.41% (Compounded)	No Deleted.
11. NSC VIII Issue (5 years)	8.6%	Exempt under Sections 80C
12. Units of UTI/Schemes of Mutual Funds	Variable	Included in 80L exemption Additional ₹ 3,000 rebated.
13. Equity Shares of Companies	Variable	1. Dividend income is not taxable for investors. 2. Provision for a tax rebate at 20% on an investment in eligible equity linked schemes of ₹ 10,000 maximum — a rebate on ₹ 2,000.
14. Convertible Debentures	Variable	Taxable

15. Non-convertible Debentures	— do —	Taxable
16. Fixed Deposits of Companies or NBFCs	Free and Variable 11% to 14%	Taxable
17. Preference Shares (Redeemable or Cumulative)	14% to 15%	Dividend deductible up to ₹ 12,000 under Sec. 80L.
18. Cumulative Convertible Preference Shares (CCP)	10%	— do —
19. Bonds of Public Sector Companies	9%-10.5%	Taxable
20. Senior Citizens' Certificates	9.3%	Taxable
21. RBI Relief Bonds (since discontinued)	8%	Not Taxable Discontinued

Note: The rates on postal instruments were lowered during 2001 to 2003. Section 80L was replaced by section 80C of I.T. Act since 2005, which is tax free upto ₹ one lakh.

INVESTMENT PROFILE OF AVERAGE HOUSEHOLD

The asset preferences of an average Indian household can be analysed from the data on the savings estimates of CSO and RBI. The data of RBI provide in particular the pattern of assets in financial form of the household sector in India.

If an average Indian saves ₹ 100, nearly ₹ 40 is set apart for investment in physical assets like consumer durables, housing, real estate, gold, silver, etc. The remaining ₹ 60 flows into various forms of financial assets, as per the latest data.

Taking savings in the financial form, the preferences of the Indian household are such that the investor keeps 13.3% of it in cash and currency and about 45% in bank deposits, which are both riskless assets but with nil return or low returns (0-9 per cent). There is also a category of contractual savings in the form of insurance. PF and pension funds, whose return is also small or moderate, but are based on the requirements of insurance coverage, contingency and precautionary requirements of individual savers. The investment in this category is about 33.6% of total financial savings.

The relatively less risky but voluntary investments relate to UTI units and Mutual Fund Schemes whose return is about 10%. The investment in this category is about one per cent of the financial savings of the household sector and these enjoy some tax benefits.

This return on investment in Government securities, P.O. savings media, PSU bonds, etc., enjoy some tax rebates. The return on these investments vary widely depending on income-tax concessions. About 24% of the financial savings are invested in this category. Among the category of most risky investments is that of deposits with companies (4%) and of shares and debentures (1 to 2%).

If all the above investments are arranged in the order of riskiness to get a picture of the risk aversion of the average Indian investor, we notice that less than 10% of savings are attracted by the high return/high risk profiles, 30% flow in the form of contractual savings and 60% as currency and bank deposits which is almost riskless investments.

If investment in public securities and private securities are taken to represent respectively, the less risky and more risky investments, the proportion of financial savings in the form of the former is as high as 80%, and the latter 10%, which clearly evidences the risk aversion of average household in India. Besides, a proportion of 10-12% of savings is held in the form of currency, which is barren in return.

Leaving aside the currency holdings, the other financial assets held by the household sector are shown in the Figure 1.3. Bulk of the investments in the public sector is indirect investment. Thus, Bank deposits, UTI units, PF and pension funds, etc. all find their way into investments in private and public securities. Leaving aside a proportion of statutory investments in Government, semi-Government and Trustee securities, the rest is invested in new issues of companies, shares and debentures of existing companies, deposits with companies, etc. Thus, although only about 10% of the direct investments of the households flow into shares, debentures and company deposits, etc., as shown in Fig. 1.3 below, there is a large component of indirect investments by the households in the private corporate sector through their bank deposits, PF, insurance, pension funds, UTI units, Mutual Funds, etc.

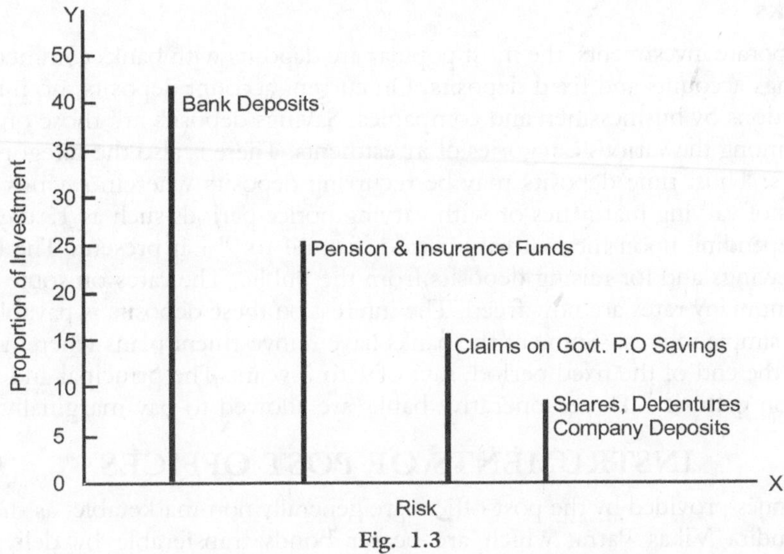

Fig. 1.3

NON-CORPORATE INVESTMENTS

In addition to securities of the corporate sector into which savings of the households flow to a minor extent, there are a number of other avenues for investment such as deposits with commercial and co-operative banks, post office savings banks, National Savings Certificates, Provident fund and pension fund contributions, insurance, deposits with companies, purchase of real estate, gold and silver etc. There are other lines of investment, more frequently resorted to by companies, financial institutions etc., such as securities of the Government and semi-government bodies, *viz.,* Treasury bills, Government bonds, public sector bonds, Semi-government bonds, etc. These investments are of many types and can be classified as follows:

1. Marketable and Non-marketable: Real estate, gold, silver, etc., are marketable and are most popular among the households. Treasury bills, bonds and Government securities are also marketable but are popular only with financial institutions and banks. Some of these like UTI units, tax-free bonds, etc., which enjoy a number of tax benefits are also popular with companies and institutions in addition to individuals. The investments in the nature of deposits with banks, companies, National Savings Certificates, etc., are not marketable as they are not transferable by endorsement.

2. Interest Payable Regularly or Reinvested: Some investments media like bank deposits pay interest quarterly or half-yearly. Some investments will have annual interest or dividends paid as in the case of M.F. units or half yearly on P.O. savings certificates. Some media will have the interest reinvested as in P.O. cumulative time deposits etc. Repayments can also take the form of annuity, that is, to say, a payment combining interest with principal.

3. Payment Linked to an Event: In the case of life insurance, payment is at the event of death, accident-insurance, at the occurrence of an accident, provident fund at the time of retirement etc. Payment out of pension funds, or out of annuities, will be spread over a number of years.

4. Regular Savings Media of Investment vs. Lumpsum Investment at a Time: Some investment media like LIC insurance premium or contributions to PF and insurance are regular monthly savings either voluntarily or compulsorily. Similarly, contributions to the recurring deposit schemes of banks and post offices are regular monthly savings media. On the other hand, purchase of NSC or a fixed deposit with a notice period or for a fixed period of time are examples of the lumpsum investments at a time. Their tax treatment varies from time to time.

CORPORATE INVESTMENTS

Ownership and Debt

The major avenues of investment among corporate securities are equity shares and preference shares, which are of ownership category. There are also debt instruments or fixed income securities such as debentures and fixed deposits from the public, which are of debt category. Of these, preference shares, debentures and deposits are having a fixed interest while equity shares are of variable dividend. The high risk is in the case of fixed deposits of companies as they are unsecured, while equity shares are of high risk and high return category.

Deposits with Banks

Among the non-corporate investments, the most popular are deposits with banks commercial and cooperative such as current accounts, savings accounts and fixed deposits. On current account deposits, no interest is paid as these are meant for regular transactions by businessmen and companies. Savings deposits are those on which interest is paid at 4%, which is the lowest among the various categories of investments. There is also the category of time deposits, which has varying characteristics. Thus, time deposits may be recurring deposits wherein savings are deposited at regular intervals or fixed deposits of varying maturities or with varying notice periods such as 15 days, etc. The interest rates on these deposits vary depending upon the maturity period, from 4 to 9% at present. The banks also provide other varieties of schemes for savings and for raising deposits from the public. The rates on some of them are fixed by the RBI from time-to-time but many rates are now freed. The interest on these deposits is payable half-yearly or quarterly calculated on the basis of simple interest. Some of the banks have reinvestment plans wherein the interest is reinvested as is accrued and paid at the end of the fixed period, say, of 1 to 5 years. The principal and the accumulated interest are paid to the investor on maturity. The co-operative banks are allowed to pay marginally higher rates of interest.

INSTRUMENTS OF POST OFFICES

The investment avenues provided by the post offices are generally non-marketable, as they are the savings media. The only exception is Indira Vikas Patra, which are bearer bonds transferable by delivery but which are now withdrawn. The major instruments of P.O. enjoy tax concessions such as exemption of investment contribution from tax or interest income from tax or both up to certain limits.

*1. **Saving Deposits:*** These are savings deposited by public up to a maximum of ₹ 1 lakh in individual account and ₹ 2 lakh in joint account. They carry interest at 4% which is tax free totally. Just as the savings deposits of commercial and co-operative banks, these accounts are operated subject to certain conditions.

*2. **Fixed Deposits:*** These accounts are open to individuals either separately or jointly for varying fixed periods of time, say 1 to 5 years. The interest rates vary from 6.25% to 7.5%. The interest is payable half-yearly and interest income is tax exempt up to a limit.

3. ***Recurring Deposits upto 5 Years:*** This is an instrument of regular monthly savings. The account-holder has to save and deposit every month a fixed amount of ₹ 5 or in multiple of ₹ 5 for 60 months. This account carries a rate 8% on the balance to the account, compounded quarterly and payable at maturity at the end of 5 years. It has its own rules of nomination, withdrawal, income and wealth tax exemption etc.

*4. **Fixed Investment with Monthly Income:*** Under this scheme, an individual can invest from a minimum of ₹ 5,000 to ₹ 1 lakh lumpsum for a period of six years. Interest at 8% is payable monthly and bonus of 10% at the end of maturity, but bonus component was withdrawn in 2006.

*5. **Six-Year National Savings Certificates (Savings Certificate VI and VII Issues):*** There are various series of this issue with slight changes with regard to payment of interest rate. These investments, as in the case of some other instruments, are exempt from income accrued up to a limit under Section 80C. The interest along with the principal is payable at the time of maturity; interest accrued is deemed to have been reinvested in the case of VI series, while the same is paid half-yearly in the case of VII series. These are now discontinued.

*6. **Six-Year National Savings Certificates (VIII Series):*** This is slightly different from other NSCs. The rate of interest payable is 8% compounded half yearly payable at maturity. Accrued interest is reinvested but is eligible for tax rebate under Section 88 of I.T. Act. Principal is also exempt from tax from 2005-06 under Section 80C.

There are a number of other avenues of savings with POs which are tax havens such as PPF and NSS, whose details vary from scheme to scheme.

Public Provident Fund (15 years)

The PPF deposits can be made in monthly instalments with a minimum of ₹ 100 and a maximum of ₹ 60,000 per annum. These deposits carry cumulative interest of 8% credited to the account. The account has a maturity period of 15 years. It is not transferable, but has nomination facility. One withdrawal per financial year can be made any time after 5 years from the end of the year in which the subscription is made. Withdrawal is limited to 50% of the balance at the end of the fourth year. All subscriptions to PPF are completely tax free and the balances in PPF are not taken into account for wealth tax purposes.

NSS

Deposits made in NSS were completely tax exempt under Section 80C of I.T. Act but income, however, is taxable at the time of withdrawal. Interest is credited to the account at the end of each month at the rate of 10% per annum now. The number of deposits that can be made are only 12 in a year and the deposits have to be in multiples of ₹ 100 and not exceeding ₹ 40,000 per annum. Only one withdrawal can be made in a year up to the maximum of the balance outstanding at the end of the fourth preceding financial year. The account can also be closed at the end of three years from the end of the year in which the last deposit is made. A passbook is given with a nomination facility. The scheme was withdrawn in 1992-93 Budget and a new NSS 1992 was introduced with slight variations, which was also withdrawn in 2002.

10-Year Social Security Certificate

These certificates are in denominations of ₹ 500 and ₹ 1,000 and mature at the end of 10 years. The maturity value of the certificate is triple the face value, giving a compound rate of interest of 10.03%. A special feature of this is life insurance coverage. In the event of death by accident or natural cause after two years from the date of purchase, the nominee or legal heirs receive the full maturity value immediately. This certificate can be purchased by individuals between 18 and 45 years of age only. These are now discontinued.

Kisan Vikas Patra

These are certificates in denomination of ₹ 1,000, ₹ 5,000 and ₹ 10,000, which will double in 8 years and seven months giving a compound rate of interest of 8.4%. These can be encashed after 2½ years for specified amounts of money. This has nomination facility but is not transferable. These are discontinued now.

Public Sector Bonds

There are two categories of these bonds, namely, tax-free and taxable. The tax-free bonds are 8% bonds issued for ₹ 1,000; interest compounded half-yearly and payable half-yearly. They have a maturity period of 7 to 10 years with the facility for buy-back sometimes provided to small investors up to certain limits. The taxable bonds yield higher, compounded half-yearly and payable half-yearly if tax rebates are considered. They have normally a face value of ₹ 1,000 and have buy-back facilities similar to taxable bonds.

Drought Relief Bonds (Relief Patra)

These are completely tax-free bonds. These carry 6.5% interest compounded annually with a face value of ₹ 1,000 and maturity period of 5 years. These investments are completely tax-free, both for wealth and income tax purposes. Interest income, either payable or reinvestible, is also tax free. This has also nomination facility. Interest rates on P.O. instruments were lowered by ½ percentage point in 2002 and 2003. These are also discontinued.

There are a large number of investment avenues for savers in India. Some of them are marketable and liquid while others are more risky and less safe. Risk and return are the major characteristics which an investor has to face and handle.

The investment avenues other than those of banks can be broadly categorised under the following heads:

(1) Corporate Shares, Debentures, or bonds.
(2) UTI and Mutual Fund Schemes.
(3) P.O. Deposits/Certificates, etc.
(4) Government and semi-government bonds/securities.
(5) P.S.U. Bonds.

The investor has to choose proper avenues from among them depending on his preferences, needs and abilities to take the minimum risk and maximise the returns. To enable investors to know the degree of risk on debt instruments. Credit rating is now made compulsory for them.

2 MARKETS FOR SECURITIES AND TAXES

We have seen what is an investment and the broad spectrum of investment avenues open to investors in the preceding chapter. The market in which these securities are dealt with is called the Securities Market. There are a number of sub-markets in the wide sense of the securities market, like debt market, equity market etc. Being markets in financial instruments, the demand for and supply of them constitute the market for each of these instruments.

The basic classification of such instruments on new issues is made on the basis of issuers of securities such as companies, public sector undertakings (PSU), Government and semi-Government bodies, and others. The investment in these new securities constitutes the primary market, while the trading in the existing securities is called the secondary market.

These markets help the issuers of securities, investors, intermediaries and the national economy, as a whole, who are all involved in the operations. Firstly, the issuers will benefit as they can raise funds through this method for financing their operations and investment. Secondly, for investors the markets provide an avenue for channelling their savings and liquidity is imparted to them for their operations of investment and disinvestment.

The financial intermediaries like bankers, brokers, etc., provide a host of services, to both issuers and investors and bring them together and enable savings and investment to meet on a common ground. The nation and the economy as a whole will benefit as these markets promote saving and capital formation in the country leading to industrial growth and economic development with a multiplier effect on income, employment and output.

These markets provide avenue for mobilisation of savings. Secondly, they activate the idle funds for productive use and conversion of savings into investment leading to growth of fixed assets and productive capacity. Thirdly, these markets provide liquidity to the investment so that public are attracted to these investments and there is a demand and supply for these instruments of investments. Lastly, these markets promote growth of the industry and economy in general and of the corporate sector in particular. The securities markets have thus a crucial role to play in the economy and the stock markets (or secondary markets) are called the windows of the economy.

LEGAL FRAMEWORK FOR SECURITIES MARKETS IN INDIA

New Issues Market and Stock Exchange are a part of the Capital Market where the shares, debentures, bonds and other securities of companies and Government are traded. The Stock Exchange provides facilities for exchange of shares into money and *vice versa*. New Issues Market is the Primary market where the issuers can sell securities, but cannot buy. Investors can buy but not sell in the primary market. They can sell in the secondary or stock market. Stock Exchange is defined as an Association of Member Brokers who assist, facilitate and regulate trading in securities. One can buy and sell in the Stock Exchange or Secondary market.

These securities are issued by the Companies under the Companies Act and by the Government under the Indian Public Debt Act which was replaced by Government Securities Act, 2006. Both these Acts are amended or replaced by new Acts. Since the public are not interested in Government Securities due to lower level of interest rates on them, the public awareness of this market is little or negligible. This market is mainly confined to banks, financial institutions etc.

The capital market comprises of two components, namely, New Issues Market where companies issue directly securities to the public and the Stock Market or the Secondary Market where the existing securities are bought and sold.

Trading in old securities is governed by the Securities Contract (Regulation) Act of 1956 and the Securities Contract (Regulation) Rules of 1957. The Act has provided for recognition to the Stock Exchanges and gave wide ranging powers to the Government to control and regulate the Stock Exchanges. It has laid down the types of contracts in securities which can be traded or purchased and sold and for listing of securities of public limited companies, whose shares are being traded. The Act and the Rules made thereunder have provided for qualifications for members, contracts to be traded, trading period, permitted deals, settlement periods, clearance and delivery of shares etc. The actual Rules and Byelaws of each Stock Exchange have enshrined these rules. The Act is applicable to Public Limited Companies, which are listed on Stock Exchanges and ensure transferability of shares and laid down the conditions, only under which transferability is denied to investors.

Companies Act

The Companies Act which regulates the activities of the companies from birth to death has provided for the sources of finance for companies and the methods of marketing the public issues which are marketable. These are in the form of ownership category, namely, Equities and Preference shares and Debt capital in the form of convertible and non-convertible debentures, fixed deposits etc. Under the Companies Act, Sections 55 to 68 provided for issue of prospectus, its contents, Registration of Prospectus, civil and criminal liabilities of the Directors for any mis-statements in prospectus etc.

The Act has laid down the methods of raising new issues, namely, through prospectus, letter of offer or statement in lieu of prospectus, Rights and Bonus. Section 58 A and B deal with the conditions for acceptance of deposits, repayments of deposits, etc., while companies (Acceptance of Deposits) Rules of 1975 laid down the period of maturity, interest rates and other conditions.

Sections 69 to 73 deal with the allotment of new issues to applicants, delivery of certificates and their listing on Stock Exchanges. The allotment is also governed by the guidelines given by the Stock Exchanges and as per the listing agreement in the case of listed companies.

The basic framework for trading is provided by the Companies Act in the form of —

(1) Marketing the shares as movable property under Section 82.
(2) Ensuring transferability of shares in respect of public listed companies under Sections 108-112.
(3) The transfer deed through which share certificates are to be transferred is provided for under Section 108.
(4) The validity of the transfer deed under Section 111 is 12 months in the case of listed companies and 24 months in the case of non-listed companies.
(5) Section 114 provides for issue of share warrants.

So far as investors are concerned, it is desirable that they know the main provisions of the Companies Act, because the issue of prospectus, the contents of it, allotment of new issues, despatch of certificates, transferability etc., are all laid down in it. The rights of shareholders and debentureholders, and different categories of creditors and debtors of companies are set out. The book-closure for accounts, presentation of Balance Sheet and Income-Expenditure accounts, payments of dividends etc., are all provided for in this Act. In particular, Section 82 provides for transferability of shares and Section 73 lays down the conditions for listing of Public Limited Companies. While these sections ensure the marketability of shares of listed public limited companies, trading in them is made possible by the Securities Contracts Regulation Act and the Rules made thereunder. The companies listed on a stock exchange are governed by a Listing Agreement.

In view of the fact that purchase and sale of shares through recognised Stock Exchanges and through licensed Stock Brokers are only legal, and those are governed by the SC(R) Act, the investors have to be familiar with this Act and the Rules made thereunder. The relation between the Brokers and Investors and in particular, the disputes if any, between them are governed by the Rules and Bye-laws of the Stock Exchanges which are formulated under this Act.

Acceptance of Fixed Deposits

A company cannot accept deposits in excess of 35% of the paid up capital and free reserves. Of this, 25% deposits can be accepted from the public and the rest 10% from shareholders of the company. The minimum period of acceptance of deposits is six months and the maximum period is limited to 3 years and 5 years in some cases. The company is under an obligation to maintain an amount not less than 10% to 15% of the company's deposit liability maturing during the course of the year, in liquid investments such as Government securities, UTI units, Semi-Government bonds etc. The maximum rate of interest that can be offered on deposits cannot exceed 12.5% per annum in the case of NBFCs, which are registered with RBI as required under the Law since 1997 and after registration with RBI since 1998, it was 11% or less depending on their credit rating. A ceiling on brokerage payable on deposits has been fixed at 1%. The interest rates on Fixed deposits by banks as well as other debt instruments are freed from fixation by the RBI and government from 1997-98 The interest earned on fixed deposits of companies does not enjoy any exemption from income tax. Neither does the amount of deposit qualify for any exemption under wealth tax. Under the existing provisions of the Income Tax Act, tax on interest paid/payable is deducted at source if the interest payment exceeds ₹ 2,500 in a financial year unless suitable declaration is furnished by the depositor in regard to the total income of the depositor not exceeding the minimum liable to tax in a financial year. (Form 15H)

The acceptance of deposits by non-bank non-financial companies is governed by the Companies (acceptance of deposits) Rules 1975 as amended from time to time. Along with the prescribed application form the terms and conditions of acceptance of deposits are required to be furnished by companies, to the RBI in the case of non-bank finance companies and a copy in case of non-bank non-finance companies to the RBI.

A careful study of either the financial data in the advertisement or the prescribed particulars as available within the application form would generally reveal the working results and the financial position of the company.

Compulsory Repayment of Deposits which have Matured for Repayment

The Companies Act, 1956 has been amended by the Companies (Amendment) Act, 1988 with effect from 1.9.1989 so as to provide for compulsory repayment of deposits which have matured for repayment (Section 58(9)). Under the amended provisions, the Company Law Board has been empowered to take cognizance of non-repayment of any deposit on maturity and to direct repayment of such deposits on such conditions as may be specified by the Company Law Board in its Order. This will help to ensure repayment of public deposits and will create confidence amongst the public.

Procedure for Making Application to Company Law Board

The person holding a matured fixed deposit which he has not renewed and which the company has failed to repay, has to make an application in triplicate in Form No. 11. The application has to be accompanied by a fee of ₹ 50 or any amount as may be specified payable by way of bank draft in favour of the Pay & Accounts Officer, Department of Corporate Affairs, New Delhi/Mumbai/Kolkata/Chennai.

The Company Law Board has four Regional Benches. The aggrieved depositors may make an application to the Bench of the Company Law Board having jurisdiction according to the Registered Office of the company. The Company Law Board would, after giving a reasonable opportunity of hearing to the company and other persons interested in the matter, make suitable orders for repayment of such deposits. Non-compliance of the order of the Company Law Board is a punishable offence attracting penalty by way of imprisonment upto 3 years and fine of not less than ₹ 50 for every day till such non-compliance continues.

Where the deposit which has fallen due for payment remains unpaid the depositor can seek remedy in a civil court, or can file an application for winding up of the company to the court after serving on the company written demand requiring the company to repay the deposit (Sections 433, 434 and 439 of the Companies Act may be referred to for the purpose).

Cases in Respect of which Applications to the Company Law Board will not Lie

It is essential to know that under Section 58A of the Companies Act, the power to order repayment of matured deposits can be exercised by the CLB only in respect of deposits accepted under the Companies (Acceptance of Deposit) Rules 1975 as amended from time to time. In other words, an application to the Company Law Board of repayment of matured deposits shall not lie in the following cases:

(i) Deposits made for booking purchases of scooter, car etc.

(ii) Deposits accepted by financial companies like, hire-purchase finance company, a housing finance company, an investment company, a loan/mutual benefit financial company, a chit fund company, which are governed by the rules made by the RBI.

(iii) Deposits accepted by companies which have been notified as 'relief undertakings' under special laws enacted by various State Governments. Court rulings point to the fact that the monetary liabilities of relief undertakings during the notified period stand suspended and any proceedings including the proceedings for compulsory repayment of deposits under Section 58A (9) shall accordingly remain stayed.

(iv) Deposits accepted by a sick industrial company covered by the Sick Industrial Companies (Special Provisions) Act, 1985 in respect of which, the Board for Industrial and Financial Reconstruction has specifically, by order suspended the operations of any contract, agreement, settlement, etc., under Section 22(3) of the Act.

COMPANIES (AMENDMENT) BILL OF 2008

This has replaced the Companies Act of 1956 in many provisions. The important provisions and changes made are brought out here.

1. One third of the Board members are to be outside independent persons as directors.
2. Restrictions were imposed on listed companies to raise public deposits.
3. Prohibition of issue of shares to promoters at a discount.
4. The key persons who should be held responsible to the investors are the CEO, Financial officer, and the Company secretary, as per the latest provisions.
5. Greater disclosures and transparency in the operations and results of listed companies.
6. A company can be of one person or of a parrtnership and a partnership firm can be of 100 persons instead of 20 persons as at present and one person company is now recognized in Law.
7. Investor protection, corporate governance and use of electronic Documents for proper disclousres are the highlights.
8. Investor Education and Protection Fund of a company is to be administered in future by a statutory authority.
9. The right of an investor to claim dividend even after a lapse of 7 years cannot be taken away under the new Act.
10. The right of intervention by the Government is now replaced by that of Investors as shareholders and owners of the company, to intervene for any offence committed by the Company. Investors can and should be more vigilant in future.
11. The rights of minority shareholders are now better protected than under the earlier Act.

INVESTORS AND STOCK EXCHANGES

Investors can deal in any of the recognised stock exchanges (23 in number) or OTCEI or on N.S.E., I.C.S.E. and The Stock Exchange Mumbai. ICSE is Interconnected Stock Exchange of India Ltd., set up in 1998, for 15 Regional Stock Exchanges for electronic trading. Delhi Stock Exchange, OTCEI and NSE are already on electronic trading system on weekly settlement basis. All the other Stock Exchanges, are now having electronic trading system. Investors should not deal with unrecognised Stock Exchanges in India.

Recognition by Government to Stock Exchanges

As referred to earlier, a Stock Exchange is recognised only after the government is satisfied that its Rules and Byelaws conform to the conditions prescribed for ensuring fair dealings and protection to investors. Government has also to be satisfied that it would be in the interest of the trade and public interest to grant such recognition. Mumbai, Kolkata, Delhi, Chennai, Ahmedabad, Hyderabad, Bangalore, Indore etc. have so far been granted permanent recognition. Others are granted temporary recognition from time to time.

The rules of a recognised stock exchange relating in general to the constitution of the Exchange, the powers of management of its governing body and its constitution (including the appointment thereon of not more than three government nominees), the admission of members, the qualifications for membership, the expulsion, suspension and readmission of members, the registration of partnerships and the appointment of authorised representatives and clerks must be duly approved by Government. These rules can be amended, varied or rescinded only with the previous approval of government. Likewise, the byelaws of the recognised exchanges providing in detail for the regulation and control of contracts in securities and for every aspect of the trading activities of members must also be sanctioned by government and any amendments or modifications must be similarly approved. Government's authority extends much further to make or amend *suo moto* any rules or byelaws of a recognised stock exchange, if it so considers desirable in the interest of trade and in public interest.

The Act empowered the government with even more drastic powers — the power to make enquiries into the affairs of a recognised stock exchange and its members, to supersede the governing body and take over the property of a recognised exchange, to suspend its business, and lastly, to withdraw the recognition granted to an exchange should such steps be deemed indispensable in the interest of trade and in public interest. Government has thus complete control over the recognised stock exchanges.

Licensed Dealers

The recognised stock exchanges are the media through which government regulation of the stock market is made effective. Where there are no stock exchanges, the Securities Contracts (Regulation) Act, 1956 empowers government to license dealers in securities and prescribe the conditions subject to which they can carry on the business of dealing in securities. These licensed dealers are now operating for OTCEI and NSE.

Securities Contracts (Regulation) Rules, 1957

Under the Act, government has promulgated the Securities Contracts (Regulation) Rules, 1957 for carrying into effect the objects of the legislation, namely, SC (R) Act. These rules provide, among other things, for the procedure to be followed for recognition of stock exchanges; submission of periodical returns and annual reports by recognised stock exchanges; inquiry into the affairs of recognised stock exchanges and their members; and requirements for listing of securities. The rules are statutory and they constitute a code of standardised regulations uniformly applicable to all the recognised stock exchanges.

Present Recognised Stock Exchanges

At present, there are 23 stock exchanges recognised under the Securities Contracts (Regulation) Act, 1956. They are located at Mumbai, Kolkata, Chennai, Delhi, Ahmedabad, Hyderabad, Indore, Bhuwaneshwar, Mangalore, Patna, Bangalore, Rajkot, Guwahati, Jaipur, Kanpur, Ludhiana, Baroda, Cochin and Pune. The recently recognised stock exchanges are at Coimbatore and Meerut. Visakhapatnam Stock Exchange was recognised for electronic trading in 1996. Both Meerut and Visakhapatnam Exchange are not operative. But the inter connected stock exchange set up by Regional Stock Exchanges, recognised in 1998 has become operational electronically since 1999. A stock exchange has also been set up at Gangtok, Sikkim early in 1986. No recognition has been sought for this body as the jurisdiction of the Securities Contracts (Regulation) Act, 1956 has not so far been extended to the areas covered by the State. A decade ago, there were hardly 8 stock exchanges in the country. With the recognition granted to OTCEI in 1989 and to NSE in 1992, there are 23 Exchanges in India.

The stock exchanges operate under the rules, byelaws and regulations duly approved by government and constitute an organised market for securities. They offer the most perfect type of market for various reasons. There is an active bidding and in the case of shares and debentures a two-way auction trading, so that purchases and sales are made in conditions of free and perfect competition. The bargains that are struck by members of the exchanges are the fairest price determined by the basic laws of supply and demand. In consequence, though gilt-edged securities represent ownership of public debt and shares and debentures of joint-stock companies represent interest in industrial property — mills and factories, plant, machinery and equipment — they become the most liquid of assets and capable of being easily negotiated.

Qualifications for Membership

The members of recognised stock exchanges should have the following qualifications. These can be amended or altered by the SEBI and now members are selected after written and oral test by the Stock Exchange.

- Age 21, Indian Citizen, not bankrupt.
- Not compounded with the creditors.
- Not convicted for fraud or dishonesty.
- Not engaged in any other business except as agent or broker.
- Educational Qualifications should be 10 + 2 (now made a graduate).
- Not connected with a company or corporation.
- Not a defaulter of any other stock exchange.

Companies and financial institutions were not members as per the earlier rules. But the government has permitted change in the byelaws of the exchanges to permit corporate and institutional members and also grant permission for a member of any stock exchange to be a member of another stock exchange during 1993 and 1994. Multiple membership of various stock exchanges is now permitted.

Members are prohibited from entering into contracts with persons other than members or from dealing with clients as principals. Spot delivery transactions are exempt from the provisions of the Act. Contracts can be passed only by the members in the notified areas where the stock exchange exists. The sub-brokers can also pass valid contract notes or confirmation notes, if they are registered with SEBI.

Organisation

The recognised stock exchanges at Mumbai, Ahmedabad, Indore are voluntary non-profit-making associations, while the Kolkata, Delhi, Bangalore, Cochin, Kanpur, Ludhiana, Guwahati and Kanara Stock Exchanges are joint-stock companies limited by shares and the Chennai, Hyderabad and Pune stock exchanges are companies limited by guarantee. Since the Rules or Articles of Association defining the constitution of the recognised stock exchanges are approved by the Central Government, there is a broad uniformity in their organisation. In fact, the Chennai Stock Exchange was reconstituted and the Calcutta Stock Exchange had to undergo a major reorganisation as a condition precedent to their recognition by the Government of India.

Governing Body

The governing body of a recognised stock exchange has wide governmental and administrative powers and is the decision-making body. It has the power, subject to governmental approval, to make, amend and suspend the operation of the rules, byelaws and regulations of the exchanges. It also has complete jurisdiction over all members and in practice, its power of management and control are almost absolute.

Under the constitution, the governing body has the power to admit and expel members, to warn, censure, fine and suspend members and their partners, attorneys, remisiers, authorised clerks and employees, to approve the formation and dissolution of partnerships and appointment of attorneys, remisiers and authorised clerks, to enforce attendance and information, adjudicate disputes and impose penalties, to determine the mode and conditions of stock exchange business and regulate stock exchange trading in all its aspects and generally to supervise, direct and control all matters and activities affecting the stock exchange. The organisation of Mumbai Stock Exchange is typical. The members on roll elect 16 members to be Directors on the Governing Board, who in turn elect a President, Vice-President and Treasurer. The Executive Director is appointed by the government on the recommendation of the Governing Board to be the Chief Administrator of the Exchange. There are also three representatives from the Government, three from the public and one from the RBI on the Board to represent their interests. As per the SEBI guidelines, the Exchanges have agreed to have 50% representation to non-members on the Governing Board.

Corporate Membership

Since 1987, individual members have been permitted to organise themselves into corporate entities. These corporate entities should have atleast two broker directors, with a minimum of two years experience as a sub-broker, authorised agent of a broker or jobber etc. The liability of member can be limited. The networth requirements which are higher than for regular individual members are to be met for each of the exchanges where they are expected to be members and operate. They can acquire multiple membership of as many Stock Exchanges as they want provided they satisfy the requirements of each of the exchanges separately and meet their networth criteria. At the same time, financial institutions and subsidiaries of banks in the public sector were also permitted to acquire the membership of Stock Exchanges.

Market Structure in India

So far as the individual investors are concerned, the market for corporate securities and Mutual funds schemes are more relevant. They satisfy the requirements of investors, namely, income, appreciation of capital, safety, liquidity, and hedge against inflation. In respect of corporate securities, leaving aside new issues market, the structure of the secondary market has undergone some changes which are depicted in the chart below:

The chart does not include the Inter Connected Stock Exchange of India (ICSEI) which was recognised only in 1999. The major Stock Exchanges are also called the National Stock Exchanges namely BSE, NSE, DSE and CSE, where only big companies with paid up capital of ₹ 10 crores and above are listed. The others are Regional Stock Exchanges like Cochin, Indore, Chennai, Hyderabad etc. where companies with ₹ 5 crores and above are listed.

SECONDARY MARKET STRUCTURE

Regular Stock Exchanges (21)	*Over the Counter Exchange of India (1)*	*National Stock Exchange (1)*
For big companies with paid up capital above ₹ 5 crores and ₹ 10 crores as the case may be — Trading ring and physical operations includes Principal exchanges like Mumbai, Kolkata, Delhi, etc. and regional exchanges like Cochin, Indore, etc. The B.S.E., C.S.E. and D.S.E., are on electronic trading and others have followed suit.	Computerised trading for smaller companies with paid up capital of ₹ 30 lakhs to ₹ 25 crores. No trading ring — started operations in Oct. '92. The upper limit of ₹ 25 crores was removed in 1997. Now all companies eligible for listing on the other exchanges can be listed on the OTCEI.	Recognised in April '93 and started operations later, only in Government securities and money market instruments. Equity Trading started in Nov. 1994 — Computerised trading, with country wide trading network. The derivatives were allowed to trading on NSE since 2001.

Chart 2.1 Contains selective presentation of marketable and non-marketable securities and those which are the issuers of the Securities. The players and intermediaries in the markets — both the primary and secondary markets are also set out.@
@ Chart 2.1 on p. 21.

INTERCONNECTED STOCK EXCHANGE OF INDIA (ICSEI)

This was registered in 1998 and got recognition from the SEBI in 1999. This was promoted by 9 regional stock exchanges like Cochin, Hyderabad, Indore etc., and was located at Vashi, Navi Mumbai, with electronic networking and computerised trading. It has about 800 members from various stock exchanges located in 131 centres spread over 25 states. The volumes were low as trading all over India was concentrated in the two major Stock Exchanges, namely BSE and NSE. The ICSEI was demutualised in 2005 under the ICSEI (Corporatisation and Demutualisation) Scheme of 2005. There was not much reporting in the press about the volumes in this exchange.

Players in the Market

The players in the New Issues market are many and the more important of them are the following:

1. ***Merchant bankers*** — their functions and working are very crucial to the operations in the primary market. They are the issue managers, lead managers, co-managers and are responsible to the company and SEBI.
2. ***Registrars*** — their functions are next to merchant bankers in importance. They collect the applications for new issues, their cheques, stock invests etc., classify and computerise them. They also make allotments in consultation with the regional stock exchange regarding norms in the event of oversubscription and before a public representative. They have to despatch the letters of allotments, refund orders and share certificates within the time schedules stipulated under the Companies Act and observe the guidelines of SEBI and the Government and RBI. Besides, they have also to satisfy the listing requirements and get them listed on one or more of the stock exchanges.
3. ***Collecting and co-ordinating bankers*** — collecting and co-ordinating bankers may be the same or different. While the former collects the subscriptions in cash, cheques, stock invests etc., the latter collates the information on subscriptions and coordinates the collection work and monitors the same to the registrars and merchant bankers, who in turn keep the company informed.
4. ***Underwriters and brokers*** — underwriters may be financial institutions, banks, mutual funds, brokers etc., and undertake to mobilise the subscriptions upto some limits. Failing to secure subscriptions as agreed to, they have to make good the shortfalls by their own subscriptions. Brokers along with their network of sub-brokers market the new issues by their own circulars, sending the application forms and follow up recommendations.
5. ***Printers, advertising agencies, and mailing agencies*** — are the other organisations involved in the new issue market operations.

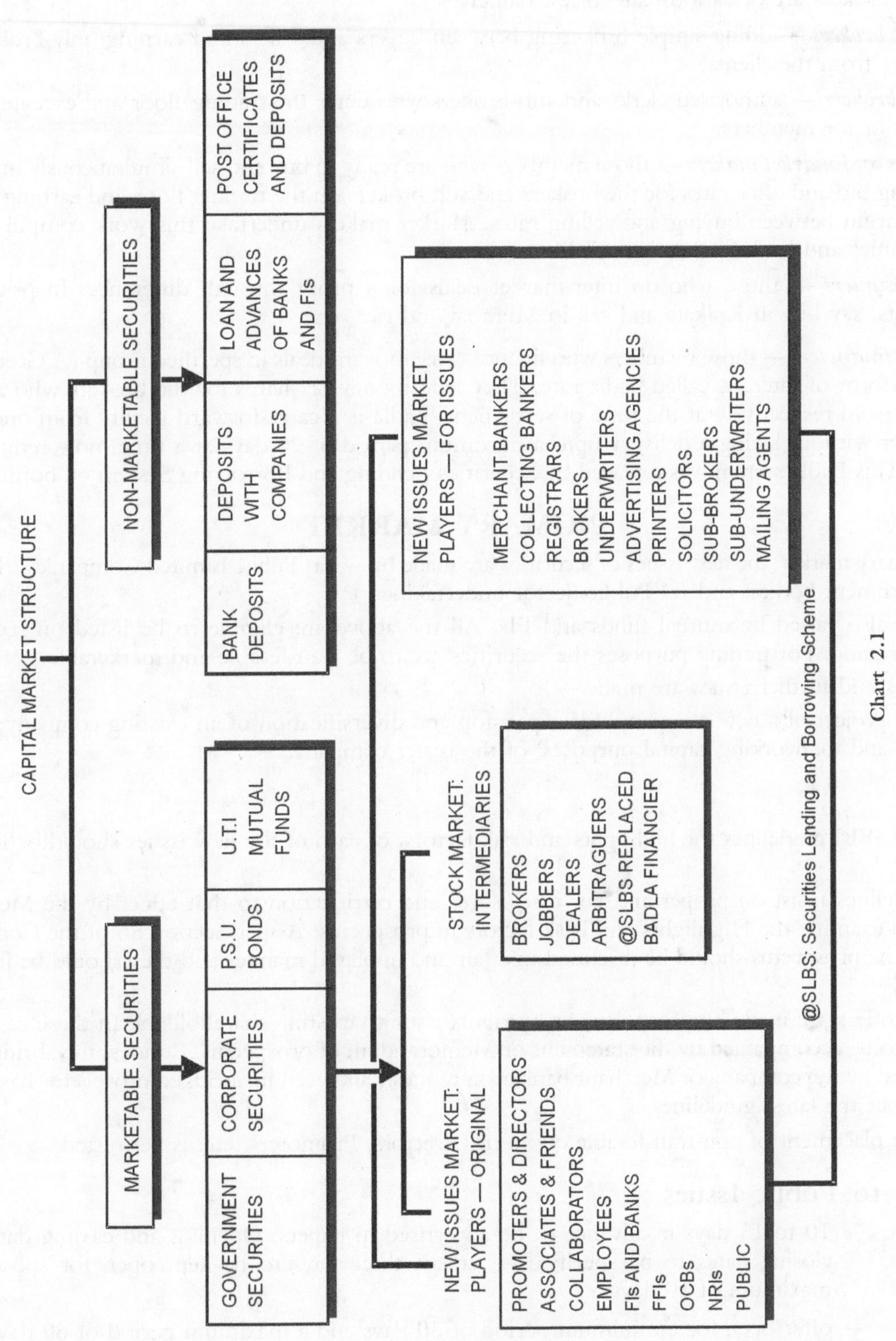
CAPITAL MARKET STRUCTURE
MARKETABLE SECURITIES
NON-MARKETABLE SECURITIES
GOVERNMENT SECURITIES
CORPORATE SECURITIES
P.S.U. BONDS
U.T.I MUTUAL FUNDS
BANK DEPOSITS
DEPOSITS WITH COMPANIES
LOAN AND ADVANCES OF BANKS AND FIs
POST OFFICE CERTIFICATES AND DEPOSITS
NEW ISSUES MARKET: PLAYERS — ORIGINAL
PROMOTERS & DIRECTORS
ASSOCIATES & FRIENDS
COLLABORATORS
EMPLOYEES
FIs AND BANKS
FFIs
OCBs
NRIs
PUBLIC
STOCK MARKET: INTERMEDIARIES
BROKERS
JOBBERS
DEALERS
ARBITRAGUERS
@SLBS REPLACED
BADLA FINANCIER
NEW ISSUES MARKET PLAYERS — FOR ISSUES
MERCHANT BANKERS
COLLECTING BANKERS
REGISTRARS
BROKERS
UNDERWRITERS
ADVERTISING AGENCIES
PRINTERS
SOLICITORS
SUB-BROKERS
SUB-UNDERWRITERS
MAILING AGENTS
@SLBS: Securities Lending and Borrowing Scheme

Chart 2.1

Stock Market Intermediaries

The players in the market are the issuers of securities, namely, companies, intermediaries like brokers, sub-brokers etc., and the investors who bring in their savings and funds into the market.

The stock brokers are of various categories, namely:

1. ***Client brokers*** — doing simple brokering between buyers and sellers and earning only brokerage for their services from the clients.
2. ***Floor brokers*** — authorised clerks and sub-brokers who enter the trading floor and execute orders for the clients or for members.
3. ***Jobbers and market makers*** — those members who are ready to buy and sell simultaneously in selected scrips, offering bid and offer rates for the brokers and sub-brokers on the trading floor and earning profit through the margin between buying and selling rates. Market makers undertake this work compulsorily for some companies and bank finance is available to them.
4. ***Arbitraguers*** — those who do inter-market deals for a profit through differences in prices as between markets, say buy in Kolkata and sell in Mumbai and *vice versa.*
5. ***Badla financiers*** — those members who finance carry forward deals in specified group (A Group) for a return in the form of interest, called badla rate. They lend money or shares for the brokers who are overbought or oversold respectively at the time of settlement. Badla is a carry-forward facility from one settlement to another without taking a delivery upto a maximum period of 90 days at a time, now reduced to 7 to 15 days. This Badla system was replaced by Securities Lending and Borrowing System on both BSE and NSE.

PRIMARY MARKET

In the primary market, the new issues of securities are made by — (a) Public Limited Companies, (b) Government and Semi Government bodies, and (c) Public Sector undertakings.

Funds are also raised by mutual funds and FIs. All the above are eligible to be listed on recognised Stock Exchanges for trading. For trading purposes the securities are to be transferable and marketable.

New issues and further issues are made —

For a new project of a new company; for expansion and diversification of an existing company; for cost over-runs of projects and for working capital purposes, of the issuer company.

Prospectus

Under the SEBI guidelines the highlights and risk factors, of each of the new issues should be incorporated in the prospectus.

SEBI guidelines insist on proper and fair disclosures and certification to that effect by the Merchant banker. Investors should examine the Highlights and Risk factors in prospectus. As per Section 56 of the Companies Act all the contents of the prospectus should be disclosed in a fair and unbiased manner and they should be factually correct and genuine.

All public offers are made by prospectus or by rights issue to existing shareholders. In these cases the form of application has to be accompanied by the statement or Memorandum of prospectus. Besides, the abridged prospectus has to be supplied by the company or Merchant banker on request, and even unabridged prospectus has to be supplied to members as per the latest guidelines.

No private placement of non-transferable quota of Directors, Promoters, etc. is permitted.

Time Limits to Public Issues

Public Offer — 10 to 15 days in advance to be advertised in papers. Opening and closing dates and earliest closing dates to be specified — atleast three days to be kept open for subscription and a maximum of 10 days.

Rights Offer — offer open for a minimum period of 30 days and a maximum period of 60 days with specific dates for closing of renunciations, split forms and other formalities.

The permitted period for rights issue to be kept open after Demat was introduced was reduced to 43 days. For initial public issues, the SEBI approved the blocking of bank funds until allotment is made from the time of closure of subscription.

Limits on Costs of Public Issues

Mandatory Costs — are to be 11% to 15% of total issue. These include, fees to managers to issue, merchant bankers, collecting bankers, underwriting commission, brokerage to brokers, fees to Registrars, press announcements, Listing fees, etc.

Other Costs — should not to exceed 2% to 5% for equity issue, and 1% to 2% for debenture issue in addition to Mandatory Costs.

The Flotation of New Issues is generally made by the following methods:

(1) Public Issue through prospectus.

(2) Private placement.

(3) Offer of sale.

(4) Rights.

Issue by prospectus:

What should be revealed in the Prospectus?

(1) Activities of company — Products.

(2) Promoters, Manager and their Reputation and their track record if any.

(3) Collaborators and Technology used and their track record.

(4) Location of the factories.

(5) Equity stake of promoters, collaborators and the method of financing.

(6) Input suppliers and Marketing arrangements.

(7) Time gap for commercial production to start

(8) Breakeven point after commercial production started for profit earnings capacity.

(9) Market Demand for the product/services and the company's share in the market.

(10) Government policy with regard to the products of the company.

(11) Capacity utilisation in the first three years.

(12) Cost of production and profit margins *vis-a-vis* other companies in the same industry line.

Pre-Issue Formalities

Project Report and Viability and Feasibility Report

— Letter of Intent, Industrial Licence or Statement in lieu of it.

— Arrangements for Financing, Agreements with Collaborators, FIs, Bankers, Auditors, Legal Advisors, Merchant Bankers, Brokers, Underwriters etc.

— Formalities for satisfying the Companies Act, SEBI Act and SC(R) Act, and FEMA.

Requirements of Section 60 of Companies Act

— SEBI permit for issue of shares to public through Prospectus.

— Meeting the requirements for listing on Stock Exchanges.

— Arrangements for issue by agreement for a common share certificate form, Draft prospectus, printing of stationery, Registrar to the issue, bankers, brokers etc.

FACTORS FOR INVESTMENT IN PRIMARY MARKET

Investors are aware that under the present free pricing environment, issuers are free to decide the issue price subject to Securities and Exchange Board of India guidelines for disclosure and investor protection. The investor guidance series was intended to educate the investors about certain aspects which they normally should look for in the memorandum containing salient features of prospectus accompanying all application forms before making investment in any issue. For any further details relating to the issue, they should make a reference to the detailed prospectus, which is available with the company or the merchant bankers managing the issue. In particular, they should look into the following:

I. Promoters Track Record

1. Adequacy of knowledge and experience in the field relating to the project.
2. Past performance particularly with reference to the companies earlier promoted by them and their track record.
3. To ascertain the reputation and integrity of the promoters with regard to their involvement in the affairs of other companies through independent inquiries with reference to financial newspapers, magazines, journals, etc.

II. Professional Management

1. The Managing Directors' background and experience in the field.
2. Composition of the Board of Directors — whether broad-based and consists of professionals.

III. Objects of the Issue

Whether the purpose of the issue is likely to result in enhancement of the profitability and growth of the company.

IV. Project Details Including Location and Raw Materials

1. To appreciate and understand the location of the project, availability of tax concessions as in case of backward areas, availability of infrastructure facilities and raw materials, etc.
2. Whether the issuing company obtained appraisal of the project by financial institutions/banks and if so whether the appraising agency has any financial stake in the project.
3. Provision for monitoring the implementation of the project by financial institutions and banks or any other agency.

V. Product/Technology/Market

1. Whether disclosure of demand-supply projection for the product has been made and whether it is based on reliable sources.
2. If the product is susceptible to fair competition, and adequate marketing arrangements for the sale of the product are made.
3. The chances of the product becoming obsolete in view of the technological developments.
4. Availability of substitutes having a bearing on the demand for the product.
5. Export potential for the product in case of an export-oriented project and whether there is any tie-up with the foreign collaborator or agency for purchase of products.

VI. Financial Data

Data relating to capital, reserves, turn-over, profits, dividend record, profitability ratios, book value, earning per share, relative percentages of profit from the operations of the company and other sources.

VII. Profitability Projections

The profitability projections as indicated by the company or by the appraising institution and likelihood of achieving the same in the light of its past performance or that of the industry.

VIII. Pricing

1. Justification for pricing with reference to the past performance and future projections; whether future projections are based on company's own estimates or independent appraisal by financial institutions, banks, etc.
2. Justification of differential pricing in case of composite issues, i.e., rights cum public.
3. In case of issues of existing companies movement of prices immediately before the issue to ascertain whether prices are fair market prices or there has been rigging of the market prices.

IX. Pending Litigations

1. Pending litigations, if any, having a bearing on the profitability of the company or likely to result in winding up of the company for inability to pay debts or any other costs.
2. The possibility of the company being construed as potentially sick or a sick company for making a reference to the Board for Industrial and Financial Reconstruction under Sick Industrial Companies (Special Provisions) Act, 1985.

X. Risk Factors

1. To ascertain specific risks and general risks relevant to each project on the basis of disclosures made in the other documents and market intelligence.

XI. Report of the Auditor/Recent Working Results

1. Auditor's report forming part of the offer document, especially with reference to significant notes to accounts, qualifying remarks on changes in accounting policies, in order to know the reliability of the figures reflected in the Balance sheet.
2. In the case of letter of offer, the recent unaudited working results given at the end of the letter of offer.

XII. Statutory/Institutional/Bank Dues

1. Whether the company is a defaulter in payment of statutory/institutional/bank dues.
2. Whether the company has been regular in payment of interest to debenture/fixed deposit holders.

XIII. Statutory Clearances

1. Whether various statutory clearances required for the implementation of the project have been obtained.
2. If not, the current status of such clearances.

XIV. Due Caution

1. The investors should weigh the risk factors against the highlights of the project. They should examine whether the price/premium fixed is reasonable as per their own assessment of the project. They should also exercise care and diligence before making any investment.

LISTING FORMALITIES AND PROCEDURES FOR THE STOCK EXCHANGES

Formalities to be completed by the Company as soon as possible and in any case within ten weeks, reduced to 30 days in 1996, from the closing of the subscription list.

1.The Articles of Association of the Company should be amended as indicated in the guidelines from the Government or the Directors should give an undertaking to amend them accordingly at the time of the next general meeting of the Company by passing a resolution in terms of the accepted draft and a certified copy thereof should be forwarded to the Exchange.

2. Specimens of the Letters of Allotment and share certificates should be filed with the Exchange. Share certificates should be in the prescribed form. A draft format thereof should be sent for approval of the Exchange.

3. It should be confirmed that letters of Allotment/share certificates would be issued in marketable lots. Such lots are also called tradable lots.

4. If there is a condition restricting of any shares, distinctive numbers of such shares as well as the date upto which they would not be transferable should be communicated to the Exchange and it should be confirmed that Letter of Allotment and share certificates of these shares would be prominently stamped with an enfacement as under:

"Not transferable upto..."

(date)

5. The Listing Agreement should be executed.

6. The Initial Listing Fees as fixed by the Exchange and the Annual Listing Fee varying depending on the paid-up capital of the company should be paid.

7. The Company should agree to make arrangement with its Bankers to receive Allotment monies, at all the centres where applications are accepted.

8. The Exchange should be advised as soon as the subscription list is closed.

9. Six copies of the Analysis Form are sent to the Exchange.

10. In the event of over-subscription, the Auditors of the Company/Practising Company Secretary should certify that allotment of shares has been made as agreed upon with the Stock Exchange concerned.

11. In the event of under-subscription it should be confirmed that the balance of the issue remaining unsubscribed has been taken up by the underwriters or their nominees.

12. The date of completion of posting of Letters of Allotment/share certificates has been filed and the Register of Members of the Company is open for registering of shares.

13. Distribution Schedules of the Equity shares be filed in duplicate and copies of Distribution Schedule are sent to the Exchange.

14. The detailed Listing Application should be submitted.

15. It should be confirmed that the cheques for brokerage and underwriting commission payable to members of recognised stock Exchange have been posted direct to them.

16. In terms of the Government Guidelines contained in press note dated the 15th October, 1985, the Auditors of the Company/Practising company secretary should certify that the certificates of shares out of promoter quota have been stamped with an enfacement as under:

"The shares will not be sold/transferred/hypothecated until...." (date)

17. The Auditors of the company should certify that the company's expenditure on the public issue does not exceed the overall ceiling fixed as per Government Letter No. F.14/1/SE/85 dated 7th May, 1985.

18. The company should obtain a certificate from the Bankers to the issue, indicating the number of applications and the amount of application money received and that all the applications have been delivered to the company.

19. Certified copies of the following documents should be filed. Agreements with Collaborators, Selling agents etc.

20. The company should furnish to the Exchange an undertaking to scrupulously adhere to the time limit of 30 days from the date of closure of the subscription list for allotment of all securities and despatch of allotment letters/ certificates and refund orders, along with a scheme incorporating the necessary details of the arrangements for such compliance. The company should file with the executive director of the exchange within five working days of the expiry of the stipulated period as above a statement signed by the chief executive that the allotment letters/securities and the refund orders have been despatched within the prescribed time limit as above. Non-compliance of the condition above will result in rejection of the company's listing application by the exchange and the consequences thereof pursuant to Section 73 of the Companies Act, for which the company will be solely responsible.

21. The company should appoint a member of the exchange as a sponsoring broker who will also act as a market maker in the company's shares after they are listed on the exchange.

SECONDARY MARKET

What is a Stock Exchange?

Stock Exchange is an organised market place where securities are traded. These securities are issued by the Government, semi-Government Bodies, Public Sector undertakings and companies for borrowing funds and raising resources. Securities are defined as any monetary claims (promissory notes or I.O.U.) and include stock, shares, debentures, bonds etc. If these securities are marketable as in the case of Government stock, they are transferable by endorsement and are like movable property. They are tradeable on the stock Exchange. So is the case with the shares of Companies.

Under the Securities Contract Regulation Act of 1956, securities trading is regulated by the Central Government and such trading can take place only in Stock Exchanges recognised by the Government under this Act. As referred to earlier there are at present 23 such recognised Stock Exchanges in India. Of these, major Stock Exchanges, like Mumbai, Kolkata, Delhi, Chennai, etc., are permanently recognised while the rest are temporarily recognised. The above Act has also laid down that trading in approved contracts should be done through registered members of the Exchange. As per the Rules made under the above Act, trading in securities permitted to be traded would be in the normal trading hours (10 A.M. to 4 P.M. on working days[1]) in the Trading Ring, as specified for trading purpose. Contracts approved to be traded are the following:

(a) Spot delivery deals are for delivery of shares on the same day or the next day as the payment is made.
(b) Hand delivery deals for delivering shares within a period of 7 to 14 days from the date of the contract.
(c) Delivery through a clearing for delivering shares within a period of 2 months from the date of the contract, which is now reduced to 15 days.
(d) Special delivery deals for delivering of shares for specific longer periods as may be approved by the Governing Board of the Stock Exchange.

1. The timings vary from exchange to exchange. But SEBI has directed that all stock exchanges should have uniform trading time. Since January 2010, the trading hours were extended by one more hour from 9 A.M. to 4 P.M.

Except those deals meant for delivery on a spot basis, all the rest are to be put through by the registered brokers of a Stock Exchange. The Securities Contracts (Regulation) Rules of 1957 laid down the conditions for such trading, the trading hours, rules of trading, settlement of disputes, etc., as between the members and of the members *vis-a-vis* their clients. The eligibility and qualifications for members, elections for Governing Board, method of administration of the Stock Exchange and all matters relating to the working of the Stock Exchange and its registered members/brokers are set out in what are called the Rules, Byelaws and Regulations of the Exchange, and as per SEBI guidelines since 1992.

Functions of the Stock Exchange

The Stock Exchange is defined as an association of member brokers for the purpose of facilitating and regulating the trading in Securities. Bulk of the trading takes place in equity shares of public Limited Companies whose transferability by endorsement is ensured under the Companies Act and under the Securities Contract (Regulation) Act. The Stock Exchange provides the service of getting shares of Public Limited Companies listed for trading purposes. Listing means making a quotation available for a company's share to be traded. Under the present regulatory system, Public Limited Companies with a minimum paid up capital of ₹ 5 crores of which 25% are issued to the public — reduced to 20% and even 10% in some cases — can list their securities for trading on a Stock Exchange. For Bombay Stock Exchange (BSE) and National Stock Exchange (NSE) the minimum paid up capital for listing purposes is ₹ 10 crores.

The equity shares of good companies which have potential for higher earnings and dividends would show capital appreciation and such shares are well traded. The Stock Exchange through their members provides facility for buying and selling of such securities listed and quoted on the Exchange.

The functions of the Stock Exchange can be set out as follows:

(a) Provides quotation for shares/stock for facilitating trading and marketability.

(b) Extends liquidity (Conversion into cash) to such stock as they are easily marketable and traded.

(c) Provides an orderly regulated market for securities whose prices are determined by free market forces of supply and demand.

(d) Promotes savings and investment in the economy by attracting funds for investment in corporate shares and securities.

Major Components in the Capital Market

As referred to earlier, the two major components of capital market are the new issues and the stock market. In the former the existing companies or the new companies raise funds from the public through issue of securities for their project financing, expansion, modernisation etc. In the latter, namely, the stock market, the existing securities are bought and sold for helping investors to disinvest and fresh investors to enter into the market. The public can only buy in the new issues market but cannot sell. But in the stock market, they can sell as well as buy the Securities. The new issues market and stock market are complementary and investors should be familiar with operations in both.

In the new issues market, brokers who are registered members of the stock Exchange help the companies issuing securities to underwrite their subscription and arrange for marketing them through a chain of sub-brokers in different parts of the country. The application forms and prospectus of companies are secured by them for distribution to prospective investors and arrange for their subscriptions through the collecting banks. The successful applicants would be allotted and the share/debenture certificates would be sent within a period of 30 days after allotment.

The brokers in the stock market take orders from the public for buying and selling of securities which they execute in the trading ring as per the rules and bye-laws of the exchange. These orders may be written or oral or sent by telex or telephone. The clients may put some limits on the prices or on the total value or leave to market rates or to the discretion of brokers.

After execution of the orders, the brokers have to confirm the execution through what are called the contract notes on the same day. These notes give the details of deals, scrips purchased/sold, rates, quantity etc. The selling clients have to deliver shares first and receive payment later. The buying clients have to pay first as per the contract note and receive the shares later. All orders should be in marketable lots which may vary from 5 to 100 shares, depending upon the face value of shares.

Players in the Market

The players in the market are the companies issuing securities, intermediaries and brokers who match buying and selling orders and finally the public at large who are the investors in the stocks.

The companies are of three categories as per the Companies Act: Public Limited Companies, Private Limited Companies and companies limited by guarantee. The shares of Public Limited Companies can be listed and traded on the Stock Exchanges and not of other categories of company as the securities of the former are freely transferable by endorsement like movable property as per the Companies Act.

Both Companies Act and the Securities Contracts (Regulation) Act have ensured that securities issued by Public Limited Companies are transferable and restrictions on transfers are an exception and free transferability is the rule. Hence, these securities are eligible to be quoted and traded on the Stock Exchanges. The Securities Contracts (Regulations) Act has provided for an organised market for trading in securities, purchases and sale and their transfers. The Rules made under that Act have provided for a market place, registered member brokers to facilitate such trading and serve the investor population by buying and selling these securities. Ultimately, the investors are the savers in the country whose funds have flowed into the corporate sector through subscriptions to new issues of shares or buying the old and existing securities. This provision of a market for securities promotes the flow of savings into investment.

Relations of Companies with Stock Exchange

The corporate sector is net borrower and needs funds for project finance, long term working capital, expansion and diversification etc. The companies can borrow from banks and financial institutions but their reliance on capital market through issue of securities to public has increased in the recent years. The companies raise the funds from the public in the following methods, which are called the external sources of funds.

1. Borrowing from banks as loans, advances, etc., and from financial institutions.
2. By attracting long-term deposits of 1 to 3 years from public.
3. By offer of sale of securities to the public.
   (a) Through prospectus and by public advertisement.
   (b) Through private offer of sale either as "right" to existing shareholders or to the general public.
   (c) Through private placement and book building process.

The first two categories of raising funds do not lead to marketable securities which can be traded, while the third category of sale of securities to the public lead to marketable securities which can be traded and has market called the stock market. This is the basis of the operations in the stock market. Thus, the companies whose shares are marketable find it convenient to get them listed on Stock Exchanges. Companies which are listed enjoy some advantages and facilities for raising larger funds.

Nearly 100 million population in India are investors in the stocks in the capital market. About ₹ 26,000 crores of capital was raised from the public either through prospectus or rights in the capital market in a peak year 1994-95 and this stood at ₹ 1,16,810 crores in 2013-14. These funds are raised either as ownership capital, say equity shares, preference shares or debt capital, say debentures or bonds. Preference shares are not attractive to investors as they are neither owners fully nor debtors fully. While equity capital provides good return in the form of capital appreciation and dividend, debt capital in the form of debentures gives only fixed interest income. More recently convertible debentures have become attractive as they give the benefits of both fixed return for sometime and the higher returns later through the conversion into equity. Convertible debentures are those which are partly or fully convertible, into the equity shares after a period of time, say a few months to few years. With the removal of ceiling interest of 15% on debentures in 1991, these instruments have also become attractive to investors. The new capital raised from the public fell to ₹ 16,171 crores, due to depressed market conditions in the year 2008-09, but revived in 2009-10. The new capital raised in 2010-11, was also lower at ₹ 27,979 crores and in 2013-14, ₹ 1,16,810 crores.

Public versus the Exchange

Stock Exchange is public institution as public funds are invested in the securities and these securities are traded on the Exchange. As trading involves money dealings and malpractices are possible in the process, the trading and settlement of deals are regulated by the law and rules as approved by the Government. The law governing the companies raising of funds is the Companies Act, 1956 and this is regulated by the Registrar of Companies. The trading in securities is regulated by the Securities Contracts (Regulation) Act, 1956 and the Regulation Rules made thereunder in 1957 by the Stock Exchange authorities which are in turn regulated by the SEBI and Ministry of Finance, Government of India. The public are savers and investors and they are motivated by the following objectives:

(a) income from investments either as dividends or interest,
(b) capital appreciation of their investments,
(c) safety of their funds, and
(d) liquidity and marketability that they can get their funds at short notice. All the above objectives are achieved by proper investment strategy of savers.

Investments in stock and capital market ensure that the above objectives are achieved. But as the trading in the securities is guided by free forces of supply and demand as if in an auction system, prices of shares can change at short notice in either direction and there is an element of risk in these investments. The public who deal in securities in the Stock Market should therefore be careful in their dealings, and be aware of the risk.

Relations of the Stock Broker and the Exchange

The Stock exchange is an association of member brokers for regulation of trading and activities of the members. It is a self-regulating body for the purpose of assisting and facilitating the securities trading, under the overall control of the stock Exchange Division of Ministry of Finance and Securities and Exchange Board of India which is overall Watch dog body of the Government to regulate stock and capital markets.

The term broker or stock broker is loosely used to denote any intermediary, but the member broker of a Stock Exchange is a registered member, licensed to trade as per the Rules, Byelaws and Regulations of the Stock Exchange. He has been given a responsibility to observe some rules, and order and a code of conduct and behave in a befitting manner to subserve the objectives of the Exchange and in the public interest. The so called brokers acting as agents of P.O., UTI, LIC, etc., are not necessarily the members of a Stock Exchange. The public are therefore advised to deal only with the member brokers or their Remisiers of a Stock Exchange and not with any broker. Only the member brokers and not others are authorised to pass Contract Notes to the clients and be bound by the regulations of the Stock Exchange.

Since May, 1992, the member brokers and sub-brokers have also to register with Securities and Exchange Board of India and the Public should deal with such brokers and sub-brokers only. These brokers are not supposed to advertise their business. Each is given a code number or a registration number. The investors should deal with only member broker, who is willing to do business for him and deal with him.

What are the Instruments Traded on the Exchange?

The instruments traded are securities which are quoted after being listed by the companies which issued them to the public. The securities issued by the Central and State Governments. Semi-Government bodies are also listed and quoted on the Stock Exchanges as per the Rules. The broker members are eligible to deal in them also. In fact some members specialise in Government securities market, but public are not in general interested in these securities, and they are less attractive to the public. Only banks, financial institutions, insurance companies etc., deal in Government securities market. But for individual investors, corporate securities are relevant as they have higher rates of interest and higher returns due to capital appreciation and dividends.

The corporate securities in which individual investors are interested and are traded on the exchanges are as follows:

1. ***Equity Shares:*** These are ownership capital and have a variable dividend, depending on the net earnings and dividend policy of the company. The prices of these shares vary widely and with a face value of ₹ 10 (₹ one to ten) they are normally quoted at a premium which leads to capital appreciation.
2. ***Preference Shares:*** These are also ownership capital but with a fixed dividend. Now-a-days, preference shares are not popular and have no public interest in them; only financial institutions hold them.
3. ***Convertible or Partly-convertible Debentures:*** The debentures are popular only if they are convertible into equity shares after a period. Non-convertible debentures carry a fixed rate of interest. But as there is now no ceiling on such interest rates, they have also become attractive to investors. They have to choose only good companies with a good credit rating, so that there would be no problem in getting their interest warrants and repayment of principal. Convertible debentures are now popular both with companies and investors as they have advantages of both fixed income up to a period and capital appreciation later on due to conversion into equity.

More interestingly, trading in equity shares constitute the bulk of the stock market activity as speculation and capital appreciation are possible only in these shares. These shares carry the advantages of "rights" and "bonus" issues declared from time to time by the companies in addition to dividends. Rights are also traded and cum rights and cum bonus quotations for shares are available on the stock market, whenever these companies have come out with these privileges.

More recently a number of new instruments are issued by companies like convertible cumulative preference shares issued at 10% or zero coupon bonds, issued with no fixed rate of interest. Similarly, secured premium notes and warrants and few other instruments of issue have come into vogue with some bigger companies to attract the investors, like discount bonds, Floating Rate Issues, Flexi bonds etc. A vibrant debt market is being developed in India by both the SEBI and the RBI, for both corporate debt and government debt.

How does an Investor Place an Order?

First of all, the investor should identify a registered broker who is willing to accept him as his client. The brokers generally show reluctance to do business with new clients and therefore require introduction or proper contact point. Therefore, the investor should approach a member broker or his remisier or sub-broker with a proper introduction.

Secondly, he should place his orders with limits or at market rates, after analysing the company's fundamentals. The investors should be well informed with practices of brokers, rules and regulations of the stock market and of companies. The investor should insist on a contract note from the broker on all the deals, done by him. Many brokers give receipts for money for orders placed by clients or for documents received from them. If they do not, investors should insist on them as written evidence.

Thirdly, investors should note the settlement schedule for trading on the concerned Stock Exchange, pay in and pay out dates for each settlement and arrange to give cheques before pay in dates. Investors should pay first before they receive the certificates. Similarly, they should deliver the certificates along with properly signed Transfer Deed, before they get the payment for sale. It takes about 15-20 days for documents to be received or payments to be made to investors for a trading cycle of one week (5 working days). The position is now different under demat form of trading and T + 2 Settlement period.

The investor should also keep a track of the book closure and record dates of companies and be familiar with the practices of companies, particularly in respect of allotment letters, share certificates, transfer deeds, transfer procedures and good and bad deliveries of shares/debentures both at the Stock Exchange level and at the Share Department level of the companies. He should know when a quotation becomes ex-dividend or cum-dividend or ex-bonus or cum-bonus.

The investors should also know that if they have to deal with the broker on a continuous basis without any problems, they have to keep his confidence and keep margins with the broker for payment to the Stock Exchange and make regular payments as and when needed.

Benefits of Investment in Shares

Shares are also called equity capital or ordinary capital, which bestows a right on the company. As owners, these shareholders who buy the equity shares of the company, will receive dividends from the residual profits of the company, after meeting all the tax and other liabilities. The residual profits are partly distributed as dividends and partly ploughed back into company's reserves for future use. The larger these ploughed back reserves, the larger is the networth of the company. All these funds belong to the shareholders or equityholders and if used productively for expansion, the profitability of the company can increase. The larger is the profit margin and the higher earnings of the company, the higher is the share price. The demand for the shares of such company will increase leading to appreciation of the share price and the capital gains to the equityholders. Thus, the equity holder gains not only through dividend increase but through capital appreciation, if he holds on to the shares for sufficiently long periods.

There are a number of other benefits also for an equity shareholder.

1. He may be entitled to bonus issue that may be made by the company out of the free reserves accumulated through retained earnings over years. Bonus shares are free shares which the existing shareholders will be given, in a ratio to the present shareholding as on a date, called the record date, as decided by the management of the company. Thus, big companies with large networth or free reserves distribute these bonus shares to existing equityholders in a particular ratio. If the ratio is say 4:1, the equityholder of 4 shares will get one bonus share free. The bonus share will be entitled to the proportionate dividend, from the date of issue for the year in which it is issued. Later, bonus shares rank equally with other equity shares and the holders can sell them and book profits.

2. *Rights:* The equity shareholders may be entitled to any further issue of capital, either as debentures, fully or partly convertible debentures or equity shares, as may be made by the company, depending on its requirements. Thus, right issue is a method of raising capital for the company for expansion, diversification or other requirements. These

are issued to existing shareholders on concessional terms, namely, at lower rates than the prevailing market prices. So the equityholders can buy the shares or debentures through rights and sell them in the open market at higher prices and book profits. It is also possible that equityholder can renounce the rights to another person and get a price for such renunciation. There is a market for such right renunciation and some quotations are published for such rights in the case of good companies whose shares are in demand.

3. The equity shareholders have also a right of vote in all meetings of shareholders either at AGM or EGM. They have other rights also such as to call for meetings, fix the terms of issue of rights or public issues etc., and even for winding up of the company under some conditions. The Companies Act has clearly laid down the rights of shareholders of a company, under its various provisions.

4. The equity shareholders being the owners of the company have the right to get the balance sheet free every year, and is entitled to receive interim and final dividends within a period of 42 days from the date of declaration of dividends.

5. The shareholders have a right to get their shares transferred to somebody else's name through gift, donation or sale. They can get their shares consolidated into marketable lots or split into certificates of smaller value freely. Thus, two certificates of 25 shares each can be consolidated freely to one certificate of 50 shares which is a marketable lot in the case of Apollo Tyres and some other companies. In the case of many companies, the marketable lot is 100 shares. Thus, transfers, splits and consolidation of shares are some of the other rights that shareholders are entitled to.

6. Any investment in shares is wealth of the investor which is free from for wealth tax. There is no limit to such investments which can be made for wealth tax purposes. But, for Income tax purposes, dividend income along with other eligible incomes are exempt; only dividend income from companies in the hands of investors is tax free as per the Budget of 1997-98. Besides investment in some new issues is also eligible for rebate of 20% from income tax upto a limit, say ₹ 10,000 under equity linked Savings Schemes of Mutual Funds. So investment in shares can be planned for tax advantages by persons subject to income and wealth taxation. Besides from March 1999, even incomes from Mutual Funds in the hands of investors are tax free. But as of now, all incomes from Companies and mutual funds are taxable in the hands of investors as any other income. There is a TDS for interest income received by them, from banks, companies etc., above a certain limit (₹ 2,500).

In addition to all the above benefits, the investor in equities enjoys some unique advantages of safety, liquidity and marketability. The investor can readily find a market for selling the equity shares in the Stock Market and encashing the investments at short notice. The investor can also benefit from his investment if made in blue chip companies in a judicious manner to protect his wealth from inflation, as such investment is a good hedge against inflation or rise in prices. The returns are good in terms of both dividend and possible appreciation of capital, if investments are made after a careful study of the companies.

SEBI AND ITS FUNCTIONS

SEBI is a short form for Securities and Exchange Board of India, which is the supervisory and regulatory authority for the stock and Capital Markets. It was set up in 1988 and was granted legal powers in February 1992.

SEBI functions are:

1. Control and Regulation of the Stock Exchanges and Stock Brokers.
2. Regulation of Merchant Bankers, Mutual Funds and other players in the Capital Market.
3. Development of Stock and Capital Markets in the right direction.
4. Licensing and authorisation of Brokers and Sub-brokers and other intermediaries operating in the Capital Markets.
5. To ensure investor protection.

This is a body set up by the Government as an autonomous organisation to regulate and develop the Stock and Capital Markets and promote investor protection.

(i) Specified Securities

These are the securities of large and good companies called blue chip companies and reputed well run companies in which the facility of carry forward of purchase and sale deals from one Trading Cycle or settlement Cycle (10 to 15 days of trading) to another cycle is provided. In these securities, no delivery need be given or taken if the member so desires, which means that speculation is permitted in them. The criteria for placing some companies in Specified Group (also called Group A) are the following:

(a) Large paid-up capital and large market capitalisation (market value of outstanding shares).
(b) Wide public distribution of shares and public interest in that company.
(c) Dividend paying and expanding company with good prospects. Only a few large Stock Exchanges in India like Mumbai, Ahmedabad, Delhi, Kolkata have such lists called 'Specified Group' of shares where clearing and carry forward facilities are provided by the Exchange. These are all well traded companies.

(ii) Non-specified Securities

These are also called Group-B securities meant for cash or hand delivery. The B.S.E. has further split this group into B_1 and B_2 with the weekly settlement and clearing facility to B_1 group. The criteria for putting some companies B_1 and other B_2 is mostly dependent on the volume of trading and number of trades per day. This means that trade in such shares results in giving delivery or taking delivery in 7 to 14 days. These securities do not have the facility of carry toward, through the provision of Badla finance for such trade carry over. Delivery has to be given or taken compulsorily in such securities depending on whether the investor is a seller or a buyer. Badla refers to carry over facility of net purchase or sales of brokers. This is now replaced by Securities Lending and Borrowing Scheme both on NSE and BSE (SLBS).

(iii) Permitted Securities

These securities are shares of such companies which are listed on some Exchange in India but are not listed on the Stock Exchange in which we are dealing. If such securities are permitted to be traded by the Board of Directors of the concerned Exchange they can also be traded like any other listed company. The listed companies pay listing fees and hence the Exchange is bound by the Rules to provide facilities for their trade. In the case of non-listed companies, the Exchange does not receive any listing fees but the Exchange on their own permit the trade in them in the interest of members of that Exchange and their investors. The BSE has no such permitted list but almost all the Regional Stock Exchanges and NSE have permitted lists.

GRIEVANCES OF THE INVESTORS IN CAPITAL MARKET

One may apply to the Securities and Exchange Board of India (SEBI) for general complaints against any party in the Capital Market, viz., Companies, Stock Exchanges, Brokers etc.

(a) ***Grievance Against the Member Broker:*** Any investor can seek redressal of his grievance with the Grievances Cell of the Stock Exchange where the broker is registered as a member.

(b) ***Grievance Against a Listed Company:*** In addition to the Securities and Exchange Board of India, the investor can apply to the Registrar of Companies or to the Grievances Cell of the Stock Exchange where the company is listed as in the Regional Exchange.

(c) ***Grievance in Respect of Debentures:*** The investor has to apply to the Debenture Trustees, appointed by the company for this purpose as per the Trust Deed terms, the details of which will be written on the back of the debenture certificate.

(d) ***Grievance in Respect of Public Deposit with a Company:*** The investor has to apply in a prescribed form to the Regional office of Company Law Board, praying for a redressal of the grievance such as non-payment of interest or of principal in respect of a Fixed Deposit.

TRADING AND SETTLEMENT

Trading in shares is allowed on the trading floor of the Exchange from 10.00 A.M. to 4.00 P.M. (now 9 A.M. to 4 P.M.) on weekdays. Settlement period of 5 days will start from Monday to Friday or Thursday and end on Wednesday of next week.[2] Thereafter the members will inform the Exchange on Thursday of their deals which will not have deliveries. Such deals will be renewed at the old prices. But if the buyer insists on deliveries, there will be auction at a later date to procure the shares and deliver them to the buyer at the expense of the seller. For outstanding sales, the members have to give delivery of shares on pay-in day and for outstanding purchases, the members have to give a cheque for the amount due on the same day. The corresponding payments for shares delivered and delivery of shares for payments made will be done on the pay-out day. The rule is to pay first and then receive later or to deliver the shares first and receive the payment later. In 1997, a weekly settlement system was introduced on BSE, to be

2. These days will vary from Exchange to Exchange as these are autonomous bodies. But the SEBI has directed all Stock Exchanges to have uniform Settlement Period to facilitate national clearing system.

followed by others and dematerialisation of securities through NSDL Depository participants. During 1999-2000, the rolling settlement system on a daily basis was introduced for selected scrips and it became compulsory rolling settlement system in 2001, and all scrips have been brought under this system by 2003.

The Stock Exchange Trading Cycle (Settlement)

(Trading days – 5)

Types of positions —				
	A –	Squared	—	bought and sold are equal
	B –	Bought	—	over bought
	C –	Sold	—	over sold
	D –	Odd lots	—	not in marketable lots of 5, 50 and 100. (not relevant now after Demat of physical certificates)

	Day@
1. First day of Trading	Thursday
2. Last day of Trading	Next Wednesday
3. No-Deliveries reports	— Do —
4. Gross position of Bought and Sold	— Do —
5. Auction for Non-Deliveries (not renewed)	— Do —
6. Net position	Thursday
7. Settlement and pay-in for members	Friday
8. Special delivery to the Exchange if pay-in does not come from members	Next Monday
9. Pay-out of Members	— Do —
10. Auction, if delivery is insisted by the buyer	Wednesday

(Normal Weekly Settlement System in B.S.E. and N.S.E.)

@ These days will vary from Exchange to Exchange as these are autonomous bodies. But the SEBI has directed all Stock Exchanges to have uniform Settlement Period to facilitate national clearing system.

New Issues Market

The following instruments can be issued in the new issues market:

(1) Equity shares through prospectus or rights issued to existing shareholders.

(2) Preference shares with a fixed dividend either convertible into equity or not.

(3) Debentures of various categories — convertible, fully convertible, partly convertible and non-convertible debentures.

(4) PSU Bonds — taxable or tax-free with fixed interest rates.

Investors should prefer debentures if they are interested in a fixed income. They may go for convertible debentures, if they want to have both fixed income and likely capital appreciation in future. If they are risk taking and aim only at capital gains, then they may invest in equity shares. Of the new issues those of well established existing companies are least risky while those of new companies floated by little known new entrepreneurs are most risky. In choosing the new issues for investment decision, the investor has to read a copy of the prospectus and note the following:

(1) Who are the promoters and their past record.

(2) Products manufactured and demand for those products at home or abroad — the competitors and the share of each in the market.

(3) Availability of inputs, raw-materials and accessories and the dependence on imports.

(4) Project location and its advantages.

(5) Prospects through projected earnings, net profits and dividend paying capacity, waiting period involved etc.

If the new issues belong to a company promoted by well-known Business Groups like Tatas, Birlas etc., they are less risky. The company should belong to an industry which is expanding and has good potential like drugs, chemicals, steel etc. The terms of offer should be attractive like conversion or immediate prospects of dividend etc.

Stock Market

As far as the stock market is concerned, investment in shares is most risky as the likelihood of fall or rise in prices is uncertain. But the returns may also be high commensurate with risk. A host of imponderable factors operate in the stock market and genuine investor has to do the following things:

(1) Study the Balance Sheet of the company and analyse the prospects of sales and profits.

(2) Analyse the Market Price in terms of book value and profit earning capacity (or P/E ratio) and use them to know whether the share is overvalued or undervalued.

(3) Study the expansion plans or tax savings plans and analyse the company's financial strength, profitability, bonus and dividend paying strength, through the mechanism of financial ratios, networth, etc.

(4) Study whether the management is professional and good and whether their accounting practices are dependable and consistent. The company becomes attractive to buy if the financial ratios support the view that the fundamentals are strong and the shares are worth buying.

(5) Lastly, if the price of the share is undervalued on the basis of the projected earnings for the coming half year or one year and its P/E ratio is below the industry average, then it is worth buying. The same is worth selling if in his judgment it is overvalued. For assessing the undervaluation and over valuation, analyst and his analytical power count for this purpose.

Guidelines for Investors in the Stock Market

1. Never buy on rumours or market gossip.

2. Buy only on the basis of fundamental analysis of companies based on balance sheet data analysis.

3. Buy a diversified list of companies and not put all money in one or two companies. All investments in the stock market are risky. The risk can be reduced by proper diversification of the portfolio into 10 or 15 companies.

4. Study the sales, gross profit, net profit in relation to equity capital employed and attempt a forecast for the coming half year or one year.

5. A declaration of bonus or low P/E ratio, along with strong fundamentals shows that the company should be a good buy.

6. The investor should also watch for low priced shares which are about to turn around for more profitability in future.

7. Investors should buy on declines and follow the principle of contrariness. This means that if everyone is buying a scrip, avoid that scrip but if a scrip is deserted and your study has shown that it has potential for expanding earnings and profitability, then such scrips should be purchased by the investor.

8. Avoid both fear and greed on the Stock Market. If investor is not afraid of the market, he generally studies the market and buys at lows and sells at highs.

9. The investor should know how to analyse the security prices of companies and pick up the undervalued shares. The valuation may be based on the net profits discounted to the present by a proper discount rate or by the book value of share, estimated on the basis of networth of the company.

10. Timing of purchase and sale is also very important. If technical analysis and the use of charts is not familiar to the investor he should follow the principle "buy low and sell high." He should see whether there is a bull market or bear market in a share by a study of the share price over a period of 15 to 30 days. In a bull phase, one can sell at one of the peaks and in a bear phase one can buy at one of troughs. If the investor is greedy to wait on to see the maximum peak: then he may be disappointed if the price shows a sudden down trend. Similarly, it is difficult to foresee the lowest price for a scrip for the buy. The investor has to use his discretion.

The investor should not do the following things:

(1) He should not put all his eggs in one basket which means that he should not put all his funds in one or two companies.

(2) Do not go by hearsay or rumours to buy or sell a scrip as that might be a dupe.

(3) Do not speculate involving the buying and selling in the same day or during the same settlement period. A long-term investor gains more than a speculator.

(4) Avoid taking undue risks or beyond the capacity of your networth. That means if capital base is ₹ 2 lakhs, put a stop loss order at ₹ 20,000/- (or $1/8^{th}$ or $1/10^{th}$ of the capital base).

(5) Do not get panicky if the scrips in which you invested go down in price. Once the investment is made after a study of fundamentals, a temporary fall in its price should not cause worry.

(6) Do not be too greedy or ambitious. Put limits to your operations and buy and sell orders in a price range and your minimum profit limit is 20%.

Margin Payment and Who Should Pay It?

The stock Exchange authorities impose margins on brokers and scripwise and the investor has to pay these margins to the broker who in turn deposits with the Exchange. This is non-interest bearing deposit to discourage speculation.

Margins imposed on a daily basis by authorities are of various categories:

1. Scripwise Margins: On the basis of price fluctuations in individual scrips, imposed daily on purchases and sales.

2. Turnover Margins: On the basis of total trade or turnover of brokers on a daily basis or settlement basis.

3. Adhoc Margins: On the basis of overtrading in any scrip by broker.

4. Carry Forward Margins: for scrips with badla facility on the basis of value of overbought or oversold position carried to the next settlement.

SEBI has asked the Stock Exchanges to impose special volatility margins from time to time on selected scrips. The margins are based on scrip prices marked to the market, and these are controlled by the SEBI directives.

Pay-in and Pay-out Days for the Stock Market

The investor has to bear in mind that he has to give specific orders of buy or sell within limits or at market rates. He should insist on confirmation notes or contract notes to be passed on the same day or on the next day after execution of orders. He should also note to take proper receipts for any cash or securities delivered to the broker. The usual practice is that here is a trading cycle of 5 days and after the last day of trading is over, there will be a day fixed to report "no deliveries" which are contracts to be renewed for the next settlement. After that, a Pay-in day is fixed by the Exchange on which all buyers have to give the cheques. After a day or two later, a Pay-out day is fixed by the exchange on which the buyers receive the shares and sellers will receive the cheque. Thus, sellers should deliver the shares first and receive the money later. If there are any disputes between the member broker and investor, the matter should be referred to the Stock Exchange authorities for arbitration or the investor should make a complaint in writing to the Investor Grievance cell of the Exchange for redressal.

PERSONAL INCOME TAXATION

In so far as securities markets and investments are concerned, the investor should be familiar with the prevailing tax system, so as to take advantage of them.

All individual income along with other eligible incomes from Mutual Funds, UTI, bank deposits etc., enjoy a tax rebate upto an income of ₹ 12,000 per annum under Section 80L. In the latest Budget, this rebate is available upto ₹ 9,000 and a separate limit of ₹ 3,000 is available for government securities and infrastructure bonds. For interest income and dividend income beyond ₹ 2,500 per annum, there is a tax deduction at source at 10% for interest income and 20% for dividend income; (tax on dividend income with investors withdrawn in 1997-98).

The following investments qualify for tax rebate:

"National saving certificates, PPF and PF, Pension Fund, P.O. Deposits, Bank deposits, Insurance, repayment of housing loans upto ₹ 10,000 per annum, contribution to equity linked scheme of mutual funds and UTI, upto ₹ 10,000 P.A. and investment upto ₹ 60,000 revised to ₹ 70,000) an any of the above categories of investment inclusive of ₹ 10,000 on equity linked schemes will enable a rebate of 20% — a total maximum rebate of ₹ 12,000 per annum." Dividend income from companies is completely tax free in the hands of investors, from 1997-98 under Section 88 of I.T. Act; investment in eligible investment like PF, NSS, LIC etc., entitled to 20% rebate; Investments in infrastructure bonds are also included in the above categories of eligible investments under Section 88.

There is no wealth tax on any investments in shares, debentures and other securities of a productive nature. Capital gains tax is at a concessional rate of 20% for long-term gains, which is reduced to 10% in 1999-2000, if the concerned securities are held for more than 12 months. There is a TDS for bank interest income beyond ₹ 5,000 at a rate of 10% and for mutual fund income beyond ₹ 10,000 at 15%. The computation of long term capital gains is based on indexing for inflation with base 1981-82 = 100 and index for each year announced by the Government and with 351 for 1998-99 used for adjusting the cost of acquisition. From April 1999, dividend income declared by Mutual Funds is also tax free in the hands of investors, if the schemes are equity oriented.

Dividends paid by companies are taxable at 20% from 2000-01. Similarly, tax payable by M.Fs and UTI on debt oriented schemes is raised from 10 to 20% from April 2000.

In the latest Budget, the debt-oriented mutual funds can invest abroad. The income distributed by them is not taxable in the hands of investors but, payable by companies and M.Fs. The service tax on brokerage income continues to be paid by brokers, who in turn collect it from customers. The tax deduction under Section 88 for investment in approved securities upto ₹ 80,000 with a rebate of 20%. Some provisions are more of a disincentive nature rather than a boost to the market. The market boost is provided by freer flow of FII and NRI funds and removal of investment limit of 24% to the FII in any company.

So far we have set out the personal tax provisions relevant to investment and portfolio management, as tax planning is an important part of the construction and revision of the portfolios. The tax provisions have been changing from year to year and latest position should be found from the latest Central Budget.

The existing tax rebates on the many savings media have been revoked and the sections 88 and 80L relating to these exemptions have been replaced by a new section 80C, granting one consolidated exemption of investment upto ₹ one lakh. (Section 80C of the I.T. Act) for those instruments which are specified in that section. Some of these are for example, insurance payments, NSC of post offices, equity linked savings schemes, Five year time deposits with banks etc.

Some exemptions which are not available are on P.O. monthly Income scheme on which the bonus was removed, and Senior citizens savings scheme being made taxable along with all interest income from banks. Debt-oriented mutual fund schemes are subject to income distribution tax, although the open ended and close ended equity oriented schemes are exempt from this. Investment in foreign equity funds and in foreign company shares under certain conditions are permitted to M.Fs.

Long-term capital gains tax was nil and short-term capital gains tax was made lower at 10% for investments in stocks and shares as in 2005-06. But since 2004-05, there was a Securities Transactions Tax (STT) on all purchases and sales in the stock market affecting all types of trading on the market. This tax rate was however nominal and was not expected to affect the volume of trade but it was raised by 25% in 2006-07. The TDS on many items of income and service tax on a wide range of services provided by Financial intermediaries, brokers, FIs and banks etc. are now applicable with the result that the burden imposed on the savers-investors using the services of banks and of the stock markets would be higher. Despite all this, the boom conditions on the stock and commodity markets continued to flourish during the years 2004 to 2008. After recession during 2009 and 2010 the share price index picked up to 18,605 in 2010-11 and then hovered around 16,000 to 18,000 during 2011-12. It stood at an average of 27,500 at end Dec. 2014, in a phase of indecision and stagnation.

Although the gifts tax was abolished, the savers/investors continue to pay wealth tax on any assets beyond ₹ 15 lakhs, if they are not shares and debentures of corporates, which are exempt from wealth tax.

As tax provisions change from year to year, depending on the changes made in the Central Budget, there is need for readers to update the tax provisions, relating to savings and investments.

3 RISK AND RETURN — CONCEPTS AND ANALYSIS

Investors have different motives for investing. Leaving aside a few who love the power and prestige of holding a major share or a minor share in a company, the majority of the investors have one of the following motives or a combination of them:

(a) Regular income either in the form of dividend or interest.

(b) Capital gains or capital appreciation.

(c) Hedge against inflation, a positive real rate of return.

(d) Safety of funds and regularity of payment of interest and principal.

(e) Liquidity and marketability in the sense that investor can convert his investments into cash or liquidity and back again into investments when cash is not needed.

Security Analysis involves an examination of expected return and accompanying risks. The first three motives of income, capital appreciation and a positive hedge against inflation refer to the expected return. The last two motives of investor lead to the risks involved in the investments. These risks are due to uncertainty of returns, regularity of returns, safety of funds, marketability or lack of it, etc.

Investors generally desire to have the maximum return possible, as they like returns, but they dislike the risk, and the extent of risk aversion varies from investor to investor. But the return depends on the extent of risk that the investor takes. The return composes of a riskless return (normally paid on a Treasury Bill or a bank deposit) plus a risk premium depending on the risk taken by the investor.

Investments are made based on security analysis and decisions involved are what securities to be brought or sold and the extent or proportion of funds to be invested in each.

COMPONENTS OF RETURN

Return is measured by taking the income plus the price change. Income is either dividend or interest and price change of the security is the capital gain or loss. The term yield is also used in respect of the fixed income securities. Thus, we buy a 12.5% Central Government bond for ₹ 95. The coupon rate is 12.5 per annum and face value is ₹ 100 but purchased for ₹ 95. Then the investor gets ₹ 12.5 by holding the bond for one year on an investment of ₹ 95. Then the yield (also called current yield) works out to 12.5/95 = 13.15%.

The expected return may differ from the realised return and the variation in return is again a risk element.

Thus, to generalise the return measurement as applicable to both variable dividend security and fixed income security, we have

$$\text{Total return} = \frac{\text{Income received} + \text{Price change}}{\text{Purchase price of asset}}$$

This return should refer to a period of time, say a year and price change is the difference between the price at the end and price at the beginning of the period. The income may be nil and price change can be both positive and negative or both can be positive and herein again lies the risk element.

Calculation of Average Returns

There are two generally used methods of calculating the average return namely the Arithmetic Average and Geometric Average. The statistical compilation of each of them is as follows:

Arithmetic Average is

$$x = \frac{\sum x}{n}$$

where x is the Arithmetic average

$\sum x$ is the summation of returns over the given member of years, namely, 'n.'

Geometric average is

$$G = [(1 + R_1)\ (1 + R_2)\ \ldots\ (1 + R_n)]^{1/n} - 1]$$

R = total return and R_1, R_2... R_n are the returns for different periods

n is the number of periods.

It is the nth root of the product resulting from multiplying a series of returns together.

R is the return and (1 + R) is the return relative. If the return is 15% or 0.15 and the return relative is 1 + 0.15 = 1.15 is the total return received at the end of the period from Re. 1, invested in the beginning. Thus, the geometric return measures the compound cumulative returns over time. Both averages have their own uses and significance.

The measurement of return on any security is generally done on the basic level of the market return, which is based on an approved index, such as B.S.E. sensitive series (of 30 scrips), Base 1978-79 = 100, which is most popularly used in India. The market return is the appreciation of the market B.S.E. sensex number, reflecting the movements in price of the most widely traded 30 scrips on the B.S.E. over any period of time. As in the U.S.A., the Standard and Poor 500 Stock index is used as the datum line for comparing the returns of the market with the individual returns, in India, investors use the B.S.E. sensex or the B.S.E. National Index of 100 scrips. The price changes measure the capital appreciation and depreciation (gains or losses) and these changes have to be taken along with the dividend income on the securities to get the total returns to compare the expected with the actuals.

RISK ELEMENTS

The components of risk are broadly two:

1. *Systematic Risk,* which refers to that portion of the total variability of the return caused by common factors affecting the prices of all securities alike through economic, political and social factors.

2. *Unsystematic Risk,* which refers to that portion of the total variability of the return caused due to unique factors, relating to that firm or industry, through such factors as management failure, labour strikes, raw material scarcity etc.

Examples of Systematic Risk

(1) Market Risk — changes in market conditions.

(2) Interest Rate Risk — changes in interest rates.

(3) Purchasing power or inflation risk.

(4) Trade cycles or Business conditions or Monsoons for agriculturally based economies like India.

Examples of Unsystematic Risk

(1) Business Risk relating to the Industries.

(2) Financial Risk due to heavy interest burden or inefficient capital management.

(3) Management Risk due to poor efficiency, faulty planning.

(4) Labour and other input risks of the company.

While the systematic risk is common to all companies and has to be borne by the investor and compensated by the Risk Premium, the unsystematic Risk can be reduced by the investor through proper diversification and planning a proper investment strategy for the purpose. The former is uncontrollable while the latter is controllable by the company concerned and the investor.

Risk Concept

All investments are risky, whether in stock and capital market or banking and financial sector, real estate, bullion, gold, etc. The degree of risk however varies on the basis of the features of the assets, investment instrument, the mode of investment, or the issuer of the security etc. Even the so called riskless assets like bank deposits carry some cost and time in realisation of proceeds or in conversion into cash.

Risk and Uncertainty

Risk and uncertainty go together. Risk suggests that the decision-maker knows that there is some possible consequence of an investment decision, but uncertainty involves a situation, where the outcome is not known to the decision-maker. But basically, whether the outcome is known or not, the investments involve both risk and uncertainty. For our discussion, the word "Risk" is used to comprise all elements of variability of return, uncertainty of the outcome, etc.

Some risks can be controlled by the investors and some by the issuers of securities by planning. Others cannot be so controlled and they are to be borne compulsorily by the Investor.

What Causes the Risks?

These Risks are caused by the following factors:

(1) Wrong decision of what to invest in.

(2) Wrong timing of investments.

(3) Nature of the instruments invested say, the category of assets like corporate shares or bonds, Chit funds, Nidhis, Benefit funds etc., are highly risky, as they are in the unorganised sector. Some instruments as bank deposits or P.O. Certificates are less risky, due to their certainty of payment of principal and interest.

(4) *Creditworthiness of the Issuer:* The securities of Government and semi-Government bodies are more creditworthy than those issued by the corporate sector and much less secure are those in the unorganised sector like indigenous bankers, shroffs, chit funds, etc. Private limited companies shares and shares of unlisted companies are more risky.

(5) *Maturity Period or the Length of Investment:* The longer the period, the more risky is the investment normally.

(6) *Amount of Investment:* The higher the amount invested in any security the larger is the risk, while a judicious mix of investments in small quantities may be less risky.

(7) Method of investment, namely, secured by collateral or not.

(8) Terms of lending such as periodicity of servicing, redemption periods, etc.

(9) Nature of the industry or business in which the company is operating.

(10) National and international factors, acts of god, etc.

SYSTEMATIC AND UNSYSTEMATIC RISKS

Reference was made to two types of Risk of investor:

*1. **Systematic Risks*** are out of external and uncontrollable factors, arising out of the market, nature of the industry and the state of the economy and a host of other factors.

*2. **Unsystematic Risks*** emerge out of the known and controllable factors, internal to the issuer of the securities or companies.

Examples of Systematic Risks

(i) Market Risk: This arises out of changes in Demand and Supply pressures in the markets, following the changing flow of information or expectations. The totality of investor perception and subjective factors influence the events in the Market which are unpredictable and give rise to risk, which is not controllable.

(ii) Interest Rate Risk: The return on an investment depends on the interest rate promised on it and changes in market rates of interest from time to time. The cost of funds borrowed by companies or stockbrokers depend on interest rates. The market activity and investor perceptions change with the changes in interest rates. These interest rates depend on nature of instruments, stocks, bonds, loans etc., maturity of the periods and the creditworthiness of the issuer of securities. But basically the monetary and credit policy which is not controllable by the investor affects the riskiness of investments due to their effects on returns, expectations, and the total principal amount due to be refunded.

(iii) Purchasing Power Risk: Inflation or rise in prices lead to rise in costs of production, lower margins, wage rises and profit sqeezing etc. The return expected by investors will change due to change in real value of returns. Cost push inflation is caused by rise in the costs, due to wage rise or rise in input prices. Demand pull forces operate to increase prices due to inadequate supplies and rising demand. The increase in demand may be caused by changing expectation of future interest rates and inflation or due to increase in money supply or creation of currency to finance the deficits of the government. This element of purchasing power risk is inherent in all investments and cannot be controlled by him.

Examples of Unsystematic Risks

(i) Business Risk: This relates to the variability of the business, sales, income, profits etc., which in turn depend on the market conditions for the product mix, input supplies, strength of competitors, etc. This business risk is sometimes external to the company due to changes in government policy or strategies of competitors or unforeseen market conditions. They may be internal due to fall in production, labour problems, raw material problems or inadequate supply of electricity etc. The Internal Business Risk leads to fall in revenues and in profit of the company, but can be corrected by certain changes in the company's policies.

(ii) Financial Risk: This relates to the method of financing, adopted by the company, high leverage leading to larger debt servicing problems or short-term liquidity problems due to bad debts, delayed receivables and fall in current assets or rise in current liabilities. These problems could be solved, but they may lead to fluctuations in earnings, profits and dividends to shareholders. Sometimes, if the company runs into losses or reduced profits, these may lead to fall in returns to investors or negative returns. Proper financial planning and other financial adjustments can be used to correct this risk and as such it is controllable.

(iii) Default or Insolvency Risk: The borrower or issuer of securities may become insolvent or may default, or delay the payments due, such as interest instalments or principal repayments. The borrower's credit rating might have fallen suddenly and he became default prone and in its extreme form it may lead to insolvency or bankruptcies. In such cases, the investor may get no return or negative returns. An investment in a healthy company's share might turn out to be a waste paper, if within a short span, by the deliberate mistakes of Management or acts of God, the Company became sick and its share price tumbled below its face value.

Other Risks

In addition to the above major risks, both in controllable and uncontrollable categories, there are many more risks, which can be listed, but in actual practice, they may vary in form, size and effect.

Some of such identifiable risks are the *Political Risks,* following the changes in the government, or its policy shown in fiscal or budgetary aspects, etc., through changes in tax rates, imposition of controls or administrative regulations etc.; *Management Risks*, due to errors or inefficiencies of management, causing losses to the company; *Marketability Risks* involving loss of liquidity or loss of value in conversions from one asset to another say, from stocks to bonds, or *vice versa*. Such risks may arise due to some features of securities, such as callability; or lack of sinking fund or Debenture Redemption Reserve fund, for repayment of principal or due to conversion terms, attached to the security, which may go adverse to the investor.

All the above types of risks are of varying degrees, resulting in uncertainty or variability of return, loss of income, and capital losses, or erosion of real value of income and wealth of the investor. Normally the higher the risk taken, the higher is the return. But sometimes the risk is caused by Acts of God and there may be no return at all.

PRECISE MEASURES OF RISK

Risk is measured by the variability of returns. The assignment of probabilities and the calculation of expected values of return are methods of taking into account the risk. But this method does not provide the decision-maker with a concrete value, indicative of the variability and therefore of risk.

The standard deviation and variance are measures of dispersion of the observations from the mean. The standard deviation is an asbolute measure, which can be applied when the mean is the same. But the coefficient of variation is the relative measure of the degree of uncertainty.

Standard deviation is defined as the square root of the mean of the squared deviations, where deviation is measured by the difference between the outcome and the expected mean value of all values.

Where C_f is cash flow and C_f is the mean of those cash flows and p is the probability of its occurence and 'n' is number of periods, the equation is

$$\alpha = \sqrt{\sum_{i=1}^{n} p_i (C_{f_1} - \bar{C}_f)^2}$$

Example

C_{f_i}	$\bar{C}_f$	$(C_f i - \bar{C}_f)$	pi	$(C_f i - \bar{C}_f)^2$ pi
C_{f_1} 10	20	−10	0.25	25
C_{f_2} 20	20	0	0.50	0
C_{f_3} 30	20	+10	0.25	25
				Variation = σ^2 =50

Standard deviation = $\sigma = \sqrt{50} = 7.07$

Coefficient of Variation

The standard deviation is misleading when comparison is to be made of two series or two projects or portfolios, if they differ in size and mean. The coefficient of variation (v) is the correct technique in such cases.

v_t is set out in the following equation.

$$v_t = \frac{\sigma}{C_f} = \frac{\text{Standard deviation}}{\text{Expected cash flow}}$$

where, C_f is the Mean of expected flows.

The higher the coefficient of variation, the more risky is the project or portfolio. In a similar vein, the conclusion comes to be the same even if we use the standard deviation. But the improvement of v is that it adjusts to the size of cash flows. Certainly, equivalents can be used to weight the cash flows or expected returns. These certainty equivalents are synonyms for the probabilities used earlier.

RISKS AND RETURNS

Investment Decision Making

Investment decision is vital for Portfolio Management.

What to Buy and Sell are the first decisions to be made and at what price? The decision to buy or sell depends on the expectations or estimations of the fair intrinsic value of the shares, overvaluation/undervaluation of the share and a number of other factors.

The objectives of investors are income, capital appreciation, liquidity, marketability, safety and hedge against inflation which are to be satified. Alternative Investment Avenues with Risk-Return relationship are set out here, in Fig. 3.1.

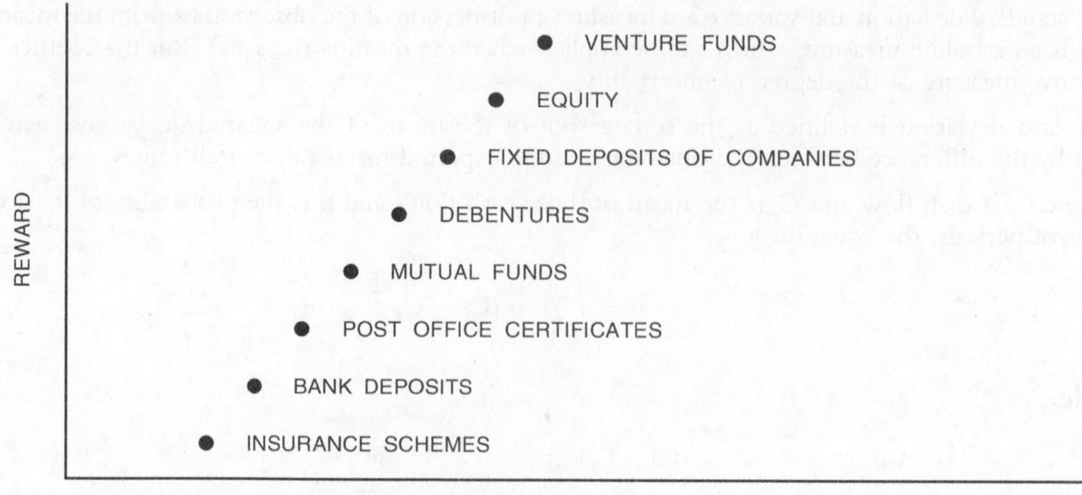

Fig. 3.1

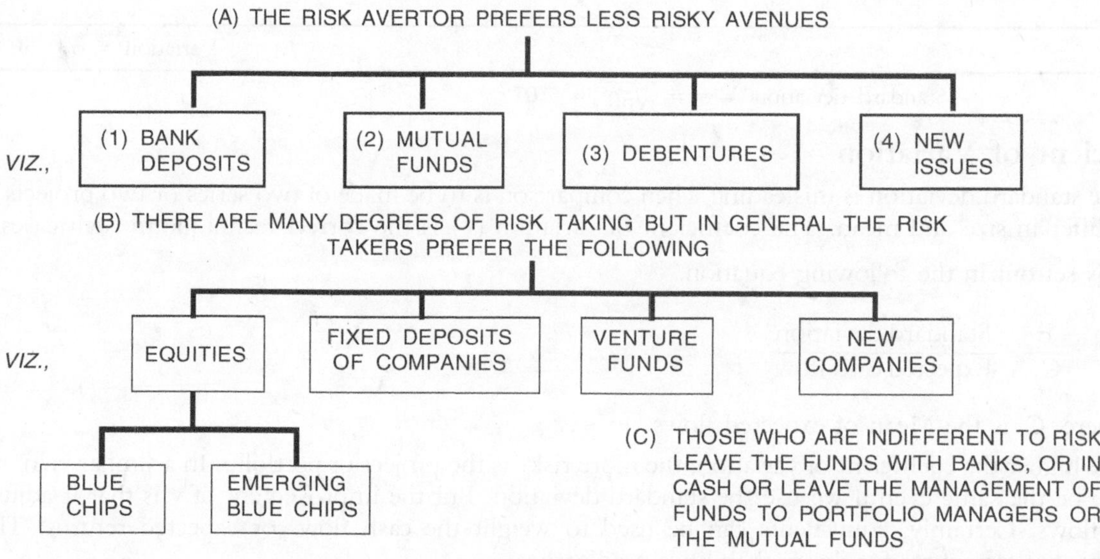

Fig. 3.2

Risk Measurement

Total Risk of any investment is total variance or volatility of returns on that investment. This can be represented by spread or range of variations or fluctuation, creating uncertainty of the return and its amount. Range is the spread or breath of variations. The concepts of variance, standard deviation, covariance and beta coefficients etc., are also used to explain the measure of risk. In the context of portfolio of assets, or investment in any assets risk is inherent in all such dealings. This risk primarily arises first out of parting of your funds or loss of liquidity. Money lent or parted is always having an element of risk. This element is the same as the concept of total risk.

Some investments in bank deposits and post office deposits or certificates or insurance, PF, etc. are less risky, but they are also not devoid of any risk. Risk may take the form of loss of time, cost involved in realisation of cash or theft of certificates etc. These are very elementary forms of risk, attached to any investment.

Range of Variation

One measure of risk is the variability or range of variability of return. If the returns for example fluctuate from zero to 20%, it is a high risk investment, which might arise due to wrong choice of companies or securities invested in. The default prone bonds, or equity shares of some sick or sick prone companies may show such a wide range of fluctuation in returns. Generally, equity investments are subject to such variability of returns, within a wide range and hence called most risky investments. The range is a relative term and can be expressed as a percentage change. Risk return assessment can be made by the investor, using CAPM.

CAPITAL ASSET PRICING MODEL (CAPM)

CAPM uses the concept of Beta to link risk with return. Using CAPM, investors can assess the risk return trade off involved in any investment decision.

Beta is a measure of non-diversifiable risk (Systematic Risk). It shows how the price of a security responds to changes in market prices. The equation for calculation of Beta is

$R_i = a + \beta_i R_m$

R_i = estimated return on i stock

a = expected return when market return is zero

β_i = Beta measuring stock's sensitivity to the market index

R_m = return on market index

Using the Beta concept, the capital asset Pricing Model will help to define the required return on a security. Normally the higher is the risk we take, the higher should be the return, as otherwise we avoid risk. So, the higher the β, the higher should be the return. The equation for CAPM is

$R_i = R_f + \beta_1 (R_m - R_f)$

R_i is the required return

R_f is the risk free return

R_m is the average market return

β_i is the measure of systematic risk which is non-diversifiable.

Risk free return is say 12% as the Treasury Bill rate or Bank rate and market return is expected to vary with the β chosen. Let us take β as 1.2 and expected market return is 18%, then the return on the stock *i* is as follows:

$$R_i = 12\% + 1.2\ (0.18 - 0.12)$$
$$= 0.12 + 1.2\ (0.06) = 0.192 \text{ or}$$
$$= 19.2\%$$

If the investor is risk taking type and chooses a Beta of 1.8, then the expected return will be higher as shown below.

$$R_i = 0.12 + 1.8\ (0.18 - 0.12)$$
$$= 0.12 + 1.8\ (0.06) = 0.228 \text{ or}$$
$$= 22.8\%$$

SECURITY MARKET LINE (SML)

When the Capital Asset Pricing Model is drawn graphically, we get the S.M.L., which is shown in the chart below. If the investor wants to decide on an investment with an expected return he would know the level of risk he has to take or alternatively given the level of risk, he has preferred to take, he would know the expected return from this chart. The investor has to assess whether it is worth taking a level of risk, if he has a target return which involves that risk, as he is assumed to be generally risk averse. Thus, CAPM and SML help the investor in evaluating risk for a return, in making any investment decision. The principle of the higher the risk, the higher is the return is embodied in this Model.

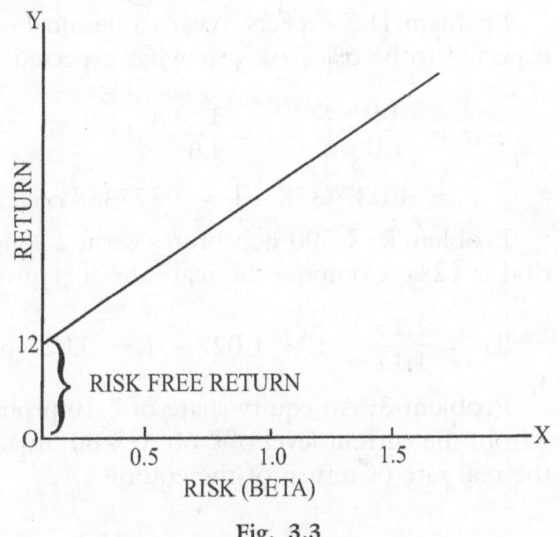

Fig. 3.3

Concept of Portfolio Models

Risks in relation to portfolios are also to be understood in the present discussion. Therefore, the concept of Risk in two Major Models used in valuation is related to systematic, unsystematic and total risk. The two models are those of Markowitz and Sharpe which go by the name of Modern Portfolio Theory.

PROBLEMS

Question: Torrent and company estimates the probability and the expected returns as returns for the five observations as follows:

Probability:	0.1	0.2	0.4	0.2	0.1
Possible return:	–10%	5%	20%	35%	50%

(a) What are the expected values of return and standard deviation?

Ans: Expected return Equation is

$$R = \sum_{i=1}^{t} R_i P_i$$

$$R = .10 \times 0.1 + 0.05 \times 0.2 + 0.2 \times 0.4 + 0.35 \times 0.2 + 0.5 \times 0.1$$

$$= 0.01 + 0.01 + 0.08 + 0.07 + 0.05 = 0.22 \text{ or}$$

$$= 22\%$$

$$\sigma = \sqrt{\sum_{i=1}^{n} (R_i - \bar{R})^2 P_i}$$

Where, R = 22 from the above

$$= [(-.10 - .22)^2 \times 0.1 + (0.05 - .22)^2 \times 0.2 + (.20 - .22)^2 \times 0.4 + (.35 - .22)^2 \times 0.2 + (.50 - .22)^2 \times 0.1$$

$$= .01024 + .00578 + .00016 + .00338 + .00784 = .0274$$

$$\sigma = \sqrt{0.0274} = 0.1655 = 16.55\%$$

Purchasing Power Risks

When inflation takes place, financial assets such as cash, stocks and bonds may lose their ability to command the same amount of real goods and services which they had in the past.

$$rr = \frac{1.0 + r}{1.0 + q} - 1$$

rr = Real Rate of Return

r = nominal rate of return

q = equals the rate of inflation

Problem 1: X expects to earn a nominal rate of 10% return on his investments next year. If the rate of inflation is expected to be 6% next year what expected real rate of return will he earn?

$$rr = \frac{1.0 + r}{1.0 + q} - 1 = \frac{1.10}{1.06} - 1$$

$$= 1.0377358 - 1 = .0377358 \text{ or } 3.77\%.$$

Problem 2: ₹ 500 debentures earns a coupon rate of 15% p.a. Inflation rate expected in the covering one-year period is 12%. Compute the real rate of return?

$$Rt = \frac{1.15}{1.12} - 1 = 1.027 - 1 = 0.027 \text{ or } 2.7\%$$

Problem 3: An equity share of ₹ 10 promises a dividend of 20% and it is expected that the price of the share rise from the current level of ₹ 60 to ₹ 80 in a years time. Inflation during the next year is estimated at 14%. What is the real rate of return of the equity?

$$\text{Nominal rate} = \frac{₹\,80 - ₹\,60 + 2.0}{₹\,60} = 36.7\%$$

$$\text{Real rate of return} = \frac{1+.367}{1+.14} - 1 = \frac{1.367}{1.14} - 1$$

$$= 1.199 - 1 = .199$$

or 19.9%

Risk and Return

Problem 4: From the following

	State of Economy				
	Boom	*Normal*	*Recession*		
Security Return %	*Probability* 0.2	0.6	0.2	X	Y
x	30	20	10	20	
y	10	20	30		20

Compute expected return and standard deviation of return if all funds are invested:

(a) One in security x or in security y.

(b) If funds are invested in the portfolio of securities x and y. (*i*) in equal proportion or (*ii*) in the proportion of 60% in x and 40% in y.

Ans:

(a) Investment in security x alone

$$R\bar{x} = (30 \times 0.2) + (20 \times 0.6) + (10 \times 0.2)$$

$$= 6 + 12 + 2 = 20\%$$

Standard deviation of return SD(x)

$$SD(x) = \sqrt{0.2\,(30-20)^2 + .6\,(20-20)^2 + 0.2\,(10-20)^2]}$$

$$= \sqrt{(0.2 \times 100 + 0.2 \times 100)}$$

$$= \sqrt{40} = 6.32$$

Investment in security Y alone

$$\bar{R}_y = (0.2 \times 10) + (.6 \times 20) + (.2 \times 30)$$

$$= 2 + 12 + 6 = 20\%$$

$$SD(y) = \sqrt{[0.2\,(10-20)^2 + 0.6\,(20-20)^2 + .2\,(30-20)^2\,]}$$

$$= \sqrt{(40)} = 6.32$$

(b) $R_x - R_y = 20\%;\ SD(x) = SD(y) = 6.32$

$$\text{Covariance (xy)} = \Sigma\, Pi\,(R_x - \bar{R}_X)\,(R_y - \bar{R}_y)$$

$$= (0.2 \times 10 \times -10) + (.6 \times 0 \times 0) + .2\ 5 - 10 \times 10)$$

$$= -20 + 0 - 20 = -40$$

(i) When the amount is invested equally in x and y, portfolio return

$$= (0.5 \times 20) + (0.5 \times 20)$$

$$= 20\%.$$

$$\text{Portfolio risk} = [(0.5^2 \times 40 + 0.5^2 \times 40 + 2 \times .5 \times .5 \times (-)40)]$$

$$= 10 + 10 + (-20)$$

$$= 20 - 20 = 0$$

(ii) When the amount invested is 60% in x and 40% in y

Portfolio Risk = $[(0.6^2 \times 40) + (0.4^2 \times 40) + (2 \times .6 \times .4 \times -40)]$

= $14.4 + 6.4 - 19.2$

= 1.60

Conclusion from the above results:

Correlation between securities X and Y

$$= \frac{Cov(R_x R_y)}{SD(R_x)SD(R_y)} = \frac{-40}{\sqrt{40} \times \sqrt{40}} = -1$$

i.e., perfectly negatively cerrelated.

Investment equally in X and Y will reduce the risk to zero.

Question: Given the data on returns of Modis and the returns on BSE index for a five year period, calcualte the Beta and Alpha

Year	*Modis*	*Market Index*
1	0.2	0.1
2	0.4	0.2
3	0.6	0.3
4	0.8	0.4
5	0.8	0.5

Use Formula for Beta

and

Formula for Alpha

$$\text{Beta formula} = \frac{\sum_{i-1}^{n} (R_{ij} - \bar{R}_{ij})(R_{mt} - \bar{R}_{mt})}{\sum_{t=1}^{n} (R_{mt} - \bar{R}_{mt})^2}$$

Alpha estimate = $\alpha_1 = \bar{R}_{1t} - \beta \bar{R}_{mt}$

Using the vlaue of Beta got above, estimate the value of Alpha.

4

ECONOMIC ANALYSIS

Economic factors play a major role in any investment decision which is formulated for making a gain and better returns. Economic Analysis and forecasting company Performance and of returns is necessary for making investments.

Any investment is risky and as such investment decision is difficult to make. Investment decision is based on availability of money and information on the economy, industry and company and on the share prices ruling and expectations of the market and of the companies in question as also on the market sentiment.

INVESTMENT DECISION

In the Stock Market parlance, investment decision refers to making a decision regarding the buy and sell orders. As referred to already, these decisions are influenced by availability of money and flow of information. What to buy and sell will also depend on the fair value of a share and the extent of overvaluation and undervaluation. For making such a decision the common investors may have to depend more upon a study of fundamentals rather than technicals, although technicals are also important. If investment is for short-term and for speculation, technicals are more important. Besides, even genuine investors have to guard themselves against wrong timing regarding both buy and sell decisions. Otherwise they will burn their fingers as happened in 1992 following the Harshad Mehta Scam. For this purpose, a study of company's performance, past record and expected future performance are to be looked into. It is necessary for a common investor to study the Balance Sheet and Annual Report and other financial statements of the company and analyse the half yearly results of the company and decide on whether to buy that company's shares or not. This is called fundamental analysis. The decision of what to buy is easier, and if investors are tuned to making fundamental analysis, then decision making becomes scientific and rational. The likelihood of high risk scenario will come down to a low risk scenario and long-term investors will not lose. They should not depend on hearsay or rumours or on vested interests, but only on fundamentals.

Criteria for Investment Decision

Firstly, investment decision depends on the mood of the market. As per the empirical studies, share prices depend on the fundaments of the company only to the extent of 50% and the rest is decided by the mood of the market and the expectations of the company's performance and its share price. These expectations depend on the analyst's ability to foresee and forecast the future performance of the company. For, price paid for a share at present depends on the flow of returns in future expected from the company.

Secondly, and following from the above, decision to invest will be based on the past performance, present working and the future expectations of the company's performance, both operationally and financially. These in turn will influence the share prices.

Thirdly, investment decision depends on the investor's perception on whether the present share price is fair, overvalued or undervalued. If the share price is fair he will hold it (Hold Decision); if it is overvalued, he will sell it (Sell Decision) and if it is undervalued, he will buy it (Buy Decision). These are general rules, but exceptions may be there. Thus, even when prices are rising, some investors may buy as their expectations of further rise may outweigh his conception of overvaluation. That means, the concepts of overvaluation or undervaluation are relative to time, space and man. What may be overvalued a little while ago has become undervalued following later developments; information or sentiment and mood may change the whole market scenario and of the valuation of shares. There are two more Decisions, namely, Average Up and Average Down of prices.

The investment decision may also depend on the investor's preferences, moods, or fancies. Thus an investor may go on a spending spree and invest in cats and dogs of companies, if he has taken a fancy or he is flooded with money from lottery or prizes. A rational investor would however make investment decisions on scientific study of the fundamentals of the company and in a planned manner.

At present, investors mostly depend on hearsay and advice of friends, relatives, sub-brokers, etc., for the investment decision, but not on any Scientific study of the company's fundamentals. In view of the increasing mushroom growth of companies and lack of any track record of many promoters, investment decision-making became more difficult now. Even otherwise, risk will increase in case of all investments made on hunches, hearsay etc. The major difficulty of individual investors is lack of information, time and cost involved in research on the fundamentals of the company.

Risk and Investment

Stock Market investment is risky and there are different types of investments, namely equity, fixed income bonds, debentures etc. Company specific risk also called unsystematic risk can be reduced by diversifying investments into 10 to 15 companies. But the systematic risk relating to the market cannot be reduced but can be managed by choosing companies with that much risk (high or low) that the investor can bear. For example, some investors can take high risk and they may invest in new ventures, turnaround companies, even when they are incurring losses, and some speculative companies like Reliance and G.E. shipping etc. But risk-averse investors will choose only Blue Chip Companies with a good track record like Colgate, ITC, ICICI, Telco, Hindustan Lever etc. It is therefore necessary for investors to be selective and discrete and analyse the risk along with return for each investment. Some companies are Blue Chips, some are emerging Blue Chips etc., and some are risky ventures. Their evaluation can be done through fundamental analysis of companies, quoted on the Exchanges.

ECONOMIC AND INDUSTRY FACTORS

As per Research studies available so far, nearly 50% of the stock price changes can be attributed to market influences which are general and are caused by the economic and industry factors. It is therefore important that any stock market investment is to be preceded by an economic analysis and industry analysis. The economy and industry are so wide and comprehensive that it is difficult to encompass all the likely factors influencing them to be captured in any set of possible indicators. Major trends in the economy, business conditions, industrial growth and a host of other factors are to be studied and a short-term forecast is to be made of the likely trends in the economy and the industries which are leaders as distinguished from laggards and forecast the likely trends in industrial growth and in particular in the industries, in which the investor is interested in.

As the stock market is supposed to be the window of the economy, the totality of forces including socio-political factors operating on the economy would influence the Stock market. Details of fundamental Analysis are given in a separate Chapter.

In the economy, some industries are expanding while others are stagnant and some contracting, depending on the demand and market conditions. The investor has to choose the growth industry and in that industry, choose the scrips undervalued as judged by his study and analysis.

Investment Objectives

The first basic objective of investment is the return on it or yields. The yields are higher, the higher is the risk taken by investors. The riskless return is the bank deposit rate of 6% at present. Here, the risk is least as funds are safe and returns are certain.

Secondly, each investor has his own asset preferences and choice of investments. Thus, some risk averse operators put their funds in bank or post office deposits or deposits/certificates with co-operatives and PSUs. Some invest in real estate, land and buildings while others invest mostly in gold, silver and other precious stones, diamonds etc.

Thirdly, every investor aims at providing for minimum comforts of a house furniture, vehicles, consumer durables and other household requirements. After satisfying these minimum needs, he plans for his future income, saving in insurance (LIC and GIC etc.), pension and provident funds etc. In the choice of these, the return is subordinated to the needs of the investor and he is risk averse.

Lastly, after satisfying all the needs and requirements, the rest of the savings would be invested in financial assets which will give him future incomes and capital appreciation, so as to improve his future standard of living. These may be in stock/capital market investments.

Cost-Benefit Analysis

In making investments of the last category, namely, in financial assets of deposits, bonds, debentures, shares, etc., investment management involves a cost-benefit analysis.

The major costs are the risk involved and major benefits are the returns involved.

Risk is measured by the variability of the returns. But the risk is of various types — non-payment of dividend/ interest, delay or non-payment of principal, variability of return or market value of investments. These risks may be classified as —

(a) Company Risk
(b) Market Risk
(c) Business Risk
(d) Commodity/Product Risk
(e) Financial Risk
(f) Economy Risk of the Nation
(g) International Factors

Among examples of International factors imports and exports and international prices of inputs of domestic goods, etc., can be cited. Among economy risks, Government Policy, Inflation, Monetary and fiscal policies etc., can be given as examples.

The other risks particularly the risk of business is relative to trade/business of the company, Product, Inputs/ Outputs etc. Interest Rate, Labour Problem, Inflation effect may lead to financial and Market risks. Company risk is unique to the company, about its own management and operations.

There are many other risks such as socio-economic factors, political and commercial problems etc. The costs are the expenses to be incurred in acquiring the assets, say registration, brokerage charges etc. In addition there will be uncertainties and risks, involved due to possible non-payment of interest or dividends or capital losses etc.

There are corresponding benefits to be assessed in terms of regular incomes (interest and dividends) — regularity and certainty of them — capital appreciation, safety and security of funds, marketability and liquidity of investments and a host of other factors. The investor has to assess the costs and benefits of each investment, in the process of Investment Management.

ENVIRONMENTAL CONSIDERATIONS

Many times, investor has to take into account the environmental factors in investment management. His past background, family requirements, the assets of neighbours or of colleagues and other external factors may influence his investments decisions.

People in rural and semi-urban areas are influenced by their immediate environment and access to avenues. The agriculturists invest in ploughs, tractors and other requirements, needed for his occupation and environment. Beyond these, he invests in gold and silver or real estate due to the influence of environment as people are rated by those factors and by the amount of gold and real estate, they hold and possess.

On the other hand, the environment in urban and metropolitan centres is different. The alternatives available to them are more varied. The funds are invested in vehicles, consumer durables, mutual funds, corporate securities and various other instruments. In many semi-urban and urban areas, housing finance companies, finance and investment companies and chit funds attract the public funds with attractive returns and incentives.

Chit Funds and Nidhis

Among the categories of investments popular with semi-urban and rural areas, there are various types of deposits kept with non-bank finance companies like hire-purchase, investment and finance companies, housing finance companies, mutual benefit funds, chit funds and nidhis. These are mostly governed by State Acts and partly controlled by the RBI in respect of their deposit raising activities.

Chit funds are of various categories, prize chits, normal and conventional chits, lottery chits, etc. They collect regularly the savings of investors on a monthly basis and lend, if necessary to members and give a lump sum money once in a year depending in the results of lottery or any other mechanism.

Mutual benefit funds and nidhis are also saving mobilisation agencies, for the benefit of members, who are saving households. These are normally registered as trusts or friendly societies and operate in mobilisation of savings and lending for the benefit of members. So long as the promoters are honest and dependable, the funds are safe and members benefit from these activities. But there are many reports, about unscrupulous elements among these promoters, fly-by-night operators who collect the funds and misuse them for trading and speculation or disappear from the scene after working for sometime. Although there are laws and rules to regulate them, the subject being a state subject, the regulation and control on them is lax and hence funds may not always be safe.

Investors have to weigh the pros and cons of making investments in such agencies. Similarly, all deposits with companies private limited or public limited are unsecured debt and hence the investors should be careful in taking this risk of investment in deposits in the chits, nidhis and even companies.

TAX PLANNING IN INVESTMENT MANAGEMENT

As investment management aims at the highest return possible, reduction in tax liability can increase returns. Tax planning is done to reduce tax liability by proper investment strategy. The elements of tax planning are as follows:

Income Tax: Interest income and dividend income upto ₹ 2,500 is not subject to tax deduction at sources. Income from dividends and Mutual funds schemes, bank deposits etc., is exempt from tax upto a limit. Dividends declared by companies are exempt from income tax in the hands of investors under Section 88 of Income Tax Act which was widened to encompass the contributions to N.S.S., P.F. etc., to be eligible for tax exemption. In 2002-03, Section 88 of I.T. Act was diluted and dividends of companies and incomes distributed by M.F.s are taxable in the hands of investors. But this was changed later on. In 2005-06, Sections 88 and 80L were replaced by Section 80C, giving a total exemption upto ₹ one lakh for approved categories of investment like insurance, NSCs, bank time deposits beyond 5 years etc.

Wealth Tax: Investment in shares and debentures are totally exempt from wealth tax without limit. The other investments in real estate, gold, housing, cars etc., are subject to wealth tax beyond ₹ 15 lakhs with some exemptions for specific purposes.

TDS: The current rate of tax deduction at source is 10% for interest income and 20% for dividend income (not of companies). Mutual funds and banks are exempt from making tax deduction at source for such income payments, but since July 1995, TDS is enforced on them also.[1]

Investments in approved Securities or P.O. certificates, are exempt from income tax, if it is upto ₹ 60,000 and the rebate is upto 20% of investment. Under Section 80L of IT Act, some P.O. certificate and bank deposit income was tax exempt upto a limit. In approved mutual fund equity linked schemes, investment upto ₹ 10,000, enjoys a rebate upto ₹ 2,000 in income tax payable for the year. This exemption or rebate for investment upto ₹ 10,000 is within the above limit of ₹ 60,000 under Section 88 of IT Act, which was raised to ₹ 70,000 by inclusion of another ₹ 10,000 p.a. for contribution to the pension scheme of LIC/GIC, and infrastructure Bonds in the Budget for 1996-97. The rebate of 20% under this Section was reduced to 10%-15% in 2002-03.

Capital Gains Tax: Long-term capital gains are taxable at 20% for individuals and 30% for corporate Units which was lowered to 20% in 1996-97 Budget. Short-term capital gains are taxable at the same rates as applicable to individual income tax payers and corporate tax payers. Long-term capital gains are those realised after 12 months in the case of shares, UTI and Mutual Fund schemes. But they should be held for more than 36 months to be considered long-term capital gains in the case of other assets like real estate etc. Since 2005-06, long-term capital gains are tax exempt, while short-term capital gains are taxed at 10%.

Gift Tax: Gifts made by NRIs to resident relatives and friends are completely exempt from gift tax. Gifts made by residents to other residents are exempt up to a limit of ₹ 30,000 p.a. Exemption limits of gifts on marriage of dependent relatives are raised from ₹ 30,000 to ₹ one lakh in the Budget for 1994-95. Gifts are treated as income in the hands of donee and taxed at normal income tax rates from 1998-99. The Gift Tax was completely abolished later in 1999.

[1] Mutual funds have to deduct tax at source for income above ₹ 10,000 p.a., at a rate of 15% for individuals and 20% plus surcharge in the case of companies. From April 1999 all dividend incomes from Mutual Funds are tax free in the hands of investors. Debt-oriented Mutual Funds have to pay Divided distributions tax, while open ended and close ended equity Funds are exempt from this since 2005-06 Banks have to collect TDS for interest income beyond ₹ 5,000 p.a. Royalty incomes are like any other income and Tax is deductible at the time of payment.

EXECUTION OF INVESTMENT DECISIONS

If investment is made in corporate securities and having chosen the scrips, to buy or sell, investor gives his orders to the broker. As per the Rules and Byelaws of the exchange, the stock broker and if sub-broker is dealing with clients, the sub-broker should accept orders in the form of entries in their inward Registers. These orders can be oral, written or by Telex or Telephone etc. The broker has to pass the contract note to the client on the same day or next day after the order is executed. If the order is executed by buying or selling on his own account *vis-a-vis* the client, then the consent of the client is necessary and the deal should be put through at the market rate, as if it is done in the Trading Ring.

The sub-broker cannot pass contract notes; but based on the contract note of broker to sub-broker, he can pass the confirmation notes to the client. The client has to check the price noted in the contract note or confirmation note with that as reported in the papers. But some variations are permissible as the broker purchases or sells at one price while market price fluctuates within a range from minute to minute. If the Stock Exchange gives the daily highs and lows and the price charged by the broker falls within that range with some margin for the broker's and sub-broker's commissions then the deal should be considered to be fair. Otherwise complaint can be made with the Exchange.

As per the latest directives of the SEBI, the contract note should show separately the price of the scrip and the brokerage charged. This ensures transparency and the client should insist on this. At present, SEBI registered sub-brokers can also pass contract notes to the clients and investors should deal with them only and insist on contract notes to be passed. From 2005-06, the service tax payable at 5% by broker has to be shown separately.

The client has to pay on or before the pay-in-day if he is a buyer and receive the Certificates on the pay-out-day. If the client is a seller, he should deliver the shares before the pay in or settlement date and receive the money on or after the pay-out-day. These pay-in and pay-out dates are fixed well in advance and the brokers know these dates and the clients should insist on this information, from the brokers and sub-brokers. Every Stock Exchange has a Trading Cycle of 5 days to 15 days for each settlement. The SEBI directed all the Stock Exchanges to have uniform period of 5 days for non-specified securities (B Group). Some Exchanges follow Trading Cycle of 5 days if they have only cash scrips or 'B' group shares and pay-in-day comes after about 10 to 15 days from the first day of trading. After a couple of days from the pay-in-day, the pay-out-day is fixed. Thus, the client has to wait for about 15 to 20 days from the date of transaction to realise the proceeds of his sale or get delivery of shares. This time period was reduced to 5 to 7 days, when electronic trading was started. Some banks lend against shares if investors need funds.

The client has to make a note of these days and insist from the sub-broker or broker for cheques or shares, as the case may be, on the due dates. The awareness of these dates and the amounts due to them will help the clients in their transactions with brokers. Similarly, knowledge of the Rules of the Stock Exchange and practices of brokers will help them to protect their interests. In the event of non-payment of cheque or non-delivery of shares on due dates, clients have to promptly take up with brokers and if they do not respond, complaints have to be made to the Stock Exchange. For making the above investment decisions, economic and industry analysis is necessary.

FORECASTING NEED

Analysis of information is to be used for forecasting the trends in economy and industry. Such forecasts may be for short periods of half year to one year or for medium-term periods of one year to 5 years. For an average investor, short-term forecasts are better as factors influencing them change quite frequently, these forecasts have to be revised. One method commonly used to analyse is the study of survey results on the economy. Forecast of GDP growth rate, inflation rate, interest rates, money supply growth rate, government deficit, food stocks, monsoon expectations, balance of payments deficits, international trade trends, international currency and economic trends, etc., is necessary. In India, the CMIE, Government FICCI and Industry Associations, C.S.O. RBI etc., publish from time-to-time these data. Government's Economic Survey and planning Commission reports are also a source for forecasting the economy and industry trends. Forecasts of many Industry Associations throw light on the trends of various industries. These are next best alternatives to a full-fledged research wing and elaborate studies. The Economic Survey before the Budget presentation and the Budget contain this information. The RBI also publishes this data on the economy in its various publications

SOURCES OF INVESTMENT INFORMATION

The Securities market is a perfect auction market where demand/supply pressures determine the price. These demand/supply pressures depend upon the available money and the flow of information. It is in this context that sources of information become relevant. Besides the market analysis and estimate of the intrinsic value around which the market price revolves, we also need an analysis of the flow of information.

Types of Information

The types of information, which are relevant for our purposes are of the following categories:

(i) ***World Affairs:*** International factors, which influence domestic income, output and employment and for investment in the domestic market by FFIs, NRIs, FII and OCBs etc. Also foreign political affairs, wars, etc., affect our markets.

(ii) ***Domestic Economic and Political Factors:*** Gross domestic product, agricultural output, monsoon, money supply, inflation, Government policies, taxation, etc., influence the market forces.

(iii) ***Industry Information:*** Market demand, installed capacity, competing units, capacity utilisation, market share of the major units, market leaders, prospects of the industry, international demand for exports, inputs and capital goods abroad, import competing products, labour problems and Government policy towards the industry are all relevant factors to be considered in investment decision-making.

(iv) ***Company Information:*** Corporate data, annual reports, Stock Exchange publications, Department of company affairs and their circulars, press releases on corporate affairs by Government, industry chambers or associations of industries etc., are also relevant for security price analysis.

(v) ***Security Market Information:*** The Credit rating of companies, data on market trends, security market analysis and market reports, equity research reports, trade and settlement data, listing of companies and delisting, record dates and book closures, BETA factors, etc., are the needed information for investment management. These data are available in stock exchange publications and credit rating agencies.

(vi) ***Security Price Quotations:*** Price indices, price and volume data, breadth, daily volatility, range and rate of changes of these variables are also needed for technical analysis.

(vii) ***Data on Related Markets:*** Such as Government securities, money market, forex market, Bullion market, etc., are useful for deciding on alternative avenues of investment.

(viii) ***Data on Mutual Funds:*** Their schemes and their performance, NAV and repurchase prices etc., are needed as they are also investment avenues.

(ix) Data on Primary Markets/New Issues, etc.

Need for Correct Information

Investors and Market Analysts depend on the timely and correct information for making investment decisions. In the absence of such information, their decisions will depend on hearsay and hunches. In order to enable the correct investment decisions to be made, investors need to know the sources of information. In the fast expansion of the markets, and increasing complexity of economies, the amount of information is also fast growing. The collection of information and its analysis is time consuming and expensive. Besides analysis of the information also requires expertise which all investors may not have. The available books on the subject deal with the theoretical aspects and not much practical analysis and down to earth operational aspects. As such the investors are left to make decisions by hunches and intuition and not on scientific analysis of the data. Those who have better information use it to make extra mileage on such information. It is also possible that insiders who have the information before it becomes public take advantage of it called Insider trading. At present, the SEBI has acquired powers to control insider trading, malpractices and rigging up of prices in the secondary markets in India, and penalise the offenders.

1. World Affairs: The day-to-day developments abroad are published in Financial Journals like *Economic Times, Financial Express, Business Line,* etc. Some foreign Journals, like *Wallstreet Journal, London Economist, Far East Economic Review* and Indian Journals like, *Business India, Fortune India* etc., also contain developments of economic and financial nature in India and abroad. IMF News Survey, World Bank and IMF Quarterly Journal, (namely, *Finance and Development*) News Letters of Foreign Banks like those of Grindlays, StanChart, etc., contain all the needed information on world developments.

2. National Economic Affairs: The daily newspapers particularly financial papers referred to above contain all the national information; Besides Journals like *Economic and Political Weekly, Business India, Dataline Business, Business Today, Fortune India* contain the material on economic developments. RBI's Annual Reports, Reports on currency and finance and monthly reports and CMIE reports all contain a wealth of information on the economy and the country. The Economic Survey of the Government of India and reports of C.S.O., D.G.T.D. and Department of companies, etc., do provide the information on economy, industry, trade sectors of the country. The reports of the Planning Commission and annual reports of various ministries also contain a lot of information.

3. Industry Information: There are various Associations — Chambers of Commerce, Merchants' Chamber and other agencies who publish Industry data. The reports of Planning Commission, government of India, publications from Industry and Commerce Ministries also contain a lot of information. The CMIE publishes various volumes and update them from time-to-time containing data on various sectors of the economy and industries, and the subscribers get these volumes and reports.

Directory of Information published by the B.S.E. also contains information on industries and companies and this is updated from time-to-time. Many Daily financial papers bring out regularly studies on various Industries and their prospects. Industry data at macro level is available in Government publications, industry wise, but in view of a large time lag involved in their reports, the monthly reports of various Associations of Industries give more up-to-date and timely information.

4. Company Information: The information on various Companies listed on Stock Exchanges is readily available in daily financial papers. Besides the Fortnightly Journals of *Capital Market, Dalal Street, Business India* contain a lot of information on the industries and companies, listed on stock exchanges. Results of equity and Market Research are also published in these Journals. As referred to earlier the B.S.E. (Bombay Stock Exchange) publishes Directory of Information on Industries and Companies, which are listed on Stock Exchanges, and the Journals of *Capital Market* and *Dalal Street* also publish these data. Computer software on these data are available with a number of software companies. The B.S.E. also publishes weekly reviews, monthly reviews giving data on various aspects of listed companies. BSE, NSE, RBI etc., have their own websites in which these data are available.

The Annual Reports of companies and their half yearly unaudited results are another source of information on the companies. The financial journalists give write ups on various companies after interviewing their executives and these are published in *Economic Times* and other financial Dailies, like *Business Line & Financial Express, etc.*

5. Security Market Information: A number of big Broker Firms who have equity research are sending newsletters on Market Information with Fundamental and Technical analysis, combined in those reports. *The Capital Market, Dalal Street, Business India* and few other Stock Market Journals like *Fortune India, Investment Weekly,* etc., contain the information on security markets. The ICFAI also publishes a monthly called *Chartered Financial Analyst,* which contains economic data, company information, and market information, Security analysis, Beta factors and a host of other items, useful for security analysis. The data on Trade periods and settlements, record dates, book closures etc., are contained in financial papers like *Economic Times, Business Line, Financial Express* etc., after they are released by stock exchanges and companies. While the newsletter of Merchant Bankers, brokers' firms, Investment Analysts, are available to subscribers or their own clients, others are available for all at stipulated prices. The collection of information is thus costly and time consuming.

6. Security Price Quotations: The daily quotations on various Stock Exchanges BSE, NSE are published in the daily papers. Each Stock Exchange is publishing its own daily quotations list, giving out opening, high, low and closing quotations of all traded securities. They also publish volume of trade for individual securities and also the total for all securities traded on a daily basis, in terms of shares and value of trades.

The price indices, for all securities, industry group wise, region wise etc., are published by the RBI, B.S.E. and major Stock Exchanges, in the country. Besides each financial Daily has its own Index published in its paper. All these indices, daily volumes, highs, lows, advances, declines etc., of well traded Companies, Gainers and Losers and such similar information, useful for both technical and fundamental analysis are available from all Stock Exchanges and published in financial Dailies and Journals. *The Capital Market* and *Dalal Street* journals also give Company information regarding their fundamentals, P/E, EPS, GPM, etc., along with the price data. Daily highs and lows, can be seen as against yearly highs/lows for each of the securities in financial Dailies, like E.T.

The pattern of share holding, distribution schedule, floating stock, past price data are available in all softwares and B.S.E. Directory. B.S.E. publishes all the data useful for technical analysis and these data are compiled by the computer specialists and floppies are available on official daily quotations and Technical charts of each of the major companies listed on Stock Exchanges. The computer software data are also sold by software companies for those who have computer facility. For others, these data can be collected from daily papers, weekly and fortnightly Journals on Stock Markets, like *Dalal Street* and *Capital Market.*

7. Data on Related Markets: Data on Money Market, Government Securities Market are available in the publications of RBI and D.F.H.I., Indian Banks Association, Securities Trading Corporation and banks. These data are published on a daily basis in the financial Dailies and journals. The publications which deal with these markets are however fewer in number compared to those on stock and capital markets. The information on Forex Market is available in RBI publications, Foreign Exchange Dealers Association (FEDAI) and foreign banks. These data are published in the form of exchange rates and cross currency rates NEER, REER, turnover data, forward premia GDR, ADRs, ECCBs, FCN,

FRA etc. in government and RBI publications and in Financial Dailies regularly. The developments in these markets are reviewed in the Dailies or weekly and fortnightly Journals.

The data on Bullion market and rates for gold and silver are available on a Daily basis in the financial press. These data are published in RBI Bulletins and are also available in CMIE reports. Many of these data on Forex Markets in countries abroad can be obtained from *London Economist, Far Eastern Economic Review,* and *Wall Street Journal.*

8. Data on Mutual Funds, UTI etc.: These are published in the Daily financial papers — atleast once in a week in the *Investment Weekly* or *Investors' Guide*. They give the Current Schemes, NAV of each scheme if quoted as against the Market price, if traded, repurchase price, redemption rate, etc., in respect of close ended funds and daily purchase and sale prices for open ended funds. Besides, however all the journals, magazines and reports on Stock Markets also contain the relevant information on Mutual funds, as many of their schemes are quoted and traded on the Stock Exchanges. Thus, the Capital Market, Dalal Street and Business India also contain information on Mutual Funds, in additon to that in the Financial Dailies. The Association of Mutual Funds of India (AMFI) bring out their data on a regular basis.

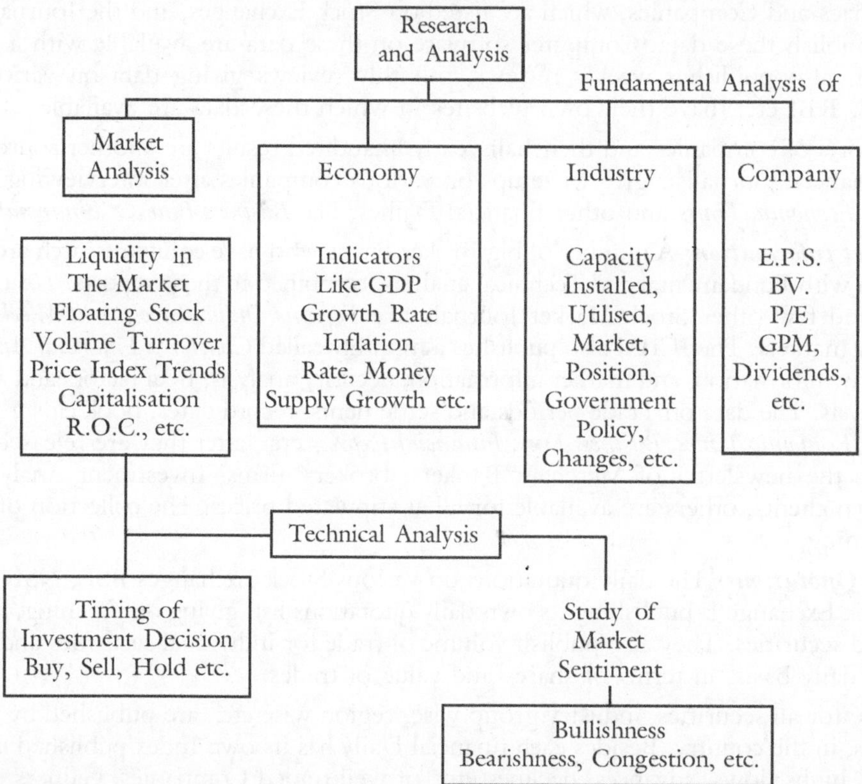

9. Data on Primary Market: New Issues in the Pipe line are first known to the SEBI as they get the Draft Prospectus for vetting and even before that, they would come to know of them from Merchant bankers' reports. But consolidation and publications of this information is done by a Magazine called "PRIME" publication. Prime publishes all information of new issues in the pipeline — industrywise and sizewise analysis and public oversubscription and undersubscription etc. The performance of companies, Merchant bankers, underwriters and brokers etc., in the New Issue Market are also analysed by them. Geographical and centrewise collection of new issues and other relevant company information is given by them.

Following them, a number of Magazines, merchant bankers, Registrars and Brokers and their Associations are publishing them. Financial Dailies are giving a write up on the forthcoming new issues as also some cable operators. The RBI and Department of Company Affairs in addition to SEBI collect and publish these data from time-to-time in their reports once in a quarter, and yearly.

Analysis of Data

The Broker firms, Investment consultancy firms, Portfolio Managers require all the investment information on Companies, industry and Economy.

Their tasks in this connection can be set out as shown in the preceding page, under Research and Analysis.

Interpretation of Information

Financial data and information is the most important factor influencing the share price and corporate decision-making. The information can be in the form of data in financial statements or in the form of verbal announcements.

The information can be classified into various types and the impact of each on the corporate performance varies both degree and direction. The chart below presents the different classes of information both Internal and External.

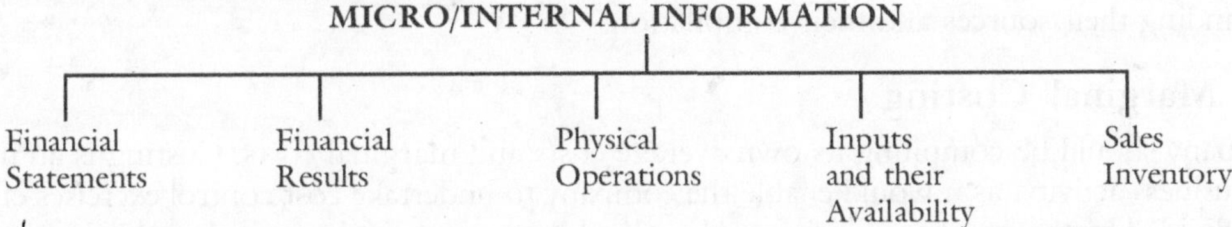

The above information is internal to the company and relates to gross block, capacity sales, cash and credit sales, inventory, purchases, costs and benefits, cash flows and funds flows and other relevant data.

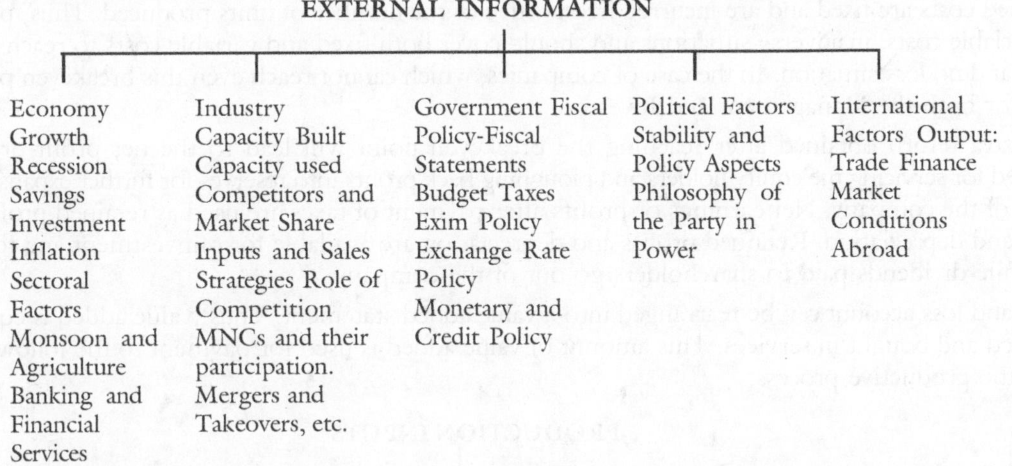

The sources of information, their collection collation and tabulation are necessary for their use and interpretation. Study of security markets will be incomplete without proper data analysis and interpretation.

Steps in Analysis and Interpretation

Data and information is to be first collected and collated. To make use of it and derive proper interpretation of the information and data, one has to follow the steps below:

(1) Collection, collation, tabulation etc.

(2) Organisation of the data into proper heads depending on their effect on the company.

(3) Study of the data through —

- (a) Cash flows and their analysis.
- (b) Fund flows and their analysis.
- (c) Average cost and marginal cost analysis.
- (d) Analysis of net operating earnings and profits.
- (e) Value added analysis.
- (f) Profit allocation and their impact.

(4) Measurement of the data and information through —

- (a) Ratio Analysis.
- (b) Trend analysis.
- (c) Use of charts and their analysis.
- (d) Common sense interpretation.

(5) Interpretation of the data and information on the company's performance, its net worth and share price and its movements.

Prior to the above analysis, analyst has to sieve out the useful from the useless data. If one sees the financial press or any daily papers or Journals, there will be plethora of information, from which one has to collect only the relevant and useful data, ignoring the useless data. Such discretion and understanding of data and information is necessary for the analyst to save time, reduce costs of analysis, and get the best out of the available data and information, full understanding and capacity to separate the grain from the Chaff. An analysis of Balance sheet is incomplete without understanding the footnotes and auditor's notes. Similarly, an analysis of cash flows and fund flows is incomplete without understanding their sources and their compilation.

Average and Marginal Costing

Every company should be compiling its own average costs and marginal costs. Costing is an important exercise for each line of business activity, as it would enable the company to undertake cost control exercises effectively. Average cost is total cost divided by the number of units produced, while the marginal cost is the additional cost of production of one additional unit. Given the price per unit it is for the company to decide to produce more or less. The costs have two components, namely variable costs and fixed costs. The variable costs vary with the number of units produced while the fixed costs are fixed and are incurred irrespective of the number of units produced. Thus, price should atleast cover the variable costs, in adverse situations and should cover both fixed and variable costs to reach a breakeven point of no profit and no loss situation. In the case of companies, which cannot reach even this breakeven point, it is a matter of concern for both the Management and Investor.

Any extra return obtained after reaching the breakeven point will lead to the net profit or net earnings (or residual), used for servicing the equity holders and ploughing back profits into reserves for further expansion, diversification and growth of the company. Net earnings or profits after payment of taxes are used as retained profits and dividends, if any paid, and depreciation. Retained profits and depreciation are available for reinvestment and for working capital purposes while dividends paid to shareholders go out of the company.

Profit and loss account can be rearranged into a value added statement. Thus, value added is equal to sales minus materials used and bought in services. This amount of value added is used for payment to the following agencies who are part of the productive process.

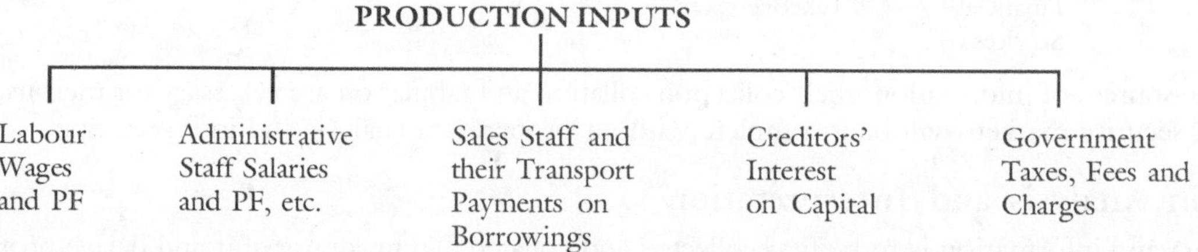

Equity holders are the last category who get their dividends, after the preference shareholders, if any, are paid. Depreciation is also an expense item for purposes arising out of net profits available for allocation to preference and equity shareholders. But the amount of depreciation is an item to write off the existing plant and machinery and is intended to be used to replace the existing ones by new ones, when needed due the lapse of life or for modernisation needed due to obsolesence.

Value Added Data

Value added statement helps the Corporate Manager analyse the efficiency of factors used, say labour and capital. Suppose there is an improvement of labour efficiency, it is reflected in a higher value added for ₹ 100 paid to employees. Similarly the cost of capital and whether it is raising or falling in relation to the value added will tell us whether any changes in strategies are needed. The investor will know how the value added is changing and whether it is due to labour, capital or management. All those interested in the company namely management or promoters, Banks and financial institutions and investors will be able to analyse the company's performance by the value added method of analysis.

INFLATION ADJUSTMENT

If rise in prices is say 10% and profits at current prices are rising by 10%, there is no net growth in the company in real terms. Similarly, if investors get a dividend of 10% in times of inflation of 10%, there is no net true benefit to investors. In times of rising inflation, debtors gain and creditors lose due to lack of inflation adjustment to the amounts paid by debtors to creditors.

The corporates are affected by the rise in input cost due to inflation and in the case of imported inputs, by imported inflation which is prevailing abroad. Since all inputs may not rise or rise by the same proportion, some companies which are efficient are able to absorb upto a point the rise input costs within the prices they charge for their output. Otherwise the prices of their output will also have to go up. There is a distributional distortion, as inflation effects different groups differently and all prices do not rise by the same proportion and users of the products whose prices rise most are affected most.

The wages and salaries of labour are in many cases adjusted for inflation by wage agreements. Only interest costs may rise with a time lag to inflation rise and residual profit shares namely the investors may or may not gain depending on a host of factors, namely the share of other factors, extent of the rise in input costs and erosion of profits due to inflation or rise in input materials.

Prima facie, three adjustments are to be made in the profit and loss account due to inflation.

1. ***Additional Depreciation:*** Needed to replace the fixed assets at higher costs.
2. ***Cost of Sales:*** Increased cost of inventory holding, purchase cost and rise in other inputs will lead to rise in both variable and fixed costs.
3. ***Monetary Working Capital:*** Rise in credit limit from banks.

CHART ON USE OF FUNDS

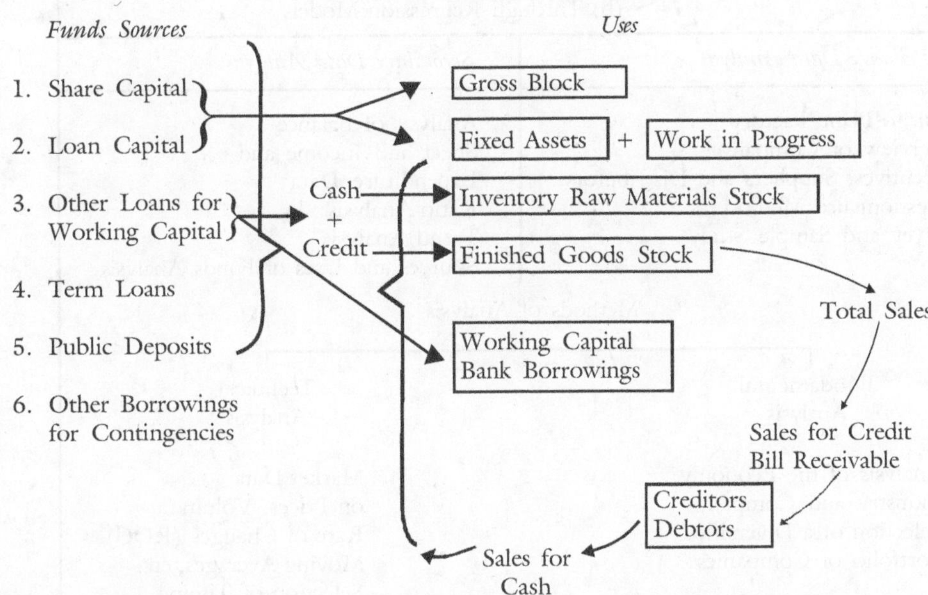

Similar to the above chart, cash flow statement can be prepared by starting with existing cash balance plus Bank balance. Then the cash inflows and outflows are all taken into account on cash receipt or payment basis and net inflow will add to cash balances while net outflow leads to reduction in closing cash balances, which may many times lead to borrowing from banks, FIs and others.

INTERPRETATION

After analysing and reorganising the data and information, understanding of the information is necessary for management control, revision and review of the annual plans and budgets and cost control and improvement of profit earnings.

Measurement and Analysis of Data is referred to earlier through approved methods namely Ratio Analysis Trend Analysis, Chart Method, Econometric Method or Statistical Method, etc., referred to elsewhere in this book.

Ernest Jones in his book on *"Business Finance"* (Pitman Publishing House) has presented some set of ratios with examples. A few are presented below:

(1) Primary Ratios: Return on net assets.

(2) Secondary Ratios: Profit margin or profits to sales.

(3) Tertiary Ratios: — PAT/Sales

— Variable Expenses/Sales

Fixed assets to sales/working capital to sales

Other ratios like Activity Ratios, Liquidity and Solvency ratios and debtors and creditors turnover ratios are examples, of the use of ratio analysis for the purpose of assessing the efficiency of capital use, sales turnover, profitability of the corporate activity. Ratios can be set for the purpose in mind of the analyst. This analysis helps the division or departmentwise activity, control of management, comparison of targets with achievements and evaluation of planing and budgeting of activities of the company.

Research Methods are very varied starting from Deskwork to plant visits.

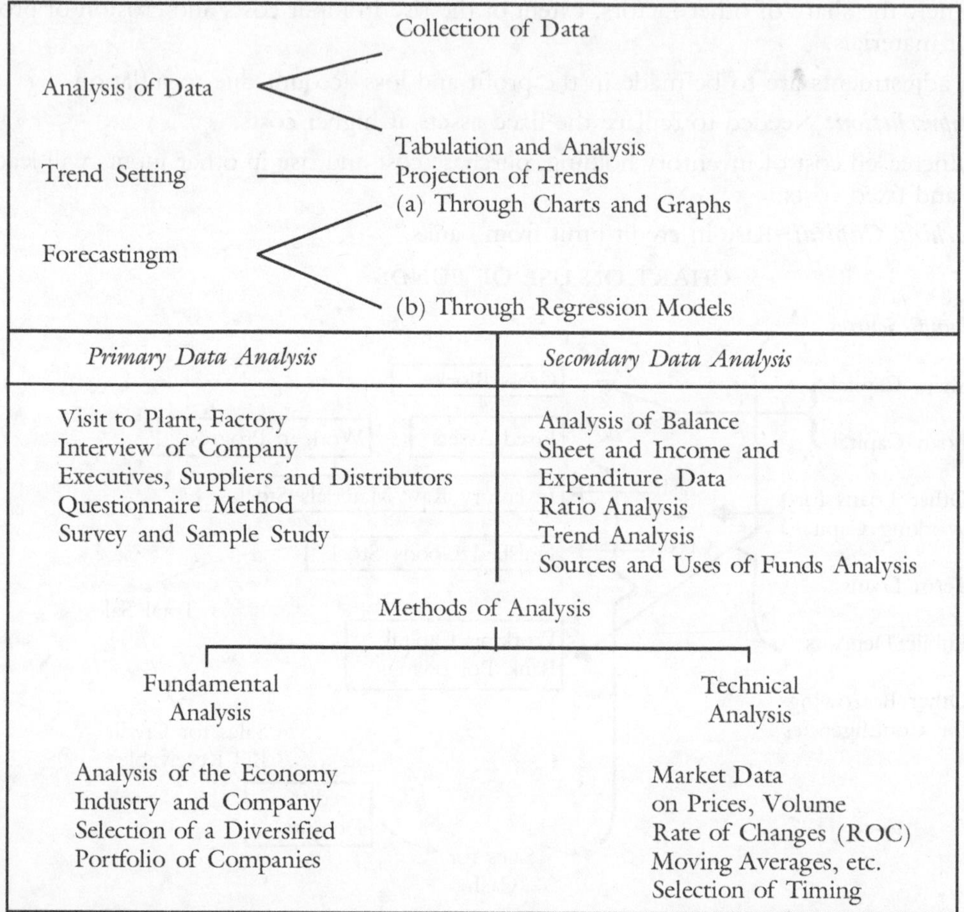

Study to be followed —

(a) Pattern of ownership of shares.

(b) Proportion of public holding.

(c) Floating stock for trading.

(d) High/Low prices for the year.

(e) Daily volatility of prices.
— Opening, High, Low and Closing.

(f) Breadth of the Market/Turnover of trade in value

(g) No. of shares traded and their volumes of the company included and *vis-a-vis* the total volume for all companies.

(h) Declines/Advances among scrips.

(i) Chart of Daily price trends, moving average trends — to get signals of buy/sell etc.

(j) Trace out the intrinsic value of the share by Fundamental Analysis — Adjust for the expectations and sentiment in the market to take a decision whether the price in the market is fair price or over valued or undervalued.

Study of the company through financial variables (BV, EPS, P/E, etc.), visit the plant and interview the chief executives of the company for knowing the expectations, as also of the merchant bankers and financial institutions, are the further steps.

Scrips chosen on all these counts are properly timed through Technical Analysis for a proper investment decision-making. An analysis of risk in terms of variability of returns (standard deviation) of each company *vis-a-vis* the market, use of Beta factor for risk which is systematic and diversification of investments into various industries and companies to reduce the unsystematic risks are the further steps in portfolio management.

Conclusion

It will thus be seen that the sources of information for investment purposes are only the first step. Collection and collation and analysis of the data are the more important next steps. The direction of analysis may be fundamental analysis or technical analysis and the emerging investment decisions are referred to in another Chapter. The data and information, set out in this Chapter are necessary for not only proper investment decision, but for portfolio management, revision and evaluation. Equity research and market analysis, so necessary for stock broking investment consultancy and portfolio management are also based on the information collection and data processing for which the sources of information referred to in this Chapter are vitally important.

5

INDUSTRY ANALYSIS

Once the Economic Analysis is made and the forecast of the Economy is known the investor will then have some idea of the likely growth of the economy and its trend. After that, the analyst would look into the industry groups which are promising in the coming year or years and then only he will be able to choose the companies in those industry groups. There is however, no perfect correlation between the growth trend of economy and industries on the one hand and of industry and the companies on the other. Economy may be in recession but some industry groups do well and *vice versa*. Similarly, an industry group may be growing faster than others but some companies in it are sick or showing slackness for some reasons or other. There is no correlation between economic growth and industry growth nor between the industry growth and the company in that industry. Despite these limitations, the investor needs to have an overall perspective of the economy and industry groups.

INDUSTRY GROUPS

In India, asset based industry groupings used to exist under MRTP Act and FERA Act. But with the economic reforms of 1991 onwards, there are no limits to the asset growth and the classification MRTP and non-MRTP companies has disappeared since then. FERA was also amended to allow foreign investment in Industrial units upto 51% normally but in some cases, it was allowed even upto 100%. So multinational companies can operate in India through their subsidiaries or they can have a majority stake in Indian industry.

The normal sizewise classification (not asset based) of industries is as follows:

(a) Small-scale Units:[1] Small-scale industries are not listed and those which are listed should be of a minimum paid-up capital of ₹ 30 lakhs. Those with ₹ 30 lakhs and above are eligible to be listed on the OTCEI at present.

(b) Medium-scale Industries: The industrial units which have a paid-up capital of ₹ 5 crores and above can be listed on the regional stock exchanges like Cochin, Coimbatore etc.

(c) Large Sized Industries: The industrial units with paid-up of ₹ 10 crores and above can be listed only on the major Stock Exchanges like B.S.E., N.S.E. etc.

Proprietary Based Classification

Industries in India have also been classified on the basis of ownership, namely, (a) private sector industries, (b) public sector industries (Government and semi-Government ownership) and (c) and joint sector (Jointly owned by private and Government). All these are at present listed on the Stock Exchanges, except some of them which are only in the public sector. Examples of joint sector companies where the government have recently divested are SAIL, NTPC and BHEL etc.

Use Based Classification

(a) Basic Industries: These are in the core sector in India and constitute the infrastructure industries which are mostly in the public sector but are now kept open to the private sector. The examples are fertilisers, chemicals, coal, cement, steel, non-ferrous metals, electricity, etc. They are mostly inputs of agriculture and industries and are basic to development.

---

1. For the purpose of the Government, an investment upto ₹ 3 crores is taken as SSI and upto ₹ 1 crore for cottage industries.

(b) Capital Goods Industries: These are both in the private and public sectors. These are highly capital intensive industries and used to produce inputs of other industries such as machine tools and equipment, agricultural machinery, electric motors, electronical equipment, railroad equipment, wires, cables, etc. In this category, there are both heavy capital goods like textile machinery and light capital goods like machine tools.

(c) Intermediate Goods: These are goods in the intermediate stage of production, having undergone some processing already but will be used for further production. The examples are Tyres, Tubes, Synthetic yarn, Cotton spinning, Dyestuffs, Automobile parts, Coal and Petrol products, bolts, nuts, manufactured metal, Dry cells, Batteries, etc. These are in both private and public sectors.

(d) Consumer Goods Industries: These are of two categories, namely, consumer durables and consumer non-durables. These are final products for consumption of households. Durables are Fans, Bulbs, Automobiles, Cycles, Two wheelers, Telephone equipment etc. Non-durables are Food products Agro based products, Tobacco, Cotton, Silk, Woollen and Jute Textiles, ready-made garments, Rubber and Paper products, Sugar, Cosmetics, Drugs and Pharmaceuticals, etc. These are mostly in the private sector.

Input Based Classification

(a) ***Agrobased products*** like jute, sugar, cotton, tobacco, groundnuts, floriculture, horticulture

(b) ***Forest based products*** like plywood, paper, teak wood, ivory, resin, honey etc.

(c) ***Marine based products*** like fisheries, prawns, pisciculture, etc.

(d) ***Metal based products*** like engineering products, aluminium, copper, gold and silver products etc., including jewellery.

(e) ***Chemical based products*** like fertilisers, pesticides, drugs, dyestuffs, paints, plastics etc.

Each of the above classifications is useful for identifying the characteristic features of the industry, its inputs and outputs or uses and the likely demand for it, constraints in production and other problems.

Mixed Economy

India has a mixed economy, where private and public sectors play a complementary role and promote planned development. Since the initiation of the reforms in 1991, even foreign enterprise and the MNCs have been given a due role to play in the development of the economy. As for the latest policy, barring about 18 Scheduled industrial groups, others are all open to both private and public sectors. Some of the core sectors are also open to foreign enterprise. Small-scale sector and co-operative sector have had deep roots in the Indian economy and some items are reserved for them. But as the securities markets comprise of only marketable securities and they are mostly from the private corporate sector and public undertakings, which are being shifted to the joint sector, their equities, bonds and other types of instruments will constitute the securities available in the markets. Insurance and many financial services are thrown open to foreign sector now.

Exemptions to the General Policy

The general policy is one of privatisation, deregulation and globalisation at present. The private and foreign participation is allowed even in the core sector and in infrastructural industries like steel, cement, fertilisers, power, oil drilling etc. Only a few strategic industries of national security like arms, ammunition, defence products, atomic energy and some mining and metal products, coal, copper, gold, etc., are kept reserved to the public sector. Similarly, some SSI and cottage industry units are kept out for foreign investment.

SOURCES OF INFORMATION FOR ANALYSIS

To make an industry analysis the statistics at Macro level are contained in the RBI Reports on currency and finance (Handbook of Statistics on Indian Economy) and in Monthly Bulletin of RBI on Industrial Production, Prices etc., sectorwise will be essential. These data on industries are published by the Ministry of Industry and by the C.S.O. Many Industry Associations, FICCI and Associations will also publish the industry data. Besides the RBI also publishes industry wise studies on corporate finance giving out the details of their financial performance. But these data are with a time lag of one or two years and will be useful only for knowing the past trends as a benchmark reference.

The CMIE publications also contain the necessary information on the industries, their production and their financial performance. From these data the analyst will get some idea of the growth prospects of the various industries, the leaders and laggards. For example, from the latest report of the RBI, it was found that the industries growing faster at the present time are food products, cement consumer goods and capital goods and pharma products, chemicals, metal products and engineering. There are some growth-oriented industries at any time and presently telecommunication equipment such as cellular phones and parts, computer parts, hotels and tourism, waste management and power sector, are the potentially growth-oriented industries. The fastest growing industries are I.T., Software Telecom and knowledge based services, multi-media and Bio-Tech Industries at present. In the Budget for 2006-07, special provision was made for development of Gems and Jewellery, cotton textiles etc. Besides, the potential growth areas are health care, financial services, education, tourism, accountancie, real estate, land and buildings, etc., and other business services etc.

Key Factors to be Examined

In industry analysis, the key factors to be looked into, by the analyst are past sales and earnings performance, stage of growth of the industry, the government policy towards the industry, labour conditions, competitive conditions and industry share prices and their relative EPS (earnings per share) etc.

Each industry has a life cycle of its own. As per the Industry Life Cycle theory, three stages of its life can be discerned, namely, pioneering stage, expansion stage and stagnation stage. The examples of the industries in the pioneering stage as also called infant industry stage are cellular phones, wind energy, computer software, Telecommunications equipment, energy and power, waste management and solar power and atomic energy for medical purposes, etc. There are some industries which are in the stage of expansion and growth, namely, finance, drugs, chemicals, engineering, jewellery readymade garments and food products, etc. The examples of industries in the stagnation stage are jute textiles, cotton textiles, leather and tobacco etc. Only the industries in the infant stage give extra profits and beat the average market performance. Many venture capital funds and new technology products in India have potentiality for growth. Diversified industry units like ITC, Reliance, Telco etc., have stable returns. At the other extreme, some industries which have reached the saturation stage, whose capacities are fully meeting the demand and market for those products is saturated or stable like tea, coffee, soaps and cigarettes etc., the investment opportunities may diminish and although the dividends may be paid like "cash cows", the growth prospects and capital appreciation will be poor. Some of the units in these categories may become sick also due to change in habits, technological growth, high labour costs and stagnant demand.

The Analyst has to be extremely careful in identifying the stage of the industry as in practice, the distinction is generally unclear and vague. Besides there may be units in a stable industry, which are doing well due to diversification, modernisation and technological upgradation. The investment analyst has to be a careful rag picker, to pick up diamonds from the waste. In judging the probable future trend of an individual stock, it is necessary not only to judge the industry group trend, but use discretion to identify the exceptions to the trend. Again within the stage of stagnation, there can be stable companies or potentially sick companies or even actual sick companies which are to be discerned and avoided by the investors.

IMPORTANCE OF GOVERNMENT POLICY

The state of the capital market depends to a great extent on the state of the economy, which in turn is a function of a number of economic and non-economic variables. The most important of these variables are *inter alia* the monsoon in the case of India and the government policies affecting industries. The monsoon although important for the Indian economy due to its predominant influence on the performance of the economy with a contribution of one-third of the national income and with two-thirds of the population depending on agriculture either directly or indirectly, is one of the fundamental factors affecting the markets referred to in a later chapter. But equally important is the direction of the government policies in regard to the economy and industry. The operations of the brokers either in the new issues market or the stock market depend on the flows of money or savings into the market on the one hand and the flows of information on the other. The information may be on the economy, industry or the company, bulk of which emanates through the PTI tickers, newspapers, journals, etc. The following flow chart represents this relationship (Chart I). This chart shows the government policies and the enabling legislation and the expected influence of these policies on the industries in the economy.

The operations of investors are thus the result of a vast number of buy and sell orders from clients and their own demand for and supply of securities which depend on the information flow on a daily, hourly and minute by minute basis. Government policies being the most important single factor influencing the economy, the market reflects and absorbs these first, and prices of shares are the result of these forces.

In choosing the company to buy or sell, a study of fundamental factors is necessary. Before the choice of company, the investor has to first select the industry and then study companies within the industry by a careful comparison of the companies within the industry with regard to their fundamentals. This is true for investment in both the new issues and stock market as the diagram will show (Fig. 5.1).

CHART I

Policy	*Enabling Act*	*Nature of Influences*
1. Industrial licensing policy (mostly scrapped in July, 1991)	1. Industries (Development and Regulation) Act, 1951	1. Governs the setting up of industrial enterprises and expansion, etc.
2. Capital Issues Control (Dispensed with)	2. Capital Issues Control Act, 1947 (repealed in May 1992)	2. Regulates the pricing and issue of shares to the public.
3. Import and Export Trade Policy	3. Trade Control Act, 1947	3. Licensing of imports and exports and their regulation in regard to price and quantum.
4. Foreign Investment Policy	4. Foreign Exchange Regulation Act, 1973 since replaced by FEMA, 1999	4. Regulation of foreign investment and technology in India and investment abroad by Indians.
5. Monopoly control on industry and trade	5. MRTP Act, 1969 cut in size in 1991	5. Control on monopoly and restrictive trade practices in industry.
6. Sick industry rehabilitation policy	6. Sick Industrial Companies Act, 1985 amended in 2004	6. Board of Industrial and Financial Reconstruction given powers to restructure and revitalise the sick units. This was wound up.
7. Labour policy	7. Industrial Disputes Act	7. Arbitration and adjudication of industrial and labour disputes.
8. Price/Distribution controls on industrial products	8. Essential Commodities Act and Maintenance of Supplies of Essential Commodities Act	8. Registration of industries with regard to their prices and distribution, stocking, etc.
9. Control and Supervision on Capital Market	9. SEBI Act	9. Registration, licensing of all intermediaries and control on capital market.

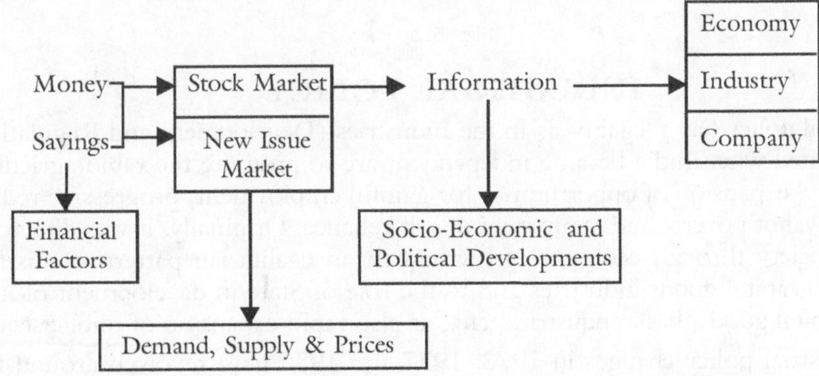

Fig. 5.1

Government Regulation — Legal Basis

There are various government policies which influence the markets; the more important of them are set out in the following Chart as having a direct effect on the market (Fig. 5.2).

In addition to those policies, the public sector policy influences the infrastructural industries, their growth, prices and distribution which account for a weight of about 28.77% of the total industrial output of the country and most of which are in the public sector. These are steel, coal, cement, electricity, petrol, petroleum products and railway freight. These industries provide the inputs to other manufacturing and mining industries which would thus influence the industrial growth in the country. The growth of infrastructural industry would thus severely affect the overall growth of the industry and hence the importance of public sector outlay and policy in this regard. More recently since 1991-92, there have been many changes in this policy to improve their working efficiency and to make them autonomous and market-oriented so that they increase their productivity and output, reduce costs and increase profits. The Competitive Act aims at improving the competition spirit among all types of Companies and the competitive commission has replaced the MRTP commission, as per the Govt. policy statements in 2006. Due to global recession the industrial growth, represented by IIP index, showed a marked fall.

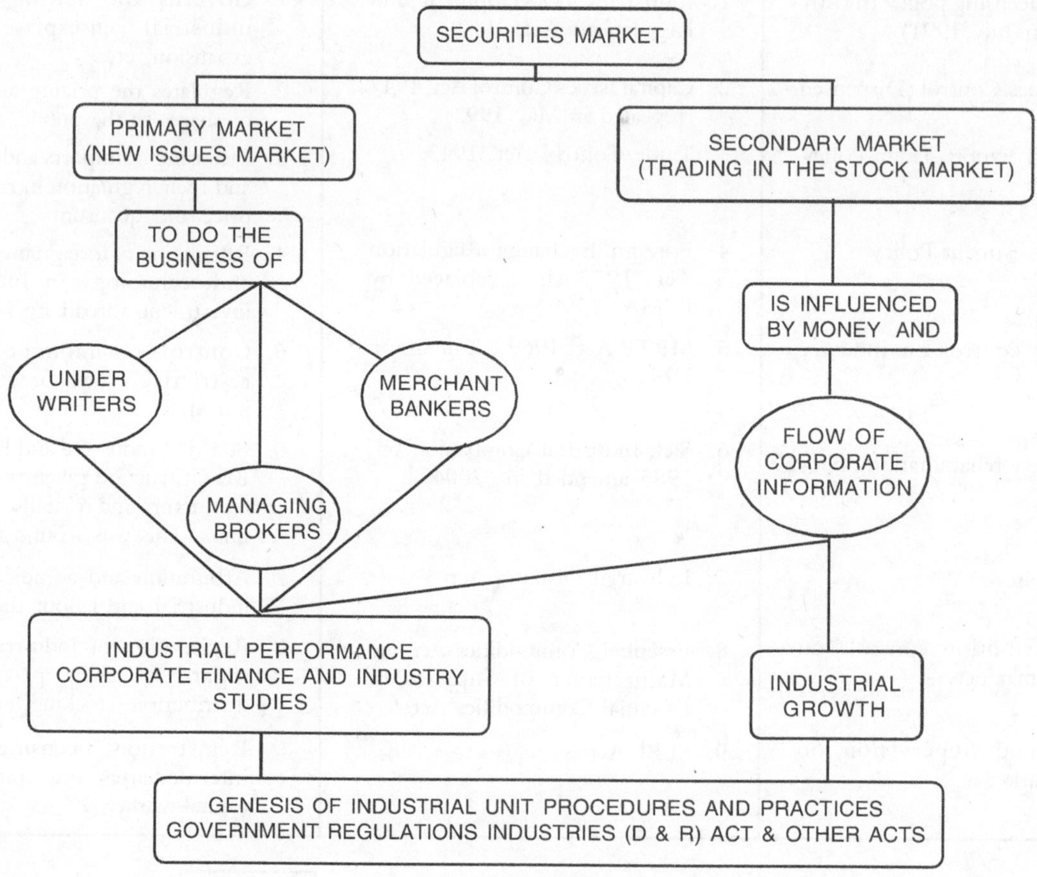

Fig. 5.2

INDUSTRIAL POLICY

In India, the industrial policy has a legal basis in the Industries (Development and Regulation) Act, 1951. The objectives of policy enunciated when India became independent are to promote the rapid agricultural and industrial development of our country, expansion of opportunities for gainful employment, progressive reduction of social and economic disparities, removal of poverty and attainment of self-reliance. Originally, it was directed to the attainment of a socialist pattern of society through economic growth with an egalitarian pattern of distribution. The 1956 Resolution gave primacy to capital goods industries and to the role of State in development of industries. This gave rise to growth of heavy capital goods, basic industries, etc., as also rapid expansion of public sector in the economy.

The subsequent industrial policy changes in 1973, 1977 and 1980 have revolved around the development of priority industries, small-scale and cottage industries and rural industries. In 1980, in particular the policy emphasised the need for competition, foreign investment, technological upgradation and modernisation as also to exports. Since 1985, a number of policy changes were made to liberalise the economy, promote competition, productivity and reduce costs and improve quality. The accent was on opening up of the economy and the domestic markets to competitive forces abroad, liberalise imports and promote exports and help the Indian industry to stand on its own in the face of international competition. Some of the price and distribution controls, as well as licensing requirements were liberalised since 1985.

The effect of these measures was that India could now boast of a wide base of infrastructural industries, a network of all capital goods and basic industries and whole range of raw materials, intermediates and finished goods are now available in India. New growth centres, industrial estates, export processing zones, etc., have been in operation. All these made India one of the top ranking industrial nations and the annual average rate of growth of industry in India was around 8.5% during the Seventh Plan period, and around 7% in the Tenth Plan period 2002-07. During the first two years of Eleventh Plan, 2007-09, the industrial growth rate was about 6% due to worldwide recession. During the subsequent two years 2010-11 and 2011-12 the growth rates were 5.2% and 8.2%, but declined in the later years.

Some of the policy measures initiated since 1985, particularly during the Seventh Plan 1985-90 have helped India to grow industrially and to broadbase its industrial structure. The liberalised licensing policy, broad banding of licensed capacities, dispensation and licensing requirements and import control requirements in many cases and cash compensatory support scheme have all helped the growth of industry. Besides, greater autonomy was given to public sector units and a memorandum of understanding was entered into with them as referred to earlier.

The government has tried to improve the efficiency and profitability of PSUs and help the private industry to grow and increase the productivity. All these efforts have not borne fruit upto 1991. There was some rise in the industrial growth rate by improving technological upgradation of industry and broadbasing the industrial structure. But the rate of growth of industry was in fact negative in 1991-92 due to foreign exchange constraint, balance of payments problem, import curbs, etc., leading to devaluation of rupee in July 1991 resulting in high cost of imports.

The year 1991-92 saw far reaching changes in the economic and financial policies. These reforms encompass the industrial policy, foreign exchange and trade policy, fiscal policy, MRTP and PSU policy etc. They aimed at deregulating the industrial sector and liberalising foreign investment and technology imports. The reforms in major areas are set out below.

Industrial Licensing

Industrial licensing was abolished for all industries except a list of 18 industries specified for compulsory licensing. Except for eight industry groups like arms, atomic energy, coal, mineral oils, electricity, mining, minerals, railways, etc., which are reserved for public sector, all the rest are thrown open to private sector. Even electricity, steel, etc., which are infrastructural industries have been kept open to private and foreign sectors. By 2015, Railways and Highways have been kept open to private sector.

Industries reserved for the small-scale sector, continue to be reserved. The existing system of registration schemes, DGTD registration, exempted industries registration etc., are all abolished. Entrepreneurs have only to file an information memorandum on new projects and substantial expansion. The convertibility clause imposed by financial institutions on borrowing companies has been withdrawn except in a few cases and facilities for broad banding and diversification continue to be available to the private sector.

Policies for PSUs

Though some reservation for public sector is being retained, a gradual opening of the area of private sector and privatisation of some PSUs is being followed. The sick PSUs like the private sector units are referred to the BIFR for necessary action. The government has aimed at professionalising the PSU management and improve their accountability and profitability by giving them greater autonomy. Many PSUs are thrown open to private sector participation and their shares are sold to mutual funds and FIs. A memorandum of understanding was entered into with many PSUs by the government to make them accountable to improve efficiency and profitability. In 2004, the BIFR Act was repealed and the Board was wound up so as to facilitate quicker rehabilitation or privatisation, mergers or acquisitions etc. both in the private and public sectors. A process of disinvestment of PSUs was started since 1992 and by end 2008, nearly ₹ 93,000 was raised through this process. Another amount of ₹ 87,000 crores was raised in three years 2009-10 to 2011-12 and ₹ 18,375 crores during 2012 to 2015.

Foreign Investment

A special empowered board comprising the top government secretaries (Foreign Investment Promotion Board) would negotiate for attracting foreign investment into India through large multinationals.[2] The government has assured automatic direct investment approval upto 51% of the total equity in Indian companies by foreigners in selected industry groups. In some cases, FDI is now allowed even up to 74% and 100%, in specified sectors. Automatic clearance for foreign investment in specified industries and for capital goods imports is also granted if the foriegn

2. For promoting foreign direct investment, a new Foreign Investment Promotion Council was set up in July 1996. A new body namely, Foreign Investment Implementation Committee was set up in 1999 to speed up the implementation process. All these measures were taken to infuse confidence in foreign investors and to promote the inflow of FDI into India.

exchange is available through collaborators. Besides the government made it clear that import of foreign technology is freely allowed in specified industries if the outgo is covered by export earnings. Besides no permission is required for employment of foreign technicians or foreign testing of indigenously developed technologies. A list of industries with 34 categories in it is provided automatic approval of foreign technology agreements by the government.

MRTP Control

The MRTP Act was amended to delete the provisions relating to the threshold limits of assets for MRTP companies. All restrictions on their expansion, acquisition and mergers etc., have gone. They are also freed for any need for government approval for establishment of new undertakings, expansion, mergers, etc. The newly empowered MRTP commission was meant to initiate investigations *suo moto* or on complaints received from individual consumers in regard to monopolistic, restrictive and unfair trade practices. Thus, the concept of MRTP companies and dominant undertakings has gone and government controls on their activities have disappeared. But emphasis is now placed on controlling and regulating their monopolistic, restrictive and unfair trade practices, and to promote competition.

Nature of Control

The nature of control on industrial enterprise used to extend from the conception of the project to the point of winding up of the enterprise. Some of these controls like a letter of intent, MRTP restrictions depending upon the size of the assets, etc., were dispensed with. The DGTD registration and other bureaucratic controls were also dropped. The Capital Issues Control Act was repealed and issues of capital of public are freed from prior permission with regard to terms and pricing of issues. But the other controls still continue. The CIC guidelines are replaced by the SEBI guidelines and control through industrial licensing is replaced by a system of reporting and submission of statements of information.

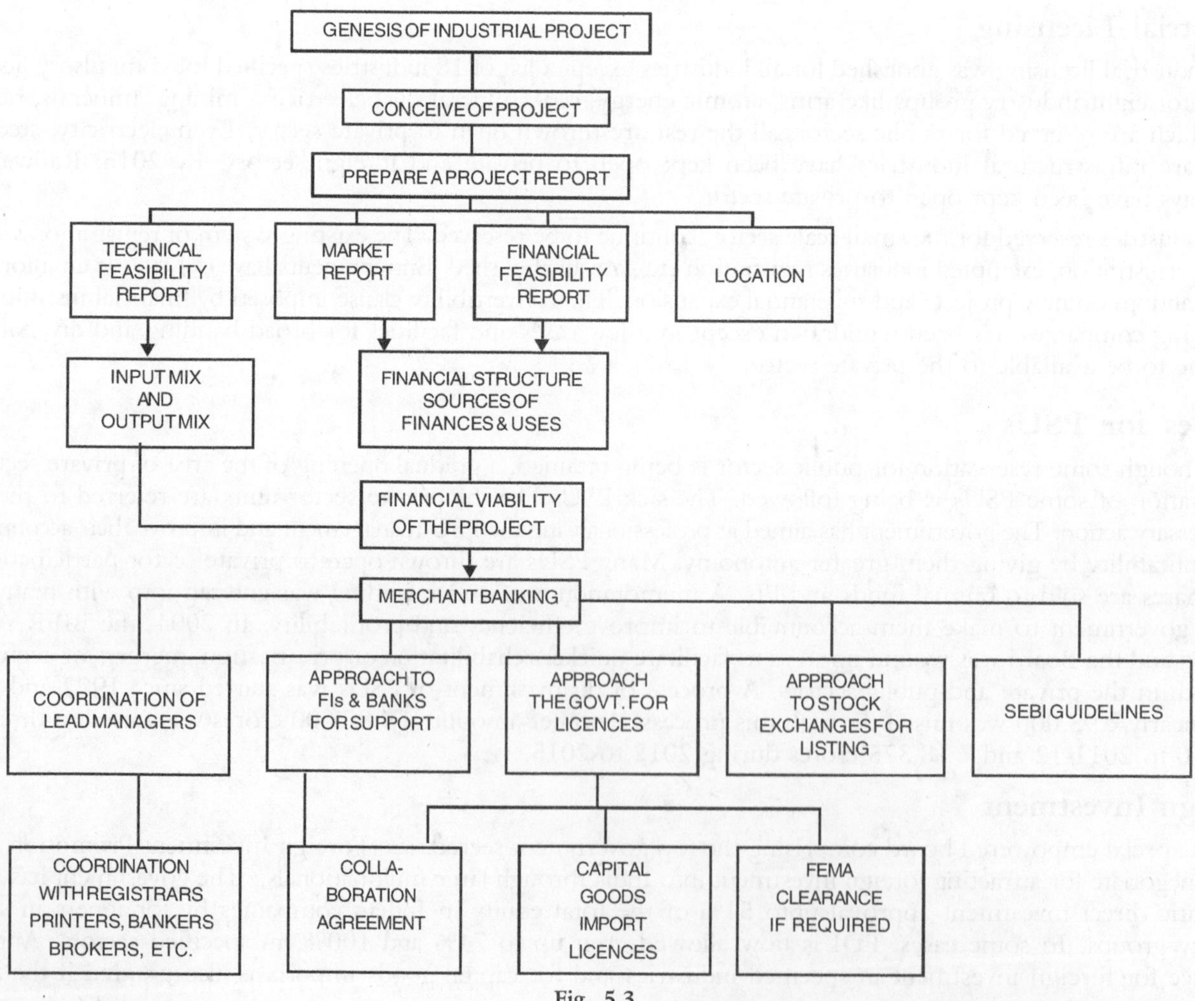

Fig. 5.3

From the genesis of the project to implementation of the idea, the project has to be vetted by the merchant banking outfits. This involves the project preparation, liaison with the government agencies, financial institutions, Registrar of Companies, stock exchange, co-managers, brokers, underwriters, registrars to the issue, bankers, etc. All these are part of the new issues activity and marketing of new issues. These are exhibited in the chart (Fig. 5.3).

The nature of the control by the government has continued to be wide ranging but more recently some discretionary controls of bureaucracy like granting of industrial licences, import licences in some cases and pricing of shares and permission to raise funds from the public etc., are dispensed with. The prevailing control system is depicted in the following diagram (Fig. 5.4). Of those depicted below industrial licensing, C.G. Clearance and foreign collaboration and technology agreement were dispensed with after the reforms started in 1991.

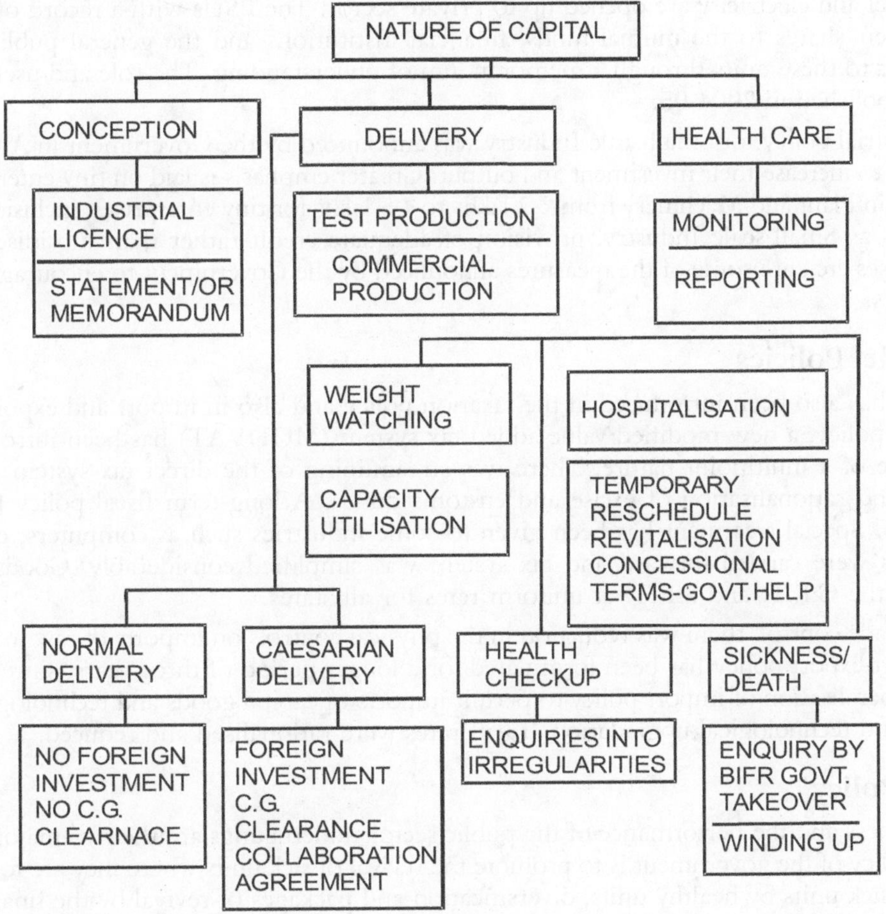

Fig. 5.4

NEW INDUSTRIAL POLICY

The New Policy initiatives were taken in July, 1991 aimed at macro economic stabilisation and structural adjustments, necessary to put the economy again on the growth process, from the relative stagnation and problems of external payments position noticed during 1990-91. The accent of new policy is delicensing, deregulation, privatisation and globalisation of industries. Industrial licensing was abolished for all industries in July, 1991, except in 18 special categories listed for the purpose. The MRTP Act was amended to remove the asset limit for MRTP companies and dominant undertakings. While the role of Public Sector is continued to be important, the emphasis is shifted to making private sector more responsive and vibrant. The reservation for SSIs was continued. Foreign direct investment through equity participation was increased to 51% in many selected industry groups and foreign exchange requirement is met through foreign equity and where the C.I.F. value of imported capital goods required is less than 25% of the total value of plant and machinery upto a maximum value of ₹ 2 crores was allowed by Govt.

Licensing would no longer be necessary for factories located in cities with population below 1 million. The mandatory convertibility clause for term loans given by financial institutions is abolished. The broad banding facility was extended to existing units producing any article without additional investment. The existing units are also exempted from licensing for expansion purposes.

In the field of foreign investment, direct foreign investment upto 51% of the equity is permitted in high priority industries. Besides the same facility is extended to trading companies primarily engaged in export business so that they can expand the export activity. Although the import of components, raw materials etc., are governed by the general import policy, the outflow of dividends through foreign investment would be governed by the RBI Policy of covering the dividend outflow by the export earning of the concerned company over a period of time. This requirement is also abolished now.

As regards the role of public sector, the main features of new policy are as follows. Areas earmarked for public sector so far like steel and electricity are opened up to private sector. The PSUs with a record of profitability will go public by selling their shares to the mutual funds, financial institutions and the general public. The management autonomy is ensured to these units through a memorandum of understanding. The role and usefulness of B.I.F.R. is now doubted and abolished in 2004-05.

The new industrial policy for Small-scale Industry was announced by the Government in August 1991. The SSIs are now encouraged to increase their investment and output. Greater emphasis is laid on tiny enterprises. Enhancement of investment limits in Plant and Machinery from ₹ 2 lakhs to ₹ 5 lakhs for tiny enterprises, inclusion of industry related service and business as Small-scale Industry, provision of adequate credit rather than subsidised credit, priority in Government purchases etc., are some of the measures announced by the Government to encourage the tiny and Small-scale Industrial Units.

Fiscal and Trade Policies

Liberalisation has also been introduced in the taxation policy and also in import and export policy since 1985. In the case of fiscal policy, a new modified value-added tax system (MODVAT) has been introduced to replace the excise duty structure of a multipoint nature. There was streamlining of the direct tax system and liberalisation of depreciation rules and rationalisation of excise and customs duties. A long-term fiscal policy framework has been initiated in 1985-86. Special treatment has been given to some industries such as computers, electronics etc. Since 1992, these reforms were carried forward and tax system was simplified considerably. Goods and services tax is expected to replace the C.E.T. and S.E.T. at uniform rates for all states.

In respect of trade control, there was reduction in the physical controls on imports of raw materials, intermediate parts etc. The import-export policy has been formulated for a longer period of three years, since 1985-88. There has been a substantial liberalisation of import policy to permit imports of capital goods and technological inputs necessary for modernisation and technological upgradation. Tariff rates were rationalised and reduced.

Sick Industry Policy

Industrial sickness and the performance of the public sector undertakings are the two major areas of concern to government. The policy of the government is to promote the revival of sick units where they are found to be potentially viable. Takeover of sick units by healthy units, diversification and packages of revival by the financial institutions are some of the proposals of the government in this regard. The establishment of Industrial and Fianncial Reconstruction Board with vast powers is another step in this direction. The government has set up the Board for Industrial and Financial Reconstruction (BIFR) in January 1987 to take the necessary preventive, ameliorative and remedial measures in respect of sick industrial undertakings and to enforce these measures expeditiously. These measures are expected to improve industrial growth by preventing sickness and helping the sick units to become viable. Even PSUs were referred to the BIFR, but the experience proved otherwise and there was only stalemate in the revitalisation and revival of sick units, referred to BIFR. So it was wound up in 2004. So far as the public sector undertakings are concerned, greater autonomy and non-interference in internal affairs of the undertakings have been granted by the government to these units. They have been permitted to borrow from the market directly. Steps have also been taken to revitalise the operation of these undertakings with a view to reduce the cost, improve the profits and profitability per employee and promote efficiency in the units. Disinvestment in the PSUs by the Govt. was also pursued since 1992.

A system of Memorandum of Understanding (MOU) and Annual Performance Plan (APP) has been introduced in the case of major public undertakings with a view to impart a greater sense of responsibility and autonomy and strike a balance between responsibilities assigned to these units, on the one hand, and the corresponding obligations of the administrative Ministry, on the other. Performance evaluation is based on four criteria of financial performance, productivity, cost reduction, technical dynamism and effectiveness of project implementation.

Backward Area Development

Industrial licensing policy was used to promote regional dispersal of industries and to initiate industrial growth of backward areas. For many years, freight equalisation scheme is operated to provide major inputs of steel, iron, cement, coal etc., at uniform prices to producers anywhere in India. In the eighties, special financial allowances and tax concessions and other facilities have been provided for industries to move into no-industry districts and backward areas.

Various criteria have been applied to identify the backward districts such as poverty, *per capita* industrial output, per capita electricity consumption etc. In 1968, the Pandey Committee and later the Wanchoo Committee laid down criteria for identification of backward States and districts respectively. A Study Group of the Planning Commission also went into the question of backward areas and incentives to be provided to them. As per their recommendations, the Planning Commission has identified 246 districts as backward in various States, based on a package of indicators. Instruments of policy to promote growth of backward districts are as follows:

1. *Infrastructure Development Strategy:* Creation of industrial infrastructure and setting up of industrial estates (examples of estates of MIDC and APIDC).

2. *Growth Centre Strategy:* Establishment of public sector projects in backward areas such as in Bhilai, Rourkela and Bokaro.

3. Capital subsidy up to ₹ 15 lakhs for investment up to ₹ 1 crore.

4. Provision of transport subsidy equivalent up to 50% of the transport costs in certain areas and states.

5. Preference in granting licences, if they are set up in backward areas.

6. Concessional finance is provided by IDBI and other financial institutions to the units set up in backward areas. These concessions related to lower rates of interest, longer amortisation period, seed capital assistance, reduction in commission charges etc., and free consultancy and other assistance.

7. Income-tax concessions, tax holidays and other fiscal incentives are also provided to units in backward areas.

8. State Governments also extended other facilities such as preferential allotment of electrical connections, provision of infrastructure, exemption from sales tax etc.

9. Provision of raw materials and other inputs and imports on a preferential basis etc.

The Department of Industrial Development provides the guidelines of policy to help the promoters and entrepreneurs. For reducing red tape and providing a single point clearance, a Projects Approvals Board was constituted in 1973 in the Ministry of Industrial Development. The Secretariat for Industrial Approvals has an Entrepreneurial Assistance unit to help applicants in the process of interpreting the guidelines of policy and in making their applications.

Progress Returns

Although no licence is required, the promoters holding licences have to submit in a prescribed form, returns every six months on the progress of the project and after the commencement of production, monthly production returns are to be submitted to the competent or concerned technical authorities. The submission of statistical returns is needed for data compilation and record.

Registration

Undertakings exempt from licensing provisions have to register with the concerned Registering Authorities.

For SSIs, it is State Director of Industries and Development Commissioner for Small-scale Industries.

For Non-SSIs it is the DGTD or Technical Authority of the Central Government such as Textile Commissioner or Iron and Steel Controller etc.

The unit has to apply for foreign collaboration agreement and capital goods import clearance, even if it is exempt from licensing. The application for registration has to be made in duplicate in the appropriate form before the firm places orders for setting up of the plant or the unit. Only delay and red tape was sought to be reduced by removing discretionary powers to Bureaucracy.

POLICY ON FOREIGN INVESTMENT AND COLLABORATION

The ceiling on foreign investment in India now is 51% of the total investment. This is relaxed in special cases for foreign equity participation in industries considered necessary by the government. The government has listed three classes of industries in this regard:

(*i*) Where foreign investment may be permitted as in hotels, hospitals, core and heavy industries,

(*ii*) Where only foreign technical collaboration and not foreign investment may be permitted as in high technology industries, electronics, pharmaceuticals, etc.,

(*iii*) Where no foreign collaboration (financial or technical) is considered necessary.

Foreign nationals require FERA clearance from the RBI for any trading, commercial or industrial activity, opening of branches/offices, acquisition of share in business or purchase of shares in Indian companies. Normally, the transfer of any share or security to a non-resident requires prior permission of RBI. Repatriation of investment, royalty and other payments also require RBI permit. But general permission is granted to companies and delegation of authority is given to banks.

Non-resident Investments

Since 1980, the government has been encouraging investment by NRIs. To clear their applications speedily, a Special Approvals Committeee was set up with the Secretary of the Department of Industrial Development as Chairman. NRIs are freely permitted to invest in Government Securities, NS Certificates, UTI units and interest/dividends on them can be repatriated through the Non-resident External Accounts (NRE - FCNRA).

NRIs can invest without repatriation benefits up to even 100% of new issues of companies, sick units, shares of existing companies, deposits with firms and companies and in convertible and non-convertible debentures, etc.

Some investments are permitted to NRIs with repatriation facility. These are:

1. Shares purchased through the Stock Exchanges, provided they are retained by NRI for a minimum period of one year, now dispended with.
2. NRIs can invest in convertible debentures up to 5% of the total paid-up value of them.
3. They can invest in Company deposits of 3-year maturity.

These investments in the secondary market under portfolio management are subject to a ceiling of 5% of paid-up equity for a single NRI and 10% of paid-up equity for total NRI investments which includes OCBs. Beyond 10% ceiling, there is need for specific RBI permission.

Investments of NRIs in new issues of Indian companies are permitted up to 40% in respect of specific areas such as hotels, hospitals etc. These are with the full repatriation rights, provided the funds come in through FCNR Accounts. In some cases, investments up to 74% to 100% with full repatriation benefits are permitted as in the case of specified priority sector industries. Some of these provisions were further liberalised in more recent years. In 1999, the government. announced its decision to treat NRIs like resident Indians only.

NRIs are also given special benefits for the setting up of industrial units in India and fast track clearance of necessary approvals were granted for import of necessary capital goods, raw materials, etc. Besides, they are given some fiscal concessions, such as lower tax rates, tax deduction at specified fixed rates on their income, dividends, capital gains, etc.

INDUSTRY GROUPS LISTED ON STOCK EXCHANGES

The C.S.O. publishes data on Industrial Production under 38 major groups. But hundreds of industry groups are there in which industries both big and small can be classified. Leaving aside the user-based classification, under which data are published by C.S.O., the three broad heads under which trends of production can be discerned are Mining and Quarrying; Manufacturing and Infrastructure industries (coal, crude petroleum, cement, steel, electricity and refinery products, having a weight of 26.7% in the total index).

The listed companies are grouped into around 80 categories by the Economic Times Industry Monitor. The financial journals like Capital Market, and Dalal Street also publish data on industry wise financial parameters like sales, earnings, E.P.S., CEPS, P/E etc., which will be useful for industry analysis. The B.S.E., Economic Times, Financial Express, Business Standard and Business India publish data on listed companies industry group wise. There are more than 100 categories under which these data are presented. The investors and analysts have to choose industry groups on a selective basis for analysis and it is preferable to concentrate on 10 to 20 major categories like Engineering, Chemicals. Cement, Electronics and Computers, I.T. Software, Steel, Sugar, Paper, Shipping. Health Care, Hotels, Banking & Finance, Food Products, Jewellery & Diamonds, Automobiles & Spares, Drugs & Pharmaceuticals, Fertilisers & Pesticides, Tubes & Tyres, Telecom, Power, etc.

Financial Data on Industries

The financial structure, operational results and profitability of these industries vary widely from industry-to-industry. The trends in production, sales, stocks and financial results, are to be studied for industry wise analysis. The past data on these parameters are available in various company finance studies, published in the RBI bulletins from time-to-time. The ICICI, CMIE and many Research bodies publish data on these industrial groups. The company wise details within the industry groups are available from the Bombay Stock Exchange Directory — a publication running into about 20 volumes giving out the details of each of the listed companies and their financial data. The history, objectives, activities, promoters and shareholding pattern, Floating Stock and a host of other data are available from this directory volumes, as also on floppies for computer usage.

The investor has to first identify the groups of industries in which he finds the growth potential and then collect the data from the above sources, referred to earlier:

Financial results can be analysed:

(1) In terms of efficiency of capital structuring, viz., gearing ratio, and leverage ratios, etc.

(2) Sources and uses of funds data such as External sources, to total funds employed, gross fixed assets as percentage of gross assets formation.

(3) Growth rates of fixed assets, gross block or total assets etc.

(4) Activity and liquidity ratios, reflecting the current operational results in sales turnover, inventory turnover, current ratio or quick ratio etc.

(5) Profitability ratios and profit allocation ratio will give net financial results, profitability, dividend distribution and Tax planning etc.

These details industry wise, and total for all the corporate sectors are published by the CMIE, RBI and other Research bodies like those of E.T., F.E, etc. From a study of these data, in the background of the overall industrial growth in the past, and projected for the current year, any analyst can discern the groups which show more than average growth, better performance and better profitability. Such groups should be examined in detail in their studies. The RBI presents the data on growth rates of 17 major industry groups, classified into those accelerating, decelerating and negative growth rates. The examples of accelerating growth rates are those of machinery, textiles, beverages, tobacco etc. (RBI Annual Report 2008-09).

These studies should aim at identifying the industry groups in which investment is recommended. For deciding on these groups, the Government policy and attitude, labour problems in the industry, raw materials and market for the industry, competitive conditions, in addition to the financial factors should also be looked into as referred to above.

Industrial Policy and Industrial Growth

The industrial growth rate in the Seventh Plan was around 9% but it fell to around 7-8% in the Eighth Plan. In the year 1997-98, the projection of the industrial growth was lower at 4% which was lower than that achieved in 1995-96 and 1996-97. There was decline in growth rates in 1997 and 1998 and it picked upto 6.7% in 1999-2000 and average rate for the period 2005 to 2012 is about 8.5%. The industries to be chosen should project a better growth rate in production. Similarly, if the growth rate of gross profits for an industry is 30% on an average, the industries showing better profitability than the average have to be selected.

The industry analysis should thus study the industrial policy statements of the Government from time-to-time and any current developments in the industry groups like technological changes, market conditions, capacity built and used, labour problems, competitions and foreign investment flows, etc. On the basis of the past performance of the industrial growth and projected industrial growth for the coming year, the industry groups showing or promising a growth rate higher than the average growth have to be chosen.

In respect of the financial parameters to be examined, some of them are the sales, gross profits, net earnings, EPS and P/E etc. These are to be studied for each of the industry groups for the purpose of using them as the parameters for examining the comparative performance of the various companies within the group. Thus, in Tubes and Tyres industry there may be 15 to 20 companies of which only three or four may be showing above average growth of the industry, as a whole in respect of sales, earnings, EPS and the projections made in respect of those companies should also be better than for the industry. Thus, the industry analysis has to be combined with Company Analysis.

EXAMPLE OF INDUSTRY ANALYSIS

Two Wheeler Industry[3]

This industry has grown by rapid strides over the recent years and stands at around ₹ 5,500 crores of market value. There are a few market leaders of which Bajaj Auto, is the oldest and leading manufacturer of two wheelers in India since the sixties and seventies. The others are TVS, Suzuki, Escorts, Hero Honda, Kinetic Honda, Majestic Auto whose shares in the overall market are shown below.

Industry Profile

	1996-97
Total demand	28.00 lakh units
Capacity utilisation	93.26%
of which the share of	
Bajaj Auto	43.3%
TVS Suzuki	15.5%
LML	9.0%
Escorts	7.8%
Hero Honda	4.2%
Total	79.8%
(Others like Majestic Auto, Kinetic Engineering and Kinetic Honda etc.).	20.2%

Growth Rate

The Industry Growth rate chart is presented below, as projected in Investors Guide (June 10, 1996). From a recession during 1991-92 and 1992-93, it has revived and reached buoyancy in 1994-95 and 1995-96. There was recession in 1996-97 and 1997-98. This industry growth rate picked up again in 2004 to 2007. Compared with 1993-94, the growth in IT by 2006-07 was two and half times more. After that, the growth was stagnant.

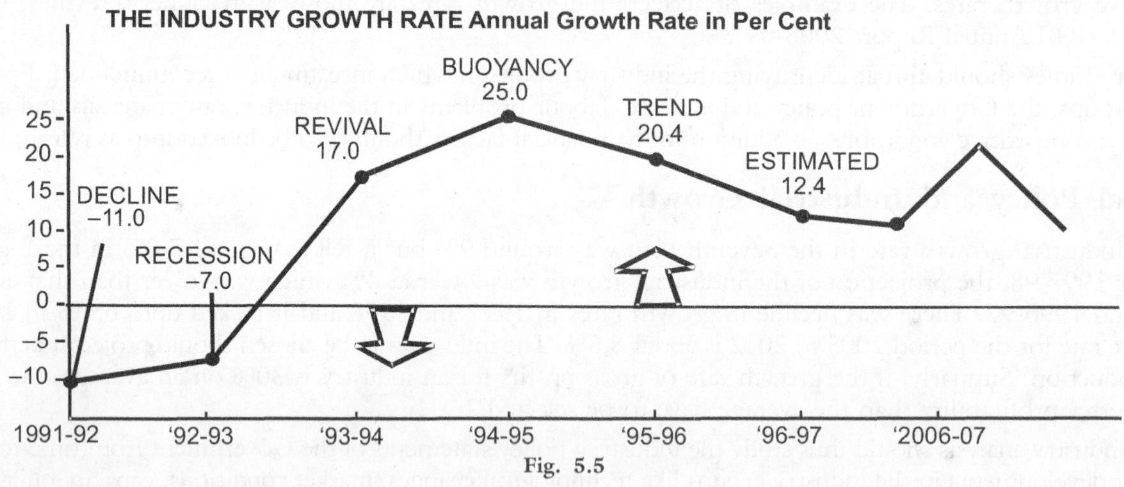

Fig. 5.5

Product Range

The major products are Scooters, Motorcycles and Mopeds. Segment wise demand shows that scooters constitute the largest component (12.25 lakh units or 46%), followed by Motor Cycles (30%) and the Mopeds for the rest. As the industry is optimistic of the growth prospects, it has projected a growth rate of about 26%. With a GNP growth rate of 6% and the consumer durable offtake at a growth rate of 20%, the middle class income group is likely to push up the demand for two wheelers to 25% or more. But the Economic Times Investors' guide has projected a growth rate of only 12-15% in the coming three years. By 1998-99, the demand should grow to around 38 lakh units from the then existing level of 27 lakh units — an annual growth rate of 14%.

All the leading manufacturers are expanding capacities from the present level of 28 lakh per annum to 44.6 lakhs per annum with an expected increase of 26% per annum. In particular Bajaj Auto is expected to increase capacity by

3. As it is illustrative, the year of data is not considered to be relevant or important.

23-25% inthe next two years in respect of both two wheelers and three wheelers, at a total cost of ₹ 400 crores, bulk of which would come from internal accruals. It has the advantages of world class plants, lower costs, low profit margins but high volumes. Its interest cost burden is low and has recently brought out new models to keep its market share against growing competitor, namely, TVS Suzuki. It has an export target of 15% of its volume of production by 2000. It has the highest gross profit and net profit ratios, cash rich and diversified into a wide product range.

Future Outlook

The industry prospects are likely to show signs of a maturing industry, with a stagnant growth of 20-25%, although the E.T. projected it at 12-15%. Of the three major products, the demand for Scooters is likely to rise by about 40% by 1998-99, Motocycles by 52% and Mopeds by 33%. These proportions may change depending upon the costs, relative profit margins, market conditions and the research component that go to improve the models. In fact the growth may be higher in respect of hybrids like scooters or low cost mobikes with better engines.

There are two areas in which the industry has to show progress, namely, cost reduction and diversification. With all the major leaders showing expansion plans, the diversification is being achieved even by single product company like Hero Honda. The expansion plans of the four major companies are as follows: As these data are only for illustration, the dates of data may not be relevant.

Table

	Installed Capacity	*Expanded Capacity*	*Cost Estimated*
(1) Bajaj Auto	12.7 lakh	20 lakh	₹ 400 crores
(2) TVS Suzuki	4.2 lakh	6.5	₹ 110 crores
(3) LML	2.5 lakh	6.5	₹ 204 crores
(4) Hero Honda	2.4 lakh	4.0	₹ 183 crores

Of these four companies, Bajaj Auto continues to be the leader, but the largest expansion is planned by Hero Honda in terms of diversification and show the largest price rise. In actual fact by 2001-2002, Hero Honda became the leader and recorded the largest sales growth. Even in 2009-12 Hero Honda continued to be the leader. Bajaj Auto is now quoted at ₹ 2,510 at end July, 2015. Its P/E ratio is 23.52.

Financial Projection

Inter Company Comparison

(*₹ crores*)

1995-96 Gross Sales ₹ crores (in brackets % age change over last year)	*Bajaj Auto 2794 (26.5%)*	*TVS Suzuki 618 (51.1%)*	*Hero Honda 633 (32.7%)*	*LML 512 (47.9%)*
Net Profits	418.12 (37.0%)	34.48 (2.2%)	26.33 (35.4%)	30.84 (16.8%)
Cash Profits	491.83 (35.1%)	43.96 (8.8%)	37.05 (32.1%)	42.04 (13.6%)
OPM	19.33	11.37	7.9	9.2
EPS in ₹	52.37	14.92	13.197	7.44
P/E multiple	19.0	24.46	20.09	10.6
Current Market Price (July 1996)	996	365	265	79
Expected Market Price in ₹ a year hence (Range of prices)	1000/1200	500/600	360/400	80/100
Actual Price range as in Jan. 2000/2010	350 – 388 400 – 1800	480 – 15 520/74	820 – 755 790/850	70 – 5 80 – 13

Market sentiment was bullish and prices were in the upswing from Nov. 1999; even so the prices of those scrips as quoted towards the end of 1999 and early in 2000 are in ranges which are disappointing. Bajaj Auto lost its importance while TVS made much headway. This historical data analysis of these companies is only for illustration, so that the reader can make his own analysis of the companies of present days.

INVESTMENT DECISION

To take an investment decision on the basis of above data is difficult, unless the following factors are also considered and the time frame of investment.

(1) Management expertise, tax planning, expansion and dynamism, as in the case of TVS.
(2) Floating stock of the company, equity base and the likely dilution of equity as in the LML.
(3) Growth prospects increase with Gross Block and operational efficiency.
(4) The financial data parameters like GPM, NPM, Profitability Projections etc.

In the short run, LML is not preferred due to likely interest burden and dilution of equity, but in the long run, it is the last bet due to expansion plans and dynamism. In the short-run Hero Honda and Bajaj Auto are to be preferred.

RESULTS OF FINANCIAL PROJECTION

In an inter-company comparision attempted above, the status of companies has been changing over years. The financial data of the companies can be compared in any proforma one of which is shown above. The data are available under corporate information — financial data — in the BSE and NSE websites. As compared to the year 1995-96, the data for 2010 is completely different. The companies BAJAJ AUTO and Hero Honda have shown relatively better performance, while the TVS Suzuki and LML Motors have resulted in worse performance as reflected in the price trends for the January 2010. This shows how the reader has to be wary about the results but should note only the mechanics of analyzing the data and arrive at his own conclusions. The performance of companies changes from year to yearand so are the financial results. The price trends reflect the fundamentals to some extent if not fully and the financial results have to be analyzed to know the performance of the company is physical operations and financial results. The objective of this chapter is only to introduce to the students to the mechanics of analysis of the fundamentals of the companies in the background of the competing firms in the same industry. The choice of the buy and sell decisions is dependent on this analysis.

PROBLEM

Lifts or Elevator Industry

This industry is one where entry is difficult due to the long time, it takes to reach a stage of worthwhile profits and production depends on the order booking and is a long drawn out process. The major players are OTIS elevators with a market share of 60% — Bharat Bijlee (9%), ECEC (7%) and Kone of France (6%) and others account for the rest. The recent entrants into this Industry are Mitsubhishi of Japan and Hyundai with collaboration of Kinetic Engineering.

Lift booking has grown at a rate of around 20% in the recent past and the depends mostly on construction industry in Metro and urban cities for commercial and residential multi-storied buildings. Make a projection for future of this industry's market demand.

In the above background of the industry the financial data of OTIS Elevator is given below. The share price quoted on NSE and BSE has a range of ₹ 466 – ₹ 245 for the latest 52 weeks in 2000. Analyse the worthwhileness of buying this share and the price, at which it can be bought.

(Caution: OTIS is not quoted now on the BSE and NSE and hence it is for illustration only)

Balance Sheet Data as at end March - (in ₹ crores)

Net worth Total	*1995 48*	*March, 96, 54*	*97, 62*	*98, 72*	*99 85*
(a) Equity	13	13	12	12	12
(*b*) Reserves	35	41	50	60	72
Debt	1	2	—	—	—
Total Liabilities	49	56	62	72	85
Gross block	32	46	61	73	78
Less: Depre.	19	22	25	30	35
Net Block	13	24	36	43	43
Investment	16	22	25	14	14
Net current Assets	18	9	1	10	25
Misc. Expenditure	2	1	0	5	3
Total Assets	49	56	62	72	85
Book Value	37	42	52	60	65
P/E Multiple@			27	22	18

(at market price of ₹ 325)

@ at end June 2002, the P/E ratio is reported as 12.6 and market price ₹ 280.

Earnings Statement

(in ₹ crores)

	1995	1996	1997	1998	1999
Gross sales	122	191	211	227	201
Net sales	112	181	201	215	248
Rate of growth	15	61	11	7	15
Operating profit	10	18	24	22	29
Other income (for maintenance contract income)	7	9	8	11	14
PBIDT	17	27	32	33	43
Finance charges	1	1	0.5	0	0
Gross profits	16	26	31	33	43
(*Less:* Depr. and Taxes)					
Net profit	9	12	15	18	22
Cash profit	11	14	20	24	27
EPS ₹	7	9	12	15	18
CEPS ₹ (Cash earnings per share)	8	11	17	21	24
Dividend per share ₹	3	4	5	6	7.5

Hints: Market price range is ₹ 245 to ₹ 466. At the peak dividend of 7.5, its retention is more, and has potential for growth. At EPS of ₹ 18, and P/E multiple of average for the last three years of 22 to 27, the market price can be 22 × 18 = ₹ 486 roughly. In terms of Book value, market price is a multiple of 3 to 7 times. Then the market price can range from ₹ 260 to ₹ 490, depending upon the Book value. Dividends, profits and book value are showing consistent rise. Then it is for the reader to decide as to whether to buy this share and at what price. If the reader wants to discount the future cash flows take the required discount rate as 20%, and the price can range from ₹ 300 to ₹ 375 as against the current market price of ₹ 290 at end of July, 1998. Its actual price early in January, 2000 was ₹ 400 and it ranged between ₹ 350-400 at the end of 1999. In June 2002, its price was around ₹ 280 and 52 week High and Low are ₹ 336 and ₹ 200 and P/E multiple is 12.6. In fact, there was no worthwhile price rise in the Scrip, despite its past significant growth due to general recession in the market. The typical way how some good companies can also become defunct and disappear from the face of the Exchange is provided by this OTIS elevators. After 2002-03, the company ceased to be quoted.

6

BASIS FOR COMPANY ANALYSIS

The Stock price has been found to depend on the intrinsic value of the company's share to the extent of about 50% as per many research studies. Graham and Dodd in their book on "Securities Analysis" have defined the intrinsic value as "that value which is justified by the facts of assets, earnings and dividends." These facts are reflected in the earning potential of the company. The analyst has to project the expected future earnings per share and discount them to the present time which gives the intrinsic value of the share. Another method to use is to take the expected earnings per share and multiply it by the Industry average P/E multiple. By any method, let the analyst estimate the intrinsic value or fair value of the share and compare it with the market price to know whether the stock is over valued or under valued. The investment decision is to buy under valued stock and sell over valued stock. The extent of variation or possible error on either side may be taken at about 10 to 20%.

The table below depicts the relationship of market price to intrinsic factors.

Some of the shares of companies may be blue chip stock or growth stocks, which are expanding and diversifying and their growth rates are higher than the market averages. Many investors, who are particularly averse to risk, prefer income stocks. These stocks are expected to give consistent dividends and with a good record of income distribution. Such companies which earn good dividends are mutual funds, unit trusts, public limited companies with a good financial record. A careful evaluation is, however, necessary to decide what undervalued scrips are to be bought.

Crudely expressed a share is undervalued, if its risk is lower than the market risk, but the return is higher than the market reward. The market price can also be compared to book value of the share or its P/E ratio can be compared to similar ratios of companies in the same industry or the industry average, to know whether the share price is

Table 1

Price Formation

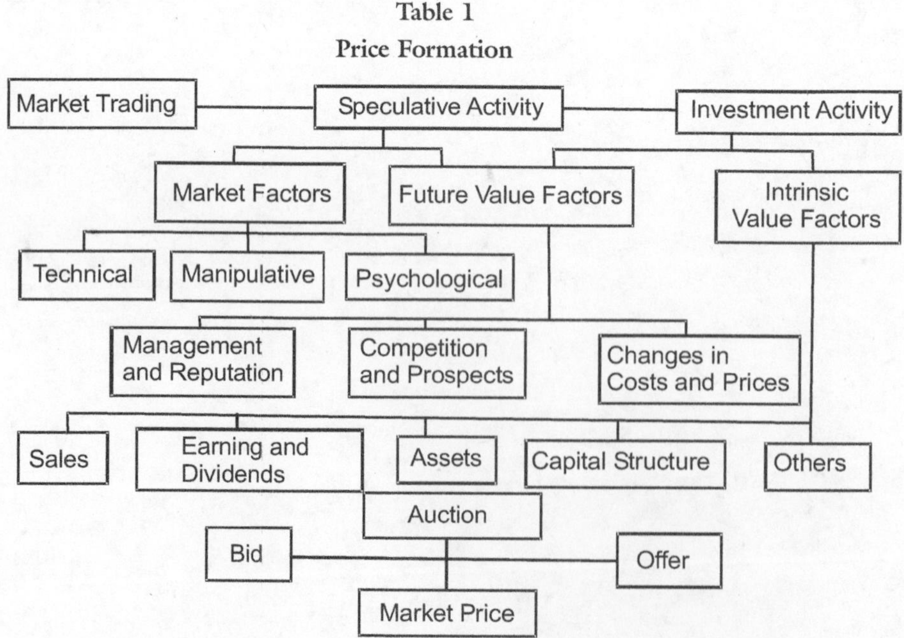

undervalued. So, it is necessary to make a Judicious mix of industry analysis with company analysis of the fundamentals. As the table below shows, the fundamentals explain the market trading comprising both the speculative and investment in the security markets.

ELEMENTS OF FINANCIAL ANALYSIS

Share price depends partly on its intrinsic worth for which financial analysis of a company is necessary to help the investor to decide whether to buy or not the shares of that company. The soundness and intrinsic worth of a company is known only by such analysis. The market price of a share depends, among others on the sound fundamentals of the company, the financial and operational efficiency and the profitability of that company. These factors can be examined by a study of the financial management of the company. An investor needs to know the performance of the company, its intrinsic worth as indicated by some parameters like book value, EPS, P/E multiple etc., and come to a conclusion whether the share is rightly priced for purchase or not. This, in short is the importance of financial analysis of a company to the investor.

What is Financial Analysis?

The financial management of a company is concerned with management of its funds which reflects how efficiently the company is managing its funds. The overall objective of all business is to secure funds at low cost and their effective utilisation in the business for a profit. The funds so utilised must generate an income higher than the cost of procuring them. Here it is to be noted that all companies need both long-term and short-term capital. The finance manager must therefore keep in view the needs of both long-term debt and working capital and ensure that the business enjoys an optimum level of working capital and that it does not keep too many funds blocked in inventories, book-debts, cash, etc. The capital structuring and average cost of capital for the company should also be examined.

Financial analysis is analysis of financial statements of a company to assess its financial health and soundness of its management. "Financial Statement analysis" involves a study of the financial statements of a company to ascertain its prevailing state of affairs and the reasons therefor. Such a study would enable the public and investors to ascertain whether one company is more profitable than the other, and also to state the causes and factors that are probably responsible for this.

Components of Financial Statements

The term 'financial statements' as used in modern business refers to the balance sheet, or the statement of financial position of the company at a point of time and income and expenditure statement, or the profit and loss statement over a period. To this is added, the profit allocation statement which reconciles the balance in this account at the end of the period with that at the beginning. Thus, the financial statements provide a summary of the accounts of a company over a period of one year, and the balance sheet reflecting the assets, liabilities and capital as at a point of time say at the end of the year.

Analysis and Interpretation: With a view to interpret the financial statements, it is necessary to analyse them with the object of formation of an opinion with respect to the financial condition of that company.

This Analysis involves the following steps:

(a) Comparison of the financial statements, over two to five years.

(b) Ratio analysis, for two to three years.

(c) Funds Flow analysis, over a short period.

(d) Trend analysis, over a period of 5 to 10 years.

The salient features of each of the above steps are discussed briefly in this Chapter.

Comparison of the Financial Statements

Comparison is the precondition for a meaningful interpretation. It may be in the nature of:

(a) figures of one year with that of another year;

(b) inter-firm comparison of figures, within the same industry;

(c) comparison of one product figures with that of another product; and

(d) comparison of budgeted figures with the actual figures.

For the purpose of analysis, the figures in the balance sheet and the income statements are to be arranged properly which will facilitate the work. The statements are prepared in single (vertical) column form as shown below for this purpose.

Balance Sheet is now presented under two heads, namely sources and uses. The sources are again Internal and External and uses refer to the application of funds into Fixed assets, Investments. Current assets – Current liabilities etc.

Balance Sheet as at . . . .

Fixed Assets

Investments

Working Capital:

Current assets *Less:*

Current Liabilities

Capital Employed Total

Less:

Funded Debts

(Debentures and Long-term liabilities)

Shareholders' Fund

Represented by:

Equity Share Capital

Preference Share Capital

Reserves and Surplus *Less:*

Preliminary Expenses

Profit and Loss Account for the year ended

Sales (Net)

Less:

Cost of Goods Sold

Gross operating Profit:

Less: Operating Expenses (Office, Selling and Distribution Expenses)

Net Operating Profit:

Earning Before Interest and Tax (EBIDT)

Minus Interest, Depreciation and Taxation

Profit After Tax (PAT) = Net Profit

Meaningful analysis can be achieved by comparing the financial data and ratios of one firm with that of another. This process is called inter-firm comparison. When the performance in various departments of a single firm is compared, the term used is intra-firm comparison.

For inter-firm comparisons, the financial statements must be made as far as practicable, comparable so as to derive reliable conclusions on anything. The stated amounts of two enterprises must be at the same price levels, and the accounting methods used by them must be similar.

RATIO ANALYSIS

The ratio is a statistical yardstick that provides a measure of relationship between any two variables. It can be effectively used as a tool of management along with Fund Flow Statements and Trend Analysis for interpretation of the financial statements. As ratios are simple to calculate and easy to understand, there is a tendency to employ them profusely.

The ratios are conveniently classified as follows:

(i) Balance Sheet Ratios which deal with the relationships between two items or groups of items which are both in the Balance Sheet, e.g., the ratio of current assets to current liabilities (Current Ratio).

(ii) Revenue Statement Ratios which deal with the relationship between two items or groups of items which are both in the Revenue Statement, e.g., ratio of gross profit to sale or gross profit margin. (Income-expenditure Statement)

(iii) Balance Sheet and Revenue Statement Ratios which deal with real relationships between items from the Revenue Statement and items from the Balance Sheet, e.g., ratio of net profit to own Funds (Composite Ratios).

Some examples of these ratios are given below:

(a) Revenue Statement Ratios:

(i) Gross Profit Ratio
(ii) Operating Ratio
(iii) Expense Ratio
(iv) Net Profit Ratio
(v) Stock Turnover or Turnover of Inventory

(b) Balance Sheet Ratios:

(i) Current Ratio
(ii) Liquidity Ratio or Quick Ratio
(iii) Debt to Equity Ratio
(iv) Asset to Equity Ratio

(c) Composite Ratios:

(i) Return on Total Resources
(ii) Return on Own Funds
(iii) Turnover of Fixed Assets
(iv) Turnover of Debtors

Usefulness of Ratio Analysis

Ratio Analysis should be based on some common standards such as comparison between two companies in the same industry and within the same assets group. Since the performance of companies varies from industry to industry and from location to location, the ratios are not comparable exactly.

What is proper for Hotel Industry which is seasonal in nature may not be true for cement and steel industry which belong to infrastructure sector.

The use of Ratio Analysis depends on the object in mind. The question to be put to oneself is what do I want to know of the company? Let us say its capital efficiency is to be examined. Then ratios such as Gross Block to equity or Fixed Assets to Share Capital or Net Profit to Capital employed are to be used. Thus, there are different ratios for different purposes.

Ratio Analysis will be meaningful to establish relationship regarding financial performance, operational efficiency and profit margins with respect to companies over a period of time and as between companies within the same industry group.

In addition to the Ratio Analysis, financial analysis involves fund flow Analysis and the Trend Analysis. Fund Flow Analysis involves the examination of sources and uses of funds. Thus, inflow of funds is due to sale, and other income, whereas uses are increases in investment or purchase of assets or for regular wage and other payments etc. Cash accruals and how they are utilised will be studied in this process.

FUND FLOW ANALYSIS

The Balance Sheet of a Company reveals its financial status at a point of time. The financial executive must know the flows of funds underlying the balance sheet changes. The operation of business involves the conversion of cash into non-cash assets which are recovered back into cash form. The statement showing sources and uses of funds is properly known as "Fund Flow Statements." It shows the ebb and flow of funds into and out of a business. It covers all movements that involves an actual exchange of assets and only transactions representing book-keeping adjustments are not reported. Thus, Funds Flow Statement is a useful tool in the kit of financial management and is a report of the financial operations of the company. The term funds should not be interpreted as literal cash, but it extends the concept to include assets or financial resources which do not effect cash or working capital. Examples are the purchase of property in exchange for issue of shares and bonds. The broader approach provides a more complete and informative presentation.

The changes representing the "sources of funds" in the business may be issue of debentures, increase in networth, addition to funds, reserves and surplus, retention of earnings.

Changes showing the "uses of funds" include:

(a) Additions to assets — fixed and current.

(b) Addition to investments.

(c) Decrease in liabilities by paying off loans and creditors.

(d) Decrease in net worth by incurring of losses, withdrawal of funds from business and payment of dividends. If the net profit for a particular accounting year is a source of funds, a net loss as shown by an income statement is an application of funds. This is so because where a loss has been incurred, funds have gone out of the business.

The changes in net working capital take place either by the decrease in current assets or increase in the liabilities as sources of funds and the reduction in current liabilities. These changes in net working capital are available from the comparative balance sheet analysis. An increase in net working capital in this manner represents a net application of funds. A statement of source and application of funds can be prepared from the two comparative balance sheets with an accompanying increase-decrease column. From the stand-point of the balance sheet, funds may come from three sources: an increase in liabilities, a decrease in assets and an increase in net-worth. The increase in networth is used to represent two sources of funds, namely, net-profits and contribution of own funds. Likewise, applications represent three uses of funds, decrease in liabilities, increase in assets and decrease in net worth. Here again, the decrease in the networth represents the uses, namely, net losses and decrease in capital funds.

The fund flow statement helps in guiding the destiny of a business by enabling the analyst to visualise the movement of funds that constantly take place. A failure to detect pattern of change can perpetuate undesirable trends and lead to financial difficulties. An extended reliance on external sources can create a top heavy capital structure. This statement helps in detecting the sources for financing the heavy accumulation of inventory and book-debts if any. It is also helpful in forecasting the flow of funds. It is used for projecting working capital requirements. It also highlights future need for funds and plays an important role in the evaluation of trade credit.

TREND ANALYSIS

Trend Analysis refers to comparison of some important ratios and rates of growth over a time period of a few years. These trends in the case of GPM or Sales Turnover are useful to indicate the extent of improvement or deterioration over a period of time in the aspects considered. The trends in dividends, E.P.S., asset growth or sales growth are some examples of the trends used to study the operational performance of the companies. Any temporary rise in inventories to sales would indicate sluggish demand for the products of the company.

Thus, the trends of the results, rather than the actual ratios and percentages, are important. Structural relationships taken from the financial statements of one year only are of limited value and the trends of these structural relationships established from statements over a number of years may be more significant than absolute ratios. Investor wants to know how well the business is operating in comparison with planned performance and if actual results are not good enough, what should the future indicate for the company. The financial results of all businesses are affected by general economic condition, by competition, and local factors relating to company.

It should be particularly emphasised that one particular ratio used without reference to other ratios may be very misleading. In other words, the combined effect of the various ratios must be considered in arriving at a correct diagnosis which will be of assistance in interpreting the financial condition and earning performance of the business. Each ratio plays its part in this interpretation.

Finally, it should be realised that ratios are only preliminary step in interpretation and must be supplemented by rigorous investigation into all aspects of operations of company before safe conclusions can be drawn from them. Trend analysis should supplement the ratio analysis to assess the good and bad aspects of working of a company.

More importantly not only the objective factual data should be analysed from Balance Sheet and Income-Expenditure Statements of the company, but a scrutiny of subjective factors indicated in the Directors' and Auditor's Reports should also be made with particular reference to any mention in footnotes to contingent liabilities, unpaid taxes, doubtful debts etc. Besides research into practical day-to-day operations of the company can be done only by a plant visit and study on the spot the prospects of the company in the coming year or two.

The Concept of Funds and Cash

While funds flow is used in the sense of working capital, cash flow is used for only cash inflows and outflows. While the former refers to long-term and medium-term funds for all activities, the latter refers to only short-term needs which are substitutable for bank balances. The cash flows are prepared from cash budgets and operations of the company. The fund flows are for total activities say operations in financial and investment and related activities. In cash flows, only cash and bank balances are involved and hence it is a narrower term than the concept of funds flows.

HOW TO PREPARE CASH FLOW STATEMENT?

The data come from the Balance sheet and Income Expenditure statement in the form of changes over a period of each in the items of these financial statements. The example of a cash flow statement is as follows:

(₹ *Lakhs*)

Sources	₹	*Use of or Decline in Cash*	₹
Cash at Bank	10,000	Increase in Inventories	20,000
Add: Cash inflows		Purchase of Fixed Assects	60,000
(a) Issue of Equity Capital as Rights	50,000	Increase in Debtors	20,000
		Payment for Expenses	30,000
(b) Issue of Debentures	20,000		
(c) Raising of Public Deposits	10,000		
(d) Increase of Creditors	10,000		
(e) Cash Trading Profits (generated)	60,000		
	1,60,000		1,30,000
		Closing Balance in Bank	30,000

Cash profits are brought forward from profit allocation statement, while the other items are derived from the Balance Sheet and income and expenditure statements. A reading of the above statement helps the cash management techniques adopted by the company and its liquidity position.

Statement of Cash Flows

The usefulness of these data for the analysts is to assess the cash generated from the operations, financial activities and investment activities and the adequacy or otherwise of these cash flows to meet the emerging obligations involved in operations. The timing of the flows and whether outflows can be met by inflows during any period reflects the ability of the company to be solvent. The cash flow statement explains how the dividends are paid, how fixed assets are financed and the cost of financing reflected in the profitability and how the working capital requirements are met including bank borrowing

If loss is shown, how is it financed? If loss is shown for tax purposes that is, as part of the tax planning, the analyst has to know the real cash flow position of the company, its liquidity and solvency which are reflected in the cash flow position and the statement thereof.

COMPANY ANALYSIS: SOURCES OF DATA

The Analyst is expected to examine two major categories of information for assessing the intrinsic worth of the company's stock. First is the factual position as revealed by the financial statements of the company, viz., *internal information.* Second is the external sources of information given by the researchers or security firms and financial journals, published from time-to-time in Dailies and Magazines or in handouts issued by the security firms.

Factual Disclosures

As per the Indian Law, disclosures in the prospectus and in the financial statements are governed by the Company Act Provisions. These disclosures ensure factual reliability, comparability and consistency and comprehensiveness. Both qualitative and quantitative aspects of the working of the company are to be revealed in the Reports. Part I of Schedule VI deals with the Balance Sheet details and Part II of Schedule VI deals with the Profits and Loss Account.

The disclosures to be made in Director's Report are laid down under Section 217 and the disclosures to be made by the Auditors Report are set out under Section 227. Besides these legal provisions, the Government has issued further guidelines and notifications in pursuance of these provisions for ensuring fair corporate disclosures and for investor protection in public interest. The SEBI and the Company Law Board (CLB) have the responsibility to ensure that those disclosures are made by the companies as per the Law and the Government notifications.

For each of the items of Assets and Liabilities, there can be schedules giving the details; as for example, take the item of capital: These details are the following

(a) Authorised Capital

(b) Issued Capital

(c) Subscribed Capital

— *Less:* Calls Unpaid

(d) Forfeited Shares

(e) Fully paid: Equity

— Preference —

In a similar way, there can be any number of Schedules for the Balance Sheet items and they form part of the Balance Sheet. Section 210 of the Companies Act requires that every limited company must prepare a Balance sheet at the end of the Accounting period and that is made uniformly for all companies as at end March. Secondly, Section 211 of the Act requires that the Balance Sheet should be prepared in a prescribed proforma as contained in Schedule VI of the Act which was given above, for illustration.

As per the Companies (Disclosures of Particulars in the Report of the Board of Directors) Rules 1988, every company has to give annexures to the Director's Report an the following items:

(I) Energy Conservation

(a) Energy conservation measures taken.

(b) Additional proposals for being implemented for energy conservation.

(c) Impact of these measures.

(II) Technology Development and Absorption

(a) Research & Development.

(b) Future Plan of Action.

(c) Benefits Derived.

(III) Foreign Exchange Earnings and Outgo

(a) Earnings.

(b) Outgo.

Law and Practice in Reporting

According to American Institute of Accountants, the financial statements "reflect a combination of recorded facts, accounting conventions and personal judgments and these judgments and conventions applied affect them materially." The Institute of Chartered Accountants of India has made it mandatory for all companies to disclose the accounting policies adopted by the companies at one place with effect from 1st April, 1991. It is also required that the auditors should qualify their report if such disclosures are not made properly.

In such disclosures or otherwise, companies with advanced practices as in developed countries can adopt human benefit accounting, inflation accounting, social cost benefit accounting, segmental reporting and value added statements etc.

By a Government Notification of Dec. 1978, the companies have been permitted to present their balance sheets in a vertical form instead of the horizontal form, allowed earlier.

Section 217 of the Companies Act makes it obligatory for every company presenting its annual accounts to the general meeting, to have the balance sheet accompanied by the Report of the Board of Directors, which should contain the following: state of company's affairs, dividend recommended, if any, surplus and problems along with factual matters relating to the company.

Under Section 227 of the Act, the auditor's report should contain whether they obtained all the information and explanations necessary, and inadequacies, changes in valuation of assets or liabilities or depreciation and inventory provisions.

In addition to the Annexures to the Balance Sheet, there will be notes to the financial statements, which will give any developments or changes not known from the statements such as:

1. Contingent liabilities not accepted or pending in litigation.
2. Options outstanding and contracted payments due but not paid.
3. Changes in accounting principles and methods such as in depreciation provision and tax provision or valuation of inventory.
4. Any other proposals for acquisition, mergers, or capitalisation changes or revaluation of assets or compounding with creditors or debtors.

There will also be an Auditor's Report and notes to that Report, which contain many details not visible from the financial statement. The notes of Auditor are very useful for better understanding of the operations or lapses or weaknesses in reporting or changes in Accounting techniques and their implication for the financial results of the company or for their comparisons as between companies or over a time period.

SEBI Directives

During the process of implementing the reforms in the capital markets, SEBI has been given all powers with regard to listed companies. The listing agreement was amended to enforce better disclosures and investor protection on listed companies. Transparency, investor protection and better services, qualitative improvement in accounting and auditing are insisted upon.

Thus the listed companies have to give flow charts, sources and uses of funds, projections *vis-a-vis* actuals in respect of statements made in the initial public offer or prospectus, etc. These companies have to present quarterly financial results in addition to half-yearly unaudited accounts, disclose all major decisions of the Board such as mergers, acquisitions take overs, splits, etc. The companies are now allowed to buy back their own shares upto a limit, adopt stock splits and stock option schemes, etc. which are to be disclosed.

During the new millennium so far corporate governance code is enforced on the listed companies. Transparency, true and fair disclosures and social responsibility, public accountability and investor protection are some of the elements of corporate code of governance, adopted for the listed companies, since 2000.

The various reports included in the Financial Statement Analysis are set out later in the chapter. The type of analysis to be done, the ratios to be used and the types of stock to be selected, as per the investor's preferences are discussed in later sections in this chapter.

Horizontal Proforma of Balance Sheet

Under the Companies Act, the proforma in which the Balance Sheet can be presented is laid down in Schedule VI as referred to earlier. This provision allows the companies to present, these data in both Horizontal and Vertical forms. An example of Horizontal Proforma is as follows:

Liabilities	*Assets*
1. Share Capital Equity capital, preference shares, if any, Deferred shares, if any, Forfeited shares etc.	*1. Gross Fixed Assets* *Less:* Depreciation Net Fixed Assets
2. Reserves & Surpluses Capital Reserves Capital Redemption Reserves Share Premium Account Other Reserves Sinking Funds, Surplus from P&L Account Proposed additions to Reserves	*2. Investments* Govt. and Semi-Government Shares, Bonds, etc. *3. Current Assets@* Inventory Sundry Debtors Loans and Advances Interest Accrued in Advance Deposits Cash & Others Bank Deposits
3. Loans (a) Secured Debentures Term loans from Banks Loans from FIs Other loans, if any (b) Unsecured Fixed deposits from Directors Working capital from banks others.	*4. Other Assets* Immovable Property Intangible Assets Others *5. Miscellaneous Assets* Work in Progress Expenditure not written off. etc Discounts, Commission, etc. *6. Profit & Loss Account* Debit Balance

4. Current Liabilities@

Sundry Creditors
Acceptances
Subsidiary companies
Advance Payments
Unclaimed dividends
Interest accrued

5. Provisions

For Taxation, Dividends
and contingencies, etc.

@ Current assets and current liabilities, in some statements are shown together to derive net current assets, used in the company.

ACCOUNTING LIMITATIONS

For accurate analysis for forecasting, the accounts in financial statements should be taken with caution, as they may contain changes in Inventory Costing, valuation of fixed assets and in method of providing for depreciation and in taxation. As the objective of the analyst is to know the real and correct position and accurately comparable earning per share and P/E multiple for security valuation, he should know the primary earnings and secondary or fully diluted earnings per share. The primary earnings show the *prima facie* earnings, divided by the number of shares issued and thus assumes that there are no options or warrants to be exercised for conversion into equity and that the earnings reflect the true earnings to be available to all equity shareholders. An example will make the difference clear between primary earnings and secondary earnings per share which are adjusted for any preferred payments or likely conversions of options and warrants.

Unadjusted Ist Method		*Fully Diluted IInd Method*	
Net Earnings:	100	Net earnings	100
Preferred Dividends	20	Stock —	
Net earnings to Stockholders	80	Stock in Preferred	40
Stock in Bonds	10	Stock in Bonds	10
Stock in Equity	50	Stock in Equity	50
No. of Total Stock	60	No. of Total Stock	100
EPS (Face value of equity is to be set out as ₹ 1 to 10)	80 ÷ 60 =1.33	EPS	100 ÷ 100 =1.00

Earnings per share are lower, if all adjustments are made for conversion and equity or stock is diluted accordingly.

Pitfalls in Use of Principles of Accounting

The investment analyst has to observe caution regarding the following Pitfalls in Accounting:

1. Expenses and revenues are improperly matched — one on accrual basis and the other on cash basis.

2. Change in methods employed over time — namely, change from cash basis to accrual basis in some years and *vice versa.*

3. Goodwill shown in revaluation of assets or due to disposal of assets under reserves or surpluses, as against intangible assets on the assets side.

4. Changes in methods of inventory costing — inventory of last year valued at current rupees is different from the same inventory valued at last year prices.

5. Observance of the comparability in the value of rupee in making comparisons over time period namely inflation accounting.

6. Changes in depreciation method from straight line method to accelerated method. In the straight line method, depreciation is calculated at original cost — Estimated salvage, divided by the estimated years of life. Declining Balance Method or Double declining Balance would permit an annual depreciation of 40% of the Balance in value every year. For example take the following data for study in their difference.

Year	*Straight Line Method (₹)*	*Double Declining Method (₹)*
1	6,000	12,000
2	6,000	7,200
3	6,000	4,320
4	6,000	3,240
5	6,000	3,240
	30,000	30,000

In the accelerated method, tax liability is lower in the initial years than under straight line method but larger in the subsequent years. But in view of the rising inflation rates future payment or postponement of payment is always preferred and hence the adoption of accelerated depreciation method is not always preferred, but change from one method to another during the life of the asset is what has to be noted with caution for consistency and comparability. Similarly, costing in old rupees cannot be compared with costing with the current rupees in the comparison of sales, earnings and net profits, as between different companies or the same company in different time periods, due to price changes, leading to changes in the value of the Rupee.

In the presentation of the data of the companies, they are obliged now to present the consolidated position of the companies along with the subsidiaries. Hence, the Balance Sheet data on all the subsidiaries owned partially or fully to the extent of the company's involvement or ownership are presented along with the data of the parent company.

In the presentation of data, tax liability or any contingent liability has to be shown separately, if not provided for in the Balance Sheet. The deferment of tax liability or contesting of any other liability is a postponement of payment, whose implications should be kept in mind by the analyst. Similarly, the Auditors' notes and their comments have to be carefully studied by every analyst.

FINANCIAL STATEMENTS

Balance Sheet Analysis in investment decision-making involves the use of the Financial Data available in Balance Sheet and Income and Expenditure statements of a Company. The objective of this analysis is to know the overvaluation or undervaluation of a share as judged by its intrinsic worth and compare it with its market price and that of the similar companies within the same industry. The Company's performance in terms of its physical operations is reflected in its Balance Sheet and Income and Expenditure Statements in terms of financial data.

Annual Reports

The main components of the Annual Reports of Companies, containing Balance Sheet and Income and Expenditure data are as follows:

1. Chairman's Speech to its Investors: This would bring out the management views of the Company's performance, in the backdrop of the economy and industrial growth, its plans for expansion or diversification if any, difficulties or problems faced by the Company and their plan of action to meet these challenges and the immediate future prospects of the Company etc.

2. Director's Report: This is a factual account of the operations of the Company during the past year and the Financial results of these operations, profits or losses, the allocation of profits for depreciation, interest, taxes, dividends etc. After allocating these sums, the residual profits are ploughed back to the reserves or losses are written off. The input availability, market for the outputs, labour problems, Government policy changes with regard to them, if any, exports or imports made by the Company etc., are all presented in this report for the benefit of its shareholders.[@]

3. Balance Sheet and Income and Expenditure Accounts: These are accompanied by the profit allocation statement and the detailed schedules for each of the items in the accounts. The method of presenting these data varies from company to company although the contents are almost the same. These data would reflect the prima facie position of the company's operations and the financial results of these operations.

4. Auditor's Report: This is a statutory report testifying the correctness of the accounts and giving their own comments on the accounting practices and procedures of the company. The real position of the company's operations is known from the footnotes to the accounts and the comments of the Auditors. They indicate the contingent liabilities, bad debts, changes in accounting practices adopted to camouflage the poor financial performance, method of providing

@ The company has to disclose information on conservation of energy, technology absorption, R&D Expenditure and benefits from it, foreign exchange earnings and outgo etc., which are also useful for investment analysis. All these are to be covered in the Director's Report.

for depreciation, provision for DRR fund and other satutory obligations, revaluation of assets if any, dividends not paid, advance calls, etc. In fact, the most vital information to be provided to Investors as per the Companies Act is contained in the footnotes. As such the analysts should examine carefully these notes and Auditors' Report to make any correct assessment of the valuation of a share.

Market Price and Corporate Performance

The market price of a share depends primarily on the Company's performance, reflected in the earnings per share or cash earning per share, dividend record and bonus payments made by the company. Besides, share price also depends on the goodwill factors which are subjective in nature such as management reputation, expansion plans, tax planning, technological set-up, reputation of collaborators and locational advantages. The management rating is subjective and is a factor contributing to the goodwill of the company. This goodwill also depends on the Government attitude to the management, Government policy with regard to the imports etc.

Honesty, integrity and consistency of management gives good rating for the company. The price of a share also depends on subjective factors like sentiment of the market, phase of the market such as gloom, fear, indecision, optimism and Euphoria etc. Thus, many non-economic and non-financial factors play a role in price formation of a scrip in the market.

To sum up, the market price of share depends on some fundamental factors like intrinsic value of the share, as also on subjective and goodwill factors and sentimental factors depending on the phase of the market. The intrinsic worth of the company is judged by the net present value, derived by discounting future returns of shares, book value of the share, earnings per share etc.

ANALYSIS OF FINANCIAL POSITION

The following financial parameters are looked into for judging the company's performance, as an illustration:

Financial Ratios	*Significance*
Equity to Networth	Strength of Owned Funds
Equity to Sales	Equity Turnover
Rights & Bonus	Expansion Prospects
MP to Book Value	Over/Under Valuation
MP to EPS	Over/Under Valuation
P/E Multiple (Market share price is relative to its face value)	Comparison with other Companies and Industry Average
GPM & NPM	Profitability
Dividend	Distribution of Profits

The above are some of the quantifiable factors derived from the Annual Accounts. But the non-quantifiable factors like goodwill and sentiment cannot be judged from the Balance Sheet data except in an indirect manner. Thus, the management policy, expansion and tax planning schemes can be known from the Chairman's speeches, Financial Press and Directors' Report.

Future prospects of the Company can be assessed indirectly from the hints given by the Chairman in his speech to the Investors in the General Body Meeting or in the Press conferences. Similarly, the genuineness and dependability of the accounting practices and true and factual disclosures as shown in the Auditors' report will reflect on the management integrity, honesty and their reputation. The Balance Sheet analysis is thus an important subject in the direction of fundamental analysis of a share price which the Analysts and Investors should undertake as part of their research for indentifying the shares to buy and the shares to sell.

TYPES OF SHARES IN THE MARKET

At any stage in the economy, there are different types of industries, some startup companies, some mature and grown, some expanding into growth industries and some showing decline in their prosperity and popularity. Some industries are seasonal, some in key or core sectors, some in export sector etc.

Similarly, in each industry there are different types of companies, some growing, some stagnant and some declining. There are thus different types of companies within the same industry and different types of Industries within the Economy. A genuine investor should try to identify the potentialities of each of these groups and concentrate on growth-oriented industries or emerging Blue Chips and established Blue Chips. Within each industry, there are some companies which are turnaround companies showing signs of emerging into Blue Chip Companies. Company characteristics also vary, viz., innovative unique product companies, leaders, single product and multiproduct companies, captive demand companies, etc.

Blue Chip Companies are in simple language, growth-oriented companies showing signs of expansion, diversification, modernisation of technology and reputation for consistent profitability and profit margins to sustain the consistent dividend distribution, growing profits and expanding networth.

The management of these companies have got a dynamic and growth-oriented policy and have a reputation for a vision for future growth and expansion and maintain a sustained growth in assets, sales turnover and profits. Emerging Blue Chip companies are those which are turn-around companies and exhibit potentiality to grow and expand in gross block, sales and net profit. The actual Blue Chip Companies like Colgate, Hindustan Lever, SPIC, L&T etc., have a consistent record of dividend pay-outs, growth in dividends, expansion and bonus from time-to-time. The main characteristics of the Blue Chip Companies may be set out as follows:

(1) These companies belong to the industry groups which are in general expanding and growing.

(2) They are market leaders as in the case of Indian hotels in the Hotel Industry, ACC in Cement Industry, Hero Honda in Scooter Industry and Colgate in mouth cleansing.

(3) These Companies show capacity to diversify and grow and generate larger gross block, higher sales turnover and growing profit margins. They continuously expand the capital base in terms of debt or equity or rights etc.

(4) They have purposeful tax planning and consistent modernisation and expansion plans. They have the capacity to meet the emerging challenges like input or labour problems.

(5) The Management outlook is dynamic and their vision is ambitious expansionism. They are highly aggressive leaders in the industry.

(6) They have also commitments to research and development and are quick to adopt new technologies and lower costs and increase profits. They may have reputed foreign collaborators to back them up.

Growth Shares

Such companies are very attractive to the long-term investors as the return to the equity shareholders in such companies are continuously expanding due to dividends, growth in dividends, networth, bonus and rights etc. Besides, in view of the consistent good performance, detailed monitoring by Investors of such companies may not be necessary. They are a good hedge against inflation and rising costs. The investor is also benefitted by capital appreciation or capital gains and by multiplying his original investment in a short period of time. The investor has only to identify such scrips and make long-term investment in them which will ensure steady return on their investment, safety, marketability and continued capital appreciation, regular dividends, rights, bonus shares etc.

The examples of such growth shares which should be included in the portfolio of every investor are Bajaj Auto and Telco in automobiles, Tisco in Steel Industry, East India Hotels in Hotel Industry, CEAT Tyres and Appollo Tyres in Tyre Industry, Tata Tea in Tea Industry, Britannia in Food Industry, HLL in consumer goods category etc.

Cyclical Shares

Other categories of shares and cyclical shares whose fortunes may depend upon the business cycle and trading like shipping, fertilisers, tea and machine tools etc. They make sometime huge profits and sometimes poor profits depending on the cycles.

Defensive Shares

Another category of companies is defensive shares whose prices are stable and do not fluctuate widely. Normally, they pay regular dividends within a narrow range and have standard practices of ploughing back profits and declaration of modest dividends. These are defensive shares whose dividends are stable and profits and profitability are expanding but at a consistent and slow rate. Many plantations and Cotton Textiles come in this category.

Discount Shares

Besides there is a category of discount shares whose prices are depressed due to low profits but with a hope of higher profitability in the immediate future due to the change in the management or in Government Policies or due to new technological changes. Among the companies in this group, there may be many undervalued groups whose potentialities for growth are high and therefore they are called Turnaround Companies, or emerging Blue Chips. The category of Blue Chips emerge out of corporate performance and can be attributed to rich parentage arising from foreign collaborators or foreign technicians, ambitious and driving promoters, unique products, special technologies, marketing strategies, management reputation, etc.

NET FINANCIAL RESULTS AND PROFITABILITY

The Company's Balance Sheet reflects the financial position of a company at a point of time, while its Income-Expenditure Account presents the picture of its physical operations over a period of say one year. So the Balance Sheet and its Income Expenditure Statement are related closely and the combined net position of the latter is transferred to the Balance Sheet in the form of residual profits or losses shown in liabilities or assets of the company.

A study of the corporate performance over a period of time is thus possible through the Balance Sheet Analysis. The assets and liabilities in Balance Sheet and of Income and Expenditure Statement are to be studied together.

It will be seen from the proforma table on Income and Expenditure that Gross Operating Profit reflects the Financial results of the Physical Operations. The Net Profits are the true residual profits after meeting the required payments of interest and taxes and providing for depreciation. But cash profits or net cash earnings include the net profit plus depreciation as the depreciation provision keeps the funds with the company only and it is only a book entry.

Income and Expenditure Statement

(For the Year Ended ....)

Income	*Expenditure*
Sales Other Income Total	Materials Consumed + Excise Duty + Manufacturing Expenses + Other Factory Expenses Like Factory Wages Total Factory Cost
Sales – Factory Cost	= Gross Operating Profit
Gross Operating Profit	Salaries & Wages of Staff + Administrative Expenses + Selling and Distribution Expenses Total Non-Factory Cost or Selling Expenses
Gross Operating Profit – Non-Factory Costs	= Earnings Before Interest, Depreciation and Taxes (EBIDT) = Gross Profit
Gross Profits (EBIDT)	= Profits after meeting Factory Cost and Non-Factory Expenses
Net Profit (PAT)	= EBIDT – Interest, Depreciation and Taxes

CORPORATE PERFORMANCE

The long-term investors prefer mostly companies with a solid past performance and continued good performance in future. Such companies are called growth companies, or Blue Chip Companies. Of the factors which influence the share prices, the most important one is corporate fundamentals, namely, company's intrinsic worth, net asset value or book value. The corporate performance is thus the single largest force, influencing share price. This is studied by the ratio analysis referred to below, funds flow analysis — namely, sources and uses of funds — and trend analysis of growth rates of important parameters like sales, gross block etc.

Corporate performance depends on a number of variables, both internal and external to the company. The major internal factors are: (i) Efficiency of capital use, (ii) Productivity of total capital employed, (iii) Growth of Gross Block and its capacity utilisation, (iv) Sales turnover and operational efficiency, (v) Profitability of the operations, (vi) Return on capital employed, (vii) Expansion plans and internal reserves built up, and (viii) Tax planning and accounting practices etc.

All the above factors are reflected and measured in Financial Ratios, referred to below — growth rates of major assets and liabilities and operational ratios measuring the profitability and profit allocation.

Selected Ratios	*Their Use*
1. *Capital Cost Ratios* Ex: Cost of Debt Capital/ Cost of Equity Capital	For Capital Structure Analysis — methods of financing the project.
2. *Leverage Ratios* Ex: Debt/Equity ratio, or Borrowed Capital/Total Capital employed.	Long-term stability of the company — leverage enjoyed by owned capital through borrowed funds.
3. *Solvency Ratios* Ex: Total long-term debt to total owned funds, Total liabilities to total shareholders' equity.	Long-term solvency and Company's Financial ability to fulfill the obligations of repayments and expenses involved.
4. *Liquidity Ratios* Ex: Current Ratio, Acid Test Ratio — Current Asset to Current Liabilities.	Company's Financial position in the short-run and the capacity to meet short-run obligations.
5. *Turnover Ratios* Ex: Fixed Assets to Sales Sundry Debtors to Sales Inventory Turnover Ratio (cost of goods sold to total Inventory).	Efficiency of the use of capital and operational efficiency in keeping high sales relative to fixed capital and management efficiency in collecting debts and keep low inventory to sales.
6. *Profitability Ratios* Gross profits to sales operating profits to sales Net profits to Equity Capital/or to total owned funds.	Measures the profitability relative to sales, and relative to capital invested indicates the efficiency of management to generate profits against sales, or capital employed.
7. *Capital Efficiency Ratios* Gross Block/Equity Sales/Equity or Sales/ Capital employed.	Measures the efficient use of owned funds or all capital employed.
8. *Debt Servicing Ratios* Interest payments to total net earnings Total debt servicing to total gross earnings.	Measures the efficiency in the use of Capital, particularly debt Capital, capacity to service Capital borrowed through earnings.
9. *Profit Allocation Ratios* Equity dividends to Net Profits All dividends to Net Profits — Tax and depreciation as % age of Gross Profits.	Management policy of dividend distribution, expansion plans, consistency in dividend distribution, bonus payments, Retention Policy etc.

10. *Overall Performance of Company*

$$\underset{\text{(Capital use)}}{\frac{\text{Gross Block}}{\text{Equity}}} \times \underset{\text{(Turnover Efficiency)}}{\frac{\text{Sales}}{\text{Gross Block}}} \times \underset{\text{(Profitability)}}{\frac{\text{Net Profits}}{\text{Sales}}} = \underset{\text{Return on Investment}}{\frac{\text{Net Profits}}{\text{Equity}}}$$

11. Comparison of Growth Rates of Gross Block, Sales, Gross Profits, etc., so as to know the efficient use of Capital and the Growth of Capital relative to sales reflecting the optimal use of capacity and profitability of operations.
12. *Investor Valuation of Company*
    Earnings per share, Book value per share, Net Asset value per share, Break down value of Equity Share, P/E Ratio, or payback period of Investments.
13. *Management Rating*
    Measured by their honesty, integrity, keeping up to schedules of project construction or fulfilling the sales target or Gross Profit margin, Consistency in dividend distribution, bonus payments, expansion plans and Tax Planning.

HOW TO LOCATE EMERGING BLUE CHIPS?

Research on the Companies' operations and their financial results is necessary for locating Emerging Blue Chips. This can be done through fundamental analysis which helps us to decide what to buy and what to sell? This research has to be both on the desk and on the field. On the desk, the financial results and Balance Sheets have to be examined to locate the potentiality of companies to emerge as turnaround companies. Prima facie, such companies, have been in losses for a year or two but due to some expected management changes leading to higher capacity utilisation or due to new projects in the last phase of completion, these companies show the potentiality for turning into profitable projects in the coming year or two. Research on the field is to interview the officers of the Companies, visit to the plant and secure the opinions of the experts, suppliers, stockists, etc. This fundamental analysis is to be supplemented by technical analysis to decide on when to buy and when to sell?

Some companies may be building up Gross Block due to expansion and diversification but sales are not rising fast enough due to low capacity utilisation. Then the company may not be making adequate profits to service investors temporarily. A few companies may have both gross block and sales rising but Gross Profit margin is low due to high costs of manufacture or sale and due to inefficiency of management. Any changes in policy to improve efficiency or improvements in technology may be expected to increase the profits and the company may be in the process of growth as a Blue Chip Company. Here are some examples of turn-around companies, or emerging Blue Chip Companies: Amar Raja Battery, Hotel Leela Venture, Wartsila Diesel etc., these are also examples of turn-around companies which have come out to be growth companies.

The expertise of the analyst lies in locating the emerging Blue Chips. Blue Chips of yesteryears are no longer the Blue Chips of today. Similarly, there is no guarantee that the Blue Chips of today will be the Blue Chips of tomorrow. Thus for long in the eighties, Scrips like Reliance, Orkay, Century etc., were the Blue Chips. In the nineties, the Essar Gujarat, Videocon, Finolex etc., took over the lead, and so on. In the new millennium, the blue chips are Infosys, NIIT, TCS etc. Informatics Robotics, Satellite communications, etc. are the leading industries in the 21st Century.

Established Blue Chips

For a conservative investor, established growth stocks with an assured return are attractive. These companies are leaders in the industry, like Reliance and Raymonds in the Textiles and TISCO in Steel etc. They have a strong capital base networth, well established financial position, organised and professionalised management. They reward the investor with uninterrupted dividends, steady rise in capital values and bonus from time-to-time or rights or other privileges. Such Companies are worth holding for long and are recommended in all the portfolios of investors. The risk of holding such scrips is low and their Betas are generally around the market Betas and their rewards are generally above average performance of the market. Investors in such Blue Chips as Reliance, HLL, Glaxo etc., have benefitted by regular dividends and bonus shares.

The characteristics of established Blue Chips are as follows and the best example of a company satisfying as these features is the Reliance (RIL).

1. *Management Rating:* Highly professionalised and efficient management. Reputed for honesty and integrity. Financial practices and accounting are consistent and dependable.

2. *Gross profit margin* and sales turnover are high and the company captured a substantial chunk of market demand. The quality and after sales service are the strong points of the company and they are some of the leaders in the industry.

3. *Dividend Record*: The company has been making continuous profits of which a reasonable dividend is declared. A prudent policy of ploughing back profits for expansion and diversification is also pursued.

4. The company's networth is high relative to equity and is expanding year after year. The leverage enjoyed by equity through long-term borrowings (debt) is also high. Their long-term solvency is rated high.

5. The current liquidity position is also strong. Their current assets cover their current liabilities including contingent liabilities by more than twice, and their sales management is such that inventory holding is always optimal. Their sales and distribution strategies are sound and cash efficient.

6. The company has expansion and diversification plans for future growth as reflected in the rise in networth and gross block. Such expansion plans are accompanied by tax planning so as to conserve resources for growth. Alternatively the company is already diversified and has still expansion plans.

7. The management has a vision for the future of the company and their policy is ambitious expansion and growth. The policies adopted are result-oriented and efficiently executed.

8. The company's networth is growing due to ploughed back profits and funds are available for bonus payments to satisfy the Investors from time-to-time.

9. The market price of such shares is rising consistently and steadily and any possible fall in price is small and temporary. The price fluctuations are narrow and the long-term trend of its price is upwards.

10. The company has earned a reputation for fair practices good corporate governance and their servicing of investors through dividends, bonus allotments, share transfer etc., is generally rated good.

HONEYWELL: A CASE STUDY

Honeywell Automation India Ltd, was chosen for this case study for the unique nature of its products and a phenomenal growth of its sales and profitability during the last few years after it ceased to be a joint venture with TATAS and became majority holder of the Honeywell International Inco with foreign technology and foreign investment of about 80% of the Equity capital. It is a company put in B1 group on the BSE. It has a history of about 22 years and has stable growth with no speculative fervour. Its registered office is at Pune, Maharashtra. It has been complying with all the listing requirements of the stock exchanges namely BSE and NSE, particularly with respect to corporate governance and compliance with the legal requirements of the land. The domestic individuals and companies hold a stake of about 15 to 20% and it has all the characteristics of an emerging blue chip among the MNCs and hence it is taken up for this case study.

The share has a face value of ₹ 10 and has a 52 week low of ₹ 619 and a high of ₹ 2,038 in April 2006. During the calendar year 2005 for which it has audited Balance sheet, the market price ranged between ₹ 532 to ₹ 1110. It was only in the year 2006 that the price shot up to ₹ 2,038. At end March 2006 it was quoted at ₹ 1,820. Such a sharp rise in price from a low of ₹ 532 in March 2005 to ₹ 2,492 in September 2012 shows the expectations of the investors of the company's performance.

What is the rationale of these expectation? Its D/E ratio indicating long term solvency has come down from 1:1.8 to 1:1.4. Its short term liquidity as judged by current ratio has also improved and stood at 1:1.2. The profitability ratio — the ratio of PAT to Sales doubled from 3.1 in 2004 to 6.9 in 2005 and as per the latest projections of the Directors' Report there are indications of improvements in sales due to larger order books and increased product range in the coming year or two. Its PAT to sales ratio stood at 6.6. It MP high/low was 3,350-1,617 in 2012.

The company's product range includes: (1) Honeywell process solutions, (2) Building solutions, (3) Access control and Fire automation, (4) Environment combustion control, (5) Electronic security products and systems, (6) Sensing and control systems and Global services etc. A lot more automation products are planned and the expansion plans are evident from the Chairman's speech.

The company's initiatives include growth, productivity, cash flow management, training of people and technology absorption, energy conservation, and product development etc. The management is professional and has wide international connections. In 2004, it has become a subsidiary of the majority stakeholder namely Honeywell International Inco and it has many fellow subsidiaries all over the world and in particular in the Asia Pacific region. It has started publishing accounts on a calendar year basis from 2004 and the table below presents the data for the years 2004, 2005 and 2011.

Table

Financial Indicators

₹ in lakhs

Indicators	*2004*	*2005*	*2011*
Equity	884	884	884
Net worth	10,603	13,200	63,025
Book Value	120	150	716
Total capital employed	17,494	16,786	63,025
Debt-equity ratio	1:1.8	1:1.4	–
Gross Block	7,747	9,415	7,690
Net Sales	26,988	49,300	1,61,256
PAT to Sales ratio	3.1	6.9	6.6
Current Assets	23,492	25,274	1,00,888
Current Liabilities	10,646	13,152	49,589
Current ratio	2.2	1.9	2.0
Profits before D.I.T. (PBDIT)	1,507	5,248	16,136
Profits after tax (PAT)	849	3,408	10,714

MP to BV	–	–	3.7
Dividend	50%	80%	100%
Earnings per share (EPS)	10	38	121.0
Average Market price (MP)	₹ 570	₹ 1,001	₹ 2,483
P/E ratio	57	26	28.3
Actual market price (H/L)	601-540/-	1,109-890/-	3,350-1,617/-

The PAT has shown a rise of four times and PBDIT has increased by nearly 3 and half times in the last one year. Sales has grown by 83%. On the basis of these trends, however, short it may be, one can estimate of EPS to rise from the present level of 38 in 2005 to 70 to 76 in 2006. The ET has given the P/E ratio as 47 in the daily price data that they publish every day as in April 2006. It was 28.3 is 2011 and EPS at 12%.

As stated above the ET gave the P/E ratio for March 2006 as 47 and 52 Week High/Low as ₹ 2,036 - 619 — which gives an average MP as ₹ 1,327. The historical EPS of 38 multiplied by the historical P/E ratio of 47 gives the expected market price as ₹ 1,786. In this context, the actual market price of Honeywell as on March end 2006 at ₹ 1,814 - 1,820 is fairly priced. Taking the estimated EPS as 76, this price can be much higher at say ₹ 2,800 by using the historical P/E multiple of 38, given above in the Table, as against the actual market price of ₹ 2,036 in April 2006. The price has stabilished at around 1,750-1,800 in August 2007, and 2,483 in Sept. 2012.

The conlcusion is that Honeywell is definitely an emerging bluechip company, with potential for rise in prices in the stock market. Its Beta is also low at 0.5, indicating less risk.

Subsequent developments show that the market price at around ₹ 2,360 in January 2010 is about 6 times the Book value. Its P/E multiple is 17 times now and as the market price of ₹ 2,360, the EPS is estimated at ₹ 138. EPS is now ₹ 93 (actuals) as against ₹ 38 in 2005. The market price is also nearly 2 times at ₹ 2,364 (52 weeks high in 2009) as compared to ₹ 1,109 (high) in 2005. There is a consistent growth in sales, PAT and EPS over the years as much as in the market price. The only drawback is sagging dividends declared which was Re. 1 per share in 2007 as against 80% in 2005 and 50% in 2004. However, the net worth and the Book value of the share are no doubt growing consistently. These features confirm our earlier conclusiont. that it is a Blue chip company Although it is listed on BSE in the B_1 category and not in "A" group, as it is not a speculative scrip; its fundamentals continue to be good.

The above case study is only for illustration. The readers are advised to take up another listed company for a similar study of market price as against its fundamentals. The market price has to be taken in conjunction with face value of the share of the company.

7 COMPANY STUDIES AND EARNINGS FORECASTS

The normal methods of assessing the stock's intrinsic worth are to measure the earning capacity, earnings in relation to networth or equity, return on investment or return on assets.

The means by which earnings are influenced are multifarious. *Prima facie*, earnings are a function of revenue and expenditure.

EBDIT = Earnings Before Depreciation Interest and Taxes.

Depreciation being retained for use by the Company, Cash earnings include depreciation also and thus EBIT, *viz.*, Earnings before interest and taxation is a better measure. Interest burden depends on the method of financing, capital structure, cost of borrowing, leverage enjoyed through debt to supplement equity and a host of other factors. Taxation depends an external factors like the Government budgetary policy, incentives available and tax planning.

FACTORS INFLUENCING EARNINGS (EBIT)

EBIT – Interest – Taxation = Net profits

EBIT itself depends on the sales and operations. The efficiency in operations and marketing will be reflected in sales. Hence, sales to gross assets and the growth rate of sales and assets are important indicators of the *capital use.* This also reflects the operational efficiency. Inventory as percentage of sales, working capital management, cost of borrowing for working capital, cost of sales and administration are also part of *operational efficiency.* Another factor is the personnel or human resources expertise used and output per man hour and *labour efficiency* are also variables influencing earnings.

Management Efficiency

Management Efficiency is the most single factor influencing the other factors affecting earnings like return on assets, capital efficiency, capacity utilisation, growth of capacity or gross block and operational efficiency and expansion and tax planning. Financing method of both long-term and short-term needs of the firm is again a management function and reflects on the efficiency of financial management of the company. All capital whether in the form of equity or debt or retained earnings have a cost either implicit or explicit. The right mixture of different methods of financing aims at lowering the costs of production through the lower interest burden or capital servicing costs.

Debt Financing and Earnings

Leverage enjoyed by a firm is another method of raising efficiency of capital use and increase the earnings per share of the company. The proportion of debt to equity and the cost of debt as against the return on total capital employed are the major determinants of the benefit of leverage. Suppose the return on total capital employed is 25% and the interest cost on debt is 20%, the additional 5% earned on capital employed is a gain to equityholders, through leverage. Suppose the return on capital varies from 20% to 30%, the return on debt being fixed at 20%, the firm becomes a high risk investment due to the possibility of variable gain or no gain due to leverage. Equityholders, being the owners of the company are the residuary beneficiaries from the profits of the company. The debt financing helps to gear up the returns, if productively used and the return on assets is more than the cost of debt.

Asset Value of a Share

Just as the book value of a share is equal to networth divided by the number of shares outstanding, there is another measure of the value of a share, namely, asset value per share.

$$\text{Asset Value Per Share} = \frac{\text{Total Assets in Value}}{\text{Number of Shares}}$$

If it is say ₹ 20, and the company issues shares at ₹ 30, there is a premium of ₹ 10 which increases the reserves and capital base of the company. The company's earnings should then be higher to service a larger equity base and secondly these returns should be stable returns on the capital without wide fluctuations. With uncertainty and fluctuations in returns the risk of the company increases for the same level of average return. In this case, the change in equity base will change the value per stock due to change in EPS. Earnings per share can also be changed as referred to earlier, by changes in composition of asset mix, liabilities mix, leverage ratio, assets and sales turnover, cost of various items of liabilities and returns on various items of assets etc.

Tax Rate Impact

The maximum corporate tax rate is say 38.5% in India, along with a surcharge but the effective rate may be lower depending on the efficiency of tax planning. The corporate finance studies show that the effective rate is lower varying from 18 to 20%; when the maximum nominal rate is 38.5%; Tax planning, and depreciation methods adopted will change the earnings per share, by increasing earnings after tax.

MECHANICS OF EARNINGS FLOW

In accounting sense, earnings are a product of operations, reflected in the *Income and expenditure* statement. To given an example:

	₹ crores
Sales	₹ 100
Plus other income	₹ 100
Total income	₹ 200
Minus Operating Expense	120
EBIT	80
Interest (I)	20
EBT	60
Taxes at 40% (maximum)	24
	36
EAT (Earnings after Tax)	36
No. of Shares 200	
Eearnings of Equity	39
Dividends Distributed	7
(Retention 20%)	

The fact that this firm has nearly 50% of its income from other sources, other than sales indicates its non-manufacturing, trading and investment activities. Then, it is necessary to examine whether it is a regular feature or a once for all phenomenon due to sale of investments or capital gains.

The sales and other income are due to utilisation of capacity built by gross fixed assets and other assets. These assets are financed by owned funds and borrowed funds which are both of short-term and long-term nature. Thus, earnings are to be examined as Return On Assets (ROA) or on owned funds or equity and absolute figures of earnings have no meaning for analysis.

Balance Sheet Analysis for ROA and EPS

Then Balance Sheet items have to be examined. Take an example:

(*₹ crores*)

Assets		***Liabilities***	
Fixed Assets	500	Borrowings	600
Current Assets	300	Long-term	400
		Short-term	200
		Equity	200
Total Assets	800	Liabilities	800

The calculations of ROA and RONW and EPS are now based on the above data. Take the earnings in the above example. ₹ 36 crores.

$$\text{ROA} = \frac{36}{800} = 4.5\% \text{ which is also called ROI}$$

$$\text{RONW } \frac{36}{200} = 18\% \text{ which is the same as Return on Equity as there are no reserves in this company}$$

Taking ₹ 200 crores as equity and the number of equity shares at 20 crores then EPS $= \frac{36}{20} =$ ₹ 1.8

The return on assets is to be viewed as the outcome of the operating cycle on the one hand and the result of utilisation of capacity built by fixed assets on the other reflecting operational efficiency and capital efficiency respectively.

Table

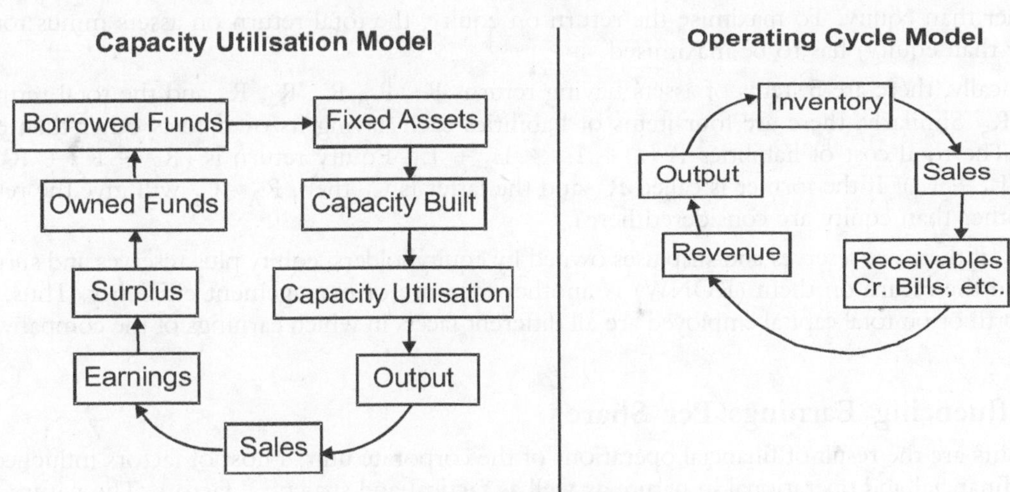

EBT MODEL

Assets generate income and liabilities lead to expenses. The return on assets (or productivity of capital) has to be used to set off the costs incurred in borrowing funds or capital (interest cost).

EBT = Return on Assets (ROA) – Interest Cost on Liabilities (IOL)

Assets = Borrowed Funds (liabilities) + Equity

$A = L + E$

Thus, $EBT = R(L + E) - I(L)$

$= RL + RE - IL$

$= RE + RL - IL$

$= RE + L(R - I)$

Where, RE is Return on Equity, R is return on assets on average and I is average interest cost on liabilities. Dividing both sides by E, we have

$$\text{EBT} = \left[\frac{RE}{E} + \frac{L(R-I)}{E}\right] \times E$$

Simplifying it, we have

$$\text{EBT} = \left[R + (R-I)\frac{L}{E}\right] \times E$$

Where $\frac{L}{E}$ is a measure of leverage.

To give a concrete example

Where,

$R = 20$

$I = 15$

$L/E = \frac{50}{50} = 1$

$E = 50$

$$\text{EBT} = [0.20 + (0.20 - 0.15)] \times \frac{L}{E}E$$
$$= [0.20 + (0.05)] \times 1] \times 50$$
$$= 0.25 \times 50$$
$$= 12.5$$

$$\text{Effective Interest Cost} = \frac{\text{Interest Expenses}}{\text{Total Liabilites}}$$

Benefit of Borrowed Money = Return on assets minus effective interest cost

Average Return on assets Minus Average outgo on liabilities will lead to net return to the company, which is to be maximised. Each of the items of assets have a return different from others and so is the cost of the various items of liabilities other than equity. To maximise the return on equity, the total return on assets minus total expense on liabilities (other than equity) has to be maximised.

Mathematically, there are 5 items of assets having returns R_1, R_2, R_3, R_4, R_5 and the total return is $R_1 + R_2 + R_3 + R_4 + R_5$. Similarly, there are four items of liabilities each having its own costs other than equity, say L_1, L_2, L_3 and L_4. The total cost of liabilities is $L_1 + L_2 + L_3 + L_4$. Equity return is $(R_1 + R_2 + R_3 + R_4 + R_5)$ — $(L_1 + L_2 + L_3 + L_4)$. If the former is called R_A and the latter is C_L then, $R_A - C_L$ will give the return to Equity Er. (liabilities other than equity are considered here).

Sometimes, if there are reserves and surpluses owned by equityholders, equity plus reserves and surpluses are total owned funds and the return on them (RONW) is another measure of management efficiency. Thus, the return on equity, or networth or on total capital employed are all different facets in which earnings of the company can be judged by the investor.

Variables Influencing Earnings Per Share

As net profits are the result of financial operations of the corporate unit, a host of factors influence these results, which are both financial and operational in nature as well as tactical and structural factors. The nature of the market, product range operational efficiency and management expertise are important variables, some of which are qualitative and subjective in nature.

In particular, the quantifiable variables readily available from financial statements can be identified as follows:

(1) Asset base and turnover of assets, as assets generate capacity and their utilisation results in output and sales. The ratios are: Sales ÷ Total Assets, or Sales ÷ Fixed Assets, Total Income ÷ Total Assets, etc.

(2) Equity base and equity to debt ratio, the long-term debt to equity and equity as a proportion of total liabilities reflect the leverage enjoyed by the company, and the capital structure reflects the costs, financial management and capital efficiency (Debt-equity ratio).

(3) Cost of total funds and cost of long-term funds and effective interest rates determine the cost of funds and the returns on assets are related to the costs for determining the net earnings of the company.

(4) Net productivity or profitability of sales — operating profits are dependent on profit margin (price minus total average cost, including fixed and variable costs).

(5) Effective tax rate, depends on the tax planning, expansion and diversification and the depreciation provision etc., which also influence the net earnings after taxes.

CAPITALISATION OR MULTIPLIER APPROACH

Capitalisation means the calculation of capital value of future flows for the present. This is the same thing as the present value of future dividend flows or earnings flows. Two models are built on the basis of this concept — one for dividend flows [D_o, D_1 ... D_n] and another for earning flows [E_1, E_2 ... E_n]. Earnings are net profit after provision for interest, depreciation and taxes, while dividend flows are a part of the net profits or the whole of net profits depending on the extent of the retention of earnings within the company to build up reserves, which are also equity holders' funds.

In actual practice, the capital market efficiency theories are not applicable to the Indian Context due to a high degree of imperfections in the market. In such cases we can adopt the more realistic earnings multiplier approach. In short, it is Earnings Per Share (EPS), multiplied by a multiplier, which gives the price of share. Thus, MP = EPS $\times$ m or $m = \frac{MP}{EPS}$, where MP is market price and EPS is projected earnings per share and m is the multiplier or also called P/E multiplier. Expected MP can be derived by using the past average multiplier multiplied by future expected earnings per share.

In the case of capitalisation model, the present value of future dividend flows and the future price of stock discounted to the present have to be estimated. For this purpose either dividend flows or earnings flows can be used, depending on the Dividend Model or the Earnings Model adopted.

DIVIDEND AND EARNINGS MODELS

Dividend or earnings models make no difference to the total share value as both reflect the owned funds of equityholders. The only difference is in time value of money in the perception of the shareholders. If investors value Re. 1 in their hands more than in the hands of the company, then a difference to the stock value can arise depending on whether the dividends are distributed or not and the proportion and amount of the distribution as against the retained earnings. If the investors perceive that the Re. 1 left with the company can have better use and higher return than Re. 1 left in their hand, then the value of the stock will increase with the increase in the retention and not payment of dividends. The proportion of dividend distributed and distribution policy has thus some variable influence on the expected EPS.

The other factors influencing the EPS are:

(a) Equity base and owned funds
(b) Total liabilities other than equity and the average cost of such liabilities
(c) Interest cost on borrowings
(d) Return on assets and the average return on assets
(e) Effective tax rates
(f) Retention rate
(g) Pattern and mix of assets and pattern and mix of liabilities.

Discounting of Cash Flows

Companies give data on expected cash flows from the project, at the time of going to public issue either for project financing, expansion, modernisation or diversification. The banks and financial institutions, which appraise the project also make projections of future cash flows, the break-even point and expected year of dividend declaration.

In the case of the existing listed company, the information on projected cash flows and actual flows, the sources and uses of funds and unaudited balance sheet data for every half year are available with the Stock Exchange and are also published. The data on P/E multiple is published in the Daily E.T. The data so available can be used for three to five years in the past for calculating the past P/E multiple (which is MP/EPS) and then project the future earnings per share for estimating the market price at a future date, say 6 months or one year hence by use of Discounting method.

The expected future dividend flows can be used along with the expected price in future to discount to the present, for the purpose of estimating the present value (Po).

Po = PVd + PVs (where PVd is the present value of future dividends and PVs is the present value of the stock price at the time period 't'.

$$PVd = \Sigma do\left(\frac{1+gs}{1+rs}\right)^t$$ (where g's is the growth of dividends and r's is the required rate of return).

$$PVs = PVt\left(1+\frac{1}{r}\right)^t$$ (PVt is the future Stock price discounted to present).

The simple formula for PVt if r and g are constants and dividends (d) grow at a constant rate.

$$PVt = \frac{dr}{rt - gn}$$

FORMULA PLANS

If none of the analytical tools are acceptable to the analyst then he may adopt formula plan to make regular and periodic investments. This scheme of action is based on the assumption that cycles exist, but follow an unpredictable pattern. As such to take advantage of these changes the best way is to follow an automatic timing pattern, independent of the expected cycles. The selection of timing is criterion in the sense that when majority of investors are selling, buy the stock and *vice versa*. This eliminates the need of forecasting, and is called the principle of contrariness.

Additionally, averaging down the purchase price has to be done by consistent purchases in small qualities when prices are falling. Averaging up the sale price has to be done by consistent sales in small quantities when prices are rising. The scheme of averaging the rupee price of stock is possible when the sum available for investment is large and the cost of the deals has to be kept low through economies of scale and the fund is to be built over a period of time and crash sales or purchases are being avoided and the funds are not needed for sometime to come.

The above scheme of automatic purchases and sales of specific timings regularly will eliminate the pitfalls of excesses and average the risks of the market. The chances of evening out the price fluctuations are large in such automatic formulas and the scheme of averaging up and averaging down. These are practical tricks of the trade, when theories do not take us far to success in stock price prediction and in making gain in operations.

The above automatic formula rules should lay down: (a) when to purchase, (b) in what quantity, (c) selection of scrips, and (d) the implementation or execution of the plan at least cost (cost of deals and incidentals).

FORECASTING EARNINGS

There are many methods by which one can estimate the Earnings before Taxes or after Taxes to estimate EPS and its projected market price. Some practical methods are set out below:

(1) *Use of Earnings Model*, for EBT, namely,

$$EBT = \left[R + (R - I)\frac{L}{E}\right]E$$, referred to earlier.

Where, R is the average return on Investments or Assets, I is the interest cost on liabilities other than equity, $\frac{L}{E}$ is the debt equity ratio or total liabilities other than equity to equity.

If we have the data on the past earnings on assets, the manner in which they are financed and the average cost of interest on the liabilities, we will have the average past trends of R, I and plug in these values for the present and future. If we know the EBT, deduct the tax payable at the effective rate in the past or the maximum corporate tax rate of 30% to arrive at EAT.

To give an example, if EAT is ₹ 1000 and equity shares outstanding are 100. Then EPS = 1000 ÷ 100 = ₹ 10. If the past average P/E multiple is 15, then the market price can be estimated at around 10 × 15 = ₹ 150. Whether investment can be made or not depends on the present price and expected future and the estimated Holding Period Yield (HPY). If price at the end is ₹ 150 and price at the beginning of holding is ₹ 120 and dividends paid ₹ 5 per share, then,

$$\text{HPY} = \frac{150-120+5}{120} = \frac{35}{120} = 29\%$$

(2) *Market Share Approach*

From an industry analysis, it is known that the share of the Company LME is 9% of the market and the demand for two wheelers will go up from 26 lakhs to 28 lakhs. Then the sales of LME can be put at 2.5 lakhs in the next year. On the basis of this sales rate and the average operating profit margin of last three years, say 35%, one can estimate the income from sales and 35% of it is taken as operating profits, from which interest and depreciation and taxes can be deducted at their normal rates and arrive at profits after taxes (PAT). Then estimate of EPS and P/E multiple and the market price (MP) at the end of next year has to be made on the same basis as demonstrated earlier. These financial data parameters are published in Economic Times and Financial Express and financial journals for calculating the past trend averages of OPM, NPM, or sales turnover.

Example[1]

Take the example of *Auto Ancillaries* industry to estimate the above parameters and of the company under analysis, stay Autolec Industries, manufacturing water, oil and fuel pumps, which are parts used in Automobile industry. The data are presented for three years for illustration, to calculate the past trend averages which are used for the projection and forecasting the variables a year or two hence. (See Table below.)

The operating profits of the company can be estimated on the basis of industry norms, say at around 18% as operating profit margin or 19% as per the past trend of the company. This type of estimates is rough and ready method, useful in practice and operationally. The data for Auto Ancillary industry is given as a bench mark for comparison of the data for Autolec Industry. The market price, estimated on the basis of P/E of 1996 will give a price of around 125 in 1997, an appreciation of around 25%, over the present 1996 price of ₹ 100-105. The yearly high is 143, as compared to the low of 85 for the share price over the past one year. This company's share thus becomes a worthwhile buy due to the likely price appreciation of 25% plus a dividend of 25% — the same as declared in the last year.

The management planned for a growth of sales of 35% per annum in 1997 and even on a conservative estimate of 28% given below in the data, profits will grow by 17%-19% and at an average return on capital employed of 25%, the fundamentals of the company are sound, particularly as the management showed dynamism in expansion plans, and have a captured market as the principal supplier of water pumps, oil and fuel pumps, to most of the automobile companies. Automobile industry and Auto ancillary industries were expected to have a boom period during 1997-2000. But, they had a boom period during 2004-08.

Table Data for Automobile Ancillary Industry

	Fy. 93	*Fy. 94*	*F. 95*
Sales to Total Assets	1.10	1.19	1.20
EBIDT To Net Sales (OPM)	19.03%	18.63%	18.81%
Debt to Net worth	1.02	0.89	0.81
Cash Profit to Equity	0.93	1.05	1.35
RON W%	13.04	15.15	19.70
Return on Capital Employed (CEP)%	27.68	28.83	30.04

Data for Autolec Industries

(in ₹ crores)

	93	*94*	*95*	*96(E)*	*97(E)*
Net Sales	22.55	26.95	40.37	53.99	66.75
OPM	11.7%	12.6%	16.6%	17.0%	17.0%
EBIDT	2.67	3.44	6.73	9.23	11.41
Net Profit (@)	0.68	1.01	3.50	4.25	4.94
Cash Profit (@)	1.35	1.76	4.35	5.96	7.24

Note: (@) Taxes and depreciation at normal rates

1. The date and year of data does not matter as it is given for illustration only.

Equity base	3.46	3.46	5.01	5.01	5.01
Book value	16.16	17.11	28.34	34.32	41.19
EPS	1.97	2.92	6.99	8.48	9.87
Cash P/E multiple			11.6	8.8	7.3
P/E multiple			15.0	12.4	10.6
Price to book value			3.7	3.1	2.5

Average Debt Equity Ratio	1.06
Average RONW	17.9%
Average ROCEP	25.0%

The actual P/E reached 11.1 in 1998-99 and a peak price of ₹ 130 in the market.

Source: *Insight Asset Management,* Monthly Report for April 1996.

Based on the above data, the expected market price a year hence can be calculated and after comparing it with the present market price, a buy or sell decision can be made.

ROLE OF FIXED COSTS AND BREAK-EVEN POINT

Some firms have high fixed costs due to large capital investment needed as in steel, Auto and other consumer durables or capital goods industries. At the other end, some firms have low fixed costs but high variable costs as in food processing, handloom, machine tools, light electronic goods, etc. The implication of high fixed costs and low variable costs for EAT is that the break-even point for profitability will be at a higher level of output, capacity utilisation and sales. This would mean a long gestation period for investors to reap the growth of earnings per share. Conversely, short gestation plants reward the investors earlier due to low fixed costs and a low break-even point. But profits or losses are both of higher magnitudes in capital intensive projects than in labour intensive projects. The rate of growth accelerates very rapidly in respect of sales and profits etc., in the case of projects with high fixed costs after the break-even period than those with low fixed costs. Investment analysts have to give weightage to the type of firms, their product range, low or high fixed costs and the level for sales and capacity utilisation at which the break-even point occurs. Thus, application of break-even analysis also becomes necessary for the analysis to make a proper investment decision, based on earnings.

Forecast of Individual Items of Revenue and Expenses

Most Scientific method of estimation of sales revenue and other revenue of a firm is to estimate separately for each division and product of the firm. Then the detailed working of the firm will come to light and items estimated should bear the imprest of better information. But this is time consuming and may miss the main objective of analysing the trends and broad parameters will be missed in the maze of confusing details.

A practical approach is to mix up a right degree of details such as sales income and other income, productwise with relative items of expenditure but yet concentrate on the overall totals in the ratio and trend analysis.

When the forecast of total revenue and total expenditure is completed, the analyst can get his forecast of earnings. From this, any perference dividend payable is deducted; interest, depreciation and taxes as applicable to the company are also provided for before arriving at the shareholder's earnings. These net earnings are divided by the number of equity shares to arrive at the EPS and deduce the expected market price by applying the historical P/E multiple of the company or the industry average P/E; the estimation of M.P. from the data on EPS and P/E multiple was already explained.

To sum up, earnings forecast is necessary for estimating the market price at a future date to make any rational investment decision. Although *prima facie,* earnings depend on the income and expenditure of the unit, the underlying factors influencing earnings are capital productivity, operational efficiency, capital structuring and financial management and profit margins and profitability. The structural and tactical factors like financial structure and technological input-output relations and current asset liquidity matching and liquidity management also influence earnings. The overall management efficiency is infact reflected in the earnings of the firm.

PROBLEMS

Caustic Soda industry was undergoing a recession in the late nineties. It is a product accounting for 75% of the domestic chloro alkalies with a turnover of ₹ 5,000 crores in India. The installed capacity was around 20-21 lakh M.T. while the capacity utilisation fell from 87% to 64% over the period 1993-98.

The outlook of this industry depends on the user industries like paper and pulp, manmade fibre, water treatment, soaps and detergents, aluminium, etc. Secondly, import prices being lower, freer imports and higher domestic costs have hit the industry. If the government policy turns positive to the industry, through higher import tariff, lower power charges etc., there is some chance for survival of this industry. International price trends show a decline in their prices which are again an adverse factor for their global competitive capacity.

Indian manufacturers are not in a position to compete globally due to high power tariffs and rising input costs, while the foreign manufacturers are pushing down the interntional prices of caustic soda.

Lowering of costs, improvement in their competitive capacity and quality improvement have to be aimed at by the industry. Thus, both Government Policy changes and the industry practices and corporate managerial efficiency have all to turn positively helpful to the industry.

Assume that the above requirements are met and the industry has some good prospects and companies with in this industry have reached low bottomlines, which company among those presented will you prefer and why? For illustrative purposes, the following data are given for the analysis of the reader and the use of his judgement.

Data for 1997 (March end)
(for 12 months)

(*₹ in crores*)

Company Name: Particulars	*Chemfab Alkalie*	*Kanoria Chemicals*	*Punjab Alkalie*	*Gujarat Alkalie*
Net Sales/Income	35.28	250.55	131.05	372.85
Other Income	0.24	4.29	1.52	7.70
Total Income	35.52	254.84	132.57	380.55
Expediture	24.62	210.00	99.04	262.80
Interest	3.79	15.47	8.37	29.75
Depreciation	3.98	7.99	7.59	29.75
Taxation	0.40	2.30	2.27	7.70
Net Profit	2.73	19.08	15.32	50.56
Equity	2.94	16.73	20.46	37.50

Hint: The choice of a company depends on the market price and a host of other considerations relating to its networth.

Calculate the EPS; Interest burden, Tax planning, if any, cost ratios of the respective Companies, Gross profit margins etc., have to be worked out with in the constraints of the data available. Then give the choice of your company for investment and explain the rationale of your choice. The limitation is lack of similar data for March 1998. Assume that market prices in 1997-98 are as follows:

Chemfab Alkalie	₹ 14-35	Average ₹ 25
Kanoria Chemicals	₹ 25-52	Average ₹ 39
Punjab Alkalie	₹ 9-39	Average ₹ 24
Gujarat Alkalie	₹ 50-82	Average ₹ 66

Give your assessment of these companies, and the price at which you will buy each of them.

Hint: All the above companies have no potential due to poor prospects of caustic soda industry and assumptions made about this industry have gone wrong. In 1999, Chemfab became a sick company.

Kanoria Chemicals ruled around ₹ 20-25 Punjab Alkalie became sick also in 1999 and Gujarat Alkalie was quoted around ₹ 15-20.

CASE STUDY ON TISCO

Tata Steel is one of the oldest companies listed on the BSE and NSE. The UBS Research Group has given a BUY rating at the current price of ₹ 848 in mid October 2007. It is therefore apt to examine this for a case study of price evaluation.... whether it is over priced or under priced. For this purpose, the fundamentals of the company need to be examined, atleast for the latest year 2006-07.

Its share price was in the range of ₹ 399-876 for the current year giving an average price of ₹ 638. For the year 2006-07, its EPS was put at ₹ 73, but the UBS group has taken it at ₹ 107-112 for the coming year, 2007-08. For, we are making the purchase for the future flows of earnings or dividends.

With proposed issue of CCPs for ₹ 5,480 crores, the fully diluted equity shares will be 822 million or 82 crores instead of 58 crores as per its last balance sheet for the year 2006-07. It was reported that the Tata Steel will sell off its Corus aluminium business for less than $100 million which will not have any perceptible difference to its financing or earnings estimates. On the basis of these assumptions, the UBS Research GROUP HAS PUT THE PRICE RANGE FOR THIS SCRIP AT AROUND ₹ 875 AND GAVE ITS RECOMMENDATION OF BUY, as in October 2007 (see Inventors Guide of E.T dated October 15th 2007).

On the basis of the last balance sheet for the full year, its EPS was ₹ 73 and P/E multiple was 8.7. Taking the EPS at ₹ 112 as estimated by UBS, and P/E as 8.7 as per the latest balance sheet data, we get a price of ₹ 974 as the outer limit. But as per the ET Financials, the P/E multiple was only 4.1 which gives a price at ₹ 459 as the lower limit. The price may be in the range of ₹ 460 to 975.

As per the UBS estimates of equity at ₹ 820 crores, its Book value will be ₹ 177 and applying the market multiple of five times, as reported by BSE for its sensex, the share price of Tisco can be ₹ 885 as against the current market price of ₹ 848. Its profitability ratio of 16.5% is good and fundamentals are strong and its current market price is undervalued. It has scope for a rise in the coming one or two years. The combined steel production capacity of both private and public sector steel plants in the country has increased from 60 million tonnes in 2008-09 to 90 million tonnes per annum in 2011-12.

For the purpose of brevity, the detailed financial analysis or the presentation of all the financial ratios is not attempted here. The reasons are clear in that, Tata steel has stood the test of time and was always a divided paying and profit earning company. It belongs to the core industry of steel and industry prospects are also good with a reported growth rate of about 11-12% at present. As such, the analysis is confined to the expected market price and buy or hold or sell decisions. Our analysis also confirms the UBS recommendation of BUY, AS AT MID OCTOBER 2007. This analysis holds good for the time and assumptions made here, there can be a different conclusion with changed assumptions and a different time. It is for the reader to make similar exercises for other companies also, to make sure of the intrinsic worth of the scrips of those companies.

The above analysis of TISCO was relevant for that period of 2007 and not for the present time in 2015. The period 2008 to 2010 was a period of recession in the economy and in the steel industry as well. In September 2012, the MP of TISCO was around 410 (₹ 456-341) with P/E ratio at 61.6. It earnings per share is only ₹ 6.6 which is very low, compared to ₹ 73 in 2006-07 and ₹ 112 in 2007-08. In the pre-recession period, P/E multiple was only 8.7 the steel industry was in recession during 2009 to 2011. Even in 2012, the industry has not fully recovered which is reflected in its financials, namely, P/E multiple (62.1), P/BV ratio (0.9), dividend (1.20%) and Beta (1.5). It is now quoted at ₹ 248 as at end July 2015.

CASE STUDY ON SUN PHARMA INDUSTRIES

Sun Pharma is a medium cap company listed on major stock exchanges in India. It is manufacturing drugs and pharmaceuticals and related items. It is a small company in its operations as compared to Ranbaxy or Dr. Reddy's Labs or Cipla, Glaxo, etc.

It is chosen for case study for its small cap, limited range of products and small size of operations. Its market price is ₹ 896 and EPS multiple is 5.4. These features are rated to be good enough for an analyst and students of research.

The data for 2013 is given below. Although the data for a later year 2014 is available, it is not given for the reason that is has shown (loss) in that year. This may be a deliberate action or a natural phenomenon due to reasons of demand or input constraints. It may be a planned effort to secure funds from its foreign counterpart, namely Sun Pharma Global Inc. along with personel and expertise or technology. It is moreover the right timing as the Government of India policy for liberalising foreign inflows and the Government slogan of "Make in India" to get entry into the vast domestic market are tavourable to the company.

For various reasons like those mentioned above, we have thought it fit for developing this company into one for case study of a small size and brief analysis. It is hoped that students chose companies of various sizes for study and analysis of the companies, listed on the stock exchanges.

Sun Pharma Industries
Listed Company
Financials Needed

	Year 2013 *(in ₹)*
Equity	1,035
Reserves	166/1
Net worth	17,647
Debt	3,025
Debt equity ratio	1:2.9
Current assets	38,372
Current liabilities	1,551
Current Ratio	1:3.7
(assets cover liabilities by 3.7 times)	
Gross Block	14,838
Gross Block to Equity	1:4 times
Profits to Sales	25% to 27%
Profits to Equity	6.4 times
Profits to Gross Block	45%

EPS Earnings (Profits) to Equity $= \dfrac{6,405}{1,035} = 64$

Face value: ₹ One

Market Price = 844 – 896 ₹ in early August 2015

Market Price Multiple of EPS 13 times

$\dfrac{844}{64} = 13$ to 14 times

PAT to Capital Employed = 3.2

Conclusion

The market P/E is 17% for 2013 and P/B ratio is 3%. The company P/E is 13% and P/B is 2.3 times.

As compared to market, the critical ratios are attractive. The scrip is moderately priced and is a good buy as it has good scope for expansion/diversification.

8 COMPANY ANALYSIS AND EQUITY RESEARCH

In the investment decision-making, analysis of the Economy, industry and company is a total exercise, which is called investment research. The objective is proper selection of the industry and the companies in that industry which are undervalued for purchase and those overvalued for sale of stock. Research is the basis of right decisions and latest techniques of research including the econometric models, linear programming, computerised programmes etc., are used by expert research staff with Mutual funds, securities firms and financial institutions. Not only the returns and the growth rate of returns, but also the variability of the returns and their growth rate are to be examined for a complete analysis of risk and return on investments. Only then, it is possible to out perform the market.

The bulk of investment and trading being in Equity in India, equity research constitutes a major chunk of investment research. Bond trading being still in a nascent stage, as the bond market is underdeveloped in India, investment in bonds is significantly low, particularly with individual investors as opposed to institutional investors.

FOUNDATION OF RESEARCH

The basis of research is the data and information relevant for the purpose. There are two major categories — one internal to the company and the other external sources. The first relates to the working operations, results, plans and financial statements of the company. The second relates to the information from outside agencies, like the Government and its policies, from the international developments, press reports on both domestic and international economic and financial developments, Industry and Commerce Chambers and Federations, Company executives' reports from security firms financial analysts and a host of developments affecting the company published in the daily financial press. The government publications, like Economic Survey and Ministry Reports and Bulletins published by the RBI, CMIE, FICCI, etc. constitute some of the examples of such information sources. Many security firms like J.M., DSP and Insight Management Company etc., are publishing reports on industry and company analysis like those of Merrill Lynch, Chase, etc., in foreign markets.

The information base is therefore the first step in Investment Research. Company wise profiles are available in the Directory of Information, published by B.S.E. and in the form of floppies from various computer firms, as software for use and analysis through personal computers. In addition to Economic Times, Financial Express, Business Line and Business Standard, which are daily financial papers, there are also fortnightly and monthly Journals like Capital Market, Dalal Street, Business India which give company reports, and sometimes detailed industry reports based on authentic interviews and research.

Techniques of Analysis

Investment Research firms adopt many techniques and methods of collecting and collating data, relevant for analysis. The more important methods are set out below, for illustration:

1. Collection from the Daily Press: Cuttings from the daily press and journals, filed in company profiles with information updated from time-to-time. Some firms like PRIME publication from New Delhi sell these updates of information through regular Weekly and Monthly Handouts and Reports. Some software companies sell these updates on floppies on a regular basis. The individual investors can collect these data from daily press.

2. Survey/Questionnaire Techniques: Data can be collected from a survey or by sending questionnaire to the Industry Associations and Companies. Many big Research organisations like Madras Institute of Financial Management and Research, RBI and CMIE adopt these techniques, in addition to sponsored research by U.G.C. and by the universities. The results of these research projects are sometimes published in journals as research articles, as in Journal of Finance or Journal of Institute of Public Enterprises, Chartered Financial Analyst.

3. Factory and Plant Visits: The research team visits the factory and the corporate office of the company and study the operational efficiency on the spot and secure oral evidence from the Departmental heads regarding the raw material and input problems, labour problems, managerial plans for expansion, diversification and for improving productivity and efficiency. The Analysts may also interview the M.D. or Chairman for their version on the assessment of the working of the factory. This can be supplemented by interviewing some executives down the line, suppliers, creditors, dealers and consumers of the products sold by the company. They can also secure the evidence from the competitors in the field or industry line and the relevant Associations in which the company is represented. Data to be collected and analysed by questionnaire and factory visit methods are given in the Appendix.

4. Desk Study of Financial Statements: Annual reports, half yearly unaudited reports etc., give the information on the companies, available from the companies themselves and are a major source of research base for the analyst. The analysis of data and information is conducted through many techniques referred to below.

FORECASTING METHODS

The traditional approaches to the forecasting of the earnings are through estimation of sales, net present value of future dividend flows and earnings per share and price earnings multiple, which were discussed in an earlier chapter. These approaches are rough and ready methods and unscientific as they consider only the expected returns, but not expected risks and risks are equally important as returns under modern portfolio analysis. The more scientific approaches are: (a) Regression and Correlation Analysis, (b) Trend Analysis, (c) Decision Tree Analysis, and (d) Econometric Models.

(1) Regression and Correlation

Simple relationship of two variables can be expressed and studied through simple linear regression equation. This is represented as y = f(x) or y = a + b(x), where y is sales and x is personal disposable income and 'a' is a constant. Graphically these relationships can be expressed as follows: a is a constant. If x is zero, y value is 'a' and later on x takes any positive value, y value will change as a multiple of x and that multiple is the slope of the graph y = a + b(x), in the above graph. The data on x and y can be rates of growth or absolute figures.

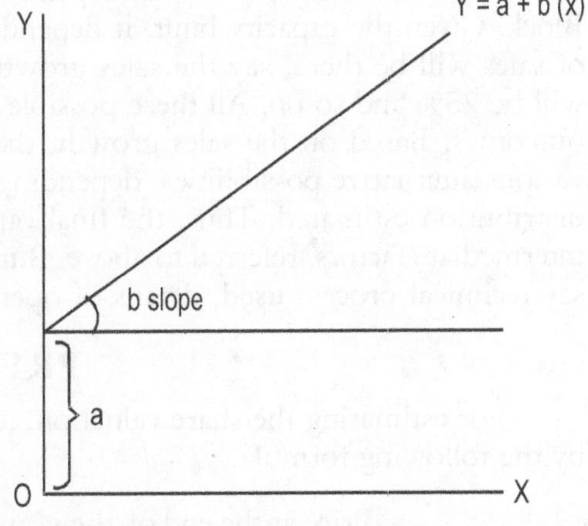

If the relationship involves more than two variables, it is called multiple linear regression and the equation may take the form of y = a + b(x) + c(z) + u. An example of multiple linear equation can be given by taking sales as a function of personal disposable income, bank credit and money supply etc. Correlation tells the analyst how well is the explanatory power of the independent variable, in relation to the dependent variable. How much of the change in "y" can be explained by "x" in the above equation? Correlation technique helps the user to test the "goodness of fit" of the equation and to change the variables or the relationship depending upon the results of the research.

(2) Trend Analysis

In Trend analysis, regression technique is used and the dependent variable, say sales is regressed over time, say months or years. Thus, earnings can be regressed over time to know the short-term and long-term trend of earnings. This can be represented graphically by taking years on the x-axis and earnings on the y-axis to fit a single straight line. If these are absolute figures, then it is a simple arithmetic graph. If it is a semi-logarithmic graph, then the growth rates of 'y' variable are taken and the 'x' variable remains unchanged, say number of years. Thus, the growth rates of earnings per share or total earnings can be taken on the 'y'-axis instead of absolute figures. The semi-logarithmic graph can be depicted as shown in the accompanying chart.

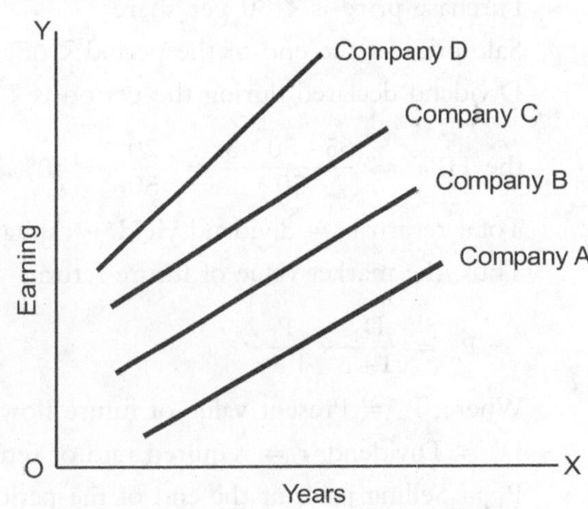

The slopes of the graph will change due to change in growth rates. They are not parallel.

These techniques require a good deal of data of the past and analysis for a length of time for experimentation. Thus, it is time consuming and subject to error of judgement in the selection of variables, the time periods or even the relationship itself. A good economic analysis and reasoning is necessary to establish relationships, logically rational, justified and dependable. Besides, the qualitative and subjective factors like the role of management, quality variations in the products affect these equations. If the error left over is large, then equations become undependable and these unaccounted variables are left in the error term. Thus, if the equation is:

y = a + b(x) + c(z) + u, where x and z are variables explaining the 'y' variable, (inventory held by the company) in the form of gross block (x) and sales (z), then u is the error term comprising of many unknown variables, which also explain the dependent variable 'y'. There are a number of statistical pitfalls and possible errors in such experiments. Even after such laborious work, and time involved in the process is undertaken, there is no surety that the predictive power of equations is 100% foolproof. There will be need for modifications in the decisions, depending on the discussions with the Management, chief executives and other concerned parties. Subjective judgements on labour quality, expansion plans, time lag, involved and the management perspective become necessary and decisions have to be modified accordingly.

(3) Decision Tree Analysis

The earlier techniques assume certainty of events for estimation; they also quantify the qualitative aspects and use statistical tools and economic rationale. Major subjective factors are not quantifiable, like the quality of management or labour efficiency. The estimates so made do not carry with them the probability of their occurrence. It is only in the Decision Tree Analysis that estimates can be made with probabilities varying with the occurrence of intermediate events and in the sequence of events or in the process of sequencing.

Specifically, growth of sales depend on the capacity built and capacity utilised which in turn depend on the Gross Block. Given the capacity built, it depends on the capacity used. If the utilisation is say 50%, one possible outcome of sales will be there, say the sales growth will be 20% and if the capacity utilisation is 80%, then growth of sales will be 25% and so on. All these possible alternatives can be examined in the decision tree analysis, along with their outcomes. Based on the sales growth, the net earnings and dividend pay outs can be decided. Even these can take various alternative possibilities, depending on the rate of depreciation and taxation assumed and the rate of dividend distribution estimated. Thus, the final outcome of share price may take various values depending on these various intermediate factors, referred to above. But this technique can be adopted if full knowledge of all alternatives is possible, say technical process used, details of operations etc.

PRESENT VALUE APPROACH

For estimating the share valuation, it is good to start with a holding period yield. This concept can be explained by the following formula.

$$\text{HPY} = \frac{\text{Price at the end of the year} - \text{price at beginning}}{\text{Price at beginning}}$$

(+) plus the dividend if any, declared during the period

To illustrate

Purchase price is ₹ 50 per share

Sale price at the end of the period ₹ 65

Dividend declared during the period is ₹ 5 per share, then

$$\text{the HPY} = \frac{65-50+5}{50} = \frac{20}{50} = 40\%$$

Total return is = dividend yield + capital gains.

Thus, the market value of future return

$$P_o = \frac{D_1}{1+r} + \frac{P_1}{1+r}$$

Where, P_o = Present value of future flows of dividend and future price

D_1 = Dividend, r = required rate of return

P_1 = Selling price at the end of the period

Putting the above values of the variables and r is taken as 40%

$$P_o = \frac{5}{1+0.40} + \frac{65}{1+0.40} = \frac{70}{1.40} = ₹\ 50$$

If the required return is only 20%. Then the selling price will be lower at ₹ 55, instead of ₹ 65 as shown below:

$$50 = \frac{5}{1+0.20} + \frac{P_1}{1+0.20} \text{ then what is } P_1?$$

then $P_1 = (50 - 4.2) \times 1.20 = ₹\ 55$

The future expected price is ₹ 55, provided the dividend is ₹ 5 and purchase price is ₹ 50.

MULTI-PERIOD HOLDING PERIOD YIELD

If the dividend payouts are growing and the periods are a few years, then the above analysis has to change as shown below:

Let P_o = price per share
P/E = price earnings multiple
e_o = earnings per share
d/e = dividend payout ratio
r = required rate of return
n = number of periods or years
g = annual growth rate

Then the equation for Po is given as:

$$P_o = \left(\sum_{n=1}^{n} \frac{(e_o)(d/e)(1+g)^n}{(1+r)^n} \right) + \left(\frac{P}{E}(e_o)(1+g)^{n+1} \right)$$

The first bracket gives the present value of all dividends received during 'n' periods and second bracket gets the present value of the selling price at the end of the holding period.

To give an illustration, let the following numbers be the values of the above variables.

$g = 6\%$, $n = 3$ $e_o = 1.90$ and $d/e = 50\%$

Dividend at present is 0.945 (½ of 1.90) $\left[e_o \times \frac{d}{e} \right]$

r = 10% (required rate of return)

The present value of future dividends is given by

$$= \frac{0.945(1.06)}{(1.10)^1} + \frac{0.945(1.06)^2}{(1.10)^2} + \frac{0.945(1.06)^3}{(1.10)^3}$$

$0.910 + 0.875 + 0.842 = 2.63$

Although over three year periods ₹ 3 was secured by the investor their present value to him is ₹ 2.63. This is the first bracket value in the above equation.

Then we have to derive the selling price at the end of 3 years. P/E is say 15 and earnings per share 1.90 and the earnings growth rate (g) is 6%.

Then the selling price at the end of period 3 is given as follows:

$Ps = 15\ (1.90) \times (1.06)^4$

$= 28.5 \times 1.26 = ₹\ 36$

Then the present value of the future selling price is

$$= \frac{36}{(1.10)^3} = ₹\ 27$$

Total present value of dividends and selling price is

$P_o = 2.63 + 27 = 29.63$

If constant growth of dividends is assumed, say at 'g' rate for an indefinite future period, then the equation boils down to

$$P_o \frac{D(1+g)}{1+r} + \frac{D(1+g)^2}{(1+r)^2} + \frac{D(1+g)^3}{(1+r)^3} \ .... + \frac{D(1+g)^N}{(1+r)^N}$$

As N approaches infinity

the above equation boils down to

$$P_o = \frac{D}{(r-g)}$$

This means that the price of a share depends on the expected dividend, divided by the difference between the required rate of return and the expected growth rate of dividends or earnings. This formula can be used as a rough and ready method to derive the price of a share, if we can forecast the dividend flow and the growth rate of dividends and the required rate of return for the investor is known.

Normal P/E Ratio and Proper P/E Ratio

Estimates of earnings of the company and EPS are arrived at by the methods referred to so far. This EPS is multiplied by appropriate P/E multiple to arrive at the expected market price. For, the market price divided by the EPS gives the P/E multiple. For using this P/E multiple, what P and what E should be used? What is the proper P/E ratio, to be applied? Can we use the closing price, or average daily price or average monthly or yearly price? What earnings per share should be used? Is it half-yearly data on an annualised basis, or yearly data or average of a few past years? Is the proper EPS the industry EPS or the past average for the company?

The above sets of data will differ significantly and the resulting outcomes will vary widely. Even the industry EPS will also vary with the time period used. This may also be different from the normal for the company, as the company may be different from the average unit in the industry, due to its wider range of products, expansion and diversification and a host of other factors. Again the normal for the company will take various values depending on the type of average taken and for the period, for which averages are taken. Many rules of the thumb are used and BSE sensex or National Index P/E multiples are sometimes used, instead of industry P/E.

FACTORS INFLUENCING P/E MULTIPLE

Normally, a three year average P/E is used to project for the next one to two years. If the company is of a normal size and the industry P/E multiple can reflect the company, the industry multiple can be used. Time horizon used for the past data is normally one to three years — averages of days and months averaged to arrive at an overall average for the year. In India, industry multiples and market multiples as reflected through B.S.E. sensex or through National Index are used for selecting the probable market price estimate at a future date. The industry and company data for EPS and P/E are available in published form in various financial journals and dailies for comparison with the actuals at any point of time. Even so, there are many practical problems in the selection of the above variables.

The P/E multiples depend on a host of factors such as:

(a) Expected sales growth.

(b) Expected earnings growth.

(c) Projected Dividend payout.

(d) Stability of the sales growth and consistency in retention ratio or dividend payout ratio.

(e) Variability of any of the above variables influencing the EPS.

(f) Variations in capital structure or in debt equity ratio.

(g) Nature of the product, market and demand for the product and company's management policy and tax planning etc.

INDUSTRY AND COMPANY ANALYSIS

In the selection of equity stocks, at one stage of investment analysis, it becomes necessary to put the industry study along with the company study together and in a comparative fashion. The selection of industry or industries among many industries has been analysed in an earlier chapter. In practice, the industries in growth stage or those emerging to be sunshine industries are favoured by the public and investors and they are necessary for the economic growth like energy conservation, waste Management, Telecommmunications etc. The Industry P/E data are compared with the Market P/E data, reflected in the BSE sensex or National Index and related P/E. These data are used to selected industries which are neither already overpriced nor reached their maximum growth or point of saturation. A high P/E multiple means that, first, the ratio is relatively higher compared to the market average and second that the scope for further rise is limited. In cases of many FERA companies in India, the P/E multiple is higher than the market average. In Healthcare, Drugs and chemicals in which there are many FERA companies, the P/E ratio is higher than 25 when the market average is only 20.

In the example here, Auto industry is chosen for its modest P/E multiple of 15 in mid-1995 and around 17-20 in mid-1996 and as its growth prospects are rated to be good in the next few years. Among the major units a few are selected representing big size companies like Mahindra and Mahindra and a relatively old company like Hindustan Motors and a newer company like Ucal Fuel, etc. Although Auto is one of the oldest industries in India, it is now rated by Research experts as one of the biggest and fastest growing markets in the world and in India. With the entry of Maruti, the scenario has changed in the last decade, while the present boom is a reaction to the recession for a few years early in the Nineties. The industry is in a recovery phase since 2000 after a recession in 1997 and 1998 with the passenger car segment taking the lead in the growth.

Growth rates in sales and gross profits are juxtaposed with the EPS and P/E multiple for the companies which are represented in the Table below. All of them are having P/E multiple lower than the average for the industry but their P/E are clearly unrelated to growth of sales and gross profits and the estimated prices are far off the actual prices. As such, estimates can be taken as rough indicators around which market prices will rule. Seen from the data in the year 2000, the only companies which might survive in the Auto industry are big sized companies like Escorts and Mahindra & Mahindras and small ones are not worth it.

Practical Example

Industry: Auto Industry

(in percentage)

Company's Name for Half Year ended Sept., 1995	*Growth Rate of Sales*	*Growth Rate of Gross Profits*	*EPS*	*P/E*	*P/E at end Feb. 2000*
1. Escorts	– 19	52	6.76	8.44	20.6
2. Ucal Fuel	67	130	7.21	10.64	3.6
3. Mahindra & Mahindra	53	74	13.0	20.22	19.6
4. Majestic Auto	– 1	3	5.2	5.81	11.2
5. Hindustan Motors	35	104	1.83	6.96	—

Industry P/E is Around 15 to 20

(in ₹)

Company	*Prices as Estimated from Above Data*	*Prices as at End Sept. 1995*	*Prices at End Dec. 1995*	*Prices at End June 96*	*Prices at end Feb. 2000*
Escorts	57	112	88	140	236
Ucal Fuel	77	133	118	138	61
Mahindras	263	373	208	360	520
Majestic Auto	30	105	79	48	22
Hindustan Motors	13	33	29	31	16

Gross profits are presented in the Table, as the depreciation, interest and taxation provisions vary from company to company and then the resultant figures will become uncomparable for inter company performance appraisal.

Objective of the Exercise

To chose a company with in the Automobile [two wheeler and three and four wheelers] Industry, which is rated in 1999-2000 as the growth industry, having emerged from a recent recession in India.

INVESTMENT DECISION

To estimate the possible price range and to select the undervalued scrips.

In practice, the data presented in the Table are not enough to make any correct decision. We should have full ratio analysis and trend analysis referred to in other chapters and a number of financial parameters both quantitative and qualitative are necessary. Taking the above data however, one has to conclude that Ucal Fuel offer good prospects from the data on growth of sales and gross profits and their modest P/E multiple. As expected in the estimates the price of UCAL Fuel almost doubled while that of Escorts has increased by 2 times between estimates and June 1996.

The above conclusion based on the estimates on the choice of companies is thus verified by the subsequent price trends and such experimentation is necessary for a rational analysis and proper investment decision. In fact, the example gives only rudiments of analysis and detailed story of all the companies in the sample as given in the chapter on fundamental Analysis is necessary for proper equity research and investment decision-making.

Equity Investment Strategy

Investment research will yield results of the following types:

(1) Scrips which are underpriced and good for buy orders.

(2) Scrips which are overpriced and good for sell orders, with the necessary margin of profit or capital appreciation.

(3) Scrips which are becoming sick and have to be disposed off immediately.

(4) Scrips which have uncertain trend and have to be set apart with neither buy or sell orders.

PASSIVE AND ACTIVE ASSET MANAGEMENT

In the case of the investment strategy, there can be two alternatives, namely, active and passive equity investment strategies. Passive investment strategy involves the holding of a diversified portfolio as per the market index, say B.S.E. sensex or NSE Nifty. The strategy is to follow the market and observe the rules of the game for Indexed funds or selected mutual funds and their portfolio of investments. In this case, one can follow the formula plan of buying a specific quantity in each month of the specified scrips, irrespective of the price but the market averages out and gives the investors market average return. Such passive strategies lead to some regular investment in selected scrips and allow the market to play its forces and give the market return for the portfolio held by the investor.

The active equity management strategy involves a different methodology of not only selection of scrips but of proper timing. Timing is discussed in the chapter on Technical Analysis. So far as the selection of scrips is concerned, the investor can have a choice of different types of scrips some of which were discussed in an earlier chapter.

1. Blue Chip Companies: These are growth-oriented companies, which give above average growth of earnings and higher return, than the market average. The examples are L&T, Reliance, SBI & ACC etc.

2. Emerging Blue Chip Companies: These companies are presently in a stagnant stage or in infancy stage, but their asset growth is good leading to a potential for increase in sales and profits in the coming few years. Examples of emerging blue chips or those which are undervalued in mid-1996 are Birla Yamaha, Ramada Inns etc. Ramada Inn has for example, a P/E multiple of 8.7 and a price range of ₹ 29 to 55, which definitely underrates the potentiality for capital appreciation, due to low P/E compared to market P/E of 20 to 25. To select proper chips of this type require a lot of equity research involving company wise analysis.

3. Small Size Companies: Investment in small sized companies, say those quoted on OTCEI or on B.S.E. and investment in similar companies on regional exchanges like Cochin, Coimbatore, etc., is another strategy of acquiring some stocks of a different calibre, where risks are high but returns can also be high. Similarly, investment in newly listed companies is also followed by some investors after examining the project report and studying the progress of project implementation, as the balance sheet of such companies may not be available immediately.

4. Defensive Stocks: Another strategy is to invest in defensive stocks which are the same as diversified industry groups or companies. Examples are I.T.C., Wipro, L&T etc. The prices may be high and P/E multiple may also be high, as in the case ITC (P/E at 29). But these investments are safe and steady and the returns are also tending to be market averages. If the investor wants to have above market average returns and to out-perform the market, investment in High risk and High return companies, Hightech Projects, newer and freshly listed companies and emerging blue chip companies is necessary. For this, a good deal of market research and equity analysis is necessary by the investment analyst.

Rumours, heresay and impulsive investments are to be avoided. Grey market quotations are no guide to investment. Investments in unlisted companies and in private placements, requires more research and study. Timing of investment is equally important.

Rupee Cost Averaging Down

In an investment strategy of regular periodical purchases, one can average down the cost of purchase per share. In an upward moving market, one generally sells and in a downward moving market one buys. When purchases are being made, assume that market continues to go down with minor fluctuations an a daily basis, then the strategy is to average down the cost per share by each instalment of purchase.

To give an example: Assume that the Tisco share moved down from ₹ 240 on April 30, 1996 to ₹ 230 in May 30; ₹ 220 on June 30, and ₹ 200 on July 30. To average down the purchase price, buy 100 shares each time as shown below by investment of a fixed amount, for a month every time.

Table

Quantity of Shares of Tisco: Held so far — nil *(in ₹)*

Date of Deal	*Purchase*	*Sale*	*Amount Paid/Received*	*Purchase Price*	*Average Price*
30/4	100	—	24000 + Brokerage	240	240
30/5	100	—	23,000 + Brokerage	230	235
30/6	100	—	22,000 & Brokerage	220	230
30/7	100	—	20,000 + Brokerage	200	222.5
Net Position	400 Shares bought		Total Amount paid ₹ 89,000		Average Price per share is ₹ 222.5

By such Rupee averaging down, the purchase price per share is bought down from ₹ 240 to ₹ 222.5. Similarly, Rupee averaging up can be done in the case of sales to realise optimum capital gain.

INVESTMENT IN FOREIGN MARKETS

Investment in foreign markets is now open to Indians. Companies, banks and Financial institutions are permitted by the Government and RBI to keep some funds in foreign markets and some foreign investments are also permitted through short-term investments in approved equity scrips, joint enterprises, collaborations, equity participation and sale of technical know-how, etc.

Assuming that a day may come, when both individuals and institutions can invest freely abroad, the following paras discuss the matter relating to foreign equities. Normally, investments abroad are chosen for two reasons:

(a) Diversification of risks among countries.

(b) Larger average returns abroad after adjusting for loss or gain on the exchange of currencies.

Major developed countries account for 90% of the total stock capitalisation in the world. The major requirements of such investment are: (a) Large floating stock of medium and large companies to enable the investor to accumulate and disinvest, as and when necessary. (b) Liquidity and depth of the market to enable the foreign investor to buy and sell easily and low cost which is possible if there is a good market of both demand and supply. The potential for appreciation should however be good.

Risks

There are many risks in foreign investment and those different from domestic investment are the following:

1. *Sovereign Risks:* Events specific to a country, say political and social developments, stability of Government and its policies, freedom of economic and financial operations, tax system and the burden of taxation, procedures and practices, etc.

2. *Foreign Exchange Risks:* Events relating to the prevailing exchange rate and the volatility of these rates in the foreign exchange market. These exchange rates fluctuate in a free market due to real interest rate differentials, relative strength of the economies, expectations regarding political and economic stability and seasonal and technical factors relating to trade and payments as between countries etc.

3. Difficulty of comparison due to presentation of accounts in local currency and at current prices.

4. Lack of timely and dependable equity research in some countries.

5. Lack of familiarity with local practices, law and arbitration procedures, in respect of some countries.

6. Inadequate liquidity and depth in trading in many developing countries.

Net Reward Calculation

Investor abroad looks into the net reward of investment, which takes into account the following factors:

(1) Gross return of capital appreciation plus dividend for the holding period (say 25%).

(2) Prevailing tax rate in the relevant country say 20%.

(3) Net post tax return (25 – 5 = 20%).

(4) Gain or loss in exchange of currencies from domestic currency to foreign currency and back from foreign currency to domestic currency (Loss of say 5%).

(5) Net gain after adjustment for currency risk (20 – 5% = 15%). If the domestic return is less than 15% then this foreign investment becomes attractive.

Appendix at the end of the chapter presents the required data and information for Equity Research.

A few examples of actual P/E ratios Oct. 2012

Scrip	Price	EPS	P/E Multiple
1. Coal India	357	23.8	15.0
2. Colgate	1,203	34.0	35.3
3. Wipro	383	23.6	16.2
4. Asian Paints	3,939	105.6	37.3
5. Apollo Tyres	93	9.39	9.9

Sources: E.T daily 2nd October 2012.

CASE STUDY

Analysis of a Mid Cap Company
Dabur India Ltd.

The Dabur India is selected for a case study of a mid cap company under FMGC category of companies which are going to be the leaders in the coming years, as per a study by the E.T (dated 14th January, 2010). The major leaders among the mid cap companies are listed by the E.T as Nestle, Godrej consumer, ITC, Asian paints, Marico, GSK Consumer Healthcare etc. Of these, the Dabur India has a modest paid up capital of ₹ 86 crores with diversified products and good fundamentals.

The Dabur India if a listed company under the category of specified shares quoted both on BSE and NSE. It has its registered office at New Delhi and corporate office at Ghaziabad., U.P. Its product range varied from food products, consumer health, personal care, to Retail Trade, etc. Being listed in "A" Group o shares, it is well traded, with well satisfied retail investors of about 30% of the total shareholders and with good corporate governance.

The financials of this company are presented in the table below for the latest years. It is particularly selected for the reason that it is modestly priced at ₹ 165 as in January, 2010 with a P/E multiple of 32 and 52 weeks high and low of ₹ 175 and ₹ 85 as given in Financial daily of E.T. The case study has the objective of finding out whether it is worth buying or selling and whether it is fairly priced. This is sought to be investigated by a study of the fundamental as presented in the latest annual reports of the company. The main financial ratios and data of the company are given in the table below.

Firstly, it is using its capital in efficient manner as reflected in the ratio of gross bloc to equity at around 6 times, and return on capital employed at around 40 to 60% which is exemplary for a mid-sized company. It has a huge built up reserves of 8.5 times its equity and a book value of ₹ 8.5 per face value of equity share of ₹ 1. It is using the debt route well with a debt-equity ratio 1:3.9. It can be said that it is using its potential of leverage of debt for its operations; it is justified by its huge resource base available internally through its large reserves built up over years. It has satisfied its investors well by giving bonus shares, dividends regularly with the latest dividend of 175% and prudent financial management.

The drawbacks of this company are in keeping the current liquidity at a poor low of about 1 to 1.4 and a high inventory ratio of about 8 to 10 times the sales. These facts can be gleaned from the data on current ratio and inventory to sales ratio in the table. But the profitability ratios are all good. The PAT to sales is around 12 to 14 and the PAT to equity is 4 and they seem to be good for a manufacturing company. Its EPS was ₹ 3.8 for 2007-08 and ₹ 4.5 for 2008-09 and is projected at around 4 for the year 2010. Taking the present P/E multiple as per the latest balance sheet at 36 times, the market price can range from ₹ 190-200. This is the position of the 52 high and low of this share as given in the E.T. at ₹ 172 and ₹ 85. The conclusion is that the share of the Dabur India is presently traded at a fair price. It is for the reader to draw his own conclusion from the analysis given here and the bundle of facts of the company given in the table below.

The actual price of share as on January 12, 2010 was ₹ 162 but fell to 125-132 during 2012. The potential price range is likely to be around ₹ 190 in the coming years, as per our study.

Financials of Dabur

in ₹ Lakhs

Indicators	Year ended March		
	2007-08	*2008-09*	*2011-12*
Equity	8,640	8,651	17,421
Net worth	52,832	73,820	1,89,639
Book Value	₹ 6.1	₹ 8.5	₹ 10.9
Reserves to Equity	5.1 times	7.5 times	8.9 times
Total Debt	1,734	13,897	68,302
Debt-Equity ratio	1:0.2	1:1.6	1:3.9
Gross Block	48,420	57,048	88,536
Net Sales	2,36,107	2,80,543	5,28,317
Sales to Gross block	4.8	4.9	5.9
Profit After Tax (PAT)	33,294	39,121	64,417

PAT to Equity	3.8	4.4	3.69
PAT to sales	14.1	13.9	12.19
Gross Block to Equity (Capital use/efficiency	5.6	6.6	5.08
Current Assets	55,281	74,504	2,29,043
Current Liabilities	58,263	66,649	1,61,175
Current Ratio	0.94	1.12	1.42
Inventory to Sales	8.5	9.3	8.73
EPS	3.85	4.52	3.68
Face Value	₹ 1	₹ 1	₹ 1
Market Price (Rough Average)	140	165	132
P/E ratio	36.4	36.0	31.4
P/BV ratio	23 times	19 times	12 times
M.P. High/low	NA	175/85	139/92
Capital employed	54,566	87,717	1,64,505
Return on capital employed	61%	44%	39%

Note: Provision was made for dividends at 175% for 2008-09. (NA: Not available). The table was compiled from the Balance Sheet and Income-Expenditure Statement as got from NSE website. Data for 2011-12 was drawn from the Balance Sheet, Published in the Economic Times dated October 29, 2012 (Quarterly results along with the previous years 2011-12). The result were not upto the expectations and the price did not rise. It fluctuated between ₹ 110 to 135 during these three years 2009 to 2012. But its Beta fell to 0.3 as per E.T mainly due to lower volubility and fluctuations which leads to systematic risk.

The actual price in 2011 was ₹ 125 and in 2012 ₹ 132. The years 2009 to 2011 were recession years for all industries. This company Dabur (I) maintained the dividend at around 130% as compared to 175% in 2009.

But the price could not rise much, as per our projection the reader may reassess the facts and figures and draw his own conclusions.

Source: www.nseindia.com

PROBLEMS

Question 1

Kirloskar Co. has published the following Profit and Loss Account for the year ended March 31, of a year.

To Opening Stock	26,000	By Sales	160,000
" Purchases	80,000	" Closing Stock	38,000
" Wages	24,000		
" Manufacturing Expenses	16,000		
" Gross Profit	52,000		
	198,000		198,000
To Selling and Distribution Expenses	4,000	By Gross Profit	52,000
" Administrative Expenses	22,800	" Land Sale	4,800
" Loss in fire Accident	800		
" General Expenses	1,200		
" Net Profit	28,000		
	56,800		56,800

Calculate the operating ratio and operating profit ratio.

Answer:

The operating ratio is also called operating expense ratio.

$$\text{Operating Ratio} = \frac{\text{Cost of Goods Sold + Selling, Administative and Distribution Expenses and General Expenses}}{\text{Sales}}$$

Cost of Goods Sold = 26,000 + 80,000 – 38,000 + 24,000 + 16,000

	= 108,000 +
Selling Administrative and Distribution Expenses	26,800 +
General Expenses	1,200
Total	136,000

Sales = 160,000

Cost of goods sold, Selling Administrative and Distribution expenses and Administrative expenses and general expenses.

= 108,000 + 26,800 + 1,200 = 136,000

Operating Expenses Ratio = 1,36,000 divided by 1,60,000 = 85%

Operating Profit Ratio = 1 – Operating Expense Ratio

= 1 – 0.85 = 0.15 = 15%

$$\text{Operating Profit Ratio} = \frac{\text{Net Proft + Non-operating Expenses Minus Non-operating Income/or Profits}}{\text{Sales}}$$

$$= \frac{28{,}000 + 800 - 4{,}800 \text{ (sale of land)}}{1{,}60{,}000}$$

$$= \frac{24{,}000}{160{,}000} = 15\%$$

Question 2

Polycom Ltd. has sales of ₹ 6 crores and an asset Turnover ratio of 6 for the latest year. Given the net profits at ₹ 12 lakhs.

(a) What is the 'Company's return on assets or earning power.'

(b) For expanding and increased efficiency the company hopes to instal a new equipment leading to an increase in investment in assets by 20% and a rise in net profit margin to 3% (from 2% earlier). If sales remain unchanged, what is the new earning power of the company.

Answer:

(a) Total Assets $= \dfrac{\text{Sales}}{\text{Turnover}} = \dfrac{6}{6} =$ ₹ 1 crores

Earning Power $= \dfrac{\text{Net Profits}}{\text{Total Assets}} = \dfrac{12}{100} = 12\%$

(b) New figure of Total Assets = 1 × 1.2 = ₹ 1.2 crores

New Earning Power = Turnover × Profit margin

$$= \frac{6 \times 3}{12} = 15\%$$

For, $\left[\text{Turnover} = \dfrac{\text{Sales}}{\text{Total assets}}\right]$ and profit margin is 3%

Question 3

Given the data for 6 companies in the same indsutry and about the same size as shown below, calculate asset turnover net profit margin and earning power.

Company	*A*	*B*	*C*	*D*	*E*	*F*
Sales (₹ crore)	10	20	8	5	12	17
Total Assets	8	10	6	2.5	4	5
Net Income	0.7	2.0	0.8	0.5	1.5	1.0

Answer:

Company A

Assets Turnover $= \dfrac{\text{Sales}}{\text{TotalAssets}} = \dfrac{10}{8} = 1.25$

Net Profit Margin $= \dfrac{\text{Net Income}}{\text{Sales}} = \dfrac{0.7}{10} = 7\%$

Earning Power = Turnover × Profit Margin

1.25 × 7 = 8.75

Company B

$$\text{Asset Turnover} = \frac{20}{2} = 2$$

$$\text{Net Profit Margin} = \frac{2}{20} = 10\%$$

$$\text{Earning Power} = 2 \times 10 = 20$$

Company C

$$\text{Asset Turnover} = \frac{8}{6} = 1.33$$

$$\text{Net Profit Margin} = \frac{\text{Net Income}}{\text{Sales}} = \frac{0.8}{8} = 10\%$$

$$\text{Earning Power} = \text{Turnover} \times \text{Profit Margin}$$

$$1.33 \times 10 = 13.3$$

$$\text{or } \frac{\text{Net Income}}{\text{Total Assets}} = \frac{0.8}{6} = 13.3$$

The reader can work out the ratios in a similar way for other companies also.

APPENDIX

Background Material to Read from Published Sources

1. Previous three years' annual reports
2. Copy of latest chairman's speech
3. Prospectus/Letter of offer
4. Latest half year results

Need to Collect following Information

1. Estimated volume, turnover, operating profit, interest, depreciation, tax, and profits after tax for
   (a) following three half years
   (b) following one or two years.
2. Anticipated foreign exchange earnings for the following two financial years.
3. Anticipated imports for the following two financial years.
4. Planned targets and expansion in the following financial year.
5. Swot analysis of the company (single most *strength, weakness opportunity* and *threat* to the company).
6. Sensitivity of the business.

(Name) . . . . Company Limited

---

1. Business Overview
2. Products — brief description of each
   — Raw materials/Costs and availability
   — Any constraints
   — Import content
   — Quality *vs.* International
   — ISO 9000
   — Technology used
   — How much value addition?
   — Application of products
   — Key customers
   — Export possibilities of product
   — Excise Duty Structure
   — Power Requirement
   — Any regulatory problems
   — R&D Expenditure
3. Industry Outlook of Major Product Lines
   — Key to success in that industry
   — Bottleneck in that business
4. Major Product Lines and Revenue of Company
5. Expansion Plans — Strategy, Timing, Advantage
   — Backward Integration
   — Forward Integration
   — Diversification
   — Time Schedule
   — Status of current projects on hand
   — Financial plan
6. Competition
   — What is its Competitive Advantage?
   — Market share
   — GPM comparison

- — Technology
- — Value addition
- — Who is their major competitor
- — Competitor's strength

7. Marketing
   - — Direct/Dealer
   - — Sister Companies
   - — Sales growth targets
8. Global
   - — Patents protection
   - — International Costs *vs.* Domestic Costs
   - — International Pricing *vs.* Domestic Pricing
   - — Quality Certification requirements
   - — Average International Plant size *vs.* The Company
9. Financials
   - — Sales projection and of inventories
   - — How to improve GPM?
   - — Credit and Receivable management
10. Cost and quality factors
    - — Costs and quality aspects of competitors
    - — Import costs *versus* domestic costs
    - — Cost reduction Techniques
    - — Quality Improvement Techniques
    - — Foreign exchange earnings and out flow
11. Distribution Philosophy
    - — Retained earnings policy
    - — Dividend policy
    - — Norms for issue of bonus
12. Is the Company's Share Underpriced? Why?
    - — What is the volume traded?
    - — What is the market lot of shares of the company?
    - — Where are shares listed?
    - — Number of public shareholders or floating stock
13. Industry/Company Specific — Cement
    - — How has liberalisation policies of the government benefited industry and company?
    - — Impact of recent budget on the cement industry and in particular to this company?
    - — Are cement bag prices likely to remain firm? Why? For how long? What are the ex-factory prices now? What is the fair estimate for the next six to twelve months?
14. Industry/Company Specific — Ceramic
    - — How has liberalisation policies of the government benefited this industry and company?
    - — What is the impact of recent budget on the ceramic industry and in particular to this company? What is the competitive advantage with mosaic tile industry, after the budget?
15. Industry/Company Specific — Paper
    - — How has liberalisation policies of the government benefited this industry and company?
    - — What are ex-factory paper prices now? How were they comparatively a year ago and six months ago? What is the prognosis for the next six months and a year?
    - — Have any of your key raw materials become expensive comparatively over a period? (Caustic soda? Chlorine? Electricity?) What are the prospects?
    - — How are international prices? Any threats of imports? Any opportunity for exports?

16. Industry Profile — Sugar
    - — How proposed sugar delicensing will help this company, sugar levy prices and free market prices and differential cyclical trends in the Industry based on sugarcane production?
    - — Capacity built and utilised by the industry.
    - — Share of this company and its main competitors.
    - — International prices of sugar and prospects of sugar exports.
    - — Is Government regulation hampering the industry?

Then the company analysis, with particular reference to the financials, has to be done as given above for the Dabur India Ltd.

9

SECURITY PRICING

Security evaluation is important to decide on the portfolio of an investor. All investment decisions are to be made on a scientific analysis of the right price of a share. Hence, an understanding of the valuation of securities is essential. Investors should buy underpriced shares and sell overpriced shares. Share pricing is thus an important aspect of trading. Conceptually, four types of valuation models are discernible. They are: (i) Book value, (ii) Liquidating value, (iii) Intrinsic value, (iv) Replacement value as compared to Market price.

FACTORS INFLUENCING VALUATION

Security price depends on a host of factors like earnings per share, prospects of expansion, future earnings potential, possible issue of bonus or rights shares, etc. Some demand for a particular stock may give pleasure of power as a shareholder or prestige and control on management. Satisfaction and pleasure in the non-monetary sense cannot be considered in any practical and quantifiable sense. Many psychological and emotional factors influence the demand for a share.

In money terms, the return to a security on which its value depends consists of two components: (i) regular dividends or interest, and (ii) capital gains or losses in the form of changes in the capital value of the asset. If the risk is high, return should also be high. Risk here refers to uncertainty of receipt of principal and interest or dividend and variability of this return.

The above returns are in terms of money received over a period of years. But money of Re. 1 received today is not the same as money of Re. 1 received a year hence or two years hence etc. Money has time value, which suggests that earlier receipts are more desirable and valuable than later receipts. One reason for this is that earlier receipts can be reinvested and more receipts can be got than before. Here, the principle operating is compound interest.

Thus, if Vn is the terminal value at the period n, P is the initial value, g is rate of compounding or return, n is the number of compounding periods, then $Vn = P(1 + g)^n$.

If we reverse the process, the present value (P) can be thought of as reversing the compounding of values. This is discounting of the future values to the present day, represented by the formula:

$$P = Vn/(1 + g)^n$$

where, the meaning of the terms used is the same as indicated above.

Security Valuation

The major factor which influences security prices is the return on equity capital to the investor. This return may be in the form of dividends or net earnings of the company. Thus, the value of a share is a function of the company's dividend paying capacity or its earnings capacity. The dividends may be different from the earnings depending on the amount of profits retained by the company for the requirements of liquidity, expansion, modernisation, etc.

Normally, the value of a share is its book value, if the shares are not quoted on the market. On the other hand, the market price of shares quoted will differ from the book value based on investors' perception of the future earning potential of the company, growth prospects and the industry prospects, quality of management, the goodwill or the intangibles of the company.

If the security is a bond or debenture and has a fixed return like 14% per annum, its market price depends upon investor's perception of the capitalisation rate which may be assumed to be 15%. In this case,

$$\text{Market Price (MP)} = \frac{\text{Earnings}}{\text{Discount rate}} = \frac{14 \times 100}{15} = ₹\ 93.$$

If the security is an equity share, its return is Dividend + Capital appreciation. Then the future dividends may not be constant or fixed as also the degree of capital appreciation.

CONSTANT GROWTH MODEL

For equity securities, the market price depends upon the discounted future dividends or earnings flows. Thus,

P = Value = D/K – g

D = Expected dividend

K = Discount rate

g = Rate of growth of earnings power.

In this simplified model, dividend flows are assumed to be constant and the rate of growth of earnings fixed.

The discount rate in the above model is subjective and is assumed to be a specific rate such as risk-free market rate or the long-term yield rate on government bonds. A few analysts[1] use the implied discount rate or internal rate of return, which is derived by equating the present value of the projected dividend stream with the current market price.

The actual selection of the discount rate as the fair rate of return on capital is a concept which is to be defined by the analysts and used as a subjective factor. Many people use a crude discounting model whereby the dividend stream is constant and the discount rate is also fixed as the internal rate of return on the project. In actual fact, the discount rate is a rate on fixed income securities, which are risk-free like government bonds. The yield on Government bonds at 7% is taken normally as the risk-free rate in India. But some use the bank rate of 6% as a risk-free return.

Book Value

Book value of a security is an accounting concept. The book value of an equity share is equal to the networth of the firm divided by the number of equity shares, where the networth is equal to equity capital plus free reserves. The market value may fluctuate around the book value but may be higher if the future prospects are good.

Liquidating Value (Breakdown Value)

If the assets are valued at their breakdown value in the market and take net fixed assets plus current assets minus current liabilities as if the company is liquidated, then divide this by the number of shares, the resultant value is the liquidating value per share. This is also an accounting concept.

Replacement Value

When the company is liquidated and its assets are to be replaced by new ones, their prices being higher, the replacement value of a share, will be different from the Breakdown value. Some analysts take this replacement value to compare with the market price.

Intrinsic Value vs. Market Price

Market value of a security is the price at which the security is traded in the market and it is generally hovering around its intrinsic value. There are different schools of thought regarding the relationship of intrinsic value to the market price. Market prices are those which rule in the market, resulting from the demand and supply forces. Intrinsic price is the true value of the share, which depends on its earning capacity and its true worth. According to the fundamentalist approach to security valuation, the value of the security must be equal to the discounted value of the future income stream. The investor buys the securities when the market price is below this value.

Thus, for fundamentalists, earnings and dividends are the essential ingredients in determining the market value of a security. The discount rate used in such present value calculations is known as the required rate or return. Using this discount rate all future earnings are discounted back to the present to determine the intrinsic value. This has been referred to earlier.

1. E.J. Elton & M.J. Gruber, *Modern Portfolio Theory and Investment Analysis.*

According to the technical school, the price of a security is determined by the market demand and supply and it has very little to do with intrinsic values. The price movements follow certain trends for varying periods of time. Changes in trend represent the shifts in demand and supply which are predictable. The present trends are the offshoot of the past and history repeats itself according to this school.

According to efficient market hypothesis, in a fairly large security market where competitive conditions prevail, market prices are good proxies for intrinsic values. The security prices are determined after absorbing all the information available to market participants. A share is thus generally worth whatever it is selling for in the market.

Generally, fundamental school is the basis for security valuation and many models are in use, based on these tenets.

EQUITY VALUATION

The intrinsic value of an equity share depends on the dividends declared by the company. These models can be broadly classified for simplicity's sake into:

(i) Single-period valuation models; and

(ii) Multi-period valuation models.

In these models, the infinite stream of future dividends are valued for the present time as price-dividend ratio. If the net earnings are assumed to be the same as dividends and no retained earnings, then the price-dividend ratio contracts to price-earnings ratio.

Single-period Valuation Models

Assume that — (i) the dividends are paid annually; (ii) the first dividend is received after one year, and (iii) the resale occurs at the end of the year. Then, the price of the share is $P_o = \frac{D_1}{(1+i)} + \frac{P_1}{(1+i)}$ where Po is the current price, P_1 is the price after an year, D_1 is the dividend after a year and i is the required rate of return.

Example

A company's equity share is expected to bring a dividend of ₹ 2 and fetch a price of ₹ 18 after an year. If the investor buys at ₹ 18, there is no capital appreciation. Assuming the required rate of return to be equal to 12%,

$$P_o = \frac{2.0}{(1+.12)} + \frac{18.00}{(1+.12)} = \frac{20}{(1.12)} = 17.86$$

If the investor purchases at ₹ 18, he incurs a loss of ₹ 0.14 on every share.

Multi-period Share Valuation Model

An investor would hold the security for more than one period. In this case, the price of the share is given by the formula

$$P_o = \sum_{t=1}^{n} n \frac{D_1}{(1+i)^t} + \frac{P_n}{(1+i)^n}$$

Where, D_i is the dividend in period i and P_n is the selling price. In case the dividends grow at a constant rate of g, the equation reduces to

$$P_o = \frac{D_1}{(i-g)}$$

In the special case of g = 0

the equation is $P_o = \frac{D_1}{i}$ where i is the required rate of return

Example

The expected earnings per share is ₹ 3 and dividend ₹ 2 respectively. If the required rate of return is 15%, what should be the share price assuming g = 0%, 5% and 10%.

Therefore, when g = 0, $P = \frac{2}{0.15} = 13.33$

when g = 0.05, $P = \frac{2}{0.15 - 0.05} = 20$

when g = 0.10, $P = \frac{2}{0.15 - 0.1} = 40$

The above example shows how the share price appreciates very high, if the company evinces growth prospects and declares rising dividends.

DIVIDEND CAPITALISATION

Sometimes, the firms do not declare dividends so as to finance their future programmes. In such cases, the dividends are non-existent, but the market prices may be high. In these cases, it is seen that the investors use earnings as a proxy for dividends in the above models. The dividend capitalisation model and the earnings capitalisation model yield the same result only when all the earnings are paid out as dividends. Then there is no growth. $P = \frac{E_1}{i}$ where the earnings (E_1) (or dividends) grow at a constant rate, then the formula is $P = E_1/i - g$.

When a portion of the earnings is retained, the dividend capitalisation model is to be used. When growth in the expected future dividends is taken as a function of retained earnings that are reinvested in profitable projects, it is double counting to include both the earnings and the future growth rate of dividends in the same model as the latter depend upon the former also, in part.

EARNINGS CAPITALISATION

It is to be noted that higher future dividends are an *alternative* to present dividends and are *not an addition* to the present dividend stream. If E = D, the firm cannot grow. Thus, the investors who use the price-earnings ratio tend to overstate the market price due to the double counting problem.

In reality, the earnings do not grow at a constant rate nor do the dividends. For theoretical nicety, these assumptions are made. But as limitations, it should be noted that the desired rate of return and the actual rate may not coincide and there is an element of subjectivity in the desired rate of return. Besides, the use of price-earnings ratio following the dividend capitalisation model, suffers from the fact that earnings data are historical but price is the present price, which already takes into account the past dividends, and the future dividend flow may not depend on the past earnings, and price is paid for the future returns.

USE OF P/E RATIO

Many practising analysts use the simple multiplier technique of P/E ratio, but not the present value models referred to above.

The ratio P/E = Current Market Price/Earnings per share.

By an analysis of the company's performance, the analyst computes the P/E multiplier (the times P is higher than the earnings per share). In this case, he forecasts the future earnings per share for the next six months or one year and uses this historical multiplier of the same company or of the industry average multiplier to arrive at the market price. The resulting market price is compared with the actual market price to find out whether it is overpriced or underpriced. If it is overpriced, it is to be sold as per the principles of trading operations based on fundamental analysis.

The valuation technique based on discounting is cumbersome and serious forecasting problems arise in the process. The discount rate to be used is a subjective factor and a number of assumptions are required to be made regarding the dividend flows in the present value models. Therefore, analysts and investors use only the P/E ratio for security valuation in practice.

To sum up, the models more commonly used for security pricing are the Dividend Discounting method/Earnings Discounting method and the P/E ratio model. These models are dealt with in detail below.

SECURITY PRICING MODELS

The Dividend Discounting Method: The expected future dividend payments by the company are discounted to the present day by the use of an appropriate discount rate, which is supposed to reflect the magnitude of risk-free return. The risk premium of stocks may have some risk element and many additional uncertainties. In this model, each of the future year's dividend up to, say, for 'n' years (10 years) is discounted with the appropriate discount rate to the present time and summed up to arrive at the worth of the stock today. Dividends are expected to remain constant and the discount rate is assumed to remain unchanged. In this simplified model, no provision is made for changes in dividend or for a variable growth of dividend/earnings. The formula is D/K – g, where D is the dividend, k is the discount rate and g is the constant growth rate of dividends. In this model, the discount rate is a matter of individual perception and is subjective. It is based on the expected depreciation of the rupee and one's own time premium of the present over the future. Thus, today one rupee may be worth ₹ 1.10 in the next year (a premium of 10 per cent inclusive of inflation).

P/E Ratio Model: The present value of the stock is also arrived at through the assumed relationship between the P/E ratio of a company and that of the average of the whole industry in which the company is. If the company's P/E ratio and the industry P/E ratio have some relationship, these can be related to derive the industry relative, which can be applied to the company's earnings per share to arrive at its price. Thus, if P/E for electronics has a P/E relative at 15, then for the company in electronics industry say TCS data on earnings per share can be multiplied by 15 to arrive at its price. If this price is higher than the market price, the security is undervalued and *vice versa*.

Other Models

Some writers speak of two supplementary guides to valuation which came into fairly wide use, namely, price-to-asset ratio and price-to-sales ratio (ref. p. 365, *Investment Analysis and Portfolio Management* by Cohen, Zinberg and Ziekel). According to the first, the stocks of a company are evaluated by reference to the true net asset values using various capital goods and inventory price indices to adjust reported book values. A number of analysts define this as the replacement cost of book value of the company. Some take it as the net working capital per share measured by current assets minus current liabilities, fixed assets minus long-term debt and preferred stock minus intangible assets divided by the number of shares. This is something like the breakdown value of the company's assets.

According to the second, the average price-to-sales ratio of the industry group is applied to the company P/S ratio to judge whether it is overpriced or underpriced. A low P/S ratio indicates a low probability of bankruptcy and hence a good buy, if other conditions are satisfied for choosing the company.

GRAHAM'S APPROACH TO VALUATION OF EQUITY

In their book on Security Analysis (1934) Benjamin Graham, and David Dodd, argued that future earnings power was the most important determinant of the value of stock. The original approach of identifying the undervalued stock is to find out the present value of forecasted dividends, and if the current market price is lower, it is undervalued. Alternatively, the analyst could determine the discount rate that makes the present value of the forecasted dividends equal to the current market price of the stock. If that rate (I.R.R. or discount rate) is more than the required rate for stocks of similar risks, then the stock is underpriced.

Graham and Dodd had argued that each dollar of dividends is worth four times as much as one dollar of retained earnings (in their original Book); but subsequent studies of data showed no justification for this. Graham and Rea have given some questions on Rewards and risks for financial data analysts to answer yes or no and on the basis of these ready to answer questions, they decided to locate undervalued stocks to buy and overvalued stocks to sell.

Such readymade formulas or questions are now out of favour due to various empirical studies which showed that earnings models are as good as or better than dividend models and that a number of factors are ably studied for common stock valuation and no unique formula or answer is justifiable.

DO DIVIDENDS MATTER?

Theoretical Approaches

The following are the theoretical approaches to the valuation of stock. The classical theory and the traditional view is that debt is cheaper than equity and that firms can increase their value by reducing the cost of capital through debt route and by raising the level of gearing (The proportion of Debt to Equity). Tax considerations also confirm this view of cheaper cost of debt as interest on debt is an expense item and not taxable like the dividend paid to equity holders. However, there is a trade off between the benefits of leverage to the company and the larger risk that this leads due to larger servicing needs of debt and the possibility of bankruptcy (or illiquidity). This theory postulates that there is an optimum level of debt for a firm at any point of time depending upon the cost of debt and the average return on capital.

Modigham and Miller (1958)[@] questioned this traditional view, as it is based on unrealistic assumptions. The assumptions are free and perfect information and competitive markets. M&M laid the foundation for Modern Theory of valuation of firms. They showed that valuation of firm is independent of the gearing or capital structure. M&M theory is called the Neo-classical Theory of Investment which showed that so long as the return on investment is higher than the cost of capital, the firm is indifferent whether it is external or internal capital. The financing decision is made independent of the investment decision. Both external sources and internal sources are viewed as substitutes and dividends paid or profits retained make no difference as source of capital does not matter.

The Modern Theories are based on cash flows generated by an investment. The "peeking order" Theory of financing states that capital market imperfections raise the cost of external financing whereby the firms first finance the new investments by resort to internal sources, then by low cost debt and finally by resort to equity from the public.

There are two approaches to the cash flow theories, normally the managerial approach and the information theoretic approach. Under the first, Managers are maximisers of the size of the firm and its profits and do not necessarily aim at the maximisation of shareholders' wealth. This approach separates ownership from control and differentiates the interests of a shareholders (ownership) from that of Management (control). Managerial Theory states that the firm relies more on internal finance as the resort to external sources leads to the firm subjecting it self to the discipline of the capital market.

The second theoretic approach is based on a symmetric information model where in the managers have the private information about the firm's return streams and investment opportunities. Myers and Majiluf (1984)[*] have showed that if the capital market is less informed than the insiders, about the value of the firm's assets, equity may be mispriced and low quality equity gets mixed up with high quality equity. The firm's preference is for internal funds, risk less debt or less costly debt, followed by external sources. But what is missed in the above approaches is the concept of *Return versus Risk*. Cash flows and investment are however closely related and hence the net present value of cash flows is the major method of valuation of the firm and Dividend Capitalisation Model and Earnings Capitalisation Model are used more frequently in the valuation of the firm in the modern literature.

Valuation of Securities in India

In India, the valuation of securities used to be done by the CCI for the purpose of fixing up the premium on new issues of existing companies. These guidelines used by CCI were applicable upto May 1992, when the CCI was abolished. Although the present market price will be taken into account a more rational price used to be worked out by the CCI on certain criteria.

Thus, the CCI used the concept of Net Asset Value (NAV) and Profit-Earning Capacity Value (PECV) as the basis for fixing up the premium on shares. The NAV is calculated by dividing the networth by the number of equity shares. The networth includes equity capital plus free reserves and surplus less contingent liabilities. The PECV is estimated by multiplying the earnings per share by a capitalisation rate of 15% for manufacturing companies, 20% for trading companies and 17.5% in the case of intermediate companies. Earnings Per Share (EPS) is calculated by dividing the three-year average post-tax profits by the total number of equity shares. Thus, if EPS is ₹ 5 and if the price earnings multiplier is 15, the price of share, which is reflected by the PECV, should be ₹ 5 × 15 = 75 (if it is a manufacturing company).

To be more specific, the Net Asset Value of a company (NAV) is equal to Total assets less liabilities, borrowings, debts, preference capital and contingent liabilities which is to be divided by the number of shares.

The (PECV) is obtained by capitalising the average profits after tax (over the past three years) by a rate varying from 15% to 20% depending on the nature of the activity of the company as already noted.

@ Modigham E. and Miller M., "The Cost of Capital ...etc.," *American Economic Review,* Vol. 48. p. 261, (1958).

* Myers S. and Majiluf N., "Corporate Financing and Investment Decision etc.," in *Journal of Financial Economies*, Vol. 13, p. 187.

The fair value of the share is the average of the NAV and PECV. This Fair Value (FV) is taken into account for comparison with the average market price over the preceding three years and the average market price should be less than the fair value by at least 20%. If the average market price is 20% to 50% of the FV, the capitalisation rate to be used is 12%. If it is 50% to 75% of the FV, the capitalisation rate is 10% and if it is more than 75% of FV, the capitalisation rate is 8%.

Example

The following example will make the above exercise clear (year 1990).

Take a manufacturing company (TISCO)

Average Market Price over the last three years = ₹ 123

Net Asset Value (NAV) computed as shown above = ₹ 68

Profit-earning Capacity Value (PECV) = Earnings per share ₹ 5.4

capitalised by 15% for manufacturing company = $\frac{5.4 \times 100}{15}$ = ₹ 36.

Average of NAV and PECV is (68 + 36)/2 = ₹ 52 which is the fair value.

The market price (₹ 123 in 1990) is more than 75% of the Fair Value (₹ 52). Hence, the captialisation rate of 8% is to be applied as referred to above to the earnings per share.

Earnings per share is ₹ 5.4.

At the capitalisation rate of 8%, the PECV = ₹ 67.50.

Book value per share or NAV is ₹ 68.

The average of the two above is ₹ 67.75.

For a share of ₹ 10 of face value, the premium is thus ₹ 57.75.

Since May 1992, with the repeal of C.I.C. Act, free market pricing of shares has been permitted. The price of new issue can be decided by the company and its Merchant banker. As per the existing guidelines of SEBI, the merchant banker need not submit the proposals regarding the share price, premium, if any, etc. of new issues to the SEBI for vetting, but the justification for the same is to be provided in the prospectus. A margin of 20% on either side is permitted to change the actual premium from the premium submitted to SEBI for record or vetting.

PROBLEMS

Problem 1

Videocon International is a B_1 Group Company listed on the BSE and NSE, with an equity of ₹ 52 crores at end March 1996. In networth is ₹ 857 crores with a total long-term debt of ₹ 594 crores, its debt equity ratio is 1:11 (Debt is 11 times the equity). Reserves are 16 times the equity. Its Book value at end Dec. 1996 was ₹ 165. Its market price was ₹ 320.

The company's operational and financial results are shown from the data below:

Data at end 1996 March
(in ₹ crores)

Profit and Loss Account

Sales	1,562	
Other Income	8	
Total Income	1,570	
Expenses	1,421	
Operating Profit	149	
Net Profit	88	
E.P.S. (net profit divided by number of equity shares)	17	and B.V. = ₹ 165

Market Price was lower than B.V at that time due to high debt and low profitability of this company.

It is now Videocon Industries quoting at around ₹ 350 in August 2007. The EPS is to be multiplied by the Industry or Market Multiplier (P/E ratio) to arrive at M.P. Similarly, the B.V. of the company is to be multiplied by the market or industry ratio of M.P./B.V. as normally M.P. is a multiple of B.V.

Problem 2

Justify the Market price in terms of the fundamentals of the company, based on the given data.

Hints: Annual Average BSE Index (sensex) Data (M.P. = ₹ 350 to 365)

1995-96 = 3,289; 1996-97 = 3,469

1997-98 = High: 4,605; Low: 3,164; Average: 3,885;

Problem 3

Dr. Reddy's Labs

Brief Data on Income and Expenditure Statement

(₹ in crores)

April to March 1995-96

Sales		196
Other Income		15
Total Income		211
Operating Profit		61
Net Profit after Depreciation and Interest and Taxes	=	50
Equity	=	26
Reserves	=	268
Net worth	=	294
Debt	=	27

Debt-Equity Ratio 1:1

$$\text{Book Value} = \frac{294}{2.6} = 113$$

$$\text{E.P.S.} = \frac{50}{2.6} = 19$$

Half-yearly Results — April-Sept. 1996-97

Sales	=	124
Other Income		2
		126
Expenditure		102
Operating Profit	=	24
Net Profit	=	16
Annualised EPS	=	12

Book Value ₹ 113

Market Price Range: ₹ 140 – 250 (in 1996)
Average ₹ 195

Market Price Range: ₹ 170 – 380 (in 1997)
Average ₹ 275.

Despite the fall in EPS and Profits in 1997, Average Market Price was higher in 1997. Explain the market in terms of intrinsic value, within the limits of data given.

Problem 4

1. ABC Ltd. has been experiencing a decline of 5% in its cash dividend growth rate for the past few years. This decline is expected to continue. The company has a current dividend per share at ₹ 2.50. If the company's required rate of return is 16%, what is the share value now. What will be its price two years hence assuming other conditions remain unchanged?

Answer:

Given $g = -5\%$

$D_o = ₹\ 2.50$

$D_1 = 20\ (1 + g)$

$= 2.50\ (1 + (-0.05)) =$

$2.50\ (0.95) = 2.375$

$$P_o = \frac{D_1}{ke - g} = \frac{2.375}{0.16-(-0.05)} = \frac{2.375}{0.21} = 11.31\ ₹$$

Price after two years:

$$P_2 = \frac{D_3}{ke - g} = \frac{D_o(1+g)^3}{ke - g} = \frac{2.50\,[1+(-0.05)^3]}{0.16-(0.05)}$$

$$= \frac{2.50(0.857)}{0.21} = \frac{2.1425}{0.21} = 10.20\ ₹$$

2. The stock of XYZ Co. has a required rate of return of 18%. The current market price of its share is ₹ 110 and its current dividend per share is ₹ 10. Calculate its growth rate.

Answer:

$$P_o = \frac{D_1}{ke - g}$$

$D_1 = D_o\ (1 + g) = 10\ (1 + g)$

$$110 = \frac{10(1+g)}{0.18-g}$$

$19.8 - 110\,g = 10 + 10g$

$120g = 9.8$

$$g = \frac{9.8}{120} = 0.082$$

$g = 8.2\%$ (growth rate)

3. An investor found that earnings of Infotech should grow at 8% for the next three years with a 50% dividend pay out ratio and that its P/E ratio should be 15 in three years. Its current EPS = ₹ 5. If he purchases the stock at a price of ₹ 70 per share, what after tax return should be earned over the three years, assuming that he is in the 40% tax bracket?

Answer:

$N = 3$ years; $g = 0.08$, $\frac{P}{E} = 15$

$P_o = ₹\ 70$, $E_o = ₹\ 5$,

$1 - b = 0.5$

ke = after tax cost of equity, T = Tax rate.

$$P_o = \sum_{t=1}^{n} \frac{E_o(1+g)^t(1-b)(1-T)}{(1+ke)^t} + \frac{(P_N - P_o)(1-T) + P_o}{(1+ke)^N}$$

$$P_N = E_o(1+g)^N \left(\frac{P}{E}\right)$$

$$P_N = 5(1.08)^3 \, 15 = 94.48$$

$$P_o = 70$$

$$70 = \sum_{t=10}^{3} \frac{5(1.08)^t (0.5)(1-0.4)}{(1+ke)^t} + \frac{(94.48-70)(1-0.4)+70}{(1+ke)^3}$$

$$70 = \frac{1.62}{(1+ke)} + \frac{1.75}{(1+ke)^2} + \frac{1.89}{(1+ke)^3} + \frac{14.69+70}{(1+ke)^3}$$

The solution is found by trial and error method and ke= 8.9017%.

4. The stock of ABC Ltd., is expected to pay a cash dividend three years from now and it will be at 25% of its earnings. The company's cost of equity is 16% and its ending P/E is 18. Its current earnings per share is ₹ 3 and its earnings is expected to grow at a rate of 10% per year. What should be the value of the stock that he is willing to pay for this stock, if he is willing to hold the stock for 4 years? No dividend will be paid in the first two years.

Answer:

N = 4 years

1–b = 0.25

ke = 16%, g = 10%, E_o = ₹ 3

and $(P/E)_4 = 18$

$$P_o = \frac{0}{(1.16)} + \frac{0}{(1.16)^2} + \frac{3(1.10)^3(0.25)}{(1.16)^3} + \frac{3(1.10)^4(0.25)}{(1.16)^4} + \frac{3(1.10)^4(18)}{(1.16)^4}$$

$$= 0 + 0 + \frac{1}{(1.16)^3} + \frac{1.10}{(1.16)^4} + \frac{79.06}{(1.16)^4}$$

= 0 + 0 + 0.64 + 0.61 + 43.67

= ₹ 44.92

Solve the following Problems

Questions

(1) ABC has issued a dividend of ₹ 2 last year. The dividend is expected to grow at 5% per year in the next 3 years; the price of stock three years hence is say ₹ 34.72 which means P_3 = ₹ 34.73 discounted at 12% rate. Calculate the present value of dividend stream and the expected future price, given above.

(2) XYZ has issued a series of 3.4% — 30 year bonds with annual interest payment in the year 1995, at a par value of ₹ 1,000. Ten years later, the price fell to ₹ 650. What is the YTM of bond in 2005. Assuming that interest rates fell again later to 2.4% by 2010, what is the price of bond in the year 2010?

(3) Mark Ltd. is paying a dividend of ₹ 3.5, which is expected to grow at 15% for the next four years and then it levels of at 8%. If the capitalisation rate is 12%, what is the market value of equity share?

(4) Orient Co. Ltd., is paying a dividend of ₹ 5 per share. The market expects the dividend to grow at 10% in the next three years and then at 5%. The market capitalisation rate is 13% for earnings of similar companies, calculate the share value of this company.

(5) Pluto Ltd., has a sales turnover of ₹ 25 crores. In the coming two years, sales are expected to grow at 20% and 10% respectivley. The company is expected to maintain a profit margin of 8% and the Dividend payout at 50%. The number of equity shares is 10 lakhs. It is expected that the share will trade at a multiplier of 15 at the end of two years. What is the intrinsic value of stock, if the investors required rate of return is 8%?

(6) Shankar sells short 200 shares of Saturn Ltd., at a price of ₹ 42. Thereafter the company declares a dividend of ₹ 1.5 per share. Later Saturn's Stock declines to ₹ 35 and at that point, the short seller covers the position. Calculate the gain or loss as percentage of his total transaction, if the transaction costs amount to 1% of the transaction.

10

FINANCIAL ARITHMETICS FOR EQUITY AND BONDS

Introduction

Investment decision is made on the basis of sound financial arithmetics. Investment involves parting with money and taking some risks. Money has many alternative uses and the returns vary with the risk taken. Thus, investment in risk free assets like bank deposit requires a minimum return, called risk free return. This is the compensation for saving by foregoing present consumption and for parting with liquidity (nearness to cash or actual cash). The risk free return is thus the minimum return for investment, required, if that investment is to be made. This minimum rate is the bank rate, or Government Bond Yield of one year maturity.

CALCULATION OF RETURNS (YIELDS)

Lending of money is for a return in the form of interest. The rates of interest vary with the purpose and maturity and a host of other factors. Thus, advances made by banks and financial institutions are at varying rates of interest and Reserve Bank has allowed freedom to banks to fix their prime lending rates, which are the rates charged for high creditworthy borrowers and the minimum basic rate for lending.

If the individuals and institutions make an investment in any asset they base their decision to invest on the basis of some financial arithmetic which takes into account the following factors, among others:

(a) Creditworthiness of the party.

(b) Time period of lending or investment.

(c) Risk of the activity of investments.

(d) Expected returns over the time period chosen.

(e) Safety and marketability of investments.

YIELDS ON BONDS/FIXED INTEREST SECURITIES

Normally, if we purchase an asset like a bond or debt instrument or debenture or lent money for any purpose the return is calculated by the formula:

$$\text{Rate} = \frac{\text{Total return}}{\text{Principal invested}} \times 100; \text{ which is also called yield.}$$

If we invest an amount of ₹ 900 on a 12% bond with a face value of 100 by purchasing 10 bonds at ₹ 90 each, then the coupon rate of bond is 12% and face value is ₹ 100, but the market price is ₹ 90. Hence, an investment of ₹ 900 got for the investor 10 bonds.

What is his yield per annum? In an investment of ₹ 90 per bond of face value of ₹ 100, he gets an annual interest of ₹ 12 being the coupon rate which is the interest rate promised for each bond of ₹ 100. Thus, if ₹ 90 can secure ₹ 12 the rate of yield for the investor is $\frac{12}{90} \times 100 = 13.3\%$.

The above is called current yield. The yield is the return on an investment as a percentage per annum.

Simple Yield or Interest Calculation

The formula is

Principal	×	interest rate	×	No. of periods
(S)	×	(i)	×	(n)

where principle is 100 and interest rate is 12%, and number of years is 3, then simple interest on ₹ 100 is ₹ 36 (12 × 3).

The formula for compound interest is $P = S \times (1 + i)^n$. With data in the above example, $100 (1 + 0.12)^3 = 140.49$.

Present value factors and future value factors are available in the published tables (given at the end of the chapter) readily and can be referred to them.

To exemplify the calculation	₹ 100
+ First year Interest of	12
	112
+ Second year Interest on 112	13.44
	125.44
+ Third year Interest on 125.44	15.05
	140.49

The same is derived through the formula given above.

This is called compounding and the reverse is disounting. If 140.49 is to be received in 3 years, what is its present value? The formula is

$$S = P \times \frac{1}{(1+i)^n}\text{; where } P = 140.49 \text{ and } S = NPV.$$

After discounting the future flows to the present (NPV) then comparison of two investments can be made and a decision about investment can be finalised.

YIELDS ON EQUITY

If the investment is in equity shares of a company, the return is in the form of dividend per annum plus capital appreciation or minus depreciation of the original investment due to fluctuations in market prices of shares. Thus, for example, an investor purchased Tata Steel at ₹ 260 per share and the company declared a dividend of 30%. But the market price of the share increased over the year to ₹ 290 involving a capital gain of ₹ 30 per annum. Thus, an investment of ₹ 260 yielded a return of ₹ 30 as dividend and another ₹ 30 as capital appreciation. The total return is ₹ 60 on an investment of ₹ 260.

The rate of return is $\frac{60}{260} \times 100 = 23\%$ p.a.

The yield on equity is generally lower if only dividends are considered. But an investor in equity shares desires not the yield only, but possible capital appreciation.

Yields are more relevant on all fixed interest yielding investments or instruments like, debentures, bonds, loans, deposits etc., with banks, companies and Government.

TIME VALUE OF MONEY AND SECURITIES

Time Preference for Money

We prefer today's money to that of tomorrow due to our pressing needs for consumption and cost of abstinence from the present consumption, fall in the value of money of tomorrow due to inflation and possible use of money when exchanged for tomorrow's money. Thus, when we lend money, we forego all the advantages of liquidity, ready usability, pressing needs, safety, etc. We abstain from present consumption when lent to somebody, or invested. All these will lead to what is called the time preference for money. To compensate for that, future money will have to be discounted to the present time, because both are not the same. Future money has to be more say 120, if the present money is ₹ 100, taking a discount factor of 20%, on one year.

Tomorrow's money or money a year hence has to be discounted to the present day by discount rate suitable as a reward for the above sacrifices. This is called discounting, used for cash flows or dividends to be received in future and to be calculated for the present.

Similarly, an investment of today, if it is to be returned after a year or so, today's money has to be compounded by a discount rate to equate to the future funds likely to be available in return. This is called compounding. Compounding and discounting are thus two major methods of analysing the time value of money.

Applications

In purchase or sale of a share, bond, or debenture, the price we pay has to be compared to the value of future flows in terms of dividends, or interest and future price realised. The principle of buy low and sell high has to be applied after an analysis of the present value of future flows of dividends, bonus, visible rights etc., as compared to the present price paid for it.

Future Value of a Single Cash Flow

Year	*Principal at the Beginning*	*Interest 10%*	*Principal at the End*
1	1000	100	1100
2	1100	110	1210
3	1210	121	1331

$FV = PV(1 + r)^n$; FV = Future value; PV = Present value; r = rate of interest; n = number of years

Future Value of an Annuity @ 10%

1	2	3	4	5	
1000	1100	1210	1331	1464	$(1+r)^4$
	1000	1100	1210	1331	$(1+r)^3$
		1000	1100	1210	$(1+r)^2$
			1000	1100	$(1+r)^1$
				1000	$(1+r)^0$
				6105	

$$= A\left[(1+r)^{n-1} + (1+r)^{n-2} + (1+r)^{n-3} + (1+r)^{n-4} + \ldots + (1+r)^{n-n}\right]$$

$$= A\frac{(1+r)^{n}-1}{r}$$

Sinking Fund Factor

$$F = A\frac{(1+r)^{n}-1}{r}$$

$$A = F \times \frac{r}{(1+r)^{n}-1}$$

$$\frac{1}{FVIFA(r,n)}$$

Present Value of an Annuity @ 10%

0	1	2	3	
909.1	1000			$\frac{1000}{(1+0.1)^1}$
826.4	909.1	1000		$\frac{1000}{(1+0.1)^2}$
751.3	826.4	909.1	1000	$\frac{1000}{(1+0.1)^3}$
2478.8				

$$\text{PVA} = \frac{(1+r)^{n-1}}{r(1+r)^n}$$

$$\text{FVA} = A\,\frac{(1+r)^{n-1}}{r}$$

$$\text{PV} = \text{FV}\,\frac{1}{(1+r)^n}$$

$$\text{PVA} = A\left[\frac{(1+r)^{n-1}}{r}\right]\left[\frac{1}{(1+r)^n}\right]$$

Doubling Period

$$\text{Rule of 72} = \frac{72}{\text{Interest Rate}} \text{ for rough estimate}$$

$$\text{Rule of 69} = 0.35 + \frac{69}{\text{Interest Rate}} \text{ for exact estimate}$$

With 12% rate of interest

Doubling period: Using Rule of 72; $\frac{72}{12} = 6$ years

Using Rule of 69; $0.35 + \frac{69}{12} = 6.10$ years

Shorter Compounding Period

If interest is credited quarterly @ 12% per annum

Quarter	*Balance at the Beginning* ₹	*Interest* ₹	*Balance at the End* ₹
1	1000	30	1030
2	1030	30.90	1060.90
3	1060.90	31.827	1092.727
4	1092.727	32.782	1125.509

Effective rate of interest = 12.551%

$$r = 1 + \left(1+\frac{k}{m}\right)^{m-1}$$

$$\text{FV} = \text{PV}\left(1+\frac{k}{m}\right)^{m \times n}$$

Where, k = Nominal rate of interest

m = Number of times compounding is done during a year

n = Number of years for which compounding is done.

Bond Valuation

Features of a Bond

1. Par Value
2. Coupon Rate of Interest
3. Maturity Period

Par Value ₹ 1000

Coupon Rate 12%

Maturity Period 5 years

Required Rate of Return 10%, 12%, 15%

At 12% value of the Bond is to be worked out:

₹ 120 × PVIFA (12%, 5) + 1,000 × PVIF (12%, 5)

= ₹ 1000 = (433 + 567) from the Tables

At 10%

₹ 120 × 3.791 + ₹ 1,000 × 0.621

₹ 1,075.92 = (454.92 + 621)

(Values of PVI FA, PVIF, FVIFA and FVIF are given in Tables at the end and Chapter 13)

At 15%

₹ 120 × 3.352 + ₹ 1,000 × 0.497

₹ 899.24 = (402.24 + 497)

If the Maturity Period is 3 years

At 12% ₹ 120 × 2.402 + ₹ 1,000 × 0.712 = ₹ 1,000

At 10% ₹ 120 × 2.487 + ₹ 1,000 × 0.751 = ₹ 1,049.44

At 15% ₹ 120 × 2.283 + ₹ 1,000 × 0.658 = ₹ 931.96

YIELD TO MATURITY

$$\text{Ytm} = \frac{\text{Interest} + (\text{Par Value} - \text{Present Price})/n}{(\text{Par Value} + \text{Present Price})/2}$$

Equity Valuation

Dividend Capitalisation Approach

Present value of the dividends expected

\+ Present value of the resale price expected

= Value of an Equity share

Basic Assumptions

1. Dividends are paid annually.
2. The first dividend is paid one year after the equity share is bought.

Single Period Valuation Model

$$P_o = \frac{D_1}{(1+k)} + \frac{P_1}{(1+k)}$$

If the price is expected to grow at rate 'g'

$$P_1 = P_o(1+g)$$

$$P_o = \frac{D_1}{(1+k)} + \frac{P_o(1+g)}{(1+k)}$$

$$P_o = \frac{D_1}{(1-k)}$$

Where, K = Rate of Interest

P_o = Present Price

P_1 = Price in Period 1

D_1 = Dividend for Period 1

Tables for PVIF, PVIFA, FVIF, FVIFA etc., are readily available and separately given.

Fundamentals of Valuation of Securities

If we need to estimate the present value of future flows, then the Discounting Method is used. If we want the future value of present investment, we have the Compounding Method. Both help the decision-making process in investment in securities.

Discounting

If the future value of the present investment is ₹ 116 at the end of 3 years and if it is discounted to the present day at 5%, then it will be equal to ₹ 100 at present.

The formula for PV (present value)

$$PV = \sum_{t=1}^{T} \frac{c_t}{(1+r)^t}$$

C_t represents the cash flows, t for period of years and r is the discount rate or is called internal rate of return in the exercises of capital budgetting.

Take an example: r = 8%, payable once a year and t is 5 years and the factor value — summation of cash flows is ₹ 100.

Then, $PV = \frac{100}{(1+0.08)^5}$ = ₹ 68 (use Log Tables).

This Formula also applies to one period return of ₹ 100 at the end of 5 years, the present value of which is ₹ 68 at a rate of return of 8%.

Compounding

If the interest rate is 5% and PV is ₹ 100, the future value one year hence will be ₹ 105, by using the formula of = $100\ (1+0.5)^1 = 105$.

In two years, it becomes $100\ (1+0.5)^2 = 110.25$

In three years it becomes $100\ (1+0.5)^3 = 115.76$ and so on.

In the case of discounting, it is the reverse of the above formula namely,

$$PV = 100 \frac{1}{(1+r)^1} + 100 \frac{1}{(1+r)^2} + 100 \frac{1}{(1+r)^3} \text{ etc.}$$

For the same three year period, at the end of 3 years, the future value should be ₹ 100 for investing ₹ 86.4 at present, when r = 0.5.

These formulae are based on some critical assumptions of constant flow of cash every period, the same reinvestment rate and the period is fixed.

Bond Prices — Factors Influencing

Bond prices fluctuate with market interest rate *vis-a-vis* the coupon rate, inflation rate, tax factors, security provided, maturity period, callable feature of the bond, credit rating of the company, etc. Some bonds, are attached with call or put options. Call means that the company can repay before maturity, if interest rates have fallen. Put means that the investor can exercise the option for selling the low yielding bond to the high yielding bond of the same characteristics as before.

Formulae

Future value of a single cash flow formula is $FV_n = PV_n \times (1 + k)^n$

This is the same thing as compounding, referred to above:

Dividing both sides by $(1 + k)^n$ we get $PV_n = FV_n \dfrac{1}{(1+k)^n}$ this formula $\dfrac{1}{(1+k)}$ is called discounting factor or the present value interest factor (PVIF, kn)

There is also similarly a Future Value Interest Factor (FVIF, kn) for compounding. (The Tables on these are presented in the Appendix).

Yield to Maturity (YtM)

Example (Short-cut Method)

$FV_n = 105$ $\quad$ k = 14% (I) Interest rate

$PV = 95$ $\quad$ N = number of years 6

$$YtM = \frac{\dfrac{(I + (F - P)}{n}}{\dfrac{F+P}{2}}$$; Putting the above values in the formula,

we have

$$YtM = \frac{14 + \dfrac{105-95}{6}}{\dfrac{105+95}{2}} = \frac{14+1.67}{100} = 15.67$$

15.67 becomes 15.67%

YtM is thus 15.67% in the above example.

VALUATION OF CONVERTIBLE BONDS/DEBENTURES

Convertibles enjoy the benefits of both debt (initially) and equity (later). The terms of conversion will decide the pricing of these convertibles, which is left to free market forces in India, now. It is the company's perception what they can sell to investors and at what price?

As per SEBI guidelines, Fully Convertible Debentures (FCDs) and Partly Convertible Bonds (PCBs) have special features and are not governed by guidelines for Non-Covertible Bonds/Debentures (NCDs). Their pricing methods, are different from bonds.

Why Convertible Financing?

(1) It will delay the issue of equity and hence dilution of earnings per share is delayed.

(2) It will give breathing time for the company for increasing its earnings, when it will be in a position to expand equity base and service them.

(3) Initial bond financing will earn leverage for the company as interest expense on debt is not taxable and the cost of debt financing is lower than that of equity for some companies.

(4) Companies in initial stages of expansion or project financing, or with low credit rating but with the potential for larger earnings in a couple of years prefer convertibles.

(5) Investors are attracted to convertibles, due to the sweeteners like premium on conversion and dividends and capital appreciation later.

Valuation of Convertibles

Whether it is FCD or PCD, the pricing of the convertible portion is complicated by the mixture of debt and equity elements. The coupon rate on debt portion will be lower than the market rate of NCD of the same duration, because of the benefits enjoyed on conversion later on.

If conversion is within 18 months, they are as good as equity for purpose of debt-equity ratio and if they are convertible within coming 12 months, they will be eligible to rights after conversion or bonus declared during the preceding 12 months.

The specification of pricing is difficult, except that the company follows the principles of what "the market can bear." What is the proportion of convertible portion to the total and the time period of waiting? The terms of offer also depend on the credit rating of the company.

Assume the conversion period is 12 months when the PCD will be converted into equity upto 50% and the rest will be NCD. Then if the expected gain on conversion is say, 2% to 5%, then the debenture will be offered at a coupon rate of 12% to 13% if the normal market rate is 14% to 15%. Coupon rate will be lower, the higher the premium permitted on conversion into equity.

Conversion Ratio

Conversion ratio is set out as so many equity shares for ₹ 100 of debenture. If the conversion price is set at ₹ 50, then the market price may be already ruling at ₹ 60 or ₹ 70 and one debenture will be converted into two equity shares. *Conversion value* is the conversion price multiplied by the number of shares given for each debenture. If conversion value is ₹ 50 and market price is say, ₹ 60, the conversion premium is ₹ 10 per share and ₹ 20 is gained by holding a debenture of ₹ 100 for one year. The debentureholder gets only say 12% as interest. The return on this investment is in fact 12% + 20% = 32%.

Conversion Premium

The company may offer a lesser premium, for one year and a larger premium for 18 months to 36 months. After 36 months, any conversion offer is subject to call and put options.

A call gives the right to buy from the company the share at the offer price if it is lower than the market price. A put option gives the right to sell the share eligibility to the company (and then buy the shares *in the market)* when the offer price is higher, than the market price. A call option is exercised if the market price is higher and put option is exercised, if the market price is lower, at the time of conversion.

VALUATION OF 'RIGHTS'

Right issue is a method of selling equity or debt securities to existing shareholders at concessional rates. Rights issues in India are governed by Section 81 (A) of the Companies Act. As these rights will give incentives or discounts on market prices or market rates, they are attractive to investors and they are given to those shareholders who are on the registers of the company at a point of time called the record date fixed by the Board of Directors. But the terms of rights issue, if made open to the public will be different from those when they are offered only to the existing shareholders.

Example of Rights Pricing

To illustrate the pricing of rights entitlements, an example is given below:

Existing Paid Up Capital (PUC) = ₹ 3 crores present issue of rights = ₹ 2 crores.

Ratio of rights issue is 3:2. That means if the investor holds 3 shares, he is entitled to 2 rights shares at a discount.

Let the Market Price (MP) = ₹ 40 and rights offer based on their book value is let us say, ₹ 30.

The market price quoted cum-rights is ₹ 40. If you buy three shares it will be ₹ 120 which when registered with the company will entitle you to 2 shares at a price of ₹ 30 (two shares will cost ₹ 60). The total cost for five shares is 120 + 60 = ₹ 180. The cost of one share is $\frac{180}{5}$ = ₹ 36.

The price of one right share thus becomes ₹ 36, while the market price is ₹ 40. The difference is only ₹ 4 per entitlement but this price of ₹ 4 will be available subject to the last date of renunciation of rights by the rightholders. When the quotation becomes ex rights, then the market price would accordingly adjust to ₹ 36, wiping out the benefit of ₹ 4. Here, the assumption is that company is a well rated company and its shares are in demand which means that there is a market for renunciations. Besides, we have not considered the brokerage costs and other incidentals involved in acquiring the rights and then selling them off.

CALLABLE BONDS

The company sometimes reserves the right to redeem earlier than the stipulated period, if the interest rates are falling. Such bonds are priced lower and discount will be more on the face value. Some bonds are redeemed in instalments, spread over 3 to 5 years. This will also be subject to risk of interest rate changes and are accordingly priced lower. Default prone bonds and junk bonds of companies with poor and falling credit rating will be substantially discounted ranging upto 50% on the face value of even short maturities.

DETACHABLE AND NON-DETACHABLE WARRANTS AND LOYALTY COUPONS

These are sweeteners attached to the debt instruments. Keeping the coupon rate at the then prevailing market rate (say, 12.5%) the company can attract investors by giving them a warrant, which will entitle the holder to buy the equity share at a discount over the market price but not lower than the intrinsic value as judged by book value or EPS.

Loyalty coupons or non-detachable warrants require the minimum holding period of say, 3 to 5 years to be eligible to this right of purchasing equity shares at face value or book value, which are much lower than the market price.

Such non-marketable warrants, attached to debt instruments are called latent warrants, which are entitled to conversion at the fixed maturity period of 3 to 5 years, while the debt portion remaining with the investor is sold in the market at a discount. However, the premium gained at conversion into equity is much more than the discount lost in the NCD portion. Some companies provide the safety net of purchasing back through their financial institutions, the NCD portion at the face value after a period of 1 to 3 years, or immediately after allotment depending on the terms.

Mortgage Bonds

Non-callable and Non-convertible bonds are to be secured by collaterals if they are to be attractive to investors and carry the market interest rates with or without clause of adjustment to floating interest rates. The bond prices in such cases depend on the equity prices and the company's performance. They are not default prone, if the company is performing well, fundamentals are strong and the share market price will be rising. Such bonds are normally near to the market prices. In fact, the rates expected on various bonds depend on their ratings by rating agencies, such as Standard and Poor, in USA. In India, credit rating is compulsory for NCDs given by companies and interest/coupon rates are decided accordingly on the basis of credit rating.

PROBLEMS

Problem 1

Problem of Discounting

Calculate the IRR for the cash flow stream given in the following Table.

Year	*Cash Flow*	*18% Discount Factor*	*19% Discount Factor*	*Present Value at 18%*	*Present Value at 19%*
0	-600	1.000	1.000	–600	–600
1	200	0.847	0.840	169.49	168.01
3	500	0.608	0.593	304.32	296.71
5	300	0.437	0.419	131.13	125.72
Total				₹ 4.94	–9.50

Answer:

The formula for calculation of IRR

$$\text{IRR} = 18 + \frac{4.94}{4.94+9.50}$$

$$= 18 + \frac{4.94}{14.44} = 18 + .34 = 18.34\%.$$

Problem 2

If the earnings per share at the end of 6 years is ₹ 7.50; P/E ratio is 8 times and the present market price is ₹ 35, what is the expected return on investment?

Answer:

Terminal value at the end of 6 years is equal to

EPS × P/E = 7.50 × 8 = ₹ 60.

The expected cash flow and their present values are shown below.

Year	*Cash Flow*	*16% Discount Factor*	*Present Value*	*17% Discount Factor*	*Present Value*
0	–35	1.00	–35.00	1.00	–35.00
1	2.3	0.862	1.982	0.855	1.966
2	2.64	0.743	1.962	0.731	1.930
3	3.04	0.641	1.948	0.624	1.896
4	3.35	0.552	1.850	0.533	1.785
5	3.68	0.476	1.752	0.456	1.678
6	64.05	0.410	26.269	0.390	24.980
			0.754		–0.765

By trial and error method, the IRR has to be estimated. It is likely to fall between 16% to 17% and hence the earlier calculations in the Table show the present values of cash inflows and outflows for the discount factors of 16% and 17% we want that rate which equates these two present values or NPV = 0 at year 0. (vide for PVDF(16,1) in the attached tables.)

Thus, we have the equation set out as follows:

$$\text{IRR} = 16 + \frac{0.754}{0.754 + 0.765}$$

$$= 16 + \frac{0.754}{1.519}$$

$$= 16 + 0.496$$

$$= 16.50$$

Problems in Time Value of Money

1. Rex is expected to retire at the end of 3 years and would get ₹ 2,00,000 as gratuity. He wants to construct a house on the basis of the present value of that amount, assuming that savings account earns 5% per annum. What is the cost of the house that he proposes to build?

Answer

$$\text{Present value } P_o = \frac{P_3}{(1+K)^T}$$

$$= \frac{2{,}00{,}000}{(1+0.05)^3} = \frac{2{,}00{,}000}{1.1576}$$

$$= ₹\ 1{,}72{,}771$$

[**Answer:** Present value and the cost of the house is ₹ 1,72, 771].

2. L.T. Co. plans for an accelerated depreciation which postpones the payment of Income Tax of ₹ 36,000 for 4 years. What is the present value of the postponed income tax, assuming the opportunity interest expense at 10% per annum.

P_4 = 36,000 K = 10%, t = 4

$$P_o = \frac{P_4}{(1+K)^T} = \frac{36,000}{(1+0.10)^4}$$

$$= \frac{36,000}{1.4641} = ₹\ 24,588.$$

What is the Discount Factor

$$\text{Discount Factor} = \frac{1}{(1+0.10)^4} = \frac{1}{1.4641} = 0.683$$

The Discount factor used is 0.683 and this given the present value to L.T. Co. of ₹ 24,588 due to postponing the payment of Income Tax. If he pays now it will be ₹ 36,000 and if he pays after 4 years, the present value is ₹ 24,588, thus ₹ 11,412 is the saving.

Appendix I FUTURE VALUE COMPOUND FACTORS FOR A SINGLE CASH FLOW

(Future value of $1 by the end of n years)

$$FVCF_{r,n} = (1 + r)^n$$

Number of years	Interest rate per year 1%	2%	3%	4%	5%	6%	7%	8%	9%	10%	11%	12%	13%	14%	15%
1	1.010	1.020	1.030	1.040	1.050	1.060	1.070	1.080	1.090	1.100	1.110	1.120	1.130	1.140	1.150
2	1.020	1.040	1.061	1.082	1.102	1.124	1.145	1.166	1.188	1.210	1.212	1.254	1.277	1.300	1.323
3	1.030	1.061	1.093	1.125	1.158	1.191	1.225	1.260	1.295	1.331	1.368	1.405	1.443	1.482	1.521
4	1.041	1.082	1.126	1.170	1.216	1.262	1.311	1.360	1.412	1.464	1.518	1.574	1.630	1.689	1.749
5	1.051	1.104	1.159	1.217	1.276	1.338	1.403	1.469	1.539	1.611	1.685	1.762	1.842	1.925	2.011
6	1.062	1.126	1.194	1.265	1.340	1.419	1.501	1.587	1.677	1.772	1.870	1.974	2.082	2.195	2.313
7	1.072	1.149	1.230	1.316	1.407	1.504	1.606	1.714	1.828	1.949	2.076	2.211	2.353	2.502	2.660
8	1.083	1.172	1.267	1.369	1.477	1.594	1.718	1.851	1.993	2.144	2.305	2.476	2.658	2.853	3.059
9	1.098	1.195	1.305	1.423	1.551	1.689	1.838	1.999	2.172	2.358	2.558	2.773	3.004	3.252	3.518
10	1.105	1.219	1.344	1.480	1.629	1.791	1.967	2.159	2.367	2.594	2.839	3.106	3.395	3.707	4.046
11	1.116	1.243	1.384	1.539	1.710	1.898	2.105	2.332	2.580	2.853	3.152	3.479	3.836	4.226	4.652
12	1.127	1.268	1.426	1.601	1.796	2.012	2.252	2.518	2.813	3.138	3.498	3.896	4.335	4.818	5.350
13	1.138	1.294	1.469	1.665	1.886	2.133	2.410	2.720	3.066	3.452	3.883	4.363	4.898	5.492	6.153
14	1.149	1.319	1.513	1.732	1.980	2.261	2.579	2.937	3.342	3.797	4.310	4.887	5.535	6.261	7.076
15	1.161	1.346	1.558	1.801	2.079	2.397	2.759	3.172	3.642	4.177	4.785	5.474	6.254	7.138	8.137
16	1.173	1.373	1.605	1.873	2.183	2.540	2.952	3.426	3.970	4.595	5.311	6.130	7.067	8.137	9.358
17	1.184	1.400	1.653	1.948	2.292	2.693	3.159	3.700	4.328	5.054	5.895	6.866	7.986	9.276	10.76
18	1.196	1.428	1.702	2.026	2.407	2.854	3.380	3.996	4.717	5.560	6.544	7.690	9.024	10.58	12.38
19	1.208	1.457	1.754	2.107	2.527	3.026	3.617	4.316	5.142	6.116	7.263	8.613	10.20	12.06	14.23
20	1.220	1.486	1.806	2.191	2.653	3.207	3.870	4.661	5.604	6.727	8.062	9.646	11.52	13.74	16.37
25	1.282	1.641	2.094	2.666	3.386	4.292	5.427	6.848	8.623	10.83	13.59	17.00	21.23	26.46	32.92
30	1.348	1.811	2.427	3.243	4.322	5.743	7.612	10.06	13.27	17.45	22.89	29.96	39.12	50.95	66.21

Appendix I (Continued)

Number of years	Interest rate per year 16%	17%	18%	19%	20%	21%	22%	23%	24%	25%	26%	27%	28%	29%	30%
1	1.160	1.170	1.180	1.190	1.200	1.210	1.220	1.230	1.240	1.250	1.260	1.270	1.280	1.290	1.300
2	1.346	1.396	1.392	1.416	1.440	1.464	1.488	1.513	1.538	1.563	1.588	1.613	1.638	1.664	1.690
3	1.561	1.602	1.643	1.685	1.728	1.772	1.816	1.861	1.907	1.953	2.000	2.048	2.097	2.147	2.197
4	1.811	1.874	1.939	2.005	2.074	2.144	2.215	2.289	2.364	2.441	2.520	2.601	2.684	2.769	2.856
5	2.100	2.192	2.288	2.386	2.488	2.594	2.703	2.815	2.932	3.052	3.176	3.304	3.436	3.572	3.713
6	2.436	2.565	2.700	2.840	2.986	3.138	3.297	3.463	3.635	3.815	4.002	4.196	4.398	4.608	4.827
7	2.826	3.001	3.185	3.379	3.583	3.797	4.023	4.259	4.508	4.768	5.042	5.329	5.629	5.945	6.275
8	3.278	3.511	3.759	4.021	4.300	4.595	4.908	5.239	5.590	5.960	6.353	6.768	7.206	7.669	8.157
9	3.803	4.108	4.435	4.785	5.160	5.560	5.987	6.444	6.931	7.451	8.005	8.595	9.223	9.893	10.60
10	4.411	4.807	5.234	5.695	6.192	6.728	7.305	7.926	8.594	9.313	10.09	10.92	11.81	12.76	13.79
11	5.117	5.624	6.176	6.777	7.430	8.140	8.912	9.749	10.66	11.64	12.71	13.86	15.11	16.46	17.92
12	5.936	6.580	7.288	8.064	8.916	9.850	10.87	11.99	13.21	14.55	16.01	17.61	19.34	21.24	23.30
13	6.886	7.699	8.599	9.596	10.70	11.92	13.26	14.75	16.39	18.19	20.18	22.36	24.76	27.39	30.29
14	7.988	9.007	10.15	11.42	12.84	14.42	16.18	18.14	20.32	22.74	25.42	28.40	31.69	35.34	39.37
15	9.266	10.54	11.97	13.59	15.41	17.45	19.74	22.31	25.20	28.42	32.03	36.06	40.56	45.59	57.19
16	10.75	12.33	14.13	16.17	18.49	21.11	24.09	27.45	31.24	35.53	40.36	45.80	51.92	58.81	66.54
17	12.47	14.43	16.67	19.24	22.19	25.55	29.38	33.76	38.74	44.41	50.85	58.17	66.46	75.86	86.50
18	14.46	16.88	19.67	22.90	26.62	30.91	35.85	41.52	48.04	55.51	64.07	73.87	85.07	97.86	112.5
19	16.78	19.75	23.21	27.25	31.95	37.40	43.74	51.07	59.57	69.39	80.73	93.81	108.9	126.2	146.2
20	19.46	23.11	27.39	32.43	38.34	45.26	53.36	62.82	73.86	86.74	101.7	119.1	139.4	162.9	190.0
25	40.87	50.66	62.67	77.39	95.40	117.4	144.2	176.9	216.5	264.7	323.0	393.6	478.9	581.8	705.6
30	85.85	111.1	143.4	184.7	237.4	304.5	389.8	497.9	634.8	807.8	1026	1301	1646	2078	2620

E.g. If the interest rate is 10 per cent per year, the investment of $1 today will be worth $1 611 at the end of year 5.

Appendix II PRESENT VALUE DISCOUNT FACTORS FOR A SINGLE CASH FLOW

(Present value of $1to be received at the end of n years)

$$PVDF_{r,n} = \frac{1}{(1+r)^n}$$

Interest rate per year

Number of years	1%	2%	3%	4%	5%	6%	7%	8%	9%	10%	11%	12%	13%	14%	15%
1	.990	.980	.971	.962	.952	.943	.935	.926	.917	.909	.901	.893	.885	.877	.870
2	.980	.961	.943	.925	.907	.890	.873	.857	.842	.826	.812	.797	.783	.769	.756
3	.971	.942	.915	.889	.864	.840	.816	.794	.772	.751	.731	.712	.693	.675	.658
4	.961	.924	.888	.855	.823	.792	.763	.735	.708	.683	.659	.636	.613	.592	.572
5	.951	.906	.863	.822	.784	.747	.713	.681	.650	.621	.593	.567	.543	.519	.497
6	.942	.888	.837	.790	.746	.705	.666	.630	.596	.564	.535	.507	.480	.456	.432
7	.933	.871	.813	.760	.711	.665	.623	.583	.547	.513	.482	.452	.425	.400	.376
8	.923	.853	.789	.731	.677	.627	.582	.540	.502	.467	.434	.404	.376	.351	.327
9	.914	.837	.766	.703	.645	.592	.544	.500	.460	.424	.391	.361	.333	.308	.284
10	.905	.820	.744	.676	.614	.558	.508	.463	.422	.386	.352	.322	.295	.270	.247
11	.896	.804	.722	.650	.585	.527	.475	.429	.388	.350	.317	.287	.261	.237	.215
12	.887	.788	.701	.625	.557	.497	.444	.397	.356	.319	.286	.257	.231	.208	.187
13	.879	.773	.681	.601	.530	.469	.415	.368	.326	.290	.258	.229	.204	.182	.163
14	.870	.758	.661	.577	.505	.442	.388	.340	.299	.263	.232	.205	.181	.160	.141
15	.861	.743	.642	.555	.481	.417	.362	.315	.275	.239	.209	.183	.160	.140	.123
16	.853	.728	.623	.534	.458	.394	.339	.292	.252	.218	.188	.163	.141	.123	.107
17	.844	.714	.605	.513	.436	.371	.317	.270	.231	.198	.170	.146	.125	.108	.093
18	.836	.700	.587	.494	.416	.350	.296	.250	.212	.180	.153	.130	.111	.095	.081
19	.828	.686	.570	.475	.396	.331	.277	.232	.194	.164	.138	.116	.098	.083	.070
20	.820	.673	.554	.456	.377	.312	.258	.215	.178	.149	.124	.104	.087	0.73	.061
25	.780	.610	.478	.375	.295	.233	.184	.146	.116	.092	.074	.059	.047	.038	.030
30	.742	.552	.412	.308	.231	.174	.131	.099	.075	.057	.044	.033	.026	.020	.015

Appendix II (Continued)

Number of years	Interest rate per year 16%	17%	18%	19%	20%	21%	22%	23%	24%	25%	26%	27%	28%	29%	30%
1	.862	.855	.847	.840	.833	.826	.820	.813	.806	.800	.794	.787	.781	.775	.769
2	.743	.731	.718	.706	.694	.683	.672	.661	.650	.640	.630	.620	.610	.601	.592
3	.641	.624	.609	.593	.579	.564	.551	.537	.524	.512	.500	.488	.477	.466	.455
4	.552	.534	.516	.499	.482	.467	.451	.437	.423	.410	.397	.384	.373	.361	.350
5	.476	.456	.437	.419	.402	.386	.370	.355	.341	.328	.315	.303	.291	.280	.269
6	.410	.390	.370	.352	.335	.319	.303	.289	.275	.262	.250	.238	.227	.217	.207
7	.354	.333	.314	.296	.279	.263	.249	.235	.222	.210	.198	.188	.178	.168	.159
8	.305	.285	.266	.249	.233	.218	.204	.191	.179	.168	.157	.148	.139	.130	.123
9	.263	.243	.225	.209	.194	.180	.167	.155	.144	.134	.125	.116	.108	.101	.094
10	.227	.208	.191	.176	.162	.149	.137	.126	.116	.107	.099	.092	.085	.078	.073
11	.195	.178	.162	.148	.135	.123	.112	.103	.094	.086	.079	.072	.066	.061	.056
12	.168	.152	.137	.124	.112	.102	.092	.083	.076	.069	.062	.057	.052	.047	.043
13	.145	.130	.116	.104	.093	.084	.075	.068	.061	.055	.050	.045	.040	.037	.033
14	.125	.111	.099	.088	.078	.069	.062	.055	.049	.044	.039	.035	.032	.028	.025
15	.108	.095	.084	.074	.065	.057	.051	.045	.040	.035	.031	.028	.025	.022	.020
16	.093	.081	.071	.062	.054	.047	.042	.036	.032	.028	.025	.022	.019	.017	.015
17	.080	.069	.060	.052	.045	.039	.034	.030	.026	.023	.020	.017	.015	.013	.012
18	.069	.059	.051	.044	.038	.032	.028	.024	.021	.018	.016	.014	.012	.010	.009
19	.060	.051	.043	.037	.031	.027	.023	.020	0.17	.014	.012	.011	.009	.008	.007
20	.051	.043	.037	.031	.026	.022	.019	.016	.014	.012	.010	.008	.007	.006	.005
25	.024	.020	.016	.013	.010	.009	.007	.006	.005	.004	.003	.003	.002	.002	.001
26	.012	.009	.007	.005	.004	.003	.003	.002	.002	.001	.001	.001	.001	.000	.000

E.g. If the interest rate is 10 per cent per year, the investment of $1 received at the end of year 5 is $ 0621.

Appendix III PRESENT VALUE ANNUITY FACTORS
(Present value of $1 received at the end of each year)

$$PVAF_{r,n} = \frac{1 - \frac{1}{(1+r)^n}}{r}$$

Number of years	Interest rate per year														
	1%	2%	3%	4%	5%	6%	7%	8%	9%	10%	11%	12%	13%	14%	15%
1	.990	.980	.971	.962	.952	.943	.935	.926	.917	.909	.901	.893	.885	.877	.870
2	1.970	1.942	1.913	1.886	1.859	1.833	1.808	1.783	1.759	1.736	1.713	1.690	1.668	1.647	1.626
3	2.941	2.884	2.829	2.775	2.723	2.673	2.624	2.577	2.531	2.487	2.444	2.402	2.361	2.322	2.283
4	3.902	3.808	3.717	3.630	3.546	3.465	3.387	3.312	3.240	3.170	3.102	3.037	2.974	2.914	2.855
5	4.853	4.713	4.580	4.452	4.329	4.212	4.100	3.993	3.890	3.791	3.696	3.605	3.517	3.433	3.352
6	5.795	5.601	5.417	5.242	5.076	4.917	4.767	4.623	4.486	4.355	4.231	4.111	3.998	3.889	3.784
7	6.728	6.472	6.230	6.002	5.786	5.582	5.389	5.206	5.033	4.868	4.712	4.564	4.423	4.288	4.160
8	7.652	7.325	7.020	6.733	6.463	6.210	5.971	5.747	5.535	5.335	5.146	4.968	4.799	4.639	4.487
9	8.566	8.162	7.786	7.435	7.108	6.802	6.515	6.247	5.995	5.759	5.537	5.328	5.132	4.946	4.772
10	9.471	8.983	8.530	8.111	7.722	7.360	7.024	6.710	6.418	6.145	5.889	5.650	5.426	5.216	5.019
11	10.37	9.787	9.253	8.760	8.306	7.887	7.499	7.139	6.805	6.95	6.207	5.938	5.687	5.453	5.234
12	11.26	10.58	9.954	9.385	8.863	8.384	7.943	7.936	7.161	6.814	6.492	6.194	5.918	5.660	5.421
13	12.13	11.35	10.63	9.986	9.394	8.853	8.358	7.904	7.487	7.103	6.750	6.424	6.122	5.842	5.583
14	13.00	12.11	11.30	10.56	9.899	9.295	8.745	8.244	7.786	7.367	6.982	6.628	6.302	6.002	5.724
15	13.87	12.85	11.94	11.12	10.38	9.712	9.108	8.559	8.061	7.606	7.191	6.811	6.462	6.142	5.847
16	14.72	13.58	12.56	11.65	10.84	10.11	9.447	8.851	8.313	7.824	7.379	6.974	6.604	6.265	5.954
17	15.56	14.29	13.17	12.17	11.27	10.48	9.763	9.122	8.544	8.022	7.549	7.120	6.729	6.373	6.047
18	16.40	14.99	13.75	12.66	11.69	10.83	10.06	9.372	8.756	8.201	7.702	7.250	6.840	6.467	6.128
19	17.23	15.68	14.32	13.13	12.09	11.16	10.34	9.604	8.950	8.365	7.839	7.366	6.938	6.550	6.198
20	18.05	16.35	14.88	13.59	12.46	11.47	10.59	9.818	9.129	8.514	7.963	7.469	7.025	6.623	6.259
25	22.02	19.52	17.41	15.62	14.09	12.78	11.65	10.67	9.823	9.077	8.422	7.843	7.330	6.873	6.464
30	25.81	22.40	19.60	17.29	15.37	13.76	12.41	11.26	10.27	9.427	8.694	8.055	7.496	7.003	6.566

Appendix III (Continued)

Number of years	Interest rate per year														
	16%	17%	18%	19%	20%	21%	22%	23%	24%	25%	26%	27%	28%	29%	30%
1	.862	.855	.847	.840	.833	.826	.820	.813	.806	.800	.794	.787	.781	.775	.769
2	1.605	1.585	1.566	1.547	1.528	1.509	1.492	1.474	1.457	1.440	1.424	1.407	1.392	1.376	1.361
3	2.246	2.210	2.174	2.140	2.106	2.074	2.042	2.011	1.981	1.952	1.923	1.896	1.868	1.842	1.816
4	2.798	2.743	2.690	2.639	2.589	2.540	2.494	2.448	2.404	2.362	2.320	2.280	2.241	2.203	2.166
5	3.274	3.199	3.127	3.058	2.991	2.926	2.864	2.803	2.745	2.689	2.635	2.583	2.532	2.483	2.436
6	3.685	3.589	3.498	3.410	3.326	3.245	3.167	3.092	3.020	2.951	2.885	2.821	2.759	2.700	2.643
7	4.039	3.922	3.812	3.706	3.605	3.508	3.416	3.327	3.242	3.161	3.083	3.009	2.937	2.868	2.802
8	4.344	4.207	4.078	3.954	3.837	3.726	3.619	3.518	3.421	3.329	3.241	3.156	3.076	2.999	2.925
9	4.607	4.451	4.303	4.163	4.031	3.905	3.786	3.673	3.566	3.463	3.366	3.273	3.184	3.100	3.019
10	4.833	4.659	4.494	4.339	4.192	4.054	3.923	3.799	3.682	3.571	3.465	3.364	3.269	3.178	3.092
11	5.029	4.836	4.656	4.486	4.327	4.177	4.035	3.902	3.776	3.656	3.543	3.437	3.335	3.239	3.147
12	5.197	4.988	4.793	4.611	4.439	4.278	4.127	3.985	3.851	3.725	3.606	3.493	3.387	3.286	3.190
13	5.342	5.118	4.910	4.715	4.533	4.362	4.203	4.053	3.912	3.780	3.656	3.538	3.427	3.322	3.223
14	5.468	5.229	5.008	4.802	4.611	4.432	4.265	4.108	3.962	3.824	3.695	3.573	3.459	3.351	3.249
15	5.575	5.324	5.092	4.876	4.675	4.489	4.315	4.153	4.001	3.859	3.726	3.601	3.483	3.373	3.268
16	5.668	5.405	5.162	4.938	4.730	4.536	4.357	4.189	4.033	3.887	3.751	3.623	3.503	3.390	3.283
17	5.749	5.475	5.222	4.990	4.775	4.576	4.391	4.219	4.059	3.910	3.771	3.640	3.518	3.403	3.295
18	5.818	5.534	5.273	5.033	4.812	4.608	4.419	4.243	4.080	3.928	3.786	3.654	3.529	3.413	3.304
19	5.877	5.584	5.316	5.070	4.843	4.635	4.442	4.263	4.097	3.942	3.799	3.664	3.539	3.421	3.311
20	5.929	5.628	6.353	5.101	4.870	4.657	4.460	4.279	4.110	3.954	3.808	3.673	3.546	3.427	3.316
25	6.097	5.766	5.467	5.195	4.948	4.721	4.514	4.323	4.147	3.985	3.834	3.694	3.564	3.442	3.329
30	6.177	5.829	5.517	5.235	4.979	4.746	4.534	4.339	4.160	3.995	3.842	3.701	3.569	3.447	3.332

E.g. If the interest rate is 10 per cent per year, the present value of $ 1 received at the end of each of the next 5 years is $ 3.791

Appendix IV FUTURE VALUE ANNUITY FACTOR
(Future value of $ 1 invested at the beginning of each year for n years)

$$FVAF_{r,n} = \frac{(1+r)\left[(1+r)^n - 1\right]}{r}$$

Number of years	Interest rate per year														
	1%	2%	3%	4%	5%	6%	7%	8%	9%	10%	11%	12%	13%	14%	15%
1	1.010	1.020	1.030	1.040	1.050	1.060	1.070	1.080	1.090	1.100	1.110	1.120	1.130	1.140	1.150
2	2.030	2.060	2.091	2.122	2.153	2.184	2.215	2.246	2.278	2.310	2.342	2.374	2.407	2.440	2.473
3	3.060	3.122	3.184	3.246	3.310	3.375	3.440	3.506	3.573	3.641	3.710	3.779	3.850	3.921	3.993
4	4.101	4.204	4.309	4.416	4.526	4.637	4.751	4.867	4.985	5.105	5.228	5.353	5.480	5.610	5.742
5	5.152	5.308	5.468	5.633	5.802	5.975	6.153	6.338	6.523	6.716	6.913	7.115	7.323	7.536	7.754
6	6.214	6.434	6.662	6.898	7.142	7.394	7.654	7.923	8.200	8.487	8.783	9.089	9.405	9.730	10.067
7	7.266	7.583	7.892	8.214	8.549	8.897	9.260	9.637	10.028	10.436	10.859	11.300	11.757	12.233	12.727
8	8.369	8.755	9.159	9.583	10.027	10.491	10.978	11.488	12.021	12.579	13.164	13.776	14.416	15.085	15.785
9	9.462	9.950	10.464	11.006	11.578	12.181	12.816	13.487	14.193	14.937	15.722	16.549	17.420	18.337	19.304
10	10.567	11.169	11.808	12.486	13.207	13.972	14.784	15.645	16.560	17.531	18.561	19.655	20.814	22.045	23.349
11	11.663	12.412	13.192	14.028	14.917	15.870	16.888	17.977	19.141	20.384	21.713	23.133	24.650	26.271	28.002
12	12.809	13.680	14.618	15.627	16.713	17.882	19.141	20.495	21.953	23.523	25.212	27.029	28.985	31.089	33.352
13	13.947	14.947	16.086	17.292	18.599	20.015	21.550	23.215	25.019	26.975	29.095	31.393	33.883	36.581	39.505
14	15.097	16.293	17.599	19.024	20.579	22.276	24.129	26.152	28.361	30.772	33.405	36.280	39.417	42.842	46.580
15	16.258	17.639	19.157	20.825	22.657	24.673	26.888	29.324	32.003	34.950	38.190	41.753	45.672	49.980	54.717
16	17.430	19.012	20.762	22.698	24.840	27.213	29.840	32.750	35.974	39.545	43.501	47.884	52.739	58.118	64.075
17	18.615	20.412	22.414	24.645	27.132	29.906	32.999	36.450	40.301	44.599	49.396	54.750	60.725	67.394	74.836
18	19.811	21.841	24.117	26.671	29.539	32.760	36.379	40.446	45.018	50.159	55.939	62.440	69.749	77.969	87.212
19	21.019	23.297	25.870	28.778	32.066	35.786	39.995	44.762	50.160	56.275	63.203	71.052	79.947	90.025	101.44
20	22.239	24.783	27.676	30.969	34.719	38.993	43.865	49.423	55.765	63.002	71.265	80.699	91.470	103.77	117.81
25	28.526	32.671	37.553	43.312	50.113	58.156	67.676	78.954	92.324	108.18	127.00	149.33	175.85	207.33	244.71
30	35.133	41.379	49.003	58.328	69.761	83.802	101.07	122.35	148.58	180.94	220.91	270.29	331.32	406.74	499.96

Appendix IV (Continued)

Number of years	Interest rate per year 16%	17%	18%	19%	20%	21%	22%	23%	24%	25%	26%	27%	28%	29%	30%
1	1.160	1.170	1.180	1.190	1.200	1.210	1.220	1.230	1.240	1.250	1.260	1.270	1.280	1.290	1.300
2	2.506	2.539	2.572	2.606	2.640	2.674	2.708	2.743	2.778	2.813	2.848	2.883	2.918	2.954	2.990
3	4.066	4.414	4.215	4.291	4.368	4.446	4.524	4.604	4.684	4.766	4.848	4.931	5.016	5.101	5.187
4	5.877	6.014	6.154	6.297	6.442	6.589	6.740	6.893	7.048	7.207	7.368	7.533	7.700	7.870	8.043
5	7.977	8.207	8.442	8.683	8.930	9.183	9.442	9.708	9.980	10.259	10.544	10.837	11.136	11.442	11.756
6	10.414	10.772	11.142	11.523	11.916	12.321	12.740	13.171	13.615	14.073	14.546	15.032	15.534	16.051	16.583
7	13.240	13.773	14.327	14.902	15.499	16.119	16.762	17.430	18.123	18.842	19.588	20.361	21.163	21.995	22.858
8	16.519	17.285	18.086	18.923	19.799	20.714	21.670	22.669	23.712	24.802	25.940	27.129	28.369	29.664	31.015
9	20.321	21.393	22.521	23.709	24.959	26.274	27.657	29.113	30.643	32.253	33.945	35.723	37.593	39.556	41.619
10	24.733	26.200	27.755	29.404	31.150	33.001	34.962	37.039	39.238	41.566	44.031	46.639	49.398	52.318	55.405
11	29.850	31.824	33.931	36.180	38.581	41.142	43.874	46.788	49.895	53.208	56.739	60.501	64.510	68.780	73.327
12	35.786	38.404	41.219	44.244	47.497	50.991	54.746	58.779	63.110	67.760	72.751	78.107	83.853	90.016	96.625
13	42.672	46.103	49.818	53.841	58.196	62.909	68.010	73.528	79.496	85.949	92.926	100.47	108.61	117.41	126.91
14	50.660	55.110	59.965	65.261	71.035	77.330	84.192	91.669	99.815	108.69	118.35	128.86	140.30	152.75	166.29
15	59.925	65.649	71.939	78.850	86.442	94.780	103.93	113.98	125.01	137.11	150.38	164.92	180.87	198.34	217.47
16	70.673	77.979	86.068	95.022	104.93	115.89	128.02	141.43	156.25	172.64	190.73	210.72	232.79	257.15	284.01
17	83.141	92.406	102.74	114.27	127.12	141.44	157.40	175.19	194.99	217.04	241.59	268.89	299.25	333.01	370.52
18	97.603	109.28	122.41	137.17	153.74	172.35	193.25	216.71	243.03	272.56	305.66	342.76	384.32	430.87	482.97
19	114.38	129.03	145.63	164.42	185.69	209.76	236.99	267.79	302.60	341.94	386.39	436.57	493.21	557.11	629.17
20	133.84	152.14	173.02	196.85	224.03	255.02	290.35	330.61	376.46	428.68	488.11	555.72	632.59	719.96	819.22
25	289.09	341.76	404.27	478.43	566.38	670.13	794.17	940.46	1136.6	1318.6	1560.7	1846.8	2184.7	2583.4	3053.4
30	615.16	757.50	933.32	1150.4	1418.3	1748.8	2155.8	2657.4	3274.7	4034.0	4967.0	6112.5	7517.7	9240.0	11349.0

E.g. If the interest rate is 10 per cent per year, the present value of $ 1 invested at the beginning of each year for 5 years will be $ 6.716 at the end of the fifth year

TABLE - 1 Compound Sum of $1

Years	*1%*	*2%*	*3%*	*4%*	*5%*	*6%*	*7%*	*8%*	*9%*	*10%*
1	1.010	1.020	1.030	1.040	1.050	1.060	1.070	1.080	1.090	1.100
2	1.020	1.040	1.061	1.082	1.102	1.124	1.145	1.166	1.188	1.210
3	1.030	1.061	1.093	1.125	1.158	1.191	1.225	1.260	1.295	1.331
4	1.041	1.082	1.126	1.170	1.216	1.262	1.311	1.360	1.412	1.464
5	1.051	1.104	1.159	1.217	1.276	1.338	1.403	1.469	1.539	1.611
6	1.062	1.126	1.194	1.265	1.340	1.419	1.501	1.587	1.677	1.772
7	1.072	1.149	1.230	1.316	1.407	1.504	1.606	1.714	1.828	1.949
8	1.083	1.172	1.267	1.369	1.477	1.594	1.718	1.851	1.993	2.144
9	1.094	1.195	1.305	1.423	1.551	1.689	1.838	1.999	2.172	2.358
10	1.105	1.219	1.344	1.480	1.629	1.791	1.967	2.159	2.367	2.594
11	1.116	1.243	1.384	1.539	1.710	1.898	2.105	2.332	2.580	2.853
12	1.127	1.268	1.426	1.601	1.796	2.012	2.252	2.518	2.813	3.138
13	1.138	1.294	1.469	1.665	1.886	2.133	2.410	2.720	3.066	3.452
14	1.149	1.319	1.513	1.732	1.980	2.261	2.579	2.937	3.342	3.797
15	1.161	1.346	1.558	1.801	2.079	2.397	2.759	3.172	3.642	4.177

In Tables 1 and 2 we summarize future and present values of a single payment of $1 for a sample of various of g and n.

TABLE - 2 Present Value of $1

Years	*1%*	*2%*	*3%*	*4%*	*5%*	*6%*	*7%*	*8%*	*9%*	*10%*
1	.990	.980	.971	.962	.952	.943	.935	.926	.917	.909
2	.980	.961	.943	.925	.907	.890	.873	.857	.842	.826
3	.971	.942	.915	.889	.864	.840	.816	.794	.772	.751
4	.961	.924	.889	.855	.823	.792	.763	.735	.708	.683
5	.951	.906	.863	.822	.784	.747	.713	.681	.650	.621
6	.942	.888	.838	.790	.746	.705	.666	.630	.596	.564
7	.933	.871	.813	.760	.711	.665	.623	.583	.547	.513
8	.923	.853	.789	.731	.677	.627	.582	.540	.502	.467
9	.914	.837	.766	.703	.645	.592	.544	.500	.460	.424
10	.905	.820	.744	.676	.614	.558	.508	.463	.422	.386
11	.896	.804	.722	.650	.585	.527	.475	.429	.388	.350
12	.887	.788	.701	.625	.557	.497	.444	.397	.356	.319
13	.879	.773	.681	.601	.530	.469	.415	.368	.326	.290
14	.870	.758	.661	.577	.505	.442	.388	.340	.299	.263
15	.861	.743	.642	.555	.481	.417	.362	.315	.275	.239

TABLE - 3 Sum of an Annuity of $1 for N Years

Years	*1%*	*2%*	*3%*	*4%*	*5%*	*6%*	*7%*	*8%*	*9%*	*10%*
1	1.000	1.000	1.000	1.000	1.000	1.000	1.000	1.000	1.000	1.000
2	2.010	2.020	2.030	2.040	2.050	2.060	2.070	2.080	2.090	2.100
3	3.030	3.060	3.091	3.122	3.152	3.184	3.215	3.246	3.278	3.310
4	4.060	4.122	4.184	4.246	4.310	4.375	4.440	4.506	4.573	4.641
5	5.101	5.204	5.309	5.416	5.526	5.637	5.751	5.867	5.985	6.105
6	6.152	6.308	6.468	6.633	6.802	6.975	7.153	7.336	7.523	7.716
7	7.214	7.434	7.662	7.898	8.142	8.394	8.654	8.923	9.200	9.487
8	8.286	8.583	8.892	9.214	9.549	9.897	10.260	10.637	11.028	11.436
9	9.369	9.755	10.159	10.583	11.027	11.491	11.978	12.488	13.021	13.579
10	10.462	10.950	11.464	12.006	12.578	13.181	13.816	14.487	15.193	15.937
11	11.567	12.169	12.808	13.486	14.207	14.972	15.784	16.645	17.560	18.531
12	12.683	13.412	14.192	15.026	15.917	16.870	17.888	18.977	20.141	21.384
13	13.809	14.680	15.618	16.627	17.713	18.882	20.141	21.495	22.953	24.523
14	14.947	15.974	17.086	18.292	19.599	21.051	22.550	24.215	26.019	27.975
15	16.097	17.293	18.599	20.024	21.579	23.276	25.129	27.152	29.361	31.772

TABLE - 4 Present Value of an Annuity of $ 1

Years	*1%*	*2%*	*3%*	*4%*	*5%*	*6%*	*7%*	*8%*	*9%*	*10%*
1	0.990	0.980	0.971	0.962	0.952	0.943	0.935	0.926	0.917	0.909
2	1.970	1.942	1.913	1.886	1.859	1.833	1.808	1.783	1.759	1.736
3	2.941	2.884	2.829	2.775	2.723	2.673	2.624	2.577	2.531	2.487
4	3.902	3.808	3.717	3.630	3.546	3.465	3.387	3.312	3.240	3.170
5	4.853	4.713	4.580	4.452	4.329	4.212	4.100	3.993	3.890	3.791
6	5.795	5.601	5.417	5.242	5.076	4.917	4.766	4.623	4.486	4.355
7	6.728	6.472	6.230	6.002	5.786	5.582	5.389	5.206	5.033	4.868
8	7.652	7.325	7.020	6.733	6.463	6.210	5.971	5.747	5.535	5.335
9	8.566	8.162	7.786	7.435	7.108	6.802	6.515	6.247	5.995	5.759
10	9.471	8.983	8.530	8.111	7.722	7.360	7.024	6.710	6.418	6.145
11	10.368	9.787	9.253	8.760	8.306	7.887	7.499	7.139	6.805	6.495
12	11.255	10.575	9.954	9.385	8.863	8.384	7.943	7.536	7.161	6.814
13	12.134	11.348	10.635	9.986	9.394	8.853	8.358	7.904	7.487	7.103
14	13.004	12.106	11.296	10.563	9.899	9.295	8.745	8.244	7.786	7.367
15	13.865	12.849	11.938	11.118	10.380	9.712	9.108	8.559	8.060	7.606

11

BOND ANALYSIS — MACRO-LEVEL

Bonds are not as attractive as equity for resasons of lack of high risk-high return profile and no capital appreciation and bonus, rights and other privileges of ownership. Bonds have fixed interest returns and less variability of returns. Bonds however have their own advantages, discussed below.

ADVANTAGES OF BONDS

1. Bonds are attractive to those who are risk averse and are happy with assured modest fixed income or interest income, and certainty of income.
2. Bonds are necessary in a portfolio to diversify assets into various alternative categories, in order to reduce risk of the total portfolio.
3. Bonds have not only lower risk but in combination with stocks or other assets, lower the total risk of portfolio due to low correlation or low tendency to vary in the same direction and to the same extent as the prices of other assets.
4. Investors, if properly trained can learn to capitalise on the bond price movement and benefit from capital gain.
5. Bonds are needed for FIs to issue debt instruments of long-term and also for investment in portfolio management.
6. Bonds are also required for duration adjustment in portfolio management.

Bond market returns are good varying between 10 to 15% in the last decade in the developed markets of UK, USA, Germany Japan and France. The Bond Index for different varieties of bonds are published abroad. The bond description of listed and traded securities is given in terms of the name of issuer, coupon rate or interest rate and year of maturity. The Government security in India is quoted for example as *12.32% Loan, 2011*.

Government and Semi-Government bonds or debentures were quoted on National Stock Exchange (N.S.E.) as follows:

Interest	*Issuer*	*Maturity*	*Yield*
12.25%	GOI	2008	10.25%
12.32%	GOI	2011	10.35%
12.65%	IFC	2005	12.65%
13.25%	WBIDFC	2007	13.69%

DEBT MARKET IN INDIA

Debt Market is not developed in India for many reasons, despite the fact that debt in terms of market capitalisation is 42% of GDP, while equity market capitalisation is 56% which has gone up to more than 109% of GDP in the peak of Frenzy on the stock market in Feb., 2000 and in 2007-08. Firstly, Government and semi-Government bodies being largest issuers of debt, the interest rates on debt are controlled historically by the Government For long, the interest rates on fixed Deposits of Companies and P.S.U.s were also fixed by the RBI, at ceiling levels. Secondly, these interest rates were kept low to facilitate Government funding at cheaper cost. The individual investors could not find these rates attractive to invest in. Thirdly, the requirements of law in respect of banks, insurance companies and financial institutions forced them to invest a proportion of their funds, in Government and semi-Government debt which led to a captive market in them. They thus used to invest accordingly in these securities and hold them, until maturity or trade in them among banks and financial institutions, only for purposes of adjustments to duration of maturity and yield. Secondary market and retail trading did emerge only after 1994-95

In the case of corporate debt also, individual investors are not attracted except through the route of fixed deposits with the companies which are not marketable. Debentures which are long-term debt, used to be sold mostly to financial institutions, insurance companies and more recently to mutual funds, UTI, etc. They also used to hold them until maturity particularly when it is privately placed or are unsecured. The secondary market in these instruments did not develop as a result. Similar is the case with P.S.U. bonds which were allowed to be issued since 1985.

Retail market and trading in these debt instruments did not develop due to these legal and structural factors. Bulk holders of the corporate debt are still the banks and financial institutions. Debt instruments used to carry lower rates than the free market rates and have no chance of capital appreciation and hence are not welcome to individual investors.

Hurdless in Debt Market

Low interest rates, institutional holding of these debt instruments, statutory obligation of holding a minimum of Government debt by banks and financial institutions and a host of other structural factors in the financial system did not allow secondary market to be developed in them. There is a stamp duty on such trade and transactions costs are high due to supply rigidities. There is also a problem of absence of liquidity as there are no ready buyers and no market makers. Both supply and demand are poor in these securities due to the above factors and in the absence of market makers, these instruments lack trading. They are therefore, not attractive investments to individual investors as they are unwilling to wait until maturity and for long periods. Debentures used to be generally issued for 7 to 9 years with a lower return than on equity.

Components of Debt Market

There are three major components of the debt market in India. They are in this order of their magnitude and importance:

(a) Government Securities and semi-Government securities or bonds.

(b) Private corporate securities in the form of debentures and bonds.

(c) P.S.U. bonds including those of public financial institutions. The Central Government and state Government issue the largest amount of debt securities, every year, followed by the corporate sector — manufacturing, finance and trading companies. The P.S.U.s and public Financial institutions have also been borrowing heavily since 1994-95 as the budgetary support to them was given up.

Data on Capital Raised as Debt

(₹ in crores)

	1994-95	*1995-96*	*2000-01*	*2004-05*	*2005-06*	*2006-07*	*2008-09*	*2010-11*	*2013-14*
1. Private Corporate Sector (Preference shares and debentures)	9,002	4,120	3,210	13,679	21,154	30,603	16,171	27,466	11,681
2. P.S.U. Bonds and those of Government sector companies	4,558	2,291	16,632	7,591	4846	10,325	13,404	60,433	50,865
3. Gross borrowings of Centre and States (Including Treasury bills)	43,231	46,783	1,28,483	1,45,602	1,81,747	2,00,198	4,36,688	5,83,521	8,97,119
4. Volume of Corporate Debt.	NIL	NIL	NIL	NIL	80,620	6,640	11,930	45,060	1,16,084

Source: RBI Handbook of Statistics.

Changing Scenario of Debt Market

The Government have raised the interest rates on Government debt to market related rates by stages since 1991-92. Secondly, the lowering of S.L.R. of banks forced institutions other than banks to contribute to Government debt. This has necessitated the RBI to announce the scheme of primary dealers, who can operate as market makers and wholesalers of the Government securities to develop the retail market. NSE was set up in 1992 with one of its objectives as development of debt market in India. A start has been made to promote wholesale debt market when RBI has directed banks to channel their trade in Government securities and Money market instruments through the NSE and is brokers. The wholesale segment is being developed by NSE and many corporate debentures series were listed for trading on the NSE. Besides, OTCEI has also some debentures listed for trading by investors at retail level and have two additional advantages of market makers and assured liquidity.

Introduction of Newer Instruments

Another development in favour of debenture trading is the freeing of interest rates on debentures in 1991 and changes in SEBI guidelines to allow debt issues to be made without vetting by the SEBI. A variety of new financial products are issued by corporates since the entry into capital market was freed in May 1992. Secured premium notes, fully convertible preference shares, premium notes, fully convertible and partly convertible debentures, convertible preference shares, discount bonds, zero coupon bonds, flexibonds, floating rate bonds etc., are some of the examples of debts instruments. As per the directive of the SEBI any instrument should not be convertible into equity within 18 months, if it is to be considered as debt instrument. Since March 1998, these are treated as debt and are to be compulsorily credit rated.

PUBLIC SECTOR BONDS

During 1995 and 1996, the largest amount of funds was raised by the P.S.U.s and public financial institutions, through the bond route. IDBI IFCI, SBI, MTPL, SAIL and NTPC are a few examples, which raised large amount of debt during the last few years. The interest rates offered were in the range of 16-18%. Although the bonds are generally issued for 5 to 7 years, they are issued by public financial institutions like IDBI, ICICI and IFCI for longer periods of 20 to 30 years with the permission of the Government. At the other extreme since companies raised debt for less than 18 months, to enjoy the benefits of debt route for equity but yet not credit rated by any agency, as the SEBI guidelines exempt these issues of less than 18 months from this requirement of compulsory credit rating; the distinction between those with less than 18 months and more than 18 months was dropped in March 1998.

ICD AND FIXED DEPOSITS

Companies borrowing through the ICD (Inter Coporate Deposit route) have to pay as high a rate as 30 to 60% in times of tight liquidity. As such they find it convenient and cheaper to raise funds from the public, individuals and institutions, at 15% to 20% through short-term debt instruments of one year in the form of deposits or some form of debentures. As per the RBI rules, Company deposits carry a maximum rate of 15 to 16% and the rest of the money out of 20% is passed on to investors the form of cash incentive and to the sub-brokers and brokers, is the form of bokerage and commisions. The above ceiling on interest rates was removed in July 1996. But interest rates have fallen since 2000 along with all debt instruments and bank rates.

An example of company issuing NCDs with a maturity of 18 months is SRF Ltd. and CEAT Financial Services. The funds so mobilised by them are at 18-20% and are used in ICD investments at 30-40% — a clean 20% gain in financial deal. SRF issued these debentures at 18% compounded on a quarterly basis and the yield to maturity works out to 20.61%. The CEAT Financial Services offered those NCDs at 19%, with interest payable on a quarterly basis and yield to maturity of 20.41%.

SOME INNOVATIVE SCHEMES

IFCI has offered four innovative schemes to raise large amounts from the public in the form of debt instruments. These are:

1. Regular Income Bonds: These carry an yield to maturity of 18%, with the coupon rate of 16%, and interest payable half yearly. They were sold at a discount of 3% and redeemable at a premium of 4%, at the end of 7 years. The face value of each is ₹ 1 lakh.

2. Step up Liquid Bonds: These bonds are having a face value of ₹ 10,000 and maturity of 5 years, The interest rate is 16% payable half yearly but increases by 0.25% every year to 17% in the 5th year. This is redeemable at a premium which increases from 0.5% at the end of first year to 3% at the end of fifth year. The yield to maturity works at to 17.51%.

3. Hi-Growth Bonds: These are Deep Discount bonds, in a different form. They carry a face value of ₹ 5,000, redeemable at ₹ 3 lakh at the end of 27 years, but with the option to redemption after 6, 11, 16 and 21 years also, at different redemption prices, but the yield to maturity works at 16.35%.

4. Lakhpathi Bonds: These are also Deep Discount bonds of a higher denomination of ₹ 48,000 each with a maturity value of ₹ 1 lakh after 5 years. But if the maturity period is raised to 10 years at the option of investor, he has to pay only ₹ 22,500 to get ₹ one lakh. The yield to maturity varies from 15.77% for 5 years to 16.07% for 10 years.

The IDBI has a triple A rating and issued in March 2000 similar bonds for ₹ 300 crores, namely 11% Regular Income Bonds, Growing Interest Bonds, Floating Rate Bonds and Tax Saving Bonds.

OMNI Bonds of IDBI

These are unsecured bonds, privately placed in two forms — one Regular return with 7 year maturity (OMNI Bonds) with a face value of ₹ 1 lakh and coupon rate of 16%, payable half yearly. There was an option of early redemption and a premium of ₹ 3,000 for holding upto 7 years. ₹ 1,250 for holding upto 5 years. IDBI has also simultaneously issued zero coupon bond with a face value of ₹ 1 lakh sold at a discount price of ₹ 33,250, redeemable at the end of 7th year, with a yield working out to ₹ 16.93%. The IDBI has raised a record amount of ₹ 1,050 crores in 1995-96 from the public and another ₹ 7,000 crores gross in 1996-97. Also, the IFCI, ICICI and SBI have also been the largest mobilisers of funds in recent years through issue of bonds.The interest rates were lowered in the early years of 21st century.

Floating Rate Notes

Here the bonds carry interest rates which are flexibly adjusted every year. These are issued by UTI in some of its income Schemes and by IDBI and ICICI. Deregulation of interest rates and frequent changes in term rates, make it necessary not to fix the rates in advance on medium and long-term bonds and have to issue these floating Rate Notes. Some companies call them flexibonds, as their rates are not fixed once for all but flexible and changeable, from time-to-time.

Discount Bonds

Like premium Notes which give a premium at the end of the maturity period and carry no interest rate, coupon discount bonds or Deep discount bonds, carry no interest coupon but are sold at a discount on the face value which itself will indicate the expected rate of return. But these bonds aim at capital gains and not interest income. For many the former is better due to lower rate of taxation on long-term capital gains at 20% as against the normal income tax rates of 20 to 30% in the case of interest income for individuals.

Indexed Bonds

The bonds sold at rates linked to the inflation rate or the price of gold are called Indexed bonds. The coupon rates are in this case variable and not fixed in advance. Government bonds and Municipal bonds in developed countries are issued on the basis of principle of indexation. They are similar to flexi bonds.

LISTING OF DEBENTURES

Debentures, which are not convertible into equity or redeemable within 18 months, should be compulsorily rated by a credit rating agency for the issue to the public. Some of those issued to the public are also listed on BSE, OTCEI and NSE. But there are some issues like those of Sundaram Finance SRF, GE Cap, Core Health, Care Dee Pharma etc., which made private placement at coupon rates of 18-19%, yielding 21-22% to the investors. As these are not listed and traded, buying and selling will be a problem and liquidity is less.

But issues quoted on OTC and NSE are now available for regular trading in retail in marketable lots and in OTCEI the facility of market makers is also available which will ensure their tradeability and a quotation. Examples of such OTC and NSE traded corporate debentures are given in the attached Tables below.

OTC Debentures

Example of OTC listed debentures show that Birla Global Finance is rated A + only, but is at a premium with ₹ 100 debentures quoting at ₹ 132.50 while Raymond with AA is quoting at a discount at ₹ 83.10. The yields to maturities varied from 15.10% in the case of BGFL to 18.36% the case of Dabur India and these yields depend on a host of factors like credit rating, coupon rate, maturity period, performance of the company etc.

NSE Debentures

The Triple "A" rated Tisco Secured promissory notes were yielding 21.39% in 1996 while Torrent Gujarat was yielding 27.09% (YTM) with only a double "A" (AA) rating.

Table 1
Bond Issues in Primary Market

Company	*Instrument Type*	*Rating*	*Min. Amt (On Appl)*	*Tenure*	*Int. (%)*	*Payable*	*Yield %*	*Put/Call*
IRFC	Tax-free bonds	AAA	₹100,000	15 years	8.50-9	Annual	–	–
IFCI	Prom. Notes	AA-/A(+)	₹100,000	10 years	13	Annual	13	None
Option 2		AA-/A(+)	₹100,000	7 years	12.9	Annual	12.9	None
Option 3		AA-/A(+)	₹100,000	5 years	12.65	Annual	12.65	None
Option 4		AA-/A(+)	₹100,000	3 years	12.2	Annual	12.2	None
Karnataka Neeravari	Regular	LA+ (so)	₹100,000	7 years	12.75	Annual	12.75	After 5 yrs.
Option II	Regular	LA+(so)	₹100,000	5 years	12.4 for 3 yrs	Annual		After 3rd and 4th yrs.
Centurion Bank	Regular	None	₹100,000	63 m	12.75-13.05	Annual		None
GSRTC	Regular	Unrated	₹100,000	7 years	13	HY	13.42	
WBIDFC	Regular	Unrated	₹100,000	7 years	13.25	HY	13.69	
HPRIDC	Regular	Unrated	₹100,000	7 years	12.25	HY	12.63	
PICUP	Regular	Unrated	₹100,000	7 years	13.4	HY	13.85	
PSIDC	Regular	Unrated	₹100,000	2 years	11.4	Annually	11.4	
MPEB	Regular		₹100,000	7 years	13.7	HY	14.17	After 4yrs. 11 mths
PSEB	Regular	Guaranteed	₹100,000	7 years	13.5	HY		After 4yrs. 11 mths
MPSIDC	Regular		₹500,000	5 years	14.4	HY	14.92	

Investor's Guide E.T. Feb. 6, 2000.

As a matter of thumb rule, the better the credit rating, the better is the safety of the debenture, but liquidity is provided by availability of market maker and trading on a regular basis. The higher the rating, the lower is generally the coupon rate, as the company can issue the security with less risk, which means lower return. The higher the risk, the higher is the return. In case of Reliance and Ranbaxy with a credit rating of AA+which means high safety, the issues were made at coupon rates ranging from 12.5% to 15%, while United Phosphorus with a lesser rating of only AA (meaning adequate safety) issued debentures at 17%. Coupon rates in general varied from 12.5% to 18.5% while the current yield, in which investors are interested varied from 15% to 20%, in 1996, and from 10 to 15% in 2006-07.

For the purpose of illustration, the actual data on Bond market in India are presented in Tables I and II. Table-I presents the data on the terms of new issues of Bonds in the primary market as in Feb., 2000. Mainly the Public Financial Institutions, banks and Semi-Government bodies have raised funds at this time in private placement, through the mode of bond issues. The data on credit rating, amount raised, maturity period, interest rates, yields, periodicity of interest payment, put and call options, if any, can be seen from the Table-I.

Table-II presents the data on the N.S.E deals in the bond market, as quoted in the daily press. These data pertain to the Wholesale Debt Segment of NSE which is the secondary market in bonds. The Table gives the data on commercial paper and government securities, issued by private, semi-Government and Government agencies, amount in ₹ crores of trade value, market capitalisation, number of trades, average daily value, etc.

Table II-Wholesale Debt Trade Growth

Business Growth in WDM Segment

Year	*Market Capitalisation (₹ Crores)*	*Number of Trades*	*Net Traded Value (₹ Crores)*	*Average Daily Value (₹ Crores)*
Jan-09	2751888.00	2218	45015.16	2250.76
Dec-08	2668915.85	2857	46864.44	2231.64
Nov-08	2442569.19	1093	23143.11	1285.73
Oct-08	2329604.27	922	19966.18	1109.23
Sep-08	2254265.46	783	19779.42	988.97
Aug-08	2225594.86	594	11507.71	605.35
Jul-08	2186726.67	815	18744.81	814.99
Jun-08	2194961.00	956	18233.37	868.26
May-08	2192183.11	1200	20656.29	1032.81
Apr-08	2168650.80	1016	19892.83	994.64
2007-2008	2123346	16179	282317.02	1138.38
2006-2007	1784801	19575	219106.47	897.98
2005-2006	1567574	61891	475523.48	1754.70
2004-2005	1461734	124308	887293.66	3028.31
2003-2004	1215864	189518	1316096.24	4476.52
2002-2003	864481	167778	1068701.54	3598.32
2001-2002	756794	144851	947191.22	3277.48
2000-2001	580835	64470	428581.51	1482.98
1999-2000	494033	46987	304216.24	1034.75
1998-1999	411470	16092	105469.13	364.95
1997-1998	343191	16821	111263.28	377.16
1996-1997	292772	7804	42277.59	145.28
1995-1996	207783	2991	11867.68	40.78
1994-1995	158181	1021	6781.15	30.41

Source: www.nseindia.com. website.Debt Segment.

Negotiated Trade Reporting Platform Business Growth
Business Growth in Negotiated Platform

Year	*Market Capitalisation (₹ crores)*	*Trading Days*	*Number of Trades*	*Net Traded Value (₹ crores)*	*Average Daily Value (₹ crores)*	*Average Trade Size (₹ crores)*
2015-2016	57,45,074	82	4,921	1,98,484.30	2,420.54	40.33
2014-2015	57,39,272	237	18,789	7,72,369.06	3,258.94	41.11
2013-2014	51,28,733	243	21,143	8,51,433.62	3,503.84	40.27
2012-2013	49,28,331	242	26,974	7,92,213.78	3,273.61	29.37
2011-2012	42,72,736	239	23,447	6,33,179.45	2,649.29	27.00
2010-2011	35,94,877	248	20,383	5,59,446.77	2,255.83	27.45
2009-2010	31,65,929	239	24,069	5,63,815.95	2,359.06	23.42
2008-2009	28,48,315	238	16,129	3,35,951.52	1,411.56	20.83
2007-2008	21,23,346	248	16,179	2,82,317.02	1,138.38	17.45
2006-2007	17,84,801	244	19,575	2,19,106.47	897.98	11.19
2005-2006	15,67,574	271	61,891	4,75,523.48	1,754.70	7.68
2004-2005	14,61,734	293	1,24,308	8,87,293.66	3,028.31	7.14
2003-2004	12,15,864	294	1,89,518	13,16,096.24	4,476.52	6.94
2002-2003	8,64,481	297	1,67,778	10,68,701.54	3,598.32	6.37
2001-2002	7,56,794	289	1,44,851	9,47,191.22	3,277.48	6.54
2000-2001	5,80,835	289	64,470	4,28,581.51	1,482.98	6.65
1999-2000	4,94,033	294	46,987	3,04,216.24	1,034.75	6.47
1998-1999	4,11,470	289	16,092	1,05,469.13	364.95	6.55
1997-1998	3,43,191	289	16,821	1,11,263.28	384.99	6.61
1996-1997	2,92,772	291	7,804	42,277.59	145.28	5.42
1995-1996	2,07,783	291	2,991	11,867.68	40.78	3.97
1994-1995	1,58,181	223	1,021	6,781.15	30.41	6.64

Source: www.nseindia.com website Debt Segment.

FIXED DEPOSITS

Like Debentures and Bonds, all debt instruments including Fixed deposits and short-term instruments like C.P., C.D. etc. are to be credit rated, as per the guidelines of RBI and SEBI. Under the present free interest rate regime the coupon rates, yields or interest rates are freely decided by the market forces.

In the table below, the FD interest rates are given as in 1999-2000.

FD Interest Rates

For the information of readers we give below the rates of interest offered by leading companies on their fixed deposit schemes. *(rates prevailing as on 27-12-99.* The rates have since declined to 6 to 9% as in 2009-2010.

Company	*Rating*	*Interest Rates*			*Interest*
		1Y	*2Y*	*3Y*	*Mode*
1. Ashok Leyland Finance	AA	—	13.00	14.00	M/Q
2. Cholamandalam Inv & Fin (R)	AAA	11.00	12.00	13.00	M/Q/Y
3. First Leasing Co of India	AAA	11.50	12.50	13.00	M/Q
4. HDFC (Individual)	AAA	9.50	10.00	10.50	M/Q/H
5. IL & FS	AAA	11.50	11.75	12.50	M/Q/H
6. Kotak Mahindra Finance	AA+	11.00	11.50	11.75	Q/H
7. Mahindra & Mahindra Finance	AA	12.00	13.00	13.50	C
8. Tamil Nadu Powerfinance	A+	12.00	12.50	13.00	M/Q
9. Ballarpur Industries	A-	14.00	14.50	15.00	Q/H
10. Carborundum Universal	AA+	9.50	10.50	11.50	Q/H

M - Monthly, Q - Quarterly, H - Half yearly, C - Cumulative
(R) - Only Renewals.

The maximum rate fixed by RBI stood at 12½% at that time but later lowered to 11%. The credit rating, terms of issue of Fixed deposits of selected companies are presented for illustration. The terms and rates of interest are those prevailing at the beginning of the new millennium in the year 2000.

It will be seen from the Table that the triple rated (AAA) companies offered a lower rate such as 9.5% by HDFC and 11.5% by First Leasing, while a single A, A+ or A– companies have offered a higher rate of 12% by T.N.P.F and 14% by Ballarpur Industries.

ASSET BASED SECURITIES (SECURITISATION)

Asset based securities and bonds issued in the place of receivables held by a company, with a highly diversified portfolio. HDFC converted its Housing loans into securities and sold them. So did the Citi Bank in December 1995 through what are called "Pass Through Certificates" (PTC). Such securities are first purchased by the Special Purpose Vehicle (SPV) which is structured as a trust company for this purpose. SPV is ready to buy before maturity, offering liquidity to these instruments. Investors get 17-18% interest. Sometimes the paper is sold as zero coupon bonds at an initial discount and they are redeemable at the end of 5 to 7 years at par. The Citi Bank was the first to get their PTC rated by a credit Agency (AAA) and have them listed on the NSE. In the case of Citi Bank securities, the SPV has a right to receive interest at 17.36% and the tenor of the security is 30 months, for these zero coupon bonds. The market maker is the Hoare Govett (India) on the NSE and the PTCs are traded on the NSE open to both residents and NREs, OCBS or FIIs. The issue price and other details of PTCs listed on NSE are seen in the chart below. HDFC, S R FF, Ashok Leyland etc., have also used the PTC, but they are not listed on any of the Stock Exchanges. In fact only the NSE, BSE, OTCEI and DSE provide the facilities for trading in bonds or debentures. Of these, the bulk of trading is on NSE which is expected to develop the debt market in India. The terms of issue of Citi Bank PTCs are shown in the following chart.

Volume of Debt Traded on NSE (Illustration)

₹ Crores / *Years*	*Corporate Debt*
2007-08	8,580
2008-09	11,930
2009-10	54,480
2010-11	45,060
2011-12	50,150

Source: NSE.

Citi Bank's Experiment

Instrument	17.36% Fixed rate auto loan through certificates
Date of Issue	7 Dec., 1995
Monthly Payout	7th of every month starting Jan.
Date of Maturity	7th March 1998 (2-3 yrs.)
Originator	Citi Bank NA
Rating	AA (+) by CRISIL
Issue Price	₹ 9.4 mn per certificate
Total Issue Size	₹ 235 mn
Listing	NSE

Source: ET Investor Guide 19th Feb. 1996.

Bond Return

Bond returns are in terms of yield and yields were discussed later in the chapter. These yields can be calculated for all fixed income securities, say debentures or preference shares etc.

In general, the current yield is given as $\dfrac{\text{Current Annual Interest}}{\text{Current Market Price}}$

In the quotations on BSE

15% Indian Hotel was quoted at ₹ 75

The current yield = $\frac{15}{75}$ = 20%

Prices vary inversely with yield. If Indian Hotel is quoted at 80, instead of 75, $\frac{15}{80}$ then the yield will fall to = 18.75%

The concepts of yield to maturity and Holding period (or yield to call period) are discussed elsewhere in this book.

Bond Risk

Risks are systematic and unsystematic Risks. In the macro sense, dealt with in this chapter there are systematic risks. The next chapter discusses them in micro sense (unsystematic risks). These risks are measured by the variability or standard deviation from the mean of the return. The source of all systematic risks are: purchasing power changes and interest rate changes, (involving price changes and reinvestment income changes). Interest rate risk has these two dimensions namely price risk and reinvestment risk.

INFLATION OR PURCHASING POWER RISK

Return expected on Government securities has two components namely riskless return plus some compensation for purchasing power risk. Inflation and expected inflation determine the second component. Riskless return is the treasury bill return of the Government, which has no risk in practice. In India, in the year 2009, the treasury bill return was around 7% and inflation rate was about 8%. Then the short-term bond should have return of 7 + 8 = 15%. But the average inflation rate in the past and expected inflation rate in the future also influence the interest rates and the yields ranged from 14% to 18% in the case of corporate bonds in India, in 2009. Inflation rate over the last decade averaged at around 8% and the riskless return plus average inflation rate will give a total return of around 20%.

Expectations also play an important part. Thus, in fiscal 2008-2009, the inflation rate was around 8%, but the expected long-term trend is 5%, due to the fact that in some years, the inflation rate touched around 3 to 5% in the past. Inflationary potential as judged by the central Government budget deficit, administered price changes, money supply changes, etc., and a host of other factors determine the expectations of inflation rates in India. Actual inflation rates were around 3% during 2001 and 2002 but the rate of growth of the economy slowed down during these years. Later the inflation ranged around 5% p.a. during 2005 to 2008.

Interest Rate Risk

Volatility of Bond prices depend on the changes in interest rates. Firstly, income and capital gain or loss will be affected, by changes in interest rates. Secondly, income from bonds reinvested will have also different income due to interest rate changes. The first is the price risk and second is the reinvestment risk, which are discussed below.

PRICE RISK — VOLATILITY OF BOND PRICES

Price changes in bonds occur due to changes in maturity of bond. Given the same coupon rate and face value ₹ 100, changes in the required yield or in interest rates will lead to different changes in prices depending upon the years to maturity. The longer term maturities will suffer larger capital depreciation with rise in yields than those with shorter term maturities. The capital appreciation will behave in the same manner, if there is a fall in interest rates. As maturity becomes larger, the greater is bond price volatility. Again, the lower the coupon rate, the greater is the volatility of bond prices. If interest rate rises, the percentage fall in prices will be larger in low coupon bonds than with high coupon bonds. If interest rate falls, the percentage rise in prices will be larger with low coupon bonds than with high coupon bonds. The starting level of yields will also influence the bond price volatility. The higher the yield level, from which yield fluctuation starts, the greater is the price volatility.

Reinvestment Risk

While the price effect from changes in yield is inverse, the reinvestment effect is positive with changes in yield. These two opposing forces will give the net effect. The higher is the reinvestment rate, the higher will be the income from the bond.

Take the example of 8% Bond due in 20 years for maturity — purchased at ₹ 100 yield to maturity is 8%. If reinvested at 8%, total realised compound rate will also be 8%. But if reinvestment rate varies from 6 to 10% what will happen? This is shown in the Table below.

Reinvestment Rate%	*Total Realised Compound Yield*
6%	6.64%
8%	8.00%
10%	9.01%

If the reinvestment rate for example goes up from 8 to 10%, the life time yield of the bond goes up to 9.01%. Reverse is the case if the reinvestment rate fell from 8% to 6%.

DETERMINANTS OF INTEREST RATES

The next question which crops up is what determines the interest rate. The bond prices being dependent heavily on interest rates, it is pertinent to note here the level of interest rates. These are dealt with separately below in the rest of this chapter.

Level of Interest Rates

The theories that explain the level of interest rates are many but two namely the Loanable Funds Theory and Liquidity Preference Theory are relevant here.

(a) Loanable Funds Theory: This theory states that the demand and supply of loanable funds determine the interest rates. The supply of loanable funds emanate mostly from household sector leaving aside the foreign factors, while the demand emerges from Government and the Business Sectors, who spend more than their income for consumption and investment. Increase in demand for funds will increase interest rates and while the increase in supply will push down the interest rates. Expectation of inflation rate rising faster than before will push up the demand for funds and this leads to rise in interest rates and the reverse is also true.

(b) Liquidity Preference Theory: Liquidity is money and demand and supply for money decides the interest rates. Demand for money balances arises for transactions purposes, precautionary purposes and for asset purposes. The higher the income and wealth, the larger is the money demand and the supply of money comes from the Reserve Bank of India and the Government of India. Given the level of money supply by these agencies, the money demand determines, the interest rates, as per this theory.

Shape of the Yield Curve

The structure of yields observed in relation to different terms to maturity is called the term structure of interest rates. The curve depicting the relationship of yields to the terms to maturity, assuming that other features remain the same, is called the yield curve. The yield curve is to be drawn at a point of time depicting yields for varying maturities of the same security or the securities of the same characteristics, except maturity.

The yield structure and the slope of the yield curve is influenced by RBI first, by the cut-off rate for auctions of securities of various maturities and secondly, by its offer of purchase and sale in its deals in Government securities (open market purchases and sales) of various maturities. The yield curve should be based on market yields of the securities of different maturities. Thus, at end March 1999 a five year bond of Government was offered at 11.55%, while a ten year bond was sold at 12.03% by the RBI. In December 2009, a five year bond was sold at 7.3% while 10 year bond was quoted at 7.5%. In 2012 a five year bond was sold at 8.2% and 10 years bond at 8.4%.

The shape of yield curve is upwards. According to theory, long-term rates are expected values of future short-term rates. This depends on the expectations of investors. If future interest rates are expected to be higher, yield curve will slope upwards, and if future interest rates are expected to be lower, yield curve will slope downwards or taper off, at least in Theory. Long-term yields may fall when short-term rates are rising relatively, when the yield curve will be inverted.

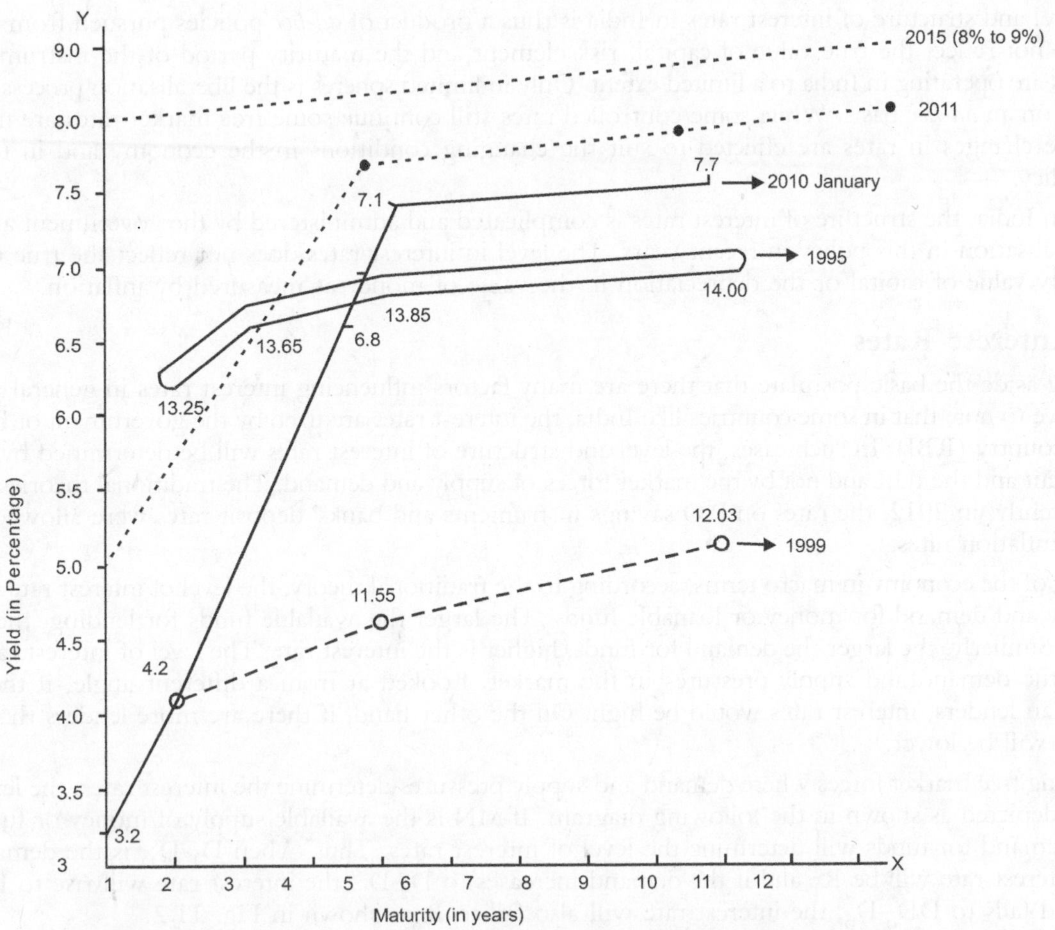

N.B: The rates for 2009-10 ranged from 3.2 to 7.7% and those for 2006-07 ranged from 6.5% to 8%.

Fig. 11.1 Yield Curve for Government Paper

Level and Structure of Rates

Table 11.1 shows that interest rates are adjusted by the government and RBI from time-to-time in tune with the requirements of the economy. The table compares the rates in 1997 and 2005 with those in 1980. There are some which were raised while others were lowered. The ceiling of 10% on call money rate was removed in May 1989. Similarly, in October 1990, the banks were given freedom to charge rates for lending at their own discretion in respect of non-priority sector advances. The government policy of lending at concessional rates to priority sectors like agriculture, SSIs, weaker sections of society etc., however, continued to be operative; but the slabs are brought down from 4 to 3.

New treasury bills of 182 days were sold on an auction basis since 1986-87 and their interest rates are determined by the market forces but this was discontinued later and re-introduced in May 1999. The short-term deposit rates varied from 6.25-7.75%. The yields on government securities were raised over the period in a significant way so as to make them attractive to investors and to bring them nearer to the free market rates. The recent liberalisation of interest rate policy in respect of banks' lending rates is also in tune with the policy of financial deregulation followed by the government and recommended by the Committee, to review the working of Monetary Policy (Chakraborthy Committee1985). The term-lending rate was, for the purpose of encouraging long-term investment, raised to 15.5% only, while the other rates were raised more. But the rate of rise was neither consistent throughout nor was it off setting the fall in the value of money through inflation. In fact, the rate payable on company deposits was lowered to 14% over the decade and 12.5% in 2001 along with a similar cut in the rate on debt capital of debentures and on ownership capital of preference shares. The only significant rise in interest rates is seen in the case of those on government securities as they were kept at artificially lower rates for a long time and hence the need for readjustment in an upward direction. The rate on company deposits was raised to 15% and the rate on debentures was freed from controls in 1991. The ceiling on deposit rates was removed in July 1996 for some categories of NBFCs. Flexible Bank rate policy and free interest rate policy was pursued thereafter, particularly early after 1999.

The level and structure of interest rates in India is thus a product of *ad-hoc* policies pursued from time-to-time. The rates do not reflect the true value of capital, risk element and the maturity period of the instrument. The free market forces are operating in India to a limited extent. Only in limited spheres is the liberalisation process implemented and that too on an *ad-hoc* basis. While some controlled rates still continue some free market rates are now available. Similarly, the changes in rates are effected to suit the changing conditions in the economy and in tune with the monetary policy.

Thus, in India, the structure of interest rates is complicated and administered by the government although there is some liberalisation in this policy in recent years. The level in interest rates does not reflect the true market forces or the scarcity value of capital or the depreciation in the value of money as measured by inflation.

Level of Interest Rates

Leaving aside the basic postulate that there are many factors influencing interest rates in general as referred to above, we have to note that in some countries like India, the interest rates are fixed by the government or by the Central bank of the country (RBI). In such cases, the level and structure of interest rates will be determined by the policy of the government and the RBI and not by the market forces of supply and demand. The traditional theories do not apply in India. Recently, in 2012, the rates on P.O savings instruments and banks' deposit rates were allowed to be raised due to high inflation rates.

Talking of the economy in macro terms, according to the traditional theory, the level of interest rate is determined by the supply and demand for money or loanable funds. The larger the available funds for lending, the lower is the interest rate. Similarly, the larger the demand for funds, higher is the interest rate. The level of interest rate, therefore, depends on the demand and supply pressures in the market. Looked at from a different angle, if there are more borrowers than lenders, interest rates would be high. On the other hand, if there are more lenders than borrowers, interest rates will be lower.

Assuming free market forces where demand and supply pressures determine the interest rates, the level of interest rates can be depicted as shown in the following diagram. If MN is the available supply of money or funds, then the amount of demand for funds will determine the level of interest rates. Thus, when D_1-D_1, is the demand curve for funds, the interest rate will be R_1 and if the demand increases to D_2-D_2, the interest rate will rise to R_2. Similarly, if the demand falls to DD_o-D_o, the interest rate will also fall to $R_o$as shown in Fig. 11.2.

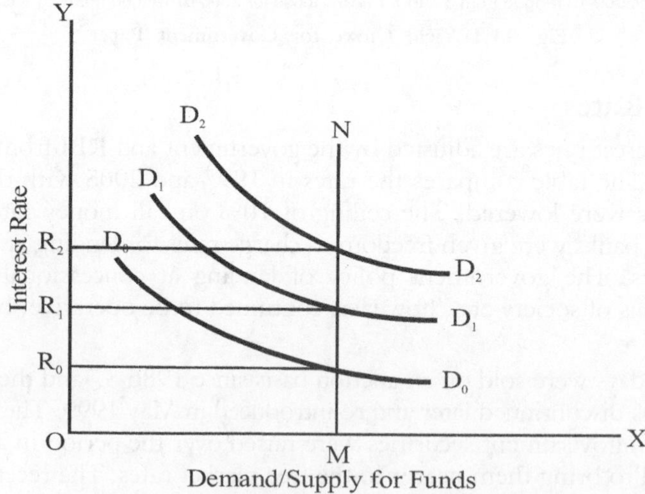

Fig. 11.2 Determination of Interest Rate

STRUCTURE OF INTEREST RATES

Leaving aside the time factor, the increase in risk in respect of banks' lending rates and the longer period involved in such lending have been reflected in the higher level of interest rates on them. As compared with the call money rates or treasury bill rates, which are for short periods, the interest rates on debentures, PSU bonds and term-lending rates by banks are higher due to the higher risk involved. Thus risk, maturity period, the safety and certainty of funds, etc., would influence the relative levels of interest rates and the structure of rates as seen from Table 11.1 which also, represents the data on the structure of rates. There are various types of instruments with varying rates of interest rates in India. These rates will depend on the characteristics of these instruments like ownership risk, variability of return, maturity period, safety, marketability, etc. The data clearly brings out the upward and downward shifts in the structure of rates depending upon the level of risk, time period of maturity and other features of the financial instruments involved.

Table 11.1
Structure of Interest Rates in India

(in percentages)

Sl. No.	*Types of Interest Rate*	*1980*	*1997 (Sept.)*	*March 2000*	*2001-02*	*2004-05*	*2005-06*	*2009-10*	*2011-12*	*2013-14*
1.	Bank Rate of RBI	9	10	8	6.5	6.0	6.0	6.0	6.0	9
2.	Auction Treasury Bill Rate (91 days)	Not applicable	6.88	9.08	9.0	4.89	6.5	3.2	5.1	8.6
3.	Auction Treasury Bill Rate (364 days)	Not applicable	8.47	10.16	9.76	5.15	6.7	4.5	8.3	9.1
4.	Call Money Rate	7.12	8.88	8.25	7.19	4.65	6.6	3.3	4.5	8.28
5.	Banks' Deposit Rate — Maximum	10	free for those above 1 year@	Free	Free	6.50	7.0	7.5-8.0%	9.25%	8 to 10%
6.	Banks' Lending Rate — Minimum (PLR)	13.50	13.00	12.0	11.0	10.25	11.25	11-12%	-10.5%	10 to 12%
7.	Term-lending Rate of FIs	14.00	14.00	Free	Free	Free	Free	12-13%	9-15%	9 to 15%
8.	Rate of Preference Shares	11.00	14.00	14-15%	—	Free	Free	Free	Free	Free
9.	Rate on Debentures	13.05	16 - 18 (free rate)	Free	Free	Free	Free	Free	Free	Free
10.	Company Deposit Rate — Maximum	15.50	16%	Free	14% - 12½%	11	11	Free	Free	Free
11.	Yields on Government Securities — Maximum (10 years)	6.44	13.05	12.40	10.05	7.25	7.5	7.54%	7.75	8.4

@ Banks are allowed to pay more than 12% for deposits above 2 years in October 1995, and more than 11% for deposits of more than one year from July 1996. But since October 1997, bank deposit rates for 30 days and above have been deregulated, and have brought down due to monetary policy changes of RBI. In mid 2012, interest rates were raised for banks and post offices on most of the saving instruments.

The change in the level of interest rates as between 1980 and 1997 and 2009 can also be seen from Table 11.1. The Bank rate rose, upto 1997 as also the banks' borrowing and lending rates and yields on government securities, etc. But the rate on company deposits and the term-lending rate of banks and FIs stood around 14% and 16% respectively in 1997. Between 1997 and 2000, Bank rate and all other rates were lowered due to free and flexible interest rate policy. Interest rates on company deposit rates, debentures and preference shares were freed from controls.

It will be seen from the table the structure of interest rates has changed over time as between, say 1980 and 2009. Generally the level of interest rates has increased over time upto 1997 to reflect the increased cost of raising funds and degree of inflation which eroded the value of money, and later on, the rates fell due to flexible interest rate policy, and deliberate lowering of rates for growth purposes.

In India, as seen above, many of these interest rates are now freed by the government. The banks' deposits and lending rates and those of financial institutions are freed by the RBI, while the rates on P.O. instruments, PSU bonds and those on government securities are only partly fixed by the government in consultation with the RBI.

The rationale of regulating interest rates in India is as follows:

(i) It keeps the interest cost low for the government borrowings and their investment. In 1999-2000 and during 2001 to 2003, the interest rates on savings media were lowered.

(ii) It promotes the socio-economic objectives of providing cheaper finance to weaker sections and priority sectors of the economy.

REFORMS

Certain adjustments may be necessary to remove the deficiencies in the interest rate structure. Firstly, interest rates in the Indian economy are to be positive in real terms so as to promote real savings in the economy. This point has been emphasised by the Sukhmoy Chakraborty Committee. The implementation of this suggestion involves a projection of the expected rate of inflation and ensuring that the basic or the minimum rates are marginally above the average inflation rate. Secondly, the short-term money markets, namely, bill market, discount market and call money market, are to be further developed and broadbased. Thirdly, in the gilt-edged market, the government and the public sector bodies should be provided finance in the form of treasury bills or of government securities and/or loans and advances at positive real rates. This would ensure that the government gets its funds at the scarcity value of capital and curtail the Reserve Bank credit to the government to the minimum.

It was felt necessary to rationalise call money rates to reflect the scarcity of inter-bank funds or stringency in the resources of the banks. Thus, the then existing ceiling of 10% was removed in May 1989. The need for a ceiling was eliminated when the supply of funds was augmented by allowing non-bank financial institutions also to operate in the market, such as IDBI, IFC, etc., mutual funds and even corporates.

In the government securities market, the interest rate reforms were already started earlier and coupon rates were adjusted in an upward direction to reflect the scarcity value of the capital in India and to improve the attractiveness of the government bonds with the primary savers and financial intermediaries. These reforms are to be carried forward to rationalise the term structure of the interest rates. The short-term debt which is of a low proportion has to be increased and long-term debt has to be reduced. The gaps between these short- and long-term yields and the gap on government debt *vis-a-vis* the private debt should be rational. Between the venture (ownership) yield and debt yields, there is a reverse gap discouraging the flow of funds to the equity market.

The existing framework of controls on bank lending and borrowing operations has been based on some justification. The reforms were in the form of reducing the various tiers of interest rate to a minimum of three or less both at the lending and borrowing ends. Interest rates on special categories like term credit, export credit, etc., may be kept out of this normal spectrum of interest rates or rebates and tax concessions should be eliminated following the reforms. The fiscal and tax benefits should be kept out of the purview of these savings instruments.

Recent Deregulation Measures

Following the recommendations of the High Level Committee on Financial System (of Shri M. Narasimham, November 1991), some measures of deregulation were initiated in the banking and monetary system. The SLR on an incremental basis stood at 25% in 1995 and the incremental CRR of 10% was discontinued. The CRR was kept at 10% of NDTL since March 1999. The Committee's recommendations on capital adequacy norms, prudential norms of income recognition and provisioning for bad debts are also being implemented in stages. The recommendations aimed at improving the functional autonomy of banks and financial institutions and enhance competition, efficiency and profitability.

Interest rates are being increasingly left to market forces since 1991. In August 1991, interest rates on debentures and P.S.U. Bonds were freed from all restrictions. The system of ceiling rates for term lending institutions was replaced by a system of minimum rates. The ceiling rate on fixed deposits of companies was raised to 15% in January 1992, but removed in July 1996.

The banks have been given greater autonomy in their lending operations and rates of interest charged subjected to a ceiling on deposit rates. New financial instruments such as Participation Certificates, Commercial Paper, Certificates of Deposits, Money Market Mutual Funds and Non-Resident (Non-repartiable) Rupee Deposit Scheme are being promoted at the market related interest rates.

New guidelines were issued in June 1992 and again in January 1998 and Jan. 2000 for Non-bank financial institutions. The interest rate payable is at monthly rests, on a compounding basis. As in the case of shares, deposits can be accepted in joint names, not exceeding three with or without either or survivor etc.

Premature repayment is permitted without penalty in the event of death of the depositor to surviving holder or the legal heirs of the deceased.

In respect of Hire Purchase and Equipment leasing companies which enjoy separate limits and conditions, it has been decided that if a company is engaged in hire purchase finance and equipment leasing activities, its business in both these lines will be taken together in determining its classification.

THE YIELD

Current Yield

The concept of yield relates to a return on investment made in any security or financial instrument. Yields may be classified into different types depending on the securities. In the case of equities, the yield refers to the current yield, which means the return on investment made at the present juncture. The yield is derived by dividing the Dividend + Capital appreciation by the purchase price of share. In the case of debentures and government securities, they are having coupon rates. Normally, the coupon rate is the rate of interest payable on a face value of ₹ 100. It is not related to the market price or the purchase price. The current yield in the case of these fixed income securities is annual interest divided by current price or purchase price of the security. Thus, if 11.5% 2008 government loan was purchased at ₹ 95, the current yield is $= \frac{11.5}{95} \times 100$, which gives 12% as current yield.

Redemption Yield

Redemption yield refers to yield to maturity. It is the average rate of return involving the return in the form of interest as well as appreciation or depreciation of capital over the period remaining to maturity. Thus, for working out the redemption yield for a government bond or a debenture, the following steps are to be taken:

1. Compute the capital gain (or loss) if it is held up to the maturity date. If the purchase price is ₹ 95 and its face value is ₹ 100, the amount realised will be ₹ 100 involving a capital appreciation of ₹ 5 at the time of maturity.
2. Allocate a capital gain for the remaining part of the maturity or life of the security. Thus, if the security has five-year maturity, an appreciation of ₹ 5 is to be distributed equally among all the 5 years, which means that there will be an appreciation of one rupee per year.
3. This annual appreciation is to be added to the annual interest rate paid on the security. If the coupon rate is 6%, an income distribution of ₹ 6 per annum is available and this is to be added to rupee one per annum as capital appreciation.
4. As a next step, add the redemption proceeds at the time of maturity and the purchase price and divide it by 2 which gives the average cost of holding the security.
5. Then divide the total return of investment, namely, (6 + 1) by the average holding cost, arrived at as above. In the example, the average cost of holding is (100 + 95) divided by 2 is equal to an amount ₹ 97.5. Then the redemption yield is arrived at by dividing the total return by the average cost of holding, namely, ₹ 7/97.5 = 7.2%.

It will thus be seen that the redemption yield is slightly different from other concepts. The redemption yield gives the actual return on investment in the form of Interest or Dividend + Capital Appreciation or Depreciation over the maturity period. The formula for deriving redemption yield is as follows:

$$V = \sum_{n=1}^{n} \frac{I_n}{(1+i)^n} + \frac{P_n}{(1+i)^N}$$

Where, *V* is the value of the bond, *I* is the interest amount paid in absolute terms, *i* is the rate of interest or yield required to be derived, P_N is the face value at maturity and *N* is the number of years to maturity.

Holding Period Yield (HPY)

Where redemption yield is not relevant, holding period yield (HPY) is used. Holding period yield brings out the possibility of purchase and sale of a security during the period of its maturity without waiting until the period of maturity. Thus, one can buy a 13.5% debenture of Reliance Petro at ₹ 80 against its face value of Rs.100. It could be sold at ₹ 85 after a year, without waiting up to the time of maturity, say, after 5 years. In this case, the holding period yield is relevant. The investor has purchased at ₹ 80 and sold at ₹ 85 after a year. The holding period is one year and the yield is interest at 13.5% that he receives during the year + an appreciation of ₹ 5 for holding it over the year, which gives a total of 18.5%. The formula for the holding period yield is as follows: The return (18.5) is divided by the purchase price (₹ 80) which gives the holding period yield (23.1%).

The formula is $HPY = \frac{(P_t - P_o) + I}{P_o}$

Where, I is interest payment, P_o is price at the beginning of the holding period and P_t is price at the end of the holding period.

Real Yield

Real yield is a different concept which takes into account the depreciation in the value of money. Thus, as opposed to nominal yield, which is the coupon rate as, for example, 6%, the real yield is adjusted for depreciation in the value of the rupee, namely, an increase in the prices of goods and services. If the price increase is represented by Wholesale Price Index (WPI), then the nominal yield is deflated by the rise in WPI over the period considered. Thus, the nominal yield of 6% if deflated by the rise in prices of, say 10% will give a negative yield of 4%. Thus, the concept of real yield presents the picture of the real return in terms of goods and services and purchasing power of the return.

Net Yield

The above concepts of yields present the picture of general yields common to any investor, irrespective of his status such as tax status or type such as an individual or institution, etc. As such, they are gross yields — yields prior to tax payment. The net yield is that after payment of tax. As tax liability varies from individual to individual or company to company, the general tax deduction rate can be applied, say 10% or 20% of the gross yield to arrive at the net yield. Interest and dividend incomes are paid without deduction of tax at source for amounts up to ₹ 2,500 per annum. These tax factors become relevant for net incomes.

Maturity and Yields

Yields vary depending not only on the type of security and interest rate, coupon rate but on the maturity of the security. Thus, the yields are higher, longer is the maturity. This is particularly true of government securities, which are issued with varying maturities.

Yield and Maturity

If yields on any security are available on a cross section basis, a yield curve can be drawn to serve for comparative purposes or for indicating the trends and for forecasting purposes. The yield curve is useful in the government securities market where yields differ mainly on the basis of maturity. It depicts the relationship of time periods to yields, as referred to earlier.

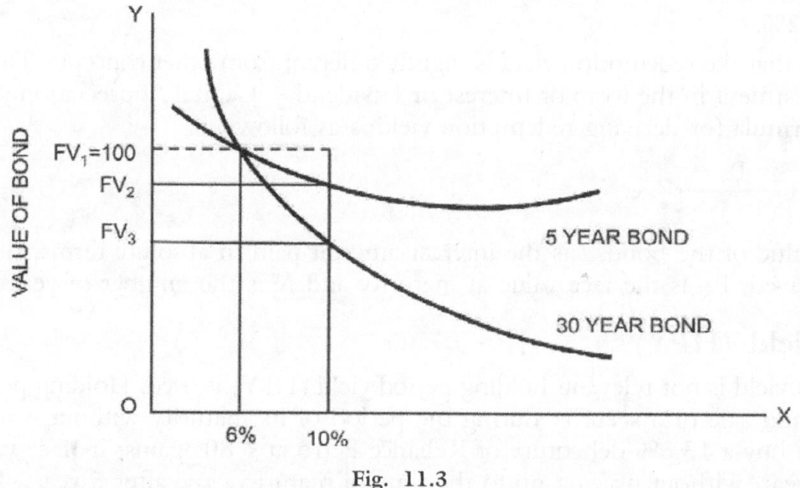

Fig. 11.3

Effect of Interest Rate changes on value of Bond.

Example: Take one bond of 5 year maturity and another of 30 year maturity — both with a coupon rate of 6%.

Required Rates of Return (r) of the Bond goes up to 10%; the fall in value of 30 year bond is steeper than a 5 year bond (that is FV_1 to FV_3, for 30 year bond as against FV_1 to FV_2 for 5 year bond).

REASONS FOR SHAPE OF YIELD CURVE

By taking Government bonds in the example, we eliminated the credit and default risks. Taking the structure of interest rates in India, long-term rates were lower over a number of years historically, when the yield curves were inverted. But normally, the longer the maturity the higher should be the return. The normal phenomena of yield curve is explained by the return risk features of the security on the premise that the longer the maturity, the greater is systematic risk of the market.

Three hypothesis explain the Term Structure:

1. Expectations Hypothesis: The current structure of interest rate is determined by the consensus forecast of future interest rates. If thus the shape of yield curve slopes upwards, investors expect hike in interest rates and flat yield curve implies that investors do not expect any change in interest rates. Downwards sloping curve augurs a fall in interest rates as per the expectations.

2. Liquidity Premium Theory: Yields on longer term should reflect a liquidity premium which means that higher risk on longer maturities should be compensated by larger premium on longer maturities. This yield curve will be upward sloping, which is the normal pattern of yields, referred to earlier.

3. Segmented Market Approach: The yields on different maturities differ due to demand and supply factors of each maturity separately. Thus, certain groups of investors like P.F., and pension funds prefer longer maturities and their yields will fall, if their supply is limited. Banks prefer short-term maturities and if their supply is limited their yields will fall due to rise in demand relative to other maturities.

Problem Solved-Example

TVS bought a bond of face value of ₹ 100 with a 5% coupon rate for ₹ 95 on Feb. 14, 1999 and sold it for ₹ 99.50 on Feb. 14, 2000. If TVS belongs to a Tax bracket of 28% average tax rate, what is his pre-tax yield and post-tax yield?

Answer:

For pre-tax yield, apply the following formula:

$$= \frac{\text{Capital gain or loss} + \text{Coupon interest}}{\text{Purchase price}}$$

$$= \frac{(99.50 - 95) + 5}{95} = \frac{9.5}{95} = 10\%$$

The gross yield before tax is 10%

To calculate the net yield after tax, apply the following formula.

$$= \frac{\text{Capital gain } (1 - \text{tax rate}) + \text{Coupon interest}}{\text{Purchase price}}$$

$$= \frac{(99.50 - 95)(1 - 0.28) + 5}{95}$$

$$= \frac{4.5(0.72) + 5}{95} = \frac{3.24 + 5}{95} = \frac{8.24}{95}$$

$$= 8.67\%$$

The bond's after tax rate of return or net yield to TVS is 8.67% while gross yield is 10%.

12

BOND ANALYSIS – MICRO-LEVEL

While at the Macro-level, the systematic risk is studied, represented by the purchasing power and interest rate risks, in the micro-level, bonds represent fixed interest securities, issued by Government, corporates and P.S.Us and Semi-Government bodies. Each of the categories of issuers and each issue of bonds, will have its own risk-return features depending on the terms of offer and the fundamentals of the company or issuer of securities, called the unsystematic risk.

(*a*) *Default Risk:* Risk of loss may be due to the fall in quality due to decline in earnings power and deterioration of fundamentals. This may lead to a fall in market value of bond of the Company and rise in yields. Default risk, arises due to non-payment or delay in payment of interest, non-provision of sinking fund instalments, delay or non-payment of principal. All these are reflected in the fall in earnings power of the company issuing bonds, caused by many factors such as business risk, inadequate revenue and increasing costs, due to poor management, weak cash flow position etc.

(*b*) *Financial Risk:* Too much of debt liability with high cost of borrowing leading to rising burden of interest. Default prone bonds are high risk instruments and early identification of such bonds and their issuers will reduce the risk and loss.

Each of the debenture issues has its own terms and as such its own yield curve. Mirco analysis thus concentrates on the individual bond analysis from the point of fundamentals and earnings power of the issuer, capacity to service the debt and other fixed income securities. Partly this in done by the credit agencies and investors can learn from the rating given to the issue.

CREDIT RATING SYSTEM

Debt Instruments are generally rated but even equity can be rated at the time of Initial Public Offer (I.P.O) based in the project appraisal and projected financial parameters. Credit rating refers to the rating of risk, involved in an instrument issued by a company. All debt instruments whether short-term or a long-term are to be compulsorily rated, if they are issued to the public. Since rating is at a point of time, it has the validity for a short period of 3 to 6 months and rating has to be updated from time-to-time.

In 1999, SEBI announced their scheme of regulating the credit rating agencies. Their minimum net worth should be ₹ 5 crores. The SEBI regulations prohibit them from rating the instruments of their promoters. There are six credit Rating agencies, at present in India which give ratings to the corporate issues and even equity issues are being rated on a voluntary basis. The more important of them are the following.

CRISIL = Credit Rating and Information Services of India, which is the oldest institution set up in 1988, with its Head quarters in Mumbai.

IICRA = Investment Information and Credit Rating Agency set up in 1991, with Head quarters in Delhi.

CARE = Credit Analysis and Research Ltd. set up in the private sector as opposed to the public financial institutions which have set up CRISIL and ICRA. This instiution was set up only in 1993.

Duff Phelps Credit Rating India Private Ltd. (DCR) is another approved credit rating agency set up in 1996-97. Many others have entered into the field. Fitch Ratings India Ltd. is another agency from the foreign sector, operating in India, as 100% subsidiary of its parent company. SME Rating Agency (India) is the sixth credit Agency set up in India.

ICRA is interested in rating of equity also. This can be either in respect of the company's issue of securities in the primary market (IPO) or in respect of their secondary market trading.

While debt rating reflects the opinion of the credit rating agency about the ability of the company to repay interest and principal in time, the equity rating assesses the company's ability to generate adequate returns to the share holders; the emphasis is on the expected return and risk associated with it. Earnings are forecast and prior claims of debt and taxation are taken into account in arriving at the net returns available to equity holders. Equity rating will help investors to judge the type of risk they are exposed to when particularly there are many fly by night operators in the primary market.

Assuming that debt only is graded the Table below presents comparative symbols used for fixed deposits by the rating agencies in India. F is pre-fixed for FDs while Pf is pre-fixed for preference shares and p for short-term instruments.

Simple Symbols

(Used for debentures)

AAA	=	Highest Safety
AA	=	High Safety
A	=	Adequate Safety
BBB	=	Moderate Safety
BB	=	Inadequate Safety
BC & D	=	High Risk and Default Prone

Comparative FD Rating Symbols

Symbols in vogue which investors must consider before placing a fixed deposit

CRISIL	
Investment Grades	
FAAA	Highest safety
FAA	High safety
FA	Adequate safety
Speculative grades	
FB	Inadequate safety
FC	High risk
FD	Default
ICRA	
MAAA	Highest safety
MAA	High safety
MA	Adequate safety
MB	Inadequate safety
MC	Risk prone
MD	Default
CARE	
CARE AAA	Best quality
CARE AA	High quality
CARE A	Adequate safety
CARE BBB	Sufficient safety
CARE BB	Speculative
CARE B	Susceptible to default
CARE C	High investment risk
CARE D	Default

RISK FACTORS

In influencing the fixed prices, there are two categories of factors to be examined namely risk factors and non-risk factors. There are broadly listed below:

In this section, risk factors are examined in respect of their influence on yields. Out of many such factors, the four listed above are discussed below in that order.

Risk Factors	Non-risk Factors
(a) Terms of issue offer or provisions in Debenture Trust Deed	(a) Legal and procedural difficulties
(b) Earnings power	(b) Market and Marketability
(c) Liquidity	(c) Incentives and call factors
(d) Management	(d) Tax factors

Terms of Issue or Trust Deed

In terms of the Company Law, debentures which are secured and registered can be issued to the public. But this requirement does not apply to Government and public sector companies and financial institutions. All debenture issues made by the companies to the public which are not convertible within 18 months should be supported by a Debenture Trustee, say a bank or financial institution and a Trust Deed to be executed within six months of the issue to the public. Such public issue of debentures has to be supported by a rating by an Indian Credit Rating Agency, as per the SEBI Guidelines. Credit rating agencies are also controlled through a code of conduct, rules and regulations by SEBI.

Debenture Trust Deed lays down the terms, rights and obligations of the trustee and the company, the security of assets against the instruments issued, sinking fund arrangements, payment of interest and principal, and action to be taken by debenture trustee in case of complaints of registered holders of Debentures for failure of the company to meet its obligation and other matters.

The Trust Deed lays down in particular the restrictions on the mortgage or further mortgage of the assets, or sale of the assets, which are constituting the security for the debenture issue, on raising the level of debt, creditor rights in the event of any arrears of interest and principal etc. These terms also include the method of repayment of principal, premium or discount at which they are to be redeemed and the exact date or dates of interest payment and principal repayment. These terms partly determine the price of the bond and yield there on, as they determine the extent of the risk, as laid/down in the original terms of issue and incorporated in Trust Deed.

Earnings Power

The earnings power is a single important factor determining the fundamentals of the corporates issuing debentures. The price of a bond is determined by the fundamentals of the issuer, through — (1) earnings level, (2) earnings variability, (3) leverage, reflected by the debt-equity ratio, (4) interest coverage of earnings, and (5) market for the debt issue, listed or not and the demand for such debt.

The earnings power also depends on the sales and the ratio of sales of gross block, operating profit margin, prior commitments through off Balance sheet guarantees and commitments, cost of debts *vis-a-vis* the earnings, current ratio, and working capital management involving current solvency, leverage enjoyed by equity through debt, extent of preferred stock having prior claims, reflecting the long-term solvency of the company, etc.

SEBI GUIDELINES

For a corporate unit to issue bonds in India SEBI has issued many guidelines since 1992. Briefly they are set out below.

(1) Minimum Debt-equity ratio should not exceed 2:1 and current ratio to be 1:1.33.

(2) The working capital debenture amount should not exceed 20% of the total gross current assets.

(3) Rate of interest paid on debenture is free to be decided by the Company since August 1991.

(4) Credit rating is compulsory for debt issues even if they are convertible into equity within 18 months and they are issued to public, through offer of sale.

(5) Debentures have to be redeemed after expiry of 7 years and a premium of 5% is permitted on NCD at the time of redemption.

(6) Buy back arrangements and price support operations are permitted for NCDs.

(7) Debentures and bonds of any type including new financial products are permitted — convertible, non-convertible, with warrants or loyalty coupons, etc.

(8) Debenture Trustee and making of a Trust deed are compulsory and to be completed within six months of the issue of debenture certificates.

(9) Debt instruments, issued with a credit rating are not to be vetted by SEBI but by the Merchant bankers only.

(10) Put and call options can be had, if their terms are specified clearly for all bonds convertible after 36 months.

Earnings potential essentially rests on the management efficiency, financial prudence and future plans, Government policy and a host of fundamental factors, discussed in another chapter. More importantly, one has to look for stability of earnings, their composition into sales income, trading income and speculative income or through sale of assets or revaluation of assets, etc. The quality of assets is a very important determinant of the solvency and liquidity of the company and hence their earning power.

EARNINGS COVERAGE FOR DEBT

The earnings coverage ratio is the ratio of charges on debt and preferred stock (Preference shares) to total income. The higher the income and lower the charges on debt and preferred stock the lower is the Default Risk of bondholders. In many cases, the average of the last few years in respect of these ratios shows the stability or volatility of these ratios and have the risk element to creditor. Earnings are represented by Earning Before Interest, Depreciation and Taxes (EBDIT). As depreciation is a commitment independent of interest and taxes, we take generally Earnings Before Interest and Taxes (EBIT).

Interest Coverage is to be measured by $= \dfrac{\text{EBIT}}{\text{Interest charges on all bonds}}$

Debt Service Ratio has to take into account the repayment of debt obligation also.

Thus, debt service coverage is given by $= \dfrac{\text{EBIT}}{\text{Interest Payable} + \dfrac{\text{Sinking Fund Payment}}{(1 \quad \text{Tax Rate})}}$

Capitalisation

Earnings power is also dependent on the capitalisation or capital structure of the corporates. This is called financial leverage. If the capital structure includes bonds, debentures and preferred stock in addition to equity, then their composition and the equity coverage of debt is an important factor for determining the financial leverage to the company and the protection to debtholders. The larger the equity base (relatively 1:1 ratio) the better is the cushion to debtholders.The higher debt relative to equity is a high financial risk and fear of default increases with every increase in debt, given the level of equity.

Default prone companies and Default free companies from the point of view of financial leverage can be illustrated as follows:

Default Prone Company				*Default Free Company*			
Total Assets	100	Total Debt:	80	Total Assets	100		
						Debt	20
		Equity	20			Equity	80
Total	100		100		1000		100

Debt is 4 times equity Debt is 1/4th of equity

The optimal ratios are as follows:

Debt in the form of bonds and Debentures	75
Preferred Stock	25
Common Stock (Equity)	100
Total Long-term Capital	200

The bondholder would consider liquidity Cushion as (125/200) = 62.5%, as preferred stock and equity are subordinate to debt in respect of repayment order.

The rates of loanable assets (Gross block or networth) to long-term debt will be another indication of the asset protection to bondholders. For this purpose, a comparison of this company with other similar companies and comparison of the company's ratio over a time period are both necessary. In taking the assets, intangible assets, revaluation of assets and depreciation should not to be considered and only long-term fixed assets for solvency and short-term liquid assets for liquidity are to be considered. These will reflect the protective shield to the bond-holders.

Liquidity

Liquidity refers to nearness to cash. In the case of a company, the liquidity ratio of current assets to current liabilities will indicate its nearness to cash. Similarly, the cash inflows in relation to cash outflows as reflected in cash flow statement would reflect the liquidity position of the company. Three sources of cash generation for the company should be considered in this respect.

(a) *Internal Cash Generation:* Net income plus depreciation and amortisation plus deferred taxes contribute to cash available to the company.

(b) *External Financing:* Through raising fresh equity from time-to-time to inject some permanent funds to avoid shortfall of working capital and thus preserve liquidity.

(c) *Sale of Fixed Assets:* It is another extraordinary method of raising cash. Capital appreciation can be booked, and unnecessary land or other fixed assets can be sold off to raise fresh cash. All these sources have to be considered as backing up cushion to the bondholders.

Management

Assessment of management efficiency is crucial to the bondholder's rating of the compay's creditworthiness. The track record of management as reflected in Earning stability, financial management, expansion plans, expertise and experience of management team, professionalisation of management should have to be examined. The assessment of management is a qualitative judgement, based on their policies, consistency, integrity and creditability and foresight, as reflected in their expansion plans, tax planning, retention and dividend policies etc.

NON-RISK FACTORS

In addition to risk factors referred to above there are other factors also which affect the bond prices. Some examples of non-risk factors which influence bond prices are terms of the issue, say issue at a discount, redemption at a premium, attached coupons, options and warrants call features etc. These affect favourably or unfavourably the bond prices. Marketability of a bond is an important feature influencing its price. The bonds, listed and well traded or those with a repurchase facility have a good demand. Bonds with a market maker have good liquidity. The laws of the land facilitating or obstructing trade in bonds is another factor to be considered. Thus, in India stamp duty on issue of debenturers and on transfers is a state subject and the rates are as high as ₹ 3 per 100 face value or market value whichever is higher. The difficulties of securing bonds in retail and in marketable lots are another set of problems. Debentures when first issued will be at a face value of say ₹ 100 and reflecting market yields after listing they fall in prices. Tax factors are another set of problems to the Indian bond market.

There will be tax deduction at source for all interest income above ₹ 2,500 per annum. The interest income is taxable at the normal rates of income tax, where the capital gains of long-term nature (after holding for more than 12 mouths) is taxable at a lower rate. But for companies, interest paid on debt enjoys the privilege of tax exemption as it is taken as an expense item. Thus, next to manufacturing expenses all the interest payments on long-term debt, bank borrowing and other short-term debt is adjustable expense item to arrive at the net profits. But the same privilege is not available to the fixed dividend payable on preference shares.

There is prior commitment to the company, before the residual profits are available to equity holders. But to serve the preference shareholders at the present fixed rate of dividend of 14%, the company will have to earn a pre-tax return of 20% at the prevailing corporate tax rate of say 30% for domestic companies. In the case of bondholders, the company need to earn only the rate of interest payable on them, which in 2009 varied from 10% to 12%, depending upon the credit rating of the company, terms of offer, conversion or warrants or other incentives and add-ons like premiums and discounts. The interest rates to be offered on debentures are now freed from any controls. The company is free to offer any rates that it thinks that investors will accept depending on their assessment of the creditworthiness of the company. To some extent, the rating of credit rating agencies will help the investors to assess the company. But to a large extent investors have to study the risk and non-risk factors that influence the market prices referred to above.

GOVERNMENT BOND MARKET IN INDIA

The Government Bond market is an important segment of Bond Market in India. This includes Central, State and Semi-Government bonds. The Central Government gross borrowings from the market was around ₹ 4.69 lakh crores in 2011-12. Total internal debt of the centre, comprising market loans, special bearer bonds,

Treasury Bills compensation and other bonds, special securities issued to RBI, international institutions and gold bonds stood around ₹ 31.10 lakh crores as at end March 2012, working out to around 42% of GDP, of India. Half of that amount is in the form of marketable loans. which can be traded. Although these bonds are default free and least risky, active trade in them did not develop at retail level. The interest rates on market loans which were very low until 1991 financial Reforms, have been gradually raised to market related rates since these reforms were started, and the Government began to depend on the market borrowings more than the RBI. During 1995-96, for example, interest rates ranged from 13.25% to 14%, as compared with 10-11.5% in 1990-91 and much lower before. The high cost of debt was due to higher coupon rates offered in the eighties and nineties and of doubling the quantum of internal debt during the years 1991-96. Due to flexible interest rate policy, the rates fell or were lowered by Government and RBI from 1998-99, on Government loans, Savings instruments, P.F. etc.

The Government of India has also entered into an agreement with the RBI to limit the former's dependence on the latter for Adhoc Treasury bills in 1994 which made the Government depend more on market borrowing. A system of auction sale of Government securities was also started in 1994 along with sale on tap basis. Sale of new instruments like flexible rate bonds, zero coupon bonds etc. was started by the RBI on behalf of the Government. The Government have agreed to discontinue their dependence on Adhocs but shift to ways and means advances from RBI from 1997-98.

The secondary market in Government. debt is encouraged by the RBI. The Securities Trading Corporation of India (STCI) was set up in June 1994 to provide wholesale trading facility as market maker. The Wholesale Debt segment of NSE is being encouraged by the RBI as also on the OTCEI.

Developmental Measures

A system of enlistment of primary dealers for allowing them to do wholesale trading and to act as market makers was started in Nov. 1995 with licensing some six firms. Banks are encouraged to sell in retail Government debt to their clients and promote the secondary market in Government securities. Delivery Versus Payment (DVP) was introduced in Mumbai for deals in Government securities from July 1995. All deals in giltedged securities are now in demat form and they can be traded on the stock market on a daily basis like any private securities.

The RBI is also publishing on a daily basis the details of all transactions in Government securities through Subsidiary General Ledger (SGL) Account with public debt office of RBI, for ensuring transparency of these deals in Government bonds. The STCI is also publishing its deals and rates at which it is prepared to buy and sell selected central Government securities on a daily basis. Repo facility with RBI in dated securities of Government was extended to STCI and DFHI. Private placement of Government securities is also done by the RBI, in addition to other methods of sale in the market, like auctions and open offer of sale. The terms of offer and methods of issue are also being revised to improve the public response to the Government debt issue. Thus some issues with flexible rates and some with instalments of contributions from the subscribers, as in the case of calls made by the companies are adopted by the RBI to raise funds for the Government of all debt items.

Government Debt Market Components

The components of gilt-edged market in India are as follows:

1. 14 days Treasury Bills	Sold on Auction basis, discontinued since May 2001
2. 91 days Treasury Bills	Sold on Auction basis
3. 182 days Treasury Bills	Sold from May 1999, discontinued since May 2001
4. 364 days Treasury Bills	Sold on Auction basis
5. Government Central and State Bonds	Sold on Auction basis or sold on offer basis
6. Semi Government and Government Guaranteed Bonds	Sold on auction or offer of sale
7. P.S.U. Bonds and Public Institutions	Sold on normal Public Offer

8. Repos, switches and swap deals in the Secondary Market.
9. Open Market operations conducted by RBI through DFHI and STCI.

Players in the Gilt-edged Market

Presently RBI, DFHI and STCI are the authorities of Government to deal in the Market. Besides the other players are:

(a) Primary dealers authorised to be wholesalers.

(b) Commercial banks, encouraged to retail trade in Government bonds.

(c) Financial Institutions like UTI, HDFC, and satellite dealers.

(d) Finance and Non-Finance Companies.

(e) Foreign Financial and Institutional Agencies.

OPERATIONS OF COMMERCIAL BANKS

The major lenders to Government are the commercial banks, as per the requirements of S.L.R. and Insurance companies, pension and provident funds and finance companies as per the requirements of their respective statutes.

Most of the commercial banks barring SBI and foreign banks do not trade in Government securities but hold them as required by law. As 50 to 60% of total Central Government securities are held by commercial banks and they do not trade to any significant extent, the secondary market in them did not develop. Pattern of ownership of the Government debt is seen from the Table below. (RBI data).

Pattern of Ownership (At end March)

Holder's Category	*Central Securities (In percentage)*								*Total Central and State*							
	1998	*2001*	*2004*	*2005*	*2006*	*2009*	*2012*	*2014*	*1998*	*2001*	*2004*	*2005*	*2006*	*2009*	*2012*	*2014*
RBI Own Account	12.8	9.2	5.0	6.5	7.0	9.7	14.4	10	10.7	7.7	4.1	5.2	5.0	7.4	10.1	10
Commercial Banks	62.3	60.7	55.3	53.2	52.0	51.1	49.2	26	63.0	60.9	56.1	52.4	47.0	47.3	59.2	44
LIC, etc.	18.7	20.0	19.4	20.2	27.0	23.2	21.1	12	18.6	18.3	19.4	20.5	22.3	22.7	20.7	28
PFs	1.5	2.1	2.0	2.8	6.0	6.7	7.5	14	2.1	2.4	2.8	3.7	4.3	5.0	4.9	13
Others	4.7	9.6	18.3	17.3	8.0	9.3	7.8	10	10.8	10.7	17.6	18.2	21.4	17.6	5.1	5
Total	100%	100	100	100	100	100	100	100	100%	100	100	100	100	100	100	100

Source: RBI Handbook of Statistics.

Only since 1994, when NSE has stated wholesale Debt market segment, there has been some growth in the secondary market trading and data is being compiled on trade volume. Trade in Government Securities stood at ₹ 2,502 crores in Sept. 1994 which rose to ₹ 1.20 lakh crores in June 2005 and to ₹ 2.70 lakh crores in June 2011. Part of the rise was due to sharp up swing in Repos transactions, which refer to sale and repurchase back after say 3 to 46 days and *vice versa*. The repurchase or Repo deals work out to around 15-20% of the total turnover in Government securities and this proportion varied from month to month. But this order of trading in this market has become very normal later on. In respect valuation of Government Bonds by the commercial banks, holdings of Government securities were classified into permanent and current assets and RBI has fixed a ratio of 30% current and 70% permanent for 94-95, for the purpose of valuation for the market price. This ratio for current holdings has gone upto 50% for 1996-97 and 75% in 1999-2000 and 100% for private sector banks, thus gradually raising the proportion of Government debt, held by banks to be marked to market value. This has forced the banks to trade more actively in the market and provide for depreciation for fall in market price due to rise in yields. The valuation norms have been laid down by the RBI from year to year and now all banks have to mark the securities to market value.

RBI AND YIELD PATTERN

For 1995-96, the RBI fixed the yield to maturity at 14% for the 10-year paper and directed the banks to value their Government securities of different maturities from one year to 10 years at market related yields. For 1999-2000, the YTM for 10 year paper was around 12.5%, and the banks have to mark the government securities to market prices based on yields fixed by the RBI. In addition, the yields for valuation purposes in respect of P.S.U. bonds was fixed at 1% above that of Government securities of the same maturity for taxable bonds and a flat 11.5% for tax free bonds. As Government bonds are risk free, banks need not set aside fresh capital for investment in gilts for the purpose of capital adequacy norms, but they have to book losses in case of depreciation of the current component of government securities. In the case of investment in non-performing assets, the banks have to provide for additional capital depending on the riskiness of the assets as per the RBI guidelines. For the purpose of valuing of Government securities, the RBI fixes the YTM figures close to the market price of the securities — sometimes yields related to the primary market if secondary market trading is not significant and sometimes yields based on secondary market prices.

It is the prerogative of the RBI to fix up the yields and quote the prices according to the STCI, which is the vehicle for its open market operations.The Banks are expected to trade actively in the market to bring the existing securities in their portfolio to the market prices and in the process make profits which may reduce the need for provision of depreciation in valuation of securities to the market.

The RBI has been giving instructions from time to time on the norms for valuation of Government securities and for portfolio management of investments. In March 1999, banks were advised that excess provision for depreciation on their investments should be appropriated to the "Investment Fluctuation Reserve Account", instead of "Capital Reserve" account and shown as a separate item in Schedule-2 "Reserve and Surpluses", under the head of "Revenue and other Reserves". This amount will be eligible for inclusion in Tier II Capital of the Bank. The amount held in "Investment Fluctuation Reserve Account" could be utilised to meet in future the depreciation requirements on investment in securities.

Commercial Banks and Retail Market

The RBI has given all encouragement needed to develop the retail market in Government Securities in India. At present the trade is confined to banks and among banks, FIs, PFs and foreign institutions. Trade at retail level among individuals, HUFs, partnerships and companies is still a long way off. To promote such trade, the RBI measures are of the following nature:

(1) If securities are held in physical form or in S.G.L. Account with RBI, in the banks's portfolio, they can be sold in retail by banks to their clients and the sold portion can be deducted from the investment Account and the S.L.R. Account of the concerned Bank.

(2) The sold portion can be repurchased after say 46 days, later reduced to 30 days in July 1996, under its Repos. (Ready forward transactions which are now permited by banks with the public also — Buy back of securities although it was confined earlier to other banks only). The lower limit of 3 days was removed by RBI to promote the use of Repo for call money adjustment purposes.

(3) Such Repo deals are also necessary because the RBI has stopped since July 1996 the provision of refinance against Government securities to banks.

(4) A system of primary dealers licensed by the RBI, has been already started in Nov. 1995 for acting as wholesalers and market makers for the giltedged market, which will impart liquidity to retail trade in Government securities. Another tier of satellite dealers and finally the branches of commercial banks to deal in retail directly with investors should help promote retail trade in gilted securities.

(5) Provision has been made for removal of Tax Deduction at Sources (TDS) on interest income earned by banks from gilts, but the same has not been extended by banks to the public.

(6) Introduction of liquidity support to Mutual funds dedicated to government securities.

Trade with and among the non-traditional investor groups is sought to be encouraged by the RBI through commercial banks on the one hand and primary dealers licenced by the RBI on the other. The latter are expected to have a network in different centres so as to promote market making and impart liquidity to the securities. The licenses granted by the RBI to some primary dealers and the Government permission granted to commercial banks to enter into repos or buy back agreement with the non-traditional investor groups are expected to prompt the commercial banks into this new area of retailing Government securities. If the yields are 12% and above for a safe investment of this type, and there is liquidity to such investments some investor clientele may be found for such retail trade.

Some legal hurdles may be there regarding the stamp duty, mode of execution of agreements, TDS on interest income to clients and procedural aspects of such operations, and the instruments to be generated thereby and their legal status. If RBI will lay down further guidelines in this direction to the banks and clear the stamp duty and taxation hurdles, some progress can be expected in this direction. In July 1996, RBI has agreed to pay underwriting commission upto 1% for gilts to primary dealers and provide them repos refinance at one percentage point less than the normal rate. RBI is also encouraging MMMFs to operate gilt fund with checking facility, to promote trade in gilted securities.

13 BOND MANAGEMENT – STRATEGIES

Introduction

Bond is an unsecured debt of the issuer, either in the Government sector or corporate sector. Bonds with special features, of zero interest or floating interest rate (as against a fixed coupon rate, normally issued) are also issued in India. Some of the bonds are however secured by collaterals, while unsecured bonds are the common feature. The Indian Companies Act does not provide for bonds, but only for debentures and warrants of various categories. Basically and in practice, both bonds and debentures are the same, and are fixed income securities like the preference shares.

Bond market in India is undeveloped and only banks, FIs and a few institutional investors trade in them for meeting with the legal requirements, such as S.L.R. The National Stock Exchange is developing this bond market in India, particularly of PSUs and Government and Semi-Government bonds.

The debentures are confined to the corporate sector and have varying features such as redeemability at a fixed date or over a period of 3 to 5 years, convertibility into equity at different time periods, etc. As per the Act, only secured and redeemable debentures can be issued in India through public offer and the registers of bondholders should be kept for effecting transfers of debentures by the investors.

Investors, mostly in the category of banks FIs, companies, PF, mutual funds, etc., hold the bonds and debentures, in India. The secondary market in these instruments is poor and underdeveloped. The normal strategy of investors in this category is passive, holding them for income and wealth purposes and not for maximisation of wealth. They hold them until maturity.

BOND MARKET IN INDIA

The wholesale debt market on NSE comprises Bank bonds, certificates of deposit, commercial paper, Corporate bonds, Government and Semi-Government bonds, and Institutional bonds, including those of IDBI, UTI, etc.

Bonds are issued by some Companies, public sector financial institutions, PSUs and semi-Government bodies in India. The secondary market in bonds is not well developed. Since 1985, PSUs have been issuing bonds and after the start of the financial reforms, and the trend of privatisation of PSUs by the Government the PSUs, public financial institutions, etc., are all encouraged to borrow directly from the public. It is in this context, that a bond market has emerged in India. Some of these are tax free and some taxable. The rates of interest are allowed to be fixed at varying levels.

The corporate sector has been issuing Non-Convertible Debentures (NCD) or Bonds (NCB). These are to be rated, if they are issued to the public and the coupon rates fixed on them vary with this rating. The details of coupon rates, face value, interest payment dates, redemption dates, current yields and Yields to Maturity (YTM) vary depending on the issuer, instrument and conditions in the market.

Special Features of Bonds

(1) They are fixed income earners with a coupon rate or without a coupon rate, as in the case of Discount Bonds or Premium Notes, giving a fixed premium at the end of maturity.

(2) Their prices move inversely with yields. Thus, if the issue price (face value) is ₹ 100 with a fixed coupon rate of 14%, then the bond may be quoting in the market at a discount say ₹ 90 if the expected market rate is higher say 16%, depending on the market perception of its risk and return in the market for similar risks.

(3) The longer is the maturity period of the Bond, the greater is the risk and larger is the percentage change in its price, relative to interest rate changes.

(4) The risks involved in Bonds to the investor are the following:

(a) *Purchasing Power Risk* with rising inflation rates, the bond redemption price being fixed, at the end of maturity of say 10 to 12 years, the real value of the redemption price will be completely wiped out by an inflation rate 10%. The only way to protect from inflation is to have accounting for real rates or yields for calculating the present bond price or to have yields, which will give risk free return plus inflation adjusted return for the risk premium. Thus, if risk free return is 6% (bank rate in the India) plus the risk premium which may be around 8-10% the total yields may vary from 14-16%, in nominal terms. Slightly higher is the rate that the equityholders of good blue chips would aim at, which will of course include dividends and capital appreciation.

(b) *Default Risk* is another risk, related to the company or agency, issuing the bonds. This is the risk of non-payment or delayed payments of interest and redemption value. For managing the default risk, the investor has to use the techniques of analysis of the financial statements of the company (including the past ratios of debt to equity, finance charge, relative gross profits, debt leverage ratios, and current liquidity ratios). The investor has to refer to the rating given to the company by a reputed credit rating agency like CRISIL, or ICRA. Now, it is compulsory for companies issuing non-convertible debentures or bonds, with or without convertibility within 18 months, to get the credit rating for these issues, of NCDs, in particular.

(c) *Interest Rate Changes:* If the bond has a coupon price, the risk of change in interest rates is high, the higher the maturity period, and lower the coupon rate. The volatility of bond price increases in response to interest rate changes, if the maturity is longer than when it is shorter, and if the coupon rate is lower and the present level of bond yields is low.

INTEREST RATE STRUCTURE

These theories of interest rates are discussed in another chapter. The required rate of return on a bond depends on the time preference for consumption, measured by risk free return, expected rate of inflation and risk associated with investment. Thus, the required rate of return

$$\gamma = \begin{pmatrix}\text{risk free}\\\text{real rate}\end{pmatrix} + \begin{pmatrix}\text{expected}\\\text{inflation}\end{pmatrix} + \begin{pmatrix}\text{risk}\\\text{premium}\end{pmatrix}$$

If the interest rates fall relative to coupon rate then, the bond price rises and the company may even call for repayment of high rate bonds with a view to issue low interest bonds. If the interest rates rise relative to coupon rate then bond price falls.

The theories that explain interest rates are many and the major ones are set out below:

1. Expectation Theory: This explains why the future level of interest rate depends on the average expectation of what future spot rate should be. The implicit forward rates reflect the market's consensus of expected future spot rates.

2. Availability of Funds: (Loanable Funds Theory): The supply of funds for lending will determine the interest rates, which will lead to changes in bond prices. Demand and supply pressures are expected to decide the interest rates

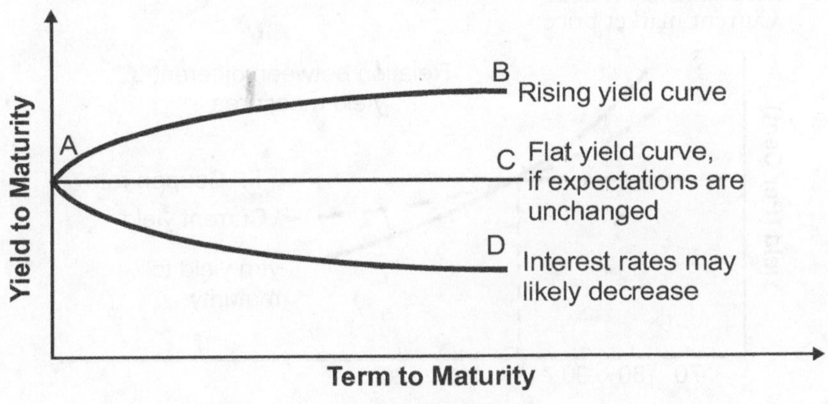

Fig. 13.1

on funds, and the supply is dependent on the money supply creation and Government fiscal deficits. The expectation of interest rates as well as the present rates depend on the business activity, prices, employment, inflation, money supply, fiscal factors and a host of other factors. Fig. 13.1 presents the yield curves for different types of expectation of interest rates. If expectations of future short-term rates are upward, the AB curve depicts the rising yield curve. If expectations of future short-term rate are downward, AD curve depicts the falling yield curve.

PROPERTIES OF BONDS AND BOND VALUE

In India, bonds have a maturity period and companies, semi-Government and Government bodies are not issuing irredeemable bonds. They are redeemable in 5 to 9 years in respect of bonds and 12 years for preference shares.

The properties of bonds can be described through the following graph. The price and yield relationship is revealed in the curve below AB which is convex to the origin. 'X' axis measures the yield and 'Y' axis the price of Bond. The relationship of yields to price and to maturity periods can be set out in the following axioms:

1. Yields will decline with rise in prices and *vice versa*.

2. If required rate of return is the same as the coupon rate, bond price is the par value.

3. If required return is lower than the coupon rate, bond price is higher than face value and reverse is true.

4. Discount or premium on face value will fall as the bond approaches maturity.

5. Interest Rate Elasticity – Sensitivity of bond price changes to a given change in interest rates will be high, if the bond is of longer maturity, and the coupon rate is lower.

6. As the YTM increases, the percentage change in price increases at a diminishing rate. The capital gains/losses on bonds will emerge on account of changes in price due to interest rate changes.

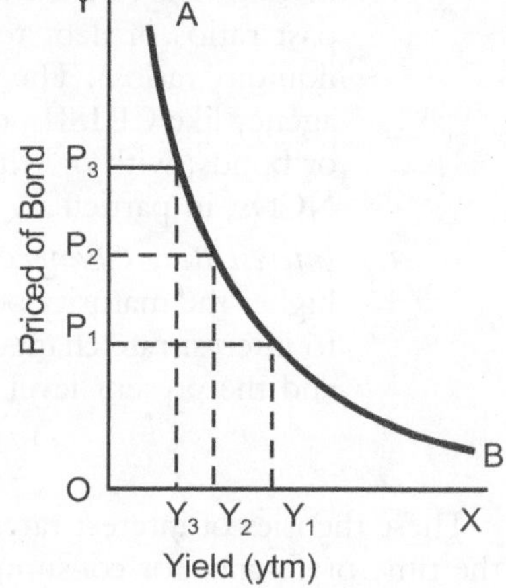

Fig. 13.2

Measures of Bond Returns

Yield is the measure of return on a bond. There are many variants in this measure:

(1) *Coupon Rate:* It is the nominal rate fixed and printed on bond certificate. It is the rate of interest fixed as say, 10% on a bond of ₹ 100, as face value.

(2) *Holding Period Yield or one Period Rate of Return:* For one period of holding, the return will depend on the coupon rate due or accrued plus or minus the capital gains or losses. The same can be presented in a formula.

$$\gamma i = \frac{\text{Capital gains or loss + coupon rate}}{\text{Purchase price of bond}}$$

(3) *Current Yield:* This will be the same as current return on any investment, if you purchase the bond at the face value of ₹ 100. But if you purchase it for any other price in the secondary market, then the

$$\text{Current yield} = \frac{\text{Coupon interest rate}}{\text{Current market price}}$$

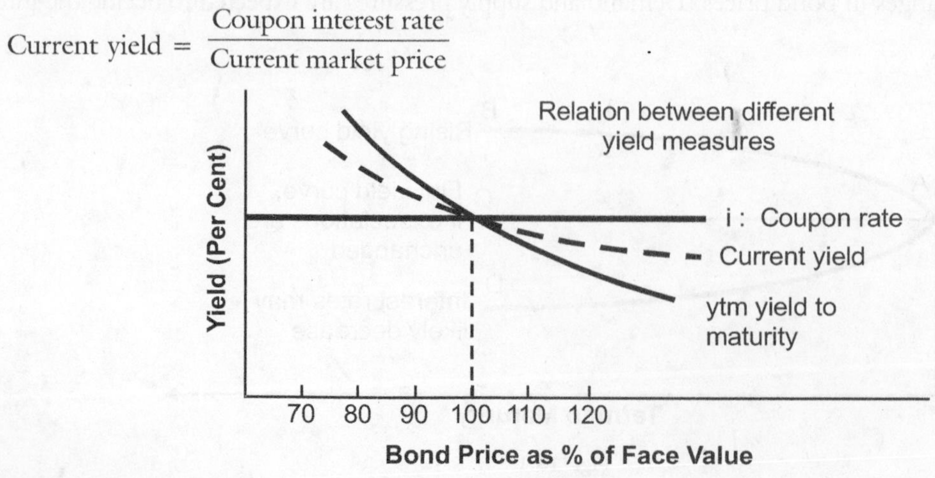

Fig. 13.3

one ₹ 100 bond is purchased for ₹ 90, which is the market price. The bond carries a coupon rate of 10%.

The current yield is $\frac{10}{90} \times 100 = 11.1\%$.

(4) *Yield to Maturity:* It is the discount rate that equates the present value of a bond's cash flows to the bond's current market price. It is the single rate with interest compounded at the specified intervals (six months) and if paid on the amount invested, would enable the investor to obtain all payments made on a security, in question.

Calculation of Yield to Maturity (YTM)

YTM is the rate of return at which NPV of a bond is equal to zero (use the AYTM method).

Par Value or Face Value = 100 (coupon rate 14%)

Current Market Price = ₹ 95 (paid annually)

YTM = Term to Maturity = 6 years; Maturity value = 105

*₹ 95 = 14 × PVIFA (Ytm, 6 years) + 105 × PVIF (Ytm, 6 years)

Assume ytm = 17%; Calculate the approximate rate. [Take values from Tables for (PVIFA) and (PVIF)]

$P_o = 14 \times 3.589 + 105 \times 0.390 =$ ₹ 91.20

Assume ytm = 15%

$P_o = 14 \times 3.784 + 105 \times 0.432 =$ ₹ 98.34

Using Linear Interpolator = $\text{Ytm} = 15 + 2\left(\frac{98.34 - 95}{98.34 - 91.20}\right)$

$= 15 + 2\left(\frac{3.34}{7.14}\right)$

$= 15.93\%$

$\text{Ytm} = 17 - 2\left(\frac{95 - 91.20}{98.34 - 91.20}\right)$

$= 17 - 2\left(\frac{3.80}{7.14}\right) = 15.94\%$

Present Market Price is ₹ 95; with ytm estimated at 17%, 98.34 and estimated at 15%, 91.20 by Interpolation, ytm works out to 15.94%.

Valuation of Bonds

The value of a Bond is simply the present value of the security's future cash flows. The buy and sell decisions depend on the estimated value of the bond as also other features of the bond. But basically, market price and expected yields are the major determinants of the bond value.

The static present value model is illustrated in the para below. This indicates the intrinsic economic value of the market asset, namely, the bond or and fixed income security.

The present value of all income flows in future during its life of maturity is called the intrinsic worth of the bond. Thus, the Present Bond Value

is expressed = $\left[\sum_{T=1}^{T} \frac{\text{income}}{(1+K)^t}\right]$

where, K is the appropriate market discount rate.

Note: These concepts are referred to in our earlier chapter.

* As the bond is below the face value at ₹ 95, ytm should be above 14%, assume 15% or 17%. See Tables at the end of the chapter for values of PVIFA and PVIF.

More specifically the present value of a bond can be set out in the following formula as a continuous model:

$$\text{Present value} = \frac{\text{Coupon 1}}{(1 + \text{interest rate})^1} + \frac{\text{Coupon 2}}{(1+ \text{interest rate})^2}$$

$$+ \frac{\text{Coupon 3}}{(1 + \text{interest rate})^3} \ldots\ldots\ldots\ldots \frac{\text{Coupon T + Face Value}}{(1 + \text{interest rate})^T}$$

Expressed Symobolically,

$$P_o = \frac{K_1}{(1 + r)^1} + \frac{K_2}{(1 + r)^2} + \frac{K_3}{(1 + r)^3} + \ldots\ldots\ldots \ldots\ldots \frac{K_T + P_T}{(1+r)^T}$$

Where, P_o = Present value and P_T is the maturity value and T is the maturity period.

K_{1toT} are coupon rates of interest paid, semi-annually or annually, by the bond issuer, r is the required rate of return, or discount rate, or yield to maturity. The investor is free to choose any of the rates of interest, referred to above and that may also depend on his expectations of the future yields. This element of subjectivity or the analyst's perception of the future rates may be the cause of the different valuations of the same bond.

Solved Problems

(1) What is the present value of a Bond with (Fv) Face value ₹ 1,000, coupon rate 8% and maturity period of 3 years and YTM = 10%

$$\text{Present value (Pv)} = \frac{\text{Coupon}_1}{(1+\text{ytm})^1} \ldots\ldots + \frac{\text{Coupon}_r + \text{Fv}}{(1+\text{ytm})^T}$$

$$\text{Pv} = \frac{80}{(1+0.10)^1} + \frac{80}{(1+0.10)^2} + \frac{80+1000}{(1+0.10)^3}$$

$$= \frac{80}{1.10} + \frac{80}{1.21} + \frac{1080}{1.331}$$

$$= 72.72 + 66.12 + 811.42 = 950.26$$

Pv = ₹ 950.26

(2) Determine the price of ZCB with a face value of ₹ 1,000, YTM of 16% and maturity period of 10 years.

$$\text{Price} = \frac{\text{Face value}}{(1+\text{YTM})^T} = \frac{1,000}{(1+0.16)^{10}} = \frac{1,000}{4.411}$$

= 226.68 (using the calculator)

The present price of ZCB is ₹ 226.68

(3) Given Face Value of ₹ 1000, YTM = 6%, and Coupon rate 3.5%, what is its present value if its maturity period in 10 years. Interest paid annually, cash flow is ₹ 35 per year.

$$\text{Present value Pv} \sum_{t=1}^{10} \frac{35}{(1+0.06)^{10}} + \frac{1,000}{(1+0.06)^{10}}$$

$$P_V = \sum_{t=1}^{10} \frac{35}{(1+0.06)^{10}} + \frac{1,000}{(1+0.06)^{10}}$$

= ₹ 816 (using the calculator)

The present value of the bond is ₹ 816

ACCRUED INTEREST

If the bond is purchased in between the semi-annual interest payment dates, the seller will receive the accrued interest from the buyer for the period he was holding since the last interest payment. Interest at the coupon rate for the number of days he held is calculated in the following formula:

$$\text{Accrued interest} = \frac{\text{Days since last interest payment}}{\text{Days between the last and next coupon payment}} \times \frac{\text{Interest amount}}{\text{Semi-Annual}}$$

for example, interest at coupon rate is 10% on ₹ 1,000 — payable on March 31 and September 30 — ₹ 50 each time; if the seller sold the bond on June 30,

then Accrued interest is $\frac{90}{180} \times 50 = ₹\ 25$

The bond price will be adjusted for the accrued interest as the buyer, the coupon holder is entitled to the interest due on the above dates.

Calculation of Accrued Interest and Value

1. Calculate the bond value using normal bond valuation model as of the next coupon date.
2. Add the coupon payment received on the next coupon payment date.
3. Discount this sum back to current date.
4. From this subtract the accrued interest.

To give an example, let us take these data:

Par value of the bond = ₹ 100

Coupon rate = 14%; half-yearly 7%

Coupon payment is half-yearly (30/6 and 31/12)

Maturity date is 31-12-1999

Maturity value = ₹ 105

Computation of bond value on 21-3-1995, assuming a ytm of 18% p.a. is as follows: (9% for half-year)

Step. 1: The value of bond on 30/6/1995 will be

= 7 × PVIFA (9%, 9) + 105 [PVIF(9%, 9)]

= 7 × 5.996 + 105 × 0.460 = ₹ 90.27

Step. 2: Add the next coupon payment, i.e., 30/6/95

₹ 90.27 + 7.00 = ₹ 97.27

Step 3: Discount this to current date (Assume half year as 180 days)

∴ the value on 21/3/95 = $97.27/(1.09)^{100/180}$ = ₹ 92.72

Step 4: Subtract the interest for 80 days (from 1-1-95 to 21-3-95),[@] i.e., an amount of ₹ 7 × 80/180 = ₹ 3.11

Hence, ex-interest value on 21/3/95

= ₹ 92.72 – 3.11 = ₹ 89.61.

In continuous models, the discount factor used is the ytm (yield to maturity) and it is used to calculate the reinvestment of coupon interest amounts. This type of model is useful only for academic interest, as in reality, the bondholder normally invests and disinvests many times before the maturity period, to take advantage of higher return, capital gains or for adjustment of duration. The immunisation process also involves frequent changes in the bonds held in a portfolio with a view to insulate the portfolio from the risks of interest rate changes and take advantage of higher reinvestment rates.

@ For simplicity, these dates are chosen in the example.

But the continuous model is useful for calculating the intrinsic value of the bond, in terms of the required rate of return. If the required rate is the same as the coupon rate, then the present value is the same as face value. There are *Bond Tables* which give the ytm for any given price and maturity. As referred to earlier, the ytm for a bond is the discount rate which equates the present value of all net cash flows to the cost of the investment.

If riskless bonds are to be valued then the discount factor, to be used is the risk free return, namely, the bank rate of 6% or Government bond yield of 7%.

DISCRETE MODELS

Bond valuation in the above discussion is based on certain assumptions:

(1) The bond is held until maturity rather than selling it at a price different from the face value before its maturity expires.

(2) All cash flows, received from coupon payments are reinvested at the same yield to maturity (ytm), promised.

(3) The coupon payments are made regularly and the principal in full at the scheduled times.

If any of the above assumptions do not hold good, then the valuation model given above becomes inapplicable. Under the conditions of limited holding periods or trading in bonds under portfolio management, the valuation of a bond has to be discrete and relevant to the current market interest rates or expected returns of the investor. In such cases, the required rate of return or the market rate for the same maturity, at the present time will be taken into account in calculating the value of bond.

Then the formula is

$P_o = \sum_{T=1}^{T} \frac{ct}{(1+k)t}$ where P_o is the present value, ct are the cash flows for the holding period of say, 1 to 3 years (t) and k is the required rate of return for reinvestment based on the present market/interest rate structure. This price will be different from the face value and varies with the values given to 'k' and 't.'

BOND PRICE THEOREMS

BP Theorem 1: Bond Face Value may be different from the Bond price in the market, if the coupon rate on bond is different from market rate.

BP Theorem 2: Bond market price fluctuations depend on the interest elasticity of the Bond price, duration, term to maturity and other bond characteristics such as callability, tax benefits, creation of Debenture Redemption Fund, security or collateral provided and a number of other factors.

BP Theorem 3: Call and put options for debentures which are convertible after 36 months, is compulsory for them as per SEBI guidelines. If the Debenture is convertible within 18 months, it is as good as equity for purposes of debt-equity ratio. This was dropped in March 1998.

BP Theorem 4: Bonds issued to the public should be compulsorily credit rated and interest rates are free to be fixed, as per market conditions and credit rating of the company, except when they are issued by public financial institutions or Government organisations.

BP Theorem 5: The percentage price change on a bond price increases at a diminishing rate as the maturity term is larger.

BP Theorem 6: The higher the coupon rate on a bond the smaller is the percentage price change for any given change in yields.

BP Theorem 7: Bond price in the market is relative to the coupon rate, and its maturity period. Bonds of longer maturity involve larger capital losses than those of short-term maturities, if the bond is sold.

BP Theorem 8: Bond prices fluctuate more widely in times of freely fluctuating interest rates and quick changes in interest rate policy.

MALKIEL BOND THEOREMS

Many Theorems were derived by B. G. Malkiel from his study "Expectations, Bond Prices and the Term Structure of Interest Rates." Quarterly Journal of Economics, May 1962. These theorems are summarised below:

Theorem 1: Bond Prices (or the present value of anything) move inversely to the yield to maturity (that is, the discount rate used).

Theorem 2: For any given difference between the coupon rate of interest and the yield to maturity of a bond, the associated price change will be greater, the longer the time, bond has to maturity.

Theorem 3: The percentage price changes described in Theorem 2, increases at a diminishing rate as term to maturity increases.

Theorem 4: For any given maturity, a decrease in yields, causes a capital gain which is larger than the capital loss resulting from an equal increase in yields.

Theorem 5: The higher the coupon rate on a bond, the smaller is the percentage change of price for any given change in yields (except for one year and perpetual bonds).

Risk Premium on Bonds

Risk premium is higher for two economic reasons: The unemployment and fear of job loss and risk aversion are more in recession. So risk premiums are higher during recessions of the business cycle. Secondly, corporations which issue bonds may be experiencing reduced sales and lower profits and hence their bonds are more risky and this requires more premium.

The non-cyclical factors, which influence risk premiums may be set out here.

Fears of future inflation, domestic political factors, fears of war or riots, foreign political factors and uncertain government policies.

YIELD CURVES — TERM STRUCTURE

The term structure of interest rates is the one major factor influencing the yields. For a given bond issuer, the structure of yields for bonds with different terms to maturity (but no other differences) is called the term structure of interest rates. *Ceteris paribus,* the term to maturity of a bond will affect its yield.

The market interest rate of the 'i' th bond at the 't' th time period is affected by varying the bond issue term to maturity.

(Market interest rate for 'i' at 't') = (real rate of return) + (Risk premium for 'i' at 't') + (Expected rate of inflation at 't')

+ (Term structure of interest rate for 'i' at 't')

The term structure of interest rates is also called the yield curve and is defined as the relationship of yields to maturities of bonds.

The following graph of yield curve can be given as an example:

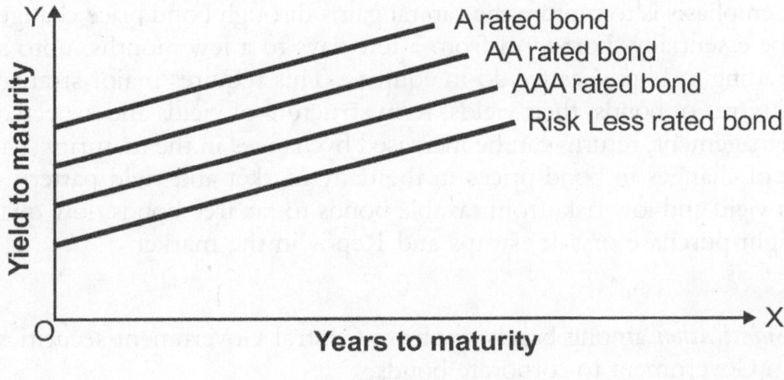

Fig. 13.4

The above Figure shows that higher the risk the higher is the return. The longer is maturity, the higher is the return.

TYPES OF BOND MANAGEMENT

Investors in bonds may adopt either the passive bond management strategy or active bond management strategy; both have their own advantages and disadvantages.

Under passive management, one can have Buy and Hold strategy or Bond Ladder strategy. These are dealt with here separately.

1. Buy and Hold Strategy: The investor ignores the expectations of future interest rate changes but selects bonds for given income with minimum risk and default free. These investors desire a fixed income and are a category by themselves, examples of which can be found among banks, P.F.s, insurance companies, retired persons and even Pension Funds in India. By holding the securities to maturity, but reinvesting income at prevailing market rates, in similar securities, the portfolio manager maximises his income. Income Funds and Index tied funds basically follow this strategy to provide diversification, lower costs and maximise income with the least research base and costs.

2. Bond Ladder Strategy: The investor under this strategy buys some bonds every year with a given amount, with a view to hold different maturities, say one to ten years; the laddering means that bonds of each group of maturity are rungs of the investment maturity ladder in which investments are made in a well diversified manner. By such regular investments market fluctuation in prices and yields can be evened out and a diversified portfolio is secured. If interest rates rise, he will invest in the higher yield bonds from the amount invested in that year. Similarly, if interest rates fall, he will have already some bonds of long maturity to provide capital appreciation.

In the Indian context, public financial institutions PSUs and government and semi-government bodies are issuing bonds with different features and maturities. The bond investor has to diversify into these securities under both Buy and Hold strategy and Bond Laddering strategy. Under the former, it is a random purchase of all default free bonds which by law of averages may contain all maturities and incorporate bonds of all features. Here, no expectations nor active buying and selling are involved. In the case of laddering strategy also, a fixed amount is used to purchase bonds of fixed income, every year, involving deliberately all maturities and diversification into all types of bonds available in the market, which are default free and with minimum of risk. In the ladder strategy, there is less randomness and some discretion, but is also automatic like the former.

3. Semi-Active Management Strategy: If the investor has time horizon, with in which investment has to fructify to give an amount of wealth to meet his obligations or liabilities, he has to follow at least a semi-active management strategy. This is necessary because in the actual market, interest rates do change frequently and reinvestment of income from interest will yield lower or higher amounts than expected and capital gain or loss will also arise due to interest rate changes. Interest Risk has two components namely price risk and coupon reinvestment risk, which move in opposite directions. If interest rates decline for example, the market price of bond will go up at the time of repayment, but the interim cash flows through coupon interest receipts will be reinvested at lower rates, which will lead to lower wealth for the investor. The reverse is what happens if interest rates rise in the interim period before maturity. Thus, investor may or may not achieve the desired wealth position at the end period due to these opposing forces. Elimination of these effects, on the Bond portfolio is called Immunisation discussed later in the chapter.

4. Active Bond Management: Increased volatility of interest rates and disappointing returns in the equity market and growing bond market, relative to equity market forced managers of portfolios to involve themselves in active Bond Management. If the major emphasis is to capture the capital gains through bond price changes, as in the case of equity, then the portfolio has to be essentially short-term from a few days to a few months, upto say one year. Active bond management is through trading in bonds, as we do in equities. This requires major strategy decisions of the type of bonds, maturity and other terms of bonds, their yields, term structure of yields and expected shape of the yield curve, etc. As a result of active management, returns can be increased bychanges in the maturity structure, coupons, and asset quality, to take advantage of changes in bond prices in the daily market and yield pattern. Shifting of bonds of low yield and high risk to high yield and low risk, from taxable bonds to tax free bonds, low quality to high quality bonds etc., is done though outright purchase or sale, swaps and Repos in the market.

Active Strategies

(*a*) *Sector and Asset Substitution* among bonds say from Central Government securities to higher yielding semi-government bonds or from Government to corporate bonds.

(*b*) *Maturity Adjustments* by shortening the maturities when interest rates are expected to rise and lengthening the maturities when interest rates are expected to fall.

(*c*) *Quality Diversification* into various grades of risk, through expected or actual ratings of bonds by Rating agencies.

(*d*) *Coupon Adjustments or Yield Substitutions:* Bonds of lower coupons are preferred when speculative capital gains or losses are aimed at. High coupon bonds are preferred to reduce the price fluctuations for higher incomes, and if expectations are for rising interest rates, the investor may prefer long-term bonds with high coupon rates. High coupon bonds, quoting above their redemption price are called cushion bonds, as they provide a cushion against sharp price declines in times of rising interest rates. To give an example in the Indian context, the Central Government resorted to short maturity bonds of three to ten years during 1994-96, with coupon rates ranging from 12½ to 14%, because of the uncertainly of future market rates, and with the intention of lowering the maturity structure of central government debt, which is heavily weighted in favour of long maturities of above 10 years.

YIELD CURVE STUDY

A study of the yield curve on a daily basis is needed for quick decisions for making active Bond Management Strategy effective. Swaps, switches, and active trading in bonds and their futures are necessary to take full advantage of yield differentials, as they emerge. Besides capital gains can be booked and capital losses can be reduced or avoided, if the investor's expectation come out to be correct.

Yield curve expectations and changes in the interest rates, short, medium and long-term play an important role in the active debt management. Mapping of expected returns, based on the expected volatility, maturity and coupon changes and likely changes in interest rates, is also necessary.

Expected return = coupon income (C) + Amortisation of premium/discount (A) + Replacement or roll of low yielding by high yielding bonds (R)

$= C + A + R$

As $C + A =$ yield,

Yield plus replacement benefit (R) will give the return expected.

Objectives of Raising Incremental Return

The component of 'R' is the one involved in active debt management. If the anticipation of yields can be made correctly or changes in interest rates are properly anticipated, R component can be positive and maximum. 'R' is the incremental return.

The strategies or tactics to be adopted for maximising the 'R' component are swapping or bond substitution and switches from one type of bond to another and Repo sale with buy back arrangements for adjusting the maturities or yields. Incremental return, reflected through 'R' component involved in active bond management can be maximised by trading in secondary market, participation in the primary market and capturing all yield advantages as they emerge in these markets. Repos and Switches are undertaken in India in government bonds by banks and FIs to adjust the liquidity or CRR requirements or for securing required maturities of bonds in the portfolio. These can be done with the RBI to a limited extent or with STCI or DFHI or with other banks and financial institutions in the market.

Need for Tax Planning

Some switches are undertaken to book losses or gains for income tax purposes not having any bearing on yield or maturity considerations. Such deals are called Washed sales, undertaken by banks and financial institutions. All these ingredients of active bond management involve expertise and large research base and it is necessary keep in touch with the market by actively trading and interacting with other market participants. Expectations of yields and interest rates are to be effectively correct to secure better results.

Tax Benefits vary from year to year in respect of the Bonds trading as much as in the portfolio management. Bond market as much as trading strategies in this market depend among others on the tax policy. The fiscal policy is tuned to promote the inflow of foreign funds for equity investment and for foreign commercial borrowings by corporates but not much for debt trading and investment in debt market in India. In particular, the corporate debt market is still in infant stage. Only in 2006-07 did the Govt. allow the raising of the limits for FII investment in debt market to $1.5 billion. Earlier they allowed their trading in the Gilt-edged market up to a limit which was raised from time to time.

The constraints to debt market trading are the need for credit rating of debt instrument, payment of the stamp duty and lack of any incentives like capital appreciation and general lowering of interest rates. Gilt edged market is being developed by the RBI through special efforts of STCI and primary Dealers, demat form of trading and role of NSE and OTCEI dealers etc. The secondary market trading in the Govt. securities has increased in outright deals and

Repo transactions and on the NSE and through the SGL account with the RBI. The same cannot be said of Private Corporate debt market.

Sequence of Steps for Bond Issues[@]

Decide on the Rate of Issue or/and Maturity: T.B. Rate, Government bond rate, LIBOR related rates, floating rate or fixed rate, frequency of interest rate payments, quarterly, half yearly, etc. and the amount of issue

Repayment Schedule: Bullet repayment, instalment schedules, bonds of perpetuity not issued, in India — short-term notes, medium-term note issuance facilities, long-term bonds — maturity schedule.

Steps in Management of the Issue

(a) Privately placed issues — Banks and investment and securities firms.

(b) Publicly placed issues — Registration with SEC. (USA) or Government or SEBI in India.

General Benchmarks in Making Issues

1. Appointment of group managers or lead managers etc.
2. Appointment of underwriters.
3. Entering into written agreements with managers and underwriters.
4. Completion of regulatory requirements, with SEBI, stock exchange, etc.
5. Pricing of the issue.
6. The actual issue.
7. A tombstone, i.e., an advertisement recording the issue of the bonds.
8. Complying with the requirements of the Government, Central Bank, etc.

Valuation of Bonds

Bond YTM varies inversely with the price. The price depends on a number of factors like:

Term to maturity

Coupon rate

Rate of return required by the investor

Credit rating of the bond

Call features of the bond, callable or not

Secured or unsecured

Part or full conversion or incentives like warrants, etc.

YTM assumes a reinvestment rate of return on intermediate cash flows equivalent to YTM. There is no default risk in respect of payment of coupon rate and the maturity value and its repayment. The bond should be held until maturity, for calculation of YTM.

Risks in Bond Holding (as it is Fixed Income Security)

Purchasing power risk: (Inflation or loss in Value of money) (Expected inflation Uncertainty of inflation rate in the years ahead)	Interest rate risk (Changes in rate of interest or required rate of return will change the bond value)	Reinvestment rate risk (When interest rate changes, the rate of reinvestment also changes which leads to Bond value changes)

Price Risk

(1) The lower the coupon rate the greater is price volatility.

(2) The higher the yield level from which fluctuation in yields starts the greater will be the price volatility.

@ The markets which are free for capital market borrowings are: U.S.A., U.K., Germany and Japan. Controls are most in Japan and less in U.K. and U.S.A. Borrowing is most in U.S. Dollars (30-38%) followed by Yen (11%) and D.M. (7-8%). Gross bond issues: $298 billion in 1991, as an example. Controls in Euro Markets are less than in domestic markets. No controls on interest rates, no reserve requirements and no Government interference in the operations, completely free market and competition prevails.

(3) The longer the maturity the greater will be the bond price volatility. As the maturity lengthens, volatility increases but at a diminishing rate.

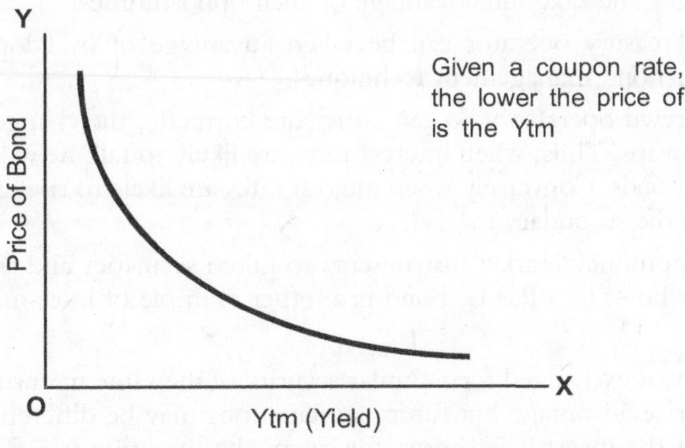

Fig. 13.5

Graph on convex shape of the price and yield relationship.

RIDING THE YIELD CURVE

Any Treasury operator in a bank or FI has to pay attention to the yield curve in order to operate in the gilt edged market, effectively. The yield curve at any point of time is drawn, based on the relationship of yields to the maturity periods. The yields may be as reflected in the primary market (new issues of gilts) or in the secondary market. The yields may be on short-term Treasury bills or medium and long dated Government securities. Towards the close of 1996, the yields, based on the primary market were as follows. Subsequently yields fell during 1998 to 2002.

Table

		March 1996		*March 1999*	*March 2002*	*March 05*	*March 06*	*March 2009*	*March 12*	*March 15*
3 Months maturity @	Yield	8.5%	Yeild	7.80	7.91	5.61	6.64	4.77	5.98	7.5
6 " " @@	"	10.5%	"	9.88	8.42	–	6.91	4.86	8.66	8.6
9 " "	"	12.5%	"	10.07	9.40	–	–	–	–	–
1 year "	"	13.5%	"	10.65	9.90	5.77	7.01	5.25	8.40	8.8
5 to 10 years "	"	14.0	"	11.5 to 12.0	11.70	7.20	7.97	6.97	8.50	9.2

@ 14 day Treasury bill was introduced in June 1997.

@@ 182 day T.Bs were reintroduced in May 1999.

Both 14 day T.Bs and 182 day T.Bs were discontinued in May 2001.

The curve depicting that relationship is as follows:

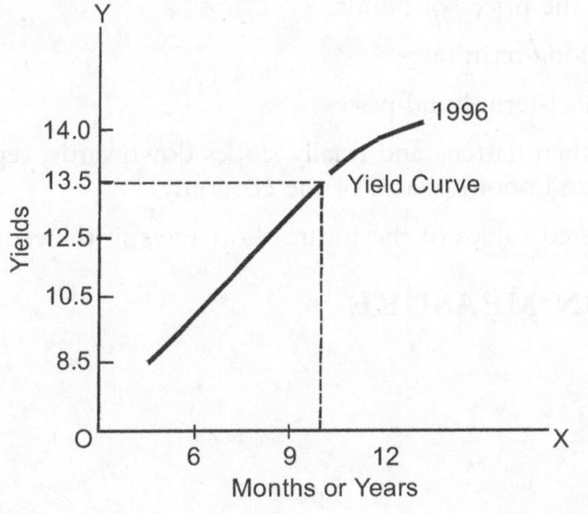

Fig. 13.6

Riding the yield curve means that the Treasury operator has to be vigilant on the emerging opportunity sets, open to him due to any changes in market demand/supply pressures, changes in interest rates, Government policy and announcements and credit policy changes and take full advantage of such opportunities.

The opportunities open to the Treasury operator can be taken advantage of by adoption of the following techniques of bond swaps, or any other bond management techniques.

(*a*) *Rate Anticipation Swaps:* A shrewd operator who can anticipate correctly, the changes in interest rates and yields, can enter into rate anticipation swaps. Thus, when interest rates are likely to fall, he will swap from long-term (or medium-term) bonds to short-term bonds. Conversely when interest rates are likely to rise, he will shift from short-term bonds to medium-term bonds, in the secondary market.

(*b*) *Inter Market Swaps:* Swap from money market instruments to gilted securities and *vice-versa* is an example. Similarly, swift from semi-Government bond to a P.S.U. bond is another example of inter-market swaps. This is to take advantage of price/yield changes.

(*c*) *Substitution Swaps:* One security, if exchanged for a similar security of the same maturity is called substitution swap. This is a perfect substitute for price advantage but future anticipations may be different for these two bonds. The one fitting with the preferences of the investor is chosen for swap; the intention is a future gain in yields.

(*d*) *Pure Yield Pick up Swaps:* This is swapping of a low yield bond to a high yield bond, if such differences in yields are noticed in the secondary market due to changes in demand and supply conditions.

In the above context, price change is split up into time effect + yield change effect; correct anticipation of yield change is critical for quick operations of advantage.

Some of Bond Value Theorems are as follows:

(1) Interest rate sensitivity is high for bonds of long maturities.

(2) Interest rate sensitivity is high for bonds of low coupon rates.

(3) The percentage change in price increases at a diminishing rate as the YTM is increased.

(4) Given the YTM, the capital gains due to fall in yield are higher than the capital losses resulting from an increase in yield.

(5) Required rate of return is the same as the coupon rate, if the value of bond is at par.

(6) If the required rate of return is higher than the coupon rate, the value of the bond is lower than the par value and *vice versa.*

(7) If the bonds are callable their values are generally lower and they depend on the call terms.

(8) As the bond approaches the maturity, the premium or discount will fall and finally disappear on the date of maturity.

(9) Some bonds have both call and put options and their pricing depend on the terms of the call and put.

(10) Term structure influences the yield curve and the prices of bonds.

(11) Short-term rates fluctuate more violently than long-term rates.

(12) Long-term bond prices fluctuate more than short-term bond prices.

(13) The normal yield curve first slopes upwards, then flattens and finally slopes downwards, representing the interest rate expectations, recession, recovery and boom phases of the economy.

(14) Long-term interest rates are the average expected values of the future short rates in the economy.

DURATION MEASURE

Risks to be Covered

1. Term to maturity.
2. Weighted average maturity.
3. Weighted average cash flow is given by.

$$= \sum_{t=1}^{n} \frac{Cft \times t}{TCF}$$ Where TCF is total cash flow at present value

Duration is measured by the weighted average maturity of a bond's cash flows and present values of these flows are used as weights. Duration is a measure of average time prior to receipt of payment.

$$\text{Duration (years)} = \sum_{t=1}^{n} \frac{PV(cft) \times t}{TPV}$$

Where Cf is Cash Flows, PV is Present Value, 't' is the time period or the number of years from the present, TPV is maturity value, or the total present value of the bond or its price.

$$\text{Duration is} = f\left(\frac{1}{ytm}\right)$$

The details on duration are referred to below.

DURATION AND IMMUNISATION

What is Duration?

Duration is a concept, which means the weighted average measure of time period of bond's life. This is valuable in understanding how bond's prices change in response to interest rate changes. Bonds with the same duration respond similarly, *inter alia* to given changes in interest rates. If the bond has no coupon rate as in the case of zero coupon bonds, duration is equal to the maturity period, or P_o = PV (Ct) for only one cash flow.

The formula for a bond's duration (D) is as follows:

$$D = \sum \frac{pv(ct) \times t}{P_o}$$

Pv (ct) is the present value of cash flow to be received at time t, that is cash flow discounted by a discount factor of yield to maturity (ytm), Po denotes the current market price and 't' denotes the remaining life to maturity.

The above equation can be rewritten as

$$D = \frac{\sum_{t=1}^{T} pv(ct) \times t}{\sum_{t=1}^{T} pv(ct)}$$

To explain this verbally, the present value of each flow [pv(ct)] is expressed as a proportion of the market price (P_o). These proportions are then multiplied by the respective amount of term until the cash flows are received. Lastly, these figures are added, with the sum equal to the duration.

To give an example of calculation of duration the table below presents the data. (7% Bond of ₹ 1,000 Face value and 3 years to maturity).

Table

Calculation of Duration

Time Until Receipt of Cash Flow	*Amount of Cash Flow Interest or Interest Plus Principal*	*Present Value Factor at 7% of Re. 1*	*Present Value of Cash Flow = 2 × 3*	*Present Value of Cash Flow × Time*
(1)	*(2)*	*(3)*	*(4)*	*(5)*
1	70	0.9346	65.42	0.065
2	70	0.8734	61.14	0.122
3	1070	0.8163	873.44	2.620
			1000	2.807

To use the formula:

$$D\ \frac{1\left(\frac{70}{(1.07)}\right)+2\left(\frac{70}{(1.07)^2}\right)+3\left(\frac{1070}{(1.07)^3}\right)}{\frac{70}{(1.07)^1}+\frac{70}{(1.07)^2}+\frac{1070}{(1.07)^3}} = 2.81$$

Use of Duration as a Concept

This calculation of duration is necessary for a study of the effect of changes in interest rates on bond prices and yields. This concept is also useful to make proper investment decision on bonds. The technique of Bond Portfolio Management (called Immunisation) involves the use of Immunisation process. Prices and duration move in the same direction, and larger the coupon rate, the smaller is the duration. Duration declines as maturity approaches and duration for a perpetual bond is equal to $\frac{1+r}{r}$, where "r" is ytm. For coupon paying bonds, duration is less than the term to maturity. Limiting value of the duration is, $\frac{1+\text{ytm}}{\text{ytm}}$ and calculation of the duration helps in investment decision-making, revision of portfolio of bonds etc.

MACAULAY'S DURATION (MD)@

Macaulay's Duration is defined as the weighted average number of years, until the cash flows occur, where the relative present values of each cash payment are used as the weights. The formula for MD is as follows:

$$MD = \frac{\sum_{t=1}^{T} \frac{Ct}{(1+\text{ytm})^t} + \frac{Ft}{(1+\text{ytm})^T}}{V_o}$$

$$\begin{bmatrix}\text{Weighted}\\ \text{Average}\\ \text{Maturity}\end{bmatrix} = \begin{bmatrix}\text{Maturities of}\\ \text{various time}\\ \text{periods of}\\ \text{payment, t and T}\end{bmatrix} \times \begin{bmatrix}\text{Proportion of}\\ \text{Bond's value}\\ \text{accounted for}\\ \text{by the payments}\\ \text{in square brackers}\end{bmatrix}$$

To give an example, let the Face value F_T = ₹ 1,000

ytm = 6%, coupon rate C = 7.0%,

Annual coupon payments= C_t = 0.07 × 1,000 = 70 = ct

No. of years to Maturity = T = 3 years

Market price = P_o = 1,026.73

Premium over face value = 26.73 (1,026.73 – 1,000)

Market price or present value is calculated by the formula

$$V_o \text{ or } P_o = \sum_{1}^{T} \frac{Ct}{(1+\text{ytm})^t} \quad \text{[put the above values]}$$

@ Note the changes in the formulas for "D" and "MD".

Year, (Na) (1)	*Cash Flow (ct)* (2)	$\frac{1}{(ytm)^t}$ (3)	*4 = 2 × 3 Vo = Present Values of Cash Flows* (4)
1	70	$\frac{1}{(1.06)^1} = 0.943$	66.04
2	70	$\frac{1}{(1.06)^2} = 0.893$	62.30
3	1070	$\frac{1}{(1.06)^3} = 0.839$	898.39
			1,026.73 = Vo

[Calculation of MD]

Year (1)	*Present Value of Cash Flow Vo* (2)	*Present Value as Proportion of Vo,* (3)	*Columns 3 × 1 =* (4)
1	66.04	0.0643	0.0643
2	62.30	0.0607	0.1214
3	898.39	0.8750	2.6250
	1026.73	1.00	MD 2.8107

Duration (Example)

Ques: An investor wants to purchase a Bond with maturity 3 years, coupon 11% and par value ₹ 100

(*a*) If the investor requiring YTM 15% of equivalent risk and maturity, what is the price he should pay.

$$P = \frac{11}{1+0.15} + \frac{11}{(1+0.15)^2} + \frac{11}{(1+0.15)^3} = 90.86$$

(*b*) If the bond is selling at a price of ₹ 97.59 what is its YTM.

YTM is to be estimated by Trial and error method. Consider 12% as YTM Then

$$\frac{11}{(1+0.12)} + \frac{11}{(1+0.12)^2} + \frac{11}{(1+0.12)^3} = 97.59$$

Hence, YTM is 12%.

(*c*) What is the duration of this Bond, if the YTM is 12% and expected return is 10.06%.

Duration	*Value =*	*% age Value*	*Weighted Duration*
1 year	$9.82 = \frac{11}{1.12}$	10.06%	0.1006 = 1 × 1006
2 year	$8.77 = \frac{11}{(1.12)^2}$	8.99%	0.1798 = 2 × 0899
3 year	$79.01 = \frac{111}{(1.12)^3}$	80.95%	2.4285 = 3 × 8095
Total	97.60	100.00	2.7087

In the case of above bond of YTM of 12% and expected return 10.06%; the weighted duration of the portfolio is 2.70.

THEOREMS EMERGING FROM MD

These theorems describe the relationship of Bond's term to maturity and M.D.

M.D. Theorem 1: A bond's duration equals its term to maturity, only if it is zero coupon bond.

Theorem 2: The maturity of coupon bond of more than one year maturity has a duration less than its term to maturity.

Theorem 3: The duration of perpetual bonds which are not permitted in India is equal to $1.0 + \left(1.0 + \frac{1}{\text{ytm}}\right)$ irrespective of its coupon rate.

Theorem 4: The duration of a coupon bearing bond selling at a market price below its face value reaches a maximum before its maturity date reaches infinity and then recedes to the limit of $\left(1.0 + \frac{1}{\text{ytm}}\right)$.

Theorem 5: The duration of a coupon bearing bond selling at or above its face value increases monotonically with its term to maturity and approaches the quantity $1.0 + \left(1.0 + \frac{1}{\text{ytm}}\right)$ as its term to maturity approaches infinity.

Theorem 6: The duration of a coupon bearing bond selling below its par value reaches the maximum value when T reaches the value indicated in the following formula:

$$T = \frac{1.01}{\log(1.0 + \text{ytm})} + \frac{1.0 - \text{ytm}}{(\text{ytm} - i)} + \frac{\text{ytm} - 1}{i(1.0 + \text{ytm})T \log(1.0 + \text{ytm})}$$

Theorem 7: The duration of a coupon bearing bond, selling below par reaches its maximum at a maturity which is directly related to the bond's coupon rate and inversely related to the bond's yield to maturity.

Theorem 8: The longer a coupon paying bond term to maturity the greater is the difference between its terms to maturity and its duration.

Advantages of M.D.

The above Theorems reflect the advantages of MD over normal measure of duration or term to maturity. Duration can be compiled for a single bond as also for a basket of bonds or fixed interest bearing securities, included in a portfolio. A bond's years of duration are considered to be a better measure of the time structure of an investment cash flow than its years to maturity T, because the duration reflects the amount and timing of every cash flow rather than merely the length of time until the final payment occurs. Further, the MD is a measure of bond's interest rate risk.

Elasticity of interest rate to the bond's price is the ratio between the change of price of bond and the change in the ytm. Bond's Price elasticity to interest rate changes is given by the formula

$$I\,\Sigma_{ii} = \frac{\text{Percentage change in price for bond i in period t}}{\text{Percentage change in yield to maturity for bond i}}$$

The bond's interest rate risk and bond's price movements are explained separately.

The graph below shows the duration and term to maturity for premium and discount.

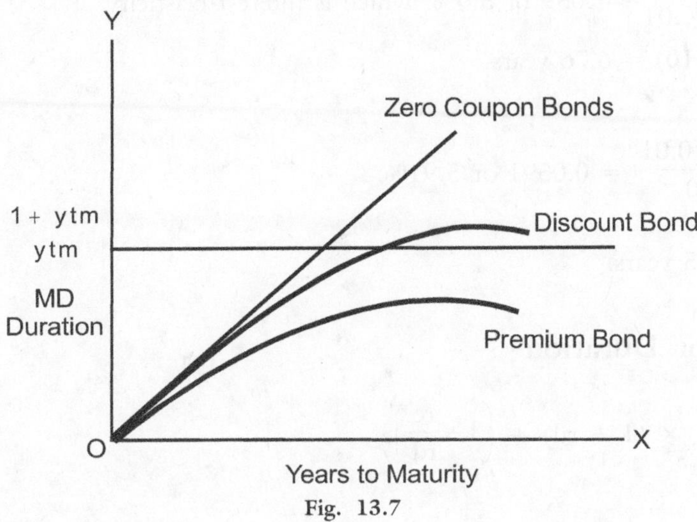

Fig. 13.7

Uses of Duration

(a) It can be used as a measure of the responsiveness of bond price to changes in market yields.

(b) It is used to immunise a bond from interest rate risk by setting the investment horizon equal to bond's duration.

Interest Rate Elasticity and Risk

$$IE_{it} = \frac{\Delta P_o}{P_o} / \frac{\Delta ytm}{ytm}$$ and it is Interest Rate Elasticity and always negative.

$$\frac{\Delta P_o}{P_o} = IE_{it} \times \frac{ytm}{\Delta ytm}$$ it is the interest rate risk.

Modified Duration (by Hicks)

$$Dmod = \frac{D}{1 + y/f}$$ where, D is Macaulay's Duration.

y is ytm in decimal points.

f is discounting periods per year.

% age price volatility using Dmod is:

$$\frac{\Delta P}{P} \times 100 = Dmod. \Delta Y$$

The following example will help understand the above formulas.

P_o = ₹ 100, C = 10%/p.a., r = 10%, n = 10 years.

For a change in r to 11%,

New P_o = 10 (PVIFA 11, 10) + 100 × (PVIF 11, 10)

P_o = 10 × (5.889) + 100 (0.352) = 58.9 + 35.2 = 94.1

Change in P_o = 100 – 94.1 = 5.9, and change in r = 11 – 10 = 1%

$$IE = \left(\frac{5.9}{100}\right) \times \left(\frac{.01}{.10}\right) = \frac{0.59}{100}$$ namely –.0059

$$\frac{\Delta P_o}{P_o} = (.0059) \times \frac{.10}{.01} = .059 \text{ or } 5.9\%, \text{ which is interest elasticity.}$$

$D = PVIFA_{10,10} \times (1 + 0.10) = 6.76$ years.

[6.145 × 1.10 = 6.76]

$$\text{Interest rate risk} = \frac{0.591 \times 0.01}{0.10} = 0.0591 \text{ or } 5.91\%.$$

$$\text{Dmod} = \frac{6.76}{1+0.10/1} = 6.15 \text{ years.}$$

Short Cut Formula for Duration

$$D = \frac{rc}{rd} \times PVIFA_{yd,n} \times (1 + rd) + \left(1 - \frac{rc}{rd}\right)^n$$

Where,

rc = Current yield (= coupon interest/bond price)

rd = YTM

n = Term to maturity

In case of a bond selling at par rc = rd the formula becomes

$D = PVIFA_{rd}\ n \times (1 + rd)$

$$D = \frac{i(1+r)\,PVIFA_{r,n} + (r-i)\,PVIF_{r,n}}{i + (r-i)\,PVIF_{r,n}}$$

Where,

i = Coupon rate

n = Term to maturity

r = ytm

(It should be noted that the short cut formula can be applied only in case of bonds redeemable at maturity. Duration of callable bonds and bonds redeemable in instalments should not be computed by this method).

IMMUNISATION

What is Immunisation?

A bondholder faces the interest rate risk and fluctuations in rates will lead to changes in bond returns. A bond which is of longer period faces larger fluctuations with a given change in interest rate than a short duration bond. Bond investor faces the interest rate risk between the time of investment and the future holding period. Interest rate risk is composed of two risks:

Price Risk and *Coupon Reinvestment Risk*: If interest rates rise in the meantime, the bond price will fall and there will be capital depreciation. Second risk is the coupon reinvestment risk, as the yield to maturity computation implicitly assumes that the coupon flows will be reinvested. Thus, if the interest income is reinvested at a higher rate, then the total end sum would be above that expected.

The above two effects are opposed to each other. While one increases the total bond return, the other decreases it, in the case of fall in interest rate. The reverse is true in the case of rise in interest rates. *The elimination of these risks is called bond immunisation.* If the realized return on investment in bonds is sure to be atleast as large as the appropriately computed yield to the time horizon, then the investment is immunised.

The maximisation is achieved by making the duration of the portfolio as equal to the desired holding period. Duration is the time period at which price risk and coupon reinvestment risk of a bond portfolio are of equal magnitude and opposite in direction.

Immunisation Process

What is Immunisation has been referred to earlier. It is a process by which the effects of changes in interest rates can be offset in a portfolio of Bonds. A change in interest rates has two effects: (1) Price effect, which is negative (as the interest rates rise, the bond prices fall) and (2) Reinvestment effect, which is positive (interest rates reinvested at higher rates lead to larger return). Immunisation attempts to offset the effects of the above on the bond portfolio — protecting the return from interest rate changes.

Immunisation Operations

It is accomplished by simply calculating the duration of the promised outflows and then investing in bonds which have identical duration. This duration of a portfolio of bonds is equal to the weighted average of the durations of individual bonds in the portfolio.

If the rate of interest rises from 9% to 11% capital loss occurs and this loss has to be made good by reinvesting, the Coupon income at higher rate of 11%. In order to earn the original target return of 9%; the duration has to be 6.79 as shown in the Table below.

Table 1 (9% Ten Year Bond)

Income Source	*Interest Rate at Time of Reinvestment*	*Holding Periods in Years* 1	3	6.79@@	10
Coupon Income	7%	90	270	611	900
Capital Gain/Loss	—	132	109	56	0
Interest on Interest		2	25	149	355
Total Return		224	404	816	1255
Total Yield		22%	12%	9%	8.5%
Coupon Income	9%	90	270	611	900
Capital Gain/Loss	—	—	—	—	—
Interest on Interest		2	32	205	495
Total Return		92	302	816	1395
Total Yield		9%	9%	9%	9%
Coupon Income	11%	90	270	611	900
Capital Gain/Loss		112	95	56	0
Interest on Interest		2	40	26	647
Total Return		20	215	816	1547
Total Yield		2%	6.7%	9%	9.8%

@@ Duration of 9% Bond purchased at par-10 years hence due is shown here as 6.79 years
Source: D.E. Fischer & R.J. Jordon:
Security Analysis & Portfolio Management (Chapter 11)
Bond of ₹ 1,000

To explain the items in the Table take the illustration of how the data of 3 years holding with 7% rate are arrived:

Coupon Income is 90 × 3 = 270

Viz., 90 is one year interest

Coupon income plus interest on interest

45 is half year interest
45 × 6.55 = 295 Where
6.55 is taken from Annuity Tables for the future value of annuity for 6 periods at a rate of 3.5% per period.

295 − 270 = 25 is interest on interest

Coupon Income = 270

Interest on interest = 25

Capital gain = Price of 9% Bond due in 7 years with a 7% market return 1109 (take from Bond Tables).

Capital gain = Market Value − Face Value

1109 – 1000 = 109

Total Return = 270 + 25 + 109 = 404

An example for effecting immunisation by matching the holding period with the duration period of a bond is given in Table 2. It is a case of holding period of 8 years, and present yield to maturity for 8 year bonds is 8%. The end period wealth required by investor is 1.8509 = $[(1.08)^8]$. If the amount required at the end of 8 years ₹ 18,500, and the present amount with them is ₹ 10,000, the immunised portfolio can be set up for 8 year period and assume a single change in interest rate (8 to 6%).

Table 2 (Maturity Strategy *vs.* Duration Strategy)

Year	*Maturity Strategy* Cash Flow	*Maturity Strategy* Reinvestment	*Accurate End Value*	*Duration Strategy* Cash Flow	*Duration Strategy* Reinvestment	*Accurate End Value*
1	80	.08	80	80	.08	80
2	80	.08	166.40	80	.08	166.40
3	80	.08	259.71	80	.08	259.71
4	80	.08	360.49	80	.08	360.49
5	80	.06	462.12	80	.06	462.12
6	80	.06	596.85	80	.06	596.85
7	80	.06	684.04	80	.06	684.04
8	1080	.06	1805.08	80	.06	1845.72

Source: Ibid.

Interest Rate fell from 8% to 6% at end of 4th year; 8% Ten year Bond, Face value ₹ 1,000 — can be sold at ₹ 1,040.64 at the end of 8 years. A ten year bond (8% 8 years) at the end of 8 years yields 1.851 from the Tables at the end of the chapter.

Expected Wealth Ratio: 1.8509

With the Duration strategy the target is achieved and uncertainty is removed for the given assumptions. Duration strategy can be used both actively and passively — actively when it is used to capitalise on interest rate change and passively to neutralise interest rate risk.

How Immunisation is Effected?[@]

Immunisation is a protection against interest rate changes and corresponding changes in yields. If yields rise, then the portfolio's losses due to selling the three year bond at a discount after two years will be exactly offset by the gains from reinvesting the maturing one year bonds along with the coupons on the three year bonds at a higher rate. If on the other hand, the yields fell, then the loss from reinvesting the maturing one year bonds and the first year coupons on three year bonds would be exactly offset by having to sell the three year bonds, after two years at a premium. The process tries to protect from the effects of interest rate changes on prices of bonds and due to reinvestment of coupons.

If immunisation is to be used, then the solution can be found by solving simultaneously a set of two equations, involving two unknowns.

$$W_1 + W_3 = 1$$

$$(W_1 \times 1) + (W_3 \times 2.78) = 2$$

Here we take a bond of 4 year maturity with a duration of 2.78 years as an example. W_1 and W_3 are the weights in which proportion the portfolio funds of ₹ 1,000 are to be invested in bonds with maturities of one and three years. The second equation states that the weighted averages of the bonds in the portfolio must equal the duration of the cash out flow which is two years. But bonds carry 10% coupon rate. The solution to the two above equations can be worked out as follows:

$W_1 = 1 - W_3$, substituting this, in the second equation, we have $[(1 - W_3) \times 1] + (W_3 \times 2.78) = 2$

$$1.78\ W_3 = 1 \text{ and } W_3 = \frac{1}{1.78} = 0.562$$

@ W.F. Sharpe & G.J. Alexander *Investments,* (Prentice Hall), p. 387.

$$\begin{aligned} \text{Then } W_1 &= 0.438 \\ \text{plus } W_3 &= \underline{0.562} \\ W_1 + W_3 & \quad 1.000 \end{aligned}$$

The investment in this example is for two years and for a target of 10%. Then the Portfolio Manager needs

$\frac{1,000}{(1.10)^2}$ = ₹ 826.0, which is distributed as ₹ 362 to buy one year bonds and ₹ 464 to buy three year bonds. This will give an immunised portfolio with duration of 2 years and target amount of ₹ 1,000. In this example, one year bonds are selling at ₹ 972 and three year bonds at ₹ 950 (approx.). The above exercise proves that the portfolio's losses due to selling 3 year bonds after 2 years will be exactly offset by the gains from reinvesting the maturing one year bonds at a higher rate.

PROBLEMS OF IMMUNISATION

The immunisation exercise is based on some assumptions: (1) Bond will not be called back by the Company, (2) There is no default risk and (3) Yield curves move horizontally and any shift in it will be parallel. In reality, the shifts in the curves may not be parallel. If the one year and three year bonds will have initial yields of 10% and 10.5%, respectively, it is possible that the yields on them will fall by 1% and 0.8% respectively after one year, which means that falls are not of the same magnitude.

Remedies are suggested for such non-parallel shifts in yield curves, namely:

1. Cash Matching: It involves the purchase of bonds, so that the cash received during each period from the bonds is identical in size to the promised cash outflow for that period.

2. Dedicated Portfolio: In the cash matching portfolio of bonds, there is no need for reinvestment of cash inflows in the future as cash outflows and inflows are matched exactly. Such a portfolio is called dedicated portfolio, which avoids the reinvestment rate risk and no interest rate risk either as the bonds do not have to be sold before Maturity.

Immunisation requires continuous and active management as some rebalancing may be required always due to changes overtime of yields, durations at different rates and emergence of non-horizontal movement of yield curves and a host of other factors.

3. "Bullet" or Focussed Portfolio: It is portfolio which has less stochastic process risk than any other. Such a portfolio is one where the bonds in it have durations, most closely matching the duration of the promised outflows.

Alternatively, the Portfolio manager may adopt both passive and active elements involving contingent immunisation.

This means that portfolio is actively managed as long as favourable returns are obtained and if unfavourable result starts falling, he will resort to the process of immunisation.

4. Bond Swaps: Swap is an exchange of one type of bond for another category. Bond swapping is to manage a portfolio actively by exchanging bonds of one category to another to take advantage of superior ability to predict the yields and prices. Substitution swap is an exchange of one bond for another of the same category to take advantage of temporary price differential due to mismatch of supply and demand factors. There are a number of other types of swaps adopted by Portfolio Managers, namely, rate anticipation swaps, inter-market spread swap or pure high yielding pick-up swap, which all aim at improving the over all yields or return on the Bond Portfolios. Some swaps will benefit tax payments and some swaps increase yields while others secure the required maturity.

BOND PORTFOLIO MANAGEMENT STRATEGIES

1. Buy and Hold Strategy.
2. Bond Ladder Strategy.
3. Semi-Active Management Strategy.

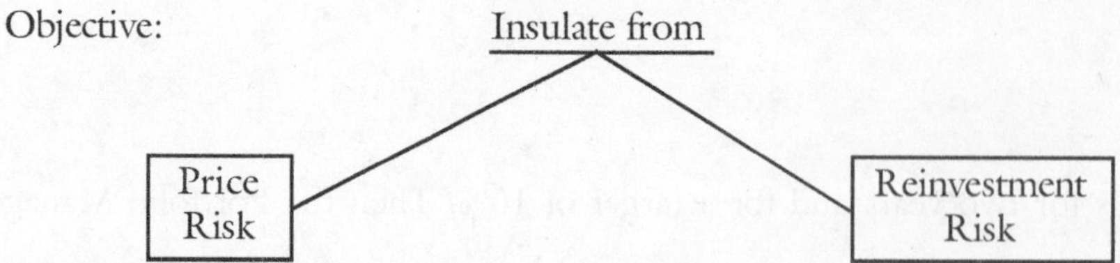

First Calculate Duration. Then use Technique of Immunisation

Example: How to Calculate Duration (D)

Data

$$D = \frac{\sum Pv(ct) \times t}{P_o}$$

Par Value = ₹ 1,000

Market Price = ₹ 50.25

ytm = 10%

Coupon Rate = 8%

Annual Coupon Payment = ₹ 80

Maturity = 3 years (T)

P_o = Present Value of all future Cash Flows

Period	*Cash Flow Amounts*	*Present Value Factors*	*Present Value of Cash Flows PV (CT)*	*Present Value of Cash Flows × Time (t)*
1	80	.9091	72.73	72.73
2	80	.8264	66.12	132.23
3	1080	.7513	811.40	2434.21
			950.25	2639.17

$$D = \frac{2639.17}{950.25} = 2.78$$

Modified duration MD = $D/1 + \frac{r}{p}$; where r = ytm and and p is number of times interest is paid, annually.

$$r = 0.10,\ p = 1,\ MD = \frac{D}{1+0.10} = \frac{2.78}{1.10} = 2.53$$

$\frac{\Delta P}{P} = -D \frac{\Delta ytm}{1+ytm}$, We can use D or MD in the equation

Bond Holding Strategies

Some of the strategies are already referred to

1. Passive Buy and Hold Strategy: This is what is adopted by many Indian Banks. This is based on Index linked investments, such as standard and poor Bond Index. These investments yield a continuous flow of fixed incomes, stable and known in advance. It needs very little planning.

2. Bond Ladder Strategy: In this strategy investments are made in bonds of different maturities, in a well planned manner, so as to constitute a ladder of maturities, reflecting a similar yield pattern, going up along with maturities. This follows a set pattern, without much discretion or active management of the portfolio.

3. Semi-Active Management Strategy: This strategy aims at insulating the bond holding from two types of risks emanating from interest rate changes namely, price change risk and reinvestment risk. These two move in opposite directions. The Bond Manager has to match them in a manner that risk of the one is offset by the risk of the other and the portfolio is then immunised from the interest rate risk.

Immunisation

Immunisation is a process, referred to earlier, whereby, the realised rate of return on investment in bonds is as large as expected and computed yield for a given time horizon, namely, the duration. Duration is the weighted average measure of bond's life, where the various time periods of it are weighted by size of the present value of cash flows from it.

CASH MATCHING (DEDICATED PORTFOLIO)

Liability matching cash flows can be generated by proper Bond Management Strategies. In a dedicated portfolio, referred to earlier, there will be exact synchronising of all cash payments or out flows by matching inflows. It should be an optimal portfolio which releases cash inflows from the coupon receipts and or principal repayment plus accrued interest from a prior balance, just sufficient to meet the next liability falling due.

This following illustration makes this matching concept clear.

Take the following data:

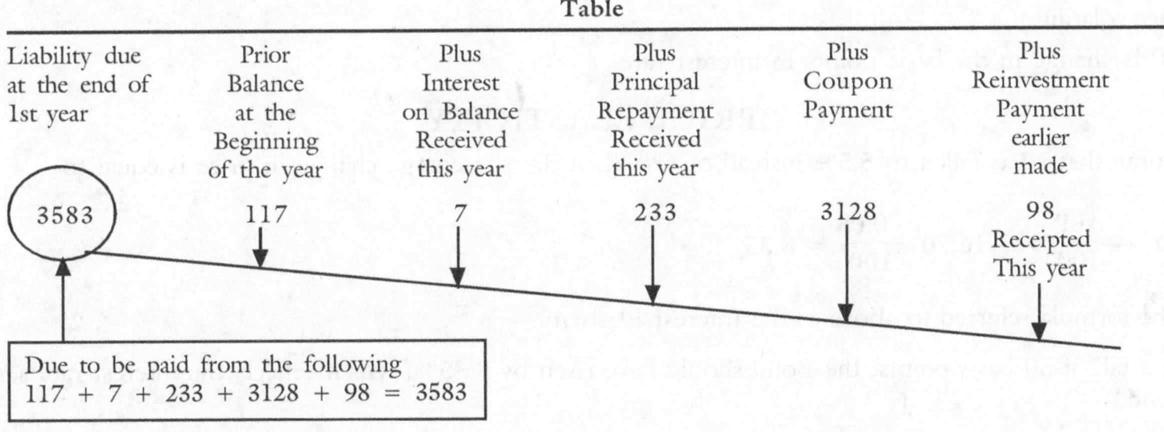

This involves many steps.

The stream of liability payments is anticipated correctly. The cash inflows due to cash expected from various sources, like coupon payments this year interest on invested portion, received this year, principal repayments, capital gains booked, if any, etc. are also to be properly planned. Then only through proper planning of duration of the Bond Portfolio can the manager achieve the dedicated portfolio.

What is Duration? This is explained by the following formula

$$D = \frac{\sum_{N=1}^{N} (n)(Cn)/(1+i)^n}{\sum_{N=1}^{N} \frac{Cn}{(1+i)^n}}$$

Numerator = sum of the weighted present values of cash flows, weighted by the time period of each of the flows.

Denominator = Sum of the present values of future cash flows or present and current market price.

where, i = ytm. N = number of periods of time.

Cn are cash flows.

Duration of the bond is bounded by

$\frac{r+p}{rp}$, where, r is ytm, p is number of times in a year that interest is paid on the bond.

If r = 6%, p is 2 times and the application of the above formula is shown by plugging in the above figures

$$\frac{0.06+2}{0.06\times 2} = \frac{2.06}{0.12} = 17.2 \text{ years}$$

It is the duration of the bond for the above values of r and p.

Modified Duration (Md)

$$MD = D/1 + \frac{r}{p} = \left(\frac{17.2}{1+\frac{0.06}{2}}\right) = \frac{17.2}{1.03}$$

MD for the above values is = 16.7

$$\text{Percentage change in price} = -\,MD \times \frac{\Delta BP}{100}$$

(Price volatility)

ΔBP is change in the basis points in interest rate.

PRICE ELASTICITY

Assume that r has fallen to 5.5% instead of 6%, then the percentage change in price is equal to

$$MD \times \frac{\Delta BP}{100} = -\,16.70\ \frac{-0.05}{100} = 8.35$$

is the formula referred to above as the Interest Elasticity.

For a fall of 50 basis points, the Bond should have risen by 8.35%, which reflects the interest rate sensitivity of the Bond.

We have already noted that there is a direct relationship between duration and interest rate risk.

Price volatility can arise due to maturity of the bond, interest rate changes, yield charges and due to reinvestment price. Time element is reflected in the duration.

Immunisation referred to earlier will help the offsetting of the interest rate risk on the Bond portfolio. A bond portfolio is said to be immunised, against interest rate risk, if the duration of the portfolio is equal to be desired holding period.

ILLUSTRATION
VOLATILITY OF BOND PRICES

I. Volatility due to maturity (6% coupon rate, face value ₹ 100)

Required Yield in %	*Number of years to maturity*			
	1 year	*10 years*	*20 years*	*30 years*
4	102	116 (13.7)	127 (9.5)	135 (6.3)
5	101	108 (6.9)	112 (3.7)	115 (2.7)
6	100	100 —	100 —	100 —
7	99	93 (–6.0)	89 (–4.3)	88 (–1.1)
8	98	86(–12.2)	80 (–7.0)	77 (–3.7)

Note: Figures in brackets refer to % changes over the previous column.

II. Volatility due to interest rate changes (fixed 20 year maturity)

Coupon Value in %	*Interest Rate Rise* 7%	8%	*% Change*	*Interest Rate Fall* 7%	8%	*% Change*
4	68	60	–11.3	68	87	27.9
5	78	70	–10.3	78	100	28.2
6	89	80	–10.1	89	112	25.8
7	100	90	–10.0	100	125	25.0
8	110	100	–9.1	110	137	24.5

III. Volatility due to yield changes (Level of rates)

6% 20 year Bond; Basis point change of 10% from original yield.

Original Yield in %	*Interest Rate Rise* Price	New Yield	New Price	% Change	*Interest Rate Fall* Price	New Yield	New Price	% Change
4	127	4.4	121	– 4.8	127	3.6	134	5.5
5	112	5.5	106	– 5.4	112	4.5	120	7.1
6	100	6.6	93	– 7.0	100	5.4	107	7.0
7	89	7.7	83	– 6.0	89	6.3	96	7.8
8	80	8.8	74	– 7.5	80	7.2	87	8.8

IV. Reinvestment Risk

Total realised compound yield over the life of 8% Bond due 20 years purchased at par (₹ 100) under varying assumptions relative to the coupon reinvestment rate: Coupon rate is 8% and reinvestment rate is 8% then the normal return is the same as the realised say 8%.

Reinvestment Rate in %	*Total Realised Compound Yield*
4	4.84
6	6.64
8	8.00
10	9.01

Immunisation

The company is required to pay ₹ 36,560.78 in 7 years show that this liability will be immunised with ₹ 20,000 of 10-year maturity 9 per cent coupon par value bonds, even if interst rates were to change immediately to — (i) 8%, (ii) 10%, (iii) remains at 9%, and stay at these assumed levels for 7 years.

Answer:

(1) Future value of ₹ 20,000 investment to be determined at all assumed levels of interest for 7 years.

(2) The future value of an ordinary annuity (FVA) is used to determine (1).

(a) If interest rate falls to 8 per cent

F.V. of Interest payments = Total interest pay × FVIFA (8%, 7)

= (0.09) × (20,000) × 8.9228

= 1,800 × 8.9228 = 16,061.04

Bond prices (end of years 7), Interest rate of 8%

$$= \frac{1{,}800}{(1.08)^1} + \frac{1{,}800}{(1.08)^2} + \frac{1{,}800 + 20{,}000}{(1.08)^3}$$

= 1666.7 + 1543.4 + 17301.5

= 20,511.6

Total = 16061.04 + 20,511.6 = 36572.6

(b) If interest rate rises to 10 per cent

PV of interest payments = Total interest pay × FVIFA (10%, 7)

= (0.09) × (20,000) × 9.4872

= 1800 × 9.4872 = 17,076.96

Bond price for end of 7 years

$$= \frac{1,800}{(1.10)^1} + \frac{1,800}{(1.10)^2} + \frac{1,800 + 20,000}{(1.10)^3}$$

= 1,636.36 + 1,487.60 + 16,378.66 = 19,502.62

Total = 17,076.96 + 19,502.62 = 36,579.58

= 36,579.58

(c) If interest rate remains at 9 per cent

FV of interest payments = Total interest pay × FVA (9%, 7)

= (0.09) × (20,000) × 9.2004

= 1800 × 9.2004 = 16,560.72

Bond prices (end of year 7)

$$= \frac{1,800}{(1.09)^1} + \frac{1,800}{(1.9)^2} + \frac{1,800 + 20,000}{(1.09)^3}$$

= 1,651.38 + 1,515.15 + 16,833.97

= 20,000

Total = 16,560.72 + 20,000 = 36,560.72

Note that with the rates of 8 per cent and 10 per cent, there is a small surplus. Duration is only exact for every small changes in interest rates. When interest rates change so do the bond's M.D., making the duration making strategy an approximated immunisation.

Immunisation

Question:

Suppose that X corporation must make a ₹ 20 lakhs pension fund payment each year for the next 4 years. Determine the average Macauly duration (MD) for this four year payment liability. Suppose that X corporation decided to immunise the payments by currently investing in zero coupon bond with 2 year and 5 year maturities. What per cent should X allocate to each zero coupon bond? What will be the accumulated face value of the bonds? Assume the yield curve is flat at 11 per cent?

Answer:

The duration of the payments can be determined for treating each payment like a zero coupon bond with a maturity date equal to the maturity date of the payment.

Year	*Payment*	*P.V. of 11%*	*Per cent of Total*	*Payments M.D. (1 × 4)*
1	2	3	4	5
1	₹ 20 lakh	18.02	.29	.29
2	₹ 20 lakh	16.24	.26	.52
3	₹ 20 lakh	14.62	.24	.72
4	₹ 20 lakh	13.17	.21	.84
	Total	62.05	1.00	2.37 = MD

[PVIF = (20 × .9009); (20 × .812); (20 × .731); (20 × .659)]; for the column (3)

To determine the immunizing asset allocation, we let 'X' equal the per cent of investment in the 2 year bonds that are needed. This implies that *(1 – x)* will be the per cent of 5 year bonds because the two weights must sum to 1.

(MD of 2 year bonds) (x) + (MD of 5 year bonds) (1 – x) = 2.37

= (2 years) (x) + (5 years) (1 – x) = 2.37

2x + 5 – 5x = 2.37; 3x = 2.63

$$X = \frac{2.63}{3} = .88 = 88\%;\ 1 - x = 100 - 88 = 12\%$$

∴ 88 per cent of the portfolio will be 2 year bonds and 12 per cent will be 5 year bonds. The duration for a zero coupon bond is equal to its time to maturity.

(A) Present value of bonds: (Total PV = 62.05)

(a) 2 years bonds — PV of 11% Bond is 62.05 as seen from the above Table.

0.88 × 62.05 = 54.60

(b) 5 year bonds

0.12 × 62 .05 = 7.45

Total 62.05

(B) Face value of bonds: (yield is 11%)

(a) 2 year bonds is

$54.6 \times (1.11)^2 = 54.6 \times 1.2321 = 67.27$

(b) 5 year bond is

$7.45 \times (1.11)^5 = 7.45 \times 1.6851 = 12.54$

Macaulay's Duration

Question:

Determine Macaulay's duration of a bond which has a face value of ₹ 1000 and 8 per cent annual coupon rate, and 4 years to go for maturity. The bonds YTM is 10 per cent.

Answer:

$$\sum_{t=1}^{4} \frac{C_t/(1 + ytm)^t + F_t/(1 + ytm)^T}{V_o}$$

C_t, is the coupon to be received in time

F_t, is the face value of the bond

V_o, is the present/market value of the bond.

$$\sum_{t=1}^{4} \frac{[80t/(1+0.10)] + 1000T/(1.10)4}{V_o}$$

The value of V_o is equal to

Year 1	*Cash flow* 2	*1/(1 + YTM) t* 3	*Present value of cash flow (2 × 3) = 4*
1	80	$.9091 = 1/(1.10)^1$	72.73
2	80	$.8264 = 1/(1.10)^2$	66.11
3	80	$.7513 = 1/(1.10)^3$	60.10
4	80 + 1000	$.6830 = 1/(1.10)^4$	737.64
			V_o = 936.58

Year	*pv of C.F.*	*pv of Cf as proportion*	*3 × 1= Duration*
1	*2*	*3*	*4*
1	72.73	.0777	.0777
2	66.11	.0705	.1412
3	60.10	.0642	.1926
4	737.64	.7876	3.1504
	936.58	1.00	3.5619

Duration 3.56 years

The Modified Duration for this bond is MMD = $\frac{MD}{1+ytm} = \frac{3.56}{1+0.10} = \frac{3.56}{1.10}$ = 3.23 years

Problems in Bonds

The term structure of interest rates is also called yield curve. This reflects the relationship at a point of time between YTMs of homogenous Bonds and years to maturity for the bonds. According to Expectations Hypothesis, long-term interest rates are the geometric mean of expected forward or future short-term interest rates. The equation for this can be set out as follows:

$$YTM_n = [(1+YTM_1)(1+F_{1,2})(1+F_{2,3})...] - 1$$

putting it in a generalised form

$$Ft, t+n = \sqrt[n]{\frac{(1+YTM_{F+n})^{t+n}}{1+YTM_t}} - 1$$

1. *To give an example.* Take the following problem. The YTM on a 7 year Bond is 9% and YTM on 10 year Bond is 10.5%. What is the implied average forward rate for a 3 year Bond, starting in 8th year.

Answer:

Using the above equation:

$$F_{7,10} = \sqrt[3]{\frac{(1.105)^{10}}{(1.09)^7}} - 1$$

$$= \sqrt[3]{\frac{2.714}{1.828}} - 1$$

$$= \sqrt[3]{1.4847 - 1}$$

$$= 1.1408 - 1 = 0.1408$$

$$= 14.1\%$$

This is the average for three years namely 8th, 9th and 10th years.

2. You are given two bonds to choose from namely ZCB of 5 years and 20 years and your target duration is 10 years. How much do you allocate to each Bond to achieve your target duration.

Answer:

ZCB or Zero Coupon Bonds have their duration equal to their maturity.

Assume that you invest X per cent in 5 year Bonds and (1 – x) per cent in 20 year bonds, then the total weight is one:

$$5x + 20(1 - x) = 10$$

$$5x + 20 - 20x = 10$$

$$15x = 10$$

$$x = \frac{10}{15} = 0.67\ (67\%)$$

$$1 - x = 0.33\ (33\%)$$

3. ICL Co. must pay ₹ 25 lakhs at the end of each of next 2 years. Bonds are correctly yielding 12%; what is the MD of this liability.

Answer:

Put the data in the following Tabular Form:

1 *Year*	2 *Liability*	3 *Present value of (2) at 12%*	4 *(3) Percentage*	5 *MD (1) × (4)*
1st year	₹ 25 lakhs	$25 \times \frac{1}{1+0.12} =$	22.32 = 53%	0.53 × 1 = 0.53
2nd year	₹ 25 lakhs	$25 \times \frac{1}{(1+0.12)^2} =$	19.93 = 47%	0.47 × 2 = 0.94
			42.25 = 100	1.47 years

In order to immunise the above portfolio a 12% ZCB with a maturity of 1.47 years (or one year 5 months and 19 days roughly) has to be purchased by the ICL Co.

4. VSTCO has to make the following payments in the next 5 years.

Year 1 – ₹ 10 lakhs, year 2 – ₹ 9 lakhs

Year 3 – ₹ 8 lakhs, year 4 – ₹ 8 lakhs, year 5 – ₹ 7 lakhs.

If the market interest rates are 9% over all these maturities, determine the duration of the above liabilities.

Answer:

Assume that all the payments could be funded by investing in ZCBs with face values equal to the deserved payments. The duration of ZCB is equal to its maturity period.

By putting the data in a Tabular Form:

Year of payment = 1	*Payment liability = 2*	*Present value of (2) AT 9% = 3*	*(3) as per cent of total = 4*	*M.D. 1 × 4 = 5*
		(from the tables)		
1.	10	0.917 = 9.17	0.28	0.28
2.	9	0.842 = 7.58	0.23	0.46
3.	8	0.772 = 6.18	0.18	0.54
4.	8	0.708 = 5.67	0.17	0.68
5.	7	0.650 = 4.55	0.14	0.70
		33.15	1.00	2.66

Weighted average MD is 2.66 years.

If you want to immunise the payments with two ZCBs of 2 years and 3 years maturities, the percentages to be invested in each is as follows: let x be invested in 2 year Bonds and (1 – x) in 3 year Bonds, Then:

2x + 3 (1 – x) = 2.66

2x + 3 – 3x = 2.66

x = 0.33 — 1/3 rd in 2 year Bonds

1 – x = 0.67 — 2/3 rd in 3 year Bonds

BONDS VALUATION — PROBLEMS

Problem:

(1) The Company x issued in 1998 bonds of 12% at face value of ₹ 1,000 for a thirty year maturity calculate its YTM.

Answer:

As the bonds are issued at par, the original YTM is the same as coupon rate of 12%.

(2) If the interest rate fell to 10% from 12% by 2003 AD five years hence, what is the price of bond. Then 30 year bond has coupon payments twice a year and it has 25 years to run.

Answer:

$$V = \sum_{t=1}^{50} \frac{120/2}{\left(1+\frac{0.10}{2}\right)^{50}} + \frac{1000}{\left(1+\frac{0.10}{2}\right)^{50}}$$

$= 60$ (PVIFA 5%, 50) + 1000 (PVIF 5% 50)

From Tables (PVIFA 5% 50) = 18.2559 (not in the Appendix).

(PVIF 5% 50) = .0872

Inserting the values given above:

V = 60 (18.256) + 1000 (0.0872)

V = 1095 + 87 = ₹ 1182.

(3) Find out the current yield and capital gains on the bond as in 2003 AD, from the data given above

Answer:

$$\text{Current yield} = \frac{\text{Annual Coupon Payment}}{\text{Price}}$$

$$= \frac{120}{1182} = 10.15\%$$

(4) With a currency of only 10 years more the company x's bonds are sold at ₹ 896.64. What is the YTM at that time.

Answer:

Using the formula

$$896.64 = \frac{60}{(1+\text{ytm}/2)^{19}} + \frac{1000}{(1+\text{ytm}/2)^{19}}$$

Take the approximate yield formula for YTM from the Author of this formula namely R.J. Rodriquez.

$$\text{viz., YTM} = \frac{1+\frac{M-V}{n}}{(M+2v)/3}$$

$$= \frac{60+(1000-896.64)/19}{(1000+1793.28)/3}$$

$$= \frac{65.44}{931.09} = 7.03\% \text{ for Semi-Annual period.}$$

Therefore, the YTM per annum is 14.06% or roughly 14% P.A.

Now let us apply this rate of 14%

$$V = I\,(PVIFA\ 7\%\ 19) + M\,(PVIF\ 7\%\ 19)$$

$$896.64 = 60\,(10.306) + 1000\,(0.2765)$$

From the Tables PVIFA (7% 19) = 10.306 and PVIF (7% 19) = 0.2765

$$896.64 = 620.14 + 276.50$$

$$= 896.64$$

This confirms that YTM as at end of 2018 — with only 10 years to run is 14%.

Bonds

Question 1

If the cash flow each year is ₹ 100 and the principal repayment at the end of 5 years is ₹ 1,000 and current market price is ₹ 960 what is its current yield and what is its YTM?

Question 2

If a bond has semi-annual coupon payments of ₹ 50 and the principal payment of ₹ 1,000 in 8 years and a price of ₹ 1,000, what is the duration of the bond, if the yield curve is a flat 10%?

Question 3

Given the following data on the three bonds and their duration, construct three different portfolios of these three bonds, each with a duration of 9 years.

Bond	Duration
A	5
B	10
C	12

YIELDS AND MACAULAY'S DURATION

Question 1

Determine Macaulay' duration of a bond that has a par value of ₹ 1,000 with a coupon rate of 8%. While the remaining period to maturity is 4 years, the YTM is 10%. Determine the modified duration also.

Question 2

Modi Rubber issued a ₹ 1,000 at a coupon rate of 12%. Interest is payable at annual intervals over a period of 20 years. What is the price of bond if the market rate of interest is 14%. What is the Modified Macaulay's Duration, using the continuous discounting model.

Question 3

A bond with maturity of 10 years has a YTM and coupon rate of 10%. Calculate Macaulay's Duration, using the continuous discounting model.

Question 4

A bond with a par value of ₹ 1,000 and a coupon rate of 8% is sold at ₹ 944.63. If the term to maturity is 4 years, calculate the current yield, AYTM and YTM.

APPENDIX

Table A.1

Future Value Interest Factor *(FVIF)*

$FVIF\ (k,n) = (1 + k)^n$

Period n	1%	2%	3%	4%	5%	6%	7%	8%	9%	10%	11%	12%	13%
0	1.000	1.000	1.000	1.000	1.000	1.000	1.000	1.000	1.000	1.000	1.000	1.000	1.000
1	1.010	1.020	1.030	1.040	1.050	1.060	1.070	1.080	1.090	1.100	1.110	1.120	1.130
2	1.020	1.040	1.061	1.082	1.102	1.124	1.145	1.166	1.188	1.210	1.232	1.254	1.277
3	1.030	1.061	1.093	1.125	1.158	1.191	1.225	1.260	1.295	1.331	1.358	1.405	1.433
4	1.041	1.082	1.126	1.170	1.216	1.262	1.311	1.360	1.412	1.464	1.518	1.574	1.630
5	1.051	1.104	1.159	1.217	1.276	1.338	1.403	1.469	1.539	1.611	1.685	1.762	1.842
6	1.062	1.126	1.194	1.265	1.340	1.419	1.501	1.587	1.677	1.772	1.870	1.974	2.082
7	1.072	1.149	1.230	1.316	1.407	1.504	1.606	1.714	1.828	1.949	2.076	2.211	2.353
8	1.083	1.172	1.267	1.369	1.477	1.594	1.718	1.851	1.993	2.144	2.305	2.476	2.658
9	1.094	1.195	1.305	1.423	1.551	1.689	1.838	1.999	2.172	2.358	2.558	2.773	3.004
10	1.105	1.219	1.344	1.480	1.629	1.791	1.967	2.159	2.367	2.594	2.839	3.106	3.395
11	1.116	1.243	1.384	1.539	1.710	1.898	2.105	2.332	2.580	2.853	3.152	3.479	3.836
12	1.127	1.268	1.426	1.601	1.796	2.012	2.252	2.518	2.813	3.138	3.498	3.896	4.335
13	1.138	1.294	1.469	1.665	1.886	2.133	2.410	2.720	3.066	3.452	3.883	4.363	4.898
14	1.149	1.319	1.513	1.732	1.980	2.261	2.579	2.937	3.342	3.797	4.310	4.887	5.535
15	1.161	1.346	1.558	1.801	2.079	2.397	2.759	3.172	3.642	4.177	4.785	5.474	6.254
16	1.173	1.373	1.605	1.873	2.183	2.540	2.952	3.426	3.970	4.595	5.311	6.130	7.067
17	1.184	1.400	1.653	1.948	2.407	2.693	3.159	3.700	4.328	5.054	5.895	6.866	7.986
18	1.196	1.428	1.702	2.026	2.407	2.854	3.380	3.996	4.717	5.560	6.544	7.690	9.024
19	1.208	1.457	1.754	2.107	2.527	3.026	3.617	4.136	5.142	6.116	7.263	8.613	10.197
20	1.220	1.486	1.806	2.191	2.653	3.207	3.870	4.661	5.604	6.728	8,062	9.646	11.523
25	1.282	1.641	2.094	2.666	3.386	4.292	5.427	6.848	8.623	10.835	13.585	17.000	21.231
30	1.348	1.811	2.427	3.243	4.322	5.743	7.612	10.063	13.268	17.449	22.892	29.960	39.116

(Contd.) Table A.1

Period n	14%	15%	16%	17%	18%	19%	20%	24%	28%	32%	36%	40%
0	1.000	1.000	1.000	1.000	1.000	1.000	1.000	1.000	1.000	1.000	1.000	1.000
1	1.140	1150	1.160	1.170	1.180	1.190	1.200	1.240	1.280	1.320	1.360	1.400
2	1.300	1.322	1.346	1.369	1.392	1.416	1.440	1.538	1.638	1.742	1.850	1.960
3	1.482	1.521	1.561	1.602	1.643	1.685	1.728	1.907	2.097	2.300	2.515	2.744
4	1.689	1.749	1.811	1.874	1.939	2.005	2.074	2.364	2.684	3.036	3.421	3.842
5	1.925	2.011	2.100	2.192	2.288	2.386	2.488	2.392	3.436	4.007	4.653	5.373
6	2.195	2.313	2.436	2.565	2.700	2.840	2.986	3.635	4.398	5.290	6.328	7.530
7	2.502	2.560	2.826	3.001	3.185	3.379	3.583	4.508	5.629	6.983	8.605	10.541
8	2.583	3.059	3.278	3.511	3.759	4.021	4.300	5.590	7.206	9.217	11.703	14.758
9	3.252	3.518	3.803	4.108	4.435	4.785	5.160	6.931	9.223	12.166	15.917	20.661
10	3.707	4.046	4.411	4.807	5.234	5.695	6.192	8.594	11.806	16.060	21.647	28.925
11	4.226	4.652	5.117	5.624	6.176	6.777	7.430	10.657	15.112	21.199	29.439	40.496
12	4.818	5.350	5.936	6.580	7.288	8.064	8.916	13.215	19.343	27.983	40.037	56.694
13	5.492	6.153	6.886	7.699	8.599	9.596	10.699	16.386	24.759	36.937	54.451	79.372
14	6.261	7.076	7.988	9.007	10.147	11.420	12.839	20.319	31.961	48.757	74.053	111.120
15	7.138	8.137	9.266	10.539	11.974	13.590	15.407	25.196	40.565	64.359	100.712	155.568
16	8.137	9.358	10.748	12.330	14.129	16.172	18.488	31.243	51.923	84.954	136.969	217.795
17	9.276	10.761	12.468	14.426	16.622	19.244	22.186	38.741	66.461	112.139	186.278	30.914
18	10.575	12.375	14.463	16.879	19.673	22.901	26.623	48.039	85.071	148.023	253.338	426.879
19	12.056	14.232	16.777	19.748	23.214	27.252	31.948	59.568	108.890	195.391	344.540	597.630
20	13.743	16.367	19.461	23.106	27.393	32.429	38.338	73.864	139.380	257.916	468.574	836.683
25	26.462	32.919	40.874	50.658	62.669	27.388	95.396	216.542	478.905	1033.590	2180.081	4499.880
30	50.950	66.212	85.850	111.065	143.371	184.675	237.376	634.820	1645.504	4142.075	10143.019	24201.432

Table A.2

Future Value Interest Factor for an Annuity

$$FVIFA\ (k_t n) = \frac{(1+K)^{n-1}}{k}$$

Period n	1%	2%	3%	4%	5%	6%	7%	8%	9%	10%	11%	12%	13%
1	1.000	1.000	1.000	1.000	1.000	1.000	1.000	1.000	1.000	1.000	1.000	1.000	1.000
2	2.010	2.020	2.030	2.040	2.050	2.060	2.070	2.080	2.090	2.100	2.110	2.120	2.130
3	3.030	3.060	3.091	3.122	3.152	3.184	3.215	3.246	3.278	3.310	3.342	3.374	3.850
4	4.060	4.122	4.184	4.246	4.310	4.375	4.440	4.506	4.573	4.641	4.710	4.779	4.850
5	5.101	5.204	5.309	5.416	5.526	5.637	5.751	5.867	5.985	6.105	6.228	6.353	6.480
6	6.102	6.308	6.468	6.633	6.802	6.975	7.153	7.336	7.523	7.716	7.913	8.115	8.323
7	7.214	7.434	7.662	7.898	8.142	8.394	8.654	8.923	9.200	9.487	9.783	10.089	10.405
8	8.286	8.583	8.892	9.214	9.549	9.897	10.260	10.637	11.028	11.436	11.859	12.300	12.757
9	9.369	9.755	10.159	10.583	11.027	11.491	11.978	12.488	13.021	13.579	14.164	14.776	15.416
10	10.462	10.950	11.464	12.006	12.578	13.181	13.816	14.487	15.193	15.937	16.722	17.549	18.420
11	11.567	12.169	12.808	13.486	14.207	14.972	15.984	16.645	17.560	18.531	19.561	20.655	21.814
12	12.683	13.412	14.192	15.206	15.917	16.870	17.888	18.977	20.141	21.384	22.713	24.133	25.650
13	13.809	14.680	15.618	16.627	17.713	18.882	20.141	21.495	22.953	24.523	26.212	28.029	29.985
14	14.947	15.974	17.086	18.292	19.599	21.015	22.550	24.215	26.019	27.975	30.095	32.393	34.883
15	16.097	17.293	18.599	20.024	21.579	23.276	25.129	27.152	29.361	31.772	34.405	37.280	40.417
16	17.258	18.639	20.157	21.825	23.657	25.673	27.888	30.324	33.003	35.950	39.190	42.753	46.672
17	18.430	20.012	21.762	23.698	25.840	28.213	30.840	33.750	36.974	40.545	44.501	48.884	53.739
18	19.615	21.412	23.414	25.645	28.132	30.006	33.999	37.450	41.301	45.599	50.396	55.750	61.725
19	20.811	22.841	25.117	27.671	30.539	33.760	37.379	41.446	46.018	51.159	56.939	63.440	70.749
20	22.019	24.297	26.870	29.778	33.066	36.786	40.995	45.762	51.160	57.275	64.203	72.052	80.947
25	28.243	32.030	36.459	41.746	47.727	54.865	63.249	73.106	84.701	98.347	114.413	133.334	155.620
30	34.785	40.568	47.575	56.805	66.439	79.058	94.461	113.283	136.308	164.494	199.021	241.333	293.190

(Contd.) Table A.2

Period n	14%	15%	16%	17%	18%	19%	20%	24%	28%	32%	36%	40%
1	1.000	1.000	1.000	1.000	1.000	1.000	1.000	1.000	1.000	1.000	1.000	1.000
2	2.140	2.150	2.160	2.170	2.180	2.190	2.200	2.240	2.280	2.320	2.360	2.400
3	3.440	3.473	3.506	3.539	3.572	3.605	3.640	3.778	3.918	4.062	4.210	4.360
4	4.921	4.993	5.066	5.141	5.215	5.291	5.368	5.684	6.016	6.362	6.725	7.104
5	6.610	6.742	6.877	7.014	7.154	7.297	7.442	8.048	8.700	9.398	10.146	10.946
6	8.536	8.754	8.977	9.207	9442	9.683	9.930	10.980	12.136	13.406	14.799	16.324
7	10.730	11.067	11.414	11.772	12.142	12.523	12.916	14.615	16.534	18.696	21.126	23.853
8	13.233	13.727	14.240	14.773	15.327	15.902	16.499	19.123	22.163	25.678	29.732	34.395
9	16.085	16.786	17.518	18.285	19.086	19.923	20.799	24.712	29.360	34.895	41.435	49.153
10	19.337	20.304	21.321	22.393	23.521	24.709	25.959	31.643	38.592	47.062	57.352	69.814
11	23.044	24.349	25.733	27.200	28.755	30.404	32.150	40.238	50.399	63.122	78.998	98.739
12	27.271	29.002	30.850	32.824	34.931	37.180	39.580	50.985	65.510	84.320	108.437	139.235
13	32.089	34.352	36.786	39.404	42.219	45.244	48.497	64.110	84.853	112.303	148.475	195.929
14	37.581	40.505	43.672	47.103	50.818	54.841	59.196	80.496	109.612	149.240	202.926	275.300
15	43.842	47.580	51.660	56.110	60.965	66.261	72.035	100.815	141.303	197.997	276.979	386.420
16	50.980	55.717	60.925	66.649	72.939	79.850	87.442	126.011	181.868	262.356	377.692	541.988
17	59.118	65.075	71.673	78.979	87.068	96.022	105.931	157.253	233.791	347.310	514.661	759.784
18	68.394	75.836	84.141	93.406	103.740	115.266	128.117	195.994	300.252	459.449	700.939	1064.697
19	78.969	88.212	98.603	110.285	123.414	138.166	154.740	244.033	385.323	607.472	954.277	1491.576
20	91.025	102.44	115.380	130.033	146.628	165.418	186.688	303.601	494.213	802.863	1298.817	2089.206
25	18.371	212.793	249.214	292.105	342.603	402.042	471.981	898.092	1706.803	3226.844	6053.004	11247.199
30	356.787	434.745	530.321	647.439	790.948	966.712	1181.882	2640.916	5873.231	12940.859	28172.276	60501.081

Table A.3

Present Value Interest Factor

PVIF (k,n) = (1 + k)

Period n	1%	2%	3%	4%	5%	6%	7%	8%	9%	10%	11%	12%	13%
0	1.000	1.000	1.000	1.000	1.000	1.000	1.000	1.000	1.000	1.000	1.000	1.000	1.000
1	0.990	0.980	0.971	0.962	0.952	0.943	0.935	0.926	0.917	0.909	0.901	0.893	0.885
2	0.980	0.961	0.943	0.925	0.907	0.890	0.873	0.857	0.842	0.826	0.812	0.797	0.783
3	0.971	0.942	0.915	0.889	0.864	0.840	0.816	0.794	0.772	0.751	0.731	0.712	0.693
4	0.961	0.924	0.889	0.855	0.823	0.792	0.763	0.735	0.708	0.683	0.659	0.636	0.613
5	0.951	0.906	0.863	0.822	0.784	0.747	0.713	0.681	0.650	0.621	0.593	0.567	0.450
6	0.942	0.888	0.838	0.790	0.746	0.705	0.666	0.630	0.596	0.564	0.535	0.507	0.480
7	0.933	0.871	0.813	0.760	0.711	0.665	0.623	0.583	0.547	0.513	0.482	0.452	0.425
8	0.923	0.853	0.789	0.731	0.677	0.627	0.582	0.540	0.502	0.467	0.434	0.404	0.376
9	0.914	0.837	0.766	0.703	0.645	0.592	0.544	0.500	0.460	0.424	0.391	0.361	0.333
10	0.905	0.820	0.744	0.676	0.614	0.558	0.508	0.463	0.422	0.386	0.352	0.322	0.295
11	0.896	0.804	0.722	0.650	0.585	0.527	0.475	0.429	0.388	0.350	0.317	0.287	0.261
12	0.887	0.788	0.701	0.625	0.557	0.497	0.444	0.397	0.356	0.319	0.286	0.257	0.231
13	0.879	0.773	0.681	0.601	0.530	0.469	0.415	0.368	0.326	0.290	0.258	0.229	0.204
14	0.870	0.750	0.661	0.577	0.505	0.442	0.388	0.340	0.299	0.263	0.232	0.205	0.181
15	0.861	0.743	0.642	0.555	0.481	0.417	0.362	0.315	0.275	0.239	0.209	0.183	0.160
16	0.853	0.728	0.623	0.534	0.458	0.394	0.339	0.292	0.252	0.218	0.188	0.163	0.141
17	0.844	0.714	0.605	0.513	0.436	0.371	0.317	0.270	0.231	0.198	0.170	0.146	0.125
18	0.836	0.700	0.587	0.494	0.416	0.350	0.296	0.250	0.212	0.180	0.153	0.130	0.111
19	0.828	0.686	0.570	0.475	0.396	0.331	0.276	0.232	0.194	0.164	0138	0.116	0.098
20	0.820	0.673	0.554	0.456	0.377	0.312	0.258	0.215	0.178	0.149	0.124	0.104	0.087
25	0.780	0.610	0.478	0.375	0.295	0.233	0.184	0.146	0.116	0.092	0.074	0.059	0.047
30	0.742	0.552	0.412	0.308	0.231	0.174	0.131	0.099	0.075	0.057	0.044	0.033	0.026

(Contd.) Table A.3

Period *n*	*14%*	*15%*	*16%*	*17%*	*18%*	*19%*	*20%*	*24%*	*28%*	*32%*	*36%*	*40%*
0	1.000	1.000	1.000	1.000	1.000	1.000	1.000	1.000	1.000	1.000	1.000	1.000
1	0.877	0.870	0.862	0.855	0.847	0.840	0.833	0.806	0.781	0.758	0.735	0.714
2	0.769	0.756	0.743	0.731	0.718	0.706	0.694	0.650	0.610	0.574	0.541	0.510
3	0.675	0.658	0.641	0.624	0.609	0.593	0.579	0.524	0.477	0.435	0.398	0.364
4	0.592	0.572	0.552	0.534	0.516	0.499	0.482	0.423	0.373	0.329	0.292	0.260
5	0.519	0.497	0.476	0.456	0.437	0.419	0.402	0.341	0.291	0.250	0.215	0.186
6	0.456	0.432	0.410	0.390	0.370	0.352	0.335	0.275	0.277	0.189	0.158	0.133
7	0.400	0.376	0.354	0.333	0.314	0.296	0.279	0.222	0.178	0.143	0.116	0.095
8	0.351	0.327	0.305	0.285	0.266	0.249	0.233	0.179	0.139	0.108	0.085	0.068
9	0.308	0.284	0.263	0.243	0.226	0.209	0.194	0.144	0.108	0.082	0.063	0.048
10	0.270	0.247	0.277	0.208	0.191	0.176	0.162	0.116	0.082	0.062	0.046	0.035
11	0.237	0.215	0.195	0.178	0.162	0.148	0.135	0.094	0.066	0.047	0.034	0.025
12	0.208	0.187	0.168	0.152	0.137	0.124	0.112	0.076	0.052	0.036	0.025	0.018
13	0.182	0.163	0.145	0.130	0.116	0.104	0.093	0.061	0.040	0.027	0.018	0.013
14	0.160	0.141	0.125	0.111	0.099	0.088	0.078	0.049	0.032	0.021	0.014	0.009
15	0.140	0.123	0.108	0.095	0.084	0.074	0.065	0.040	0.025	0.016	0.010	0.006
16	0.123	0.107	0.093	0.081	0.071	0.062	0.054	0.032	0.019	0.012	0.007	0.005
17	0.108	0.093	0.080	0.069	0.060	0.052	0.045	0.026	0.015	0.009	0.005	0.003
18	0.095	0.081	0.069	0.059	0.051	0.044	0.038	0.021	0.012	0.007	0.004	0.002
19	0.083	0.070	0.060	0.051	0.043	0.037	0.031	0.017	0.009	0.005	0.003	0.002
20	0.073	0.061	0.051	0.043	0.037	0.031	0.026	0.014	0.007	0.004	0.002	0.001
25	0.038	0.030	0.024	0.020	0.016	0.013	0.010	0.005	0.002	0.001	0.000	0.000
30	0.020	0.015	0.012	0.009	0.007	0.005	0.004	0.002	0.001	0.000	0.000	0.000

Table A.4

Present Value Interest Factor for an Annuity

$$PVIFA = (k,n) = \frac{1 - \frac{1}{(1+k)^n}}{k}$$

Period n	1%	2%	3%	4%	5%	6%	7%	8%	9%	10%	11%	12%	13%
0	1.000	1.000	1.000	1.000	1.000	1.000	1.000	1.000	1.000	1.000	1.000	1.000	1.000
1	0.990	0.980	0.971	0.962	0.952	0.943	0.935	0.926	0.917	0.909	0.901	0.893	0.885
2	1.970	1.942	1.913	1.886	1.859	1.833	1.808	1.783	1.759	1.736	1.713	1.690	1.666
3	2.941	2.884	2.829	2.775	2.723	2.673	2.624	2.577	2.531	2.487	2.414	2.402	2.361
4	3.902	3.808	3.717	3.630	3.546	3.465	3.387	3.312	3.240	3.170	3.102	3.037	2.974
5	4.853	4.713	4.580	4.452	4.329	4.212	4.100	3.993	3.890	3.791	3.696	3.605	3.517
6	5.795	5.601	5.417	5.242	5.076	4.917	4.765	4.623	4.486	4.355	4.231	4.111	3.998
7	6.728	6.472	6.230	6.002	5.786	5.582	5.389	5.206	5.033	4.868	4.712	4.564	4.423
8	7.652	7.235	7.020	6.733	6.463	6.010	5.971	5.747	5.535	5.335	5.146	4.968	4.799
9	8.566	8.162	7.786	7.435	7.108	6.802	6.515	6.247	5.995	5.759	5.537	5.328	5.132
10	9.471	8.983	8.530	8.111	7.722	7.360	7.024	6.710	6.418	6.145	5.889	5.650	5.426
11	10.368	9.787	9.253	8.760	8.306	7.887	7.499	7.139	6.805	6.495	6.207	5.938	5.687
12	11.255	10.575	9.954	9.385	8.863	8.384	7.943	7.536	7.161	6.814	6.492	6.194	5.919
13	12.134	11.348	10.635	9.986	9.394	8.855	8.358	7.904	7.487	7.103	6.750	6.424	6.122
14	13.004	12.106	11.296	10.563	9.899	9.295	8.745	8.244	7.786	7.367	6.982	6.628	6.302
15	13.865	12.849	11.938	11.118	10.380	9.712	9.108	8.559	8.060	7.606	7.191	6.811	6.462
16	14.718	13.578	12.561	11.652	10.838	10.106	9.447	8.851	8.312	7.824	7.379	6.971	6.604
17	15.562	14.292	13.166	12.166	11.274	10.477	9.763	9.122	8.544	7.022	7.549	7.120	6.729
18	16.398	14.992	13.754	12.659	11.690	10.828	10.059	9.372	8.756	8.201	7.702	7.250	6.840
19	17.230	13.678	14.324	13.134	12.085	11.158	10.306	9.604	8.950	8.365	7.839	7.366	6.938
20	18.050	16.351	14.877	13.590	12.462	11.470	10.594	9.818	9.128	8.514	7.963	7.469	7.025
25	22.023	19.523	17.413	15.622	14.094	12.783	11.654	10.675	9.823	9.077	8.422	7.843	7.330
30	25.808	22.397	19.600	17.292	15.373	13.765	12.409	11.258	10.274	9.427	8.694	8.055	7.496

(Contd.) Table A.4

Period n	14%	15%	16%	17%	18%	19%	20%	24%	28%	32%	36%
0	1.000	1.000	1.000	1.000	1.000	1.000	1.000	1.000	1.000	1.000	1.000
1	0.877	0.870	0.862	0.855	0.847	0.840	0.833	0.806	0.781	0.758	0.735
2	1.647	1.626	1.605	1.585	1.566	1.547	1.528	1.457	1.392	1.332	1.276
3	2.322	2.283	2.246	2.210	2.174	2.140	2.106	1.981	1.868	1.766	1.674
4	2.914	2.855	2.798	2.743	2.690	2.639	2.589	2.404	2.241	2.096	1.966
5	3.433	3.352	3.274	3.199	3.127	3.058	2.991	2.745	2.532	2.345	2.181
6	3.889	3.784	3.685	3.589	3.498	3.410	3.326	3.020	2.759	2.534	2.339
7	4.288	4.160	4.039	3.922	3.812	3.706	3.605	3.242	2.937	2.678	2.423
8	4.639	4.487	4.344	4.207	4.708	3.954	3.837	3.421	3.076	2.786	2.540
9	4.946	4.772	4.607	4.451	4.303	4.163	4.031	3.566	3.184	2.868	2.603
10	5.216	5.019	4.883	4.659	4.494	4.339	4.193	3.682	3.269	2.930	2.650
11	5.453	5.234	5.029	4.836	4.656	4.486	4.327	3.776	3.335	2.978	2.683
12	5.660	5.197	5.197	4.988	4.793	4.611	4.439	3.851	3.387	3.013	2.708
13	5.842	5.583	5.342	5.118	4.910	4.715	4.533	3.912	3.427	3.040	2.727
14	6.002	5.724	5.468	5.229	5.008	4.802	4.611	3.962	3.459	3.061	2.740
15	6.142	5.847	5.575	5.324	5.092	4.876	4.675	4.001	3.483	3.076	2.750
16	6.265	5.954	5.669	5.405	5.162	4.938	4.730	4.033	3.505	3.088	2.758
17	6.373	6.047	5.749	5.475	5.222	4.990	4.775	4.059	3.518	3.097	2.763
18	6.647	6.128	5.818	5.534	5.273	5.033	4.812	4.080	3.529	3.104	2.767
19	6.650	6.198	5.877	5.584	5.316	5.070	4.844	4.097	3.539	1.109	2.770
20	6.623	6.259	5.929	5.628	5.353	5.101	4.870	4.110	3.546	3.113	2.772
25	6.873	6.464	6.097	5.766	5.467	5.195	4.948	4.147	3.564	3.122	2.776
30	7.003	6.566	6.177	5.829	5.517	5.235	4.979	4.640	3.569	3.124	2.778

14

OPTIONS TRADING

What is Options

It is a derivative security used for the purpose of risk management in the investment market, based on some security. Futures, forwards, swaps, options etc., are all examples of hedge against risk. Investors are risk averse and want to reduce the risk. Individuals and corporations have a strong urge to reduce or manage risk and this is secured by trading in derivative markets.

The volatility in share prices require to be hedged. Thus, the larger the volatility the larger is the hedging demand. This is secured through the options and futures. Thus, the volume of future trading and volatility may be correlated but this does not mean that futures or options can cause higher or lower volatility in underlying shares/securities. These are all tools of risk management and no correlation is empirically found for options to increase or reduce volatility of share prices.

Characteristics of Options

Derivatives have many distinctive characteristics.

1. Their origin is from some other security, commodity or a reference point, (such as indexes).
2. They are instruments of hedge against risk of undue volatility.
3. They are leveraged instruments for risk management based on original security or instrument.

Calls and Puts

The two major types of stock options are calls and puts. A call gives the investor the right to purchase shares of a particular stock at a fixed price until a specific date. An investor who purchases a call option locks in a price on shares of stock for a predetermined time. A put option gives an investor the right to sell shares of a particular stock at a fixed price until a specific date. A put locks in a price at which to sell stock rather than a price at which to buy stock. Both puts and calls provide the investor with the right, but not the obligation, to use the option. Stock options are created, or "written" by Member Brokers who wish to earn income from selling the options. The writers then become obligated to sell (if a call has been sold) or purchase (if a put has been sold) the stock if and when the owner of the option decides to exercise the put or call.

Puts and calls derive their values from the values of the stock that they are used to sell or purchase. Stock options pay no dividends or interest and expire without any value if not used by the expiration date. The value of a call option is directly related to the value of the underlying stock (*i.e.,* the option value increases when the stock value increases) and the value of a put is inversely related to the value of the underlying stock (*i.e.,* the option value increases when the stock value decreases). Option values are also affected by the time remaining until expiration, the price volatility of the underlying common stock and the market rate of the interest.

Types of Derivatives

The security or asset classes on which the derivatives depend are:

(1) Debt or Bonds, (2) Equities, (3) Indexes, (4) Commodities, (5) Currencies.

Categories of Derivatives

Derivatives can be divided into two general categories

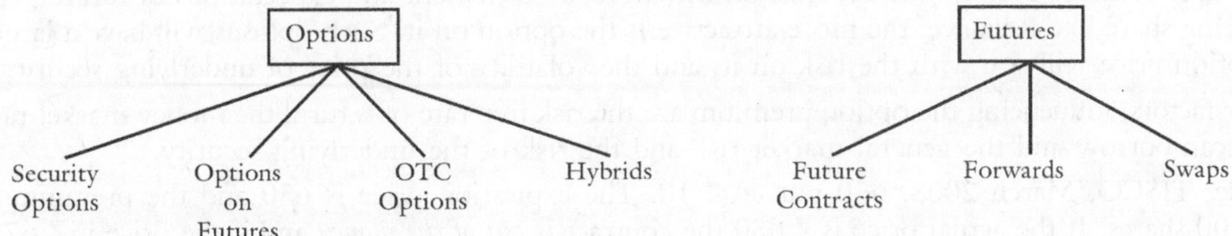

There are now traded options in India on Index and Securities and so are the futures on index and securities.

I. Why Options for Corporations/Government?

(a) Hedging Inventory
(b) Hedging Currency Rate
(c) Hedging Interest Rate Risk
(d) Lowering Borrowing Costs

II. Why Options for Individuals?

(a) For Speculation
(b) For Hedging
(c) Yield/Return Enhancement
(d) Asset Relocation or Allocation
(e) Arbitrage Operations

Investors and Dealers

Investors are individuals, mutual funds, pension funds, trusts, endowments, portfolio managers, companies, etc. The dealers in these markets are security firms, banks, financial institutions, market makers etc.

Option Price

The option price is in the form of premium paid on a contract. The rupee amount of the premium is the price paid (debit) for an option when purchased or received (credit) for the option when sold. The actual amount paid for a contract is quoted price times the number of underlying shares, normally 100 shares, for each contract. The premium is determined by buying and selling pressures in the auction type of market. The exercise or striking price is the price to be paid or received for the underlying shares, when option is exercised.

Suppose, the exercise price of HLL is ₹ 250 for a call option and the actual market price is ₹ 240 then the call is said to be *out-of-the money*. If on the other hand, the market price of HLL is ₹ 260 which is above the exercise price (₹ 250) then the option will have an intrinsic value or real worth and the call is said to be *in the money*. The reverse is true in the case of put options.

The premium for an option is almost always greater than the intrinsic value of the option. This excess value, namely premium minus intrinsic value is called the time value which is the speculative value of the premium paid on the option contract. This is what the buyer is willing to pay above the real worth for the expectation of future profits based on the underlying share. It is this time value which reflects the speculative element in option trading.

Factors explaining the premium of an option are as follows:

(a) Movements in exercise price relative to market price.
(b) Time remaining for expiration.
(c) Volatility of the underlying security.
(d) Market's expectations for the underlying security.
(e) Quality and yield of the underlying security.
(f) Interest rates in general.
(g) Supply and demand position for the option.

As referred to above, the intrinsic value depends on the share price of the underlying security and the exercise price of the option. This intrinsic value = actual share price — exercise price (call option).

The excess of the option premium over the intrinsic value is called the time value of option. The time value depends on length of the time to maturity or expiration date and optimistic expectations of a rise in price of the intrinsic security. The time value of option thus depends on the speculative element and expectations of future. The more risky the underlying share like Reliance, the more attractive is the option on it. Such options will have a larger time value and the option price will rise with the risk on it, and the volatility of the price of underlying security.

Among the other factors, influencing the option premium are the risk free rate of return, the money market rate at which the investor can borrow and the general market risk and the risk of the underlying security.

Take for example, TISCO, March 2008, 650 put @ ₹ 10. The expiration price is 650 and the premium is ₹ 10 per contract of 100 shares. If the actual price is ₹ 630 the contract is *out of the money* and if the price is ₹ 675, *it is in the money*. The premium of ₹ 10 will vary depending upon the price of the underlying security and its risk and a host of other factors. If the actual price is above say ₹ 680 then the option contract will have intrinsic worth and the buyer may exercise his option to sell at ₹ 650 and after deduction of the premium paid ₹ 10 the buyer of the option gains ₹ 20 (680–650) per share. If the market price of the underlying security is the same as the exercise price, it is said to be trading At-the-Money.

Take the example of put option. TISCO 650 put @ ₹ 5 March 2008. The expiration price is ₹ 650 and premium paid is ₹ 5, multiplied by 100 shares per contract, namely ₹ 500.

If the actual price fell to less than ₹ 645 before the expiration, the buyer of the option may exercise the right to sell as he will gain by selling at ₹ 650 instead of at say ₹ 645. Depending upon whether the option is a call or put, the premium will vary with the price. Take the example of TISCO given earlier, namely TISCO 650, March 2008 is sold as call option at a price of @ ₹ 10 for 100 shares. If you buy a contract, the minimum shares to be purchased are 100 and to purchase a contract, one has to pay ₹ 10 × 100 = 1,000. But the actual cash price of underlying securities if purchased will be ₹ 640 × 100 = 64,000 at that time. If the investor is bullish and expects the rise in price much more than ₹ 10, he will purchase the call option at ₹ 1,000. If the price of TISCO does not rise at all, he will lose only ₹ 1,000 but if it rises beyond ₹ 650, he will gain and the gain will depend on the extent of the rise in TISCO price beyond ₹ 650; its exercise price is ₹ 640 and premium paid is ₹ 10.

The terms used in options markets are as follows:

Writer of Options

	Call	Put
Long	Right to Buy	Right to Sell
Short	Obligation to Sell	Obligation to Buy

The uncovered options are called naked options. To cover calls buy the underlying security or go long in a put of equal or higher premium maturity. To cover puts, go short in the underlying security or go long in a put.

Normally option contracts are settled on the next day. If you exercise an option, settlement takes place in T + 5 days. The OCC@ makes arrangements for the settlement of these contracts in the U.S.A. The collection of margins and regulation of writing of contracts in options and in their trading and related matters, including settlement and clearance are the responsibility of the regulatory authority, namely, the Options Clearing Corporation, in the U.S.A.

Price Changes

The price of an option is the premium paid per 100 shares of the underlying security. The purchase of an option involves the payment of the price per contract, of 100 shares, multiplied by the number of such contracts purchased. In the event the price of the underlying security goes against the option price, fixed at the time of writing the option, the loss to the buyer is only the premium paid by the contracts purchased. The gain will be in the rise in option price, depending on the price movements of the underlying security.

Thus, each contract of 100 shares will have a price, which varies with the price of the underlying security and the unexpired time to maturity. The maturity of the option contract is generally a 3 or 4 months and as the time goes on the price varies from day-to-day and even minute to minute during trading time depending upon the demand and supply pressures.

@ OCC is Options Clearing Corporation

The value of option has two components.

(a) Intrinsic value, based on the underlying security.

(b) Time value based on the time available before expiry.

Risks of Buying and Selling Options

Depending on how options are used, investors can be subject to substantial risks or reduced risks. Losing the entire amount spent to purchase a call option or a put option is not an unusual event. Investors who write options are subject to the possibility of losing substantially more than the premium received. Option prices are volatile to the point that their relative values change by a multiple of the change in the underlying stock. Thus, anything that can bring about a change in the price of the underlying stock in a short period of time has the potential for producing great losses (or profits) for the owner of a stock option.

If an option position is established in combination with another investment that is purchased or is already owned, the result may be that an investor's risk is reduced. For example, an owner of 500 shares of TISCO may purchase five puts on this stock and guarantee a selling price in the event that the market price of the stock declines. Thus, the puts act as price insurance on the investment position. So is the case of call options. Likewise, investors will frequently write calls on stocks that they own to generate additional income. Because the stock is already owned by the writer, the required shares can be delivered in case the option buyer exercises the call.

While options can be used in conjunction with other securities to reduce the overall risk of an investment position, it is unlikely that this is the use to which most individual investors put options. The speculative investor satisfying his urge may however prefer this derivative market, which does not involve delivery.

Brokers and investment advisors frequently make the case that options expose investors to less risk than an investment in the underlying common stock, because the potential losses are smaller. This is true only for the rupee amount of the loss. An investor stands to lose less on options only because less money is initially invested. From this standpoint, the investor also generally stands to make less than would be the case if the underlying stock was purchased. An investment in options is substantially riskier than an investment in the underlying stock, unless this is combined with other investment or option combinations.

The bottom line for investors is that stock options should be avoided by anyone who dosen't have a thorough understanding of the fundamentals and potential risks of these volatile investments. The short-term nature of options frequently results in heavy trading and high commissions and only intelligent traders should get into this trade.

Growth of Derivative Markets

Derivative markets in the US, UK and Europe have been started in the seventies. In 1988 Japan has started its Topix Options and in 1993 Hongkong had its first options contracts. The European style options are based on the principle that the buyer can only exercise the right on the expiry date but not before. But in the US style of options, it can be exercised on any of the specific times before the expiry date. The rapid growth of derivatives was due to need for hedging in trade, increased volatility in cash markets, improved technology and deregulation in the markets. In India, options are now permitted by a change in law and NSE and BSE have started trading in them since 2001.

Market Structure

The options markets may have three different types of structures.

(a) Auction market with jobbers or market makers (as the present one).

(b) Order matching electronic trading.

(c) Dealer markets as in government security.

Auction markets require a trading floor which the present system of stock exchange can adopt. Even dealer markets can also be developed as in the gilt edged market or money markets in India. It is based on telephonic, telex and fax systems of communications.

Only in the case of order driven marketing system, computer aided trading is needed as in the OTC.

Types of Options

Options are of two types namely call options and put options as referred to earlier. Call option gives a right to buy without any obligation to buy; put option gives a right to sell without any obligation to sell.

Options have varying characteristics depending on the underlying securities and indexes. The writer of an option is a stock broker member or a security dealer. The buyer of an option pays only a premium or a price depending on the risk of the underlying security and he is an investor or a dealer or trader.

Advantages of Derivative Markets

1. Diversion of speculative instinct from the cash market to the derivatives.
2. Increased hedge for investors in cash market.
3. Reduced risk of holding underlying assets.
4. Lower transactions costs.
4. Enhance price discovery process.
6. Increased liquidity for investors and growth of savings flowing into these markets.
7. It increases the volume of transactions.
8. It leads to faster execution of trades and arbitrage and hedge against risk.

Globalisation and World Market Integration

The derivative markets also help the process of globalisation and spread of technology across the markets. The available supply of capital will increase at a given level of risk due to the provision of hedge in this market for the investments in the cash markets.

The competition will increase among the world markets, encourage openness of the economies and spread of capital across the borders in the world. The growth of technology and the revolution in the informatics will provide the avenue for such capital flows across borders and this is aided by the available options markets.

Salient Features of Options

The longest option period is 9 months but it can be for a shorter period of 30 days to 90 days. The expiration date is generally for March, June, September, and December, normally fixed for the second Friday of the month. The contract unit can be of 100 shares or stocks.

The trading in these contracts can be fixed for a specific time period say 9 a.m. to 11.15 a.m. and 1.00 p.m. to 3.15 p.m. as in Tokyo or just for a couple of hours in a day. The last day of trading will be the business day prior to the second Friday in the expiration month. The contract unit being 100 shares, the minimum trading unit can be fixed at 100 contracts. Instead of one exercise price, there can be many exercise prices at 50 point intervals of the index or of the underlying security price. The contract unit in Tokyo is 10,000 Yen multiplied by Topix.

There can be margin requirements for both customers and members. Customers may have to deposit transactions value of the option contract plus some percentage of the exercise price. Members have also to deposit some margins depending upon the option contracts sold. If trading is done on margin account instead of cash account margins are imposed by the Regulators. There is unlimited risk on uncovered short options. These risks are generally covered by hedges and actual possession of securities. The amount of margin payable depends on premium, market price and volatility of the scrip and a host of other factors.

Transactions in Options

The index options are traded during the permitted time period on auction principles. Only regular authorised members can trade in these options on their own account or on account of their clients. There can be jobbers or specialists who deal with the authorised members as market makers. In most developed markets as in Tokyo or New York, trading in options is routed through the computer-assisted order Routing and Execution System (CORES-O).

Contract Unit

The contract multiplier can be fixed at 100, 1,000 or 10,000. In Tokyo, the contract multiplier is 10,000. If the contract is a three month call option priced at 30 and the underlying index is 2,480 and the exercise price 2,500. The actual price paid by the call buyer is 30 × 10,000 = 300,000 Yen.

The Exchange can set an upper or lower limit for the price fluctuation at say 60 to 120 points depending upon the closing price of the previous day. The expiration cycle is 3 or 4 months in Tokyo. The expiration dates are second Friday, which is the day prior to the second Friday of the expiration month.

In Tokyo, there are five exercise prices for both call and put options. First a central exercise price is set by rounding the current value of the index to the nearest 50 or 100. Then two upper and lower exercise prices are set at 50 point intervals to bracket the central exercise price. The Exchange may when necessary change the number of exercise prices and their intervals.

Terms of Contracts

(a) Underlying Security can be any index or marketable security.

(b) Term to expiration is one day to 9 months in the U.S. There are standard expiration dates such as Second Friday of every month.

(c) Exercise price is the current market price — normally standardised by OCC.

(d) Premium is negotiable.

The Options clearing corporation of the U.S. (OCC) has standardised the following items in respect of Options.

(a) Exercise prices, based on the prices of underlying securities.

(b) Expiration cycles and expiration dates of the options contracts.

(c) Trading pattern and trading times.

(d) There are both an initial or maintenance margin calculation and a minimum margin calculation, standardised by the OCC.

Exercise Dates

Exercise is the act of converting a call option into a purchase and a put option into a sale of the underlying security. The holder has a right of such conversion but no obligation. Normally, options are not exercised but brought and sold through the auction system. The premium is the price paid for the option. If the option is held upto the last day of trading, and as the expiration date is the next day to the last day of trading it becomes worthless on the day following the third Friday of the expiration month.

Regulation of options rests with the OCC. The issuer of writer of options should be a member of the OCC which provides the service of guarantor and middleman between the issuer and the trader. In return the issuer has to keep margins in the form of underlying securities with the OCC.

Options vs. Badla

The age old method of badla financing facilitates the carry forward transactions in the stock market and serves almost the same purposes of helping speculation and imparting greater volume and better liquidity, as in the case of options. In both methods, no delivery of securities is envisaged and both depend on some underlying securities traded on cash/delivery basis. Then why did SEBI and other influential sources advocate the substitution of badla by options in India? Their perception is that badla adds to speculation and it is better to separate the speculative market from real investment market, so that genuine investors are protected from the effect of excessive speculation. Options would have the same effects and objectives as badla trading. Both increase liquidity, cater to the instinct of speculation and provide a hedge against risk. Both are tools of risk management and based on some rules and regulations, margins and other terms.

The differences between them and the advantages of option over Badla may be set out as follows:

The risk can be limited and kept with in a range both in upward and downward direction in the case of options. Transparency in operations is possible due to well organised trading in contracts in options. No manoveuvrability of terms, margins, expiration dates and no flexibility in operation are possible. Cash outlay is limited to the premiums paid and risk taken can be kept in limits. But once the contract period is over the right to exercise option ceases and no advantage can be taken of any favourable change in price. But in the case of badla, money lending is used as a tool. There is flexibility of margin fixation, and in fixation of carry forward prices. Badla terms can be bargained and the trader has the chance to adjust his purchase and sale position depending on the price movements after settlement, which is not possible for the option purchaser once the contract period is over.

Thus, options and badla have both advantages and disadvantages. The edge of options over badla will come in due to electronic trading possible through the use of computer network and this will also ensure greater transparency to trading in options. Otherwise, the time tested method of badla is by itself not inferior as a method of facilitating speculative trading and to increase the volume of trade and liquidity in the securities markets.

Options for Investors

To give an idea of how an investor benefits from the options, it is necessary to know the plus and minus features of these options. This can be demonstrated for two specific objectives of speculation and hedging, which are the common major use of options for investors. Options are a tool for the management of risk. A risk taker prefers the options to take advantage of speculation in the stock market. A risk averter also resorts to option as a hedge against risk. Options can also be used for inclusion in a portfolio by portfolio manager for diversification of risk by the investor for a given level of return.

For simplicity, two examples can be given for its use for speculation and hedging.

Options for Speculation and Hedging

Let us say that Reliance is quoted at ₹ 300 at end of November 2007. A call option is written for ₹ 300 RIL February, 2008 at a premium of ₹ 30. The investor purchased the call option at ₹ 30 and paid ₹ 3,000, for 100 shares. If he would have purchased the actual shares, the cash amount paid would be ₹ 30,000. The interest on this amount for three months at a rate of 20% p.a. would work out to ₹ 1,500. The premium/price paid on option would work out to ₹ 3,000. The loss for this investment would be limited to ₹ 3,000 if the price has fallen below ₹ 300 per share.

The Payment and Settlement System Act of 2007, gave powers to the RBI for the regulation and supervision of the payments system in India. Accordingly, the Payments and Settlement Systems Regulation, 2008, came into effect. The electronic clearing system was already in operation under the supervision of the RBI. All the payments and clearings have to pass through the banks.

In case the amount is borrowed, and invested in the cash market the loss would be ₹ 1,500, plus the actual price fall. Thus the loss is now limited and risk is known and calculated. But if the price goes beyond ₹ 300 let us say ₹ 330 before end of February, 2008 the option buyer has no profit or no loss. He paid for the option ₹ 30 and the exercise price of ₹ 300 plus premium paid ₹ 30 would just be covered by the actual price of ₹ 330. But if the actual price of Reliance went upto ₹ 350 as compared to his price of ₹ 330 paid for the option, he will make a gain of ₹ 20 per share without taking delivery of share and without shelling down ₹ 30,000 for the actual purchase of shares. This gain of ₹ 20 per share will give a gain of ₹ 2,000 per contract of 100 shares and on an investment of ₹ 3,000. This is clear speculative gain of 66% on a calculated risk.

The investor can look into the market behaviour of the share and of the high/lows of the past month and year. Thus, over year Reliance recorded a price range of ₹ 204 (low) to ₹ 452 (high). In this background if the investor is bullish, he will buy the call option of RIL ₹ 300 at a price of ₹ 30.

Suppose the investor is bearish and wants a hedge against future fall in price, as he holds Reliance in his portfolio, then he buys a put option. Let us say RIL February, 2008 is quoted say ₹ 300 at a premium of ₹ 20. If the contracted shares of 100 are sold in cash market he gets ₹ 30,000 but if he buys a put option he pays only ₹ 2,000. If the actual market price is, let us say ₹ 260 the investor can exercise his option to sell and get ₹ 300 per share and after deducting the premium paid ₹ 20 per share, he still gains ₹ 20 per share in this deal. Here the investor has protected his portfolio from a further loss if Reliance share prices fall more, before end of February, 2008.

An investor can buy both a call option and put option for limiting his risk and trade in options market. Thus, RIL call ₹ 300 February 2008 @ ₹ 30 (premium). Bought 100 calls and RIL put ₹ 300 February 2008 at ₹ 20 (premium) bought 100 puts.[@]

The range of price in which he is protected from risk is ₹ 330 at high and ₹ 280 at low. He paid ₹ 50 per share for this option position. Alternatively an investor may buy in the cash market at ₹ 300 per share and cover his risks by buying a put option RIL 320 February 2008 at a price of ₹ 20.

Various combinations of puts and calls along with or without deals in the cash market can provide the necessary hedge to the investor. Hedging in the options market can be got by taking the opposite position in the cash market. Hedging in the options market itself is called spreading (Bull spread or Bear spread).

Thus, an investor can plan for speculation pure and simple or for calculated hedge of risk or for portfolio management, if he is operating in the options market.

Settlement and Clearance

An agency like Options Clearing Corporation (OCC) was set up and the members of which can write options and trade in them. Members are normally registered stock brokers or security firms. The OCC laid down the rules

@ The scrip prices are not current prices but selected for illustration. The Payment and Settlement Systems Act of 2007, gave powers to the RBI for the regulation and supervision of the payments systems in India. Accordingly, the Payment and Settlement Systems Regulations, 2008, came into effect. The electronic clearing system was already in operation under the supervision of the RBI. All the payments and clearings have to pass through the banks.

and regulate the trading in options through imposition of margins, deposit of underlying securities and settle disputes. The OCC also provided the facilities for settlement and clearance in the contracts in options, as in the case of the stock exchange for contracts for hand delivery and those for clearing as at present regulated.

The OCC will govern the terms for writing the contracts, trading hours, expiration dates, exercise dates and related matters for the options. Finally, at the end of trading on last day, the settlement and clearance facilities are also extended by this corporation through computerised EDP and netting procedures.

Reference was made earlier of what all the authorities can control and standardise in terms of option contracts. The rules governing the writing of the options trading in such contracts, exercise dates, expiration dates etc., are all governed by such controlling body. In India, the control rests with the SEBI, and the RBI

As in the case of the regular stock exchange activity involving the regulation of trading and of the members' activities in securities trading, the control of options trading is to be entrusted to a separate body regionally or on an all India basis. The final control of all the self-regulatory bodies such as options control corporations rests with the Securities and Exchange Board. The regular stock exchanges, the NSE and the BSE have formulated the rules for implementing them in India, and SEBI has approved them. SEBI remains as the final Controlling Authority in India.

REPORT ON DERIVATIVES

Derivatives Market

As part of financial market reforms, new instruments and financial reengineering have been introduced in India since 1991. One area where the growth and innovation is slow is in the introduction of derivatives. What are the factors which hindered the introduction and growth of derivative markets in India? Infrastructural difficulties, poor clearing and settlement procedures, differences in practices among Stock Exchanges and low level of expertise among brokers, sub-brokers and investors in absorbing new technologies and low level of electronic trading network.

Although National Securities Clearing Corporation (NSCC) was created by NSE in 1996, some headway was made in the introduction of NSE 50 Index limited futures market, NSE with slow in the process but due to unpreparedness of member brokers, insufficient funds with brokers and inadequate infrastructural support. The Government also wanted to go slow in this process.

The L.C. Gupta Committee on Derivatives (1998) reportedly favoured the introduction of derivative market in a phased manner in India. As a first step, Index futures are recommended and trading in derivatives is to be strictly regulated by the Exchange authorities, as per the Rules to be made by the SEBI. But the scope and the need for such derivative market is undoubtedly accepted by the committee. Index futures can be followed by other derviative markets like those in Interest Rates and Foreign Exchange rates, in a phased manner.

Experience in Developed Countries

The committee has drawn heavily on the experience of derivative markets in the Developed Countries. In India, the experience of this type of trading will be found to be riddled with hurdles of poor regulatory enforcement, malpractices and failures of the system. The experience in badla trading is felt to be completely different from that of derivative markets although the intent and purpose are the same. The separation of cash market from speculative market and provision of a different venue for the operation of speculative forces is no doubt laudable. But the fact that it is closely linked to the cash market cannot guarantee the separation of these markets and the interlinkages are bound to create problems and the effect of one on the other. In this context, when badla is already providing a venue for speculative instinct, the need for futures and options is felt less impending. But, the Government is determined to replace the badla system by a more modern and sophisticated electronic trading system in the derivatives in India for the benefit of trading by FIIs and FFIs, who are more used to these markets.

The government was only biding the time for the broker members and investors to get ready for the introduction of the futures trading in India. The BSE members being used to Badla trading wanted a phased introduction of futures, while NSE is more willing and ready for the trading in the futures. The experience of developed countries succintly proved that the success of the future trading depends on how effectively the rules are enforced, dematerialisation of physical certificates and effective and efficient system of clearing and settlement.

Experience in Emerging Countries

China, Singapore and Hongkong have successfully introduced the Derivative markets. Countries, which introduced derivatives after 1990 among the developing countries are Brazil, Korea, Philippines, Malaysia, Argentina, Spain, in addition to China, Singapore and Hong Kong, referred to above. Many other developing countries are working towards setting up derivative markets as in the case of Turkey, Colombia, Greece, Poland, Thailand, Indonesia etc. In the category, mention may be of India, whose efforts in this direction are laudable.

The SEBI has decided on the introduction of derivatives in a phased manner and L.C. Gupta report on the subject is being implemented. The greatest hurdle in India as per this Report is regulation in which all the regulatory bodies like SEBI, RBI and Ministry of finance are seriously concerned. The derivative markets opens up the gates of greater competition, globalisation and speculation. The areas of concern are the possible manipulation, inadequate expertise and concern with the efficiency of clearing house and settlement procedures. The securities industry derivatives start with equity and go to debt instruments and spread, to all markets like foreign exchange, commodities and real estate and make these markets exposed to global forces where efficiency and manipualtion are both forces to reckon with. Among equities index derivatives were the first to be started followed by those of stocks.

Gupta's Report on Derivatives

L.C. Gupta Committee Report on Derivatives was submitted to SEBI in March 1998. The panel took an year to complete the drafting of the Report. The Committee is of the view that introduction of Derivatives trading is an important component of modernising the capital markets. The trading in derivatives will provide a much needed hedge mechanism to the big players and institutional investors in the Market. The derivative segment should have a minimum of 50 Members.

The Committee wanted a phased introduction of derivative trading in India under strict controls and rules. The Committee has also set out a Model Set of Rules and guidelines. Models of derivative trading as existing in some well developed markets have been set out by the committee. The capital or networth requirements for the trading members and clearing members are set out.

The future capital market should be sophisticated with well developed segments of all types namely cash market, forward market, options and futures etc. These segments will attract more foreign funds to come in through the FFIs and FIIs in particular who are familiar with this type of trading in developed countries and will be at home in these markets and make them popular with the Indian counterparts as well. The individuals and small investors may be out of this market due to strict capital adequacy norms and high margins.

Section 2 (H) of S.C. (R) Act has been amended by a notification of the Government to give recognition to derivatives as a security and promote trade in the segment of the Market. In March 2000, the forward trade in securities has been permitted with the result that it opened up the gates for trading in derivatives.

Derivative Trading

The BSE has started derivatives trading in the Index Futures, based on the sensex series, with effect from June 9, 2000. The NSE has started this trading in Index Futures contracts, based on S & PCN X Nifty with effect from June 12,2000. These contracts are for one to three months and mature on the last Friday of the contract month. Each contract would be valued as the sensex value on a particular day, multiplied by ₹ 5, per each Index point. Stock options and futures were started in mid 2001. Trading in option and futures contracts of one to three months are now taking place. The data reported in the press relate to standard or exercise price, premium, traded quantity, Notional value, no. of contracts, open interest and expiration dates of contracts, etc.

The final settlement will be done on the last trading day. The method of settlement and the other terms are as approved by the SEBI. The BSE has developed the on line derivatives Trading and Settlement Software (DTSS) to facilitate trading. The DTSS software covers trading settlement, risk management, default handling, and collateral management.

The BSE has made mandatory for broker members of its Derivative Segment to have minimum of two approved users for operating Derivative work station. The users are required to pass the Derivatives certification test which is being conducted in coordination with NIIT and BSE.

The Derivative Trading is open to all institutional and individual/corporate members, subject to some networth, requirements and passing the above test. This made the Indian Capital Market one of the sophisticated markets in the world.

The minimum contract value on BSE was pegged at around ₹ 2.25 lakh, with an initial margin of 10%. Trading volume was low in the starting period but has picked up, as experience is gained in this line. Options are quoted in daily trade and the published data contain the open, high low, close, open interest and number of contracts etc. for each of the contracts.

National clearing and settlement system was set up and electronic clearing and funds flows accelerated the trading in derivatives. The NSE is leading over the BSE in this trade. The turnover in derivative market was more than twice the turnover in the cash market despite the fact that derivative trade was started only in 2001. Besides, the derivative trade on NSE is far surpassing that on BSE, in terms of both of value and volume of trades.

Options Valuation

Problem 1

The market price of Wipro is ₹ 28 at present. Six month call option is written on the stock with an excercise price of ₹ 30. Presently, the option has a market price of ₹ 3. Expected market price of stock and their probabilities are as follows:

Price	₹ 24	28	32	37	43
Probability	0.1	0.2	0.4	0.2	0.1

Answer:

Expected value V of share price is given by a formula. (weighted average)

24 (0.1) + 28 (.2) + 32 (.4) + 37 (.2) + 43 (.1)

2.4 + 5.6 + 12.8 + 7.4 + 4.3 = 32.5 = ₹ 32.5

At share prices less than ₹ 30, which is the exercise price, the option has zero value. The Theoritical value of the option.

(28 – 30) = 0

Hedge Ratio: This is explained in detail in the next chapter.

Problem 2

$$\text{The Hedge ratio is } \frac{uV_o - dV_o}{uV_s - dV_s}$$

Two possible values of Equity Stock — highest and lowest: one is higher than the current value of the stock say uVs and the other by dVs the lower one. Coxton's share price is ₹ 60, it will be ₹ 75 six months hence with a probability of 0.7 and ₹ 50 with a probability of 0.3. A call option exists on the stock that can be exercised at the end of six months at ₹ 65; illustrate its hedged position.

Answer

$$\text{Hedge Ratio} = \frac{10-0}{75-50} = \frac{10}{25} = 0.4,$$ The numerator is explained by

option value at the highest point 75 – 65 = 10

option value at the lowest point 60 – 65 = 0

Exercise price is ₹ 65 and the maximum price is ₹ 75 and minimum price is ₹ 60.

The hedged position can be illustrated under the two possibilities as follows:

Stock Price	*Value of Long Position in Stock*	*Value of Short Position in Stock*	*Value of Combined Hedge Position*
₹ 75	2 (75) = 150;	–5(10) = – 50;	₹ 100
₹ 50	2 (50) = 100	–5 (0) = 0	₹ 100

Here the value of the Hedged position is the same irrespective of the Stock value possibility.

What is the expected value of option price?

EV of option price = (75 – 65) (.7) + 0 (.3)

= 10 × 0.7 + 0

= ₹ 7

BIBLIOGRAPHY

1. Gastineau Gary., *Options Manual.* McGraw-Hill Publishing House.
2. McMillan Lawrence G., *Options as a Strategic Investment, NYIF.*
3. Mesler Donald T., *Stock Index Options, PROBUS.*
4. Yates James W., *Options Strategy Spectrum,* Dow Jones Irwin.
5. *TOPIX — Tokyo Stock Price Index, T.S.E.*

15 VALUATION OF RIGHTS, WARRANTS AND CONVERTIBLE CLAIMS

Introduction

Normally, any Company follows the accounting norms in valuation of all the assets and liabilities, as laid down by the Institute of Chartered Accountants. Subject to these guidelines, the accounting practices vary from company to company. When a company is due to pay interest or repay the principal, these become contingent liabilities, due at specified future dates. They are paid out of current revenues if it is interest and out of profits or Debenture Redemption Reserves fund, created for this purpose if it is repayment of principal of debt.

If the contingent liabilities are some dues to be paid to the excise, customs or income tax authorities, or other claims pending, they are shown in the Balance Sheet under Notes or Auditor's Comments. These have to be met as and when they fall due for payment, and sometimes provisions are made, for them in advance by prudent companies and kept in special accounts. Normally a company is healthy and liquid if its current assets are two times the current liabilities so that if the current assets are sold as they are atleast 50% of the book value or market value of current assets can be realised and liabilities can be met in full. Then in the investors' perception, the company is rated as fully solvent for current purposes.

What is Contingent Claim?

Contingent claims due to options, warrants, convertible debentures and similar instruments are different from the ones referred to earlier. These claims arise in the event of the holders of debt instruments opting for equity — a right or option given to them in the above instruments by the company. Then the claim of debtor is to become owner with the following implications:

(1) Tax benefits for interest income as a deductible expense will disappear for the company with its impact on net profits.

(2) The leverage enjoyed through the debt for equity capital may also vanish to the extent that the return on total capital employed is higher than the interest burden on debt and that privilege to trade on borrowed funds will not exist.

(3) Conversion of debt into equity will increase equity base and larger profits have to be earned for servicing this larger equity base.

(4) The cost of servicing equity is higher than servicing debt with the result that the company will have to earn larger profits through larger sales and/better profit margins.

The above factors lead to changes in capital structure, average cost of capital and profitability. On the other hand, a company with larger equity and less debt has the following advantages: (1) Dividends or equity need not be paid if profits are not adequate but interest to creditors has to be paid, (2) The riskiness of the venture will come down due to reduction of debt burden and credit rating will improve for the company, (3) With a larger equity base, the potential for borrowing from banks and financial institutions and even from public at any future date will increase and company can expand and diversify better than before. These are the plus and minus points in the case of contingent claims.

Pricing of Such Claims

There is no standard method of pricing of such contingent claims. But the erstwhile CCI used some guidelines for fixing the pricing of securities, particularly for equity shares. But in the case of debentures, bonds and debt instruments, they are issued at par, with a face value of ₹ 100, normally except in the cases of discount bonds or Premium Notes.

It is also laid down that if conversion facility is offered, the company has to justify the premium or the price fixed to the SEBI before they are issued to the public, but no formulas are presented by the SEBI.

If such claims are partly or fully convertible into equity shares as warrants and loyalty coupons, etc., then the issue of their pricing becomes relevant. The non-convertible part of pure debt instruments is taken at par, while the convertible part is priced as per the normal pricing mechanism of equity shares. This in essence involves first a decision on the part to be converted or the terms of the warrants such as period of time etc. The pricing of warrants and the convertible part of bonds are freely decided by the company and SEBI does not interfere, except for seeking disclosures and justifications for the premium or price fixed.

Free Market Pricing

This is dealt with in a separate chapter but under the current policy of Government free market pricing is permitted for any category of ownership funds. But the norms used by companies or merchant bankers can be set out as follows:

(1) SEBI has permitted differential pricing if the company is going for rights cum public issue, with separate prices for rights to the existing shareholders from that offered under public issue.

(2) In case of FCD, PCD etc., with convertibles or warrants pricing for convertible portion is again freely decided by the company, subject to their confidence of acceptability by the public and justification to the SEBI. The principle adopted, as in foreign markets, is what the market can bear, or what investors perceive as reasonable for investment.

(3) In practice, the price fixation is based on the past price record of the share and its future projection based on some bench marks like EPS and P/E multiple.

(4) The average of the market prices for the last three years is one criteria if it is already listed and traded.

(5) The book value and earnings per share (EPS) and projection of its future price based on P/E multiple for the industry or for comparable companies are also sometimes taken into account. This is shown in same case studies, presented in this book.

What is a Convertible Security?

A convertible security is a bond or debenture or preferred stock that can be converted into equity of a company. The original security is a debt instrument, which can be converted into an ownership instrument, after a time. The period of holding necessary for conversion, the ratio of conversion and other terms including the price are to be laid down in the beginning itself. Once the conversion terms are stated, they cannot be altered by the company unilaterally.

The SEBI guidelines cover all the categories of convertible instruments and new financial products like warrants, loyalty coupons etc. As per these guidelines, a company can issue three types of debentures as debt instruments, *viz.*:

(*a*) *Fully Convertible Debentures:* These are fully convertible into equity in phases at predetermined times, say 6 months or 12 or 18 months etc., and the terms of conversion including the conversion price are to be spelt out in the beginning itself including the compulsory nature of conversion. The company decides the periods and prices, at which they will be converted into equity. They may be converted in instalments or all at one instalment. Thus, fully convertible debentures can be converted in two instalments of 50% for 6 months hence and the other 50% at the end of 12 months or in three or more instalments such as 25% of the total each time.

If the conversion period is within 18 months, these amounts will be treated as good as equity, as per the SEBI guidelines, for the purposes of debt equity ratio and other legal and procedural requirements since withdrawn in March 1998. They do not have to follow the guidelines applicable to debt, namely, bonds or debentures, which are not convertible. FCDs with a conversion period of more than 36 months are not permissible to be issued except under special terms. Instruments of less than 18 months have to be treated as debt and rated by Credit Rating Agencies.

(*b*) *Partly Convertible Bonds:* These are the second category of debt which are convertible in part while the rest is non-convertible. Thus, a debt instrument can have a face value of ₹ 100 of which ₹ 60 is convertible at the end of 12 months at a specified price and in specific convertible ratio such as two equity shares for ₹ 60, each of ₹ 30, (for a share of face value of ₹ 10 and with a premium of ₹ 20). As the market price may be ruling higher than ₹ 30 per equity share, the conversion facility will appear attractive to the investors. During the first year, the bondholder gets interest at a fixed rate of say 14% and after that ₹ 60 out of ₹ 100 (for each bond) will become two equity shares on which dividend will be paid, if declared out of profits at the end of second year. Thus, it has the advantage of both debt and equity.

The rest of 40% will remain as debt only and will continue to get interest at the specified coupon rate of 14% for the rest of its life, until redemption. As per the Companies Act and the Rules made thereunder all debt instruments say, bonds or debentures can have a maturity period of 5 to 7 years, extendable upto nine years in some cases, after which redemption becomes compulsory. Any such non-convertible bonds can be renewed, if the company wants after maturity at the specific written consent of the investors only.

(c) *Non-convertible Bonds (NCDs):* The third category of debt instruments is the non-convertible debentures called N.C.D. (also called khokhas for the non-convertable portion). This category will have to be held until the maturity or redemption date after 5 to 9 years. It is entitled to only interest per annum, payable half yearly or once in a year. This category is pure debt while the first category of fully convertible debentures is as good as equity and the second category is partly debt and partly ownership capital. All the above categories are to have specific terms, spelt out in the beginning itself before investors decide to put in their funds. No debt instrument or bond can be issued in India without redemption, under the law.

Valuation of Rights Shares

Companies can also issue rights shares which are a right to buy the equity shares of the company given at par or a premium to the existing shareholders in a particular proportion to their holdings. Under Section 81 of Companies Act, companies issuing further capital after two years of the formation of the company or after one year of the first allotment of the shares have to offer the same as rights to the existing shareholders.

The premium used to be fixed on the basis of the average book value of the company and post-tax earning capacity of the shares normally capitalised at 15% and even at 8% if the market price is substantially higher than the fair price. The average of the two prices worked out on the basis of book value and the earning capitalisation model is accepted. If earnings for share is ₹ 3 and capitalisation rate is 15%, then the fair price is $3/15 \times 100 = 20$ according to the earnings capitalisation formula. The price on the basis of book value is, say, ₹ 30.[1] Then the average of these two prices ₹ 20 and ₹ 30, namely, ₹ 25 is taken as the fair price for fixing the premium (namely, ₹ 15 on a share with the face value of ₹ 10).[2]

The rights are quoted in the market. The price of the rights will depend on the ratio on which they are issued. If the ratio is 1:3 and the market price is ₹ 50, then valuation of rights is done as follows:

Let the premium be ₹ 15, then,

$$\frac{50 \times 3 + 25}{4} = \frac{175}{4} = 44$$

The value of one right is ₹ 44 – 25 = 19 which is got for three shares (₹ 6.33 for one existing share).

Rights can be issued only if authorised by a special resolution of the company. The company making the rights has to inform the existing shareholders as to the use to which the additional funds are put, the future earning capacity of the company and other financial indicators such as sales, estimated gross profit or loss, etc. This information would enable the shareholders to decide to opt for the rights or not.

Preference Shares

Preference shares are of a hybrid category having ownership rights like equity and also a fixed income like creditor capital. They have preferred rights for payment of dividend, along with arrears, if any, if such provision is made in the Articles of Association. They are paid their fixed dividend before any dividend is declared to the equityholders. Besides they have also similar preferential right over equity to payment of capital and their share of assets in the event of winding up of the company. This right is, however, subject to the claims of creditors.

This instrument is suitable to some investors who would like to take some risk but not as much as equityholders but more than debenture-owners. They get an income which may, however, fluctuate depending upon the profits of the company but fixed, if profits are adequate to service all preference and equityholders. They may also get back their capital after a fixed period like debentures as per the present law.

The return on preference shares is fixed by the Government at 14% since April 1987 although some companies offer a higher or lower rate with the permission of the government. The preference shareholders do not enjoy any voting rights except in respect of resolution affecting their rights or when their dividends due are in arrears for the past two financial years.

---

1. Book value is net worth of the company divided by the number of equity shares.
2. The method of premium fixation adopted by the erstwhile CCI is given already.

There are various types of preference shares like redeemable and non-redeemable, cumulative and non-cumulative, participating and non-participating and convertible and non-convertible.

Preference shares are redeemable generally after 12 years and for this purpose, the company is required to provide for transfer out of profits a sum to the reserves called Capital Redemption Reserve. If there is no provision to redeem these shares, they are non-redeemable. As these non-redeemable shares were not popular, they were abolished by the Companies Amendment Act of 1988.

Preference shares which have a right to receive dividends in a cumulative fashion are called cumulative preference shares. These enjoy the right to receive dividends in all the years in which the dividends are skipped, as profits were inadequate in those years. The fixed dividend on preference shares should be paid later in a cumulative way when profits are adequate before any dividends are declared for equityholders. Those which have no such right are called non-cumulative preference shares.

Preference shares are convertible, if there is a provision for their conversion into equity after a specified period in a particular ratio to the existing equity shares. Preference shares may not be convertible if no such provision is made. Preference shares are participating, if they can share in profits in excess of a guaranteed fixed return, if such a provision is made in the Articles of the company and specify the level of profitability such as an equity dividend of 20%. If these are not so participative, they are called non-participating.

CCP

A new instrument called Cumulative Convertible Preference Shares was introduced by the Government in 1985, the features of which are as follows:

(1) The CCPs can be issued by any public limited company to raise finance for new projects, expansion and diversification, etc.

(2) The amount of issue of CCP will be to the extent of the equity issue to the public for subscription.

(3) The dividend payable is fixed at 10%.

(4) The entire issue of CCP would be convertible into equity shares between three and five years.

These issues have not proved popular with the companies as the dividend on their shares is not a tax deductible item as in the case of interest on debentures. Besides, the dividend of 10% for the first 3 to 5 years has not proved attractive to investors.

But preference shares as a class are attractive to institutions and individuals in the high income brackets as the dividend income on them is tax exempt under Section 80L unlike interest income on debentures and company deposits. But companies themselves do not find these preference shares as an attractive alternative to raise funds, except in the special conditions when the company is unable to raise funds from fresh equities from the public or in the form of rights.

Legal Provisions

The Companies Act provides for issue of debentures, warrants and other bearer certificates, under Sections 114 to 120. These instruments may provide for an entitlement to the holder a specified number of equity shares. If these debentures or bonds are not convertible into equity or are not converted, the debenture or bondholder has no voting rights in the company and does not become an owner. But debentureholders are represented by the debenture Trustee in the meetings of equityholders (AGM or EGM). They are entitled under the Act, for asking for transfers and for Copies of Annual Reports. In respect of registers to be maintained under Sections 15 and 152 of the Companies Act, the debenturesholders are treated alike as shareholders. The closure of registers, the procedure for transfers of debentures are all similar to those of equity shares.

The SEBI has also laid down that in the event of declaration of bonus by a company with convertible debentures or bonds, due for conversion within 12 months, provision has to be made to protect the rights of such holders to equity and subsequently to bonus, declared during the year. Convertible bonds thus enjoy some specific privileges and incentives.

Norms for NCD and Non-convertible Portion of PCD

These are pure debt instruments and are governed by norms of issue laid by SEBI. Briefly all debentures are to be credit rated for risk element involved and the capacity of the company to redeem the principal and service the creditors with interest etc.

These debt instruments can be issued subject to the following conditions:

(a) They are to be compulsorily redeemed. Debentures issued for working capital should not exceed 20% of total current Assets.

(b) Debt to equity ratio should normally be 2:1 ratio, except for some capital-intensive projects.

(c) They are creditors of the company and cannot therefore attend the AGMs of the company. But their interests are protected under a debenture Trust Deed.

(d) All debt or debenture issues should be covered by a Trust Deed and a debenture Trustee is appointed to operate under the Trust deed, which governs the relations of the company and debentureholders. The Trust deed and debenture Trustee have to be approved by the SEBI.

(e) The company has to complete the above formalities within 6 months from the date of allotment of debentures and/or despatch of debenture certificates.

(f) The company has to create a Debenture Redemption Reserve Fund (DRR), out of the profits of the company, after the commercial production started. These reserves should reach a stage of 50% of the total debenture amount, before it can be used to redeem the debentures. Besides, their use can be started for repayment purposes, after the company has already redeemed at least 10% of the outstanding amount due from out of the current profits.

Conversion Value

Conversion value of a convertible security is the conversion ratio[@] of the security, times the market price, per share. Conversion price is the price at which the debenture will be converted into equity. If it is a convertible debenture, it has to be compulsorily converted at the specific price and time which should have been specified in the terms of issue.

If the present market price of Cipla is ₹ 260 and the conversion price is fixed at ₹ 250, the premium on conversion is ₹ 10 (260 – 250). The minimum period of holding or conversion time is fixed at the beginning of issue and normally converted on allotment, six months hence etc. If the actual price is ₹ 280 in the market, the investor gains a premium of ₹ 280 – 250 = ₹ 30 per share. If the debenture amount is ₹ 500 and is to be converted into equity shares at ₹ 250 each, two equity shares will be allotted to him and his total premium or gain is ₹ 60 per debenture.

If the debenture is a convertible one, the right to call before conversion by the company is not given, but the call provision may be incorporated in case of N.C.D. or bonds.

In the case of NCD, or non-convertible bond, the company is allowed to offer a premium upto 5%, on the face value, at the time of redemption, as an incentive for holding the debenture until maturity.

Conversion Premium

As already referred, convertibles enjoy the benefit of a premium on conver-sion. If market price is say ₹ 280 and conversion price is ₹ 250, the premium enjoyed is ₹ 30. If suppose the market price has fallen to ₹ 220, there is no incentive to holders of convertibles on conversion. To offset such contingencies SEBI has permitted conversion only at an incentive price and not at a disincentive. Thus, whatever the market price, a company can offer conversion at the book value/face value or at a discount of ₹ 20 or so on market price.

In some cases, the option of Call and Put is given to the holders of convert-ibles, if the period of conversion is after 36 months. Compulsion of conversion is only provided for, if it is made immediately on allotment, so that the market price and intrinsic value of share are all known and the premium on conversion is ensured. For all conversions, after the allotments, substantial discounts are provided for in the conversion terms. If the debenture is NCD, provision for buy back at face value through a financial institution or a lead bank is made, so that investors do not lose in the capital value of bond due to fall in its price, after allotment.

PRICING OF CONVERTIBLES

Valuation of Convertibles

Whether it is a bond or debenture with an option of convertibility or compulsory conversion at the end of a perid of time, the value of that bond or debenture is related firstly to the value of *equity* into which it can be converted and secondly to the value of residual non-convertible portion of the debenture instrument, which remains as debt instrument.

@ Conversion ratio of 1 : 2 means that a holder of one debenture is given two equity shares. Then market price of equity shares is to be multiplied by two to arrive at Conversion Value.

Both the above components vary with the market conditions, time to expiry of the bond, prevailing interest rates or yields, etc. Let us take the first component of convertible bond convertible into equity (say C_1). This C_1 depends on the number of equity shares into which that convertible portion can be converted. The face value of bond say ₹ 75, convertible into 5 equity shares at ₹ 15 each. The bond face value is, normally ₹ 100 of which ₹ 75 is convertible at the end of three years into 5 equity shares at ₹ 15 per share, the residual ₹ 25 will remain as bond and carry coupon rate of 12%, payable annually (here denoted as C_2). Thus, Bond face value ₹ 100 consists of two components namely $C_1 + C_2$.

For the First Three Years ₹ 100, the face value of the Bond carries with it an interest return of 12% per bond. At the end of three years, ₹ 75 is converted into 5 equity shares. If the market price is ₹ 20 and exercise price for converion is ₹ 15, then the convertible portion gains by ₹ 5 per share, say a total gain of 25 (5 × 5). Besides for the next two years, equity shares may show capital gains or losses plus dividends, if any declared for the rest of the period to maturity. The non-convertible portion of the Bond earns 12% per year namely ₹ 4 on ₹ 25 of the Bond of ₹ 100.

Graphical Presentation

The price of the convertible bond and the conversation value of the bond are related by the equation $C_1 = \frac{F}{Pc} \times Ps$, where, F is the principal value of the Convertible Bond Pc conversion price into equity. Ps Market price of equity.

Upto ₹ 15, the exercise price or the conversion price is the same as the market price. Thus, Pc = Ps; then C_1 = F and the value convertible bond is the same as the market price.

If Ps is greater than Pc, that is, if market price is more than conversion price, then C_1 is greater than F. If Pc > Ps, that is, if conversion price of 15 is more than the market price (say ₹ 10), then the C_1 < F. In the graph below, conversion value is shown on the Y-axis and price of equity share is represented on the X-axis.

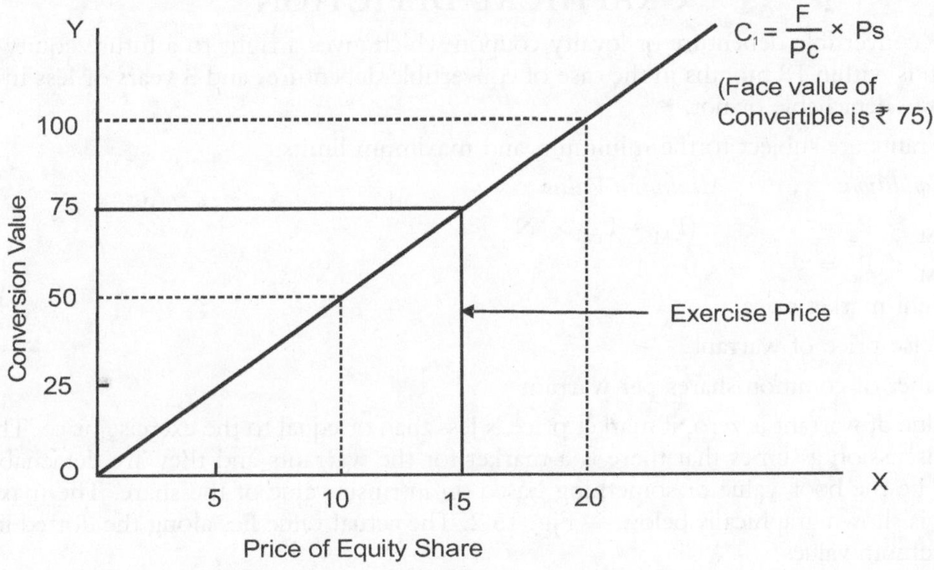

Fig. 15.1

If the price of equity in the market is ₹ 20, then the conversion value is ₹ 100 as against the face value of ₹ 75. During the first three years, when conversion has not become exercisable, it is as good as debt but the conversion value of the convertible bond will go up and down over the face value of ₹ 75 and after that, it depends on the market price of equity for 5 equity shares.

Suppose the conversion portion of the Bond is ₹ 75 and the non-conversible bond is ₹ 25; the total bond value can be ₹ 125, as against face value of bond of ₹ 100. The conversion value of convertible debenture sets the minimum market price of the convertible bond. If actual market price is higher, then arbitraguers operate and buy equity shares and short sell the convertible bond. If the actual market price of the bond is less than its value as equity, the Arbitraguers will purchase the bond and sell short the equity and the shares later purchased through the bond would cover the short sale of equity.

To give an example, the convertible bond may be selling at ₹ 60, when the equity based price is ₹ 75 based on ₹ 15 as exercise price for 5 equity shares, then arbitraguers will buy the convertible bond at ₹ 60 and exercise the option to get 5 equity shares at ₹ 15. The short position taken by the buyer will be covered by conversion option in which he makes a profit of ₹ 15.

The supply and demand factors operate to determine the price of the convertible bond, but is basically dependent on the conversion value of the convertible bond. Normally the convertible has also a debt component, namely ₹ 25 and hence its actual price will be ₹ 60 + 25 = ₹ 85 and at the exercise price of ₹ 15, the bondholder gets ₹ 75 + 25 = 100. Then the conversion bond quotes at a premium over its face value, if the conversion value of the bond is less than the market price of corresponding equity shares.

Role of Interest Rate

As regards the convertible bond, the coupon rate offered on it is generally lower than the market rate offered on non-Convertible bonds of comparable maturity. The reason is that such bonds are quoted at a premium due to the value added incentive following from the conversion facility. The value of bond as debt, is lower than that of the convertible bond which includes partly equity component and partly debt component. Since interest paid on convertible debenture is fixed, the value of this bond varies inversely with interest rate. The higher is the interest rate, with coupon rate fixed at say 12½%, the lower is the value of the convertible bond, for the same degree of risk and maturity. The market operators would buy convertible bond to attain the higher yield, if its price is lower than that floor. The operators can not force down the price any more beyond the floor price of the non-convertible debt, even if the value of the equity into which the convertible portion is to be converted were to decline. The reason is that at the floor point the whole Bond value is treated as equal to debt which sets the floor, but at the peak level, the limit is set by the market price of equity and conversion value of the convertible bond plus the face value of the non-convertible portion of the convertible bond. There is thus insurance at the floor level but with opportunity of gain the upper end of the bond price.

GRAPHICAL DEPICTION

A warrant or convertible debenture or loyalty coupon which gives a right to a future equity is like non-voting share, if conversion is within 18 months in the case of convertible debentures and 3 years or less in the case warrants, loyalty coupons, etc., detachable or not.

Prices of warrants are subject to the minimum and maximum limits.

Condition	*Minimum Value*
$P_M > P_e =$	$(P_M - P_e) \times N$
$P_M < P_e =$	0

P_M = Current market price

P_e = Exercise price of warrant

N = Number of common shares per warrant

Minimum value of warrant is zero, if market price is less than or equal to the exercise price. The maximum value is $P_M \times N$. The discussion assumes that there is a market for the warrants and they are detachable. The minimum exercise price may be the book value or something based on intrinsic value of the share. The maximum price is the market price. This is shown graphically below — Fig. 15.2. The actual value lies along the dotted line in between the minimum and maximum values.

Convertible bond is assumed to be tradeable and has a market value. So is the case with convertible preference shares. It has both investment value and conversion value. Investment value (straight value) is based on the ytm in respect of a bond and dividend on preferred stock, in respect of Convertible Preference Share. Investment value is the face value for bonds; which is the minimum payable to bondholders. The investment value of CPS is $V = \frac{D}{\gamma}$, where D is dividend for preferred stock, and γ is the current yield or appropriate discount rate. For Bonds, we take ytm, instead of γ, for straight value. The conversion value will change with the market price. If the bond can be exchanged for 20 shares, and market price of each is 55, then the conversion value = 55 × 20 = ₹ 1,100.

Investment value = ₹ 1,000

Market Stock price = ₹ 55 and

Market Bond price ₹ 1,200.

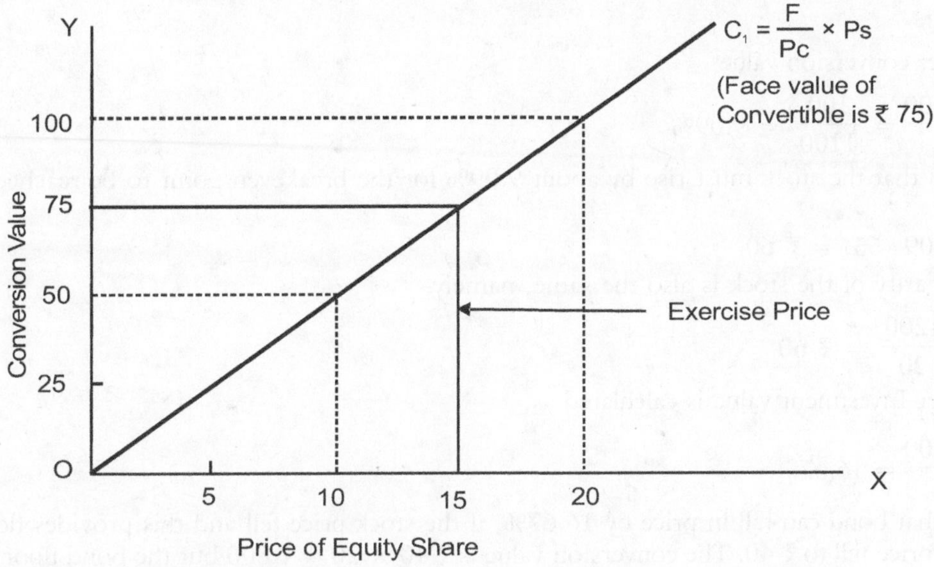

Fig. 15.2. Slope of Pe depends on the number of shares exchanged

Graphically, the values and market premium for a convertible bond are shown below:

(*i*) Premium over conversion value is

$$= \frac{\text{Bond Price} - \text{Conversion Value}}{\text{Conversion Value}}$$

(*ii*) Premium over Investment value is

$$= \frac{\text{Bond Price} - \text{Investment Value}}{\text{Bond Price}}$$

(*iii*) Conversion parity price of stock

$$= \frac{\text{Bond Price}}{\text{No. of shares on conversion}}$$

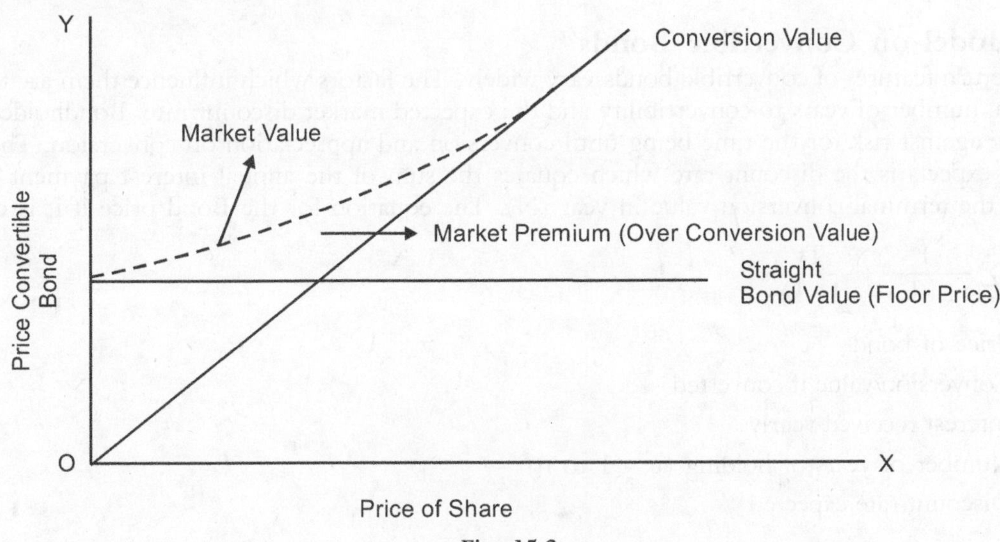

Fig. 15.3

Examples

Premium over conversion value

$$₹ \frac{1200 - 1100}{1100} = \frac{100}{1100} = 9.09\%$$

This suggests that the stock must rise by about 9.09% for the breakeven point to be reached. If stock price is 55, then

₹ 55 + 0.0909 (55) = ₹ 60

Conversion parity of the stock is also the same, namely,

$$= \frac{1200}{20} = ₹ 60$$

Premium over Investment value is calculated as,

$$\frac{1200 - 1000}{1200} = 16.67$$

This means that bond can fall in price by 16.67%, if the stock price fell and this provides floor price of bond. Suppose the stock price fell to ₹ 40. The conversion value is ₹ 40 × 20 = ₹ 800 but the bond floor price may remain at ₹ 1,000.

In the trading of convertibles, one has to look into the current yields on stock and bonds. Suppose the underlying stock is selling at ₹ 55 and annual dividend is ₹ 1.65, then

Current yield on stock $= \frac{1.65 \times 100}{55} = 3\%$. Interest on Bond is 6% and the current price of bond is ₹ 1200.

Current yield on Bond $= \frac{60 \times 100}{1200} = 5\%$

If the current yield on bond is higher than on stock, why do people buy convertibles? The bond will fall to ₹ 1,000 only and not to ₹ 800 [as 40 × 20 is ₹ 800] even when the stock falls to ₹ 40. This means there is a downward protection for bondholder in capital losses. For the strategy of principal amount the bond is preferable; while the stock can fall to any extent, but not the bond. Besides, a convertible offers both the advantages of debt and ownership. However, if there is a capital appreciation the equity stock provides a better scope for appreciation than for bond.

It will thus be seen that the investor preferences or the portfolio objectives are the guide for a decision to invest in Common Stock, bond or a convertible bond. In periods of falling prices, bonds and convertible bonds, and in times of rising prices equity or convertible bond will be chosen depending upon the expectations of interest rates and market prices.

Brigham's Model on Convertible Bonds[@]

The risk-return features of convertible bonds vary widely. The factors which influence them are the coupon rate until conversion, number of years to convertibility and the expected market discount rate. Bondholder invests in the bond as a hedge against risk for the time being until conversion and appreciation on conversion. The return which the bondholder expects is the discount rate which equates the sum of the annual interest payment till the year of conversion and the terminal conversion value in year (N). The equation for the Bond price if it is convertible is

$$M = \sum_{t=1}^{n} \frac{I}{(1+k)^t} + \frac{Tv}{(1+k)^n}$$

M = Price of bond

Tv = Conversion value if converted

I = Interest received yearly

n = Number of years of holding (t = 1 to n)

k = Discount rate expected

@ Brigham: "An Analysis of Convertible Debentures: Theory and Some Empirical Evidence" — *Journal of Finance*, March, 1966.

This is graphically explained by Brigham, as shown below:

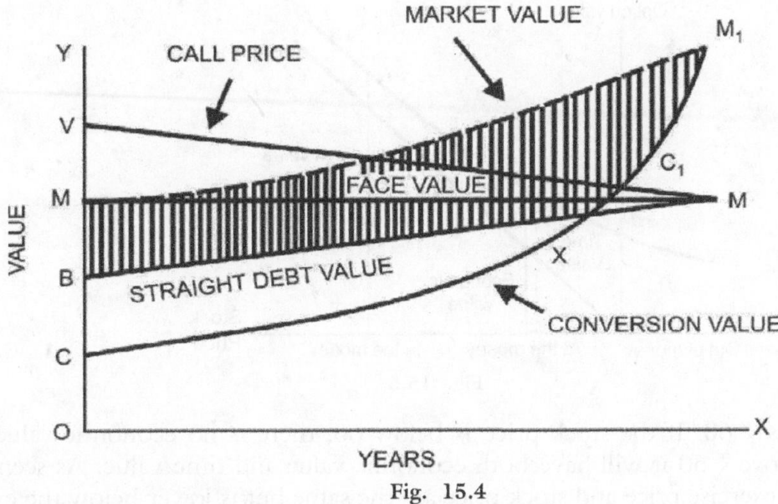

Fig. 15.4

Take 12% Convertible Debenture of Tatas — 14% Market Return

MM = Face value = 100

B × M = Straight Debt value

M is Maturity Date

MM_1 Market Price

$C \times C_1$ is conversion value of convertible bond. It is assumed that equity stock price of the corresponding bond is growing at a constant price and $C \times C_1$ rises accordingly every year, until bond is called for conversion — MM_1 is the market price of bond, and this will rise with time in a similar manner as conversion value, $C \times C_1$, but the latter rises faster as time approaches for call or conversion.

Premium is shown by the shaded area say $B \times M_1$ (as shown in the graph).

VM is the call price to be paid if the company redeems before maturity and not converted. VM line falls, as it approaches maturity and joins M, on the final date and disappears. Call price is more than the face value, to give incentive for the bondholder to surrender bonds before maturity and not converted. VM line falls, as it approaches maturity and as maturity approaches, the difference narrows down to zero on the date of maturity. On the call date, market value and conversion value become the same. If the bond is not called, it is paid at maturity or converted into stock. Both these alternatives are not as good as call.

The decline in call premium shows VM is downward sloping.

Premium is shown by the shaded area in the graph, Bx, or straight debt value. The premium on the bond will disappear, if it is to be called or if it is converted. The graph shows that the conversion value goes sharply up, as it approaches the conversion time (M_1).

In practice premium on conversion from bond to equity will offset the lower interest rate offered on convertible bonds and hence they are more attractive than bonds which are not convertible.

It will thus be seen that there is no simple formula for fixation of price for warrants, loyalty coupons and incentives offered by companies, selling debt instruments to public. Some salient features can however, be stated. First, the warrant will entitle the holder to equity shares at a price lower than the market price — allowing a conversion premium. Second, warrant gives an option to the holder to buy the shares for a specified amount of money. These warrants have only rights and no obligations and will not put the holder to any loss. It has only incentive value and disincentive is not allowed as per the SEBI guidelines.

VALUATION OF OPTIONS

Basically, the value of option is related to the value of the underlying security. The value differs with time before the expiration and at expiration. The value of the stock option has three different zones, as shown below:

(*i*) *Out of the Money:* Where the stock price is below the exercise price.

(*ii*) *At the Money:* Where it is close to or at the exercise price.

(*iii*) *In the Money:* Where the stock price is above the exercise price.

These zones are depicted in the chart below — Fig. 15.5.

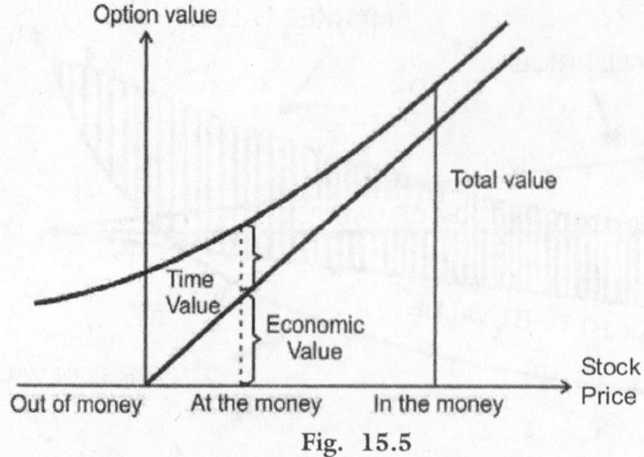

Fig. 15.5

Say the exercise price is ₹ 60. If the stock price is below 60, there is no economic value. There is only time value; if stock price starts above ₹ 60 it will have both economic value and time value. As seen from the chart time value is maximum, when the exercise price and stock price are the same but is lower below the exercise price or above it. If the actual price is lower than the exercise price there is less chance of profit on the call. If the actual price is above the exercise price, then there is a chance of profit, and there is less reason to pay a premium over the economic value (intrinsic value).

Factors Affecting the Option Value

There are normally several factors which influence the option value. The more important of them are: (1) expected variance in price or return of the underlying stock, (2) the time to expiration, (3) the level of interest rates, and (4) the dividends and fundamentals of the stock. Leaving aside the fundamentals of the stock and dividends paid, which will generally be reflected in the actual stock price, the influence of other factors are explained in the diagrams below:

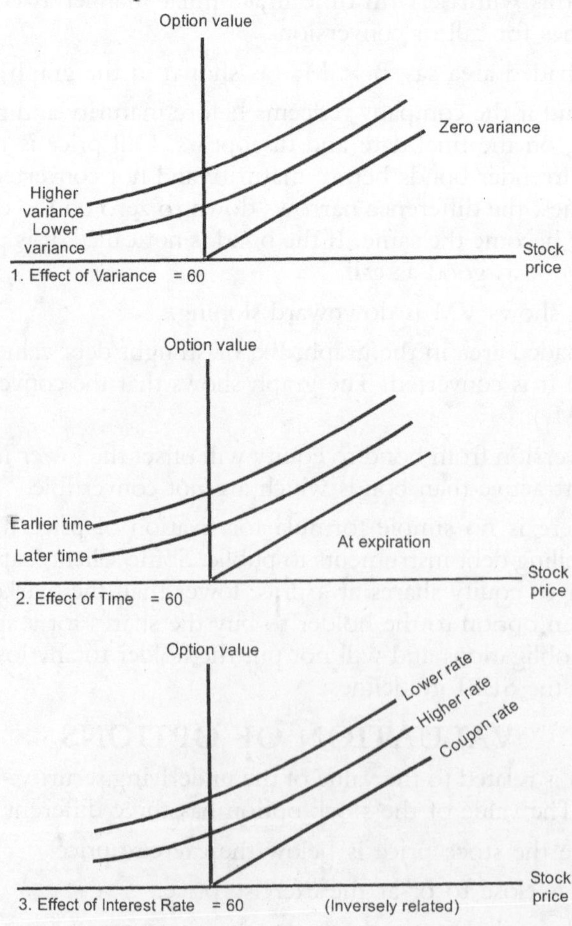

Fig. 15.6

Call and Put Options

A call option is a right to buy and a put option is a right to sell. Their valuations will differ, although the factors referred to above are the same.

The graph below depicts the value of a call and put:

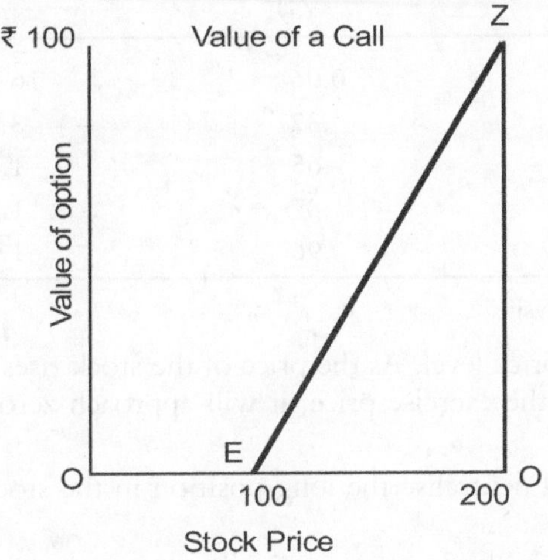

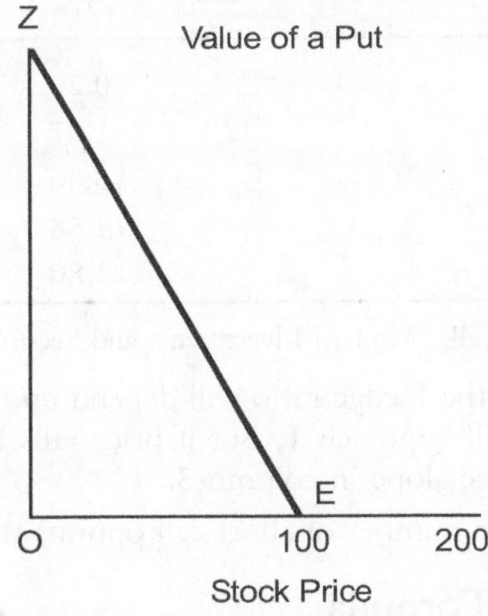

Fig. 15.7

For the call option, if the stock price is less than ₹ 100 (exercise price) option is worthless when it expires. If the price is above, the call option gains by the amount above ₹ 100. For the put option, if the stock price is above ₹ 100, then the option is worthless, when it expires. If it is below, the option can be exercised and he will gain as he can sell at ₹ 100 but buying in the market at a lower price and profit is the difference between the market price and exercise price. In either case he need not buy or sell, but can take the difference as gain. The angled parts of EZO and OZE are called intrinsic values of the options. Thus the option value has two components, as referred to earlier, namely, intrinsic value (or economic value) and Time Value (time to expiration).

The intrinsic value depends on the price of the underlying security and time value depends on the time available before expiry.

Hedge Ratio (Black-Scholes Model)

Take numerical example to explain the hedge ratio. The option values for each stock price are given in the Table below.

Option Value — Exercise Price ₹ 60

Stock Price	*Economic Value*	*Time Value*	*Total Option Value*
₹ 40	0	0.22	.22
50	0	1.97	1.97
60	0	6.86	6.86
70	10	4.58	14.58
80	20	3.80	23.80

Hedge Ratio Data

Stock Price (1)	*Total Option Value* (2)	*Slope of Hedge Ratio* (3)	*Calls to Neutralise Stock* (4)
40	0.22	0.06	16.67
50	1.97	.32	3.12
60	6.86	.65	1.54
70	14.58	.87	1.15
80	23.80	.96	1.04

Source: Fuller & Farrell. "Modern Investments and Security Analysis."

The slope of the Hedge ratio will depend upon the price level. As the price of the stock rises above the exercise price, the slope will approach 1, But if price falls below the exercise price, it will approach zero. The column 4 is the reciprocal of the slope in column 3.

It will tell the number of short call options that will neutralise the long position in the stock.

Black-Scholes Formula

The operations involving the hedge is the vital part of the Black Scholes Option Valuation Model. The long position in the option can be hedged by a short position in the stock and *vice versa*. By hedging perfectly, any profit resulting from an instantaneous increase in the price of the stock would be exactly offset by an instantaneous loss on the option position and *vice versa.*

Black Scholes formula can be used to hedge the market risk of stock portfolio by proper option strategy. Because we can reach a theoretically riskless position, one can earn a risk free return, by such hedging — that is, the short-term interest rate is the fair value of the option. The option price would adjust to the fair value under equilibrium conditions.

What is Black-Scholes Formula?

If C is the equilibrium value of option, the formula given by Black-Scholes is as follows:

$$C = SN(d_1) - E\,(e^{-rt})\,N(d_2)$$

Where, $$d_1 = \frac{\ln\left(\frac{S}{E}\right) + \left(rt + 0.5\sigma^2\right)t}{\sigma\sqrt{t}}$$

$$d_2 = d_1 - \sigma\sqrt{t}$$

and where,

S = Current market price of underlying stock

E = Exercise price of the option

r = Risk free rate of return (Continuously compounded)

N(d) = The value of the cumulative normal distribution evaluated at 'd'.

t = Time remaining before expiration

σ = Risk of the underlying common stock measured by standard deviation. $N(d_1)$ cumulative density function of d_1 and similar is $N(d_2)$, $N(d_1)$ and $N(d_2)$ denote the probabilities that deviations of less than d_1 and d_2 respectively will occur in a normal distribution that has a mean of '0' and a standard deivation of 1.

Mathematically 'e' is the base of natural logarithms and is approximately equal to 2.71828. This means that E/e^{RT} is the present value of the exercise price, when a continuous discount rate is used (it is analogous to $E/(1+R)^T$ or E (e^{-rt}) used in the formula — the present value of the exercise price, using a discrete discount rate.

The Table on N(d) Values is set out at the end of the chapter.

The quantity in $\left(\frac{S}{E}\right)$ is the natural Logarithm of $\frac{S}{E}$.

Note: Values of N(d) for various levels of d_1 and d_2 can be had from the Table at the end and a pocket calculator for estimating the fair value of option is necessary to use Black-Scholes Formula.

The B/S Model can be used by reference to Table at the end for values of $N(d_1)$ and $N(d_2)$, with given values of d_1 and d_2. This model is also based on the following assumptions

(1) Stock returns are expected to follow a log normal distribution.

(2) These are no costs of transactions and no taxes.

(3) The stock will not pay dividend during the life of the option.

(4) The underlying asset value and the risk free rate are constant during the life of the option.

Implications

Black-Scholes formula is a static analysis. The formula shows that the fair value has the following major inputs:

Common stock price, exercise price, time to maturity, market interest rate and standard deviation of annual price changes. The implications of the formula are:

(1) The higher the price of the underlying stock, the higher is the value of call option.

(2) The longer the time to expiration date (t) the higher is the value of the call option.

(3) The higher the exercise price, the lower the value of call option.

(4) The higher the risk free rate, the higher is the value of call option.

(5) The greater the risk (σ) of the common stock, the higher is the value of the call option.

Black and Scholes: The pricing of options and corporate liabilities, JPE May-June, 1973.

Solved Problem (B/S Model)

Given the following values, calculate the value of call option under the B/S Model:

σ = .3, R = .10, S = ₹ 25, T = 0.3 years and E = ₹ 28.

$$D_1 = \frac{\text{In}\left(\frac{25}{28}\right) + [.10 + 0.5\,(0.3)^2]0.3}{0.3\sqrt{0.3}}$$

$$= \frac{-0.1133 + (.10 + 0.045)\,0.3}{0.3 \times 0.5477}$$

$$= \frac{-0.1133 + (0.145)\,0.3}{0.16431} = \frac{-0.1133 + 0.0435}{0.16431}$$

$$D_1 = \frac{-0.0698}{0.16431} = -0.425$$

$$D_2 = -\ 0.425 - (0.3)\ (0.5477)$$

$$D_2 = -0.4250 - 0.1643 = -0.5893$$

$$C_1 = 25\ N\ (-.43) - e^{-10(.3)}(28)\ N\ (-0.59)$$

From the Table at the end of the chapter the values of N (–.43) and N (–.59) are taken.

$$C_1 = 25 \times (0.336) - 0.9704\ (28)\ (0.2776)$$

$$C_1 = 8.34 - 7.54 = 0.80$$

$$C_1 = ₹\ 0.80$$

Note : Reading of the N(X) Table or N(d) Tables is as follows: Say if 'X' is –.43, go to column under –.4 and then turn to rows: under the row of 3, we will get the value of –.43.

Thus, N(X) = –.43 = .336

Similarly, if N(X) = N (–.59), go to column under –.5 and then turn to rows and under row 9, we will get the value of –0.59 = which is .2776.

Problems

Question 1

Keys Co. Ltd. has EPS at ₹ 3 with 5,00,000 shares outstanding. Then the company issued 40,000 shares of 7% convertible preferred shares at ₹ 50. Each preferred share is convertible into 2 shares of equity, which has a market price of ₹ 21 per share.

(a) What is the preferred share's conversion value?

(b) What is the conversion premium?

(c) Assuming the total earnings to remain the same what will be the effect of the issue on primary earnings per share before conversion?

Answer:

(a) Conversion value = Conversion ratio × Market price per share = 2 × 21 = ₹ 42

(b) Conversion premium = $\frac{50}{42} - 1 = 19.05\%$

(c) **Effect on primary earnings per share**

With EPS at 3 and total shares outstanding at 5,00,000.

Then 3 × 5,00,000 = 15,00,000 = Total Primary earnings

Less preferred share dividend

₹ 7% per bond of ₹ 50

₹ 7 per ₹ 100 and 3½ × 40,000 = 1,40,000

Then 15,00,000 – 1,40,000 = ₹ 13,60,000

(₹ 3½ per ₹ 50)

Total Earnings	₹ 13,60,000
No. of Shares	5,00,000
Net earnings per share before conversion	(13,60,000 ÷ 5,00,000) = ₹ 2.72
Total after tax earnings	15,00,000
No. of shares after conversion (5,00,000 + 80,000)	5,80,000

Conversion rate is 2 for one and 40,000 shares of preferred stock. This gives 40,000 × 2 = 80,000.

$$EPS = \frac{15,00,000}{5,80,000} = 2.59$$

EPS after conversion = ₹ 2.59.

Question 2

The current rate of interest on 4 year ZCB of Government of India is 10% and that on 5 year securities is 9.8%

(a) What is the implied forward rate on a one year loan 4 years in the future?

Answer:

$$\text{Implied forward rate, } \frac{(1.098)^5}{(1.10)^4} - 1$$

$$= 1.089 - 1 = .089$$

which is roughly 9.00%.

(b) What happens to the forward rate if interest rates decline so that 4 year security yields 8% and 5 year security 8.4%.

Answers:

Implied forward rate $= \dfrac{(1.084)^5}{(1.08)^4} - 1$

$= 1.104 - 1 = 0.104$ what is roughly 10%.

Question 3

Goldwan needs to borrow in the bond market three months hence; As he expects the interest rates to rise, he needs hedging. The Company has the option on government bond futures.

(a) Should the company buy a put or call option.

(b) If the present futures contracts trades at ₹ 100, and a 3 month put option involves, a cost of 1½% based on the strike price. During the three months, interest rates rise and the price government bond went down to ₹ 95. What is the gain or loss on the option per ₹ 1,00,000 contracts.

Answer:

(a) To protect against upward movement in interest rates, price movements will go down and the Co. should ask for a put option.

(b) Gain on option = (1.00 – 0.95) × 100,000 = 5,000

Premium = 1½% × 1,00,000 paid = 1,500; 5,000 – 1,500 = 3,500

Net gain = ₹ 3,500.

Question 4

Flexico has outstanding warrants with a right to conversion of 2 equity shares at ₹ 24 per share. The data on market price of equity and warrant price are given; the theoretical value of warrant can be estimated by the equation.

NPs – E = theoretical value

where, N = no. of shares that can be purchased per every warrant, Ps market price of the Equity share and E is the exercise price of the conversion of warrant into equity.

	Observation Numbers					
	1	2	3	4	5	6
Market Price	18	20	24	27	32	38
Warrant Price	3	5	8	12	20	29

Applying the above formula, the theoretical values for these obserations can be set out as

	1	2	3	4	5	6
theoretical values	0	0	0	6	16	28
premium of warrant	3	5	8	6	4	1

(Warrant price-minus-theoretical values = premium)

Premium is the highest at 8 when the market price is ₹ 24, which is the same as exercise price and theoretical value is zero. Here there is the greatest leverage and the premium over the theoretical value is the greatest at this point, since volatility is what gives the option value.

Observation 1

Theoretical values 2 × 18 = 36 – 48 (which is the exercise value for 2 shares × ₹ 24).

= negative value or Zero

Observation 2

Theoretical value = NPs – E.

$2 \times 20 - 48 < 0$

Observation 3

$2 \times 24 - 48 = 0$

Observation 4

$2 \times 27 - 48$

$= 54 - 48 = 6$

Observation 5

$2 \times 32 - 48$

$= 64 - 48 = 16$

Observation 6

$2 \times 38 - 48$

$= 76 - 48 = 28$

Premium of warrant = Warrant price – Theoretical values

Observations

Premium (1) $3 - 0 = 3$; (2) $5 - 0 = 5$; (3) $8 - 0 = 8$

(4) $12 - 6 = 6$; (5) $20 - 16 = 4$; (6) $29 - 28 = 1$

The highest premium is at observation 3 at ₹ 8 as the premium.

Question 5

Kalyan Steel has EPS of ₹ 3 with 5,00,000 shares outstanding, the company issued 40,000 shares of 7% convertible preferred stock at par of ₹ 50. The preferred stock is convertible into two shares of equity for each preferred share. The equity stock has a current market price of ₹ 21 per share. What is the conversion value of preferred stock. What is its conversion premium?

Answer:

Conversion value = conversion ratio × market price per share

₹ 2 × 21 = ₹ 42

Conversion premium $\frac{50}{42} - 1 = 1.19 - 1 = 19\%$.

Self-help Problems

Question 1

Phillips has warrants oustanding which will allow the holder to buy 3 shares of equity for a total of ₹ 60 per warrant. The market price of equity share is ₹ 18 at present. The holders believe the following probabilities about the equity stock six months hence,

Market Price	₹ 16	18	20	22	24
Probability	15	20	30	20	15

(a) What is the present theoretical value of the warrant?

(b) What is the expected value of stock price 6 months hence from now?

(c) What is the theoretical value, expected of the warrant 6 months hence?

Question 2

Determine the value of the following call option making use of the Black-Scholes formula given in the Text.

So = Current Market Price = ₹ 95

E = Exercise price = ₹ 105

t = Expiration period to go = 8 months

γ = Riskless rate of interest = 8%

σ = Instantaneous standard deviation of the stock return is 0.6.

$$\text{Then } d_1 = \frac{\ln\left(\frac{95}{105}\right) + \left[0.08 + \frac{1}{2}(.36)\right](0.66)}{0.6\sqrt{0.66}}$$

$$d_2 = d_1 - \sigma\sqrt{t}$$

Hint

Calculate

$N(d_1)$ and $N(d_2)$ and plug in the formula for current value of the option.

$$C = SN(d_1) - \frac{E}{e^{rt}} \cdot N(d_2)$$

If the actual value of C is less than the C as calculated above, it is undervalued. Otherwise it is overvalued.

Question 3

Shanker has a share warrant that can buy 5 shares at an exercise price of ₹ 40 each. At share prices of ₹ 35, 45 and 50, and with respective premiums at 0, 2 and 4, determine the market values of the warrant.

Question 4

Calculate the floor value of the convertible bond, if the following data are given to you.

Par value	₹ 1,000
Coupon rate	10%
Maturity period	20 years
YTM of NCB of	8%
Similar nature	
Conversion price	₹ 40
Market price	₹ 50

Question 5

The exercise price of an option stock is ₹ 50 with the market value of ₹ 60 the option contract has an expiration period of 120 days. If Rf (Riskfree rate) is 7%, the variance of return is 0.144. What is the value of the call option under the Black-Scholes Model?

Question 6

The exercise price of option stock is ₹ 10, which is also the market price. The option contract has an expiration period of 4 years. While the riskless rate of return on the stock was estimated at 9% (continuously compounded) and the expected variance of return on the stock was estimated at 9%. Determine the value of call option under the Black-Scholes Model.

Table: Value of N(X) for Given Values of X for a Cumulative Normal Distribution with Zero Mean and Unit Variance

X	*0*	*1*	2	3	4	5	6	7	8	9
-3.	*.0013*	*.0010*	*.0007*	*.0005*	*.0003*	*.0002*	*.0002*	*.0001*	*.0001*	*.0000*
-2.9	.0019	.0018	.0017	.0017	.0016	.0016	.0015	.0015	.0014	.0014
-2.8	.0026	.0025	.0024	.0023	.0023	.0022	.0021	.0021	.0020	.0019
-2.7	.0035	.0034	.0033	0032	.0031	.0030	.0029	.0028	.0027	.0026
-2.6	.0047	.0045	.0044	.0043	.0041	.0040	.0039	.0038	.0037	.0036
-2.5	.0062	.0060	.0059	.0057	.0055	.0054	.0052	.0051	.0049	.0048
-2.4	.0082	.0080	.0078	.0075	.0073	.0071	.0069	.0068	.0066	.0064
-2.3	.0107	.0104	.0102	.0099	.0096	.0094	.0091	.0089	.0087	.0084
-2.2	.0139	.0136	.0132	.0129	.0126	.0122	.0119	.0116	.0113	.0110
-2.1	.0179	.0174	.0170	.0166	.0162	.0158	.0154	.0150	.0146	.0143
-2.0	.0228	.0222	.0217	.0212	.0207	.0202	.0197	.0192	.0188	.0183
-1.9	.0287	.0281	.0274	.0268	.0262	.0256	.0250	.0244	.0238	.0233
-1.8	.0359	.0352	.0344	.0336	.0329	.0322	.0314	.0307	.0300	.0294
-1.7	.0446	.0436	.0427	.0418	.0409	.0401	.0392	.0384	.0375	.0367
-1.6	.0548	.0537	.0526	.0516	.0505	.0495	.0485	.0475	.0465	.0455
-1.5	.0668	.0655	.0643	.0630	.0618	.0606	.0594	.0582	.0570	.0559
-1.4	.0808	.0793	.0778	.0764	.0749	.0735	.0722	.0708	.0694	.0681
-1.3	.0968	.0951	.0934	.0918	.0901	.0885	.0869	.0853	.0838	.0823
-1.2	.1151	.1131	.1112	.1093	.1075	.1056	.1038	.1020	.1003	.0985
-1.1	.1357	.1335	.1314	.1292	.1271	.1251	.1230	.1210	.1190	.1170
-1.0	1587	.1562	.1539	.1515	.1492	.1469	.1446	.1423	.1401	.1379
- .9	.1841	.1814	.1788	.1762	.1736	.1711	.1685	.1660	.1635	.1611
- .8	.2119	.2090	.2061	.2033	.2005	.1977	.1949	.1922	.1894	.1867
- .7	.2420	.2389	.2358	.2327	.2297	.2266	.2236	.2206	.2177	.2148
- .6	.2743	.2709	.2676	.2643	.2611	.2578	.2546	.2514	.2483	.2451
- .5	.3085	.3050	.3015	.2981	.2946	.2912	.2877	.2843	.2810	.2776
- .4	.3446	.3409	.3372	.3336	.3300	.3264	.3228	.3192	.3156	.3121
- .3	.3821	.3783	.3745	.3707	.3669	.3632	.3594	.3557	.3520	.3483
- .2	.4207	.4168	.4129	.4090	.4052	.4013	.3974	.3936	.3897	.3859
- .1	.4602	.4562	.4522	.4483	.4443	.4404	.4364	.4325	.4286	.4247
- .0	.5000	.4960	.4920	.4880	.4840	.4801	.4761	.4721	.4681	.4641
3.	0013	.0010	.0007	.0005	.0003	.0002	.0002	.0001	.0001	.0000
.0	.5000	.5040	.5080	.5120	.5160	.5199	.5239	.5279	.5319	.5359
.1	.5338	.5438	.5478	.5517	.5557	.5596	.5636	.5675	.5714	.5753
.2	.5793	.5832	.5871	.5910	.5948	.5987	.6026	.6064	.6103	.6141
.3	.6179	.6217	.6255	.6293	.6331	.6368	.6406	.6443	.6480	.6517
.4	.6554	.6591	.6628	.6664	.6700	.6736	.6772	.6808	.6844	.6879
.5	6915	.6950	.6985	.7019	.7054	.7088	.7123	.7157	.7190	.7224
.6	.7257	.7291	.7324	.7357	.7389	.7422	.7454	.7486	.7517	.7549
.7	.7580	.7611	.7642	.7673	.7703	.7734	.7764	.7794	.7823	.7852
.8	.7881	.7910	.7939	.7967	.7995	.8023	.8051	.8078	.8106	.8133
.9	.8159	.8186	.8212	.8238	.8264	.8289	.8315	.8340	.8365	.8389
1.0	.8413	.8438	.8461	.8485	.8508	.8531	.8554	.8577	.8599	.8621
1.1	.8643	.8665	.8686	.8708	.8729	.8749	.8770	.8790	.8810	.8830
1.2	.8849	.8869	.8888	.8907	.8925	.8944	.8962	.8980	.8997	.9015
1.3	.9032	.9049	.9066	.9082	.9099	.9115	.9131	.9147	.9162	.9177
1.4	.9192	.9207	.9222	.9236	.9251	.9265	.9278	.9292	.9306	.9319
1.5	.9332	.9345	.9357	.9370	.9382	.9394	.9406	.9418	.9430	.9441
1.6	.9452	.9463	.9474	.9484	.9495	.9505	.9515	.9525	.9535	.9545
1.7	.9554	.9564	.9573	.9582	.9591	.9599	.9608	.9616	.9625	.9633
1.8	.9641	.9648	.9656	.9664	.9671	.9678	.9686	.9693	.9700	.9706
1.9	.9713	.9719	.9726	.9732	.9738	.9744	.9750	.9756	.9762	.9767
2.0	.9772	.9778	.9783	.9788	.9793	.9798	.9803	.9808	.9812	.9817
2.1	.9821	.9826	.9830	.9834	.9838	.9842	.9846	.9850	.9854	.9857
2.2	.9861	.9864	.9868	.9871	.9874	.9878	.9881	.9884	.9887	.9890
2.3	.9893	.9896	.9898	.9901	.9904	.9906	.9909	.9911	.9913	.9916
2.4	.9918	.9920	.9922	.9925	.9927	.9929	.9931	.9932	.9934	.9936
2.5	.9938	.9940	.9941	.9943	.9945	.9946	.9948	.9949	.9951	.9952
2.6	.9953	.9955	.9956	.9957	.9959	.9960	.9961	.9962	.9963	.9964
2.7	.9965	.9966	.9967	.9968	.9969	.9970	.9971	.9972	.9973	.9974
2.8	.9974	.9975	.9976	.9977	.9977	.9978	.9979	.9979	.9980	.9981
2.9	.9981	.9982	.9982	.9983	.9984	.9984	.9985	.9985	.9986	.9986
3.	.9987	.9990	.9993	.9995	.9997	.9998	.9998	.9999	.9999	1.0000

Source: "Theory and Problems of Investments", Schaurn's Outline Series. p. 214.

16

FUTURES TRADING

Futures trading in stock and shares was prohibited in India for a long time, until March 1995, when they were permitted again alongwith options. Futures, in commodities like cotton, jute, tea, tobacco, etc., are still in vogue. For example, Cochin pepper per quintal March 2000 was quoted at ₹ 20,800 while the same for. May 2000 was ₹ 21,250 (quotation on March 10, 2000). Generally, these quotations are available for one to three months futures delivery, based on their present quotations and expected future demand and supply position and stock position.

What is Futures?

A futures contract is a firm legal commitment between a buyer and seller in which they agree to exchange something say pepper for a specified money at the end of a designated time period, say three months hence. Delivery is necessary and the price is known in advance. The risk is borne by both buyer and seller. Only the risk of uncertainly is not there for the buyer, as the seller bears it, for a reward. The possible risk attached to the upward and downward changes in the actual price at the future stipulated time is there for both buyer and seller. If prices fall below the stipulated price, the buyer loses and if they rise above the stipulated price, the seller loses due the contracted stipulated price. The loss of one is the gain of the other and it is a zero sum game. Here in lies the speculative element in futures.

How Futures Differ from Options?

In options, the delivery is optional for buyer but obligatory for seller of the option. The buyer pays the seller a premium in the beginning itself while there is no premium paid on the future contract. Future contracts can be performed only at the settlement date but not before that. The buyer of the options has a right to exercise the option either at the expiration date or prior to that. Deliveries and execution of contracts are enforced by the organising authorities.

Index Futures

Suppose the future contracts are based Nifty Index. The NSE 50 is quoting early on March 10, 2000 at 1,646. Each point in the index is valued at ₹ 50, one futures contract on NSE Index will cost ₹ 60,000; if at the end of one month, the index rose to 1,666 then on the settlement day a cash payment of ₹ 50 × 20 = ₹ 1,000 is to be paid by the seller to the buyer. All the traders in the futures are to be members and each trader is expected to put in "good faith" margin deposit depending upon the value of the total contracts. These margin moneys are marked to the market value or a daily basis. The margins to be kept on futures are less than for normal deliveries, as index futures do not involve full value payments. Thus, an index futures contract is an obligation to deliver at settlement an amount of cost, equal to a number of times (say 100 or 500) of the difference between the stock index value at the close of the last trading day (1,666) of the contract and the price at which the future contract was originally struck (1,646). The terms of the contract, underlying the futures trading will determine the number of times the difference is to be multiplied. Margin money has to be kept and other conditions are to be observed for any contingent event of failure to make the additional deposit marked to the market value of the contract and the possible failure to honour the contract by either party. The trading hours, and contract months (normally 3, 6, 9 and 12 months are allowed) minimum price fluctuation and the last day of trading and settlement date etc., are all set out in the original futures trading system; as laid down by the controlling authority, say the NSE authorities or the BSE authorities, and SEBI.

Valuation of Index Futures

If an investor invests in BSE 30 index he will collect dividends on the scrips he holds and his principal value may go up or down depending on the index. In the case of the futures index, the investor will get the same outcome as if he invests all his money in riskless Treasury bills and enters into a futures contract for future delivery of the index. The futures then must sell at a price equal to today's price of the index plus a premium *equal* to risk free return plus dividend on the index shares.

To show this symbolically let F_e be the price of the futures, F_B is today's price of futures I_B current price of the Index and D is dividend on the index shares, and I_E is the index price at the expiration date.

Return to Index = Index price at Expiration – Current Index Price + Dividend

$$= I_e - I_B + D \quad \ldots. (1)$$

Return to futures = Futures price at Expiration – current futures price + Interest on Risk free asset.

$$= F_e - F_B + R_F \quad \ldots. (2)$$

As I_E will equal F_e at expiration, using the above equations, we can derive, F_B as $= I_B + (R_F - D)$.

The above equation means that the present price of futures, will equal present price of Index plus the *"cost of carry"*, which equals $(R_F - D)$, namely the interest obtainable on risk-free asset (R_F) minus dividend on Index Shares (D). The cost of purchasing the Index Shares is substantially higher than the cost of buying the futures contract for the same index. The money used to buy the futures will involve interest cost and by not buying the shares, dividends are lost. Assume that the money used to purchase the index shares is invested in Treasury bills to give risk free return (R_F). If R_f is less than the dividends lost, the futures price will be below the Index price (that is $F_B < I_B$) and $(R_F < D)$.

Arbitrage or Basis Trading

Arbitrage is the simultaneous purchase and sale of the same commodity in two different markets in order to make profits from the price difference between the two markets. Inter-market differentials are eliminated by operations of the Arbitrage. Thus, stock index futures arbitrage involves the buying of a basket of stocks and selling futures when mispricing is perceived by the investor or the reverse operation of the same. These operations require expertise in program trading and a large amount of capital to be used. Arbitrage reduces the risk involved in markets by lowering and eliminating the price differential as between markets.

Hedging

Hedging occurs mostly in Treasury bill futures markets to reduce the risk of the portfolio which may be an existing investment in money market or anticipated future investment. The exposure to interest rate risk depends on the mismatch of assets and liabilities of short-term nature. Specific or general interest rate risk exposure can be covered by the futures in Treasury bills. The major use of the futures market lay either in the risk coverage of the specific market risk or the interest rate risk. The most common way of covering the interest rate risk is to hedge on Treasury bill futures. A short position in futures will cover the long position in the spot market.

Example of Topix Price Index Futures

Let us take the Topix futures of Tokyo Stock Exchange. The terms of the futures contracts are generally as follows.

Contracts are based on Topix-Tokyo stock price index, covering all shares listed in first section of T.S.E. It represents the market as a whole, comprehensive and weighted by the number of shares outstanding in each stock and is quoted every minute of trading session and is the most suitable bench mark for behaviour of the market.

Contract Months: March, June, September, December — five contract months are traded at all times covering exactly 15 months at any time. Basic trading unit is yen 10,000 times Topix Point (decimals not considered). Minimum price change: one full point in Topix value of minimum Move = 10,000 yen. Daily price limit: Around 3% an either side, last trading day: Trading starts on the second Friday in each new contract month and last trading day is the second Friday of the succeeding month.

Settlement Day	: T + 3, — Thursday after the second Friday of the month.
Margin Requirements for Customers	: 9% of the Transaction value or 6 Million yen.
Margin Requirements for Members	: 6% or More of the first trading day's closing price of each contract month.
Trading System	: Pure auction, order driven system through Computer assisted Order Routing and Execution System (CORES).

Futures and Speculation

Longs and shorts take positions in the futures markets. Being a zero-sum game, the loss of one set is a gain of another set. As such it is pure speculation, based on the expectation of the spot price of an asset security or index on the delivery date. The longs in a futures contract gains, if the observed spot price on the delivery date is greater than the expected spot price that has reflected in the futures price of the asset or index at the time of initiation. Correspondingly, those in the short position in the futures gain, when the observed spot price on the delivery date is lower than the expected spot price at that date.

All members in futures trading are controlled by the Exchange authorities as per the terms of the contracts. Margins are collected from Members as well as their customers and these margins are marked to daily market values. The clearing House of the exchange becomes the counter party to ensure orderly trading and default-free system. For the buyer, the Exchange becomes the seller and for the seller, the exchange is the buyer.

ADVANTAGE OF FUTURES INDEX

It is a risk hedge and caters to speculative instinct of investors. It is a more efficient method of controlling risk on a portfolio, as it reduces the transactions costs, trading costs and price pressure. Neither the buyer nor the seller pays the full value of the underlying assets but deals only in differences, in cash without involving delivery of the assets. The futures smoothens the asset reallocation, provides hedge to future inflows or outflows of cash and reduces the impact of bullish and bearish trading as futures do not involve full payment or receipt of the underlying assets but is a dealing in differences.

Operation of Hedge of Risk

To illustrate the coverage of risk, assume that you expect a future cash inflow of ₹ 50,000 a month hence, which you wish to invest in equities. But the market is bullish and prices are expected to rise. Then you buy an index future contract to cover the expected rise in price. you can also sell short if the market is expected to fall in prices. Suppose, you have the securities in your portfolio and expect the market to fall then you can sell the futures, instead of the securities. If the actual fall is more than the expected price, you will receive the difference in cash. A bullish expectation makes you buy the futures contract and a bearish expectation makes you sell the futures contract. If your expectations are correctly realised, you can make money on the deals without actually buying and selling the underlying securities. This will enable you to trade on a smaller investment as the margins you have to keep for trading in Futures is generally 6 to 10%, and the loss of interest money is less expensive than the loss of interest on a bigger outlay involved in buying and selling for deliveries of underlying securities or shares or bonds.

Futures on Bonds

While stock index futures provide low cost and efficient method of insuring against systematic risk of the portfolio, futures on bonds and Treasury bills provide the risk coverage to interest rate risk, which is the largest source of systematic risk in holding fixed income securities.

In the case of index futures, delivery is in cash settlements only but in the case of futures on Treasury bills or bonds, delivery is in bills or bonds. In the U.S., Treasury Note futures are more popular and easy to understand and operate. These contracts are available for delivery dates in March, June, Sept. and Dec. and for delivery dates of upto two years from the current date. Yields are basic unit on which prices are determined.

Thus, Annual discount rate =

$$= \frac{\text{Face Value} - \text{Price}}{\text{Face Value}} \times \frac{\text{No. of Days to Maturity}}{360}$$

Treasury Bill futures price is decided on the basis of change in the discount rate.

Price paid at delivery = 100 – Discount Rate (as a per cent of face value) × $\frac{90}{360}$; if discount rate is 6%, for example,

$$100 - 6 \times \frac{1}{4}$$

$$100 - 1.50$$

$$= 98.50$$

Deliverable grade is also set out in the terms of the contract as for example 8% coupon bill with a maturity period of 6.5 years to 10 years.

There are some futures on long-term bonds, like Mortgage Bonds, U.S. GILT bonds, Municipal Bonds etc. The bond that is cheapest to deliver is used for delivery by traders.

Bonds sell in the cash market at varying prices, some above and some below the converted price of the futures contracts (futures prices × conversion factor). The conversion factors are equal to the ratio of the actual price of the deliverable bond, to the delivery price of the futures contract; the bond that is cheapest to deliver is used for delivery by traders and that is decided by the bond, for which the difference between the invoice price and market price is the most positive.

Futures price = cash price + carrying costs

Carrying costs depend on the interest at which money can be borrowed by the investor and the period of financing, say 3 months to delivery.

Duration Effect

Using the above futures on fixed income securities, the duration of the portfolio can be changed. Instead of buying in the cash market, it is cheaper to hedge in futures. If interest rates are likely to increase, the investor should shorten the duration of the portfolio and *vice versa*. He then uses in technique of buying or selling the futures to lengthen or shorten the duration, respectively. This effect on portfolio is called duration effect of futures.

Portfolio can have reduced duration by selling short in futures and increased duration by buying futures. If cash is expected and interest rates are likely to fall pushing up the prices of bonds, then investor can go long in futures and when funds come in, the futures can be converted into cash purchase of bonds or the underlying security. The opposite stand can be taken if an outflow of cash is expected at a specific time period in future.

Hedging Effect

Hedging in futures can be done to reduce the interest rate risk. A futures position can be taken to offset the risk in the cash market. Thus, a ten year bond is likely to suffer capital loss due to rise in yields and that is held in the portfolio of the investor. The risk can be hedged by an appropriate sale of that security-backed future. If the loss on the existing security is offset by the gain in the futures contract then it is called a perfect hedge. The difference between futures price and cash price is called the basis and the risk of variance of this basis is called basis risk.

The above basis risk is substantial when the cross hedging is done. Cross hedging is hedging in a bond futures, which is not identical with the bond to be hedged and held in the portfolio. A hedged position thus creates a basis risk which can be reduced or eliminated by taking extreme caution and use of expertise in anticipation of the proper time and bond to be hedged.

Yield Enhancement Effect

The futures on fixed income security, say a bond, can be used to improve yields also. What hedging has done is to reduce the risk on the portfolio by holding a long-term bond for a short maturity. As the price of the futures is fixed, the risk is nil on this period of the futures say 3 months, and the ten year bond of 10 years, purchased will have greater risk than a riskless bond of 3 months in futures plus a 9 year 9 month bond in the portfolio. The holding of a riskless bond for short periods of time in the futures, reduces the risk. This process may, or may not increase the yields, however.

To enhance the yields, the yield on the synthetic security should be higher than on the cash market security. This synthetic security is created by being short in a three months futures Treasury bill along with a long position in the cash market. If the yield on the three month Treasury bill is higher say 6.6% as against the Treasury bill yield in cash market of 6.4%, then the portfolio will benefit, from higher yield of 0.2% on the synthetic security, in the futures market.

Options in Futures Contracts

Another financial derivative product traded in New York and London for example is options on future contracts. These contracts are presently traded in Europe and America, in Treasury bonds, Treasury Notes and Euro-dollar deposits. Calls and puts in the above futures are traded. A call position if exercised, will lead to a long position in the cash market. A put option if exercised will lead to a short position in the cash market. If not exercised, only cash differences are paid and received by the buyer and seller respectively. The cost of such deals include the premium paid and the limited margins that have to be deposited for dealing in Futures. By using options trading, the futures market provides high risk speculation for those whose speculative instinct is high. Futures market has an element of speculation although lack of delivery by itself is not speculative but that futures prices may differ widely from its price in cash market at the time of settlement, is itself risky and speculative.

NSE Proposal for Futures

The NSE has proposed to start Futures and options by end of the year 1996, (O&F Section) but started in June 2000 and 2001. This section is for corporate members only. Members trading only and those who will write options are the two classes of members in O&F Section. The former will have a networth of ₹ 3 crores and the latter ₹ 5 crores. They have to pay additional cash deposits with NSE and National Securities Clearing Corporation (NSCCL) separately.

The membership of O&F Section is also thrown open to non-NSE members, if they satisfy all the requirements of networth and cash deposits with NSE and NSCCL. The new O&F members have to be members of the Equity market of NSE also, as they can take positions in the cash and futures markets at different times.

Existing NSE members opting as trading members in the O&F Section will have to hike their networth from ₹ 1 crore to ₹ 3 crores and make an additional cash deposit of ₹ 28 lakhs. For NSCCL, they will have to pay cash deposit of ₹ 25 lakhs and provide a bank guarantee of ₹ 25 lakhs.

Existing members of NSE opting to be writers of "Futures" or "Options", will hike their networth to ₹ 5 crores and pay a cash deposit of ₹ 56 lakhs to NSE. For NSCCL, they would make a cash deposit of ₹ 50 lakhs and provide a bank guarantee of ₹ 50 lakhs. The other terms and details are finalised by the NSE, and approved by SEBI. These terms and conditions are variable.

Even by end March 2000, NSE did not succeed in starting futures due to teething problems in starting futures and due to the difficulties of members to bring in additional funds. Reference was already made to the recommendations of the Committee on Derivatives, set up by SEBI. In March 2000, when the ban on Forward Trading on Securities was lifted, both the NSE and BSE wave considering the launch of the Futures, based on the Index of securities to start with. Index futures and options were started in 2000 and in stocks in 2001.

DERIVATIVE TRADING IN SECURITIES

The Securities Laws (Amendment) Act of 1999 has allowed the trading in derivative products in India. As a further step to widen and deepen the securities markets the government have notified on March 2, 2000 that with effect from March 1, 2000 the ban on forward trading in shares and securities was lifted to facilitate trading in forwards and futures.

It may be recalled that the ban on forward trade in securities was imposed in 1968 to curb certain unhealthy trade practices and trends in the securities market and unhealthy speculation by unscrupulous operators. During the past few years, thanks to the economic and financial reforms, there have been many healthy developments in the markets which necessitated sophistication and fine tuning of the capital and stock markets.

The Government notification delineated the areas of responsibilities between the RBI and SEBI. "The contracts for sale and purchase of government securities and gold related securities, money market securities and securities from these securities and ready forward contracts in debt securities will be regulated by the RBI. Such contracts will however be regulated by SEBI in a manner that is consistent with the RBI guidelines."

The RBI has notified that forward trading in gilted securities will not be allowed except Repos. Trade Cycles of T and T + 1 for direct deals and T + 5 for NSE deals will however continue. Repos are now allowed for varying periods for one day to 14 days. These are in the form of ready forward contracts in Treasury bills and government securities.

The lifting of the ban a forward deals in securities helped to develop index futures and other types of derivatives and futures on stocks in India. This is a step in the right direction to promote sophicated market segments as in Western Developed Countries. Sensex futures and Nifty futures for one to three months are now regularly traded and their quotations are published in the Daily Press. The traded quantity, number of contracts and their value are the details of data published. Futures trading in selected scrips both on BSE and NSE is also taking place and their details are also published in the Daily Press, under the head of Derivatives Trading.

17

FUNDAMENTAL ANALYSIS

Influence of the Economy

Companies are a part of the industrial and business sector, which in turn is a part of the overall economy. Thus, the performance of a company depends on the performance of the economy in the first place. If the economy is in recession or stagnation, *ceteris paribus,* the performance of companies will be bad in general, with some exceptions however. On the other hand, if the economy is booming, incomes are rising and the demand is good, then the industries and the companies in general may be prosperous, with some exceptions however.

In the Indian economy, the matters to be considered in the first place are the behaviour of the monsoon and the performance of agriculture. As agriculture is the mainstay of about 60% of the population and contributes nearly 18% of the output of the economy, it is important for the assessment and forecast of industrial performance which again constitutes about 25% of the total output. If the monsoon is good and agricultural incomes rise, the demand for industrial products and services will be good and industry prospers. Although services sector contributes 60-65% of the output of the economy, its prosperity depends on the performance of the agricultural and industrial sectors in the economy.

Secondly, India has a mixed economy, where the public sector plays a vital role. The Government being the biggest investor and spender, the trends in public investment and expenditure would indicate the likely performance of the Indian economy. Concomitant with this, the government budget policy, tax levies and government borrowing programme along with the extent of deficit financing will have a major influence on the performance of the Indian economy, as these influence the demand and incomes of the people. The changes in excise and customs duties, corporate taxes, etc., are all relevant to assess the trends in the economy as they have an impact on the industry and the companies.

Thirdly, the monetary policy and trends in money supply which mainly depend on the government's budget policy, its borrowing from the public and credit from the banks and the RBI, have a major impact on the industrial growth through the cost and availability of credit, the profit margins of the companies etc. The monetary situation along with the budgetary policy influences the movement in price level (inflation) and interest rates. The tight money position, increasing budget deficits and RBI creation of currency lead to an inflationary spiral. Although the interest rates in the organised financial system are controlled, this is being changed to a free market economy and the bazar rates in the unorganised market do reflect the availability of funds in the free markets. So interest rates in the free markets and the degree of inflation do have a major influence on the economy and the performance of the industries. Although a mild inflation is good for business psychology, higher degrees of inflation, particularly in two digits, will defeat all business planning, lead to cost escalations and squeeze on profit margins. These will adversely affect the performance of industry and companies.

Fourthly, the general business conditions in the form of business cycles or the level of business activity do influence the demand for industrial products and the performance of the industry. In India, there are no business cycles but outputs do fluctuate depending upon the state of the economy, performance of agriculture, availability of power and other infrastructural outputs, imported inputs and a host of other factors. These factors do influence the costs and profit margins of companies from both demand and supply sides. The business earnings and profits are affected by such changes in business conditions.

Fifthly, the economic and political stability in the form of stable and long-term economic polices and a stable political system with no uncertainty would also be necessary for a good performance of the economy in general and of companies in particular. The Government regulations being all-pervasive in India, the government policy has to be known in advance in all its aspects and there should be no uncertainty about the political system as economic and political factors are interlinked. Political uncertainties and adverse changes in government policy do adversely affect industrial growth. Government policy relating to projects, clearance for foreign collaboration and foreign investment policy and distribution controls, and listing requirements on stock exchanges and a host of other matters like import restrictions do affect the performance of companies. The foreign exchange position and the balance of payments situation at any time would also indicate the rigours of government policy with regard to imports, exports, foreign investment and related matters.

All the above factors of the economy influence the corporate performance and the industry in general. In any investment analysis, a broad picture of these factors and a forecast of the growth of the economy and of industry would be necessary to decide when to invest and what to invest in.

Economy vs. Industry and Company

At any stage in the economy, there are some industries which are growing while others are declining. The performance of companies will depend among other things upon the state of the industry as a whole and the economy. If the industry is prosperous, the companies, within the industries may also be prosperous although a few may be in a bad shape. The performance of a company is thus a function not only of the industry and of the economy, but more importantly, on its own performance. The share price of the company is empirically found to depend up to 50% on the performance of the industry and economy. The economic and political situation in the country has thus a bearing on the prospects of the company. With the opening up of the economy in the new millennium, the international factors, trade and business conditions play a more vital role.

There are different phases in the economy such as boom, depression, recession, etc. The performance of the economy in India is not cyclical as in the case of developed countries exhibiting business cycles, as the Indian economy depends basically on the monsoon and the growth rate of agriculture. Besides, with a huge public sector in our mixed economy, the performance of the five-year plan, yearly public investment, government expenditure and a host of other factors influence the economy, industry and company. Thus, one important factor is the fiscal policy which incorporates government expenditure and taxation, borrowing, deficit financing, etc., and which influences both the public and private sectors in the economy. The industrial growth in general and of infrastructural industries in particular influence the corporate performance.

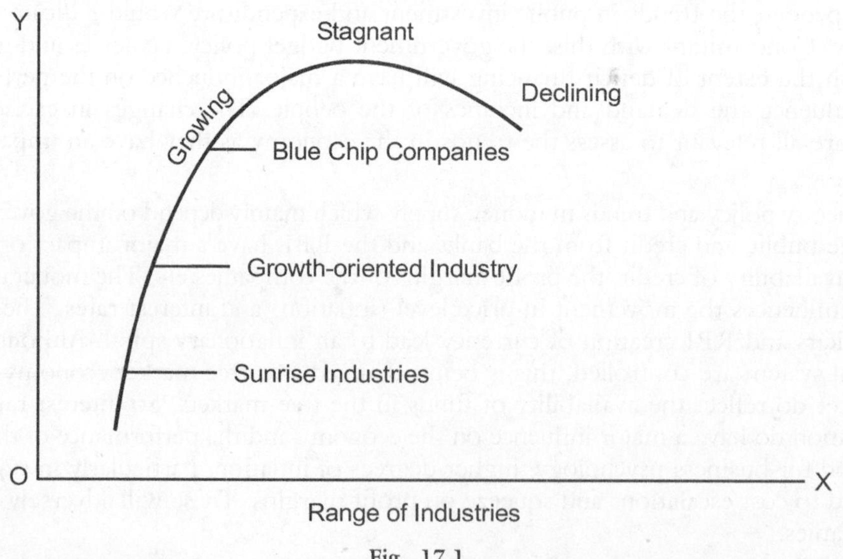

Fig. 17.1

As referred to earlier at any stage in the economy, there are some industries growing fast while others are declining. The performance of companies will depend among other things upon the state of the industry as a whole. If the industry is prosperous, the companies, within the industries may also be prosperous, if the economy is also doing well. The performance of a company is thus a function of the industry and of the economy, in addition to its own performance (Fig. 17.1).

As referred to earlier, the share price of the company is empirically found to depend upto 50% on the external factors such as the performance of the industry and economy. The economic and political situation in the country has thus a bearing on the prospects of the company. The industries in different stages of growth are shown below (Fig. 17.2).

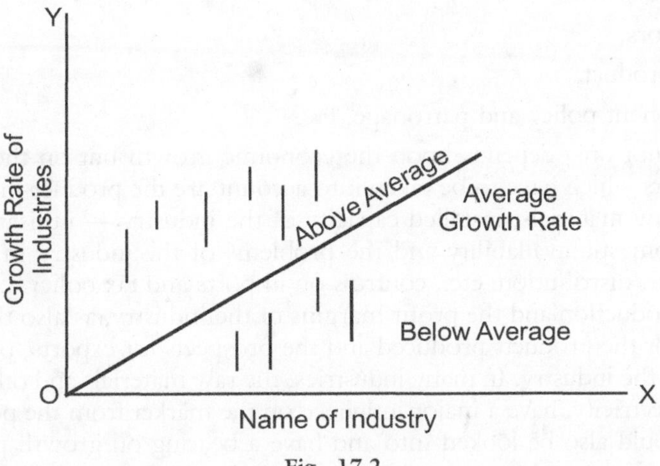

Fig. 17.2

Even in industries of above average growth, there may be some companies of poor growth or no growth at all. The fundamentals of the company will explain this. The Market Price (MP) is a function of intrinsic factors to the extent of about ½ of it and the rest is accounted by the expectations, psychological and sentimental factors (Fig. 17.3). A poorly performing company namely Finolex Industries is analysed at the end of the chapter.

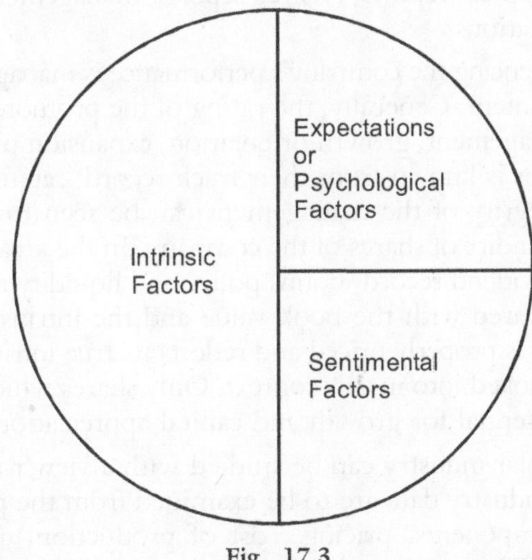

Fig. 17.3

In the above context, any particular industry can be studied with a view to assess the problems, prospects, etc., of the company in the industry. The industry data are to be examined from the point of view of the product-mix, raw materials, components, pricing, cost of production, etc., profit margins and related data juxtaposed with those of the company. The capacity utilisation of the industry in general and of the company in question within the industry are to be compared. The demand and supply, the market conditions and the share of the company in the market are to be studied before making a projection of its future growth, keeping the industry prospects in mind. The future profitability can be assessed from the quarterly half-yearly and annual reports, press releases, AGM's reports, market reports, management interviews and Industry and Commerce Association's publications. The share of the company in which investment is sought is to be analysed in terms of the fundamentals of the company in the background of the industry's performance. The decision to buy has to be on the basis of whether the price of the share is proper and the future profitability is good based on a rational forecast for the future.

We have to consider the quantifiable factors and qualitative factors of the company. Among the quantifiable factors we have to consider the capital efficiency and the sales turnover and the profitability margins. The quantifiable data are based on financial statement analysis.

The qualitative factors are:

(a) Management efficiency,

(b) Rating of promoters,

(c) Rating of collaborators,

(d) Uniqueness of the product,

(e) Location — government policy and patronage, etc.

The industrial position not only depends upon the economic growth but on the nature of the industry itself. Within the industry, the factors which have to be taken into account are the product-mix, the various outputs, nature of the products, inputs and raw materials, installed capacity of the industry — utilisation of capacity — the market nature of the inputs, their domestic availability and the problems of the industry in general. The pricing and the Government controls on prices, distribution, etc., controls on imports and tax policy, excise and customs duties, etc., would influence the cost of production and the profit margins of the industry, as also the prospects of growth. In the area of market, the demand for the products produced and the prospects for exports, protection or tariff preferences, etc., influence the prospects of the industry. In many industries, the raw materials and other inputs and their availability domestically, particularly of electricity, have a major influence on the market from the point of view of supply. Labour conditions in the industry should also be looked into and have a bearing on growth prospects.

In the company analysis, the financial highlights of the companies, which are influenced by the industry and the economy are the capacity utilisation, demand, cost and profit margins. The state of the capital market and the capacity to raise capital from the market not only depend on the performance of the company but of the economy and the industry as well. The fundamentals of the company are to be analysed in terms of its financial structure, leverage, liquidity and profitability, financial viability, etc. The information for this purpose is to be secured from the annual reports of the company, balance sheets, press reports, AGM's reports, management's press releases and the publications of the Industry and Commerce Associations.

The most important variable influencing the company's performance is management, namely, the quality, capability, popularity and integrity of the management. Generally, the rating of the promoters and management has to be looked into through their plans, financial management, growth-orientation, expansion plans, tax planning, R&D, technology, etc. The popularity of the management is known from their track record, retention policy, distribution of dividends and bonus, etc. The honesty and integrity of the management can be seen from the shareholding pattern and the availability of floating stock and the liquidity of shares of the company. In the area of financial management, companies' financial structure, retention policy, dividend record, bonus policy and liquidity ratios, etc., are to be looked into. The market price of a share is to be compared with the book value and the intrinsic worth of the company. The share has to be examined to know whether it is properly priced and reflects its true intrinsic value. The P/E ratio and earnings per share, book value, etc., are to be looked into in this context. Only shares which are underpriced are to be generally purchased, provided they have the potential for growth and capital appreciation.

In the above context, any particular industry can be studied with a view to assess the problems, prospects, etc., of the company in the industry. The industry data are to be examined from the point of view of the installed capacity and its utilisation, raw materials, components, pricing, cost of production, etc., profit margins and related data juxtaposed with those of the company. The capacity utilisation of the industry in general and of the company in question within the industry are to be compared. The demand and supply, the market conditions and the share of the company in the market are to be studied before making a projection of its future growth, keeping the industry prospects in mind. The future profitability can be assessed from the half-yearly and annual reports, press releases, AGM's reports, market reports, management interviews and Industry and Commerce Association's publications. The share of the company in which investment is sought is to be analysed in terms of the fundamentals of the company in the background of the industry's performance. The decision to buy has to be on the basis of whether the price of the share is proper and the future profitability is good based on a rational forecast for the future.

To examine the financial highlights, we have to consider among other things, the capital efficiency and the sales turnover and the profitability margins. For this purpose, the following components may be taken into account:

$$\underset{\text{(Capital turnover)}}{\frac{\text{GB}}{\text{Equity}}} \times \underset{\text{(Sales turnover)}}{\frac{\text{Sales}}{\text{GB}}} \times \underset{\text{(Profitability)}}{\frac{\text{GP}}{\text{Sales}}} = \frac{\text{GP}}{\text{Equity}}$$

Normally, a company uses capital efficiently by having a high turnover of equity. Similarly, the use of capital is efficient if there is a high sales turnover to gross block. The company may have only a small profit margin but if the sales turnover is high, the profits will also be high. Gross profts-to-sales ratio measures the profit margins. In this context, the growth of gross block, sales, equity, and gross profits are to be analysed in respect of each company within the industry. On this basis, these ratios of companies within the industry are to be compared with the industry's overall operating performance in respect of the variables referred to earlier. The Gross Profit (GP) is also to be examined in relation to the market capitalisation. The riskless return is 7% and a reasonable return is 15%. Depreciation, taxes, etc., may account for another 15%. A total return in the form of gross profit of not less than 30% is, therefore, necessary for any company to start with. If a company in any industry is less profitable than that, it is not worth the purchase. Similarly, gross profit to gross block and the dividend policy, earning per share and bonus payouts are all to be examined from the point of view of the future prospects of the company in the background of industry performance and possible capital appreciation of the shares.

Industry Analysis

At any point of time, there may be industries which are on the upswing of the cycle called sunshine industries and those which are on the decline called sunset industries. In India, there are some growth industries like electronics and computers which are the key industries. The engineering, petrochemicals and capital goods industries are in the core sector. A few industries like diamonds, engineering, etc., are in the export sector. Jute and cotton textiles are the decadent industries. At present, Telecommunications, Computer Software, Solar Energy, Media and Biotechnology, waste management are some examples of Sunrise Industries.

As referred to earlier, performance of a company has been found to depend broadly up to 50% on the external factors of the economy and industry. These externalities depend on the availability of inputs, like proper labour, water, power and inter-relations between the economy and industry and the company. It is, in this context, that a well-diversified company performs better than a single product company, because while the demand for some products may be declining, that for others may be increasing. Similarly, the input prices and cost factors would vary from product line to product line, leading to different margins and a diversified company is a better bet for investor.

The industry analysis should take into account the following factors among others as influencing the performance of the company, whose shares are to be analysed:

*1. **Product Line:*** The position of the industry in the life cycle of its growth — initial stages, high growth stages and maturing stages are to be noted. It is also necessary to know the industries with a high growth potential like computers, electronics, chemicals, diamonds, etc., and whether the industry is in the priority sector of the key industry group or capital goods or consumer goods groups. The importance attached by the government in their policy and of the Planning Commission in their assessment of these industries is to be studied. Product may be new one or an import substitution product which has good future.

*2. **Raw Material and Inputs:*** Under this head, we have to look into industries depending on imports of scarce raw materials, competition from other companies and industries, and the barriers to entry of a new company, protection from foreign competition, import and export restrictions, etc. An industry which has a limited supply of materials domestically and where imports are restricted, for example, will have dim growth prospects. Labour is also an input and industries with labour problems may have difficulties of growth.

*3. **Capacity Installed and Utilised:*** The demand for industrial products in the economy is estimated by the Planning Commission and the government, and the units are given licensed capacity on the basis of these estimates. If the demand is rising as expected and the market is good for the products, the utilisation of capacity will be higher. If, however, the quality of the product is poor, competition is high and there are other constraints to the availability of inputs and there are labour problems, then the capacity utilisation will be low and profitability will be poor.

*4. **Industry Characteristics:*** Whether the industry is cyclical, fluctuating or stable, has to be looked into first, as the prospects for growth will depend on this to an extent. If the demand is seasonal as in the case of fertilisers, pesticides, etc., their problems may mar the growth prospects. If it is consumer product or a pharma or a food product and the demand is all over India, freight charges are an important component of the cost of production. The scale of production and the width of the market would also determine the selling and advertisement costs. The nature of the industry would thus be an important factor for determining the scale of operations and profitability. The growth prospects would depend on raw materials, easy access to inputs, particularly power, transport and other infrastructual facilities.

*5. **Demand and Market:*** The demand for the product should be expanding and its price should not be controlled by the government, if the industry is to have good prospects of profitability. If the demand is income-elastic and price-elastic, the supplier should be able to sell the goods at a growing rate and the prospects of growth are good. It is also important that the prices of raw materials and other input costs like freight, electricity, etc., should not be controlled by the government. The demand should also be growing and there should be export demand for the product. If the nature of the product is such as drugs, fertilisers or other consumer goods, whose price and distribution are controlled by the government, the growth prospects would be less. Thus, decontrol of cement recently has helped the cement industry to grow and expand. Similarly, the reduction of the regulations on pharmaceuticals after the reforms has helped the Drug industry.

6. Government Policy with Regard to Industry: The government policy is announced in the Industrial Policy Resolutions and subsequent announcements from time-to-time by the government. The policy can also be seen from the strategy as laid down in the five-year plans and importance given to the industry by the Planning Commission and the expected demand in the economy. The Plan priorities for the industry, the physical and financial targets of investment and foreign collaboration in that industry are important variables affecting its fortunes. The government has powers of control over industry in terms of output, price and distribution of the product and a number of other aspects. The government policy with regard to granting of clearances, installed capacity and reservation of the products for small industry, etc., are also factors to be considered for industrial analysis.

7. Labour and Other Industrial Problems: The industry, whether it is capital-intensive or labour-intensive, has to use labour of different categories and expertise. The productivity of labour as much as the capital efficiency would determine the progress of the industry. If there are problems of labour, strikes, lockouts and poor productivity, that industry should be unwelcome for the investors. The best example is coal, where presently labour productivity is poor, and there are labour problems.

There are some decaying industries, like jute and cotton textiles, whose shares are to be avoided by the investors unless such companies are diversified into other lines as in the case of Birla Jute. Certain industries with problems of marketing like high storage costs, high transport costs, dependence on foreign markets etc., as in the case of fertilisers may have poor growth potential and investors have to be careful when investing in such companies.

8. Management: An industry with many problems may be well-managed, if the promoters and the management are efficient and capable of steering the company through difficult days. Such management like Tatas, Birlas, Ambanis etc., who have a reputation, built up their companies on strong foundations. The management has to be assessed in terms of their capabilities, popularity, honesty and integrity. In the case of new industries and new managements, there will be no track record and the investors have to carefully assess the project reports and the assessment of financial institutions in this regard. The capabilities of management will depend upon tax planning, innovation of technology, modernisation, expansion of R&D, etc. A management with a broad vision will plan for the expansion and diversification, make tax planning, increase the retained earnings with a consistent dividend policy so that the future expansion plans are put on a sound basis. A good management will also ensure that their shares are well distributed and liquidity of shares is assured and trading is fair and just in the market with no malpractices like cornering of shares or insider trading.

9. Future Prospects: Many of the factors of operation in industry are interlinked such as capacity utilisation, demand and markets, government policy, availability of inputs, infrastructure, etc. It is, therefore, necessary to have an overall picture of the industry and to study these problems and prospects. After a study of the past, the future prospects of the industry are to be assessed. For this purpose, the projected demand, input availabilities, unutilised capacities, the alternative growth strategies, methods of reducing of cost, economies of scale and the position of competitors in the market are to be probed into. The scope for diversification horizontally or vertically and the management's willingness and ability to diversify should also be examined *inter alia.* A company has to be assessed in terms of its strategies to meet the challenges as they emerge and its future prospects should be assessed before an investment is made. The growth and growth prospects and capacity utilisation of major industry groups are published in their Annual Reports.

In fundamental analysis, intrinsic worth as reflected by BV or EPS or GPM, etc., is expected to indicate the market price. But in actual practice it is not so. Take the Tyres/Tubes Industry for example. The table below shows how the market prices of similar companies in the same industry do not bear any perceptible relationship to BV, EPS or GPM. A number of non-economic factors, psychological factors and expectations play an important role at any point of time.

Tyres/Tubes Industry

(In rupees)

Name of the Company	*Book Value (BV)*	*Market Price (MP)*
Apollo	50.41	150
Govind Rubber	50.13	90
Modi Rubber	63.87	50
Dunlop Rubber	45.83	65

Name of the Company	*EPS*	*MP*
Ceat	10.17	78
J.K. Industry	10.24	128
Dewan Rubber	11.41	55
Apollo Tyres	11.84	150
Vikrant Tyres	11.86	40

Name of the Company	*GPM*	*MP*
Premier Tyres	7.8	300
Falcon Tyres	7.7	15
Dewan Rubber	7.9	55
Ceat Tyres	7.1	78
MRF Tyres	6.9	625

(***Note:*** Data relate to 1993, but date is immaterial for illustration).

EXAMPLE OF AN INDUSTRY ANALYSIS

Petrochemicals

Product Nature: Petrochemicals are derived from petroleum and natural gas. The product groups are aromatics, plastics, surfactants, etc.

Raw Materials: Coal tar, intermediates, etc., calcium carbide, alcohol, etc.

Market (Users): Food processing, clothing, housing, health care, automobiles, etc.

Demand Scenario: The first enterprise in the public sector was Indian Petrochemicals Corporation Ltd. (IPCL) set up in 1979. Demand was poor until 1983. After the pioneering work of IPCL to promote uses, the demand picked up. As per the demand projections of the government, demand and supply gap has persisted and necessitated imports costing more than ₹ 1,000 crores per annum.

Policy of Government: The government has placed petro-chemicals under the core sector as being vital to the national economy. The Planning Commission's study group headed by Abid Hussain has estimated the need for an investment of ₹ 22,000 crores to achieve self-sufficiency by 2000 A.D. The government has sanctioned a number of new projects which were in the pipeline such as those of Hindustan Lever, Nirma Chemicals, etc. Already RIL and TNP have set up projects and there are others in the pipeline.

Problems of the Industry: (a) Long delays in government clearances and project cost escalations; (b) Projects established were not of economic size in many cases; (c) High prices of main feed stock, namely, Naptha; (d) Need for R&D and introduction of new technologies which are most cost effective; and (e) High excise duties on Naptha.

Competition: What is the share of the company in question in the total market demand? Soon after IPCL, ABS Plastics began production whose capacity is currently 2000 tonnes p.a. and is expected to be raised to 5000 tonnes p.a. The main competitors are Polychem with a 30% share in the market. There are others such as Indo-Nippon, Bansali Engineering, etc. The companies in this line with strong fundamentals are ABS Plastics, Gujarat Petrosyl, PIL, NOCIL, Polychem, etc.

Cost Comparisons: The cost per tonne of the Bansali Engineering is three times that of ABS Plastics. ABS and Polychem are leaders in cost-effectiveness. The industry is asking for protection from foreign competition. The ban on exports of petrochemicals may help some units.

Process Comparisons: Mysore Petrochemicals uses Oxelene Oxidation route; Tirumalai Chemicals adopts the benzene route; Rama Petrochemicals uses the alcohol as feedstock, while competitors are using propylene.

Company Analysis

In the case of company analysis, the balance sheet data should be first analysed for:

(1) Efficient use of capital;

(2) Leverage enjoyed in the use of capital;

(3) Return on networth; and

(4) Return on equity.

The capital structure and the cost of different types of capital and the problems of servicing the borrowed funds are to be taken into account. For this purpose, the interest burden, tax and depreciation provision are to be examined. The cash profits and profit after depreciation should be considered in relation to equity and networth.

The sales turnover is an important indicator of the activity of the company and an assessment of gross profits in relation to sales is to be made. Sales to equity would be high to indicate a good turnover of sales for equity (or NW) employed in the business. The profit margins, earnings per share and P/E ratios will indicate the earning potential of the company for the equityholders.

A fair return on capital employed can be assumed to be 10-15% as the government and public sector bonds give a return of around 10-11%. A provision for tax and depreciation has to be made at around 15%. These together would account for about 30% as gross profit for a company to be eligible for investment. The gross profits as well as net profits are to be related to the market capitalisation for each company. Besides, the performance of the company analysed has to be compared with that of its competitors in the industry under the following heads:

(1) Cost per unit;

(2) Profit margins;

(3) Earnings per share and P/E ratio;

(4) Bonus payments;

(5) Dividend distribution policy; etc.

The variables to be studied for each company and the relative ratios are set out below:

(1) Capital Efficiency $= \frac{\text{GB}}{\text{Equity}}$ and $\frac{\text{Sales}}{\text{GB}}$ (GB = Gross Block)

(2) Leverage Employed $= \frac{\text{Debt}}{\text{Equity}}$; $\frac{\text{Borrowed Capital}}{\text{Net worth}}$

$$\frac{\text{Total Borrowed Capital}}{\text{Total Capital Employed}}$$

(3) Size for the Company — The expansion and growth of the company has to be judged by the growth of sales, assets, gross block and net block.

The growth of the company can also be judged by the rate of growth of any of the above variables while the size of the company has to be judged in terms of its sales, installed capacity utilisation with a view to see that the company is of an economic size.

The profitability of the company is to be judged by the net profits (PAT) or cash profits in relation to sales, equity or networth, dividend distributed, etc.

The following variables are also to be analysed for a company analysis:

(1) Company's share in industry — its capacity utilisation *vis-a-vis* the utilisation in the whole industry.

(2) Modernisation and expansion plans — reflected in tax planning, retention policy, bonus policy, etc.

(3) Turnover of capital: $\frac{\text{Sales}}{\text{GB}}$ or $\frac{\text{Sales}}{\text{Trading Assets}}$

(4) Leverage $= \frac{\text{GB}}{\text{NW}} = \frac{\text{Total Assets}}{\text{NW or Equity}}$

(5) Profitability: $\frac{\text{PAT}}{\text{GB}}$; $\frac{\text{PAT}}{\text{Sales}}$

(6) Earnings per share, cash earnings per share and P/E ratios, and its intrinsic worth as judged by Book Value per share (BV).

Need for Forecast

The disadvantage of the above type of analysis is that it is based on the past performance and that it may not be an indicator of future performance. So a forecast is necessary for the coming six months or one year for making an investment. Such a forecast can be made on the basis of some assumptions of costs, prices and demand for its products. The earnings, gross and net profits, the EPS, etc., can be worked out and an assessment can be made whether the scrip is worthwhile purchasing judged by its prospects a year hence.

For making a forecast, some subjective weights may be given to management (50%), expansion and growth (25%), prospects of bonus (15%) and other subjective factors like Government patronage or changes in market conditions (10%). These give a total weight of 100%. Companies in the same industry group can be studied by using the above weights to decide on which scrips to purchase depending on their rating. These weights and cosequent judgement will be subjective and the result would depend on the ability and expertise of the analyst.

Guidelines for Investment

A company which has a high intrinsic worth is not necessarily the best stock to buy. It may have no growth prospects or it may be overpriced. Similarly, a company that performs well during any one year may not be the best to buy. On the contrary, a company which has been doing badly for sometime might have turned the corner and it may be the best buy, as its shares may be underpriced and it has good prospects of growth. So an analyst should not be guided by one or a few indicators but has to consider the performance of the whole company, and over a period of time, say, 5 years. Besides a company is to be judged in the background of the industry's performance, product nature, prospects of the industry, etc. A study of the industry factors constitutes the industry analysis. Next to economy's performance, industry's performance is vital for an assessment of a company's prospects and growth.

Example of Company Analysis

It is necessary to analyse the financial data of the company in the background of the industry performance as shown below:

Company	*Debt Equity Ratio (D/E)*	*Gross Profit to Sales (GPM)*	*Profit After Tax to Net Worth*	*Book Value*	*Rate of Dividend %*	*EPS (₹)*	*P/E Ratio*	*Market Price*
Industry		10.6	32.3	—	—	—	10.4	—
ABS Plastics	1.82	12.74	45.45	21.0	21%	9.5	8.5	81
Cochin Refineries	0.89	5.25	54.45	275.0	36%	120	6.8	810
NOCIL	0.78	16.14	27.16	405.0	40%	89	13.8	1255
Reliance Petro	7.84	25.56	4.62	10.1	15%	0.5	53	25

Only selected companies are studied above. The debt-equity ratio representing leverage is good for NOCIL and Cochin Refineries. But PAT to NW is higher and the actual market price is covered by book value three times in the case of Cochin Refineries. As compared to the industry averages, although the gross profit margin is lower, capital efficiency is higher, and P/E ratio is lowest indicating that a multiple of 7 of price to earnings exhibits some potential for capital appreciation in the case of Cochin Refineries. Besides, examine the data of Gross Block, NW, Sales, Gross and Net Profits and their growth rates over a period of 5 years. Then assess whether the company's EPS and P/E ratios are better than the average industry performance and whether the scrip is underpriced or overpriced and buy only if it is underpriced with growth prospects or is fairly priced for its fundamentals. In the above example, Cochin Refineries is the best buy at its price.

How to Pick up Growth Shares?

The growth companies are also called blue chip companies. The blue chips of yesteryears are not necessarily the blue chips of today. The investor has to review and assess the companies from time-to-time to locate the blue chips, based on fundamental analysis.

In order to enable one to identify these blue chips of tomorrow, one should know the nature and characteristics of these companies. A few guidelines in this regard are set out below.

Firstly, the management should be professional, experienced and efficient; they should have the honesty, integrity and vision for expansion and growth. Such is the case with Ambanis, Tatas and Birlas.

Secondly, the market share of the company should be substantial and at least more than one-third. The larger the share, the better the prospects of controlling the market and profit margins and expanding the operations. Bajaj Auto and Hero Honda have a share of two-thirds in the two-wheeler and three-wheeler market. So is the case with Asian Paints, Laxmi Machine Works etc., in their respective industry groups.

Thirdly, the company must be well-diversified into areas of growth potential. The growth potential changes from time-to-time. At present, industries with a growth potential are cement, paper, petro-chemicals, etc. Thus, a company with a good diversification into such growth areas would do well in sales, profits, and earnings. Some of the consumer product industries producing soaps, cosmetics, toothpaste and powders etc., would generally record a consistent growth. A well-diversified company like ITC, Hindustan Lever, or L&T is a good buy at any reasonable price.

Fourthly, the company's policy of expansion should be consistent and has a long-term perspective. Its assets growth should be reasonably good, reflecting its expansion goals. Growth helps the industry to stabilise its earnings from undue fluctuations and helps the diversification process. The companies with a good asset growth are Reliance, L&T, Ranbaxy etc.

Fifthly, the company should have a consistent and stable distribution policy with good profit margins. The company should distribute a reasonable proportion of its profits as dividends bonus etc. Such companies like Ponds, Colgate, Glaxo etc., would be in good demand, as investors prefer regular dividend-paying companies.

Sixthly, such a company services the investors well with bonus or rights issue or convertible debentures, from time-to-time in addition to increasing dividend payments. The financial structure and utilisation of capital are efficient. The profit margins are growing and the company is growing in financial strength.

Lastly, the industry or industries in which the company is operating should have good growth prospects. The products should be in continuous demand like food products, paper soaps, etc., or consumer non-durable goods. The future outlook of the company and prospects of the industry are interlinked. The prospects would depend also on the government policy and whether it is subject to price and distribution control or any restrictions or regulations. The prospects of the industry in which the company is operating should be assessed from all points of view.

Thus, in the choice of blue chips, the investor has to examine the fundamentals of the companies through balance sheet analysis for a period of at least five years before finally selecting the shares. The time of purchase should be decided on the basis of technical analysis referred to later. But for a layman, the purchase time should be in the bearish phase of the market, when an all-round decline in prices is recorded. At such times, the companies with strong fundamentals should be picked up at low prices for long-term investment if they can be classified as blue chips as per the above guidelines.

New Millennium Trends

In the new millennium, starting with the year 2001, the New Economy and the new Government policies are under the need for a review of analysis and interpretation. In this context a new Industry Study and Company analysis are presented here. The sectors which come to limelight in this new Millennium are knowledge based industries, Satellite Telecommunications, Internet trading business and e-commerce, Multi-media, Robotics, Informatics, Bio-Tech and Hi-Tech Industries. Of these the fastest growing sector is I.T. Software Sector in the year 2000, and in 2008-09 dispite the general global recession, consumer durables and non-durables, beverages, tobacco etc. showed steady acceleration in 2007-08 and 20011-012.

KNOWLEDGE-BASED INDUSTRIES

A Case Study on I.T. Industry

For Industry analysis, I.T. industry is chosen. In India, Software sector and I.T. Industry is a leading example of knowledge-based industries. Globally, this sector is a leading growth sector in the economies of the many countries. There are different types of business within this sector companies that provide custom solutions and export project services, pure technology companies, providing packaged solutions, companies in the Internet trading, Infrastructure business, e-commerce business Internet providing services, B.P.O. service, I.T. Education and Training Services etc. Each of these lines of business is different in the sense that they differ in the customer profile, revenue profile, level of technology, cash flow profile etc.

The National Association of Software Services Companies (NASSCOM) has pioneered the case of these companies with the government in 1999-2000 and I.T. capital and entreprenurship is being encouraged by the government as a leading growth sector and an I.T. Venture Capital Fund was set up and the government has assured the industry of all assistance for capital, and technology promotion.

I.T. Sector is the leader of new Economy, in the 21st century. In 1998, U.S. accounted for 75% of Internet based commerce and is expected to account for 50% in 2003. U.S. will once again emerge as the leading technology country, as compared with Japan and EU. This would mean that traditional labour and capital would not be leading factors of production but the Information technology and knowledge would be the source of growth in the New economies. Internet Age will be the harbinger of a new era of global growth. The key to the next stage of Internet era is whether and how fast the financial innovations will be spread the world over as technological innovations.

INDUSTRY PROFILE

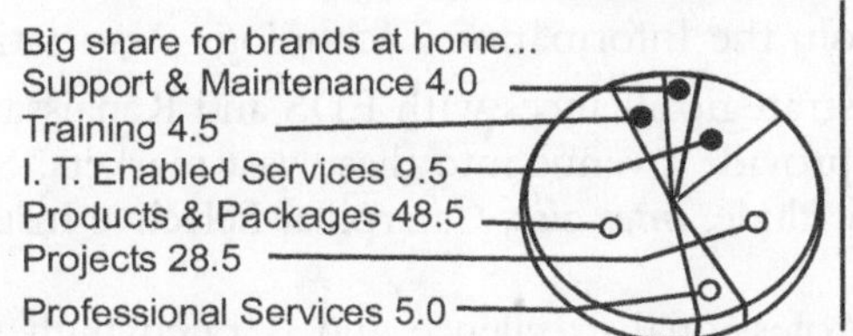

India: The Emerging Software Giant

	Software industry in India		*Domestic Software market*		*Software exports*	
	US $ mn	*₹ mn*	*US $ mn*	*₹ mn*	*US $ mn*	*₹ mn*
1995-96	1124	41,900	490	16,700	734	25,200
1996-97	1755	63,100	670	24,100	1085	39,000
1997-98	2700	100,400	950	35,100	1750	65,300
1998-99	3900	158,900	1250	49,500	2650	109,400
1999-00 (est.)	5700	245,000	1700	73,000	3900	172,000

It will be seen from the attached Table that the growth of software industry was rapid from 1995-96, rising in value terms by about six times over the quinquennium of 1995-2000. The domestic software market grew from ₹ 16,700 million in 1995-96 to ₹ 73,000 million in 1999-2000 and the rise in exports was much higher in 1999-2000 at ₹ 172 billion.

The main categories of Brands in software industry and their relative shares are shown in the charts attached. The main brands are products and packages and projects accounting for about 77% of the total brands sales in the domestic market but they account for only 44% of the total export sales. In the markets abroad software exports are mostly in the form of projects and professional services, which together accounted for about 81% of the total export market for Indian software industry.

There are a few hundred High Tech stocks quoted on the Stock Exchanges. Some of them have market prices sky high, running into a few thousand rupees for a share of ₹ 10. Thus in March 2000 (10th March), Aptech was quoted at ₹ 2,300 with a P/E multiple of 54. Dig Equipments is quoted at ₹ 965 with a P/E multiple at 50. Global Tel has a price of ₹ 3,300 and P/E multiple of 118. Infosys was quoted at ₹ 11,700 with P/E at 318. This boom in I.T. industry was burst in 2001 and their Stock Prices crashed to more modest levels and this position continued thereafter.

Growth Potential

Over the last few years, particularly from 1995-1996, we have seen in India a fast growth of I.T. Companies to emerge from nowhere and show the annual growth rates of 60% to 70% per annum. Some of them including Wipro, Infosys and Satyam could end up as home grown MNCs, operating in a large number of countries. It is found that some have P/E and high as 300 or 400 and valuations have reached sky high levels. On the other hand some have only modest P/E like ₹ 21 in the case of Higher Software.

Many software companies have set up shops in software Technology parks (STP) which enjoy some tax benefits. Similarly, many have Software Technology Development Centres (SDC), which enjoy the STP status such as Aptech, BFL, DSQ, HCL, etc. Thus, Infosys has 11 centres all enjoying STP status. Similarly, Wipro has 16 SDCs of which 14 have STP status. Satyam has five SDCs and all enjoy STP status. Many other I.T. Companies like Maars Software, Mastek, NIIT, Pentasoft, Pentamedia, PSE Data, RS Software, Silverline, Sonata Software, Sierra Optima, Vasual Soft etc. have Software Development Centres. Many of them were set up in the last couple of years which enjoy tax holiday of 100% tax free status for 10 years from the commencement of commercial production. For units set up till March 31, 1988, exemption is available for 5 consecutive years in a block of 8 assessment years from the date of commercial production. For units set up till March 31, 2000 exemption would be available for 10 years from the date of commencement of commercial production, as per section 10(A) of the Income Tax Act providing for newly established undertakings set up in Free Trade Zones and Soft Ware Technology parks.

Case Study of Satyam Computers

Satyam has its registered office at Hyderabad. It has developed strong domain knowledge in the fields of insurance, manufacturing, banking and financial services Nearly 60% of its turnover emanates from mainframes including Y2K business and the balance from open system. It has also developed some productised services under the caption of products and packages. Nearly 70% of its business comes from offshore markets and the rest from on site business. Besides nearly 80% of its billing comes from business on time and material basis and the balance 20% from Fixed price contracts.

Satyam has a joint venture with DBSS of the U.S. and this has given Satyam International recognition as a quality software house. Its offshore solution (SOS 2000) to Y2K problem is the first methodology from an Indian Company to have received the prestigious ITAA 2000 certification from the Information Technology Association of America.

The U.S. is a major contributor to its revenue. It has strategic alliances with EDS and Renaissance world-wide in U.S. and Jasdic Park Company in Japan. These alliances provide a venue into these vast markets. Satyam has long relationship with Ford, GE, and First Data. Its other clients include, *inter alia,* Caterpillar Selective Insurance, Sandgeo Data and Boeing

Satyam has earned international recognition in its professional excellence and is rated high for its business strategies and long-term planning. Satyam has started separate business units for specialised ventures. It has kept with itself its core business of software development.

Satyam Computers — Company Profile

Satyam Computers is quoted at ₹ 6,700 on March 10, 2000 with a P/E multiple of ₹ 295; as against this Wipro has a wobbling high P/E multiple of 520 and Infosys has 318 and Zee Telefilm has 624. But Satyam is chosen for its potential. Satyam was quoted at hardly ₹ 50-60 during 1996, but rose to around ₹ 400-500 by 1998 and went sky high of ₹ 7,000 early in 2000 recording quantum jumps all throughout. The annual turnover recorded a high rate of growth of 100% and above during 1996 to 2000 with expenses rising by an average growth rate of less than 50% and operating profits rose by an average growth rate of 35-40%. It has a consistent growth record.

Ratio Analysis on Satyam Computers

(₹ in Lakhs)

At end March:	*31.3.1998*	*31.3.1999*	*31.3.2001*
Equity	2602	2602	5,623
Reserves & Surplus	7668	14090	75,666
Net Worth	10,270	16,692	81,289
Debt Capital	12,050	24,828	—
Book Value	₹ 39.5	₹ 64.2	₹ 28.9
Debt Equity Ratio	1:1.17	1:1.49	—
Current Ratio	4.0	4.6	N.A.
Gross Block	17477	29376	N.A.
Sales (Total)	19,013	37,845	124,167
Gross Block to Sales Ratio	1.09	1.29	—
P.B.I. DT (Operating Profit)	7854	14,669	46,671
Interest	1198	2643	3451
Interest to Operating Profits	15.25	18.02	7.39
Net Profit After Tax	3908	7280	31,616
EPS	15.0	28.0	11.24
Enterprise Value (Market Value of Equity & Debt)	76031	4,46,857	N.A.
Return to Capital Employed	₹ 31.69	₹ 32.50	₹ 34.65
Return to Networth	₹ 40. 72	₹ 54.01	38.9
M.P. to Book Value	6.26	25.28	15.5
P/E Multiple	16.47	58.00	24.46
Market Price	Around ₹ 240	Around ₹ 1600	₹ 275

Note: The face value of share was ₹ 2 only since 2001 and has quoting around ₹ 450 in September 2007. At end Sept. 2012, the MP was ₹ 110, year H/L – 116/73, P/E = 8.6, P/B.V = 4.4, Beta = 0.7, EPS = 12.8, From October 1, 2012, it was listed in "A" group on BSE, under the name "Mahendra Satyam".

Satyam is recording an above average rate of growth in the industry during the last few years. Satyam's growth strategy is penetration into new areas of value chain with a set of centres and branch offices in U.S.A. and other foreign countries like Japan and E.U. During 1998 and 1999, U.S. continued to be a major market for its products with its turnover there accounting for around 70% of its total business.

Satyam has got ISO 9001 certification and SEI level 4, which gives it an entry into the select brand of quality software companies, world wide. It has set up its own power plants and is aggressive in Y2K business. It has impressive client profile with respect orders constituting 75% of its total business and a record of consistent growth performance. It has four fully owned subsidiaries each with a specific business goal and specialised product line.

The stock of Satyam was having a maximum price of ₹ 100 only in June 1997, and ₹ 613 in June 1998, which rose to ₹ 1,700 by March 1999 and ₹ 6,600 by March 2000. The I.T boom was burst in 2001 and prices fell thereafter. In 2006-07, the share price of Satyam was having a high of ₹ 525 and a low of ₹ 396 and as on Sept. 16, 2007, it was quoted at ₹ 435-440. It has a P/E multiple of 20, which is market average for BSE in 2005-06.

Latest Position of the Company

During the years 2005 to 2007 when this company was studied, this was a blue chip company quoted in specified group and well traded and respected both in India and abroad where its ADRs are traded. Now in 2009 and 2010, the position of the company is completely different. It is down graded, removed from the "A" Group and from the Sensex composition and kept in the B1 group of other shares. It is no longer a blue chip company. Its present market price is ₹ 116, P/E multiple is 6.3 and has a 52 week high and low of ₹ 126 – ₹ 6, as on January 7, 2010. As per these data, its EPS is only ₹ 16 to 18 and not even 20 or 24, as in 2005 to 2007.

The fortunes of the Satyam has seen a phenomenal rise and also an abysmal fall during the last few years. In 2001, it was quoted at ₹ 6,700 for a face value of ₹ 10. Later in 2001, its face value was brought down to ₹ 2 and the share price was quoted at a high of ₹ 525 as in September 2007. At that time, its P/E multiple was 20 and it was quoted and traded well. It was only after that during the years 2008 and 2009, the fortunes began to fall, mainly due to the reported crimes committed by the Promoters, namely, Ramalinga Raju and associates in the form of corruption, diversion of funds, wrong accounts and falsification of facts, for which a CBI enquiry was held and the company was taken over by Mahindra Tech for its salvage from extinction.

It was revived by the new managers and continued to be quoted in the B1 category of shares. Its market price began to fall and reached a level of ₹ 116 as on January 20, 2010 and ₹ 96 on Feb. 5, 2010. Its P/E ratio is 6.3 and its yearly market high and low as in Jan.-Feb. 2010 was ₹ 129-23.

The investors of this company have lost crores of Rupees during the last two years of 2008 and 2009 as its market price fell form a high or ₹ 525 in 2007 to a low or ₹ 23 per share at one time. To add fuel to the fire, the markets were also in a bearish phase. Even at the low price of ₹ 116, there are not many takers in this counter as it may not have the fundamentals to support this price. It is for the readers to assess the fundamentals again when its annual financial data for March 2010 will be out in or before September 2010.

This case study has become unique for the exceptional rise in fortunes and equally abysmal fall in its values. Therefore, this case study was kept here as an example of this type of companies in the market.

The Details of Subsidiaries of Satyam

Company		*Business*
Satyam Rennaisance	—	Consulting
Satyam Enterprises	—	Total I.T. Solutions
Satyam Infoway	—	e-Commerce
Satyam Spark	—	Software Products

Relative Comparison with Competitors

	Satyam	*NIIT*	*DSQ*	*Infosys*
Wage per Employee ₹	4.2	2.1	2.0	4.3
Revenue per Employee ₹	10.3	13.0	11	12
Equity ₹ crores	26	26	20	16
EPS ₹	15	33	12	38
NW ₹ crores	103	186	69	173
Net Profits (NP) for the quarter ₹ crores (Oct-Dec. 1999)	36.19	18.52	14.63	73.79
Annualised EPS	₹ 55	₹ 28	₹ 30	₹ 185

Satyam Mahindra was taken over by Tech MM whose price is quoted at ₹ 538 at end July 2015.

In the case of Satyam computers, the estimated Annualised profit for 3rd quarter (Oct.-Dec. 99) was ₹ 144 crores as against annualised profit (NP) for the half year at ₹ 112 crores and the actual for 1998-99 was ₹ 73 crores a growth of 100% over 3 quarters. In 1997-98, its net profits after tax was only ₹ 39 crores. As this is only for illustration, the time period of the data may not be significant.

Satyam seems to have shown a greater rise in market price due to better performance in 1999-00.

	Satyam	*NIIT*	*DSQ*	*Infosys*
Early Jan. Market prices (4.1.2000)	₹ 2,500	Rs.3,500	₹ 950	₹ 16,000
14.3.2000	₹ 6,600	₹ 2,500	₹ 2,300	₹ 12,000

The boom in I.T. Stocks was burst in 2000 and their stocks fell steeply thereafter. Many internet opportunities stocks have disappointed their investors. The market price of Satyam comp was hovering around ₹ 290-300 in March 2004. Infosys was however much higher at around ₹ 4,900 in the same period.

This case study is now provided with the latest data on the company which is now available. These data confirm the trends seen in the years last presented in 2001. These data may be studied, for its share valuation on the basis of the fundamental analysis referred to in this chapter. Satyam computers falls in the category of NEW ECONOMY STOCKS in the Services Industry. It is also unique in that it has become a bluechip company within less than a decade. Leading financial data and financial ratios are to be analysed to come to any reasonable conclusion about the state of the correct valuation of its share as compared to its market price. An attempt is made to present some data in support of this bluechip nature of this company.

The reasons why this company is chosen for this case study illustration are many unique features that it has got, some of which are set out below:

1. It has shown a marked growth in assets and networth in less than a decade.
2. It has a good amount of daily trading and has acquired a substantial market capitalisation with in a short span.
3. It has been included in the elite few companies for good corporate governance and has been included in the BSE Sensex and NSE Nifty.
4. It has been quoted and traded both in the BSE and NSE and has become a favourite scrip for the FIIs, FFIs and mutual funds and for derivative trading.
5. It has been included in the "A" Group scrip quite early in its history and is on a Rolling settlement system showing its good public holding and its liquidity for investors.
6. It has ADRs, quoted on New York Stock Exchange and also well traded there.
7. The number of shareholders is also large at 1,10,684 and has a large public holding.
8. The number of shares traded on NSE was high at 1,38,30,21,473 followed in that order by lower amounts on the BSE and NYSE.

This share has a face value of ₹ 2 but its market price was ₹ 770 in February 2006. As at end FEB 2006, its 52 week high and low were given as ₹ 780 and ₹ 364 giving an average of ₹ 572. Its P/E multiple was placed at 24 implying that its market price was 24 times the EPS. The lower the P/E multiple the more attractive it becomes for buyers. Its volume of trade was higher in NSE at 28 lakh shares as against 8.8 lakh shares on the BSE. The number of trades on the NSE was nearly three times that on the BSE. It is also quoted and traded on the New York Stock Exchange.

The company's net worth and assets showed an impressive rise. For example its net worth was ₹ 53.43 crores in 1996 which rose to ₹ 3,217.02 crores in 2005. Over the decade ended March 2005, the Gross Block grew from ₹ 58 crores to ₹ 1,002 crores. Its EPS rose from ₹ 0.61 to ₹ 23.61 — which is nearly 24 times over the same period. On the basis of data of March 2005 its P/E multiple would work out to about 15 but with the data as in February 2006, it is placed by the E.T. Daily in its daily reports at 20 times.

The following Table presents some data on financial indicators over the decade 1996-2005 with particular reference to the year 2004-05.

Table

(*₹ in crores*)

March end	*1996*	*2000*	*2005*
Equity	22.30	36.23	63.85
Networth	53.43	350.05	321702
Gross Block	58.01	438.63	1002.38
Book Value (in ₹)	4.50	12.45	100.75
EPS (in ₹)	0.61	4.89	23.61
P/E Multiple	81.9	—	17.00
Dividend	—	—	250%
PAT (Profits after Tax)	13.58	134.86	750.26

The Table above shows how this company became a growth oriented Blue chip company with in a decade. The equity base rose by only by about three times while its networth grew by about 60 times and PAT by about 54 times. Its EPS and Dividend pay outs were also impressive. It is suggested that the reader prepares such time series data for any company studied by him and analyse its valuation. Only some snapshots are given here for illustration. It is for the readers to judge whether the present market price of ₹ 770 in February 2006 is over valued in the above context.

The financial results just announced for 2005-06 particularly in respect to PAT to confirm the major expectations about the scrip by market operators. It is also to be considered why its share price fell to ₹ 440 a by mid September 2007 with in a high and low of ₹ 525-396 during the last one year and whether it is worth a buy order, or hold order? This company had become defund due to corruption conspiracy and personal diversion of funds by the promoters namely Ramalinga, Raju and his friends as revealed early in 2009. This company was taken over by Mahindra Tech Company to revive and run it on the diluted net worth.

EXAMPLE: FUNDAMENTAL ANALYSIS OF FINOLEX INDUSTRIES

We have seen fundamental analysis of a high profile company namely SATYAM COMPUTERS In the I.T. Industry – its ups and downs, booms and bursts, and its latest position. Now it is proposed to present an analysis of a low profile company-also listed in the specific group of BSE and NSE – for a contrast – namely the FINOLEX INDUSTRIES.

FINOLEX is a 26 old company manufacturing pvc resins and pvc pipes and fittings. It has captive power plant at Pune for 43 MW which is expected to be expanded. It is also proposed to set up a new plant for pvc pipes at URSE with an installed capacity of one lakh MT per annum. Even so, the COMPANY did not show so far, any signs of expansion and diversification or plans for growth. Its share has a face value of ₹ 10 and market price of ₹ 75 or so in October, 2007, its price has a range of ₹ 65 to 110 over the last one year, as per the latest financial daily.

The objective of the study is to analyse fundamentals of the company to know its intrinsic worth and whether it is overvalued or undervalued or whether it is worth buying at the present price.

As regards the economy, it is growing at an impressive rate of 7% during the last quinquennium with even at 9% in the last two years. The Industry in general is growing at a rate of 6.5% with the consumer durables to which the Finolex Industries belongs growing faster at 9% to 10% during the same period. The economy and industry fundamentals are strong during this period with the stock market booming since 2004. and the SENSEX reaching a new peak of 19,276 in October 2007. The FII and FFI inflows into our economy are growing and foreign advices are positively bullish.

It is in this context that the FINOLEX INDUSTRIES is studied for its intrinsic worth for the latest period. Selected financial ratios are presented below:

Table
Financial Ratios of Finolex

	2006-07 (*₹ in million*)	2011-12
1. Equity paid up capital	1240	1240
2. Net worth	5287	6621
3. Book Value (₹)	42.6(43)	53.35
4. Debt-Equity ratio	1:3.9(1.4)	1:0.29
5. Current ratio	1:1.55 (one and half times)	1:0.93
6. Gross block to Equity	5 times	13 times

7. Sales to Gross block	one and half times	1.4 times
8. Profitability Ratio	6.5%	3.2%
9. Dividend ratio	30%, same as last year.	30%
10. EPS in (₹)	₹ 5.6	6.06
11. P/E multiple	10 as per ET 14 as per the balance sheet	10

It will be seen from the above table that the solvency and liquidity ratios are poor for the company. Its capital turnover as measured by the G.B/Equity is also not satisfactory nor the sales turnover as measured by the Sales/GB which is 1.5 times. The current ratio and the Debt to Equity ratio are reflecting the poor financial management. Its profitability and dividend record is also not worth the mention. Its profitability ratio at 3.2% is very disheartening.

Its book value is ₹ 43 and market price is ₹ 75 which means that MP is less than two times, while the market average is five times. Judged by the market average trends, its book value should support a market price of ₹ 215. Unfortunately the maximum price reached in the market was only ₹ 110 for this share. As judged by the P/E multiple, its EPS supports a price of 5.6 multiplied by 10 namely ₹ 56 only. Using the P/E multiple of the market average of 20, the MP could be ₹ 112 which it has recorded at one time. The actual market price was in the range of ₹ 65 to 110 in Sept.-Oct. 2007 and ₹ 71 – 25 in January 2010, and around 55 in 2012.

The price range as per the fundamentals of the company should be around ₹ 110 to 220 which has not fructified. This is due to the poor expectations and sentiment about the company's performance. The present market price range of ₹ 65 to 110 in 2007 is therefore a reflection of the poor expectations of the fundamentals of the company. The present market price of ₹ 65 is grossly undervalued at the time of January 2010 but sentiment and expectations played a greater role here, than fundamentals. Consideration has to given to factors like poor solvency and liquidity, lack of dynamism and planning at the management level and inefficient use of capital and poor profitability, etc. These adverse factors led to the pessimistic expectations and unfavourable sentiment on the share of this company. It has P/E ratio of 6.7 which is lower than those in March 2006, 2007 and 2008.

Conclusion

Looked at from all angles, FINOLEX is a mediocre company worth not more than ₹ 65 to 110. It has recorded no capital appreciation and a dividend of ₹ 3 per share of ₹ 10 will give a yield of only 4% at the market price of ₹ 75 (3/75 multiplied by 100). This does not even give the investor a risk free return of 7% at present, not to speak of the risk premium of 10 to 15% over above the risk free rate — a total return of 20 to 25% on average equity. Hence, the reader should conclude that this is not worth the purchase or hold decision in this portfolio management.

Latest Position of the Finolex Industries

In the year 2008-09, it had a loss before tax itself of ₹ 59 crores and deferred tax liabilities of ₹ 76 crores respectively as against a profit before tax of ₹ 101.7 crores in 2007-08. The profits after tax in 2007-08 was ₹ 71 crores and Earnings per share of ₹ 5.74. Now in the latest year with closed and audited accounts of 2008-09, the earnings per share was a loss of ₹ 3.06 with a total loss for the company of ₹ 59 crores in the year of 2008-09 which explains a fall in the market price from ₹ 75 in the last year to ₹ 56-57 this year as on February 5, 2010. The current EPS as reported in the ET was 6.1 times as against the market ratio of 23 times. This confirms the conclusion drawn already that it was not a good company to buy or hold for any rational investor. The reasons are the lack of profit planning and tax planning on top of lack of any expansion and diversification plans with a vision for the future. Earnings have increased no doubt but the expenditure rose more than the income which reflects on the poor efficiency of the management. The position improved after 2008-09, but the trend of declining profitability and greater rise in expenses than income was a drag on the company. Price to B.V. was low at 1.1 and market price 2012 was only hovering around 60, while the book value was around ₹ 50-55.

Latest data Sept. 2012, MR = 63, P/E = 16.7, P/BV = 1.2, Beta = 0.7, 52 week, High/Low = 73/54. Our estimate was correct. It has good fundamentals. Its price has risen sharply to ₹ 296 by July end 2015.

CASE STUDY OF INDIAN BANK

Indian Bank is one of the oldest banks among the 39 listed scheduled commercial banks. The P/E ratio of nine out of 39 banks was lower as compared with others. The volatility of BSE Bankex was higher than that of BSE Sensex indicating the higher risk in bank stocks than others in general.

Risk-Return Scenario

	2008-09	*2009-10*	*2010-11*	*2011-12*
Return on Bankex —	41.8	37.2	24.9	–3.6
Return on BSE Sensex —	37.9	80.5	10.9	–2.3
Volatility (Risk) on BSE Bankex	23.0	16.8	10.3	4.3
Risk on BSE Sensex	24.2	11.9	6.3	3.3

Banks capitalisation as a share of total capitalisation stood at around 10-12% during the past three years. The government shareholding of total paid up capital was roughly 57% to 85% as against the statutory requirement of 51%. The government and RBI hold together the highest share of 85.5 in United Bank of India. The Government share in Indian Bank is 80%. The prices of shares in Bankex reflected a slowdown in growth due to global recession and their exposure to foreign business.

In the case of Indian Bank, the share prices were quoted lower during the recession period of 2009 to 2009 at around ₹ 83 in 2008-09 and ₹ 163 in 2007 and ₹ 176 in 2009-10. But the fundamentals are strong in the case of this bank.

The credit deposit ratio is 71.6% as against Industry average of 77% in 2010-11. But the growth rate of credit was 2.6 times, as against deposit growth rate was only 2.2 times over the quinquennium 2007 to 2011. Its profitability was 15-16%. Bulk of the rise in profits was due to increased labour productivity. The number of employees have come down and the business per employee rose from ₹ 364 lakhs to ₹ 930 lakhs over the same 5 year period 2007-2011.

Gross NPA were brought down from 1.85% in 2007 to 0.98% in 2011. Net worth and book value have shown remarkable growth rates.

Indian Bank share price ranged from a high of ₹ 316 in October 2010 to a low of ₹ 168 in September 2012. In December, the share price of Indian Bank was at ₹ 221 in 2011 and ₹ 261 in December 2012. On the basis of our estimates of EPS of 51, the estimated market price is about ₹ 51 × 5.5 = Around ₹ 275 – 280 (EPS × Multiplier = 5.5).

It has potentiality of appreciation in price. Its Deposits and Advances growth are higher than the averages for the banking sector as a whole. The financial ratios given below show the picture of good fundamentals. But it is not reflected in M.P. This bank lacks the trust and marketmanship like ICICI or SBI.

Financial Ratios

	31-3-07	*31-3-2011*
Equity	430	430
Reserves	2792	7497
Net worth	3622 (inclusive preference capital of 400)	8327
Book value	₹ 75	₹ 184
Dividend	30%	75%
EPS	₹ 20	₹ 39
M.P.	₹ 163	₹ 193
PAT	760	1714
Income	5018	10543
Profitability	15.1%	16.2%
BV/Price	1.5	1.1
P/E	7.2	5.9
C.D. Ratio	62.6%	71%
CRR	Not Available	6.5%

CRAR – capital adequacy ratio was 12.83% in March 2011.

For bank shares the Debt-Equity ratio and Current Asset ratio are not relevant. Its CPR, SLR and CD Ratio and others are more relevant. It comes under Financial Services Sector.

Source: Annual Report 2010-11.

The data for the latest date – Sept. 2012.

Indian Bank – M.P. – 193; Dividend 75%, P/E ratio = 4.5, $\frac{P}{BV}$ = 0.9; Beta 1.02.

52 week High/Low – 199/151.

As of end July 2015, it is priced at ₹ 151. It may be an old quotation as no trading takes place in this scrip and its public holding is only 20% of the total net worth.

18

TECHNICAL ANALYSIS

Importance of Timing in Investment

While fundamental analysis and security evaluation explain why share prices fluctuate, how they are determined and what to buy or sell, the technical analysis will help the decision making when to buy and sell. The traditional theory of capital market efficiency postulates that entry into the market at any time would lead to the same average return as that of the market. But in the real world of imperfections, there are investors who have burnt their fingers by entering the market at the wrong time. Investment timing is, therefore, crucial as the market is continuously jolted by waves of buying and selling and prices are moving in trends and cycles and are never stable. The Stock market is different from other markets, as there is a continuous buying and selling and bid and offer rates as under a system of auctions. The resultant prices, led by the sheer force of the market, may fluctuate either way and may exhibit waves or trends. Entry and exit in the market will, therefore, make all the difference to the spread between buying and selling prices and the profits or losses. Timing of investment is, therefore, of vital importance for trading in the stock market.

Basic Tenets of Technical Analysis

Technical analysis of the market is based on some basic tenets, namely, that all fundamental factors are discounted by the market and are reflected in prices. Secondly, these prices move in trends or waves which can be both upward or downward depending on the sentiment, psychology and emotions of operators or traders. Thirdly, the present trends are influenced by the past trends, and the projection of future trends is possible by an analysis of past price trends. Analysis of historical trends confirmed the above principles and the Random Walk Theory explaining the randomness of price changes has been found to be not applicable by the technical analysts in practice.

Tools of Technical Analysis

1. Daily Fluctuation or Volatility: Open, High, Low and Close are quoted. Changes between Open and Close or High and Low can be taken in absolute points or in percentages to reflect the daily volatility. Such fluctuation can be worked out on weekly, monthly or yearly basis also to reflect the general volatility of the market. The use of this indicator is to caution the investor against high volatility in any scrip. But a stable uptrend or downtrend can be discerned from these changes for the investor to interpret the market.

A Bar chart as given below can be used to depict the daily variations:

High	High	High
Close	Open	Close
	Close	Open
Low	Low	Low

An yearly High-Low indicates the possible levels within a range that the prices may move which helps to locate entry and exit points.

2. Floating Stock and Volume of Trade: Floating stock is the total number of shares available for trading with the public and volume of trade is effected in any part of that floating stock. The higher this proportion, the higher is the liquidity of a share which is to be purchased or sold. Volume trends are also a supporting indicator to the price trends to interpret the market.

3. Price Trends and Volume Trends: The Chartist method and Moving average method can be used to depict these trends.

4. Rate of Change of Prices and Volumes or the ROC Method: This is useful like the moving average method to indicate more clearly the buy and sell signals. The Chartist method is useful to indicate the directions and the trend reversals. ROC is calculated by dividing the today's price by the price five days back or few days back. It can be expressed as percentages or positive or negative change. Thus, they can be moving around 100, in the case of percentages or zero line, in the case of positive and negative percentage changes.

5. Japanese Candlestick Method: There are three main types of Candlesticks with each day's trade being shown in the form of candlesticks. Each stick has the body of the candle and a shadow. The body shows the open and close prices while the shadow shows the high and low prices. The three main types are as follows:

(a) Closing price is higher than open price (White candlestick).

(b) Closing price is lower than the open price (Blackstick).

(c) Open and Close are at the same level (Doji candlestick).

6. Dow Theory: There are three major trends in this theory. Minor, inter-mediate and major trends representing daily or weekly, monthly and yearly trends in prices comparing the price trends to waves, tides and ripples.

7. Elliot Wave Theory: The market is unfolded by a basic rhythm or pattern of 5 waves up to be corrected by three waves down with a total of 8 waves — a philosophy of price trends.

***8. Theory of Gaps*:** Gaps in price between any two days causing a discontinuity is called a gap. The high of one day may be lower than the low of the previous day when prices are falling.

Gaps are of different categories, namely:

(a) Common gaps — When prices move in a narrow range, a gap can occur in prices.

(b) Breakout gaps — When price trend is likely to change, a gap can occur in either direction. This gives a break to congestion in any direction.

(c) Runaway gaps — These gaps occur continuously in a downward phase or an upward phase, accelerating or decelerating the trends.

(d) Exhaustion gaps — Occur when the rally is getting exhausted. When the runaway gap is coming to an end, there can be exhaustion gap to indicate the likely completion of the uptrend.

9. Advance Decline Line or Spread of the Market: The ratio between advances to declines will indicate the negative strength of upward or downward phases. When the advances are increasing over declines it is an upward phase and the reverse indicates the downward phase.

10. Relative Strength Index (RSI) of Wells Wilder: It is an oscillator used to identify the inherent strength or weakness of particular scrip.

Thus, $\text{RSI} = 100 - \left(\frac{100}{1+\text{RS}}\right)$ where

$$\text{RS} = \frac{\text{Average gain per day}}{\text{Average loss per day}}$$

RSI is calculated for one scrip while RSC or the relative strength comparative, is the ratio of two prices of two different scrips, used for comparison of two or more scrips. RSI can be calculated for any number of days say 5 or 10 etc., to indicate the strength of price trend.

Dow Theory

The Dow Theory postulates that prices of industrial securities tend to move in tune with business cycles of the boom, depression etc. in the economy. As the corporate performance depends on the industrial growth and the tone of the economy, prices of shares should broadly reflect the overall trends in the economy, which in developed countries are dependent on the business cycles and business expectations. If the business conditions are good, demand increasing, industrial performance will be good and the corporate share prices will be on the upswing. The reverse is true in times of recession and depression in the economy. The trends in the economy are reflected in the market average prices of shares. All fundamental factors are thus discounted by the market, and get reflected in average prices. It will thus be seen that factors affecting these supply and demand conditions in the market are summed up in the average prices in the market. A study of these average market prices is what is attempted in technical analysis and its trends are in the form of peaks, troughs and cycles.

Major Trends

The trends in stock prices are divided under three heads — primary, secondary and minor. The primary trend is a long-term trend of a year or more reflecting the basic mood of the market showing upward or downward movement. The secondary or intermediate trend represents the correction to the primary trend and is of a short duration of a few weeks to a few months. The minor trends may be in either direction on a daily or weekly basis, but pointing to the underlying primary trend either upward or downward. These three trends are comparable to the tides, waves and ripples of the sea respectively. If the successive waves move further inland towards the beach than the preceding ones, then the tide would reflect the upward trend through higher peaks and troughs. On the reverse side, if the tide is moving inwards into the sea, then the trend is downwards and prices tend to decline on average. Each successive minor trend and intermediate trend result in a net downward movement and support the primary market trend in the downward direction.

In the Dow Theory, the major trends, namely, bullish or bearish trends, have three phases. In the first phase of bullish trend, called the accumulation phase, only a select elite of investors who perceive the coming things first start buying shares. In the second phase, the followers of trend notice a distinct uptrend and begin to participate in the buying and then the mass buying starts. The third phase is the end of the uptrend when the first elite group who initiated the first phase should dislodge their shares for profit-taking. Then there will be a reversal of the trend. The fall in the prices in a bull phase is a technical reaction and a rise in prices in a bear phase is a technical rally. The concentration in the hands of bull is called accumulation, which when sold off gets distributed and there will be a decline in prices.

So far as the volume of trade is concerned, it should expand in the direction of the major trend. During the uptrend period, the volume would expand when prices rise and decrease when prices decline. During the downtrend, there will be a reversal of the trend and the volume will expand when prices drop and contract when they start rising.

The only problem which is a grey area in the Dow Theory is the signal for reversal of the trend. The first symptom of a change would call for "buy or sell" decision and those who perceive the change first would gain in speculation. As the primary trend continues, the gain from speculation decreases. The fact of the matter is that it is not easy, except for the expert eyes, to detect a change in direction in the existing trend and the first leg of the new trend in the opposite direction. For knowing the reversal point, a lot of experience and expertise is necessary in this line.

The reversal pattern is explained below. A, B, C are the successive peaks during the upswing, but M is a point of trough which is lower than the earlier troughs of D and E. The point S_1 is the point of sell signal. This is called the failure swing diagram (Fig. 18.1).

In the non-failure swing diagram, M is below E but the peak is still above peak B. So it is not certain whether the point S_1, or S_2 should be the sell signal. Whether the point of reversal has set in or not is not clear from the diagram. Such occasions arise in both upswing and downswing diagrams (Fig. 18.2).

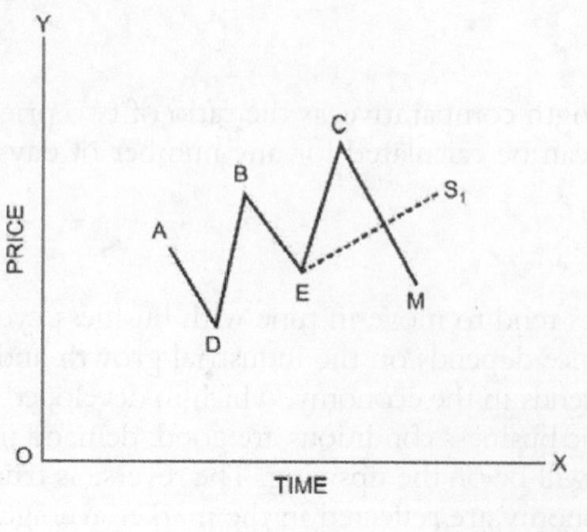

Fig. 18.1

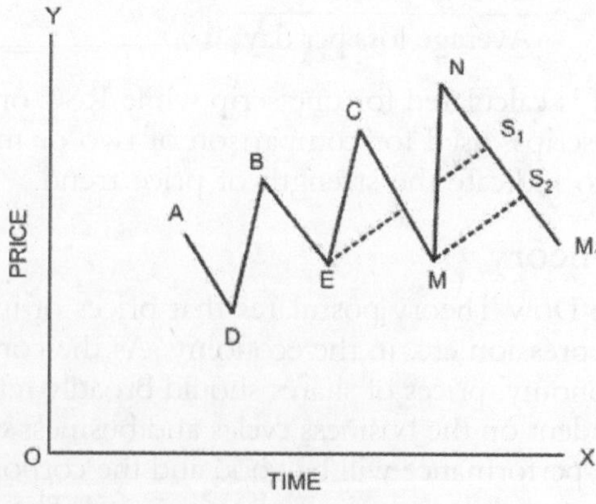

Fig. 18.2

Chartist Method

As referred to earlier, technical analysis is a study of the market data in terms of factors affecting supply and demand schedules, namely, prices, volume of trading, etc. A study of the historical trends of market behaviour shows the cycles and trends in prices which may repeat as the present is a reflection of the past and the future of the present. This is the basis for forecasting the future trends which are used for deciding on the basis of the buy or sell signals. For forecasting, analysts use charts and diagrams to depict the past trends and project the future. But these methods are rough and ready methods and there are no foolproof methods of forecasting the stock prices. The technical analysis only helps to improve the knowledge of the probabilities of price behaviour (upswing or downswing) and help the investment process. The technical analysis does not claim 100% chance of success in predictions that are made for investment.

In view of the limitations inherent in the technical analysis, this analysis is generally juxtaposed with fundamental analysis of the market and the scrips. It was the past experience that the receipt of information and the actual price absorption of the information would not coincide and there is a time lag between them. As a result, the current price changes would give a clue to the subsequent price changes, if properly analysed and interpreted.

In the market analysis, the variables to be taken into account are the breadth of the market, volume of trading etc. Market breadth is the dispersion of the general price rise or decline, which means daily cumulation of a net number of advancing or declining issues. Breadth analysis focuses on change rather than level in prices. Breath of price changes in terms of the number of gainers or losers among the scrips is analysed to know the width of rise or fall in prices.

Breadth of the Market

The breadth of the market analysis is based on the nature of stock market cycles. Bull markets are viewed as long-drawn-out affairs, during which individual stock reach peaks gradually with the number of individual peaks accelerating as the market averages rise to the turning point. Thus, the turning point for a bull phase is at that point where a larger number of stocks are falling when the averages are still rising. In the bear market, there is a large number of stocks falling in a period of time. The end of the bear market is near when there is a selling climax and a large number of sellers rush to sell all at once. The breadth is measured by the number of scrips rising or falling to the total number. In a bull phase, there will be a large number of net rises and in a bear phase, a large number of net falls.

Normally, the breadth and the market average (BSE Index) lines move in tandem. In a bull phase, if the breadth line declines to successive new lows, while the market average is going up, it means that a larger number of scrips are declining although blue chips included in the BSE Index continue to rise, but the suggestion is that there is an approaching peak in the averages and a major downtrend is in the offing later.

Volume of Trading

The above trends of the breath of the market are to be examined along with the supporting data on volume of trading. Price trends follow the volume trends in general.[1] Historical data analysis of price and volume movements indicate that in a normal market, the price rise is accompanied by an expanding volume. If the level of volume is declining more than in the previous rally in times of bullish trend, it warns of a potential trend reversal. Termination of a bearish phase is often accompanied by a selling climax. Following a decline in prices, a heavy volume of trade with little price change is indicative of accumulation and is normally a bullish factor. A strong bull market can exist only as long as buying pressure continues to be strong. These indications are to be studied carefully before a final decision is taken on the state of the market, whether bullish or bearish, the phase of the uptrend or downtrend and look for buy and sell signals at the start of the reversal trends.

Both the price spread and volume trends are the result of demand and supply pressures. In the short-run, or on a day-to-day basis, the demand and supply for each scrip is based on a host of fundamental, technical and other factors. Trading in futures, options and arbitrage activity would distort the pure demand and supply analysis. The money flow analysis of the market generally adopted by the analysts is also distorted by the dynamics of insider trading, short sales, margins and controls on trading "buying on weakness" and "selling on strength", etc.

Tripod of Technical Analysis

1. Market prices are determined by a host of fundamental, technical and other factors which are both rational and irrational. It is possible that the market prices may be overvalued or undervalued always.

---

1. "If you can predict volume, you can predict the movement of the Stock Market" (in *Investment Analysis and Portfolio Management* by Cohen, Zinbarg and Zeikel, p. 257).

2. Average market price discounts all developments and is a reflection of the sum total of all forces operating on the market.

3. History or past trends have a role in the shaping of the future and as such an analysis of the past helps the projection for the future.

The above tripod leads to a science of recording in a graphic form, the price trends. The actual history of trading on the stock market is recorded in terms of price changes, moving averages of prices, velocity of price changes, namely, oscillators, and the volume of transactions in any scrip together. Based on the past behaviour, the future trends are predicted and investment suggestions are made based on such predictions of trend changes. The timing of an investment when to buy or sell is facilitated by a study of these charts and graphs. These are no doubt subjective factors based upon the behaviour and psychological aspects of human beings which influence the market. As opposed to fundamental factors, which are statistical incorporating the financial and physical variables of corporate units and economy, the market is also influenced by the non-statistical information such as behaviour aspects, emotions, etc.; for the latter factors, technical analysis assumes importance in the investment strategy. In particular the decision to buy or sell is a fundamental decision, but the decision when to buy or sell is a decision arising out of technical analysis of the market.

Principles of Technical Analysis

The principles involved in technical analysis and in particular in the Dow Theory analysis, can be summarised as follows:

(1) Principle of wave motion and trends leads to different types of price trends.

(2) Action and reaction resulting from buying and selling pressures lead to corrections and rallies to the major uptrends and downtrends respectively.

(3) Principle of congestion involving support and resistance lines results in a phase of activity, in which the market is undecided, hesitant and the trend undermined. The prices move within a band of resistance and support lines, and the trends involve up and down movements in a more or less horizontal path, until the prices are driven up or down.

In congestion, the continuous pressures of buyers are met equally. But when the buyers exceed the sellers, both in volume and value of deals, then the price emerges from the bottom of the range and there will be an up breakout. When the sellers predominate, there will be a down breakout in the price level, the resistance and support lines are broken in either case. When buyers are increasing their purchases and the volume increases, then there is said to be accumulation. When sellers are increasing their sales and the volume rises, then there is said to be distribution. When buying exceeds selling and persists, then there is a breakout of prices from the congestion into a bull phase. On the other hand, when selling exceeds buying and continues to persist, the congestion is broken out into a bear phase.

Charts and Trend Lines

The use of charts for analysis of prices in technical analysis was referred to. Fitting a trend line for price changes on a daily basis is the first step in the analysis of charts. These changes may be pointing upwards or downwards or stable over a horizontal one. The movements are such that there are both peaks and troughs in these price changes — peaks showing an upward trend troughs or reactions to the uptrend, *viz.,* line joining the lowest points or troughs pointing up. If this line is pointing downwards, then it is a bearish phase (Fig. 18.4). If the movements are downwards generally, then there will be rallies moving up the prices. These upper peaks, if they are joined, give the trend line as much as the lowest troughs. The bull phase depicts the rising peaks successively (Fig. 18.3), while the bear phase shows the falling peaks successively (Fig. 18.4).

When the share prices are rising or falling, there will be a resistance level above which the prices may not pierce in the upward direction or a support level, below which the price may not fall.

These support lines and resistance lines are clearly noticed when the prices are moving in a narrow band for sometime. When the price pierces the resistance line, this is the first indication of the reversal of the trend in the upward direction. So also in a bull phase when the price line falls below the support line, a reversal of the trend is indicated.

Various configurations of price movements like stable pattern, M and W patterns, head and shoulders etc., are formed. It is possible that various triangles, flags, pendants, etc., can be described by the price trends. The basic analysis involves the deciphering of the trend identifying of the reversal and fixing up of buy and sell signals in these price movements. The stable price pattern is ideal for genuine investors to enter the market.

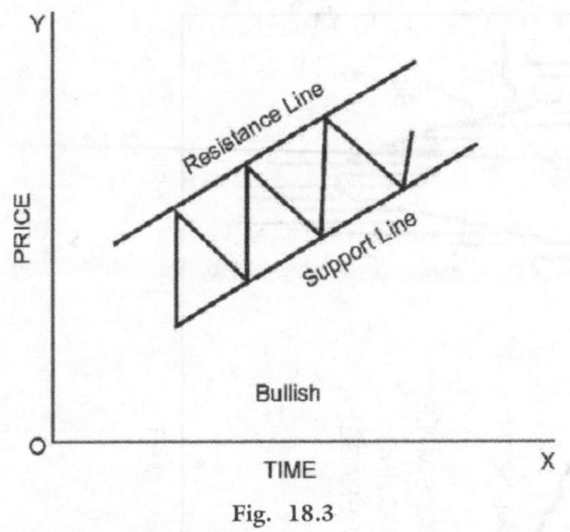

Fig. 18.3

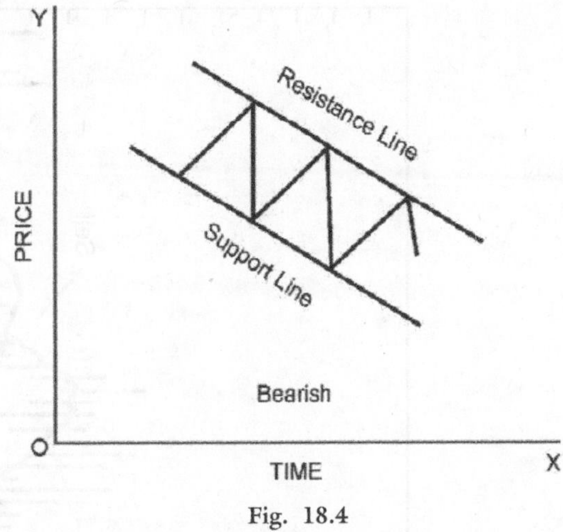

Fig. 18.4

Moving Averages

The analysis of the moving averages of the prices of scrips is another method in technical analysis. Generally, 7-day, 10-day and 15-day moving averages are worked out in respect of scrips studied and depicted on a graph along with similar moving averages of the market index like BSE Sensitive Index. There will then be two graphs to be compared and when the trends are similar, the scrip and BSE market index will show comparable average risks.

The theory of moving averages also lays down the following guidelines for identifying the buy and sell signals. Whenever the moving average price line cuts the actual price line of the scrip or of the market index from the bottom, it is a signal to sell shares. Conversely, when the moving average line cuts the actual price line from above, it is the right time to buy shares. Here, the comparison can be made separately for the BSE market index moving average with its actual price index and the moving average price of any scrip with its actual price.

Advantages of Moving Averages

Since the price fluctuations are wide and frequent, reflecting the volatility of the market and the scrips, some amount of smoothing can be achieved by taking the moving averages of the prices. Generally, the closing prices of these scrips are taken for the moving averages. The usefulness of this will also depend on the number of days (7 days, 10 days, 20 days, etc.) for which these averages are worked out. These averages can be represented in a graphical form to help identification of buy and sell signals. The first indication is that when the actual scrip price crosses the short-term moving average line (or, say, 7 or 10 days). This is to be supported by other evidence of a reversal of the trend to justify the buy signal. The short-term moving average of 7 or 10 days should cross the longer-term moving average of 15 or 20 days, which in turn should cross the further long-term moving averages (of, say, 30 or 40 days) to finally confirm the buy signal. In other words, the buy signal is to be given when the moving average line cuts the actual price line from above. If it cuts from below, then the signal is to sell. This signal of moving averages can also be confirmed by further analysis of other technical factors like the trend reversal shown in the chart-graphs referred to above. (Fig. 18.5)

Criticism of Dow Theory

The Dow Theory is subject to various limitations in actual practice. Dow has developed this theory to depict the general trend of the market but not with the intention of projecting the future trends or to diagnose the buy and sell signals in the market. These applications of the Dow Theory have come in the light of analytical studies of financial analysts. This theory is criticised on the ground that it is too subjective and based on historical interpretation; it is not infallible as it depends on the interpretative ability of the analyst. The results of this theory do not also give meaningful and conclusive evidence of any action to be taken in terms of buy and sell operations.

Charts

The drawing of charts, diagrams, graphs, etc., is a method by which the technical analysis is made. These charts depict the trends in prices, rate of changes in prices, volume of tradings, etc.

There are various types of charts, namely, point charts, line charts, vertical bar charts, etc. All these would depict the trends in prices and breadth of trading which are both indicators of buying and selling pressures and the market behaviour.

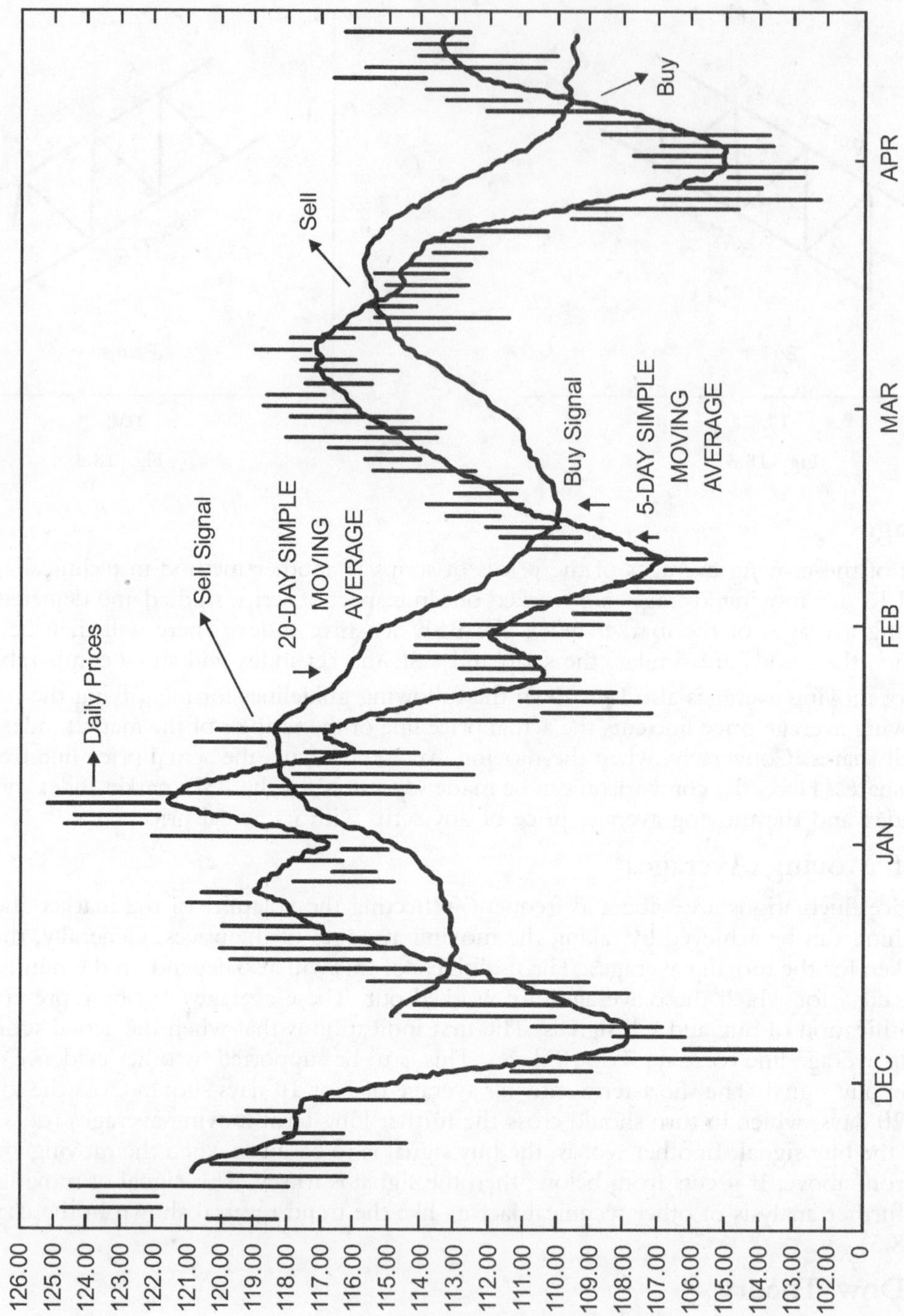

Fig. 18.5: Daily actual prices are dashed lines. When the daily price line cuts the moving average of 5 days and the line of 5 days cuts the line of 20 days, from above, these are sell signals. The buy signals are when the actual prices cut the moving average lines from below.

Head and Shoulders

The configurations emerging from the charts show different patterns. Of these, the most important is the "Head and Shoulders." It depicts a top and a reversal pattern in either the bull phase or the bear phase (Fig. 18.6).

The left shoulder is formed when the prices reach the top under a strong buying impulse and trading volume becomes less than it did during the upswing to reach the top. Then there is another high volume advance which takes the price to a higher top than in the case of the left shoulder. This is called the "Head" top and followed by another reaction on less volume which takes prices down to a bottom near to the earlier recession. The third rally which takes the prices up reaches a height of less than that of the head and results on the right shoulder, which has a comparable height as the left shoulder. This type of configuration occurs under a bull phase and the exactly reverse configuration occurs in a bear phase. This is indicative of a likely reversal of the trend.

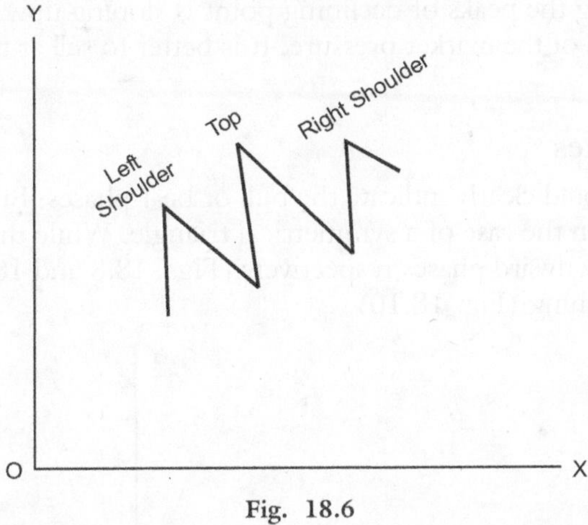

Fig. 18.6

Breaking the Neckline

If the prices are having an uptrend movement in a bull phase and the configuration of the head and shoulders is noticed, then the analyst has to look for a possible trend reversal indicator. This can be noticed when the third recession cuts the support line down across the bottoms of the two reactions between the left shoulder, head, and the right shoulder (called the neckline) and the actual price line should go below the neckline by about 3 to 5 points of the market price (Fig. 18.7).

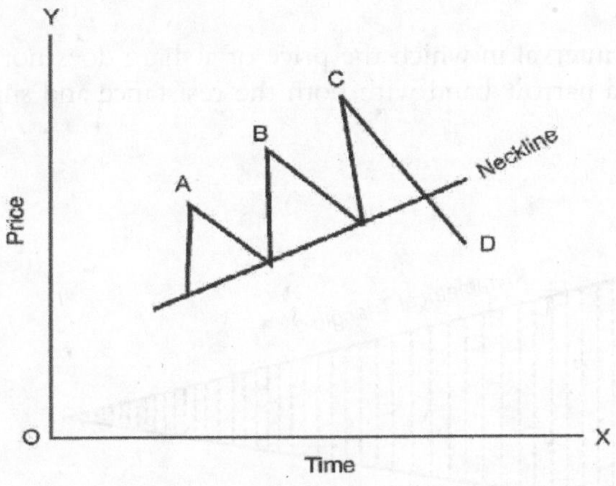

Fig. 18.7

There are a number of other patterns which are to be looked into by analysts, if they are doing an indepth analysis. These patterns are useful to identify the primary or secondary trends. Some signs of reversal can be seen in the "rounding turns" and triangles and gaps. However, some gaps are attributed to ex-dividend, ex-bonus, etc., or due to symptoms of consolidation and acceleration or exhaustion and reassessment or it may be a break away gap of the market. Some insight into the future movement of prices can be had by a close study of the pattern that prices are making. Thus, forecasting is a practical use to which the charts in general and these configurations in particular can be put to.

The bull market indicators are as follows. The bear market has been in progress for a long time. The peaks of advancing points are still sloping upwards. The number of advancing points is substantially higher than the number of declining points. Then if the stock establishes certain levels of accumulation and consolidation over a number of days or weeks and if the volume of trading slows down, then it is certain that distribution is taking place and it will meet with the resistance level soon. So, as a rule, it is safe to buy at the top or three points below or around the old bottom.

The bear market indications may be set out as follows. A bull market has been in progress for a long time. The recovery is occurring on low volume and the number of advancing points is only slightly higher than the number of declining points. The line connecting the peaks of declining point is sloping upwards but the price line may cross the support level soon due to exhaustion of the market pressure. It is better to sell at the previous high to peak or 3 points around that high.

Resistance and Support Lines

The point and figure charts should clearly indicate the bull or bear phases. But some configurations do not clearly indicate the definite signals such as in the case of a symmetrical triangle. While the ascending triangle and descending triangle indicate the upward and downward phases respectively (Figs. 18.8 and 18.9), the symmetrical triangle drawn below does not clearly indicate anything (Fig. 18.10).

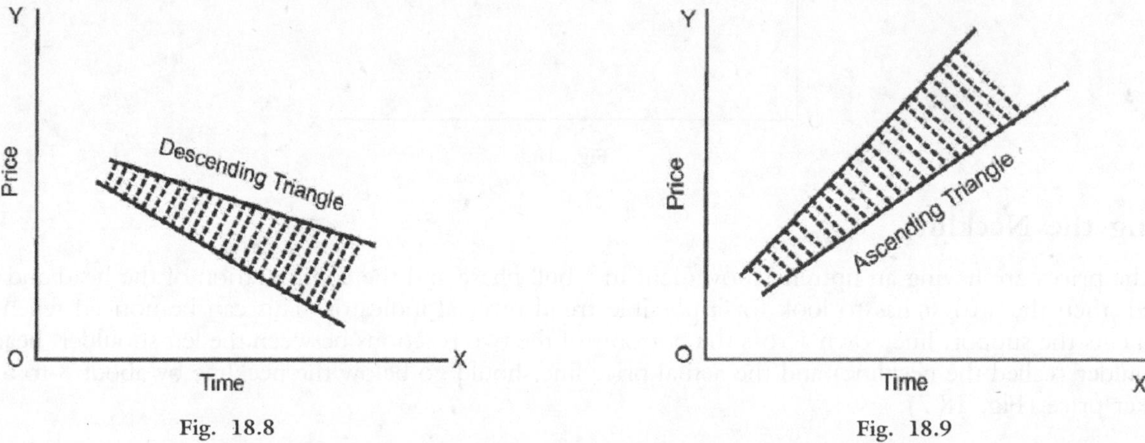

Fig. 18.8

Fig. 18.9

Consolidation refers to time interval in which the price of a share does not break through in either direction. Then the price movements are in a narrow band with both the resistance and support lines moving horizontally.

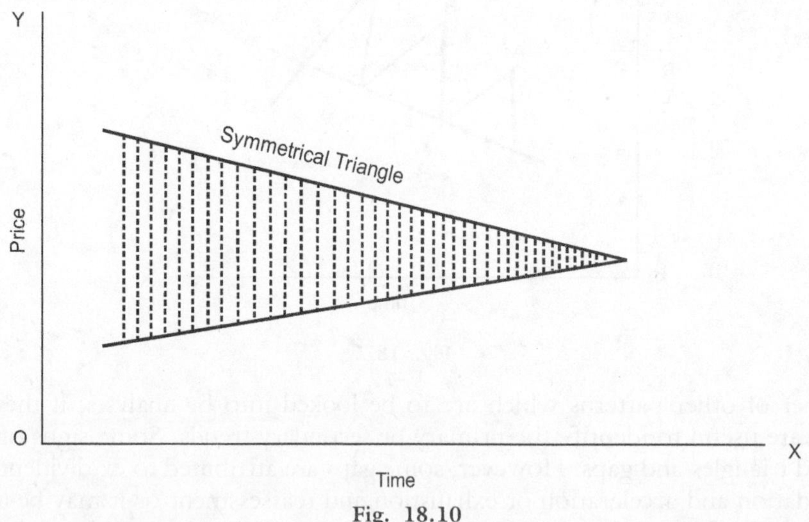

Fig. 18.10

Speculative Trading and Technical Analysis

Timing of purchase and sale is very important particularly for speculative trading. The basic rule is to follow the daily chart of highs/lows or tops/bottoms. When the long-term trend is bullish and price trend is pointing up, the advance line must make higher tops and higher bottoms. One can enter the market any time so long as the uptrend is continuing as indicated by the higher tops and bottoms. The best buy point is when the prices decline by 50% of the higher ever peak achieved or at a level of 50% between the extreme low and high. The best points to sell are when prices rise to the old top levels or near to those levels or when the prices start advancing after being below the 50% point between the extreme high and extreme low. There is no sanctity of these levels, as they are set by experience and observation. Experience and analysis are the best guides in these matters.

Before taking the buy and sell decisions, one has to observe the rules of the game:

(i) Put stop loss order at, say, 10% of one's capital at any time. This will protect the extent of losses possible in speculation.

(ii) Draw the daily, weekly, monthly charts separately and observe the highs and lows and the mid-points and turning points carefully.

(iii) The buy and sell signals can be located at 3 points below the highs or 3 points above the lows, etc.

Elliot Wave Theory

There are a number of theories which seek to explain the behaviour of the market. In the area of technical analysis, one such theory is that of Ralph Elliot. According to this theory, the market is unfolded through the basic rhythm or pattern of 5 waves up and 3 waves down to form a complete cycle of 8 waves. This wave principle is derived from empirically tested rules from the studies on stock market price trends. The basic pattern of waves is reflected in various cycles and waves. One complete cycle consists of waves made up of two distinct phases — bullish and bearish. Thus, the wave 1 is upwards and wave 2 corrects the wave 1. Similarly, waves 3 and 5 are those with an upward impulse but are corrected by waves 4 and 6 respectively. An entire sequence of 1 to 5 waves is corrected by the sequence of bearish waves, namely, A, B, C. Thus, in a complete cycle, there are 5 bullish phases and 3 bearish phases, as shown in Fig. 18.11. The impulse waves are the waves in the direction of the main trend and the corrective waves are less in number but reverse the earlier trend. This is based on the principle that action is followed by reaction. Once the full cycle of waves is completed after the termination of the 8-wave movement, there will be a fresh cycle starting with similar impulses arising out of market trading, change of sentiment in the market etc. Again there will be 5 cycles upwards constituting the bullish trend and 3 waves downward constituting the bearish trend. According to the followers of Elliot wave theory, accuracy and timeliness of the waves is the basis for their usefulness in identifying the buy and sell signals in the market. A lot of empirical work has gone into the study of the waves and cycles of prices. It has been found that the behaviour of prices on the stock markets conforms to the cycles and waves and it is possible to use these data for predicting the price change and deciding on the buy and sell signals. As the upward waves of 5 are more than 3 downward waves, the net trend is upward in the long term which explains why an investor waiting for long will always be a gainer from the share market.

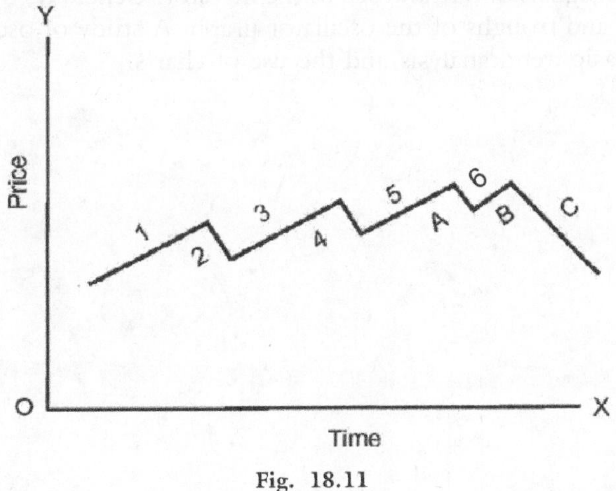

Fig. 18.11

Operation of Wave Theory[2]

The wave is a movement of the market price from one change in the direction to the next change in the direction. The waves are result of buying and selling impulses emerging from the demand and supply pressures on the market. If the demand exceeds supply, there is pressure of overbought position leading to a rise in prices. If the supply exceeds demand, there is an oversold position in the market leading to a downward trend in the prices. Depending on the pressure of the oversold and overbought position, the waves are generated in the prices.

The stock market has been found to behave in a consistent manner giving rise to a basic rhythm and a wave movement in prices. The basic rhythm is reflected in 3 impulses in one direction followed by 2 waves of corrective

2. R.R. Prechter Jr. (Ed.): *The Major Works of R.N. Elliot.*

nature with a total of 5 in the wave phase and 3 cycles in a reverse phase. These 3 waves correct the entire movements of 5 major upward movements.

The personality of each wave is an integral part of the reflection of mass psychology that it embodies. Although sometimes these wave counts are not clear, the shape and length may vary depending on the buying and selling pressures. But the analysts who have the experience and expertise can discern the waves in both upward and downward directions and also the impulse waves and corrective waves. These will help the analyst to learn what the chart tells regarding the phase and turning points. The wave principle offers the tools of identifying the market turns and their approach. As a limitation, however, it should be noted that the wave theory is not perfect and there are many limitations in its practical use. The rhythm as well as the count number of the waves may not be consistent and it may not be possible to clearly discern the turning points and take proper decision on buy and sell. But on the whole, it should be accepted as one of the tools of technical analysis for the investor and trader to decide on the timing of investment.

Oscillators (Rate of Change or ROC)

Oscillators refer to the velocity of price changes reflecting the market momentum which is measured by the rate of change of prices. This rate of change may be over the short period of 5 to 10 days or a longer period of 3 to 6 months. These oscillators may also be based upon the daily market prices when the volatility of the market spread is measured on a daily basis. Most oscillators would move in the same direction, either positive or negative, depending on the trends of the market. A positive reading reflects on overbought market and negative reading reflects oversold market. These oscillators in the form of velocity of price changes are plotted around a zero line to reflect both positive and negative values of the graph. The shape of the oscillator will depend on the period for which it is calculated say 5, 10, or 20 days. If the oscillator is for a longer period, it will become a smoother curve and if it is compiled on a daily basis, it will be widely fluctuating.

Usefulness of the oscillator graph depends on a proper reading of the graph. As a general rule, if the oscillator reaches the extreme lower end, it is suggested to buy and if it is at the upper end, then the suggestion is to sell. The crossing of the zero line may also be understood as the first indication of buy and sell signals.

The crossing of the zero line is an important indicator of the price trends and its direction. The market is said to be overbrought when the oscillator is at the upper extreme and is oversold when the oscillator is in the lower extreme. These points provide the signals of buy and sell to the investor. Generally, the peaks and troughs in the actual price chart also reflect the peaks and troughs of the oscillator graph. A study of oscillators is thus useful to confirm the conclusions arrived by the basic trend analysis and the use of charts.

19

EFFICIENT MARKET THEORY (Random Walk Hypothesis)

Valuation of a security is the basis for making an investment decision, as referred to in earlier chapters. The method of evaluation is shown to be Fundamental Analysis, in chapter 17 and Technical Analysis, in chapter 18. What to buy and sell and when are decided by these two approaches, so far, which are both exclusive. But a third theoretical approach is the Random Walk Theory, where in the price is determined by independent market forces, which absorb all the information efficiently.

What is Security Valuation?

Security analysis refers to the analysis of securities from the point of view of their prices, returns and risks. All investments are risky and the expected return is related to the risk. Their analysis will help in understanding the behaviour of security prices and the market and in decision-making for investment. If it is an analysis of only one scrip, it is called micro-analysis of a company. If it is an analysis of market of securities, it is referred to as a macro-picture of the behaviour of the market.

Information Flows

Markets are influenced by information flows, on the one hand, and money flows, on the other. If the information flows are perfect and free, and the markets adjust to these flows quickly and effectively, the markets are said to be perfect. If the information is imperfect or partial, the markets will be imperfect and the price formation will be unpredictable, haphazard and volatile.

The information whether perfect or imperfect has to be analysed to know its impact on the market prices and forecast prices. For this purpose, analytical tools and forecasting ability are necessary. If information is not perfect, a few with inside information would gain at the expense of others. If information is free and unbiased, the markets behave rationally and nobody can gain extra profits and normal returns are available to all whenever they enter the market.

Savings or Money Flows

The markets are also influenced by the flows of savings and money. The micro level flows would depend on the following objectives: income, capital appreciation, hedge against inflation, liquidity and safety to investors, etc. These are the criteria by which individual savers would enter the market for investment.

At the macro level, savings flows determine the level of investment in the corporate sector and in the economy and lead to capital formation and growth of fixed assets. The introduction of technology would also depend on these investment flows. The fixed capital formation would promote growth of output and income by a multiplier process. This leads to the theory of savings and investment of Keynes and also to Modern Monetarist Theory linking money flows to the growth of output and income in the economy.

Factors Influencing the Market Behaviour

Many of these factors relate to the economy, industry and company, which constitute the fundamental factors.

(1) Factors external to the company like environmental factors, economic and political developments.

(2) Internal factors of the company or of the market. These relate to the physical and financial performance of the company or companies.

(3) Size of paid-up capital and pattern of distribution of shareholding among the public.

(4) Investment habits and trading habits of the people.

A host of other factors, psychological and emotional, also play a role in the market operations.

Trading

The market in securities is influenced by the forces of supply and demand which in turn are influenced by the above factors. These forces of supply and demand determine the volume of trading-turnover and also the prices. These two indicators, namely, volume and price of the market, are macro-indicators for studying the market behaviour used in the technical analysis.

The volume of trading is reflected in the number of deals per day or hour, number of days in a year in which the company's share is traded or the number of shares traded in a day or a year. Our empirical studies show that the liquidity of shares, which depends on trading, is confined to a few scrips on the stock exchange, namely, 20-30% of the total. The liquidity is closely related to the spread of shareholding, size of capital and pattern of holding of share capital. It is also related to the intrinsic worth of the company and other financial indicators like P/E ratio. Nearly 50% of the performance of the share price is explained by the internal factors of the company like its earnings per share, debt servicing, book value, etc. The rest of the factors are external to the company such as demand conditions, government policy, environmental factors, etc.

The *main constituents* of and players in the markets are as follows:

(1) Instruments traded.

(2) Institutions and investors.

(3) Intermediaries.

The *indicators* of the market operations are as follows:

(1) Quantity raised from the new issues market and quantity traded in the secondary market.

(2) No. of issues made in the new issue market.

(3) No. of scrips traded in the stock market.

(4) Prices of instruments.

(5) Velocity of price changes.

(6) Intensity of trading and turnover of trading. (Volume changes)

Instruments

The instruments traded and their characteristics are set out in an earlier chapter. There are equity and preference shares in the category of ownership capital and debentures, bonds and P.S.U. Bonds, and Government securities in the category of debt capital. In the hybrid variety, there are convertible debentures and cumulative convertible preference shares which although have the characteristic of debt capital would eventually be ownership capital. A number of new instruments like warrants, Zero Coupon Bonds etc., are also being issued at present.

Players

The institutions or players in the market are the issuers of capital, namely, corporate units, government and semi-government bodies and public sector undertakings which are the major borrowers, in addition to the investors and intermediaries such as banks, financial institutions and brokers. More recently, a number of Mutual Funds, FFIs, NRIs, OCBs have also started as players in the markets.

Intermediaries

As referred to earlier the intermediaries are the brokers, merchant bankers, financial institutions, financial and investment consultancy firms etc. These are active in both the primary and secondary markets.

What is Market Analysis?

The security market analysis refers to the analysis of markets and securities traded there in terms of the risk-return, quantities raised or traded, price trends and other indicators of the market referred to above. The market analysis is made in terms of fundamental macro factors in the economy and technical factors like price and volume trends in the market. As regards the risk-return factors, the expected return varies with the risk attached to the instruments. Some instruments like government securities, P.S.U. Bonds or UTI units are least risky but have a cost in realisation. The cost of conversion or realisation of funds is zero in the case of bank deposits. The relationship between the risk and return in respect of various assets can be set out in macro terms as in Fig. 19.1.

A, B, C etc., are denoted to represent the various instruments with different combinations of risk-return characteristics. OM is risk free return. The higher the risk, the higher will be the return as shown in Fig. 19.1.

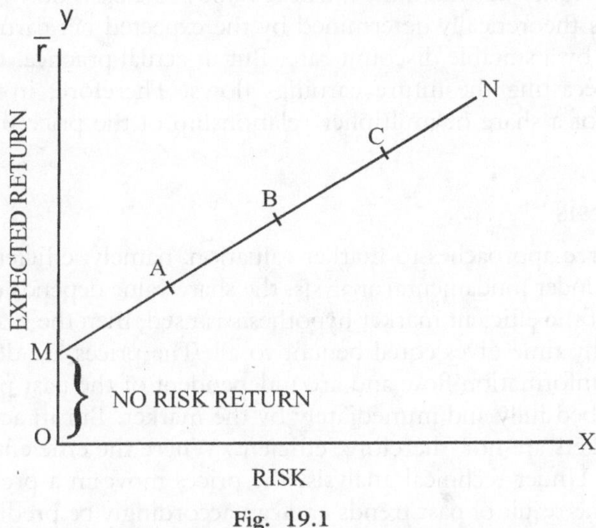

Fig. 19.1

In respect of individual scrips in the market, the security is valued in terms of the returns or earnings it fetches. The valuation is, therefore, an important aspect of security analysis. The market price depends on the supply and demand forces but basically veers around its intrinsic value, which in turn depends on the financial performance and fundamental factors of the company. These inter-relations can be represented as in Fig. 19.2.

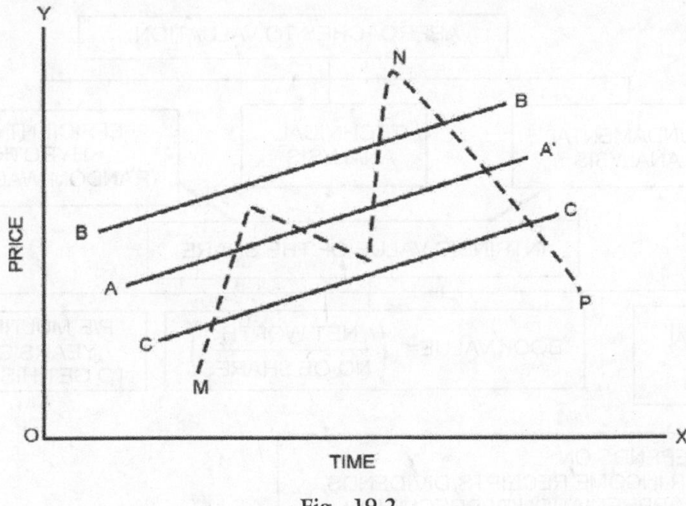

Fig. 19.2

AA′ = Intrinsic Value. BB and CC provide the range of error around the intrinsic value. MNP is the actual price curve in the market. This chart shows the importance of intrinsic factors under the Efficient Market Theory.

Valuation

The basic objective of market analysis is to know the fair valuation of shares for buying and selling. The market comprises hundreds of securities whose prices change from day-to-day and from time-to-time. The investors should have information of fair prices for making their decisions of buying and selling. It is, therefore, necessary to make security valuation an important part of market analysis. Besides, the trends of prices and volume of trading are inter-connected. Therefore, the market indicators of price, volume of trading, velocity of price changes and intensity of trading, etc. (volume of trading per hour) should all be examined together to have a correct picture of the market.

The valuation analysis in particular has two components, namely, the market valuation at the macro level and the individual security valuation at the micro level. The macro level analysis is done with the help of suitable price indices of the leading scrips in the market and their price-earning ratio. Thus, the BSE National Index of Security Prices has 100 scrips in it and their P/E ratio represents the market valuation of the securities. These are published by the BSE on a daily basis, and by ET once in a week.

As regards the individual security valuation, the intrinsic value is the basis on which overvaluation or undervaluation is judged. The intrinsic value is theoretically determined by the expected net earnings flows over a number of years discounted to the present time by a suitable discount rate. But in actual practice, this method is not followed due to the practical difficulties of forecasting the future earnings flows. Therefore, in practice, the P/E ratio is used to represent the pay back period of a share or multiplier relationship of the price to its earnings per share. These are explained in earlier chapters.

Random Walk Hypothesis

There are theoretically three approaches to market valuation, namely, efficient market hypothesis, fundamental analysis and technical analysis. Under fundamental analysis, the share value depends on the intrinsic worth of the shares, namely, its earnings potential. If the efficient market hypothesis is used, then the market becomes perfect and the entry into the market by buyers at any time gives equal benefit to all. The prices are determined in a random manner by competitive forces and perfect information flow and are independent of the past prices. This information is not only free and perfect, but it is absorbed fully and immediately by the market. But in actual practice, the information flow is not free and perfect and markets are not, therefore, efficient. Where the efficient market hypothesis does not hold, technical analysis is applicable. Under technical analysis, the prices move in a predictable manner and in waves and trends. The present prices are the result of past trends and can accordingly be predicted. Thus, by the use of analytical tools of charts and curves, the price trends can be studied and future trends can be predicted to decide on when to buy and sell.

In Fig. 19.3, the schematic presentation of valuation approaches and the three major methods of valuation of shares are depicted. The methods of valuation which are explained in detail later also are: (*i*) Discounted value of future income streams or dividends, and (*ii*) No. of years of payback period (P/E ratio).

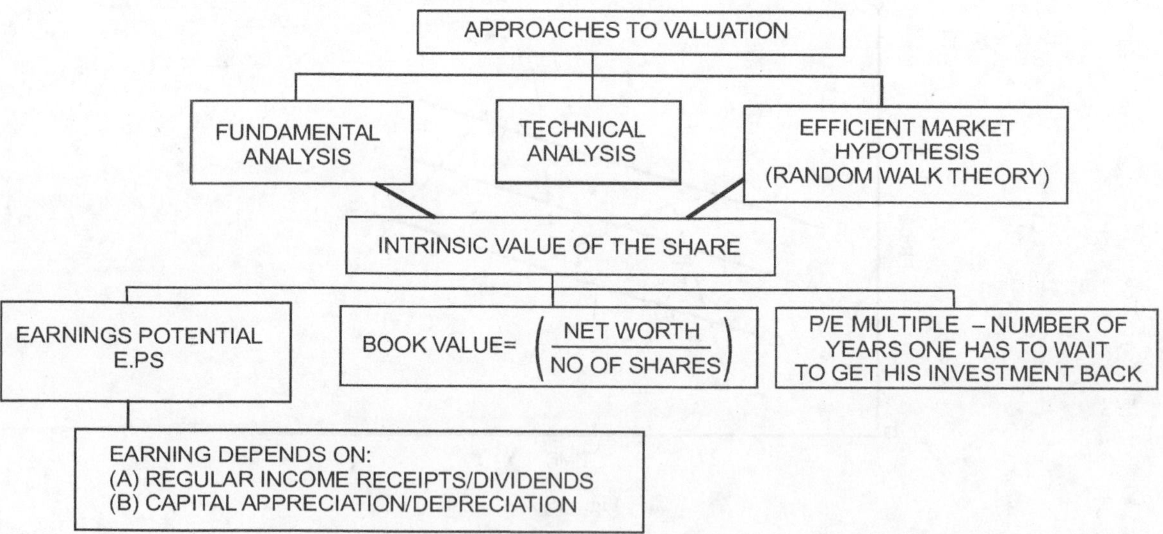

Fig. 19.3 Approaches to Valuation

Theoretical Framework

Investment refers to purchase of claims on money or financial assets used in the productive process in the economy. Investment, if it is in productive assets, should lead to an increase in output and income in the economy. In the macro sense, the investment income multiplier of Keynes operates whereby additional investment leads to an addition to output and income. Investment and income are related by a constant, namely, investment income multiplier or incremental capital-output ratio, which is the ratio of additional output due to the additional capital used in the productive process.

Besides, the aggregate capital-output ratio should be distinguished from the incremental capital-output ratio. While the former relates to the output created through a given capital input, the latter refers to the incremental output generated through a given increase in capital input. Corresponding to these two concepts, there are two multipliers namely aggregate investment multiplier and incremental investment multiplier. These refer to the increase in incomes due to a given increase in investment.

Mathematically, multiplier M = DY/DI where Y is income and I is investment. An increase in I (DI) will lead to a rise in Y (DY), as a multiple of I. This multiple is called investment multiplier by Keynes. A clear understanding of this concept will also explain the capital-output ratio. An increase in capital is investment itself while an increase in output as a result of an increase in capital input will lead to an increase in output and thus income in the macro sense.

If the incremental capital-output ratio is given by K, then the increase in output ΔO can be set out as follows: $\Delta O = K \times \Delta I$.

Thus, $K = \Delta O/\Delta I$, which is similar to the equation set out above for the investment multiplier.

Thus, the first theoretical tool is the Savings Investment Theory, which postulates that savings flow into investments which in turn leads to a multiple increase in output and income through what is called the capital-output ratio or investment multiplier. Thus, savings promote capital formation and economic growth through increase in output and incomes of the country. The mobilisation of savings for capital formation is through the capital market comprising the new issues market and the stock market. The role of capital market is thus primarily to promote economic growth. The instruments through which this process is carried out is through the sale of corporate securities, which are claims on financial assets. These instruments are issued by the corporate sector to raise capital through such securities, as equities, preference shares, debentures, etc. The purchase and sale of these securities is carried on in the stock and capital markets, which impart liquidity to these investment instruments and thus promote the flow of public savings into these financial markets.

Secondly, the market behaviour also depends on the players and their role in trading. An analysis of the market price behaviour is thus possible through the number of buyers and sellers available and the free flow of correct and unbiased information into the market. The Market Efficiency Theory or Random Walk Theory and many other theories explain how prices behave in the market in the macro sense. Competitive market conditions with a large number of buyers and sellers and with free and perfect flow of information will result in correct price formation in which prices tend to move near to their true intrinsic values of shares. In the absence of the above conditions, the share price movements may be erratic and biased; they may be overvalued or undervalued at any point of time. The insider information, rumours, cornering of shares and semi-monopoly conditions would all lead to imperfections in the market and price formation would be unrelated to the prevailing fundamentals of the company and its shares. The theoretical analysis of the market for its price behaviour would enable the investor to understand the market and make the right investment decisions regarding corporate securities.

The third theoretical tool in investment analysis is the fundamental analysis which explains why prices are what they are. This is an analysis of fundamental factors affecting the market in the macro sense, namely, economic, industry and company analysis. In the micro sense, the price of a share can be analysed through security valuation to find out the intrinsic value of a share and to examine whether a share is overvalued or undervalued. In the security valuation, the most important tool is the ratio analysis or examination of the balance sheet and profit and loss accounts of the company, whose share is being examined. The examination of these fundamentals will enable us to locate the undervalued shares and overvalued shares and to decide what shares to buy and what to sell.

The next question is when to buy and when to sell. This leads to the fourth theoretical tool, namely, technical analysis, which is an analysis of the price behaviour of the aggregate market and of individual shares with the help of charts on price, trading volume and moving averages of prices. An analysis of the price behaviour of the individual scrip historically in the background of the market price index behaviour will help to locate the turning signals indicating the likely changes in trends and suggesting the buy and sell points in the charts. The Dow Theory and Elliot Wave Theory are some of the theories in this analysis, which explain the price behaviour in the past and help us forecast the likely behaviour in the immediate future.

Yet another type of analysis is the analysis of risk and return which are the two major characteristics of any investment. This is sought to be achieved by the use of portfolio theory and portfolio management. In this analysis, the choice of scrips is decided by an analysis of risks involved in relation to the return in the background of the market risk and market return. A diversified portfolio of scrips is decided by an analysis of risk involved in relation to the return in the background of the market risk and market return. A diversified portfolio of scrips with varying degrees of risks in the upward and downward directions would lead to a minimisation of risk for the selected basket of scrips in the market. The degree of risk of the whole basket would, of course, depend upon the asset preferences, income requirements and other investment characteristics which an investor would choose, given his likes, preferences, needs etc. Broadly the modern portfolio theory depicts the choice of scrips in terms of its risk-return characteristics and maximisation of returns and minimisation of risks involved. The greater the risk taken the larger is the reward. Capital Assets Pricing Model is a hypothesis explaining the valuation of assets in a portfolio.

Schematic Presentation of Theory

In Fig. 19.4, all the theories are integrated to help decision-making by investors. Firstly, the basis of markets is the money flow, which is represented by the funds flow theory, resulting in the emergence of stock and capital markets. Looked at from a different angle, the savings of the public are channeled into investment, which for an individual at micro level leads to claims on money and future cash flows. For the country as a whole, the savings flow into investment, which helps the growth process in the economy. This is explained by the Savings Investment Theory.

Secondly, an investor to make a right decision to purchase or sell shares has to know the correct and fair value of a share. To explain why share prices fluctuate and what are the fair prices, the theories used are Market Efficiency Theory or, Random Walk Theory and Capital Assets Pricing Theory. All these presume that markets are efficient due to free and perfect information flows and their absorption by the markets. In actual practice, information is not perfect and markets are not efficient. Prices depend *inter alia* on a host of psychological and emotional factors. The theory of Trend Walkers explain the market trends as set by a few trend setters or leaders followed by a mass of trend walkers.

Thirdly, the market prices and individual share prices are explained by the fundamental factors, namely, economy, industry and company analysis. This leads to factors determining the market prices and their movements around the intrinsic worth of the shares. This process is helped by the balance sheet analysis of companies and application of ratio analysis and other tools of financial management.

Fourthly, an investor should know the timing of investments, when to buy and sell. This decision is helped by the technical analysis of markets, incorporated in the Dow Theory and moving averages, Elliot's Wave Theory, etc.

Lastly, the portfolio theory provides the linkage of markets to investment. An efficient portfolio is to be developed by the investor by making proper investments to minimise the risks and maximise the returns. The portfolio management helps the investment process by applying the principles of Portfolio Theory to build up an efficient portfolio through a diversified basket of scrips and by using the concept of Beta.[@] Security evaluation and risk return assessment are linked to the investment process. What securities to buy and when to buy so as to build up an efficient portfolio are all interlinked to result in the buying and selling of shares in the market and trading.

Thus, the whole theoretical framework results in a practical application to the buying and selling and savings and investment process in the market. The various theories are provided inter-linkages, *inter se* by the schematic representation in the Fig. 19.4.

Investment and Time Value of Money

A bird in hand is worth two in the bush. Money today is more valuable than the same tomorrow or a few days hence. This is because money has alternative uses and opportunity costs. If it is invested, it would bring a return and better the investment, the better is the return. To part with money is a risk which should be rewarded by a return. The present value of a delayed pay off may be found by multiplying the pay off by a discounting factor, which is expressed as the reciprocal of 1 plus a rate of return. Thus, the discounting factor is $= 1/1 + r$, where r is the rate of return that investor thinks adequate for his parting with money. Money has also a psychological satisfaction and value and to part with money is to part with a value which can only be compensated by a return.

Present Value Method

Thus, the present value (PV) $= \frac{1}{1+r} \times C$, where, C is the expected cash flow or pay off in the period. If there are more than one periods, then

$$PV = \frac{C_1}{(1+r)} + \frac{C_2}{(1+r)^2} + \frac{C_3}{(1+r)^3} = \Sigma \frac{C_t}{(1+r)^t}$$

@ Beta concept is explained in later chapter.

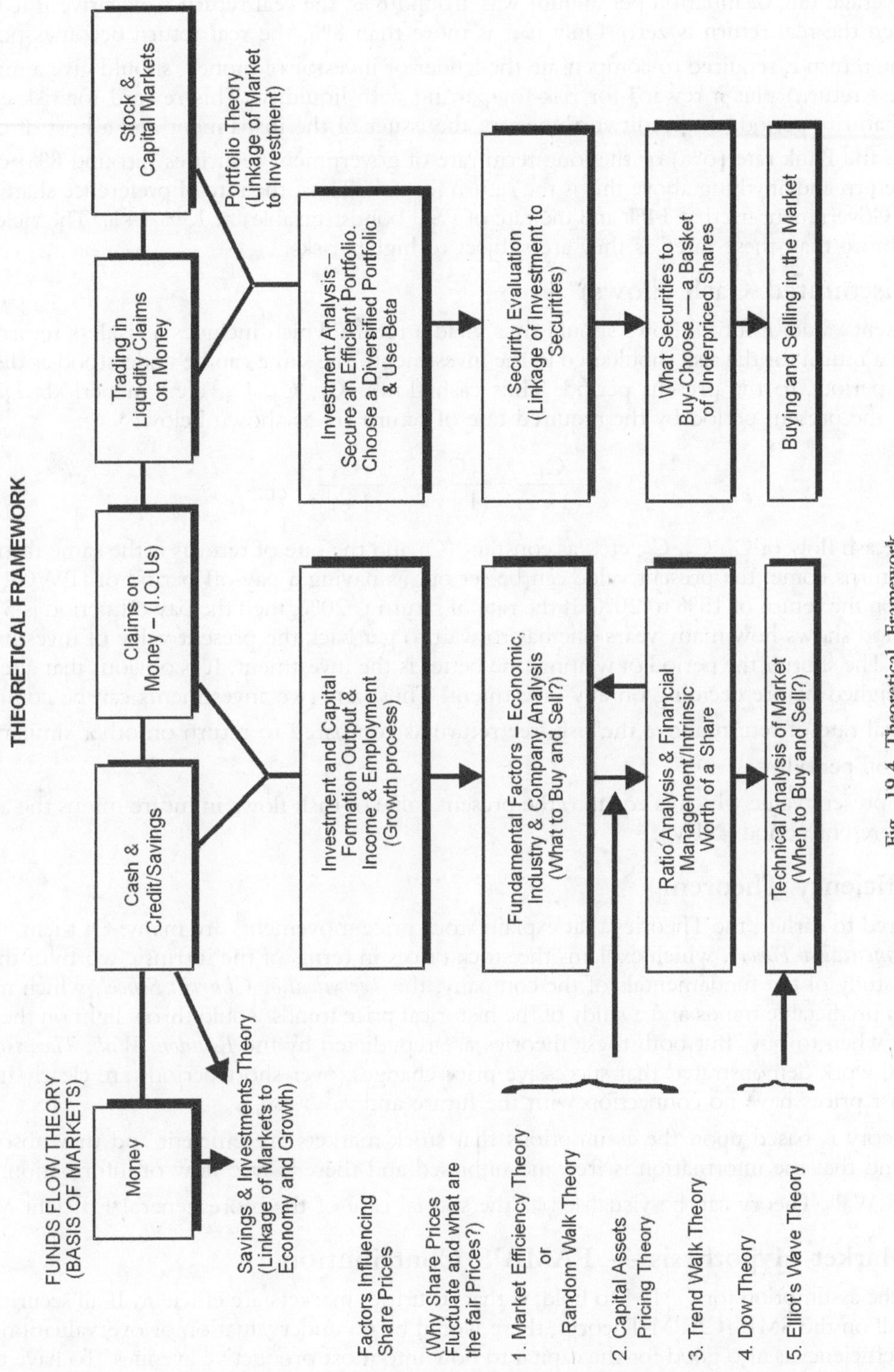

Fig. 19.4 Theoretical Framework

where, C_1, C_2 etc., are returns in periods 1 and 2 etc., and r remains as the same rate of return during all these periods. If r is the required rate of return or reward for the risk of parting with money and it remains the same throughout all the periods considered, and C_1, C_2, C_3 etc., are the cash receipts in all the periods, then PV = C/r or PV × r = C. Thus, given the required rate of return, the needed cash flow can be derived.

In the above equation, r refers to the nominal return. The real return is the nominal return divided by the rate of inflation or rise in prices. Money is losing its value by the degree of inflation, year after year. In the eighties and nineties the average rate of inflation per annum was around 8%; the real return is negative if it is less than 8% and if r is 8%, then the real return is zero. Only if it is more than 8%, the real return becomes positive.

Thus, the return r, required to compensate the lender or investor of money, should give a minimum of inflation rate (or riskless return) plus a reward for risk for parting with liquidity. This reward for risk element varies from instrument, maturity period, the creditworthiness of the issuer of the instrument and a host of other factors.

In India, the Bank rate (6%) or the long-term rate of government securities (around 8%) could be considered the risk-free return and anything above this is the return for risk. Thus, the rate of preference shares and fixed deposits is kept by the Government fixed at 14% and the rate of PSU bonds (taxable) at 13%-14%. The yield on equities should be definitely more than these rates as they are subject to higher risks.

D.C.F. (Discounted Cash Flows)

The present value of future flows should thus yield a return which includes a riskless return (for the degree of inflation) plus a return for the risk shouldered in the investment. The same can be understood as discounted cash flows of the future periods to the present period. Thus cash flows (C_1, C_2, C_3, etc.) in periods 1,2,3 etc., should be discounted to the present period by the required rate of return (r) as shown below:

$$\frac{C_1}{(1+r)} + \frac{C_2}{(1+r)^2} + \frac{C_3}{(1+r)^3} \text{ etc.}$$

Assuming the cash flow of C_1, C_2, C_3, etc., as constant (C) and the rate of returns is the same throughout the periods when these returns come, the present value can be set out as having a pay-off period of [PV/C], say, 6 to 10 years, depending upon the return of 15% to 20%. If the rate of return is 20%, then the pay-off period is 5 years. This concept of pay-off period shows how many years one has to wait to get back the present value of investment at the required rate of return. The shorter the period of waiting, the better is the investment. It is obvious that alternative investments have to be weighed before deciding on any investment. Thus, any two investments can be compared in terms of:

(1) Actual rate of return above the risk-free return as compared to return on other similar assets;

(2) Pay-off period;

(3) Net present value which is equal to the present value of cash flows in future minus the actual investment in the present period (NPV).

Market Efficiency Theorem

As referred to earlier, the Theories that explain stock price movements are many. Of them, the more important are the *Fundamentalist Theory,* which explains the stock prices in terms of the intrinsic worth of the company's share, based on the study of the fundamentals of the company, the *Technical or Chartist School,* which maintains that stock prices move in predictable trends and a study of the historical price trends would throw light on the forthcoming prices which tells us, when to buy. But both these theories are repudiated by the *Random Walk Theorists*, who based upon their empirical work demonstrated that successive price changes, over short periods are clearly independent of each other. The past prices have no connection with the future and *vice versa.*

This Theory is based upon the assumptions that stock markets are efficient and they absorb all the available information and that the information is free and unbiased and there is free flow of information, into the market.

Random Walk Theory can be visualised as the special case of the more general Efficient Market Hypothesis.

Efficient Market Hypothesis — FAMA'S Contribution

One of the assumption for CAPM to hold, is that securities markets are efficient. If all securities would be priced so that they fall on the SML (CAPM Theory), there would be no undervaluation or overvaluation of securities. Then the allocative efficiency is also good for the capital to flow into most productive avenues. To have this type of efficient markets, it is necessary to have both internal and external efficiency.

Internal efficiency refers to markets where the transactions costs are low and speed of transactions is high. This matter refers to market conditions on which investor has no control. External efficiency refers to absorption of information by the market in an unbiased manner and reflected in the price formation. If investors are rational and markets are efficient, the price adjusts quickly to new information. Fama (1970) has provided three classifications of efficiency which depended on the extent of absorption of information and the time taken for absorption and the type of information absorbed.

A market is efficient with a given set of data or information, if it is impossible to have abnormal returns adjusted for risk and transactions costs by trading on the basis of that available data and information.

The three classifications of efficiency as set out by Fama are:

(1) weak form of efficiency; which absorbs only past price and volume data, and those on returns of the market,

(2) semi-strong form of efficiency, which absorbs all publicly available information,

(3) strong form of efficiency which absorbs all publicly and privately held information.

This Hypothesis postulates that the market is efficient under free market conditions and it absorbs all the information through demand and supply forces. This absorption is of different degrees. In particular, three forms of efficiency are discussed, in this context.

Weak Form

The weak form states that the current market prices of shares already reflect all the available information that is contained in the historical sequence of prices. This weak form of efficient market hypothesis holds that all historical and past information is absorbed in the market forces. They hold that prices move in a random fashion, independent of the past and hence there is no benefit in examining the past prices. This hypothesis contradicts the statements of Technical Analysts, who state that historical price movements can help the forecast the future price trends and prices move in a predictable manner.

Semi-strong Form

The semi-strong form of the efficient market hypothesis postulates that current prices of stocks not only reflect all the information contained in the historical prices but also reflect all *publicly available knowledge* about the companies. To analyse public information on corporate reports, policy statements on dividends, rights, bonds and other corporate information will not yield consistently superior returns to the analyst. The reason is that as soon as such information is publicly available, it is absorbed and reflected in stock prices. Even if the market absorption is imperfect, it will not be possible for the analyst to obtain superior returns on a consistent basis. The absorption even if it is incomplete or incorrect, it will not continue for long and it will not take place in the same fashion and in a consistent manner. There can be over adjustments and under adjustments and in the absence of any consistency, the results are not predictable and the analyst cannot take advantage of the fundamentals and the information on them, to gain superior investment returns.

Strong Form

The strong form of efficient market hypothesis maintains that not only is publicly available information useless to the investor but all information is useless to gain superior investment returns. This means that no information, be it public, private, or inside can be used to consistently earn superior investment returns by the analyst, because the market absorbs all the information by itself. The market absorbs efficiently all information whether past, published and present or insider information.

To counter the above arguments it is stated that mutual funds with their better and inside information gain more and earn superior returns. Besides, the brokers and sub-brokers who are in the trading ring with insider information can gain excess profits and empirical tests have proved the same.

The strong form states two conditions to be met: first that successive price changes or returns are independent and second these successive price changes or return changes are identically distributed, like Random Walk Theory. This Theory is not interested in price or return levels as such, but in changes between successive levels.

Empirical Tests

In the real world, imperfections are there; transactions costs and information costs may lead to non-availability of information to all participants equally and at the same time which may lead to pockets of better absorption and poor absorption. These may lead to less than or more than the equilibrium profits, namely, excess profits or losses. Thus, the efficient market theory has been found to have some limitations in application to the real world. The results have been almost unanimous in supporting the weak form of *Efficient Market Hypothesis.* If so, the Random walk hypothesis holds good in the real world.

If markets are truly efficient, then the fundamentalist will be successful only when he has insider information, or he has the superior ability to analyse publicly available information and gain insight into the future of the firm or he uses the above insider information or his superior ability to reach long-term buy, sell and hold investment decisions, to benefit by a gain larger than the market average return.

Test of Random Walk Theory (Mutual Fund Performance)

One of the tests of the validity of Random walk hypotheses is that of the Mutual Funds, because they are expected to have better access to insider information or atleast have better information due to their research expertise. But evidence shows that mutual funds do not out perform the market normally. But there are exceptions. The normal return of Mutual Funds in India is around 15% to 20% and most of the them are quoted at a discount on Net Asset Value (NAV) during past few years. Thus, the mutual fund performance in India partially supports the efficient market hypothesis, in a weak form.

Serial Correlation Tests

A number of researchers like FAMA, FISCHER, JENSEN, etc., in the USA and many experts in India have conducted tests for serial correlation of the price changes. These tests are run to find correlation between the present price changes and the price changes in any past period, with a lag of one day to a few days. The average daily price changes for stocks, in B.S.E. Sensex are not found to be significantly correlated with any lagged series.

Run Tests

Run Tests are also conducted in which the absolute numbers are replaced by signs. These merely count the number of runs, namely consecutive price changes or signs in the same direction and their repetition at a later date. These tests revealed their distribution in random manner.

Filter Tests

In this analysis, filters are fixed at some percentage change and price movements are observed. Some mechanical trading strategies run on these filter levels on the premise that once a movement in prices has exceeded a fixed level of price movement called resistance or support levels, the security price will move in the same direction.

Thus, if the closing price of a security on a daily basis has moved up atleast by 5%, then strategy calls for buying that security until the price starts moving down then, the investment strategy is to sell and go short, until the price fell by the same percentage (5%) and then start covering up the short position. The selection of filter levels from 0.5% to 20% was adopted by Researchers and it was found that the results, of this filter strategy are no better than those with buy and Hold strategy or simple formula plan of buying at regular intervals. This is particularly true, if the total transactions costs are also included in the prices. All the above tests mildly confirm the validity of the Random walk Hypothesis. Under Indian market conditions, the strong form of Market efficiency Theory does not seem to have validity but a weak form of this hypothesis has been found to be applicable to our conditions.

Even in the developed markets like the U.S., research results do not give any unambivalent conclusion regarding the validity of the semi-strong and strong forms of market efficiency Theory.

ESSENCE OF RANDOM WALK THEORY

There is a lot of misunderstanding of this Theory. This is identified firstly with market Efficiency Theory. Perfect market efficiency is taken as the basis for random walk of prices. Random Walk Hypothesis says nothing of the reasons for price movements or the valuation of stocks. It does not depend on perfect market conditions or perfect market absorption of all information. What only this Model postulated on the basis of empirical tests is that successive price changes are independent of the past changes. That means by implication that prices will average out and reflect the intrinsic value of a security.

The implication of the validity of this Theory is that Technical analysis is relegated to a secondary position and analysis of fundamentals is brought to greater focus in the valuation of securities. Security Analysis should therefore concentrate more on the intrinsic worth of a share, its fundamentals, like E.P.S. P/E, etc. The developments in the field of fundamentals like dividend annoucement Earnings Reports, Bonus or Rights announcements and financial results will have influence on stock prices and they need to be studied to the extent that this hypothesis supports the market efficiency theory and asserts that the markets are efficient to some extent in the absorption of all information, or superior expertise in analysis and better understanding of the affairs of the company in question. Better information and expertise in analysis and interpretation can give better results or enable one to outperform the market in India, as some analysts have shown. Hence, the Fundamentalist school has more relevance in India.

Gordan's Hypothesis

M.J. Gordan has postulated a hypothesis called *Bird — in the Hand Model*, in which dividend policy becomes relevant, in the real world, as dividends today are more valuable than dividends in future. That means that internal rate of return = r and appropriate discount rate = k may or may not be equal. If r = k, the introduction of risk in the model, makes $K_t > K_{t-1}$ and K cannot be held constant. If this factor is also taken into account, namely, today's dividends are taken as more valuable than tomorrow's, then two possibilities occur: (*i*) r > k or r < k rates of return r, on each successive investment goes upto a point and then drops, due to operation of Laws of Returns, and (*ii*) K is itself changing due to the principle that dividends today are more valuable than those in future due to the introduction of risk.

Walter Model

The Model of Walter is based on the hypothesis that dividends as well as earnings effect the share price. The reasoning is that the firm's internal rate of return (r) and its cost of capital (k) may be different. If it is cheaper to raise funds from external sources, then it is better to pay out dividends and raise resources from outside. If the internal rate of return (r) exceeds cost of capital (k) then the firm should payout the earnings as dividend. Since these two sources of funds have different returns, dividend payouts do matter and the value of the firm is affected by dividend payout policy. Investor prefers to invest funds outside the company, if r > k.

Walter's formula

As referred to earlier, Walter's equation can be set as follows: where P_o is the present price

$$P_o = \frac{E}{K} + \frac{(g-k)(E-D)}{K^2}$$

E = earnings, D = dividends per share

K = market discount rate or required rate of return

g = growth rate of dividends or earnings.

Walter took into account both dividends and earnings, as they both affect the share prices.

Walter *vs.* M.M. Hypothesis

M.M. Hypothesis postulates that dividends are irrelevant to the value of the firm. The arbitrage process operates to bring about equality of costs of capital, whether raised from issuing new shares or by borrowing from external sources. Payment of dividends from the earnings involves borrowing from issuing new shares or borrowing from external sources. The investment policy lays down the method of financing and whatever is the method of financing investments, the arbitrage process brings about the equality in the cost of capital raised.

The firm makes investments so long as the internal rate of return (r) is higher than the cost of capital (k). The firm earns more than the cost of capital raised, and so long as this is true, the shareholders are indifferent whether dividends are distributed or not. The investors are indifferent between dividends and capital gains. In this scenario, distribution of dividends has no effect on the value of the firm.

The assumptions for M.M. Hypothesis are the following:

Perfect markets, no transaction costs, free flow of information, investors are rational, no taxes, the internal rate of return is independent of the method of financing investors are certain of the flow of earnings, the returns and cost of capital. If dividends are paid out, capital has to be raised through sales of new shares or through retained earnings and investors are indifferent as between dividends and capital gains. If invested by raising equity, the firm raises capital by borrowing loans or issue of bonds, there will be no difference between debt and equity because of leverage and the real cost of debt is the same as the real cost of capital. The cost of capital is not affected by the method of raising of capital, in the light of the above assumptions.

On the other hand, in Walter's model, dividend pay outs and capital gains, if any influence the value of the Firm. Thus, the value of a share is the present value of all dividend flows expected in future and present value of expected capital gains. The relevance of Dividends is due to the relationship between the return on Investment or internal rate of return (r) and its cost of capital (k). A firm should retain earnings only if r > k, as it is then making profitable investments and investors are happy as they cannot earn more by having their dividends reinvested elsewhere outside the company. If k > r, *viz.,* cost of capital or *required* rate of return is more than the *expected* rate of return on investment, then the company should pay out dividends, as the company cannot use funds profitably and shareholders can use the dividends paid out more profitably than the firm.

The dividend pay out policy and the maximisation of the value of the firm are interlinked. The connecting link is the relationship between r and k. The proportion of dividends paid out depends on how much is to be retained by the Firm for investment which is done as long as r is greater than cost of capital (k). The pay out ratio may thus vary from 0 to 100%, depending upon available investment opportunities and the proportion of investments, whose r is greater than k and the firm's investment policy.

Walter model is criticised as unrealistic as r and k are assumed to be constant. Besides, the model is applicable to equity firms whose financing is done by retained earnings only, which is again a limitation. This model ignores the effect of risk on the value of the Firm, arising out of debt financing. Cost of capital in reality varies with the method of finance. The existence of taxes, transaction costs, cost of raising new issues of equity or debt etc., make this model unrealistic in the practical world.

M.M. Hypothesis*

Miller & Modigliani Hypothesis postulates that dividend payout has no effect on share prices. What is relevant for share valuation is its earnings capacity. Whether earnings, cash flows and/or dividends are taken the result is the same for the above purpose. If dividends are not paid they are used in the firm for investment and total return on capital employed is more relevant for valuation of the firm than what is paid as dividend for the shareholder. But this hypothesis is based on some assumptions.

(a) Perfect markets, and no uncertainty.

(b) No taxes and no transactions costs.

(c) Fixed investment policy of the firm.

(d) Return on capital employed is the same as the cost of capital acquired from outside say r = k, which means that internal rate of return is the same as the cost of capital.

Under the above assumptions arbitrage process operates in a way that it is the same for the company (or for investor) if they use the retained earnings or external funds for investment. This approach is cost of capital approach.

Equation for M&M model is

$$V_o = \frac{D_o}{K - g}$$

Where, D stands for dividends or earnings, K for required rate of return, and g is the rate of growth of dividends.

Earnings Model

The market value of a share is determined by the present value of all anticipated future earnings flows.

$$pt = \sum_{t=1}^{n} \frac{E_t - I_t}{(1+k)^t}$$

E_t is earnings per share during various periods. I_t is investment per share during the period and the other variables are the same as above.

Graham and Dodd Model

According to Graham & Dodd, the dividends of a firm determine its share value and the equation can be set out as:

$$P = M\left(D + \frac{E}{3}\right) + A$$

M = Total earnings of firm

E = Earnings per share

A = Adjustment for Asset Values (say Book value per share)

D = Dividend per share

* F. Modigliani & M.H. Miller, *The Cost of Capital* ... AER, 1958.

$\frac{P}{E}$ *Ratio and its Determinants:*

$\frac{P}{E}$ ratio is the market price divided by the earnings per share.

$\frac{P}{E}$ ratio is one of the models used for comparing prices of shares, like the Dividend discount model or earnings.

Dividend Model

Consider the Dividend Discount Model which is given as:

$$P_o = \frac{D_1}{r-g}$$

Dividend D can be written as Eb, where, E is earnings and b is payout ratio, then

$$P_o = \frac{Eb}{r-g}, \text{ and rearranging, we have}$$

$$\frac{P}{E} = \frac{b}{r-g}$$

Then $\frac{P}{E}$ ratio can be taken as a function of three variables — ***payout ratio (b), Discount rate (r)*** and ***growth rate*** of earnings (g).

The ***Whitbeck and Kisor Model*** has calculated the undervalued and overvalued portfolios for 1960-61, quarterwise. As per their study (V.S. Whitbeck and M. Kisor — "New Tool in Investment Decision Making," *Financial Analyst Journal*, May-June 1963) one method of "beating the market" is to estimate the undervalued portfolios compared with the market portfolio as given by Standard & Poor 500 Index and choose such companies in the portfolio. The undervalued portfolio is calculated on the basis of P/E ratios, estimated and the actuals. The performance of each portfolio is compared with that of the Standard and Poor market index. Undervalued portfolio gives the above market return, called "Beating the Market."

Malkiel and Cragg Regression Model

Malkiel and Cragg used the regression model to suggest that the cross sectional regression models explain a good deal of the cross sectional variance in P/E ratios at any particular point of time. The dependent variable in the regression equation is P/E, the three independent variables were ***expected earnings growth rate (g), expected payout ratio (b) and the risk measure (β).***

The regression equations* for 5 years, studied by them are shown below:

Table

Year	*Equation*	R^2
1961	$\frac{P}{E} = 4.73 + 3.28g + 2.05\,b - .85\beta$	.70
1962	$\frac{P}{E} = 11.06 + 1.75g + 0.78\,b - 1.61\beta$	.70
1963	$\frac{P}{E} = 2.94 + 2.55g + 7.62\,b - .27\beta$	.75
1964	$\frac{P}{E} = 6.71 + 2.50g + 5.23\,b - .89\beta$	.75
1965	$\frac{P}{E} = 0.96 + 2.74g + 5.01\,b - .35\beta$	.85

* B.G. Malkiel and J.G. Cragg: *Expectations and The Structure of Share Prices,* A.E.R., Sept. 1970. R.J. Fuller and J.C. Farill: *Modern Investments and Security Analysis,* McGraw-Hill.

As for each year, the R^2 ranged from 0.70 to 0.85. The authors have concluded that there is a good relation between P/E and the independent variables g, b and β. Similarly, one can use ROE and other variables like ROA (ROE is return on equity and ROA is return on assets, etc.).

Cootner's Price-Value Interaction Model

Stock valuation Models take into account future cash flows discounted to the present time. The Standard Model can be represented in the following equation:

$$\text{Present Value} = \frac{\text{Income}_1}{(1+i)^2} + \frac{\text{Income}_2}{(1+i)^2} + \frac{\text{Income}_3}{(1+i)^2} \text{ ... and so on}$$

(P_o)

where t = 1,2,3...etc. (time periods)

i = Discount rate expected

If these incomes or cash flows vary in every period, then Cf_1, Cf_2, Cf_3... etc. will be discounted to the present time.

Paul Cootner[@] had suggested that security prices can be viewed as series of constrained random fluctuations around their intrinsic value. There are two classes of investors. Of these, the more important *professional investors* who have better avenues to get information and analyse them make estimates of intrinsic value and if its market price goes very much off the intrinsic value, they start buying or selling. The second class of investors, whom he calls *Naive Investors* follow the 'hot tips' or the mass media and buy and sell following the path set by the professionals.

Actual prices in the market move around the intrinsic value, for which the trend is set by the professionals and naive investors follow them. Buying and selling pressures emenate from the mass of the naive investors but the professionals snatch the cream of the gains, as they have the better information to foresee the changes in intrinsic value and book profits when necessary. This market is then called the intrinsic value random walk market.

Limitation of Random Work

According to Random Walk Theory, security's intrinsic values change and market prices move randomly around these intrinsic values. The new information affecting the market arrives at random intervals. This new information will force the analysis to reestimate the intrinsic value and again the stock prices move randomly around the new intrinsic value.

This Theory thus states that security prices move randomly in a continuous fashion to set new equilibriums. There may be upward or downward movements and changes take place in a random manner. If the trade barriers are imposed, by the Stock Exchange authorities then there may be lower reflecting barriers (support lines) or upper reflecting barriers (resistance lines) etc. The movements in share prices thus move generally within a narrow band, in a random fashion and these trends are changed from time-to-time with the flow of new information. These random steps are based on the market absorption of the information. With perfect absorption, there will be continuous moves to equilibrium and this is what Samuelson had in mind when he referred to continuous or dynamic equilibrium model, under perfectly efficient market conditions leading to perfectly efficient prices. This is based on the assumption of continuous flow of market information, which will change the stock prices, following the changes in the estimates of intrinsic value of the company's shares.

Random Walk Assumptions

The price movements under Random Walk Theory are randomly distributed, in such a way that the present steps are independent of past steps and in view of such random movements entry into the market any time gives same returns for the same risk to the investors.

This theory is based on the following assumptions:

(1) Market is perfect and free without trade restrictions.
(2) Market absorbs all the information quickly and efficiently.
(3) Information is free and costless and is quickly available to all at the same time.
(4) Information is unbiased and correct.
(5) Market players can analyse the information quickly and the information is absorbed in the market through buy and sell signals.
(6) Demand and supply pressures are absorbed in the market through price changes. Such absorption leads to quick and prompt movements in prices which are random in fashion.

@ P.H. Cootner: *Random Character of Stock Prices,* Cambridge Mass, MIT Press, 1964.

20 INTRODUCTION TO PORTFOLIO THEORY

INTRODUCTION

So far we dealt with analysis securities for assessing the fair price of an asset and investment in such assets as suits the requirements and preferences of the saver or investor. What for is it needed? It is for choosing the portfolio of assets, which will maximise his wealth, subject to minimum of risk. This is the subject of further discussion in this chapter and the rest of the following chapters.

Two basic principles of finance form the basis of portfolio theory, namely *Time value of money* and the *safety of money.*

Rupee today is worth more than rupee of tomorrow or a year hence and as parting with money involves the loss of present consumption, it has to be rewarded by a return commensurate with time of waiting. Secondly, a safe rupee is preferred to an unsafe rupee at any point of time. Due to risk aversion of investors, they feel risk is inconvenient and has to be rewarded by a return. The larger the risk taken, the higher should be the return.

Present values and future values are related by a discount factor comprising firstly the interest rate component and secondly the time factor. The future flows are to be discounted to the present by a required rate of discount to make them comparable and equal in value. This time value factor is discussed in a separate chapter.

As regards the risk factor, there is a direct relationship between the expected return and unavoidable risk. Avoidable risk can be reduced or even eliminated by measures like diversification, referred to in detail in another chapter. Risk and return concepts are also explained in an earlier chapter, while these are discussed separately in relation to Portfolio Theory in chapter 22.

As the book deals with the securities and investor puts his money or savings into these securities, investment and disinvestment activities should be examined. The basis for these activities is the income and consumption of these economic units. If Y is income and E is expenditure then savings is (Y – E) and borrowing is (E – Y) lending of savings arises if Y – E is positive.

Investment Activity is based on three components, namely the following sources of investment.

Table 1

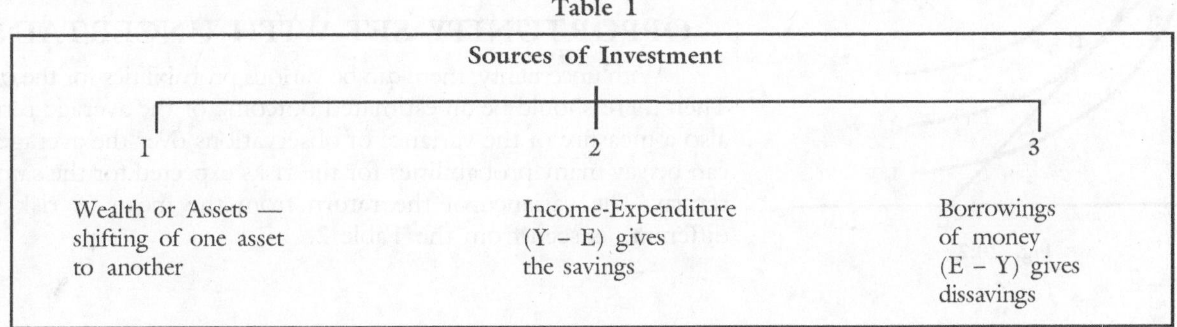

Investment choice depends on firstly the available alternatives, opportunity set, and secondly, the preferences of investors reflected in their indifference curves. The objective of all investors is to achieve the maximum level of utility or consumption during any period. The constraints are set by the above three sources. The available opportunities are set by the alternatives open to him, given his preference. Some of them are riskless and with certainty and others are risky and uncertain.

Let us take the case of choices with certainty first. The investor has an income of ₹ 10,000 per annum in each of the two years. As the savings Account in Bank pays 4%; assume that he can also borrow at the same price, as he can lend. Then what are the alternatives open to him?

In a two period simplified model, he has three alternative choices open to him: (a) consume in both periods ₹ 10,000 of income, (b) consume less in the first period to save and lend, and (c) consume more in the first period by borrowing and reduce consumption in the subsequent period.

Conditions of Certainty

Graphically the opportunity set and investor preferences or utility curves under certainty can be shown as follows. Assume that his income is ₹ 10,000 per period. (1) Alternative is to abstain from consumption in period (1) and consume all ₹ 20,000 in period (2) Alternative is to borrow and consume in the period (1) and consume less and repay borrowings in the second year.

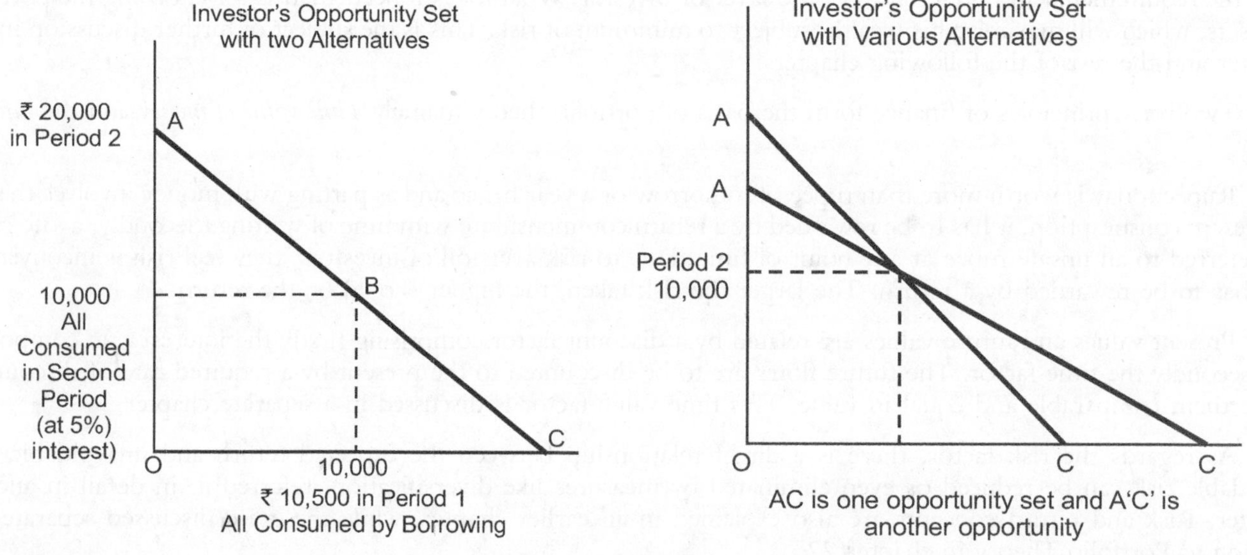

Fig. 20.1

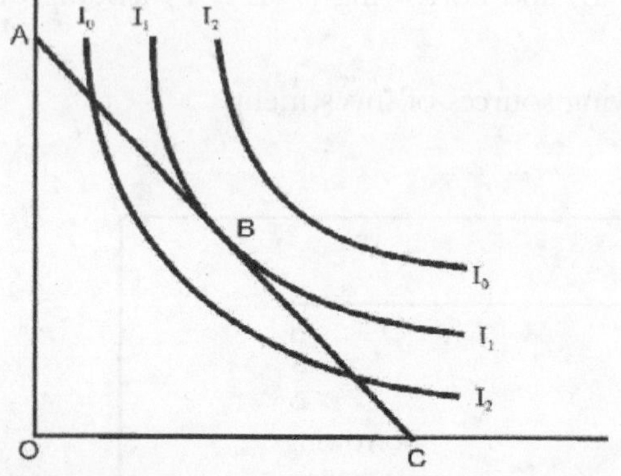

The equilibrium point is at the point of intersection between the Indifference curve (investor preference) and the opportunity set, as shown below:

The equilibrium point is set at B on the Indifference curve I_1, the point which is maximum possible for the given opportunity set, given by the line AC.

Fig. 20.2

OPPORTUNITY SET WITH UNCERTAINTY

With uncertainty, there can be various probabilities for the outcome. Then there should be an estimated outcome or the average return and also a measure of the variance of observations over the average. There can be say many probabilities for the risks expected for the same mean return. The variance of the return from the mean or risk may be different, as seen from the Table 2.

Table 2

	Asset 1	*Asset 2*	*Asset 3*
Mean Return	10	10	10
Variance	24	54	24
Standard Deviation	4.9	7.35	4.9

Average return is the mean, which is generally used to measure the expected value. If we know the returns probable for each of the outcomes or events and their probabilities, we can calculate the average, by giving the weights to the returns by the probabilities assigned to them.

Take the following example.

Table 3

Event	*Probabilities*	*Asset I*	*Asset II*
A	$\frac{1}{3}$	9	12
B	$\frac{1}{2}$	6	8
C	$\frac{1}{6}$	3	6

Weighted Average for Asset I $= \frac{1}{3} \times 9 + \frac{1}{2} \times 6 + \frac{1}{6} \times 3)$

$= 3 + 3 + \frac{1}{2}$

$= 6\frac{1}{2}$

Simple Average $= 6$

Weighted Average for Asset II $= \frac{1}{3} \times 12 + \frac{1}{2} \times 8 + \frac{1}{6} \times 6$

$= 4 + 4 + 1 = 9$

Simple Average $= 8^2/_3$

Let the portfolio be of three securities and the market conditions are good, indifferent and bad. Under each of the market conditions expected returns, their mean and derviations can be calculated to derive their covariance. The Table below gives an illustration.

Table 4

Market Condition	*Deviation of Asset (1)*	*Deviation of Asset (2)*	*Product of Deviations*
Good	15-9	16-10	36
Indifferent	9-9	10-10	0
Bad	3-9	4-10	36
		Sum of the Deviations	72

Similar Tables can be set out for deviations between Asset (1) and (3) and (1) and (4) and so on. The above table gives only for Assets (1) and (2).

If the sum of derivations is 72 and there are 3 securities, then the covariance is $\frac{72}{3} = 24$, and coefficient of correlation is $= \frac{24}{\sqrt{24} \times \sqrt{24} = 24} = +1$

Let the sum of deviations of security (1) and (3) be = 108, then covariance is $\frac{-108}{3} = -36$ and sum of deviations of 1 is 24 and of 3 is 54, then the coefficient of correlation is $\frac{-36}{\sqrt{24} \times \sqrt{54} = 36} = -1$ (see next page for explanation)

Thus, the coefficient of variation changes between + 1 and –1 and a matrix of covariances between 1 and other assets and between 2 and other assets etc., can be worked out and presented.

The formula for variance is as follows:

$$\sigma^2 = \Sigma P_{ij} (R_{ij} - R_i)^2 \qquad \sigma^2 \text{ is variance and } \sigma \text{ is standard deviation}$$

($\sqrt{\sigma^2}$ or standard deviation = σ)

$$\text{variance} = \frac{\text{sum of squared deviations}}{\text{N = number of assets}}$$

For illustration take the following table for deviations between assets (1) and (3)

Table 5

Market Condition	*Deviation of Security 1*	*Deviation of Security 3*	*Product of Deviations*
Good	15 – 9	1 – 10	– (6 × 9) = –54
Average	9 – 9	10 – 10	9 × 0 = 0
Bad	3 – 9	19 – 10	– (6 × 9) = –54
			–108

Total of squared deviations for security (1)

is = 36 + 0 + 36 = 72

$$\text{variance} = \frac{72}{3} = 24$$

Total of squared deviations for security (3)

81 + 0 + 81 = 162

$$\text{variance} = \frac{162}{3} = 54.$$

Let us study covariance now.

The sum of deviations between assets 1 and 3 in –108. Then

$$\text{covariance is } \frac{-108}{3} = -36$$

Correlation coefficient between (1) and (3)

$$\text{is} = \frac{-36}{\sqrt{24} \times \sqrt{54} = 36} = \frac{-36}{36} \ -1$$

Risk Measure of Dispersion

The variability of returns can be from zero to infinity, which is most risky and on the other hand, a safe and fixed income is least risky.This variability or dispersion is measured by the deviation of the actual or expected from the mean or average.

If average is R and observations are R_1, R_2, R_3.... R_n, then

$$\text{Variance is given on } \sigma^2 = \sum_{1}^{N} \frac{(R_j - R)^2}{N}$$

Standard deviation is the square root of it, namely $\sqrt{\sigma^2} = \sigma^2$

Another factor which influences the portfolio risk is the covariance of returns R_i to R_n, where R_i is the expected return on asset 1 and so on. Covariance is a measure of how returns on two or more assets move together or their inter-relations. If it is positive, they move in the same direction and if it is negative they move in opposite directions. If the positive and negative deviations are unrelated or offset covariance is zero.

Symbolically, Let P_i be Correlation Coefficient, then

$$P_i = \frac{\sigma_{ij}}{\sigma_i \sigma_j}$$; where, i and j are the assets and σ is the standard deviation and σ_{ij} is covariance.

The numerator σ_{ij} is the covariance and σ_i is the standard deviation of i and σ_j is the standard deviation of i asset. Thus, P_i value can vary from +1 to –1.

The return on a portfolio is the weighted average of the return on individual assets. Suppose if the investor has three assets x_1 x_2 x_3 in his portfolio, in which the returns and the proportion of his investment is given as in the following Table.

Table 6
Portfolio A

Assets	*Proportion of Investment*	*Relative Weights*	*Return Expected*	*Weighted Return*
1	2	3	4	5 = 3 × 4
x_1	20%	0.2	10%	2.0
x_2	50%	0.5	20%	10.0
x_3	30%	0.3	15%	4.5
				16.5%

In a similar manner the investor has to assess the expected returns on different portfolios and in different combinations of assets to arrive at the proper choice of the portfolio suitable to him. All these combinations will give him the opportunity set. He chooses one set among them with the least risk.

Risk, as referred to earlier, is measured by variance or standard deviation for an individual security and for the portfolio the covariances among securities are taken into account.

In terms of symbols,

Let σ_i^2 be the variance of Asset 1

σ_2^2 be the variance of Asset 2

and so on

x_1 is the proportion invested in Asset 1

x_2 is the proportion invested in Asset 2 and so on.

σ_{12} is the covariance of Assets 1 and 2

σ_{13} is the covariance of Assets 1 and 3 and so on.

In our example, let us take two Assets only then the formula for variance (Risk) of portfolio is

$\sigma_P^2 = x_1^2 \sigma_1^2 + x_2^2 \sigma_2^2. + 2 x_1 x_2 \sigma_{12}$

If we plug in some figures, given in the above illustrations, in the chapter, and the proportion invested are assumed is 60% and 40%. in Asset 1 and 2 respectively, then

$x_1 = 0.6.\ \sigma_1^2 = = 24$ and $\sigma_{12} = -36$

$x_2 = 0.4\ \sigma_2^2 = 54.$

Then the risk or variance of portfolio is given as σ_p^2

$$\sigma_P^2 = \left(\frac{0.60}{1.00}\right)^2 \times 24 + \left(\frac{0.40}{1.00}\right)^2 \times 54 + 2 \times \frac{0.60}{1.00} \times \frac{0.40}{1.00} \times (-36)$$

$$= (0.6)^2 \times 24 + (0.4)^2 \times 54 + 2 \times 0.60 \times 0.40 \times -36$$

$$= 8.64 + 8.64 + (0.48) \times -36$$

$$= 17.28 - 17.28 = 0$$

By the above combination of asset (1) and asset (2) we arrived at a zero Risk portfolio, which happened so due to the compensating positive and negative covariances, which exactly coincided in values. Otherwise, by such exercise we can arrive at combinations of various degrees of risk and choose the least risk combination. The combinations with the same degree of risk will give the investor's utility or indifference curve. Risk also varies with the number of scrips in a portfolio due to possible diseconomies of scale.

No. of Securities in a Portfolio

There is no rigid rule on the optimum number of scrips or assets in a portfolio. That depends on the amount of fund, investor's or fund's goals, risk tolerance and their preferences, and a host of other factors. The unsystematic risks relating to the company can be reduced as shown above, by inclusion of securities, whose covariances among themselves would offset each other, so as to reduce the risk even to zero; that is an extreme case, but normally proper diversification can reduce the risks to the minimum of any portfolio.

Normally for individuals, the risk return management is optimum for 10-15 companies, as studies on the Portfolio Management have revealed. In the case of medium size funds of investment companies, portfolio managers, Mutual Funds etc., B.S.E. 30 N.S.E. 50 or even National Index 100 should be enough for a proper management of the fund. The economies of Management of fund reach the optimum for such a number as 10 for individuals and 100 for bigger size funds of investment companies. After that diseconomies short operating due to unwieldiness of operation in an efficient manner.

RISK AND RETURN IN PORTFOLIO THEORY

What is the Objective?

The objective of portfolio management is to maximise the return and minimise risk. A portfolio is a basket of investments or assets held by an individual or a corporate body. The wealth maximisation is ultimate goal of any investor and portfolio management is a tool for that purpose.

What is Risk?

Risk is uncertainty and variability of the income/capital appreciation or loss of both. The two major types of risk are: Systematic or market related risks and unsystematic or company related risks. The systematic risks are the market problems, raw material availability, tax policy or any Government policy, inflation risk, interest rate risk and financial risk. The unsystematic risks are mismanagement, increasing inventory, wrong financial policy, defective marketing, etc.

How to Minimise the Risks?

The company specific risks (unsystematic risks) can be reduced by diversifying into a few companies belonging to various industry groups, asset groups or different types of instruments like equity shares, bonds, debentures etc. Thus, asset classes are bank deposits, company deposits, gold, silver, land, real estate, equity shares etc. Industry groups are tea, sugar, paper, cement, steel, electricity, electronics, computer software etc. Each of them have different risk-return characteristics and investments are to be made, based on individual's risk preferences. The second category of risk (systematic risk) managed by the use of Beta of different company shares.

What is Beta?

In simple language, Beta is percentage change in the scrip return divided by the percentage change in market return. Here the appreciation in the scrip price relative to the market price index is considered. Leaving aside the mathematical formulae for calculating the Beta over the period of time, one can take readily available betas of well traded companies from Financial Journals and Dailies like ET, Capital Market, ICFAI Journal etc. If Beta is 1, the scrip risk is the same as the market risk. If Beta is greater than 1, the scrip risk is more than the market risk, and if Beta is less than 1, the scrip risk is less than the market risk. The Defensive or risk averse investors should invest in scrips with Beta less than 1. Aggressive risk takers would prefer scrips with Beta greater than 1.

Risk-return Analysis

All investments are risky. The higher the risk taken, the higher is the return. But proper management of risk involves the right choice of investments whose risks are compensating. The total risks of two companies may be different and even lower than the risk of a group of two companies if their risks are offset by each other. Thus, if the risk of Reliance is represented by Beta of 1.90 and of Dr. Reddy's at 0.70 the total of these two is 1.30, on average. But the actual Beta of the group of these two may be less than that due to the fact that covariances of these two may be negative or independent.

Degree of Risk and Risk Free Return

Risk on some assets is almost zero or negligible. The examples are Bank deposits, where the maximum return is 7.5%. Similarly, investments in Treasury bills, Government Securities etc., are also risk-free or least risky. Their return is about 7%-7.5%. The riskiness of assets can be represented diagrammatically as in Fig. 20.3.

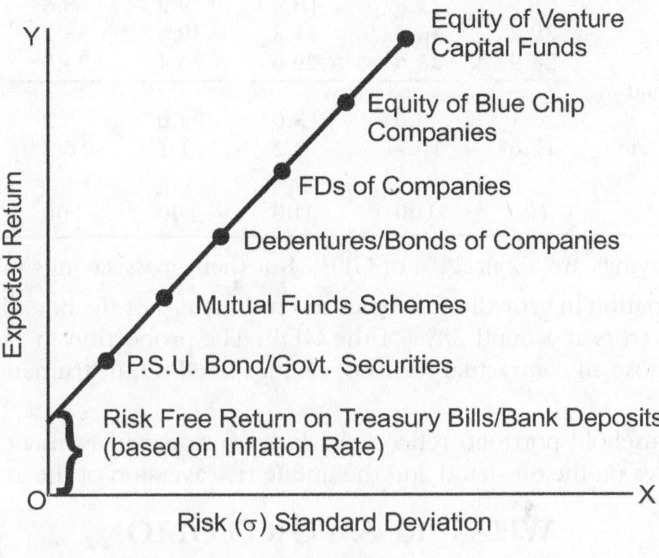

Fig. 20.3

Capital Market Instruments

The main capital market instruments, one can invest and include in his portfolio are as follows:

(a) Equity shares.
(b) Preference shares.
(c) Debentures, convertible and non-convertible.
(d) Secured premium notes.
(e) Zero coupon bonds.
(f) Discount bonds and deep discount bonds, etc.

Money Market Instruments

The main money market instruments, available for investment include:

1. Treasury bills.
2. Commercial paper.
3. Commercial bills.
4. Certificates of deposits.
5. Participation certificates.
6. Repos.
7. Inter-bank money etc.

The above instruments are discussed in other chapters.

Macro Profile of Households in India – Household Savings in Financial Assets (RBI data)

(in percentage to total financial assets)

In Forms of	*1992-93*	*1994-95*	*1998-99*	*2004-05*	*2006-07*	*2008-09*	*2011-12*	*2012-13*
1. Cash/Currency	8.9	13.3	10.9	9.2	8.6	12.5	11.3	10.2
2. Deposits	39.2	43.4	44.3	39.4	55.7	58.5	52.8	56.2
3. Insurance PF Pension Funds	28.9	23.6	29.6	26.4	24.5	29.6	38.7	21.4
4. Claims on Government PO and	–							
Government Bonds	5.4	9.0	13.0	24.0	5.2	–3.2	–2.1	9.8
5. Shares and Debentures, UTI, etc.	17.6	10.7	2.2	1.1	6.3	2.6	0.7	2.1
								0.3
	100	100	100	100	100	100	100	100

Total household sector savings are about 24% of GDP. But their gross savings in financial assets are 12% only.

Due to inflation and stagnation in growth of incomes the real savings of the household sector stagnates at around 24% of the GDP and for all sectors at around 38% of the GDP. The proportion in cash and deposits and insurance and PF have increased while those an contractual forms of savings like P.O. instruments and Government bonds and shares etc., declined.

The above picture of household portfolio reflects the lack of proper investment expertise and appreciation of portfolio management principles on the one hand and the undue risk aversion of the average household on the other.

WHAT IS A PORTFOLIO?

As the investors acquire different sets of assets of financial nature, such as gold, silver, real estate, buildings, insurance policies, post office certificates, NSC or NSS etc., they are making a provision for future. The risk of each of such investment is to be understood before hand. Normally the average householder keeps most of his income in cash or bank deposits and assumes that they are safe and least risky. Little does he realise that they also carry a risk with them — the fear of loss or actual loss or theft and loss of real value of these assets through the rise in price or inflation in the economy. Cash carries no interest or income and bank deposits carry a nominal rate of 4% on savings deposits, no interest on current account and a maximum of 9.5% on term deposits or fixed deposits of banks. The liquidity on Fixed deposits is poor as it has to wait for the period to maturity or take loan on such amount but at a loss of income due to penal rate. Generally risk averters invest only in banks, P.O. and UTI and mutual funds. Gold, silver real estate, Nidhis, and chit funds are the other avenues of investment for average Householder, of middle and lower income groups. If the investor desired to have a real rate of return which is substantially higher than the inflation rate he has to invest in relatively more risky areas of investment like shares and debentures of companies or bonds of Government and Semi-Government agencies or deposits with companies and firms. Investment in Chit funds. Nidhis, company deposits, and in private limited companies has the highest risk. But the basic principle is that the higher the risk, the higher is the return and the investor should have a clear perception of the elements of risk and return when he makes investments. Risk-return analysis is thus essential for the investment and portfolio Management.

Definition of Portfolio

Many times the investors go on acquiring these assets in an *ad-hoc* and unplanned manner and the result is high risk, low return profile which they may face. All such assets would constitute his portfolio and the wise investor not only plans his portfolio as per his risk return profile or preferences, but manages his portfolio efficiently so as to secure the highest return for the lowest risk possible at that level of investment. This in short is the portfolio management.

Speculative Instinct

Out of available savings, many investors first start with making application for new issues in the capital market. By chance if they get allotment, they are in the market and they accumulate such investments or sell them in the stock market immediately after listing. This is possible if the price quoted after listing is higher than the initial offer price and if the investor is interested in speculation and not investment. If the issue is not appreciating after listing, or if he is a long-term investor, he will keep such investments. In cases where he accumulates the shares of many companies without any plan or design, such investors, if they are not well informed about the market, will end up with a dead weight of paper certificates, without much worth. When they really want money back and if their investments turn out to be trash, they lose their wealth and burn their fingures, particularly in a bearish phase, where prices are on downtrend.

Precautions for Investment

All investors should therefore plan their investments first to provide for their requirements of comfortable life with a house, real estate, physical assets necessary for comforts and insurance for life, and accident, and make a provision for a provident fund and pension fund etc., for a future date. They have to take all needed precautions for a comfortable life, before they enter the stock market as it is most risky. But rarely any such plan or design is noticed among investors as they start investment in these markets on the advise of friends, relatives and agents or brokers, without much of premeditation or preparation.

There is a trade-off between risk and return. If you want more return, you take more risk but the art of portfolio management is that you plan to get more return without taking more risk.

21

CAPITAL MARKET THEORY

Valuation of assets or investments is the subject-matter of security analysis, which the book deals with. In valuation of investments, one has to consider his assets in the portfolio as a part of his total investments. In considering the portfolio, not only returns are to be considered as in the case of single investment but their risks also. Two plus two will not make it four in the aggregation of risks, as shown by famous Author, Markowitz. So the risks in a portfolio of assets will not be the total of individual risks of investments, made; it can be more or less than the total. The objective of investor is to minimise the risk for a given return and capital market theory deals with that subject.

Content of Capital Market Theory

Capital market theory is an extension of the portfolio theory of Markowitz. The portfolio theory explains how rational investors should build efficient portfolio based on their risk-return preferences. Capital Market Asset Pricing Model (CAPM) incorporates a relationship, explaining how assets should be priced in the capital market.

Assumptions of Capital Market Theory are:

(1) Investors are expected to make decisions based solely on risk-return assessments (expected returns and standard deviation measures).

(2) The purchase and sale transactions can be undertaken in infinitely divi-sible units.

(3) Investors can sell short any number of shares without limit.

(4) There is perfect competition and no single investor can influence prices, with no transactions costs, involved.

(5) Personal income taxation is assumed to be Zero.

(6) Investors can borrow/lend, the desired amount at riskless rates.

Efficient Frontier

The above assumptions, although some of them are unrealistic provide a basis for an efficient frontier line common to all. Different expectations lead to different frontier lines. If borrowing and lending is introduced the efficient frontier line can be thought of as a straight line. Lending is like investing in a riskless security say of R_f in the Fig. 21.1.

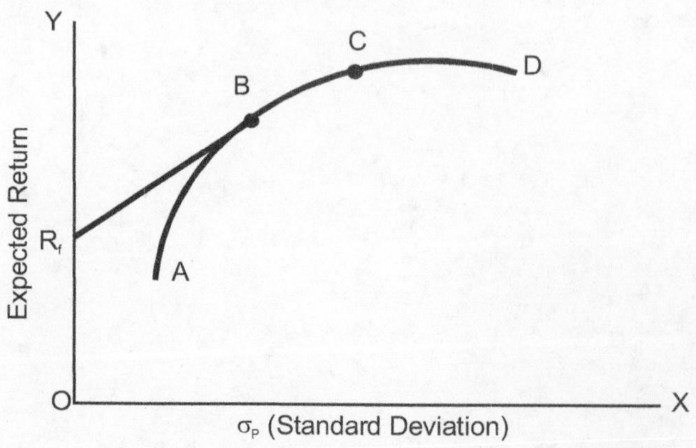

Fig. 21.1 Efficient Frontier with Introduction on Lendings

R_f = Risk free investment. If he places part of his funds in Risk free assets (R_f) and part of his funds in risky securities (B) along the efficient frontier, he would generate portfolios along the straight line segment R_fB.

$R_p = XR_m + (1 - x) R_f$

where, R_p = expected return on portfolio

X = percentage of funds invested in risky portfolio

$(1 - x)$ = percentage of funds invested in riskless asset

R_m = expected return on risky portfolio

R_f = expected return on riskless asset

and $\sigma_p \times \sigma_m$

σ_p = expected standard deviation of the portfolio

σ_m = expected standard deviation on risky portfolio

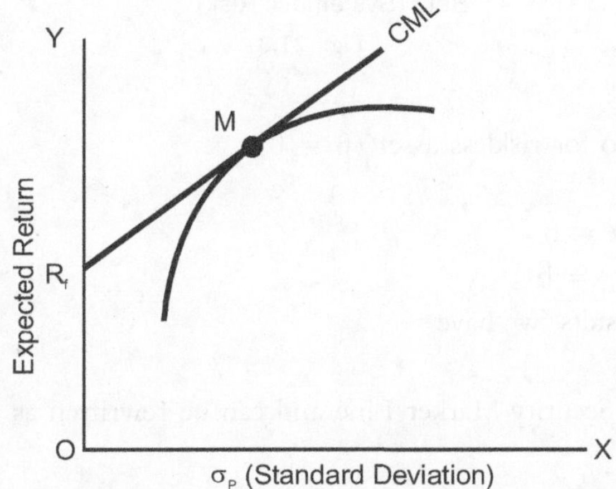

Fig. 21.2 Efficient Frontier with Borrowings and Lending

Introduction of both borrowing and lending has given us an efficient frontier that is a straight line throughout as shown in the Fig. 21.2. M is the optimal portfolio of risky investments. The decision to purchase at M is the investment decision and the decision to buy some riskless asset (lend) or to borrow (leverage the portfolio) is the financing decision.

Capital Market Line

If all the investors hold the same risky portfolio, then in equilibrium, it must be the market portfolio. In that sense RfM straight line is the *Capital Market Line* (CML). All investors choose along this line and efficient portfolios will be on this line. Those which are not efficient will however fall below the line. The equation of the capital market line connecting the riskless asset with a risky portfolio is

$$R_e = R_f + \frac{R_M - R_F}{\sigma_M} \sigma_e$$

Subscript (e) denotes the efficient portfolio. $Rm - Rf/\sigma_m$ can be thought as the extra return that can be gained by increasing the amount of risk on an efficient portfolio by one unit. Thus, $\frac{R_M - R_F}{\sigma_M} \times \sigma_e$ can be taken to represent the market price of risk times the amount of risk in the portfolio. R_f is the riskfree return for abstaining consumption for period one. Thus, R_f is the price of time. σ_e is risk on the portfolio.

Security Market Line

In case of portfolios involving complete diversification, where the unsystematic risk tends to zero, there is only systematic risk measured by Beta (β) the only dimension of a security, which concerns us are expected return and Beta. We have seen earlier that all portfolios of investments lie along a straight line in the return to Beta space. To determine this line we need to connect the Intercept (where Beta is zero as it is riskless security), and the market portfolio (Beta of one and return of R_M). These points are R_f and M in the graph below (Fig. 21.3). The equation of that straight line is Security Market Line (SML):

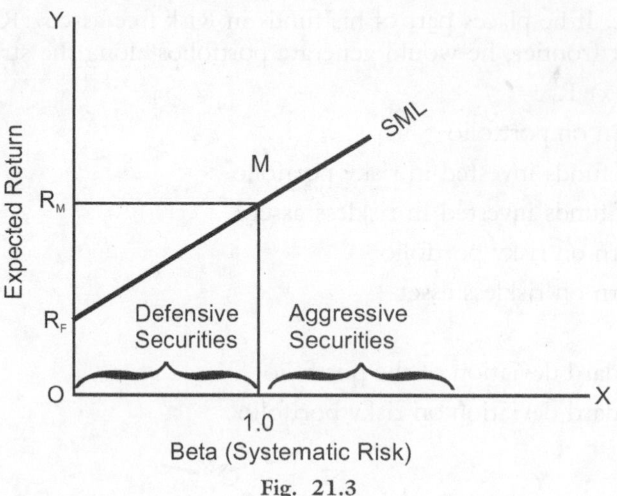

Fig. 21.3

$R_i = \alpha + b\,\beta_i$

$R_F = \alpha$ as $b\,\beta_i$ becomes zero for riskless asset ($\beta = 0$)

where, $\beta = 1$

$R_M = \alpha + b\,(1)$ or $R_M - \alpha = b$

Since $R_F = \alpha$, then $R_M - R_F = b$

Combining the above two results, we have

$R_i = R_F + \beta_i\,(R_M - R_F)$

This is the key equation for Security Market Line and can be rewritten as $R_i - R_F = \beta_i\,(R_M - R_F)$

CAPM

As Betas differ according to the market proxy, that they are measured against, then in effect, CAPM, has not been and cannot be tested. We may recall that CAPM states that

Total Return = Risk free rate + Beta (Market Return – Risk free rate)

A security with a zero Beta should give a risk free return. In actual results, these zero beta returns are higher than the risk free return indicating that there are some non-Beta risk factors or some left over unsystematic risk.

Besides, although, in the long-run, high Beta portfolios have provided larger returns than low-risk ones, in the short-run, CAPM Theory and the empirical evidence diverge strikingly and sometimes the relationship between risk and return may turn out to be negative which is contrary to CAPM Theory.

It can thus be concluded that CAPM Theory is a neat Theoretical exposition. The CML and SML are the lines reflecting the *total risk* and *systematic risk* elements in the portfolio analysis, respectively. But in actual world, the CAPM is not in conformity with the real world risk-return trends and empirical results have not always supported the Theory atleast in the short-run.

Market Efficiency and CAPM

The theory of Market Efficiency and Random Walk Theory explain the price formation through the absorption of information in a perfect manner and postulate that prices move in a random fashion independent of past trends. The market is said to be efficient, if price is determined by competitive forces of supply and demand based on the free flow of correct and full information. In the real world, information is not free and complete. There are trends in which prices move and technical analysis is the answer and the Dow Theory is applicable here. If the market absorption and information flows are not perfect, market prices move around the intrinsic worth of the shares but may not reach them. The actual pricing of shares is to be evaluated in terms of its earnings potential (EPS), Book value, dividend distribution, P/E ratio and a host of other financial ratios and a forecast of the prices is to be made to assess whether the share is overpriced or underpriced. Then the principle of buying underpriced shares and selling overpriced shares is adopted by the investor. If the random walk theory is disproved, then the markets are not efficient. CAPM depends on the assumptions of market efficiency, competition and free play of forces in the market.

According to the capital assets pricing model, there is an efficiency frontier for each investor and following the Markowitz model, the capital market line and efficiency frontier line can be drawn to arrive at an efficient portfolio for each investor. The efficient portfolio minimises the risk for a given level of return or maximises the return for a given level of risk. The risk-return analysis under portfolio theory helps the construction of an efficient portfolio.

In modern portfolio theory, the risk is represented by the concept of Beta in substitution of the standard deviation of expected returns in CAPM. This Beta relates the specific risk of a company to market risk and is represented by the slope of the capital market line. The scrips with a high Beta are aggressive such as L&T and Reliance. They are more risky and give a higher return than the market average. The scrips with a low Beta are defensive and have lower returns but are less risky than the market average like ITC or HDFC on ICICI. If the specific risk of a company is the same as that of the market risk, the company's risk premium (Beta = 1) is equal to the risk premium of the market. By using a proper Beta, consistent with the investor preferences, an efficient portfolio, can be constructed. Portfolio management is a dynamic process, based on portfolio theory, involving constant review of the purchases and sales of scrips and market operations, revision of the portfolio and reshuffle of investments, etc.

Thus the portfolio theory and portfolio management constitute the rational ground to base the purchases and sales of the investor. The fundamental factors of financial and physical performance of the company, provide the basis for the forecast of the prices of shares. The technical analysis of the market helps the determination of time for purchase or sale. All these together constitute the theoretical framework for investment analysis and market operations.

Risk and Portfolio

The choice of a portfolio aims at reducing the risks which are broadly of two categories, namely, systematic risk and unsystematic risk. The elements of systematic risk are external to the firm and cannot be controlled by the firm. The examples are changes in economic conditions, interest rate changes, inflation, recession, changes in the market position, etc. These risks are classified as interest rate risk, purchasing power risk (inflation) and market risk.

The unsystematic risk is the controllable variation in earnings due to the peculiar characteristics of the industry, and company management efficiency, consumer preferences, labour problems, raw material problems, etc. These are classified as business risks, financial risks, etc. The total risk is defined as the total variability of returns, which is the summation of systematic and unsystematic risks referred to above.

For a scientific basis for investment, the analyst or investor has to make a rational analysis of the market and the scrips in which he would like to invest. For this purpose, he should be familiar with factors that influence the market prices and the rationale of price formation. One should ask, what determines the prices? Why is the present price of a scrip of Tata Power at ₹ 830? Why is Tisco scrip quoted at ₹ 750 today? Is it overpriced or underpriced? Is it worth buying at this level or not? These and other questions should be analysed and understood by the investor and trader. The theoretical basis for this price formation is therefore important.

Random Walk Theory

This theory holds that no one can predict the prices of shares based on the past or historical trends. As the market is assumed to be efficient, all information is quickly absorbed in the prices, which move in a random manner and history does not repeat itself. The prices today do not depend upon the prices of yesterday. The prices have the equal capability of going up or down and it is, therefore, impossible for an average investor to earn more than the average profits except by chance. The prices move in a random manner depending upon the flow of information and any combination of shares is as good as any other combination to secure fair returns. For Indian conditions, where the markets are not perfect, Random Walk model is less relevant then Trend Walk Theory.

Trend Walk Theory

As opposed to the Random Walk Theory, the Trend Walk Theory postulates that the investor goes by the past trends and buys those which others are also buying. The trend is set by the so-called trend-setters and the investor follows the trends and is called the trend-walker. He goes by what he thinks is the trend set by the majority in the market. This behaviour is rational and justified by the logic that the market is determined by the past trends. The present is the offshoot of the past and the market absorbs the information imperfectly and as such random movements are not logical and consistent with reality. The market pattern is set by the majority and the trend-walkers follow the market trends on a day-to-day basis. In contrast to the Random Walk Theory, this theory is more realistic as the information flows are often incorrect and biased and the market absorption is imperfect. The early bird or the trend-setters who are the first to realise the changes or are better informed would start the trends in the market and generally they are the gainers. The trend-walkers are the average investors who may sometimes get beaten up in the market when the trends change suddenly against them.

Capital Asset Pricing (CAP) Theory

Under this theory, the return on each security is related to the total risk inherent in that security. This risk is made up of systematic risk related to the market and unsystematic risk related to the company. If the risk is spread over a number of securities in the market, then the company-related risks are covered, reduced or eliminated. In a diversified portfolio, the unsystematic risk is eliminated but only the market-related systematic risk remains. In this model, the return is the same on different portfolios, if they are diversified in the sense that the risk is reduced. The traditional theory that the higher the risk, higher the return is not true under this theory. The reward is related to risk and high risk scrips provide high returns under normal conditions. Under CAPM, even if a high risk security is clubbed with a low risk security, risk in total need not be increased but even reduced.

In the Capital Asset Pricing Theory, the company risk is eliminated and only the market risk remains. The market should be a free market with a large number of players who are influenced fairly and accurately by the demand and supply forces generated by the free flow of correct and perfect information. This information is digested by the market from time-to-time and the resultant prices are fair and competitive. Thus, the price of a share is determined as in an auction system and the market is the best performer and no individual can out perform the market.

This model postulates that the company risk and the market risk are related by a variable called "Beta." The following equation for security valuation presents the concept of "Beta":

$$(R_i - R_f) = \beta_i \, (R_M - R_f)$$

where, R_i is the rate of price appreciation on the scrip i (return on it).

R_f = Risk-free rate or return.

R_M is the market risk or average market rate of return and β_i is the constant, which relates the premium of the market rate over the risk-free rate to the company's risk premium $(R_i - R_f)$. While $(R_i - R_f)$ is the risk premium of the i scrip, $(R_M - R_f)$ is the risk premium of the market and these concepts are related by the multiplier named "Beta", which is thus a measure of the company's risk relative to the market risk.

Modern Portfolio Theory

This theory is closely related to the above CAP Theory. Under this theory, the companies have different types of risks. These risks cannot be eliminated completely in any investment in shares on the stock market. But the investors are generally risk averse. They would like to choose a portfolio, which is least risky but with high returns. In the portfolio theory, the risk is reduced or eliminated by choosing companies in the portfolio whose covariance is negative, which means that they are not dependent upon the same economic variables. Thus, companies manufacturing autos should be combined with companies manufacturing its competitive products like scooters, cycles, etc. In this context, it is necessary that one should classify the companies into those with positive covariance (complementary) and negative covariance (competitive). Industries and companies, which move differently to the same economic variables, should be chosen in a portfolio in order to reduce the risk.

As referred to earlier, the risk is of two types, namely, systematic risk (market-related) and specific risk (company-related). Systematic risk reflects the behaviour of individual scrip to the market behaviour. Some shares move along the market more closely than others. This relative measure of volatility of individual scrip relative to the market behaviour is given by "Beta".

Concept of Beta

This concept of Beta as a measure of systematic risk is useful in portfolio management. The Beta measures the movement of one scrip in relation to the market trend. Thus, Beta can be positive or negative depending on whether the individual scrip moves in the same direction as the market or in the opposite direction and the extent of variance of one scrip *vis-a-vis* the market is being measured by Beta. The Beta is negative, if the share price moves contrary to the general trend and positive if it moves in the same direction. The scrips which are having a high Beta of more than 1 are called aggressive, and those with a low Beta of less than 1 are called defensive. The portfolios with aggressive scrips will out perform the market. It is, therefore, necessary to calculate Betas for all scrips and choose those with high Betas for a portfolio of high returns. But aggressive scrips are also risky as they out perform the market in uptrend as well as downtrend and fluctuations are wide. If the B is 1.5, this security is more risky by 50% than the market portfolio. If B is 1, the risk of the security is the same as that of the market.

Calculation of Beta

The calculation of "Beta" is explained below:

The concept of B is defined commonly as that part of the variability of the return of a scrip which is relative to the overall variability of the market return.

The formula is $R_j = a + B_j R_M + u$

Where R_j is the return on security j, R_M is the return on market index, B_j is a measure of the risk, a is the intercept term and u is the error term introduced to estimate this regression equation. This model is commonly known as market model and Beta can be derived from the equation. For example, if the risk free rate is 10%, the expected market return is 15% and B is 1.5, the expected return on the security should be worked out as follows:

Risk free rate + B [expected return on market Portfolio – Risk free rate] = 10 + 1.5 (15 – 10) = 10 + 7.5 = 17.5%.

While the market rate is 15%, the rate on the security considered gives a larger return of 17.5%, as it is more risky than the market average.

Let α be risk free rate of 10% and market return R_M is 15 and the scrip return is 17.50% (TISCO). Then β can be worked out as follows:

$17.5 = 10 + \beta\ (15 - 10)$ and then $5\ \beta = 17.5 - 10 = 7.5$

$5\ \beta = 7.5$

$\beta = 7.5 \div 5$ or $\beta = 1.5$

$$\frac{7.5}{5} = 1.5$$

Example of Beta Values

In the Indian Stock Markets, the listed companies carry less risk than non-listed companies. Among listed companies the risk of specified shares is more than that of non-specified shares, due to larger speculation in the former category because of availability of carry forward facility, and margin trading. The variation between the high and low prices indicates the range of fluctuations, which is larger in general in the case of specified shares. The volumes and volatility of prices are also higher in their case.

Beta values are calculated over a number of years and as such changes in any one year may not reflect the degree of volatility of a scrip. High risk and high volatility go together and that is seen in the case of speculative scrips like Reliance (with a Beta of 1.87) and TISCO (with a Beta of 1.52) which have got high Betas of more than one 1. But it is to be noted that even in non-specified shares, there can be high Beta values as in the case of I.G. Patro (Beta of 1.42) and Femnor Minerals (Beta of 1.94) for the simple reason that they turn out to be speculative due to some vested interests in those scrips.

Table
Volatility of Stock Price (Specified Shares)

Company	*Price as on in ₹*		*Price*	*Percentage*	*52 Week*		*Beta*	*Beta*
	1996 (Feb. 14)	*2000 (Feb. 14)*	*2012 Sept. end*	*Change (1996-2000)*	*High*	*Low*	*Value (Feb. 2000)*	*Value (Sept. 2012)*
Arvind Mills	124	18	80	–85.5	47	18	0.81	1.3
A.C.C.	373	204	1470	–45.3	303	91	1.15	0.8
Bajaj Auto	816	354	1830	–56.6	650	325	0.73	0.6
East India Hotel	640	147	–80	–77.0	304	135	0.75	0.4
Essar Guj.	40	11	50	–72.5	19	6	1.07	1.5
GE Shipping	56	18	247	–67.8	30	17	1.08	0.9
HDFC	282	356	774	+26.2	372	192	0.64	0.9
ITC	289	1043	272	+260.9	1145	603	1.12	0.5
IPCL	161	101	484	–37.3	148	83	1.12	0.4
ICICI	107	150	1058	+40.2	180	40	0.51	1.7
L&T	269	473	1596	+75.8	630	166	1.14	1.4
Reliance Cap	91	172	–431	+89.0	190	28	1.72	2.0
R.I.L.	235	352	837	+49.8	380	116	1.87	1.2
SBI	248	268	2240	+8.1	295	48	1.17	1.4
Sterlite	329	734	99	+123.1	893	141	0.96	1.8
Telco	436	170	190	–61.0	326	127	0.90	0.5
Tisco	213	140	400	–34.3	183	75	1.52	1.5

Source: BSE publication.

It is seen from the above Table that there is no significant relation between volatility and Beta values and that Beta values of the past may not reflect the present or future volatility of prices. This conclusion holds good for the data of 2012. There is a large variation in the prices in 2000 and 2012, this has no relation to the Beta values. The conclusion is inevitable that past Betas are no predictors of the future prices, nor of volatility.

The above Table present the data on selected Company Scrips, their prices in 1996 and 2000, and 2012 their more recent 52 week high and low prices and their Beta values.

12/10/2012 Latest Period
Comparison of Beta with Volatility

Scrip.	*M.P.*	*A/L Volatility*	*% Change*	*Beta*
1. Appollo Tyres	88	102/52	1.96	1.1
2. Asian Paints	3995	4170/2551	1.63	0.4
3. Cipla	360	395/283	1.40	0.4
4. Dr. Reddys	1704	1818/1493	1.21	0.3
5. Infosys	2531	2930/2180	1.37	0.8
6. Sun Pharma	722	729/466	1.56	0.4
7. Tata Steel	420	501/331	1.51	1.5
8. ICICI Bank	1058	1098/541	2.02	1.7
9. L&T	1649	1657/971	1.71	1.5
10. Wipro	358	453/326	1.39	0.6

Source: Latest ET. Dailies (October 2012).

Highly volatile scrips like ICICI Bank and L&T have high Betas. So is the case with Tata Steel, Appollo Tyres, with Betas more than are. This is only a Random Sample out of the "A" group specified scrip quoted on the BSE and NSE, given for example.

Limitations of CAPM

Capital assets Pricing Model is the model tested under Capital Market Theory. This model helps the investor build his portfolio of assets through investments. Although it is theoretical, the practical application of this is the use of market Beta and individual scrip Betas to select the scrips suitable to the preferences of investors, so that the returns are maximised for the given level of risk.

The CAPM has serious limitations in real world, as most of the assumptions, are unrealistic. Many investors do not diversify in a planned manner. Besides, Beta coefficient is unstable, varying from period to period depending upon the method of compilation. They may not be reflective of the true risk involved. Due to the unstable nature of Beta it may not reflect the future volatility of returns, although it is based on the Past history. Historical evidence of the tests of Betas showed that they are unstable and that they are not good estimates of future risk. But the Betas of a portfolio may be stable. Beta values vary with the period chosen and method of compilation.

Empirical evidence showed that there is positive relationship between systematic risk and realised returns. Besides the relation between risk and return is linear. Although CAPM focuses attention on market related risk (systematic risk), total Risk has been found to be more relevant and both types of risk appear to be positively related to the returns. Another limitation is that investors do not seem to follow the postulation of CAPM although this does not invalidate the theory as such. The analysis of SML is also not applicable to the bond analysis, although bonds are a part of a portfolio of investors. The factors influencing bonds in respect of risk and return are different and the risk of bonds is rated and known to investors. The conceptual nicety of CAPM is thus broken by the less practical nature of this model and complexity and difficulty of dealing with the Beta values. Lastly, the fact that Betas may not reflect the total risk of the security but only systematic risk is another limitation of CAPM.

Investor's Wealth Maximisation

The investors prefer more wealth to less wealth. Their happiness in having wealth is measured by utility or in other words some subjective index of preferences. It is assumed here that the utility is measurable by an numerical number and the one with a higher numerical value is preferred to one with a lower numerical value under conditions of certainty, the utility function is known and the investor preference for higher utility as compared to that of lower utility is the notional behaviour of investor. In the world of uncertainty, the returns on alternative portfolios are random variables but probabilities can be attached to various possible outcomes and the weighted average can be taken. The weights are the probabilities of occurrence, associated with each of the outcomes. This treatment of the behaviour of investor through expected utility hypothesis is based on the utility Model, developed by Von Neumann and Mergenstern.

Based on some assured values of expected return and their probabilities, one can draw a graph depicting their relationship. The investor will choose that alternative with the highest value of Pu (di) – a utility maximising function. The following figure explains this.

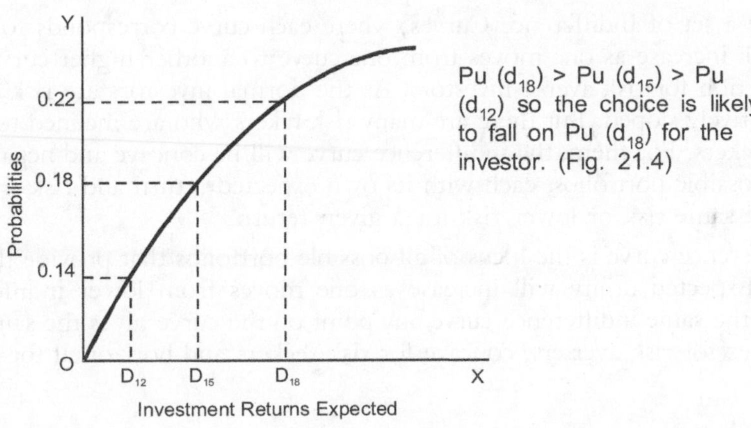

Fig. 21.4

The basic assumptions of the Utility Analysis are:

(1) Utility is measurable although it is subjective.

(2) Investor always prefers more terminal wealth to less terminal wealth — principle of non-satiation is accepted.

(3) Investors are normally risk averse.

(4) Investors behave rationally so as to maximise expected utility consistent with their risk tolerance.

(5) Normally investors put some money in the riskless assets whose expected returns are less but distribute the rest of the money in a stochastic manner in assets which yield positive expected returns, so that the investors make choices involving risk that maximise their expected utility.

There will be positive but diminishing marginal utility of wealth and decreasing absolute risk aversion. Generally such functions are positive monotanic functions which are concave toward wealth axis. As marginal utilities are decreasing with increasing investments, the investor will invest in each of the assets upto the point that marginal utilities in each of the lines of investment are equal and positive.

It is seen from the above that the Investor's expected utility could be expressed as a function of risk, measured by standard deviation of returns and expected returns. Given the vlaue of σ_2 (risk) and r_i (return) for a number of alternative portfolios, the investor can depict his choices giving equal satisfaction on what is called the Indifference Curve.

Indifference Curve Technique

Investor's expected utility can be expressed as a function of risk, measured by the Standard deviation of returns. The indifference curve is a locus of points on which the investor is indifferent between utility as return expected and its expected risk. This curve reflects the relationship of r_p with σ_p. r_p is drawn on the y axis and σ_p on the x axis, as shown below. Indifference curves can be derived from the investor's utility function and used to represent investor's preferences for risk and expected return.

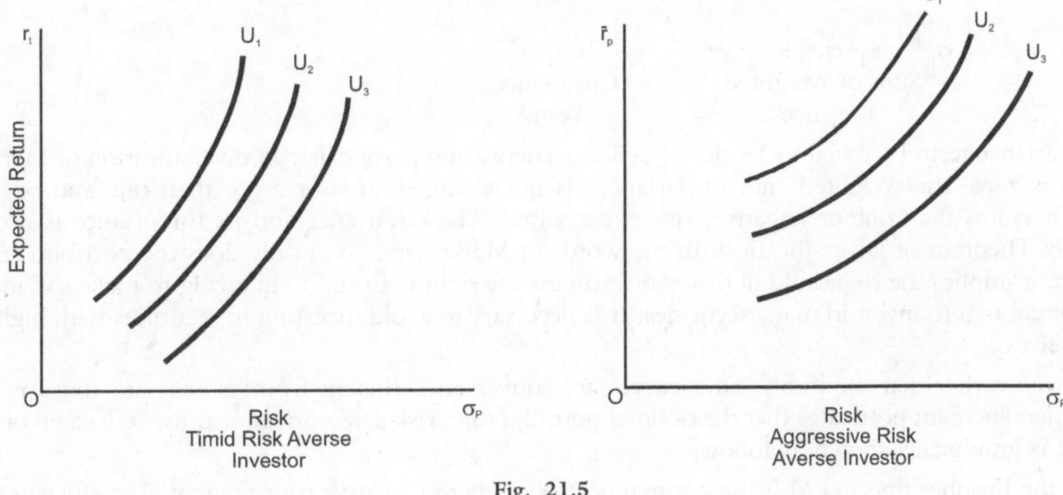

Fig. 21.5

An investor can have a set of Indifference Curves, where each curve corresponds to a given level of expected utility. Expected utility will increase as one moves from one curve to another higher curve, in the sense that it lies in the north westerly direction for risk averse investors. As the normal investors are risk averse, their indifferences curves are convex and positively sloped. But there are many risk takers who are inclined to take higher levels of risk and these are called risk seekers. For them, the indifference curve will be concave and negatively sloped, the investor can have any number of possible portfolios, each with its own expected return and risk. He prefers that one which gives higher return for the same risk or lower risk for a given return.

To sum up, an indifference curve is the locus of all possible portfolios that provide the investor with the same level of expected utility. Expected utility will increase as one moves from lower indifference curve to a higher indifference curve. But on the same indifference curve any point on the curve gives the same utility. Such curves are positively sloped and convex for risk averters, concave for risk seekers and horizontal for risk neutral investors.

Efficient Frontier

Each security has an expected return (r) and risk (σi) value and connecting these securities with lines representing all possible combinations constituting the portfolios generates the opportunity set for the Investor. With in the opportunity set, are all individual securities as well as portfolios. The outer boundary of an opportunity set is called the efficient Frontier line and with in the boundary are all possible sets.

G.J. Alexander and J.C. Francis define an Efficient Portfolio as: "one which has greater expected return than any other portfolio in its risk class or one which has less risks than any other portfolio with the same level of expected return."

The Curvature of efficient frontier is concave which follows from the covariance effect in that if one moves to higher values of portfolio (Er that will reduce the number of securities that can be held in combination so as to lower σ (risk). If the curvature is not concave, one can move from a lower return to a higher return for a given level of risk. At the outer points of the concave curve, one gets the most efficient points. This curve has to be concave only under the given assumptions, just as the Indifference Curve has to be convex to the origin for a rational risk averting investor:

The assumptions may be summarised as follows:

(1) A rational investor is risk averse.

(2) He tried to maximise his expected utility.

(3) He chooses the optimal portfolio on the basis of lowest risk (σ) or standard deviation of returns (r).

(4) Markets are perfect and information is free with no transactions costs and no taxes.

(5) The time horizon is known and fixed.

Importance of Covariance Term

For a portfolio of securities, it is not only the expected returns and variances that matter but the covariances as between these securities in the portfolio. The variances of a weighted sum is not always simply the sum of the weighted variances, since the covariance term, shown below may increase, or decrease the total sum. Thus, the equation is as follows:

$$\underbrace{\sigma_p^2 = x_1^2\sigma_1^2 + x_2^2\sigma^2}_{\text{Sum of weighted variances}} + \underbrace{2x_1x_2\sigma^{12}}_{\text{Covariance Term}}$$

The covariance term is crucial to Modern Portfolio Theory and particularly in diversification of Markowitz type. If covariance is zero, the weighted sum of variances is not changed. If it is more than one and positive, risk is increased. If it is less than one or negative, risk is decreased. The covariance and its importance is brought out in the Markowitz Theorem of Diversification. In the words of Markowitz, "Not only does the portfolio analysis imply diversification, it implies the right kind of diversification for the right reason....... in trying to make variance of returns small, it is not enough to invest in many securities. It is necessary to avoid investing in securities with high covariances among themselves.

It was seen earlier that the indifference curves are convex and efficient frontier lines are concave and that the efficient Frontier Theorem postulates that the optimal portfolio for a risk averse investor must be located on the efficient frontier. This is graphically shown as follows.

EMF is the Frontier line and M is the optimal portfolio where I_2. Curve runs tangential to efficient frontier line.

The point M maximises the utility, for a given level of risk. Any point below M is feasible but gives less return for the same risk (σ_p). Any point above M is not feasible due to wealth constraint. Investor prefers to be on a higher Indifference curve I_1 than on I_2 but it is not feasible, as it does not touch any of the possible efficient sets of portfolios. The point of tangency of the utility curve (or I_2) with the efficient frontier line EF determines the choice of the portfolio which is optimal for his given choices and preferences.

In the above graph, it is assumed that there is no lending and borrowing and that the investor invests all his funds in risky securities, as this model does not take into account the possibility of risk free investment and borrowing and lending at risk free rates.

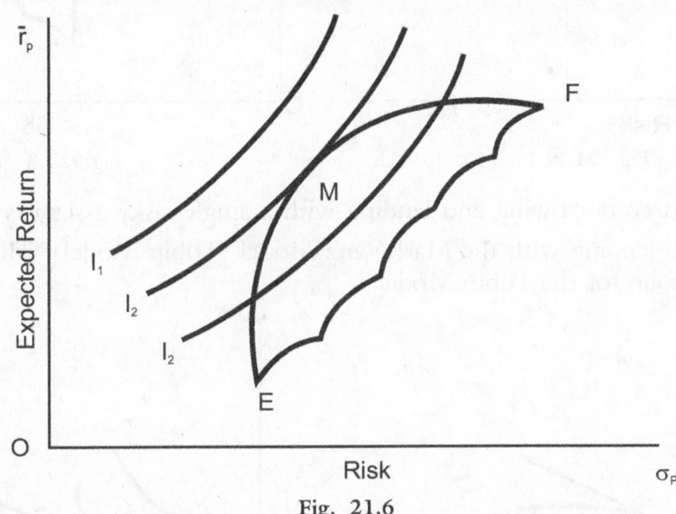

Fig. 21.6

The importance of covariance in the language of common man is the relative interdependence in terms of risk of the securities within the given portfolio. Thus, one can diversify into three companies in steel which will have more risk than three companies in three industries, say steel (Tisco), cement (Indian cement) and pharmaceuticals (Dr. Reddy Labs). The reason is that in the former case all the scrips have similar risks and the sum of the risks is say y ($x_1 + x_2 + x_3$) and the covariance between x_1 and x_2, x_2 and x_3 and x_1 and x_3 is positive and high, which makes the total sum of all risks higher than ($x_1 + x_2 + x_3$). In the latter case, the risk in cement industry is different from that of steel and pharmaceuticals. Even if steel and cement are complementary, that of pharmaceuticals will be different and covariance between cement (y_1) steel (y_2) and pharmaceuticals (y_3) may be low or negative which will reduce the sum of the total risks to less than ($y_1 + y_2 + y_3$). Thus, covariance as between the scrips included in a portfolio makes a lot of difference to the diversification Technique.

As per Markowitz diversification, the term covariance makes all the difference to the sum total risk of all risks in a portfolio because the covariance may increase or decrease the sum of the risks of scrips in a portfolio. Tobin introduced the possibility of existence of a security with no risk.

For a two security portfolio, the standard deviation can be calculated by using the following equation.

$$\sigma_f = \sqrt{x_f^2\sigma_f^2 + (1-x_f)^2\sigma_f^2 + 2x_f(1-x_f)\sigma f_i}$$

If one is a riskless asset, $\sigma^2{}_f = 0$ and $\sigma f_i = 0$ then the above equation becomes

$$\sigma_p = (1 - x_f)\ \sigma_f^2$$

If r_p is related linearly to σ_p.

$$r_p = r_f + [[r_i - r_f]/\sigma_i]\ \sigma_p$$

If $r_f = 0$ then

$$r_p = \frac{r_i}{\sigma_i} \times \sigma_p$$

The graph in the case of only one risky asset x_i and risk free borrowing and lending, is shown below:

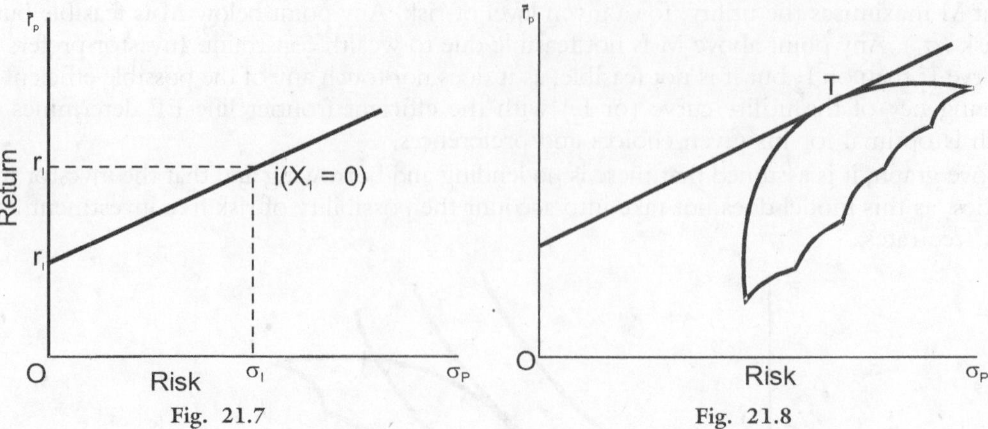

Fig. 21.7 Fig. 21.8

The position with Risk free borrowing and lending with a single risky asset i is shown in the graph below.

Risk free borrowing and lending with the Markowitz Model (Tobin Model). The following graph shows the identification of optimal portfolio for the Tobin Model.

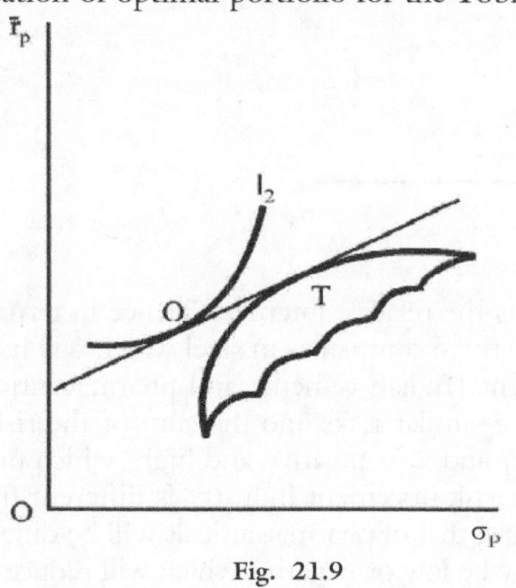

Fig. 21.9

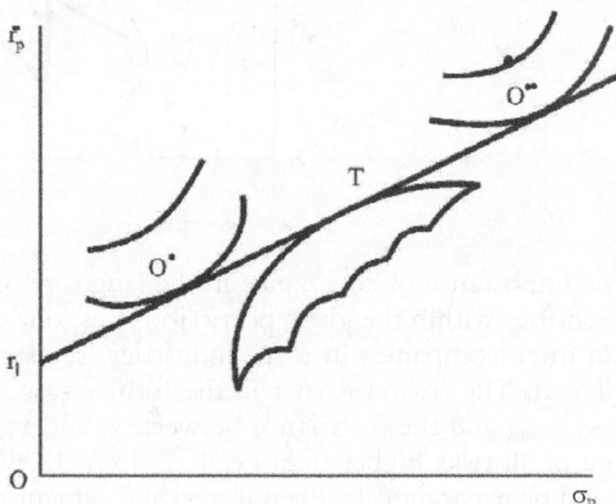

Fig. 21.10 Identifying the optimal portfolio for the Tobin Model.

Any efficient frontier line can be combined with the risk free asset or risk free borrowing and lending.

At O* this portfolio involves investing 50% of the investor's funds in risk free asset and 50% in portfolio T. Next at point O**, this portfolio involves borrowing an amount equal to 50% of investor's own funds and investing the borrowed funds and investor's own funds at point T. In that case and in general, efficient lending and efficient portfolios above T involve risk free borrowing.

Example

If you invest 60% of wealth in market portfolio and 40% in risk free asset, expected return of market portfolio is 15% and Sd is 25% and risk free rate is 10%, what is the expected risk and return of the 60-40 lending portfolio.

(Return) $E(r_p) = X_r R + (1 - x_r)\, Er_m$
$= 0.4 \times 10 + 0.6\ (15) = 4 + 9 = 13\%$

(Risk) $\sigma_p = (1 - x_r)\, \sigma_m$
$= 0.6 \times 25\% = 15\%$

where, x_r is the proportion invested

R is risk free rate (10%).

Er_m is expected market return (15%) σ_p is Standard deviation (Sd) or risk of the portfolio of investor.

σ_m is risk of the market portfolio.

RISK AND RETURN IN PORTFOLIO MANAGEMENT

What is the Objective?

The objective of portfolio management is to maximise the return and minimise risk. A portfolio is a basket of investments or assets held by an individual or a corporate body, or any economic unit.

What is Risk?

General concepts of risk and uncertainty were already discussed in the earlier chapters. Risk is uncertainty of the income/capital appreciation or loss of both. The two major types of risk are: Systematic or market related risks and unsystematic or company related risks. The systematic risks are the market problems, raw material availability, tax policy or any Government policy, inflation risk, interest rate risk and financial risk. The unsystematic risks are company related risks like mismanagement, increasing inventory, wrong financial policy, defective marketing, etc.

How to Minimise the Risks?

The company specific risks (unsystematic risks) can be reduced by diversifying into a few companies belonging to various industry groups, asset groups or different types of instruments like equity shares, bonds, debentures etc. Thus, asset classes are bank deposits, company deposits, gold, silver, land, real estate, equity shares etc. Industry groups are tea, sugar, paper, cement, steel, electricity, electronics, computer software etc. Each of them have different risk-return characteristics and investments are to be made, based on individual's risk preferences. The second category of risk (systematic risk) is managed by the use of Beta of different company shares.

Return

What is return? Investors are interested in an income from their investment either in the form of interest, dividend or capital appreciation. This is called the return. It is the key variable, influencing the investment decision and is the motivating force for people to save and invest. Returns are used to evaluate the performance of assets, in which the investments are made.

In this context, two terms used namely realised return and expected return have to be distinguished. Realised return is actually earned income of the past, while the investment decisions are made on the basis of expected returns. Thus, expected return is more important than the realised return although the latter is dependent on the former. Expected return is the return on an investment anticipated by the investor. It is that level or amount that induces the investor to invest. This level or rate may or may not be realised, which leads to Risk in Investment.

Measurement of Return

The two elements of return are cash inflows due to an investment called generally income, and the price changes leading to appreciation or depreciation of the value of the asset invested in.

Total Return = Income + price change; the total return is a measure in respect of a time period, say an year or a holding period. The income is the expected or actual cash inflows over this period and the price change is the difference between the purchase price (or the price at the beginning of the period) and sale price (or the price at the end of the period).

As an illustration, assume that you purchased a 12½% NCD of Tisco at ₹ 95 and at the end of the period you got an interest warrant of ₹ 12.5 on an investment of ₹ 95 and the price bond went up to ₹ 96 leading to a capital appreciation of Re. 1 over the period. Thus, total return in this case is ₹ 12.5 + 1= ₹ 13.5 on an investment of ₹ 95 — an yield rate of 14.2% = (13.5 ÷ 95).

It will thus be seen that the concept of total return is an acceptable measure of return for a given period of time. But the statistical measures of return for longer periods of more than one year are average returns. These are measured by taking arithmetic average or geometric average. The arithmatic average normally given by the symbol $\overline{X}$ is shown as

$\overline{X} = \frac{\sum x_i}{n}$ where, x_i is the return for the period i, during the given periods of time and 'η' is the number of years.

This measure of Arithmetic average is useful as a measure of central tendency of a number of returns calculated over a period of time. But arithmetic average is not always suitable when the growth rates are required to be measured; geometric average return is more useful as a measure of compound cumulative returns over a period of time. It is defined as the η th root of the product resulting from multiplying series of returns in the form of rates of growth. This can be represented as follows:

$$G = [(1+r_1)(1+r_2)\ldots\ldots(1+r_n)]^{\frac{1}{n}} - 1$$

Where, G is the geometric average and r is the total return or rate of return and n is the number of years.

By adding 1.0 to each return (r), we get the return relative. Thus if the return is 10%, the return relative is (1 + 0.10) = 1.10 Return relatives are useful in the calculation of geometric means because the negative rates of return can be taken into account by this method. If the first year return is 10% and the second year return is –5%, both can be used in the calculation of geometric average as follows.

Return relative for period 1 = 1 + 0.10 = 1.10

Return relative for period 2 = 1 – 0.05 = 0.95

Using the above formula, we have the following:

$$G = [(1.10)(0.95)]^{\frac{1}{2}} - 1$$

$$G = \sqrt{1.045} - 1 = 1.0225 - 1$$

$$G = 0.0225$$

$$G = 2.3\%$$

Meaning of Risk

Risk in the securities markets is associated with a number of uncertainties of possible outcomes. The realised returns may vary from the expected returns in direction as also in degree. The degree of variance may be anything from Zero to Infinity. The words risk and uncertainty are not the same in the strict sense. Risk is a wider term and decision maker may know the possible consequences of his decision. The possibilities of the outcomes may be known in some cases. But the burden of such possibilities has to be borne by him. In the case of uncertainties, the outcomes are not known or the possibilities cannot be predicted. Risk can be there under both certainty and uncertainty of outcome.

The risk may arise out of a host of factors both internal and external and some controllable and some non-controllable. The risk is associated with all types of assets in the securities in the market, whether it is bonds, equity or any other asset like convertibles or callables etc. The risk is measured by the variance or standard deviation, dispersion of the actual from the expected or the mean of the series. Thus the variability of the return is a risk measure, normally used. The risk associated with holding equity is the likelihood of expected return to materialise. The variation in dividends or earnings per share and the possible outcomes of the final price of stock as compared with that at the beginning of the period may lead to the risk of investor. Since so many economic and non-economic factors play a role on these variables, risk is inherent in any investment.

WHAT IS A PORTFOLIO?

As the investors acquire different sets of assets of financial nature, such as gold, silver, real estate, buildings, insurance policies, post office certificates, NSC or NSS etc., they are making a provision for future and building up a portfolio of assets. The risk of each of such investments is to be understood before hand. Normally the average householder keeps most of his income in cash or bank deposits and assumes that they are safe and least risky. Little does he realise that they also carry a risk with them — the fear of loss or actual loss or theft and loss of real value of these assets through the rise in price or inflation in the economy. Cash carries no interest or income and bank deposits carry a nominal rate of 4% on savings deposits, no interest on current account and a maximum of 9.29% on term deposits of one year. The liquidity on Fixed deposits is poor as one has to wait for the period to maturity or take loan on such amount but at a loss of income due to penal rate. Generally risk averters invest only in banks, P.O. and UTI and mutual funds. Gold, silver real estate, Nidhis, and chit funds are the other avenues of investment for average Householder, of middle and lower income groups. If the investor desired to have a real rate of return which is substantially higher than the inflation rate he has to invest in relatively more risky areas of investment like shares and debentures of companies or bonds of Government and Semi-Government agencies or deposits with companies and firms. Investment in Chit funds. Nidhis, company deposits, and in private limited companies has the highest risk. But the basic principle is that the higher the risk, the higher is the return and the investor should have a clear perception of the elements of risk and return when he makes investments. Risk-Return analysis is thus essential for the investment and portfolio management.

Definition of Portfolio

What a portfolio means is discussed many times before in this book. Many times the investors go on acquiring these assets in an *ad hoc* and unplanned manner and the result is high risk, low return profile which they may face. All such assets would constitute his portfolio and the wise investor not only plans his portfolio as per his risk return profile or preferences but manages his portfolio efficiently so as to secure the highest return for the lowest risk possible at that level of investment. This in short is the portfolio management.

Speculative Instinct

Out of available savings, many investors first start with making application for new issues in the capital market. By chance if they get allotment, they are in the market and they accumulate such investments or sell them in the stock market immediately after listing. This is possible if the price quoted after listing is higher than the initial offer price and if the investor is interested in speculation and not investment. If the issue is not appreciating after listing, or if he is a long-term investor, he will keep such investments. In cases where he accumulates the shares of many companies without any plan or design, such investors, if they are not well informed about the market, will end up with a dead weight of paper certificates, without much worth. When they really want money back and if their investments turn out to be trash, they lose their wealth and burn their fingures, particularly in a bearish phase, when prices are on downtrend.

Precautions for Investment

All investors should therefore plan their investments first to provide for their requirements of comfortable life with a house, real estate, physical assets necessary for comforts and insurance for life, and accident, and make a provision for a provident fund and pension fund etc., for a future date. They have to take all needed precautions for a comfortable life, before they enter the stock market as it is most risky. But rarely any such plan or design is noticed among investors as they start investment in these markets on the advise of friends, relatives and agents or brokers, without much of premeditation or preparation.

The following chart shows the trade off between risk and return. If you want more return, you take more risk and if no risk is taken, only bank deposits are used.

At R_0 risk, the reward is only OM. If we take a higher risk of R_1, the reward will increase to ON. Reward is desirable, risk is undesirable. Hence, the investor who wants the risk taken to be only R_o; but return to be ON he has to plan his Investments in Portfolio. This is what in essence is called Portfolio Management (Fig. 22.1).

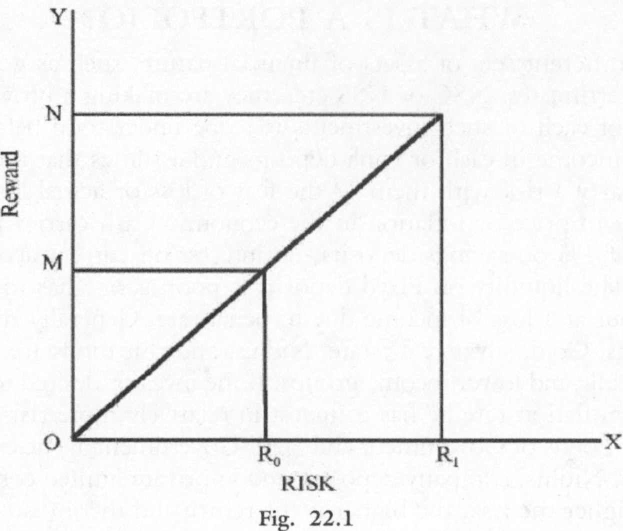

Fig. 22.1

Decomposition of Return

The portfolio return is related to risk. There is also a risk free return, which is secured by any investor by keeping his funds in say commercial or cooperative bank deposits or post office deposits or certificates. Beyond the risk free rate, the excess return or premium depends on many factors like the risk taken, expertise in selectivity or selection, return due to diversification and return for expertise of portfolio Manager.

Fama has presented the decomposition of actual returns into its components. Thus, there is risk free return, excess return, risk premium for taking risk, etc. There is also a return for selecting the proper assets and extra return for the expertise of the portfolio Manager.

An example will make the above statement clear, for which the following values can be taken:

Return an Portfolio $R_p = 8\%$

Return on Market Portfolio = 9%

Risk free Rate = 2%

Risk related to SML (Diversification) = 6.5 (RSML)

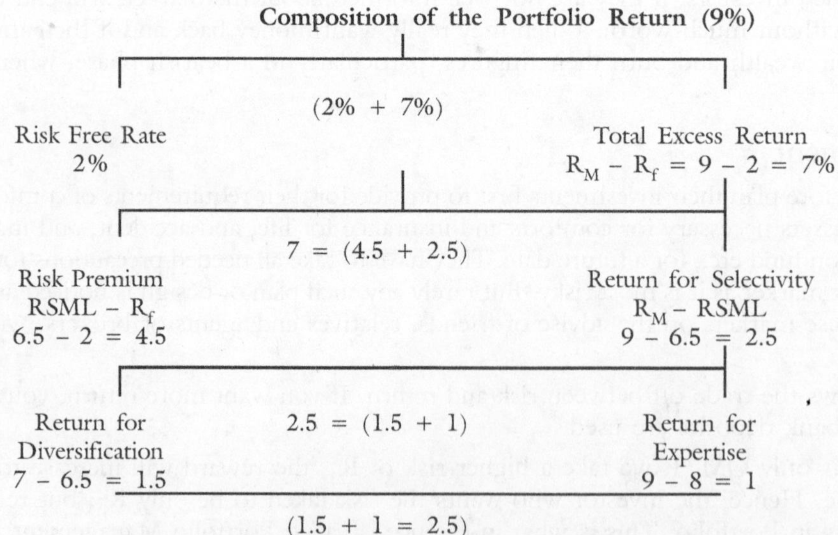

The formula for return is as follows:

$R_i = R_f + \beta(R_M - Rfs)$, where, β is Beta of the Company and β is the systematic risk.

Problem

Given $R_f = 10\%$ and $R_m = 15\%$ where, R_f is risk free rate and R_m is the market return and the Expected return and Betas of 4 companies are given below.

	Company	Expected Return	Expected Beta
	1	17.0%	1.3
	2	14.5%	0.8
	3	15.5%	1.1
	4	18.0%	1.7
Answer	Ri_1 =	10 + (15 – 10) 1.3 =	16.5
	Ri_2 =	10 + (15 – 10) 0.8 =	14.0
	Ri_3 =	10 + (15 – 10) 1.1 =	15.5
	Ri_4 =	10 + (15 – 10) 1.7 =	18.5

Compared with the Expected return given above, those calculated on the basis of formula for return premium companies 1 and 2 are under valued. Number 3 company is fairly valued and Number 4 Company is overvalued. The calculation of Return and Risk in a portfolio is explained with the following example.

Question

(1) The equity of Orient and Crompton have expected returns of 15% and 20% and the standard deviations (risk) of 20% and 40%. The coefficient of correlation of these two stocks is 0.36.

(a) What is the expected return and standard deviation of portfolio consisting of 40% of Orient and 60% of Crompton?

(b) What is r and s of the portfolio consisting of 60% of Orient and 40% of the Crompton?

Answer:

(a) $R_p = 0.4\ (.15) + 0.6\ (.2)$

$= .06 + 0.12 = 0.18 = 18\%.$

Variance, $\sigma^2_p = [(0.4)^2 \times (1.0) \times (0.2)^2] + [(0.6)^2 \times 1.0 \times (0.4)^2]$

$+[2 \times (0.4) \times (0.6)(0.36) \times 0.2 \times 0.4]$

$= [0.16 \times 1 \times 0.04] + [0.36 \times 1 \times 0.16] + [2 \times .006912]$

$= .0064 + .0576 + .0138$

$= .0778$

$\sigma^2_p = 0.0778$

SD or $\sigma_p = \sqrt{0.0778} = 27.9\%$

What is used to multiply the first and second terms namely $(0.4)^2\ (1.0) \times (0.2)^2$ and $(0.6)^2 \times 1 \times (0.4)^2$ represent? The correlation coefficient for their own variance terms which is 1.0 and the third term represents the covariance.

(b) $R_p = 0.6\ (0.15) + .4 \times (0.2)$

$= 0.09 + 0.8 = 0.17 = 17\%$

$\sigma^2_p = [(0.6)^2 \times 1 \times (.2)^2] + [(0.4)^2 \times 1 \times (0.4)^2] + [2(0.6)\ (0.4)\ (0.36) \times (0.2)\ (0.4)]$

$\sigma^2 = 0.36 \times .04 + 0.16 \times 0.16 + .013824$

$= .0144 + 0.0256 + .013824$

$= 0.0538$

$\sigma = \sqrt{.0538} = 23.2\%.$

	Return	Standard Deviation (Risk)
Orient	18	27.9
Crompton	17	23.2

Crompton has lesser risk and lesser return.

CAPITAL ASSET PRICING MODEL (CAPM)

The CAPM was developed to explain how risky securities are priced in market and this was attributed to experts like Sharpe and Lintner. Markowitz theory being more theoretical, CAPM aims at a more practical approach to stock valuation.

It is no doubt based on the mean-variance approach to risk for assessment of investment as developed by Markowitz. It explains the behavioural pattern of investors in building up portfolios.

CAPM Assumptions

The CAPM is based on certain assumptions some of which are common to CAPM and MPT. CAPM is in fact developed as part of MPT (Modern Portfolio Theory). The assumptions are first set out below:

1. The investor aims at maximising the utility of his wealth, rather than the wealth or return. The difference between them is that individual preferences are taken into account in the utility concept. While some have preference for larger risk who will have increasing marginal utility for wealth, for others, with less preference for risk, the incremental wealth will be less attractive if it is attached with more risk. Thus, the preference of investors for risk return will be taken into account in this model.

2. Investors have similar expectations of Risk and Return. Without these consensus standards, the estimates of mean and variance may lead to different forecasts with the result that the efficient portfolio of each will be different from that of the others. There will be innumerable efficient frontiers, each dependent on the set of preferences of individuals for risk and return. If investors do not have similar expectations, there will be no homogeneity in their conception and no single efficient frontier line will apply to all.

This in turn will imply that the price of an asset, which is the best estimate of the present value of future returns will be different for different investors. This assumption is therefore unrealistic for application in the real world. But this is exactly the reason why there are always some buyers and others as sellers of the same scrip. Different persons have different valuations of the same scrip, depending on their preferences and estimates.

3. Investors make investment decision on a rational basis, depending on their assessment of risk and return. Risk is measured by two factors, mean and variance. In the CAPM, we assume that rational investors diversify away their diversifiable risk, namely, unsystematic risk and only systematic risk remains which varies with the Beta of the security. While some use the beta only, as a measure of risk, others use both Beta and variance of returns (total Risk) as the source of reward or expected return. As these perceptions of risk and reward vary from individual to individual, under CAPM we get a series of efficient frontier lines while in the case of MPT, there will be a single efficient frontier line, for the conception of risk and return expectation is assumed to be homogeneous in the latter.

4. Investors will have free access to all available information at no cost and no loss of time. If the information is not the same for all, no common efficient frontier line can be drawn. Besides even if the information is not available at the same time different conclusions can be drawn regarding expected return and risk and no single price of the capital asset can be conceived.

5. Investors should have identical time horizons which again is highly unrealistic. Investors have different time horizons and their estimates of stock value will therefore differ, even as the estimated earnings are the same per year. Continuous time models are sometimes used to get over the above difficulty or again one can approximate a single

period model as a proxy to multiperiod model on the assumption that returns are the same over time and time has no relevance to expected returns and that expected returns are again independent of the past and current information.

While the above assumptions are common to both CAPM and MPT, some assumptions are specific to CAPM. Thus, there is a risk free asset, which gives risk free return. Investors can borrow and lend unlimited amounts at the same price. This assumption of risk free asset transforms the curved efficient frontier line to a linear one. Risk can be reduced by adding a risk free asset, or borrowing at the risk free rate.

Besides, it is also necessary to assume in CAPM that total asset quantity is fixed and all assets are marketable and divisible. This assumption implies that the liquidity requirement of investors is ignored and there will be no new issues, which are both unrealistic.

After the brief review of the above assumption we can summarise the requirements for CAPM as follows:

Risk is measured by variance of expected returns. There are two components of Risk — systematic (non-diversifiable) and unsystematic (diversifiable). For diversifiable risk, the investor makes a proper diversification to reduce the risk and for the non-diversifiable portion, he uses the relevant Beta measure to adjust to his requirement or preferences. Due to the possibility of risk free asset and lending and borrowing at the free rate, the investor has two components of the portfolio — risk free assets and the risky market assets. His total return is summation from the above two components.

Under CAPM, the equilibrium situation arises when all frictions, like taxes, divisibility, transaction costs and different risk-free borrowing and lending rates are assumed away. Equilibrium will be brought about by changes in prices due to changes in demand and supply.

CML

Figure below depicts the capital market line with riskless rate of return. Point P is the riskless interest rate. Preferred investments are plotted along the line PMZ, by combination of both risky assets and risk free asset along with the borrowing and lending. The slope of the PMZ is the measure of the reward for Risk taking. OP is the risk free return, Em — T is the measure of the risk premium — a return for the risk taking. The reward for waiting is the risk less interest rate, OP, and second reward is the return per unit of risk borne measured by the slope 'a' of the PMZ line. *The internal rate can be considered as price of time and the slope of capital market line as price of the risk.*

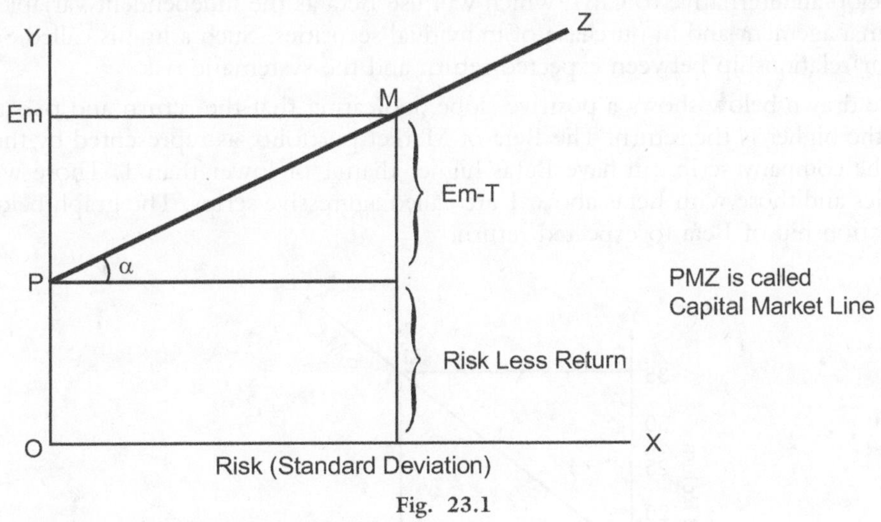

Fig. 23.1

The equation of CML, connecting the risk less asset with the risky portfolio is:

$$R_e = R_f \frac{R_M - R_f}{\sigma_m} \times \sigma_e$$

If the borrowing and lending rates are different, then OQ becomes the borrowing rate and OP will be the lending rate, as shown below in Fig. 23.2. The efficient frontier line with differential borrowing and lending rates will be as shown below:

QMN is with the borrowing rate of OQ and PMN is with the lending rate of OP and ABC is the efficiency frontier line without borrowing and lending. The curved line will become linear; if once the riskless asset of borrowing and lending at fixed riskless rate is introduced.

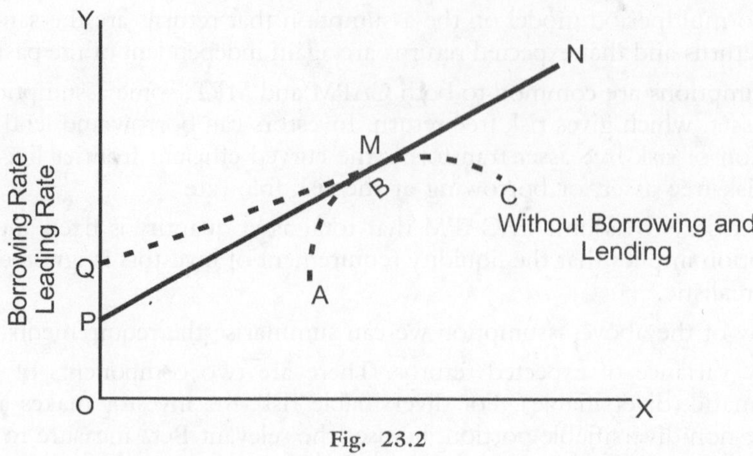

Fig. 23.2

The CML as described above reflects the relationship of total risk and expected return. Total risk includes both systematic and unsystematic risks. It may also include the risk free assets to reduce the total risk. The CAPM has two components of the capital market return, which are reward for waiting or riskless return, and the reward per unit of risk borne as measured by the slope of the CML line.

The investors will have their choice of efficient portfolio somewhere along the line of CML, as all efficient portfolios would be on it. Those which are less efficient will be below the line PMN, in the chart above. The risk free rate can be thought as the price of time and the slope of the capital market line as the Price of Risk.

Security Market Line (SML)

Unlike the CML, which considers the total risk as a measure of variability of returns, SML takes into account only the systematic risk, which is market related and is not possible to reduce or eliminate by diversification. Beta is the measure of risk of a security relative to the whole market, and is used in the SML.

Since the unsystematic risk is already taken care of by diversification in the construction of an efficient portfolio, it is desirable to develop an alternative to CML which will use Beta as the independent variable and can be adopted for use in portfolio management and in purchase of individual securities. Such a line is called Security Market Line, which depicts a linear relationship between expected return and the systematic risk.

The SML curve drawn below shows a positive slope, indicating that the return and risk are positively related. The higher the risk the higher is the return. The Beta of Market portfolio, as represented by the BSE or NSE index is always one. But the company scrip can have Betas higher than 1 or lower than 1. Those with Betas less than 1 are defensive securities and those with Betas above 1 are called aggressive scrips. The graph below shows these types of scrips and the relationship of Beta to expected return.

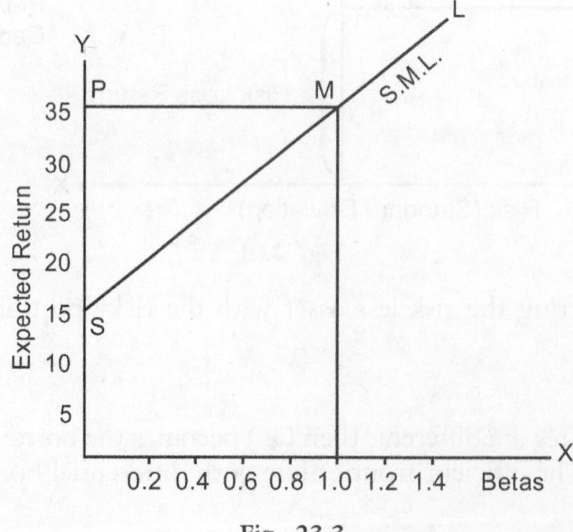

Fig. 23.3

SML is Security Market Line, OS is the risk-free return, OP is the return of the market, whose Beta is 1; those below Beta 1 are defensive and others are aggressive scrips in the market.

SML can be represented symbolically by an equation as

$R_i = R_f + \beta_i (R_m - R_f)$

R_i is the return on the security, i,

R_f is Risk-free return

R_m is Market Return.

β_i is Beta of Scrip i related to Market Risk

If $R_f = 10$, $R_m = 20$ $\beta_i = 1.5$, which is more risky than the market average, then

$R_i = 10 + 1.5 (20 - 10)$

$= 10 + 15 = 25.0\%$ which is higher than the market return

Suppose the β_i is less risky than the market at 0.75 then

$R_i = 10 + 0.75 (20 - 10)$

$= 10 + 7.5 = 17.5\%$, which is lower than the market return

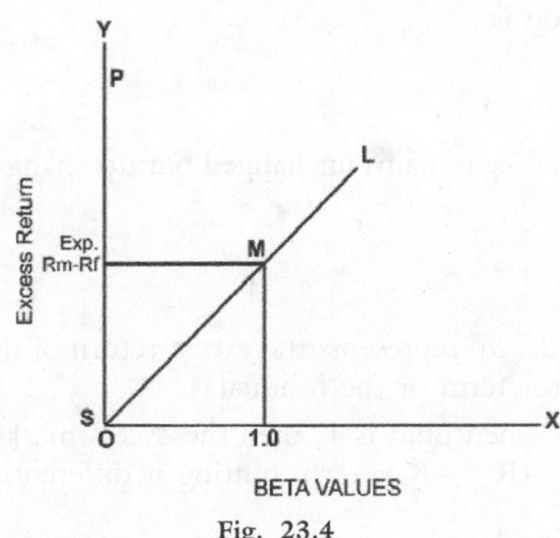

Fig. 23.4

From the above equation, we can estimate the expected return on a security. It is represented as something like a premium or discount on the market return and can be compared. It can be a return on a security as distinguished from a portfolio. If the security is correctly priced it will have $R_i = R_f = 0$ and SML curve goes through the origin (see chart below) $R_i - R_f$ measures the excess return which varies with the risk taken. Within the chart it is seen that $R_m - R_f$ is excess return if market Beta = 1. The security market line implies that the individual assets and portfolio should be on SML, if they are correctly priced. Beta values should then correctly represent the contribution to the risk of the security to the portfolio. All assets lying above the SML are undervalued and those below the SML are overvalued. If we buy undervalued securities, the returns will be more and *vice versa.* It will thus be seen that SML curve assumes a critical importance in portfolio selection and individual investment decision.

CAPM Analysis

The expected return of a portfolio in equilibrium is equal to risk free rate R_f, plus risk premium which is related to its Beta. Thus, $R_p - R_f$ = risk premium and this is equal to $\beta_{PM} (R_m - R_f)$ where R_p is expected rate of return and R_f the risk free return.

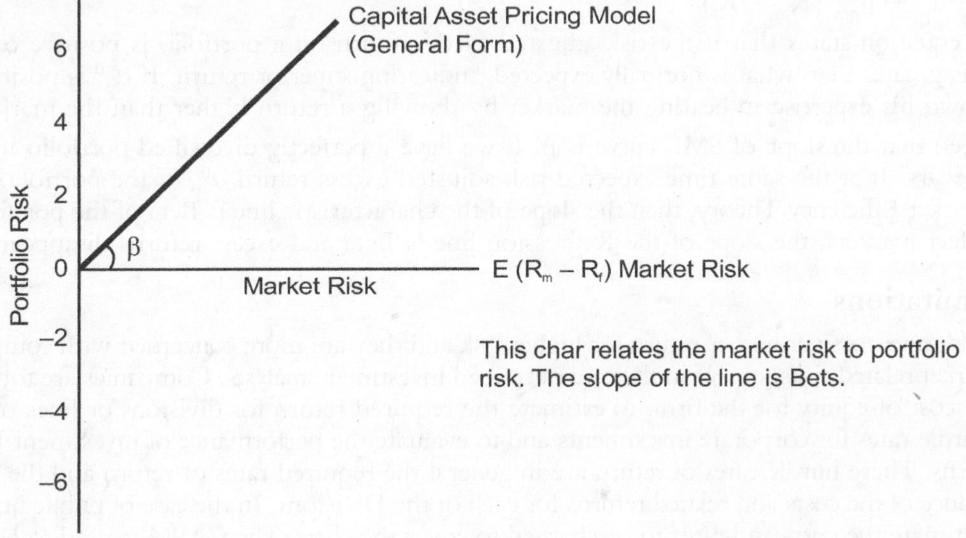

Fig. 23.5

These symbols are the same as explained above. This leads us to the market model, which relates the expected excess return of the portfolio to the excess return of the market. This is an explanation of the risk premium which gives excess returns. The chart below presents the relation of E $[(R_m) - (R_f)]$, to the E $(R_P - R_f)$ viz., in words, excess returns on a portfolio to the portfolio's excess risk over the market risk. This chart presents CAPM in a general form with expected excess market risk related to expected excess return.

Market Model

Risk Premium form is the one shown above and the equation for this is

$$\begin{matrix} R_pT \\ \text{(Premium} \\ \text{for portfolio)} \end{matrix} = \begin{pmatrix} \beta_{pm} \\ \text{Beta} \end{pmatrix} \times \begin{pmatrix} R_m - T \\ \text{Premium} \\ \text{for market} \end{pmatrix}$$

Beta relates the portfolio premium to market risk premium. If Beta is one they are the same.

Market Model can be presented in the form of a regression equation. Taking the above equation for Risk premium of the portfolio, let us introduce a new concept of risk adjusted excess return which is generated by the expertise of the portfolio Manager, represented by the $\alpha^0{}_p$. This can be graphically represented as the y-axis intercept for the regression line. $\alpha^0{}_p$ can be zero, positive or negative, depending on the performance of the portfolio.

When this model is presented in the Risk premium form, the equation is

$$R_p - R_f = \alpha_p - R_f(1 - \beta_{pm}) + \beta_{pm}(R_m - R_f) + rp$$

$$\alpha_p{}^0 = \alpha_p - R_f(1 - \beta_{pm})$$

As the risk of the portfolio remains unaffected, β_{pm} of the characteristic line remains unchanged but αp changes to $\alpha_p{}^o$ as follows:

$$\alpha_p{}^0 = \alpha_p - R_f(1 - \beta_{pm})$$

$\alpha_p{}^0$ is risk adjusted excess return

α_p is return on portfolio when the market return is zero. In other words, αp represents the excess return of the portfolio, when the market return is equal to riskless rate and rp is the error term or the residual.

$\alpha_p{}^0$ can be the same as αp, when $R_f(1 - \beta_{pm})$ is zero which happens when βpm is 1; then the excess market return disappears. The above equation now becomes; $R_p - R_f = \alpha_p + \beta_{pm}(R_m - R_f) + rp$; putting it differently,

$$R_p = \underset{\text{(Riskless Return)}}{R_f} + \underset{\text{(Risk Adjested Excess Return)}}{\alpha_p} + \underset{\text{(Systematic Risk Premium)}}{\beta_{pm}(R_m - R_f)} + \underset{\text{Error Term}}{rp}$$

If error term is dropped then the equation becomes

$$R_p = R_f + \alpha_p + \beta_{pm}(R_m - R_f)$$

The above equation states that if the risk adjusted excess return on a portfolio is positive $\alpha_p{}^0 > 0$, then the portfolio return is greater than what is normally expected, indicating superior return. If $\alpha_p{}^0$ is positive, the Portfolio Manager has shown his expertise in beating the market by showing a return higher than the market return.

We have seen that the slope of SML curve is β. If we have a perfectly diversified portfolio in the CAPM, the error term disappears. If at the same time expected risk adjusted excess return $\alpha^0{}_p$ of the portfolio is zero which is assured under Market Efficiency Theory, then the slope of the characteristic line is Beta of the portfolio. Thus, under condition of perfect markets, the slope of the Regression line is Beta and excess returns disappear $(\alpha_p{}^0 = 0)$.

Uses and Limitations

In real world, investors get higher return for higher risk and they are more concerned with company related risks than with the market related risks, except in the case of trained investment analysts. Companies are found to use CAPM to determine the cost of equity for the firm, to estimate the required return for divisions or lines of business and to determine the hurdle rates for corporate investments and to evaluate the performance of investment Division in terms of costs and returns. These hurdle rates of return are in general the required rates of return and the corporates assess the past performance of the costs and related returns for each of the Divisions. In the case of public utilities, the CAPM can be used to estimate the costs and rates to be charged to cover the costs. The CAPM is used to regulate the public utilities from the point of view of costs.

Historical return and Betas are used to select the proper risk in investments in the portfolio. CAPM is applied to select securities, construct portfolios and evaluate the performance of the portfolio. It is thus a useful tool for investment analysis and portfolio management.

The limitations of the theory are also pointed out by many critics. This theory is unrealistic for any average investor, who goes by the fundamental factors influencing the company, its earnings, dividend and bonus record. Empirical tests of the Model have not proved very useful. The Model is built *ex-ante* factors while in reality the expectations of the future vary from person to person. Data and analysis is to be based on *ex-post* factors while anticipations of future risk and returns are *ex-ante* and both may not be related. The CAPM is in fact not testable exactly as the exact composition of the market is known and is used in testing. The empirical tests conducted by Richard Roll and others were only tests on samples whether the proxy market portfolio was efficient or not. The use of surrogatives and proxies have not proved the theory as really useful and practical.

CAPM theory is thus a nice theoretical exposition but in actual world, it does not conform to the real world risk-return trends and empirical tests have not given unequivocal support to the theory. It is also found that there are many non-Beta factors influencing the returns. The calculation of Beta is itself of doubtful validity as the historical Betas may not reflect the future risks or returns. In the short-run in particular, projections on the basis of Betas on returns and risk have been found to be unreliable and results contrary to CAPM Theory were noticed. Thus, CAPM is a good theoretical tool but with its own limitations in practical applications.

Capital Asset Pricing Model

The assumptions of CAPM are that the market is in equilibrium and the expected rate of return is equal to the required rate of return for a given level of risk or Beta. CAPM presents a linear relationship between the required rate of return of a security and the market related risk or Beta, which cannot be avoided. The equation for the CAPM Theory is

$$R_J = R_f + B_J (R_M - R_f)$$

R_J is expected rate of return on security 'J', R_f is risk free return.

B_J is Beta coefficient — a risk measure for the non-diversifiable part of total Risk. R_M is return on Market Portfolio and $R_M - R_f$ is the excess return for the extra risk.

Limitation of CAPM

It is not realistic in the real world. This assumes that all investors are risk averse and higher the risk, the higher is the return. Investors ignore the transactions cost, information costs, brokerage, taxes etc., and make decisions on the basis of single period horizon. The investors are given a choice on the basis of risk-return characteristics of an investment and they can buy at the going rate in the market. There are many buyers and sellers and the market is competitive and free forces of supply and demand determine the prices.

CAPM establishes a measure of risk premium and is measured by B_J $(R_M - R_f)$ Beta coefficient is the non-diversifiable risk of the asset, relative to the risk of the asset.

Suppose Tisco Company has a Beta equal to 1.5 and the risk free rate is say 6%. The required rate of return on the market (R_M) is 15%. Then, adopting the above equation, we have

$$\begin{aligned} R_J &= R_f + (B_J)(R_M - R_f) \\ &= 6 + 1.5\,(15 - 6) \\ &= 6 + 13.5 = 19.5\% \end{aligned}$$

If the market rate is 15% then the return on Tisco should be 19.5%, because the larger risk on Tisco than on the market.

SML Security Market Line

SML plots the relationship between the Required rate of return R_J and non-diversified risk, Beta, as expressed above in CAPM.

Example

Market Expected Return = 12%

Market Risk Premium $(R_M - R_f)$ = 7

Risk free Return = 5 (R_f)

$R_M - R_f = (12 - 5) = 7$

If security x has Beta of 1.20

$$\text{Then } R_J = R_f + B_J (R_M - R_f)$$
$$= 5 + 1.2 (7)$$
$$= 5 + 8.4 = 13.4 \text{ (Aggressive Scrip)}$$

If security y has Beta as 0.80, then it is a defensive scrip. Thus,

$$R_J = 5 + 0.8 (7)$$
$$5 + 5.6 = 10.6$$

These can be represented as follows:

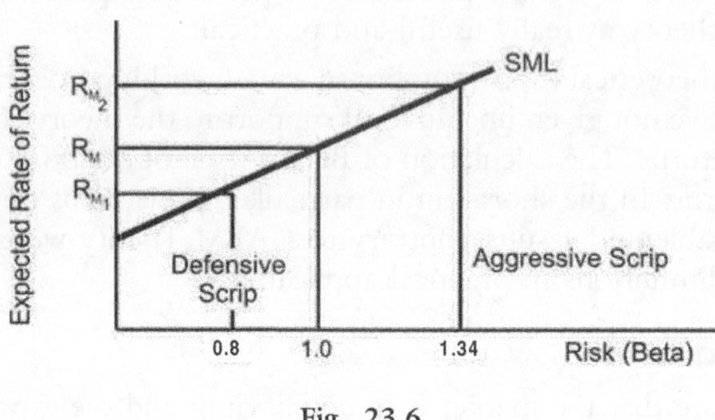

Fig. 23.6

The actual prices of securities may fall above or below the SML. The over-valuation and under-valuation can be seen from the above chart.

When we estimate the expected return after an year, in the absence of historic data on returns and probabilities the following formula which is derived from the basic formula given above is useful.

$$\text{Expected return } R_J = \frac{D_o(1 + g)}{P_o} + g$$

Where, D_o = last paid dividend

P_o = current market price

g = Growth rate of dividends.

If the above return is higher than the equilibrium rate effecting the equilibrium price — a position on the SML — both the stocks, above the SML and below the SML have undergone some changes. The expected rate has to be equated to the required rate of return, when the point of equilibrium is reached on the SML. When the expected return is higher than the required rate, the demand for that security will rise and the price will also rise, bringing down its return to the equilibrium level. If the expected return is lower than the required return, the demand will fall leading to a fall in its price, bringing it to the equilibrium level. In the former case, the investors will buy securities and in the letter case, they will sell securities.

Thus, the CAPM is useful to provide insights for the finance manager to maximise the value of the firm. Following the principle of the higher the risk, the higher is the return, the finance Manager will keep the risk level at the optimum level in performing the investment function or financing function by keeping in mind the return that shareholder expects to take at a given level of risk at the company.

The Finance Manager has to keep in mind the expected returns of the shareholders and the returns he provides should be commensurate with the risk. This risk is reflected in his investment and financing decisions. The SML provides a bench mark reflecting the equilibrium position in the relationship between the risk and return. The risk that is reflected in the non-diversifiable or systematic risk is that the company is exposed to in its operations, financing and investment decisions.

Problems

Q. An investor wants to purchase a Bond with maturity 3 years, coupon rate 11% and par value of 100.

(A) If the investor is requiring YTM 15% of equivalent risk what is the price he should pay?

$$\text{Ans:} \quad P = \left(\frac{11}{1+0.15}\right) + \frac{11}{(1+0.15)^2} + \frac{111}{(1+0.15)^3} = 90.9$$

(B) If the bond is selling at a price of ₹ 97.59 what is its YTM.
YTM is to be estimated by Trial and error method. Consider 12% as YTM.
Then

Ans: $\frac{11}{(1+0.12)} + \frac{11}{(1+0.12)^2} + \frac{111}{(1+0.12)^3} = 97.59$

Hence, YTM is 12%

(C) What is the duration of Bond, if the YTM is 12% and expected return is 10.06%?

Duration		*Value*		*% age Value*	*Weighted Duration*
1	Year	9.82	$= \left(\frac{11}{1.12}\right)$	10.06	0.1006 = 1 × 0.1006
2	Year	8.77	$= \left(\frac{11}{(1.12)^2}\right)$	8.99	0.1798 = 2 × 0.0899
3	Year	79.01	$= \left(\frac{111}{(1.12)^3}\right)$	80.95	2.4285 = 3 × 0.8095
	Total	97.60		100.00	2.7089

The duration in the case of value bond of YTM of 12% and expected return 10.06% was shown above. Then the weighted duration of the portfolio is 2.7087.

The Market Model and CAPM may not give similar results as expected excess returns and risk premiums, in the two models are not identical.

Say $\alpha_p = 4\%$, $R_f = 6\%$ (riskless return)

β Beta = 2, R_m (expected market return) = 10%.

Expected Risk Premium $(R_p - R_f)$ For, $\alpha_p{}^0 = \alpha_p - R_f(1 - \beta_{pm})$

Market Model $= \alpha_p{}^0 + \beta_{pm}(R_m - R_f) = 4 - 6(1 - 2)$

$(R_p - R_f) = 4 - 6(1 - 2) + 2(10 - 6)$

$4 + 6 + 8 = 18\%$

Where, $\alpha_p{}^0 = \alpha_p - R_f(1 - \beta_m)$

$= 4 - 6(1 - 2) = 10$

CAPM

$(R_p - R_f) = \beta_{pm}(R_m - R_f)$

$= 2(10 - 6)$

$= 20 - 12 = 8\%$

In the exceptional case when the portfolio is in equilibrium, the expected risk premium of the portfolio under both models should be identical. That happens when $\alpha_p{}^0 = 0 = \alpha_p - R_f(1 - \beta_{pm})$

Then under Market Model

The excess Premium $= 0 + 2(10 - 6)$

$= 2 \times 4 = 8\%$

and under CAPM

$R_p - R_f = 2(10 - 6)$

$20 - 12 = 8\%$

Problems

If the risk free rate is 10%, expected return on NSE Index is 18%, standard deviation is 5% (SD). Construct an efficient portfolio to secure 16% return. The efficient portfolio consists of market securities and risk free securities invested in the proportion of W and 1 – W respectively, then

$$R_p = W(R_m) + (1 - W)R_f$$
$$16\% = W(18\%) + (1 - W)10\%$$
$$16 = 18W + 10 - 10W$$
$$16 - 10 = 6 = 18W - 10W = 8W. \text{ Thus, } 8W = 6$$
$$\text{and } W = \frac{6}{8} = 75\% \quad 1 - W = 25\%$$

Investment in market securities is 75% of the amount and 25% in risk free securities. The portfolio risk in this case is

$$R_p = R_f + \frac{(R_m - R_f)}{\sigma_m}\sigma_p$$
$$16 = 10 + \frac{18-10}{5}\sigma_p$$
$$16 - 10 = \frac{8}{5}\sigma_p$$
$$6 \times 5 = 8\sigma_p$$
$$\sigma_p = \frac{30}{8} = 3.75$$

If now an amount of ₹ 10,000 is to be invested and expected return is 20%, construct a portfolio and calculate its risk

$$R_p = 20 = W \times 18 + (1 - W)10$$
$$20 = 18W + 10 - 10W \; (\textit{viz.}, 10 + 8W)$$
$$20 - 10 = 10 = 8W$$
$$W = \frac{10}{8} = 1.25$$

Since it is more than 1, borrow 0.25 or 25% of ₹ 10,000 to invest in market portfolio. Thus own funds are ₹ 10,000 and borrowed funds are ₹ 2,500, with a total of ₹ 12,500.

Risk on the portfolio is calculated as follows:

$$20 = 10 + \left(\frac{18-10}{5}\right)\sigma_p = 10 + \frac{8}{5}\sigma_p$$
$$20 - 10 = \frac{8}{5}\sigma_p$$
$$\sigma_p = \frac{10 \times 5}{8} = \frac{50}{8} = 6.25\%$$

Types of Diversification

The traditional theory laid down diversification as a technique of selection of securities in a portfolio. This is called "Random diversification" or "Simple diversification," on the basis of straight rule of "two is a better than one." Simple diversification on Random basis was found to be more remunerative by researchers and these number of scrips in a portfolio of individuals is to be around 10-15 securities.

Rational basis of why diversification and how to achieve optimal diversification were studied by later researchers, of which Markowitz is reputed to be the pioneer. "Naive diversification" or "Superfluous diversification" may result from random and indiscriminate selection of securities, which does not lead to any reduction of risk. Thus, cycle and tubes are related industries and one invests in those two types of industries which are highly correlated in a positive manner, the risk will be increased by diversification rather than reducing. Naive diversification thus means that diversification in name only which does not reduce the risk. Thus, an investor may have 10 scrips in steel, mini steel and ferrous metals, which will only increase risk. But an investor having 10 scrips spread in cycles, electronics, sugar, steel, auto, etc., will have less risk as these industries are not auto correlated and their risks are independent of each other or even negatively related.

It is thus left to Markowitz and later researchers to show that diversification is a tool to reduce unsystematic risk and how it can be reduced by a study of variances and covariances of securities return, as against the market returns.

Why Diversification?

It is never prudent to put all ones' eggs in one basket, as it may lead to total ruin if the basket itself is broken or lost. The human behaviour is normally risk averse which means that for psychological reasons, he distributes his assets in a variety of risk classes, some in cash, some in bank deposits, insurance, provident fund, pension fund etc. These are all examples of the normal human behaviour of diversifying the asset holdings to reduce risk, provide for contingency and take all precautions against total loss.

(a) Thus, the average investor never puts all his savings in one form or in one security for self-protection and for psychological reasons.

(b) Money kept idle or in some investments which do not give adequate return will be a loss to investor, as he loses the value of money over time. By logic of common sense, investors try to satisfy most of their objectives of savings by putting money in various avenues and that means diversification. The various objectives are income, capital appreciation, safety, marketability, contingency, liquidity and hedge against inflation and for future provision of larger incomes. His choice of investments will cater to these requirements which lead to diversification of investments.

Even without the theoretical basis of covering or reducing the unsystematic diversifiable risk, the investor in the traditional Theory used to adopt some methods of Diversification.

Example on Measurement of Risk

Calculation of Standard Deviation and Variance

As diversification is meant for reduction of risk, its measurement is relevant here.

DCM			*Escorts*		
Return	*Probability*	*Weighted Average Return*	*Return*	*Probability*	*Weighted Average*
8	0.15	1.20	9	0.30	2.70
9	0.20	1.80	10	0.40	4.00
10	0.30	3.00	11	0.30	3.30
11	0.20	2.20			
12	0.15	1.80			
		10%			10%

Average return is the same in both cases but risk is different. DCM has a range of variation from 8% to 12% while the Escorts has a variation from 9 to 11.

Calculation of Standard Deviation

Example DCM

Return	*Mean*	*Difference (d)*	*Square of Deviation (d^2)*
8	10	– 2	4
9	10	– 1	1
10	10	0	0
11	10	1	1
12	10	2	4
			$\Sigma d^2 = 10$

σ = Standard deviation is $\sqrt{\dfrac{\Sigma d^2}{N}} = \sqrt{\dfrac{10}{5}} = \sqrt{2}$

σ standard deviation $= \sqrt{2} = 1.41$

σ^2 = variance is 2

Example Escorts

Return	Mean	Deviation	Square of Deviation
9	10	1	1
10	10	0	0
11	10	1	1
			$\Sigma d^2 = 2$

$$\sigma = \text{standard deviation} = \sqrt{\frac{\Sigma d^2}{N}} = \sqrt{\frac{2}{3}} = \sqrt{0.66}$$

$$\sigma = \sqrt{0.66} = 0.82$$

$$\sigma^2 = \text{variation} = 0.66$$

Risk on the Escorts is lower in the above example, referred to above.

Example of Simple Diversification

Take two securities of TISCO and Reliance

Security	Expected Return	Proportion of Investment
TISCO	20%	25%
Reliance	25%	75%

The return on the portfolio by combining them would be $R_p = W_1R_1 + W_2R_2$. Rs are returns and W_1 and W_2 are weights of two investments.

$$R_p = 0.20\ (.25) + 0.25\ (0.75)$$

$$= 5\% + 18.75\% = 23.75\%$$

Here no consideration is given for risk and covariance of risk among the securities, invested in the portfolio. This can be demonstrated by taking an example of Markowitz diversification.

Markowitz Diversification

Before discussing the Markowitz diversification, what the researches of investors and investment analysts have found is to be set out briefly. Firstly, they found that putting all eggs in one basket is bad and most risky. Secondly, there should be adequate diversification of investment into various securities as that will spread the risk and reduce it; if the number of them say 10 to 15 it is adequate to enjoy the economies of time, scale of operations and expertise utilised by the investor in his analysis.

Reference was already made to Naive diversification, which is a spread of investments into many securities but will not reduce the risk, like buying ten securities all in the shipping industry, which is risky industry in itself. Besides some researchers have found that there is an optimisation process for diversification to reduce the unsystematic or company related risk by choosing such companies which are not closely related or not owned by the same family group in the same industry group. For individuals, this optimisation process leads to an investment in 10-15 companies well chosen for differences in their characteristics, nature of the product market, pattern of production etc.

Example

What is the expected return of a portfolio, comprising of the following securities:

Security	Expected Return	% of Fund, Invested
1. DCM	10%	25%
2. Shriram Fibres	15%	25%
3. J.K. Synthetics	20%	50%

$$R_p = W_1R_1 + W_2R_2 + W_3R_3$$

Rs are expected returns and Ws are weights

$$R_p = (10 \times 0.25) + 15\ (0.25) + 20\ (0.50)$$
$$= 2.5 + 3.75 + 10.0$$
$$= 16.25\%$$

Example

Given the following data on two stocks Tisco and Reliance and their returns, calculate the required measures of expected returns, etc.

Security	*Year*	*Return*	*Proportion Invested*
TISCO	1	10%	40%
	2	16%	
Reliance	1	12%	60%
	2	18%	

$$R_p = \text{Expected Return} = \frac{40}{100} \times \frac{10+16}{2} + \frac{60}{100} \times \frac{12+18}{2}$$
$$= 5.2 + 9.0$$
$$= 14.2\%$$

Calculation of Standard Deviation

$R = \sqrt{\dfrac{X^2}{n}}$ for R stock (Tisco)

Return	$(x - \bar{x})$	$(x - \bar{x})^2$
10	− 3	9
16	+ 3	9
26		18

$\sigma^2 = \Sigma \dfrac{(x-\bar{x})^2}{n}$

$\bar{x} = \dfrac{26}{2} = 13$ $\sigma = \sqrt{\dfrac{18}{2}}$ and $\sqrt{9} = 3$

SD = 3; variance $\sigma^2 = 9$

$\sigma_s = \sqrt{\dfrac{X^2}{n}}$ = for S stock (Reliance)

	Return	$(x - \bar{x})$	$(x - \bar{x})^2$
	12	−3	9
	18	+3	9
Total	30		$\Sigma(x - \bar{x})^2$ 18

$\sigma = \sqrt{\dfrac{\Sigma(X-\bar{X})^2}{N}}$

$\sigma^2 = \dfrac{\Sigma(X-\bar{X})^2}{n}$

$\left[\bar{x} = \dfrac{30}{2} = 15\right]$ (S.D.) − $\sigma = \sqrt{\dfrac{18}{2}} = \sqrt{9} = 3$

variance $\sigma^2 = 9$, SD = 3

Calculation of Covariance

Given, $\sigma r = 3$ $\sigma s = 3$

Rx = Expected Return on security x

Ry = Expected Return on security y

N = number of observations

Covariance, Cov x. y = $\frac{1}{N}$ (Rx – R$\bar{x}$) (Ry – R$\bar{y}$)

Cov. x. y = $\frac{1}{N}$ (Rx – R$\bar{x}$) + $\frac{1}{N}$ (Ry – R$\bar{y}$)

	Return	*Expected*	*Deviation*	*Product of Deviations*
Stock R	10	14.2	– 4.2	4.2 × 2.2
Stock S	12	14.2	– 2.2	= 9.24
Stock R	16	14.2	+ 1.8	1.8 × 3.8
Stock S	18	14.2	+ 3.8	= 6.84

$$\text{Cov.} = \frac{1}{2}\,(10 - 14.2)\,(12 - 14.2) +$$

$$\frac{1}{2}\,(16 - 14.2)\,(18 - 14.2)$$

$$= \frac{1}{2} \times (-4.2)\,(-2.2) + \frac{1}{2}\,(1.8 \times 3.8)$$

$$= \frac{1}{2} \times 9.24 + \frac{1}{2}\,(6.84)$$

$$= 4.62 + 3.42 = +\,8.04$$

Correlation Coefficient

$$r_{xy} = \frac{\text{Cov. XY}}{\sigma_x \sigma_y} = \frac{8.04}{3 \times 3} = 0.893$$

$$= 0.893$$

If the coefficient of correlation is high as 0.893, nearer to one, then the degree of risk in the portfolio is also high

SML Example – Security Returns

	Expected Return	*Beta*	*Sd*
BSE Index (Market)	.12	1.00	20
Riskless Treasury Bill	.08	0.00	0
Scrip A	.32	1.70	50
Scrip B	.30	1.40	35
Scrip C	.25	1.10	40

Equation for SML is as follows:

Calculate the SML?

$R_i = R_f + \beta_i\,(R_m - R_f)$

Scrip A = .08 + 1.70 (.12 – 0.08)

= .08 + .068 = 0.148 = 14.8%

Scrip B = .08 + 1.40 (.12 – .08)

= .08 + 0.056 = .136 = 13.6%

Scrip C = .08 + 1.10 (.12 – 0.08)

= .08 + 0.044 = .124 = 12.4%

CML

All investors have to choose for a combination of two components of the portfolio: (1) Market Risky Portfolio. (2) Riskless Securities. The straight line tangent to the Efficient Frontier Line is called the Capital Market Line. On this line all the efficient portfolios would be lying. The CML chooses the most efficient portfolio and this indicates the market price of risk represented by the formula.

The Return, *viz.*, $R_p = R_f + \dfrac{R_M - R_F}{\sigma_m} \sigma_p$

The term $R_m - R_f/\sigma_m$ is the extra return over the risk free rate by increasing the level of risk (Sd) of the efficient portfolio by one unit.

SML

Taking non-systematic risk as zero for a well diversified portfolio, the only relevant risk is systematic risk measured by Beta. If Beta is zero, it is riskless security. For Market Portfolio, the Beta is one. The straight line called SML is represented by the equation $R_i = \alpha + b\beta_i$ . . . . Equation 1

if $\beta i = 0$, then the first point of the line is

$R_f = \alpha + b\ (0)$

$R_f = \alpha$

the second point of the line is

$R_M = \alpha + b\ (1)$ Where $\beta_M = 1$

As $\alpha = R_f$, $R_M - \alpha = b$

then $R_M - R_f = b$ . . . . Equation 2

Combining the above two results, we have the equation of SML

$R_i = R_f + \beta i\ (R_M - R_f)$

Example

Elecon stock is expected to sell at ₹ 70 a year hence and pay a dividend of ₹ 4 per share. If the Stock's correlation with portfolio is –0.3.

σ_x 40%, $\sigma_m = 20\%$, R_f (Risk free Rate) = 5%

$$\beta_x = \frac{\sigma_x}{\sigma_m} \times \text{Correlation coefficient}$$

$$= \frac{40\%}{20\%} \times -.3 = -0.60$$

$$ERp = R_f + \beta_x R_f$$

$$ERp = 5\% + (-0.6 \times 5\%)$$

$$5 - 3 = 2\%$$

Stock price a year hence will be ₹ 70

Present selling price $P_o = \dfrac{70 + 4}{1.02}$ = ₹ 72.55

Example

Given the following data, answer the question below:

Correlation Matrix

Category of Assets	*Total Market*	σ	*RE*	*E*	*D*	*Total*
RE	₹ 10,000 (50%)	20%	1.0	—	—	0.65
E	₹ 6,000 (30%)	30%	0.3	1.0	—	0.60
D	₹ 4,000 (20%)	15%	0.3	0.3	1.0	0.30

Portfolio Mix is 50: 30: 20.

What is its S.D.? Following the formula used earlier we have,

$$
\begin{aligned}
\sigma^2 &= (0.5)^2 (0.20)^2 + (0.3)^2 (.30)^2 + (0.2)^2 (0.15)^2 \\
&\quad + 2 (0.3) (0.5) (0.3) (.2) (.3) \\
&\quad + 2 (0.3) (0.5) (0.2) (.2) (.15) \\
&\quad + 2 (0.3) (0.3) (0.2) (.3) (.15) \\
&= 0.01 + .0081 + 0.0009 + .0054 + .0018 + 0.00162 \\
\sigma_p^2 &= .02782 \\
\sigma &\quad \sqrt{0.02782} = 0.1667 \\
\sigma &= 16.7\%
\end{aligned}
$$

CAPM

Example

If the risk free rate is 8%

Market Risk premium 6%, Market SD is 10%

Calculate the variance of two portfolios —

(1) Risk free investment 30%, Risky Fund 70%.

(2) Diversified portfolio with Beta of 1.5.

Portfolio (1)

$$
\begin{aligned}
\sigma_1 &= 0.7 (10.0\%) + 0.3 (0) \\
&= 7.0 + 0 = 7\%
\end{aligned}
$$

Portfolio (2)

$$
\begin{aligned}
\sigma_2^2 &= \beta_2^2 \sigma_m^2 + 0 \\
\sigma_2^2 &= (1.5)^2 (10)^2 = 2.25 \times 100 = 225 \\
\sigma_2^2 &= 225 \\
\sigma_2 &= \sqrt{225} = 15\%
\end{aligned}
$$

Example

IndFund has three Investment strategies as given below. Find out the plan with greater risk

Strategy	*Investment in % Bonds*	*Investment in Stocks*	*Beta of Stocks*
A	0	100	1.0
B	20	80	1.0
C	30	70	1.0

Strategy	*Portfolio Beta Calculation*
A	00.0 (0.0) +1.0 (1.0) = 1.0
B	0.2 (0.0) +0.8 (1.0) = 0.8
C	0.3 (0.0) +0.7 (1.0) = 0.7

Strategy A has the largest Risk, as the portfolio Beta is highest at 1.0, as compared to B and C.

Problems

Republic Forge has a beta 1.45, the risk free rate R_f is 10% and r_p expected return on market portfolio is 16%. This company pays a dividend of ₹ 2 a share and expected growth in dividends is 10% per annum.

(a) What is the stock's required rate of return according to CAPM?

(b) What is the stock's Market price, assuming the required return?

Answer:

(a) $R_p = 10 + 1.45\ (16 - 10) = 10 + 8.7 = 18.7\%$

(b) Following the perpetual Dividend Growth model, we have

$$P_o = \frac{D_1}{R_p - g} = \frac{2(1.10)}{(0.187 - 0.10)} = \left(\frac{2.20}{0.087}\right)$$

$$= \frac{2.20}{0.087} = 25.29$$

The Numerator is the present value of Dividend stream and denominator is the required rate of return or expected rate minus the growth rate of dividend.

Asset Pricing Implication of SML

One of the major assumptions of the CAPM is that the market is in equilibrium and that the expected rate of return is equal to the required rate of return for a given level of market risk or beta. In other words, the SML provide a framework for evaluating whether high-risk stocks are offering returns more or less in proportion to their risk and *vice versa*.

$$\text{Expected Return} = D_t + \frac{(P_t) - (P_t - 1)}{P_{t_1}} = \frac{\text{Expected Income}}{\text{Market Purchase Price}}$$

In the absence of historic data, the following formula may be used.

$$\text{Expected Return} = \frac{D_o\ (1 + g)}{P_o} + g$$

D_o = Last dividend paid

P_o = Current purchase/market price.

g = Growth rate.

To reach equilibrium and their required rate of return points on the SML, both stocks have to go through a temporary price adjustment.

In practice, how does the price of say stock "X" get pushed up to its equilibrium price? Say Investors will be interested in purchasing security "x" if it offers more than proportionate returns in comparison to the risk. This demand will push up the price of x as more of it is purchased and correspondingly bring down the returns. This process will continue till it reaches the equilibrium price and expected returns are the same as required returns.

Equilibrium Price (SLM)

Problem

Short-term Government securities yield 7% and the expected market return is 12%. Stock X's beta is 0.8, its growth rate is 4% and its last dividend was ₹ 2.0. what would be the stock's equilibrium price?

Answer:

$R_x = R_F + \beta_x (R_M - R_F)$ and $P_x = D_o (1 + g) [R_x - g]$

R_x = Rate of return required on stock x

R_F = Risk free rate of interest.

R_m = Return on Market Portfolio.

β_x = Beta co-efficient of stock x.

g = Growth rate of dividend

D_o = Last dividend per share

We are given R_M 12%; $\beta_x = 0.8$; $D_o = 2.00$; $g = 4\%$: $R_F = 7\%$

$R_x = 7 + 0.8 (12 - 7) = 7 + 0.8 \times 5 = 7 + 4 = 11\%$

Equilibrium price can be worked out as given below.

$$R_x = \frac{D_o (1 + g)}{P_o} + g$$

$$11 = \frac{2(1+0.04)}{P_o} + 4$$

$$11 = \frac{2.08}{P_o} + 4$$

$$11 - 4 = 7 = \frac{2.08}{P_o}$$

$$P_o = \frac{2.08}{.07} = 29.71$$

Problem

The beta co-efficient of standard company is 1.2. The company is maintaining a 5% rate of growth in earnings or dividends. The last dividend paid was ₹ 2 per share. The risk-free rate of return and the return on market portfolio are 10% and 15% respectively. The current market price of the company is ₹ 14. What will be the equilibrium price per share of standard company?

Answer:

According to CAPM, the expected Rate of Return E (R) is equal to $R_F + \beta(R_M - R_F)$

Given $R_F = 10\%$; $\beta = 1.2$; $R_M = 15\%$.

$\therefore E(R) = 10 + 1.2 (15 - 10)$

$= 16\%$

$$E(R) = \frac{D_1 (1+g)}{P_o} + g$$

$$0.16 = \frac{2(1.05)}{P_o} + 0.05$$

$$\frac{2(1.05)}{P_o} = 0.16 - 0.05 = 0.11$$

$$P_o = \frac{2(1.05)}{.11} = \frac{2.10}{.11}$$

P_o = ₹ 19.09

Calculation of β

Problem: Calculate β_1 and β_2 from the data given:

Year	R_s	R_B	R_M	R_f *(TBrate)*	y_1 $(R_s - R_f)$	$(y_1)^2$	y_2 $(R_B - R_f)$	$(y_2)^2$	x $(R_M - R_f)$	x^2	xy_1	xy_2
1993	15	10	11	6	9	81	4	16	5	25	45	20
1994	–6	–2	–5	5	–11	121	–7	49	–10	100	110	70
1995	17	13	12	7	10	100	6	36	5	25	50	30
1996	18	9	11	6	12	144	3	9	5	25	60	15
1997	22	11	13	7	15	225	4	16	6	36	90	24
					$\bar{y}_1 = 7$	$\Sigma(y_1)^2 = 671$	$\bar{y}_2 = 2$	$\Sigma(y_2)^2 = 126$	$\bar{x} = 2.2$	$\Sigma(x)^2 = 211$	$\Sigma xy_1 = 355$	$Exy_2 = 159$

From the above Data $\quad \Sigma y_1 = 35 \quad \Sigma y_2 = 10 \quad \Sigma x = 11$

Systematic Risk =

$$\beta_1 \frac{N\sum xy - \sum x \times \sum y}{N\sum x^2 - (\sum x)^2} = \frac{5 \times 355 - 11 \times 35}{5 \times 211 - 121} = \frac{175 - 385}{934} = 1.48$$

$$\beta_2 \frac{5 \times 159 - [795\ (11 \times 10)]}{5 \times 211 - 121} = \frac{795 - 110}{1055 - 121} = \frac{685}{934} = 0.73$$

Problem on CAPM

$$V_o = \frac{D_1}{K_c - g}$$

$$D_1 = D_o (1 + g)$$

$$D_o (1 + g)^n = D_n$$

Problem

Given the following variables

D_1 = Dividend per share = 3.5%

g = growth rate = 6%

K_c = Required rat of return = 18%

R_f = Risk-free Return = 9%

β = Beta (Systematic risk measure) 1.3

$R_i = R_f + \beta (R_m - R_f)$

Where, R_f = 9%, R_M = 16% and β = 1.3.

Thus, $R_i = 9 + 1.3 (16 - 9) = 18.1$

Applying the value of R_i as the required rate of return K_c. We have the formula

$$V_1 = \frac{D_1}{K_c - g} \text{ or } \frac{D_o(1+g)}{K_c - g} = 3.5 (1 + 0.06) = 3 \times (1.06) = 3.71$$

$$= \frac{3.5(1+0.06)}{0.18-0.06} = \frac{3.5 \times 1.06}{0.12} = \frac{3.71}{0.12}$$

P_1 or V_1 = 30.92 and D_1 = 3.71, $K_c - g = 0.12$

Given P_1 as 30.92 ₹

and P_o as 20 ₹

$$\text{Return } R_i = \frac{D_1 + (P_1 - P_0)}{P_o} = \frac{3.71 + (30.92 - 20)}{20}$$

$$= \frac{3.71 + 10.92}{20} = \frac{14.63}{20} = 7.3\%$$

Problem on SML

Security	E (R)	β
1	14%	1.20
2	15%	0.75
3	20%	1.50

Given R_f as 9% and R_M = 15%

Calculate the Return on the securities 1 to 3 and compare them with the expected return security line or SML is given by the formula.

$$R_1 = R_f + \beta_1 (R_m - R_f)$$
$$= 9 + 1.20 (15 - 9)$$
$$= 9 + 7.2 = 16.2\%$$

$$R_2 = 9 + 0.75 (15 - 9)$$
$$= 9 + 4.5 = 13.5\%$$

$$R_3 = 9 + 1.5 (15 - 9)$$
$$= 9 + 9 = 18\%$$

Security 1 only could secure 16.2% which is higher than the expected return E(R): 14%.

CAPM

Question 1

Given the following Security Market Line $R_i = 0.07 + 0.09\ \beta_i$

What are the returns on the two stocks whose βs are 1.2 and 0.9.

Question 2

If the CAPM line is as shown below:

$R_i = 0.04 + 0.10\ \beta_i$

What is the excess return of the market over the risk free rate and what is the risk free rate?

Question 3

Using the formula for SML, in equilibrium namely.

$R_i = R_f + \beta_i\ (R_M - R_f)$

and Given

$R_1 = 6\%\ \beta_i = 0.5$

$R_2 = 12\%\ \beta_2 = 1.5$

What is the expected return on an asset with a Beta of 2?

PROBLEMS

(1) The following characteristic lines are given for three mutual funds namely Kothari Pioneer Templeton and Morgan Stanley.

Kothari Pioneer $r_1 = -0.5\% + 1.25$ rm, P = 0.8

Templeton $r_2 = 1.25\% + 0.95$ rm, P = 0.75

Margon Stanley $r_3 = 0.75\% + 1.35$ rm, P = 0.7

(a) Which fund has the most systematic risk?

(b) What percentage of each Fund's risk systematic and unsystematic?

Answer:

(a) The Fund which has the higher Beta of 1.35, *viz.,* Margon Stanley has the most systematic risk.

(b) The percentage of systematic and unsystematic risk in the total risk can be worked by taking the correlation coefficient squared P^2 which gives the systematic risk (β) and 1-systematic risk is the unsystematic risk.

Kothari Pioneer: Systematic Risk = $(0.8)^2$ = 64%

Unsystematic Risk = 1 – 0.64 = 0.36 or 36%

Templeton: Systematic Risk = $(0.75)^2$ = 56.25%

Unsystematic Risk = 1 – 0.5625 = 0.44 or 44%

Morgan Stanley: Systematic Risk = $(0.7)^2$ = 0.49 = 49%

Unsystematic Risk = 1 – 0.49 = 0.51 or 51%

(2) If Risk free Rate (R_f) is 5%, and market return 14% and Beta is 1.5 for the security.

(a) determine the expected return for the security.

(b) what happens to expected return if Rm or market return increases to 16%, assuming that other variables do not change.

(c) what happens to expected return if the Beta falls to 0.75, assuming that other variables do not change.

Answer:

(a) $R_i = R_f + (R_m - R_f)\ \beta$

$= 0.05 + (.14 - .05)\ 1.5$

$= 0.05 + 0.\ 135 = 0.\ 185$ or 18.5%

(b) $R_i = 0.05 + (0.16 - 0.05)\ 1.5$

$= 0.05 + 0.165 = 0.215$ or 21.5%

(c) $R_i = 0.05 + (0.14 - 0.05)\ 0.75$

$= 0.05 + 0.0675 = .1175$ or 11.75%.

(3) given $R_f = 8\%$, $R_m = 15\%$ and $R_A = 18\%$

(a) Find out the beta for stock A.

(b) What is stock A's return if its Beta falls to 0.75

Answer:

(a) $R_A = R_f + (R_m - R_f)\ \beta$

$18 = 8\% + (15 - 8)\ \beta$

$18 = 8 + 7\ \beta$

$7\ \beta = 10$

$\beta = \frac{10}{7}\ 1.43$

(b) $R_A = R_f + \beta\ (R_m - R_f)$

$= 8 + 0.75\ (15 - 8)$

$= 8 + 5.25 = 13.25$

$= 13.25\%$.

(4) Given $R_f = 6\%$, $E\ (R_m) = 15\%$ and expected returns and expected Betas are as follows.

Stock	*Expected Return*	*Expected Beta*
A	14%	1.20
B	15%	0.75
C	13%	1.50
D	20%	1.60
E	10%	0.80

Which stock is overvalued and which is undervalued, relative to expected return?

Answer:

$E\ (R_I) = R_f + \beta\ (E(R_m) - R_f)$

$E\ (R_A) = 6 + 1.20\ (15 - 6) = 6 + 10.8$

$= 16.8\%$ (overvalued)

$E\ (R_B) = 6 + 0.75\ (15 - 6) = 6 + 6.75$

$= 12.75\%$ (undervalued)

$E\ (R_C) = 6 + 1.50\ (15 - 6) = 6 + 13.5$

$= 19.5\%$ (overvalued)

$E\ (R_D) = 6 + 1.60\ (15 - 6) = 6 + 14.4$

$= 20.4\%$ (overvalued)

$E\ (R_E) = 6 + 0.80\ (15 - 6) = 6 + 7.2$

$= 13.2\%$ (overvalued)

(5) An investment company manages an Equity Fund consisting of five stocks, with the following market values and Betas.

Stock	*Market value*	*Betas*
A	₹ 1,00,000	1.10
B	₹ 25,000	1.20
C	₹ 50,000	0.75
D	₹ 1,25,000	0.60
E	₹ 1,65,000	1.30
Total	4,65,000	

If $R_f = 7\%$, $E(R_m) = 14\%$,
What is the portfolio's expected return?

Answer:

W_s are the weights given to five stocks

$$W_A = \frac{1,00,000}{4,65,000} = 0.22$$

$$W_B = \frac{25,000}{4,65,000} = 0.05$$

$$W_C = \frac{50,000}{4,65,000} = 0.11$$

$$W_D = \frac{1,25,000}{4,65,000} = 0.27$$

$$W_E = \frac{1,65,000}{4,65,000} = 0.35$$

Total weight 1.00

Beta of the portfolio $= \Sigma W_i \beta_i$

$$\beta = 0.22\ (1.10) + 0.05\ (1.20) + 0.11\ (0.75) + 0.27\ (0.60) + 0.35\ (1.30)$$

$$\beta = 0.242 + 0.060 + 0.0825 + 0.162 + 0.455$$

$$\beta = 100.15$$

$$E(rp) = R_f + (R_m - R_f)\ \beta$$

$$= 7 + (14 - 7)\ 100.15$$

$$= 7 + 7.0105 = 14.0105$$

$$= 14.01\%$$

24

PORTFOLIO ANALYSIS

Return on Portfolio

Each security in a portfolio contributes returns in the proportion of its investment in security. Thus, the portfolio expected return is the weighted average of the expected returns, from each of the securities, with weights representing the proportionate share of the security in the total investment. Why does an investor has so many securities in his portfolio? If the security "ABC" gives the maximum return why not he invest in that security all his funds and thus maximise return? The answers to this question lie in the investor's perception of risk attached to investments and his objectives of income, safety, appreciation, liquidity and hedge against loss of value of money etc. This pattern of investment in different asset categories, security categories, types of instruments, etc., would all be described under the caption of diversification, which aims at the reduction or even elimination of non-systematic or company related risks and achieve the specific objectives of investors.

Assuming that investor puts his funds in four securities, the holding period return of the portfolio is described in the Table below:

Security	*Proportion of Funds Invested in Each Security (1)*	*Expected Return of Holding Period (2)*	*Contribution of Each Security to Return (3) = (1) × (2)*
A	30	15%	(30 × .15) = 4.50
B	25	20%	(25 × 0.20) = 5.00
C	25	25%	(25 × 0.25) = 6.25
D	20	10%	(20 × .0.10) = 2.00
	Weights = 100	Weighted return 17.75%	

The above describes the simple calculation of the weighted average return of a portfolio for the Holding period.

Risk on a Portfolio

Risk on a portfolio is different from the risk on individual securities. This Risk is reflected in the variability of the returns from zero to infinity. The expected return depends on the probability of the returns and their weighted contribution to the risk of the portfolio. There are two measures of Risk in this context — one is the absolute deviation and the other standard deviation. These can be explained with following illustrations. The assumed probabilities of each of the returns and the estimation of absolute deviation and standard deviation, based on them are given for illustration:

Event	*Probability*	*Return*	*Probability × Return*	*Absolute Deviation*	*Probability × Absolute Deviation*
(1)	(2)	(3)	(4)	(5)	(6)
			(2) × (3)		(5) × (2)
1.	.20	– 10	– 2.0	– 25	+ 5.0
2.	.30	20	+ 6.0	5	+ 1.5
3.	.40	25	+ 10.0	10	+ 4.0
4.	.10	10	+ 1.00	– 5	+ 0.5
	Expected Return		15.00	Average Absolute Deviation	11.0

Column 5 is deviation of the Returns under colum 3 from the expected return 15 (Thus – 25 = (– 10 – 15). Column 6 is the result of multiplying deviation under column 5 with the probability in column 2 without considering signs. Thus, one measure of risk is absolute deviations of returns under column 6.

Another measure is the standard deviation and or variance

Standard deviation $= \sqrt{\Sigma}\ (x - \bar{x})^2$

Variance $= \Sigma\ (x - \bar{x})^2$

The summation of all deviations from the mean and then squared will give the variance. The square root of variance is standard deviation (sd)

x is the expected return on security.

$\bar{x}$ is the mean or the weighted average return. If two Risks are compared, then standard deviations divided by their means are compared. This is the coefficient of variation, namely $\left(\frac{SD}{X}\right)$.

Example of Standard Deviation

Take a Portfolio XYZ

Possible Outcome	*Return*	*Probability*	*Weighted Return*	*Return Deviation from Mean*	*Weighted Deviation Squared*
1	5%	.25	0.0125	–.04	.0004
2	9%	.50	0.0450	.00	.0000
3	– 13%	.25	0.0325	.04	.0004
		1.00	.090		.0008

Average Expected Return .09 or 9%. (Mean)

The last column of weighted squared deviations are derived by multiplying by the weights of probabilities with squared deviations. Thus, $(.04)^2$ = .0016 and this multiplied by the probability of it 0.25 gives .0004 and so on.

Now, the variance is sum of the weighted squared deviations, namely, .0008

$\sigma^2 = .0008$

SD $\sqrt{.0008} = 0.028$ or 2.8%

When the return of company XYZ is compared with that of company ABC, we have to take into account, their expected return and standard deviation of the return.

Say Company A and B have the following characteristics.

	A	B
Expected Return	0.115 (or 11.5%)	0.09 (or 9%)
Standard Deviation	4.9	2.8

Which company do you prefer? The Company with a higher return of 11.5% has a higher risk than the other company.

Return and standard deviation and variance of portfolios can also be compared in the same manner. Companies can be ranked in the order of return and variance and select into the portfolio those companies with higher returns but with the same level of risk.

Regression Equation

The basic equation for calculating risk can be formulated as a regression equation

Thus, $y = \alpha + \beta X + E$

Where, y = Return in the security in a given period and

X is the market return

α = the intercept where the regression line crosses the y axis

β = The slope of the regression line

E = Error term containing all residuals

Take the following graph to illustrate the above

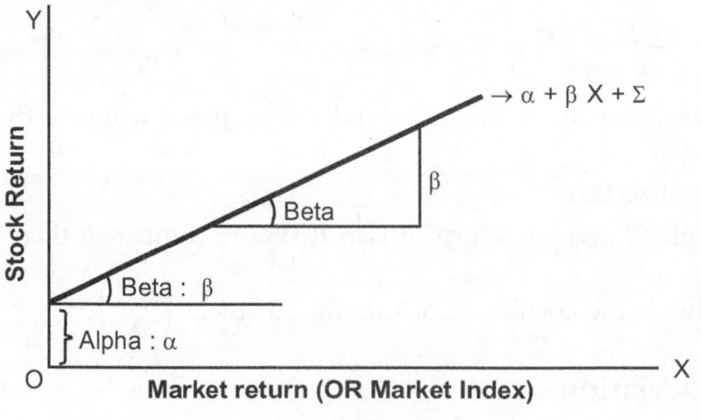

Fig. 24.1

Alpha

α or Alpha is the distance between the horizontal axis and line's intersection with y-axis. It measures the unsystematic risk of the company. If a is a positive return, then that scrip will have higher returns. If a = 0, then the regression line goes through the origin and its return simply depends on the Beta times the market return.

Beta

β or Beta describes the relationship between the stock's return and the Market index return. This can be positive and negative. It is the percentage change in the price of the stock regressed (or related) to the percentage changes in the market Index. If Beta is 1, a one percentage change in Market index will lead to one percentage change in price of stock. If Beta is zero, stock price is unrelated to the Market index. If the Beta is minus one, it indicates a negative relationship with the Market Index and if the market goes up by a +1%, the stock price will fall by 1%. Beta measures the systematic market related risk, which cannot be eliminated by diversification. If the portfolio is efficient, Beta measures the systematic risk effectively. On the other hand, Alpha and Epsilon ($\alpha + \Sigma$) measures the unsystematic risk, which can be reduced by efficient diversification. More details of Beta are discussed elsewhere in the book.

Rho or Correlation Coefficient (Covariance)

Rho measures the correlation between two stocks say i and j. If the correlation coefficient is one (+1), an upward movement of one security return is followed by a direct upward movement of the second security. If on the other hand, Rho is –1, the direction of the movement will be opposite as between the stock price and market index. If there is no relation between them, the coefficient of correction can be zero. It can normally vary from –1 to +1.

The equation for Rho is

$$P = \frac{Cov(XY)}{\sigma_X \sigma_Y} = \sum_{X=1}^{n} \frac{R \times i - R_i}{\sigma_i} \frac{R \times J - R_J}{\sigma_j} P \times i_J.$$

$R \times i$ = xth possible return for security i
$R \times j$ = xth possible return for security j
R_i and R_j are expected returns for i and j
$P \times i_J$ = Joint probability that $R \times i$ and $R \times j$ occur simultaneously
n = total number of joint observations.

An Example for Covariance and Correlation

Given the standard deviation of X and Y as 13.23 and 9.75 in the portfolio of two securities the covariance between them has to be estimated.

Event	*Probability* (1)	*Deviation for x* (2)	*Deviation for y* (3)	*Product of Deviations* 4 = (2) × (3)	*Probability Times Product of Deviations* 5 = (1 × (4)
1	.10	– 5.0	– 10.0	50	5.0
2	.30	5.0	00.0	0	0.0
3	.40	10.0	10.0	100	40.0
4	.20	– 25.0	– 15.0	375	75.0
				Covariance	120.0

The covariance in the above data is 120

$$r_{xy} \text{ coefficient of correlation } = \frac{\text{Covariance}}{(\text{SD of x})(\text{SD of y})}$$

$$r_{xy} = \frac{120}{13.23 \times 9.75} = \frac{120}{128.99} = 0.93$$

The relationship between coefficient of correction and covariance is expressed by the equation below.

$$r_{xy} = \frac{C_{XY}}{S_X S_Y}$$

Where, r_{xy} = Coefficient of correlation
C_{xy} = Covariance between x and y
S_x = Standard deviation of x returns
S_y = Standard deviation of y returns

Problem

Calculate the covariance and coefficient of correlation from the following data

Stocks are x and y and their returns and expected returns are given below:

	Return	*Expected Return*
Stock X	14	18
Stock Y	26	18
Stock X	22	18
Stock Y	10	18

Sd First calculate standard deviation σ

X	*Y*	d_x *Deviation*	d_y *Deviation*	d_x^2 *Squared*	d_y^2 *Deviations*
14	26	– 4	+ 8	16	64
22	10	+ 4	– 8	16	64
Σx 36	Σy 36			32	128

$$\overline{X} = \frac{36}{2} = 18 \quad \overline{Y} = \frac{36}{2} = 18$$

Sd Calculation

$$\delta_X = \sqrt{\frac{32}{2}} = \sqrt{16} = 4$$

$$\delta_Y = \sqrt{\frac{128}{2}} = \sqrt{64} = 8$$

Covariance (CV)

1	*Return* *2*	*Expected Return* *3*	*Difference of expected and actual return* *4 = (3–2)*	*Product of (4)* *5*
Stock X	14	18	–4 }	–32 = –4 × 8
Stock Y	26	18	+8	
Stock X	22	18	+4 }	–32 = 4 × –8
Stock Y	10	18	–8	

$$CV = \frac{1}{2}(14 - 18)(26 - 18) + \frac{1}{2}(22 - 18)(10 - 18)$$

$$CV = \frac{1}{2}(-4 \times +8) + \frac{1}{2}(4 \times -8)$$

$$CV = \frac{1}{2}(-32) + \frac{1}{2}(-32) = -16 - 16 = -32$$

Correlation. The formula is

$$r_{xy} = \frac{Cov.XY}{\sigma_X \sigma_Y}$$

r_{xy} = coefficient of correlation

Cov X Y = –32

$\sigma_x = 4 \ \sigma_y = 8$

$$r_{xy} = \frac{-32}{4 \times 8} = \frac{-32}{32} = -1$$

Correlation coefficient is negative and they are perfectly negatively correlated with a value of 1.

Expected Returns

If we know the ratio in which investments are made in x and y stocks say, that the ratio is 40:60, then investment in X is 40 and investment in y is 60 out of 100

Actual Returns on portfolio are as follows:

In portfolio (1) =

14 and 26 in first year and
the returns are
22 and 10 in second year.

$$X = \frac{14+22}{2} = \frac{36}{2} = 18$$

$$Y = \frac{26+10}{2} = \frac{36}{2} = 18$$

Expected Return

$R_p = R_1X_1 + R_2Y_1$

$R_p = 18\ (.40) + 18\ (.60)$

$= 7.2 + 10.8 = 18$

R_p = Expected Return on the portfolio is 18

Problem

Given the data below on two companies A and B, calculate the expected return from companies and standard deviation as a risk measure of companies. Which one is better for Return and Risk estimates?

	Company A		*Company B*	
Outcome	*Expected Return*	*Probability*	*Expected Return*	*Probability*
1	6	0.3	8	0.2
2	10	0.5	14	0.5
3	12	0.2	18	0.3

Solution:

Company A Return (1)	*Probability (2)*	*Weighted Probability Return (3) = (1) × (2)*	*Company B Return (4)*	*Probability (5)*	*Weighted Probability Return (6) = (4 × 5)*
6	0.3	+ 1.8	8	0.2	1.6
10	0.5	+ 5.0	14	0.5	7.0
12	0.2	+ 2.4	18	0.3	5.4
Expected Returns		9.2			14.0

Company A (Expected Return 9.2)

Outcome (1)	*Weighted Probability Return (2)*	*Deviation from Expected Return (3)*	*Squared Deviations (4)*	*Weighted Deviations Squared Weighted by Probability (5)*
1	1.8	9.2–6 = 3.2	10.24	3.072
2	5.0	9.2–10 = 0.8	0.64	0.320
3	2.4	9.2–12 = –2.8	7.84	1.568
				4.960

Expected Return 9.2%

Standard Deviation $\sqrt{4.960} = 2.23\%$

Company B (Expected Return 14.0)

(1)	(2)	(3)	(4)	(5)
1	1.6	14 – 8 = 6	36	7.2
2	7.0	14 – 14 = 0	0	0
3	5.4	14 – 18 = –4	16	4.8
				12.0

Expected Return = 14.0%

Standard Deviation $\sqrt{12}$ = 3.46%

Risk of Company B is higher, but the return is also higher.

Problem

Given below are the returns on IBM and BSE sensex for a five year period. Calculate Beta, Alpha Residual variance and Correlation:

Year	*Return on IBM (Y)*	*Return On BSE Sensex (X)*
1	0.2	0.1
2	0.3	0.2
3	0.5	0.3
4	0.4	0.4
5	0.6	0.5

Solution:

Year	*X*	*Y*	*XY*	*X*²	*Y*²
1	0.10	0.2	0.02	.01	.04
2	0.20	0.3	0.06	.04	.09
3	0.30	0.5	0.15	.09	.25
4	0.40	0.4	0.16	.16	.16
5	0.50	0.6	0.30	.25	.36
	$\Sigma X = 1.50$	$\Sigma Y = 2.0$	$\Sigma XY = 0.69$	$\Sigma X^2 = 0.55$	$\Sigma Y^2 = 0.90$

$$\overline{X} = \frac{1.5}{5} = 0.3;\ \overline{Y} = \frac{2.0}{5} = 0.4$$

Calculation of Beta

β slope of the Regression line is given by

$$\beta = \frac{\eta\Sigma XY - (\Sigma X)(\Sigma Y)}{\eta\Sigma X^2 - (\Sigma X)^2} \text{ is the Equation}$$

$$= \frac{(5\times.69)-(1.5\times 2.0)}{(5\times.55)-(1.5)^2} = \frac{3.45-3.00}{(2.75)-(2.25)} = \frac{0.45}{0.50}$$

$$\beta = 0.9$$

Calculation of Alpha

The formula is $\alpha = \overline{Y} - \beta\overline{X} = 0.4 - (0.9)(0.3)$ [$\overline{X}$ and $\overline{Y}$ are as given above]

$= 0.4 - 0.27 = 0.13$

Calculation of Residual Variance

The formula is $e^2 = \dfrac{\Sigma Y^2 - \alpha\Sigma Y - \beta\Sigma XY}{\eta}$ = is the Equation

$$e^2 = \frac{\Sigma Y^2 - \alpha\Sigma Y - \beta\Sigma XY}{\eta}$$

$$= \frac{0.9 - 0.13 \times 2.0 - 0.9 \times 0.69}{5}$$

$$= \frac{0.9 - 0.26 - 0.621}{5} = \frac{0.019}{5} = 0.004$$

Method of Calculation of (r)

$$r = \frac{\Sigma XY}{\sqrt{\Sigma X^2 \times \Sigma Y^2}} = \frac{0.69}{\sqrt{0.55 \times 0.90}} = \frac{0.69}{\sqrt{0.495}}$$

$$r = \frac{0.69}{0.703} = 0.983$$

Coefficient of Determination = $r^2 = (0.983)^2 = 0.966$

Variance of IBM

$$\bar{y} = \frac{\Sigma Y}{\eta} = \frac{2.0}{5} = 0.4.$$

Y *Return*	*dy* *Deviation*	*dy²* *Deviation Squared*
0.2	−.2	.04
0.3	−.1	.01
0.5	+.1	.01
0.4	0	.0
0.6	+2	.04
n = 5 $\bar{y}$ = 0.4		Σdy^2 .10

Variance $\sigma^2 = \dfrac{.10}{5} = .02$

Standard Deviation $\sqrt{.02}$ = 0.141

Explained systematic variance (.02) × 0.964 = .0193

Unexplained Residual/unsystematic variance = .0007

Total Variance = .02

$$Sd = \frac{\text{Covariance}}{\sigma x \sigma y} = \sqrt{.02} = .141$$

Variance of BSE Index

Return	dx (deviation)	dx²
0.10	.20	.04
0.20	.10	.01
0.30	0	0

0.40	.10	.01
0.50	.20	.04
		$\Sigma dx^2 = .10$

$$\bar{X} = \frac{\Sigma X}{n} = \frac{1.5}{5} = 0.3$$

$$\text{Variance} = \frac{0.10}{5} = .02 = \frac{\Sigma dx^2}{n}; \qquad sd = \sqrt{\frac{dx^2}{n}}$$

$$\text{S.D. } \sigma = \sqrt{.02} = 0.141$$

$$\text{Coefficient of Correlation} = \frac{\text{Covariance}}{\sigma x \sigma y}$$

Coefficient of correlation can also be worked through the above formula.

CALCULATION OF ALPHA & BETA

Given the following data, calculate the A and B (Alpha and Beta) of Birla Fund.

Years	*Birla Fund*	*Risk free Rate*	*Market Return*
1995	7	5	5
1996	–5	9	–4
1997	13	7	10
1998	11	6	9
1999	15	8	12

Risk free Rate is that of 91 days TB rate for the year. Market Return is that of S & P. CNX 500 for the year; use the Risk premium formula, namely.

$$(r_{it} - R_t) = \alpha_i + \beta_i (r_{mt} - R_t) + u_{it}$$

Keeping aside the residual (error) term u_{it} we have,

$$(r_{it} - R_t) = \alpha_i + \beta_i (r_{mt} - R_t)$$

y variable = Alfa + Beta (x variable)

$$y = \alpha + \beta (x)$$

$$\alpha = y - \beta x$$

$$\beta = \frac{N\Sigma xy - \Sigma x \Sigma y}{N\Sigma x^2 - (\Sigma x)^2}$$

Y is dependent variable (Birla fund)

X is independent variable (Market returns).

Answer:

Year	R_{mt} *Market Returns*	R_{it} *Birla*	R_t *+ or* R_f *Risk Free Rate*	x $(R_{mt} - R_t)$	y $(R_{it} - R_t)$	$x.y$	x^2
1995	+5	7	5	0	2	0	0
1996	– 4	–5	9	–13	–14	182	169
1997	10	13	7	3	6	18	9
1998	9	11	6	3	5	15	9
1999	12	15	8	4	7	28	16
				$\Sigma x = -3;$	$\Sigma y = 6;$	$\Sigma xy = 243$	$\Sigma x^2 = 203$

$$\beta = \frac{N\Sigma xy - \Sigma x \Sigma y}{N\Sigma x^2 - (\Sigma x)^2} = \frac{5 \times 243 - (-3) - (6)}{5 \times 203 - (-3)^2}$$

$$\beta = \frac{1215+18}{1015-9} = \frac{1233}{1006} = 1.226$$

$$\bar{Y} = \frac{6}{5} = 1.2$$

$$\bar{X} = \frac{-3}{5} = -0.6$$

$$A = \bar{Y} - BX$$

$$A = 1.2 - 1.226\ (-0.6)$$

$$A = 1.2 + 0.736 = 1.936$$

As A is positive at 1.936, Birla Fund has out performed the market on a risk adjusted basis over the period 1995-99.

Problem

1. Given the following data for a two security portfolio, find the minimum variance portfolio. Also calculate the return and Risk of the portfolio.

Security	*Return*		*Standard Deviation*	*Correlation between C and D*
C	26.9	—	22.3	−0.12
D	17.5	—	51.0	

Answer:

$$W_C = \frac{\sigma_D{}^2 - \sigma_C\sigma_D r_{CD}}{\sigma_C{}^2 + \sigma_D{}^2 - 2\sigma_C\sigma_D r_{CD}}$$

$$= \frac{(0.51)^2 - 0.223(0.51)(-0.12)}{(0.223)^2 + (0.51)^2 - 2(0.223)(0.51)(-0.12)}$$

$$W_C = \frac{.027374}{0.33712} = 0.812$$

$$W_D = 1 - W_C = 1 - 0.812 = 0.188$$

The proportion of investment in W_C is 81% and that in W_D is 19% of the portfolio.

Return on the portfolio is calculated as follows:

$$\sum_{i=1}^{N} W_i\, R_i = 0.812 \times 26.9 + 0.188 \times 17.5$$

$$rp = 21.84 + 3.29 = 25.13$$

Risk on the portfolio to calculated as follows:

$$\sigma p = \left[\sum_{i=1}^{N} W_i{}^2\sigma_i{}^2 + \sum_{i=1}^{N}\ \sum_{j=i+1}^{N} W_i\, W_j C_{ij}\right]^{\frac{1}{2}}$$

$$= \left[\begin{matrix}(0.812)^2\,(0.223)^2 + (0.118)^2\,(0.51)^2 + \\ 2(0.812)(0.118)(0.223)(0.510)(-0.12)\end{matrix}\right]^{\frac{1}{2}}$$

$$= \sqrt{0.03769} = 0.1945$$

2. A company and B company have the following risk – return statistics, calculate the minimum risk portfolio, if P_{ab} = 0 and P_{ab} = –1

$E(r_a) = 14\%$ $E(r_b) = 16\%$

$\sigma a = 22\%$ $\sigma b = 25\%$

Answer:

(i) When $P_{ab} = 0$

$$W_a = \frac{\sigma b^2}{\sigma a^2 + \sigma b^2} = \frac{(0.25)^2}{(0.22)^2 + (0.25)^2}$$

$$W_a = \frac{0.0625}{0.0484 + 0.0625} = \frac{0.0625}{0.1109} = 0.56$$

$W_a = 0.56$ or 56%

$W_b = 1 - Wa = 1 - 0.56 = 0.44$ or 44%

(ii) When $P_{ab} = -1$

$$W_a = \frac{\sigma b}{\sigma b + \sigma a} = \frac{0.25}{0.25 + 0.22} = \frac{0.25}{0.47} = 0.53$$

$W_a = 0.53$ or 53%

$W_b = 1 - W_a = 1 - 0.53 = 0.47$ or 47%

3. ABC Co and XYZ Co., have the following probability distribution of returns. Determine the expected covariance of returns.

State of Market	*Probability (P)*	R_{ABC}	R_{XYZ}
Recession	0.1	10	20
Boom	0.2	–12	–30
Normal	0.2	–7	–20
Slow Growth	0.1	20	40
Recovery	0.4	30	35

Answer:

$\bar{R}_{ABC} = \sum_{i=1}^{N} = PR_{ABC}$, where P is probability

$= (0.1)\ 10 + (0.2)\ (-12) + (0.2)\ (-7) + (0.1)\ (20) + (0.4)\ 30$

$= 1 - 2.4 - 1.4 + 2.0 + 12.0 = 11.2$

$\bar{R}_{XYZ} = (0.1)\ (20) + (0.2)\ (-30) + (0.2)\ (-20) + (0.1)\ (40) + (0.4)\ (35)$

$= 2.0 - 6.0 - 4.0 + 4.0 + 14.0 = 10$

The covariance is calculated as follows:

$$\begin{aligned} Cov_{ABC,\ XYZ} &= (10 - 11.2)\ (20 - 10)\ (0.1) + \\ &\quad (-12 - 11.2)\ (-30 - 10)\ (0.2) + \\ &\quad (-7 - 11.2)\ (-20 - 10)\ (0.2) + \\ &\quad (20 - 11.2)\ (40 - 10)\ (0.1) + \\ &\quad (30 - 11.2)\ (35 - 10)\ (0.4) \\ &= (-1.2)\ (10)\ (0.1) + (-23.2)\ (-40)\ (0.2) \\ &\quad +(-18.2)\ (-30)\ (0.2) + (8.8)\ (30)\ (0.1) \\ &\quad +(18.8)\ (25)\ (0.4) \\ &= -1.2 + 185.6 + 109.2 + 26.4 + 188 \\ &= 508 \end{aligned}$$

4. The annual rates of return for XYZ Co., and the market returns for these years are given below.
   (a) Determine the Beta coefficient for the company
   (b) What part of total risk is systematic.

Year	XYZ Co. Return	Market Return
1995	– 5%	– 6%
1996	14	16
1997	10	12
1998	12	14
1999	17	20

Answer:

(a) $\beta = \dfrac{N\sum xy - \sum x \sum y}{N\sum x^2 - (\sum x)^2}$ where

N is the number of observations

X is the return on the market or independent variable.

Y is the return of security Y or dependent variable.

Year	R_m	R_{co}	R_m^2	R_{co}^2	$R_{co}\,R_m$
1995	-6	-5	36	25	30
1996	16	14	256	196	224
1997	12	10	144	100	120
1998	14	12	196	144	168
1999	20	17	400	289	340
	Σ s = 56	48	1032	754	882

N = 5

$$\beta = \frac{5 \times 882 - (48)(56)}{5(1032) - (56)^2} = \frac{4410 - 2688}{5160 - 3136}$$

$$\beta = \frac{1722}{2024} = 0.85079$$

(b) Correlation Coefficient (P^2) tells us percentage of systematic risk. The formula for P is as follows.

$$P = \frac{N\sum xy - \sum x . \sum y}{\{[(N\sum x^2) - (\sum x)^2][N.\sum y^2 - (\sum y)^2]\}^{\frac{1}{2}}}$$

$$= \frac{(5)(882) - (48)(56)}{\{[5(1032) - (56)^2][5 \times 754 - (48)^2]\}^{\frac{1}{2}}}$$

$$P = \frac{1722}{[(2024)(1466)]^{\frac{1}{2}}} = \frac{1722}{1722.5516} = 0.999$$

P = 0.99968 and

$P^2 = (0.99968)^2 = 0.9936$ or 99.94%

ЮЮЮ

DIVERSIFICATION AND TECHNIQUES OF RISK REDUCTION

What is Diversification?

Diversification is a technique of reducing the risk involved in investment and in portfolio management. This is a process of conscious selection of assets, instruments and scrips of companies/Government securities, in a manner that the total risks are brought down. This process helps in the reduction of risk, under category of what is known as "Unsystematic Risk" and promotes the optimisation of returns for a given level of risks in portfolio management.

We have seen that in the case of unsystematic risk, the method of lowering the risk is to diversify into a number of companies and a number of industries, for selection of scrips in the portfolio. This diversification may take any of the following forms:

(1) Into different *types of assets,* like gold, real estate, Government securities, corporate securities, etc.

(2) Into different *instruments* or security type bonds, stocks, debentures, Government securities, etc.

(3) Into different *industry lines,* namely, plastics, chemicals, engineering, cement, steel, fertilisers, etc.

(4) Into different *scrips of companies,* viz., new companies, growing companies, new product companies etc.

Principles

The principles involved in diversification are as follows:

A single company/industry is more risky than two companies/industries. Two companies in say, steel industry are more risky than one company in Steel, and one in Tyres and Tubes.

Two companies, one in steel and the other in chemicals are less risky than two in either steel or chemicals. Similarly, two companies or two industries which are similar in nature of demand or market etc., are more risky than the two in dissimilar industries. Statistically speaking, their variance/covariance should be different. It is proper diversification which involves two or more companies/two or more industries whose fortunes fluctuate independent of one another or in different directions.

Random Diversification

The traditional belief is that diversification involves "not putting all eggs in one basket." This policy involves as many baskets as possible; carried to the extreme, it is good to have as many companies as possible, and as many industries as possible in one's portfolio. But this is a misconception as economies of scale operate in the reverse direction (involving diseconomies) with the result that monitoring and review of the portfolio become inefficient, costly and cumbersome and outweigh the benefits of diversification.

There are some accepted methods of effecting diversification:

1. Randomness in Selection of Companies and Industries: The probability of reducing risk is more with a random selection as the statistical error of choosing wrong companies will come down due to randomness of selection which is a statistical technique. This involves placing of companies in any order and picking them up in random manner.

2. Optimisation of Selection Process: Given the amount of money to be invested there is optimum number of companies, where money can be invested. If the number is too small, risk cannot be reduced adequately and if the number is too big, there will be diseconomies and difficulty of supervision, analysis and monitoring will increase risk again. There is thus an optimum number of companies to be chosen for a given amount of investment.

3. Adequate Diversification: Many traditional approaches emphasise on the need for adequate diversification. This involves as many industries and companies or securities as possible to get the best results. This principle believes in the possibilities of readucing risk to even zero, if there are adequate number of companies and industries. Markowitz emphasised however that what is needed is not only the number of securities to be chosen but the right kind of securities to be chosen. Thus, even if there are a large number of companies they may not reduce risk adequately if they are positively correlated with each other and the market, in which case, they all move in the same direction and many risks will not be reduced and may even increase.

4. Markowitz Diversification: Markowitz emphasised the need for a right number of securities — not too many or too less — and securities which are negatively correlated or not correlated at all. The purpose of diversification is to reduce the unsystematic risk arising out of company's policies and performance. Thus, many of such risks can be reduced by a proper choice of companies and industries. Neither random selection, nor adequate number of securities can guarantee this. One can see from the graph below that for an individual investor a number of around 10-16 companies can secure reduction of risk to an optimum level if they are properly selected as per Markowitz. For Mutual funds or finance companies this number may be higher. The graph shows both systematic and unsystematic risks and the horizontal line of systematic risk cannot be reduced by diversification, but to a large extent unsystematic risk can be reduced by a right choice of companies and to a limited number (Fig. 25.1).

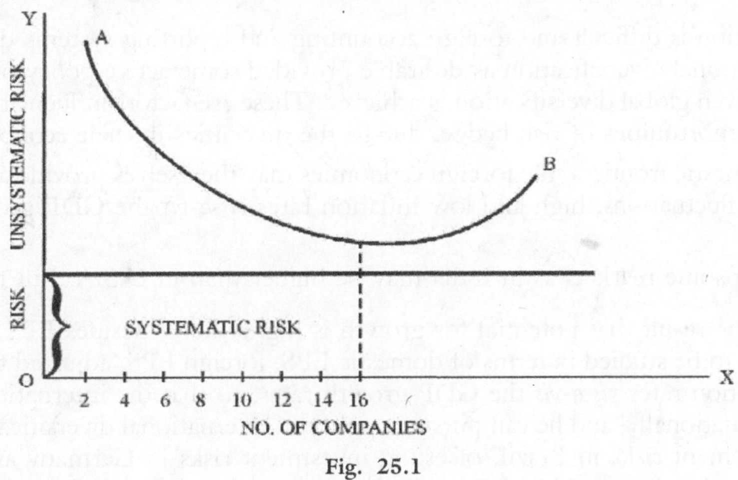

Fig. 25.1

International Diversification

The benefits of deversifcation are well perceived by Portfolio Managers, that many in developed countries, started investing in Foreign bonds, stocks and other instruments. They found that they can extend diversification principle to foreign stocks, bonds etc., to improve returns for a given risk by adopting proper techniques of diversification.

Why International Diversification?

(1) The size and character of International Equity and bond markets are widely varying that it will increase the scope for larger investment and larger diversification.

(2) The returns in local currencies of some foreign countries are higher than in domestic markets. Thus, for example in Singapore, Malaysia, Taiwan and India the returns in local currencies are higher than in U.S. economy.

(3) The economic trends, business conditions and local profitability and earnings ratios differ widely among countries that the EPS in some developing countries is higher and give opportunity for better diversification and higher returns, through international investments.

(4) International investment is advantageous due to larger investment avenues now open in the first place and secondly due to the imperfect correlation among the international markets. The total risk of a portfolio including the international investment will be lower than with only domestic investment. The degree of volatility, and all risk measures, indicate that these risks vary among the countries and in different degrees and the possibility of covariance, or high correlation will be low.

The frontier of efficient portfolios can be widened, by inclusion of foreign investments in a portfolio. Thus, many International Portfolio Managers prefer to invest in India and so will be the case of Indian Portfolio Managers, if they can diversify into International Investments. There are some directions however which will increase risk in such investments.

Risks in Foreign Investments

(1) Political and social developments may create problems in an unpredictable manner.

(2) Economic and monetary policies may change to their disadvantage.Foreign exchange controls, double taxation, appropriation of foreign assets etc., stand in the way.

(3) Risks of currency fluctuations may pose danger to larger profits depending upon the management in exchange rates. The currency risks are important because the foreign investor when he wants to take home his profits, the desired currency is his local currency, and this has to take into account the exchange rates. The gains or returns out of foreign investments might be offset by opposite and adverse movements in exchange rates. These factors create more risks.

(4) Unforeseen international developments such as wars, political and ideological conflicts etc., might create additional risks.

(5) Foreign information is difficult and foreign accounting and reporting systems differ. All the above factors make the international diversification as desirable provided some active policy of management of portfolio is preferred and even global diversification is achieved. These are factors influencing the global diversification which provide opportunities of risk hedge, due to the diversities in their economies and markets:

Thus, leaving the domestic frontiers, the foreign economies may themselves provide a picture of varying degrees of economic and business fluctuations, high and low inflation rates *vis-a-vis* the GDP growth rates, etc.

Thus, $\frac{P}{E}$ multiple of some markets as in India may be higher than in U.S.A. But the growth rate of India is higher than U.S.A. with the result that potential for growth is higher here. Besides EPS in different countries may vary widely and these have to be studied in terms of domestic EPS, foreign EPS, adjusted for forward exchange rates, foreign interest rates, inflation rates *vis-a-vis* the GDP growth rates, so that the international investor knows which markets are attractive internationally, and he can pursue a policy of international diversification to secure offsetting of risks — risks that is investment risks in Brazil, ofsetting investment risks in Germany and yet the returns in total portfolios are higher, when taken back in U.S. dollars. The various markets behave with different degrees of risk/return features such that when the U.S. returns are lower, the Companies' total returns may be higher in foreign markets thus reducing the total risk of portfolios including foreign investments.

FFI'S INVESTMENT IN INDIA

FFIs were permitted to operate in the Indian capital market since Sept., 1992, in a bid to globalise the markets. Since Jan. 1993, FII investment started in India. By March 2006, there were 898 FFIs registered with the RBI/SEBI, operating in India. The cumulative amount of their investment upto March 2001 was more than ₹ 49,000 crores. During 2000-01 to 2004-05, FII net investment amounted to a cumulative figure of more than ₹ 1,21,120 crores. During 2005-06 to 2007-08, the FFI portfolio investment an amount of ₹ 1,96,761 crores flowed in, but this was offset by an outflow of ₹ 43,337 crores in 2008-09, due to worldwide recession. Further, FDI inflows continued unabated, despite recession. These inflows have almost doubled during the latter period. Net investments by FIIs in the Indian Capital Market picked up again to ₹ 1,14,901 crores in 2009-10 and ₹ 1,90,718 crores in 2010-11 and stood at ₹ 21,59,650 crores in 1914-15. In a study published in RBI's Annual Report, 1995-96 it was revealed that BSE Sensex is significantly related ($\gamma = 0.49$) to lagged net investment by FFIs. Such studies are also available in World Bank studies and IMF Studies, which also revealed the significant impact of foreign flows into capital markets of developing countries.

(Ref. Claesseus S. and S. Gooptu, Eds. (1993) "Portfolio Investment in Developing Countries". W.B. Discussion paper No. 228 and Schadler S. and Carkovic M. Eds. (1993) "Resent Experiences with Surges in Capital Inflows" IMF occasional paper No. 108, IMF.)

These flows influence the market through demand pressures, affecting the interest rates and stock prices, money supply, domestic savings and investment activity in the domestic economies.

NRI Investment in India

NRI Investments in India can take any of the following three forms:

(a) Avenues for Personal Investment.

(b) Direct Investment Schemes.

(c) Portfolio Investment Schemes.

A. Personal Investments Scheme

NRI or Foreign Citizens of Indian origin can acquire any of the following investments in India without RBI's prior permission. These are:

Government Securities, P.O. Savings and National Plan Certificates, UTI units, and their schemes, company deposits Mutual Fund schemes new issues of equity, equity shares, debentures, both on repatriation and non-repatriation purposes, immovable property for residental purpose, India Development Bonds, Housing and Real estate development to the extent of even 100%.

The Investee Company and not NRI has to take prior permission of the RBI in the above cases, Repatriation is permitted if only funds have come from NRE/FCNR accounts and not NRO accounts. The shares of companies, their deposits and debentures and commercial paper are all available for investment on a non-repatriation basis, under this scheme.

B. Direct Investment Scheme

There are two schemes of 40% and 100% of investment. Under this category of 40% scheme is investment in shares and debentures in companies engaged in Industrial and manufacturing activity, Hotels, Hospitals, Shipping Companies, Computer Softwear, oil exploration, etc. There is no ceiling on the amount of remittable dividend, but the investee company has to take the RBI permission in this regard.

100% scheme is for Real Estate Development, Township development, Construction of residential buildings, houses etc., development of roads, building materials, bridges and infrastructure facilities, house finance and Air Taxi operators. They can invest upto 100% in debentures (NCDS), sick industrial undertakings without repatriation. The 100% investment is also permitted for OCBs (overseas corporate bodies with 60% participation of NRIs). They can make investments, in 100% export oriented units, EPZ, and high priority industries with foreign equity participation of 51% with the rest to be left (49%) to NRIs.

Original investment can be repatriated after 3 years from the date of the issue. Actual income or dividends, can be freely repatriable, subject to payment of tax (at a flat rate of 20%). OCBs are permitted to repatriate after 3 years at 16% net profit and Air Taxi operators only after 5 years and out of accumulated foreign exchange earnings only.

NRIs can invest in High priority industries listed in Annexure II to the latest statement on Industrial Policy. The general guideline is that FIIs and FFIs etc. can invest in any corporate upto 51% of equity, subject to changes of permitting their investment upto 74% of equity in certain cases and in certain sectors as in Telecom, Aviation etc.

C. Portfolio Investment Scheme

NRIs can freely invest and disinvest without any lock in period in the cases of the investment in Domestic Mutual Funds, without any limit, and in paid up capital and debt capital upto 5% for each individual subject to an overall ceiling of 10% for all NRIs and OCBs, which can be raised upto 24% if the company passes a Resolution to that effect in the General Body Meeting.

The ADs who have the accounts of NRIs can be used as the medium for portfolio investments on the stock exchanges. RBI's approval is to be secured by the NRI through that particular AD. There is no lock in period and RBI's approval is valid for 5 years. Capital gains and dividends etc., can be repatriated after payment of taxes (at a flat rate of 20%), if the funds have come through NRE and FCNR accounts.

Sale and Transfer of shares is also permitted by the RBI without prior permission in respect of Government securities, debentures of corporates, and those on non repatriation basis. However, RBI prior permission is required for transfer to other NRIs, Residents, either by private placement or through any private agency. Those on repatriation basis require permission of the RBI. Rights entitlements and bonus issued are subject to RBI's permission which has to be sought by the company. General permission of RBI is available only for those on non-repatriation basis.

These provisions are subject to constant changes, and there have been many liberalisations in recent years.

Passive International Investment Strategy

In passive strategy, an International Index fund is the ideal method of investing abroad. Thus, the offshore funds of India, or other International funds of China, Brazil, Mexico, etc., can be used as the index funds, for passive investment. They can alternatively trade in only major world markets, like U.K., Japan, Germany, France, and Switzerland, after a study of their market behaviour. This strategy of investing in balanced portfolio of a large number of countries, with a high degree of diversification may improve the returns on such positions.

Risk in a foreign portfolio in terms of standard deviation of the continuously compounded annualised return is

$V_t = [V_l m^2 + V_c^2 + 2PV_c\ V_{lm}]^{1/2}$

V_c = Exchange Rate risk, V_{lm} is total portfolio risk in local market terms, fully hedged, V_t = total portfolio risk in base currency terms, without currency hedging, p = correlation between exchange rate return and portfolio return in local market terms. The above formula indicates that total portfolio risk in foreign markets is lower, if there is a good negative correlation between local currency returns and local market returns in stock market.

The factors influencing such foreign portfolios are: (i) Foreign asset local returns, (ii) Foreign currency returns, (iii) Domestic asset returns, and (iv) Correlation Coefficient between these variables.

The return on a fully hedged foreign investment is

$R = Lr + F_p/d$

R = Return an foreign investment fully hedged.

Lr = Local asset returns, F_p/d is the Forward Premium/discount (U.S. Short-term rate and foreign short-term rate).

Active International Investment Strategy

Active strategy is oriented to identifying relatively attractive and unattractive national markets. Such identification is followed by ranking these markets abroad and weightage in one's portfolio is given by such ranking in terms of the attractiveness of the local markets. This identification involves some analytical and predictive powers both in the investment markets and currency markets. The operation of such active strategy is depicted below.

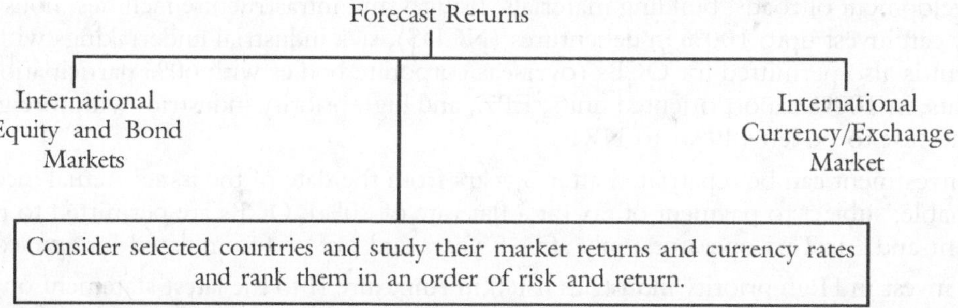

Adjust for hedging of currency rates and Market returns so that an optimum portfolio with higher return and lowest risk is built. International Rating Agencies like Moody's provide country and currency ratings and publish investment grades of countries.

Return Forecasts

An exercise of importance in active Portfolio Management is to forecast the returns in equity market and in currency markets.

If say the foreign equity return is 20% as against 10% of domestic return, foreign investments may look attractive but if that 20% return is lost by adverse currency rate fluctuations or high local tax rates then it is not worthwhile investing abroad.

Example of return forecast Table is given below:

Country	*Currency Forecast Return*	*Equity Market Forecast Return*	*Net Return %*
UK	1.1	18.2	19.3
France	1.0	13.6	14.6
Germany	4.7	13.9	18.6
India	–5.0	20.0	15.0

Equity market returns are high in India but tax rates and currency rate variations create negative return so that investment becomes unattractive in India, as seen from the above Table. In considering various markets the Portfolio Manager takes into account various economic and political factors and not merely equity returns. A few examples are given here:

(1) EPS market index and $\frac{P}{E}$ multiple.

(2) Relative growth of the economy and the market. If market earnings growth is higher than the growth rate of GDP it is potentially good market.

(3) If the market capitalisation is low relative to GDP and potentiality of growth of MC is high, such markets are again attractive to foreign investors.

(4) Monthly volatility and annual volatility of prices, which should not be very high, for attracting foreign investment.

(5) Liquidity and settlement process in the markets — whether deliveries are prompt and enough scrips are available for delivery at the international standards of T + 3 Delivery.

(6) Good floating stock of companies and wide public holding so as to promote trading in such securities in domestic markets of those countries.

(7) Free and floating currency without current and capital account controls. If the county has only capital account controls but no current account controls, it is partly attractive as in the case of India.

(8) Stable exchange rates or facilities for hedge and cover for forward exchange position are available in these markets.

If the above features are prevailing in a good measure, such countries are worthwhile and attractive for foreign portfolio Management. The breadth of the market in terms of the available number of traded companies and their floating stock are also considered in addition to the expected returns and risks involved in trading in such markets.

The optimisation process with international diversification is more complicated and active investment strategy will give better returns than passive strategy. Some prior conditions should also be satisfied for optimisation process.

Advantages of Diversification

Advantages of diversification are seen in both returns and risk. Returns can be improved and risks lowered by proper diversification of securities, in those which have negative covariance or are independent. In the chart below, stocks 4 and 5 and portfolio 4 and 5 are having the same expected return of 14% but the standard deviation (σ) of the portfolio 4 and 5 is less than the standard deviation of 4 or 5 alone. By combining 4 and 5 into a portfolio, the investor has reduced the risk without any loss of return.

Take stocks 5 and 6, and a portfolio of 5 and 6. Since the return of any portfolio is the weighted average of individual security returns, the expected return of the portfolio is 12, while that of stock 5 is 14% and of Stock 6 is 10% [average is ½ (14 + 10) = 12.] But the risk or standard deviation of a portfolio is not simply a weighted average of individual securities. Standard deviation, portfolio 5 and 6 plots to the left of a straight line connecting 5 and 6 — which means that there is less risk in the Portfolio than in the weighted average combination (linear line).

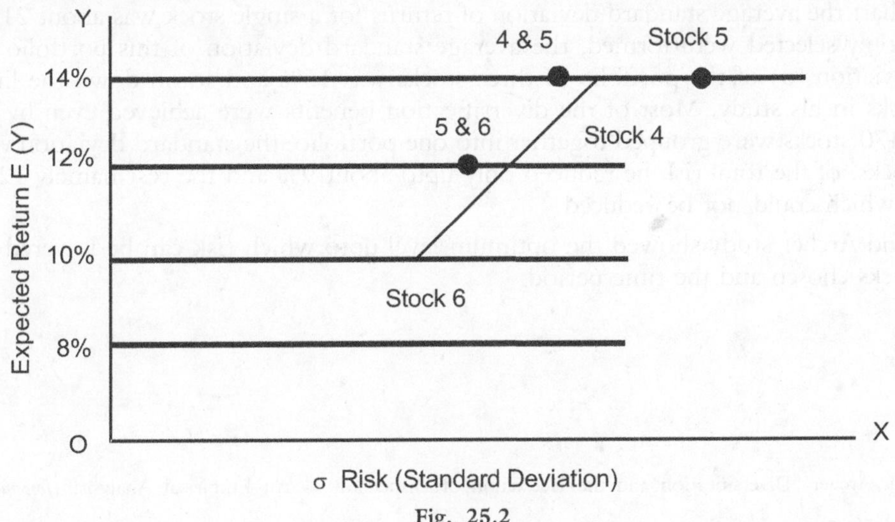

Fig. 25.2

Besides, the securities need not be equally weighted as in the above example. If one can design different combinations, he may reach the efficient Frontier line which has least risk for a given return.

In this chart, as seen above, returns can be improved and risk reduced by diversification. The optimum points of different combinations, giving the least risk for a given level of return will constitute the efficient frontier. Beyond the frontier line, one cannot reduce the risk further, due to diseconomies or difficulties of reducing the risk further. Reduction of risk takes place due to the fact that securities' returns are not perfectly correlated in the portfolio.

Naive Diversification

This refers to the diversification by simply picking stocks at random. This may or may not reduce risk to the optimum level. As the number of stocks in a portfolio is increased randomly, it is possible to reduce the risk upto a point and that too only in respect of the non-systematic risk. The market related systematic risk cannot be reduced by diversification. Even the diversification cannot be achieved by naive diversification.

Evans & Archers' Study[@]

Evans & Archer studied the data of 470 NYSE firms during 1958-67 and showed that if the maximum risk of a single stock is 21%, it can be reduced to the extent of approximately 9% and the rest of 12% representing the systematic risk, cannot be diversified away. That is the market risk which the investor has to bear and by using the concept of Beta referred in another Chapter, he can take that much risk, that he can tolerate as per his preference or aversion.

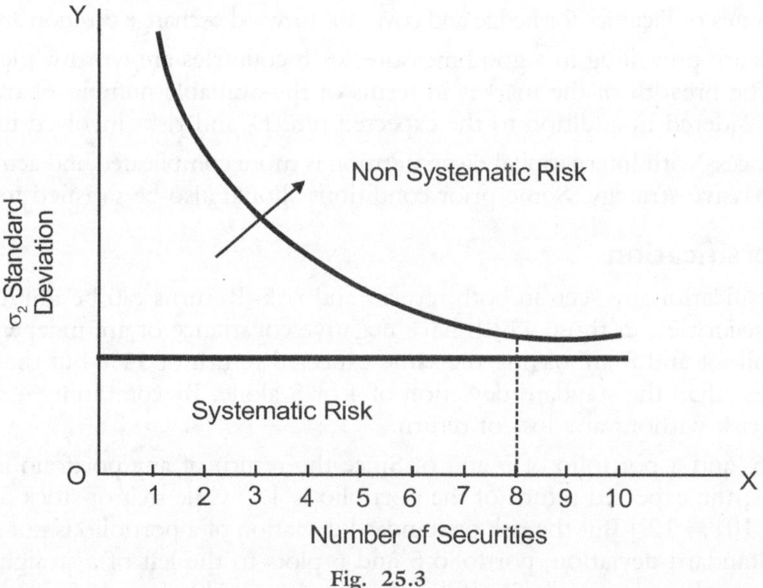

Fig. 25.3

In the above chart the average standard deviation of returns for a single stock was about 21%. When portfolios of two stocks, and only selected were formed, the average standard deviation of this portfolio is about 16%. The average standard deviation (σ) of the portfolio of three stocks was 15% and so on down the line, until, the risk is reduced upto 8 stocks in his study. Most of the diversification benefits were achieved even by the use of 8 stocks portfolio. If all the 470 stocks were grouped together into one portfolio, the standard deviation was 11.6%. Thus, in his study of 470 stocks, of the total risk he reduced only upto about 9% and the rest namely 12% is the systematic risk or market risk which could not be reduced.

Thus, Evans and Archer study showed the optimum level upto which risk can be lowered and that will lower depending upon stocks chosen and the time period.

@ J.L. Evans and S.H. Archer "Diversification and the Reduction of Dispersion — An Empirical Analysis," *Journal of Finance* (December 1968).

26 BASICS OF PORTFOLIO MANAGEMENT IN INDIA

In India, Portfolio Management is still in its infancy. Barring a few Indian banks, and foreign banks and UTI, no other agency had Professional Portfolio Management until 1987. After the setting up of public sector Mutual Funds, since 1987, Professional Portfolio Management, backed by competent research staff became the order of the day. After the success of Mutual Funds in Portfolio Management, a number of brokers and Investment Consultants some of whom are also professionally qualified have become Portfolio Managers. They have managed the funds of clients on both discretionary and non-discretionary basis. It was found that many of them, including Mutual Funds have guaranteed a minimum return or capital appreciation and adopted all kinds of incentives which are now prohibited by SEBI. They resorted to speculative over trading and insider trading, discounts, etc., to achieve their targetted returns to the clients, which are also prohibited by SEBI.

The recent CBI probe into the operations of many market dealers has revealed the unscrupulous practices by banks, dealers and brokers in their Portfolio Operations. The SEBI has then imposed stricter rules, which included their registration, a code of conduct and minimum infrastructure, experience and expertise etc. It is no longer possible for any unemployed youth, or retired person or self-styled consultant to engage in Portfolio Management without the SEBI's licence. The guidelines of SEBI are in the direction of making Portfolio Management a responsible professional service to be rendered by experts in the field.

SOME ASPECTS OF PORTFOLIO MANAGEMENT

Basically Portfolio Management involves:

(A) A proper investment decision making of what to buy and sell;

(B) Proper money management in terms of investment in a basket of assets so as to satisfy the asset preferences of investors;

(C) Reduce the risk and increase returns.

Investment Strategy

In India, there are a large number of savers, barring the 26% of the population who are below the poverty line. In a poor country like this, it is surprising that its saving rate is as high as 34% of GDP per annum and investment at 37% of GDP. But the return in the form of output growth was as low as 7 to 8% per annum. One may ask why is it that high levels of investment could not generate comparable rates of growth of output? The answer is poor investment strategy, involving high capital output ratios, low productivity of capital and high rates of obsolescence of capital. What is true of the nation at that Macro level is also true at Micro level of individuals and institutions. The use of capital in India is wasteful and inefficient, dispite the fact that India is labour rich and capital poor. Thus, the Portfolio Managers in India lack the expertise and experience, which will enable them to have proper strategy for investment management.

Secondly, the average Indian Household saves around 45% in financial form and 55% in physical form as in 2012-13. Of those in financial form, nearly 66% is held in cash and deposits, as per the latest RBI data and they have negative real returns or return less than the inflation rates. Besides, a proportion of 29% of financial savings is held in form of Insurance, P.F., Pension Funds etc., while another 1 to 2% is in Certificates like Post Office Deposits, N.S. Certificates, Public Provident Funds, National Saving Scheme etc. The real returns on Insurance, P.F., etc., are low and many times lower than the average inflation rates. With the removal of many tax concessions for investments in P.O. Savings instruments, Certificates, etc., they also become less attractive to small and medium investors. The only investments, statisfying all their objectives are capital market instruments. These objectives are income, capital appreciation, safety, marketability, Liquidity and hedge against inflation, and investments by average household in shares and debentures and MF Schemes is only around 4% of the total financial savings.

Objectives of Investors: The return on equity investments in the capital market particularly if proper investment strategy is adopted would satisfy the above objectives and the real returns would be higher than any other saving instruments. It is in this context, the art and science of investment and of Portfolio Management became the *sine-qua-non* of success.

All investments involve risk taking. However, some risk free investments are available like bank deposits or P.O. Deposits whose returns are called risk free returns of about 4 to 9% but the inflation on rate is high at 8 to 10%. So the returns on more risky investments are higher than that, having risk premium. Risk is variability of return and uncertainty of payment of interest and repayment of principal. Risk is measured by standard deviation of the returns over the mean for a given period. Risk varies directly with return. The higher the risk taken, the higher is the return, under normal market conditions.

Although Indian markets are imperfect and are developing, all the basic principles and theory of portfolio management would apply and these are recapitulated below. The principles and theoretical concepts involved are reproduced here, at the risk of repetition.

Risk and Beta

Risk is of two components — systematic market related risk and unsystematic risk or company specific risk. The former cannot be eliminated but managed with the help of Beta (β), which is explained as follows:

$$\beta = \frac{\text{\% age change of Scrip return}}{\text{\% age change of Market return}}$$

If $\beta = 1$, the risk of the company is the same as that of the market and if $\beta > 1$, the company's risk is more than the market risk. If $\beta < 1$, the reverse is the position.

Specific Risk: If risk is company specific risk it can be reduced by diversification into different industries and companies of different types and nature and whose covariances are different and whose performances are disparate.

Types of Risk

Unsystematic Risk	*Systematic Risk*
Company related risks due to higher costs, mismanagement, defective sales or inventory strategy, insolvency, fall in demand and company specific recession, labour problems, inputs problems etc.	Market related risk due to demand problems, interest rates, inflation, raw materials, import and export policy, Tax policy etc., Business Risk, Market Risk, Financial Risk, Interest Rate Risk, Inflation Risk, etc.

Modern Portfolio Theory (MPT): This postulates that public generally are risk averse. In a perfect market, information is free and quickly absorbed by the market. Given the return, risk can be reduced by diversification of investment into a number of Scrips. Each Scrip has its own risk profile. The risks of any two Scrips are different from the risk of a group of two companies together. Thus, if the risk of Reliance (β) is say 1.90 and that of Dr. Reddy's is 0.70, the total of these two units is 1.30 as the average. But the actual 'β' may be less at say 1.00 the reason being that the covariance of these two may be zero or negative (less than 1).

CAPM & SML: (Capital Asset Pricing Model and Security Market Line) CAPM postulates that in a perfect market, where shares are correctly priced, every security will give a return commensurate with its risk. "β" is a measure of the risk. The market risk is different from the risks of individual Scrips comprising the market. CML relates to the total risk of the market. But SML refers to the risk, which is undiversifiable market related risk. Total risk is measured by the standard deviation, while the undiversifiable risk is measured by Beta (β). CML, is Capital Market Line and SML is Security Market Line.

Risk premium of portfolio is the excess of the expected portfolio return over the risk free return. Similar is the definition in respect of risk premium of the market, namely, expected Market Return minus Risk Free Return. CML passes through the risk free rate, which represents the true time value of money or the reward for waiting by savers.

Time Value of Money

In portfolio management and investment decision-making, time element and time value of money are very relevant. Savings are automatic or induced. If induced, it requires a return enough to induce them to part with liquidity. Thus, savings and liquidity will be parted by the investors if only their time preference is satisfied by proper return.

Why time preference? Why savers prefer today's return to tomorrow's return? "A bird in hand is worth two in the bush", as the adage goes.

(1) More money is to be received after a year, if he has to lend to the user of funds today. He forgoes consumption which has to be compensated.

(2) Money lent today can produce something more than before and hence present money is more valuable than money tomorrow. This premium is needed for waiting.

(3) Money is losing in value due to rise in prices. Hence, moneylenders lose and borrowers gain in times of inflation. Premium given is to compensate the lenders against loss due to fall in value of money.

Compounding

Future Value Factor (FVF) is $(1 + r)^n$ where (r) is the rate of interest required and (n) is the period of years of waiting.

$Fn = P\ (1 + r)^n$, or

Future Value = Present Value × (Future Value Factor)

So the return required by savers is related to the waiting period, loss of consumption at present, or liquidity and risk of loss of money or variance of returns.

Discounting

If the future flow of money is known as C_1, C_2, C_3, etc. What is the present value of them and how much is he prepared to pay for them? If he deposits today ₹ 100 he gets ₹ 110 at the end of 1 year and ₹ 121 at the end of 2 years, the interest rate is 10%. This process of finding the present value for future money flows is called discounting. Present value of future amounts is:

$$P = F\ (n)\ \frac{1}{(1+r)^n}$$

The multiplier $\frac{1}{(1+r)^n}$ is called PVF or Present Value Factor. We should know the amounts of cash flows, (Fn) number of years (n) and the required rate of return (r).

Perpetuity

When we receive a fixed sum of money every year upto infinity, it is called perpetuity. Suppose we want to receive ₹ 100 every year for infinity and interest rate is 10%, we have to deposit ₹ 1,000 and the equation is $PV = \frac{a}{r}$ where PV is Present Value of perpetuity, "a" is fixed periodic cash flow and r is the rate of interest.

Annuity

Annuity is a constant cash flow for a finite time period of say 5 years (n). Examples of annuity are found in the case of lease rentals, loan repayments, Recurring deposits, etc. More detailed discussion is given on *time element* in a separate chapter.

Application to Porfolio Management

Portfolio Management involves time element and time horizon. The present value of future returns/cash flows by discounting is useful for share valuation and bond valuation. The investment strategy in portfolio construction should have a time horizon, say 3 to 5 years, to produce the desired results of say 20-30% return per annum.

Besides Portfolio Management should also take into account tax benefits and investment incentives. As the returns are taken by investors net of tax payments, and there is always an element of inflation, returns net of taxation and inflation are more relevant to tax paying investors. These are called net real rates of returns, which should be more than other returns. They should encompass risk free return plus a reasonable risk premium, depending upon the risk taken, on the instruments/assets invested. (Tax factors are discussed in another Chapter).

Portfolio Construction, Revision and Evaluation

Portfolio Manager has to use all the tools of research like fundamental analysis and technical analysis in addition to Risk-Return analysis to decide on the investment, buying and selling etc. After the design of the Portfolio Strategy, the construction and allocation of funds will lead to the building up of the portfolio. Thereafter the portfolio thus built requires a constant review and revision with the result that operations on it are a continuous process. This is also called Monitoring. Finally, once in a quarter or half year, the portfolio performance is evaluated, for its success by comparing the actual achievements with the targets fixed. This throws light on the efficiency of the investment strategy of Portfolio Manager and helps the revision of portfolio.

MPT and Dominance Concept

The Modern Portfolio Theory (MPT) is based on assumptions of *free and perfect information flow* and the *notion of dominance.* This means that if the market is able to absorb the information, fully and efficiently, price reflects the risks involved given the same return, the investor can choose the scrips with the lowest possible risk. This is possible by diversification into a number of companies of say 10 to 15, which have diverse characteristics of risk. Thus, when any two Scrips behave differently to given changes in the economy and industry and when the co-efficient of correlation between them is less than 1, such scrips can be joined in a portfolio so as to reduce the combined risk of the portfolio.

The notion of dominance tells us that no investor should invest in one company alone and if there are two or more companies with the same risk, then he has to choose the one with higher return and if both have the same return he has to choose the one with lower risk. The investor can reduce the risk by distributing his funds in a diverse variety of companies with varying risks and returns which do not have much auto correlation. Thus, the investor has not only to make proper investment decision of what to buy and when to buy, but has a proper investment strategy through diversification and choice of a proper 'B' for the scrips selected so that the total risk of portfolio is the lowest possible.

Diversification Process

The process of diversification has various phases involving investment into various classes of assets like equity, preference shares, CDs, NCDs, P.S.U. Bonds and Shares, Money market instruments like commercial paper, inter-corporate investments, deposits etc. Within each class of assets, there is further possibility of diversification into various industries, different companies etc. The proportion of funds invested into various classes of assets, instruments, industries and companies, would depend upon the objectives of investor, under portfolio management and his asset preferences, income and asset requirements. The subject is further elaborated in another chapter.

A portfolio with the objective of regular income would invest a proportion of funds in bonds, debentures and Fixed Deposits. For such investments, duration of the life of the bond/debenture, quality of the asset as judged by the credit rating and the expected yield are the relevant variables.

Bond market is not well developed in India but debentures, partly or fully convertible into equity are in good demand both from individuals and Mutual Funds. The Portfolio Manager has to use his analytical power and discretion to choose the right debentures with the required duration, yield and quality. The duration and immunisation of expected inflows of funds to the required quantum of funds have to be well planned by the Portfolio Manager. Research and high degree of analytical power in investment management and bond portfolio management are necessary.

The bond investments are thus equally challenging as equity investments and more so in respect of money market instruments. All these facts bring out clearly the needed analytical powers and expertise of Portfolio Manager. Bond market is discussed in a separate chapter elaborately.

SEBI Guidelines for Portfolio Managers

It will thus be seen that Portfolio Management is an art and requires high degree of expertise. The merchant banker has been authorised to do Portfolio Management Services, if they belong to Categories licensed by the SEBI. This classification of merchant bankers into different categories was dropped in 1996 and only the category I merchant bankers is allowed to operate in India. Others who want to provide such services should have a minimum networth of ₹ 50 lakhs and expertise, as laid down or changed from time-to-time by the SEBI and would have to register with the SEBI. The SEBI have set out the guidelines in this regard, in which the relations of the client *vis-a-vis* the Portfolio Manager and the respective rights and duties of both have been set out. The code of conduct for Portfolio Managers has been laid down by the SEBI. The job of Portfolio Manager in managing the client's funds, either on discretionary or non-discretionary basis has thus become challenging and difficult due to the multitude of obligations laid on his shoulders by the SEBI, in respect of their operations, accounts, audit etc.

It is thus clear that Portfolio Management has become, a complex and responsible job which requires an in-depth training and expertise. It is in this context that the regulations of SEBI on Portfolio Management become necessary so that the minimum qualifications and experience are also ensured for those who are registered with SEBI. Nobody can do Portfolio Management without SEBI registration and licence.

The SEBI has given permission to Merchant Bankers to do Portfolio Management. As per the guidelines of September, 1991 a separate category of Portfolio Managers is also licensed by SEBI for which guidelines were given in January 1993. A code of conduct was also laid down by SEBI for Portfolio Managers.

Portfolio Management Service

As per the SEBI norms, it refers to professional services rendered for management of Portfolio of others, namely, clients or customers with the help of experts in Investment Advisory Services. The latter involves the advice regarding the worthwhileness of any particular investment or advice of what to buy and sell. Investment management on the other hand involves continuing relationship with client to manage investments with or without discretion for the client as per his requirements.

Who can be a Portfolio Manager?

Only those who are registered and pay the required licence fee are eligible to operate as Portfolio Managers. An applicant for this purpose should have necessary infrastructure with professionally qualified persons and with a minimum of two persons with experience in this business and a minimum networth of ₹ 50 lakhs. The Certificate once granted is valid for three years. Fees payable for registration are ₹ 2.5 lakhs every year for two years and ₹ 1 lakh for the third year. From the fourth year onwards, renewal fees per annum are ₹ 75,000. These fees payable are subject to change by the SEBI.

The SEBI has imposed a number of obligations and a code of conduct on them. The Portfolio Manager should have a high standard of integrity, honesty and should not have been convicted of any economic offence or moral turpitude. He should not resort to rigging up of prices, insider trading or creating false markets, etc. Their books of accounts, are subject to inspection and audit by SEBI. The observance of the code of conduct and guidelines given by the SEBI are subject to inspection and penalties for violation are imposed. The Manager has to submit periodical returns and documents as may be required by the SEBI from time-to-time.

Method of Operation

The Professional Portfolio Manager can be approached by any individual or organisation with a minimum amount of investible funds of ₹ 1 lakh or ₹ 2 lakhs. If the Manager is willing to accept him as his client, a contract is entered into for management of his funds either on discretionary basis or non-discretionary basis, specifying the objectives, risk to be tolerated, composition of assets/securities in the Portfolio and their relative proportion, fees payable and time period of management, as per the preference of the client etc. The client's data base is collected, namely, his available income and assets, his needs, his risk preferences, his choice for income or growth or both and host of personal details of the client so as to enable the Manager to design a Proper Investment Strategy for him.

SEBI Norms

SEBI has prohibited the Portfolio Manager to assume any risk on behalf of the client. Portfolio Manager cannot also assure any fixed return to the client. The investments made or advised by him are subject to risk which the client has to bear. The investment consultancy and management has to be charged at rates which are fixed at the beginning and transparent as per the contract. No sharing of profits or discounts or cash incentives to client are permitted.

The Portfolio Manager is prohibited to do lending, badla financing and bills discounting as per SEBI norms. He cannot put the clients' funds in any investment, not permitted by the contract, entered into with the client. Normally investments can be made in both capital market and money market instruments.

Client's money has to be kept in a separate account with the public sector bank and cannot be mixed up with his own funds or investments. All the deals done for a client's account are to be entered in his name and Contract Notes, Bills etc. are all passed in his name. A separate ledger account is maintained for all purchases/sales on client's behalf, which should be done at the market price. Final settlement and termination of contract is as per the contract and for the time period agreed upon. Notice of termination of contract is also as per the contract. During the period of contract, Portfolio Manager is only acting on a contractual basis and on a fiduciary basis. No contract for less than a year is permitted by the SEBI.

27

MARKOWITZ MODEL

Harry M. Morkowitz is credited with introducing new concepts of risk measurement and their application to the selection of portfolios. He started with the idea of risk aversion of average investors and their desire to maximise the expected return with the least risk. Morkowitz model is thus a theoretical framework for analysis of risk and return and their inter-relationships. He used the statistical analysis for measurement of risk and mathematical programming for selection of assets in a portfolio in an efficient manner. His framework led to the concept of efficient portfolios. An efficient portfolio is expected to yield the highest return for a given level of risk or lowest risk for a given level of return.

Markowitz generated a number of portfolios within a given amount of money or wealth and given preferences of investors for risk and return. Individuals vary widely in their risk tolerance and asset preferences. Their means, expenditures and investment requirements vary from individual to individual. Given the preferences, the portfolio selection is not a simple choice of any one security or securities, but a right combination of securities. Markowitz emphasised that quality of a portfolio will be different from the quality of individual assets within it. Thus, the combined risk of two assets taken separately is not the same risk of two assets together. Thus, two securities of TISCO do not have the same risk as one security of TISCO and one of Reliance.

Risk and Reward are two aspects of investment considered by investors. The expected return may vary depending on the assumptions. Risk index is measured by the variance or the distribution around the mean, its range etc., which are in statistical terms called variance and covariance. *The qualification of risk and the need for optimisation of return with lowest risk are the contributions of Markowitz. This led to what is called the Modern Portfolio Theory, which emphasises the trade off between risk and return.* If the investor wants a higher return, he has to take higher risk. But he prefers a high return but a low risk and hence the need for a trade off.

A portfolio of assets involves the selection of securities. A combination of assets or securities is called a portfolio. Each individual investor puts his wealth in a combination of assets depending on his wealth, income and his preferences. The traditional theory of portfolio postulates that selection of assets should be based on lowest risk, as measured by its standard deviation from the mean of expected returns. The greater the variability of returns, the greater is the risk. Thus, the investor chooses assets with the lowest variability of returns. Taking the return as the appreciation in the share price, if TELCO shares price varies from ₹ 338 to ₹ 580 (with variability of 72%) and Colgate from ₹ 218 to ₹ 315 (with a variability of 44%) during a time period, the investor chooses the Colgate as a less risky share.

As against this Traditional Theory that standard deviation measures the variability of return and risk is indicated by the variability, and that the choice depends on the securities with lower variability, the modern Portfolio Theory emphasises the need for maximisation of returns through a combination of securities, whose total variability is lower. The risk of each security is different from that of others and by a proper combination of securities, called diversification, one can arrive at a combination wherein the risk of one is offset partly or fully by that of the other. In other words, the variability of each security and covariance for their returns reflected through their inter-relationships should be taken into account. Thus, as per the Modern Portfolio Theory, expected returns, the variance of these returns and covariance of the returns of the securities within the portfolio are to be considered for the choice of a portfolio. A portfolio is said to be efficient, if it is expected to yield the highest return possible for the lowest risk or a given level of risk. A set of efficient portfolios can be generated by using the above process of combining various securities whose combined risk is lowest for a given level of return for the same amount of investment, that the investor is capable of. The theory of Markowitz, as stated above is based on a number of assumptions.

Assumptions of Markowitz Theory

The Modern Portfolio Theory of Markowitz is based on the following assumptions:

(1) Investors are rational and behave in a manner as to maximise their utility with a given level of income or money.

(2) Investors have free access to fair and correct information on the returns and risk.

(3) The markets are efficient and absorb the information quickly and perfectly.

(4) Investors are risk averse and try to minimise the risk and maximise return.

(5) Investors base decisions on expected returns and variance or standard deviation of these returns from the mean.

(6) Investors prefer higher returns to lower returns for a given level of risk.

A portfolio of assets under the above assumptions is considered efficient if no other asset or portfolio of assets offers a higher expected return with the same or lower risk or lower risk with the same or higher expected return. Diversification of securities is one method by which the above objectives can be secured. The unsystematic and company related risk can be reduced by diversification into various securities and assets whose variability is different and offsetting or put in different words which are negatively correlated or not correlated at all.

Markowitz Diversification

Markowitz postulated that diversification should not only aim at reducing the risk of a security by reducing its variability or standard deviation, but by reducing the covariance or interactive risk of two or more securities in a portfolio. As by combination of different securities, it is theoretically possible to have a range of risk varying from zero to infinity.

Markowitz theory of portfolio diversification attaches importance to standard deviation, to reduce it to zero, if possible, covariance to have as much as possible negative interactive effect among the securities within the portfolio and coefficient of correlation to have –1 (negative) so that the overall risk of the portfolio as a whole is nil or negligible. Then the securities have to be combined in a manner that standard deviation is zero, as shown in the example below. Possible combinations of securities (1) and (2) are as follows:

Security (1)	*Security (2)*	*S.D.*
80	20	0.8
70	30	0.4
66	34	0.0
20	80	0.8
10	90	0.9

In the example, if $^2/_3$rds are invested in security (1) and $^1/_3$rd in security (2), the coefficient of variation, namely $= \frac{\text{S.D.}}{\text{mean}}$ is the lowest.

The standard deviation of the portfolio determines the deviation of the returns and correlation coefficient of the composition of securities in the portfolio, invested. The equation is:

$$\sigma^2_p = \sum_{t=i}^{N} \sum_{j=1}^{N} x_i\, x_j\, r_{ij}\, \sigma_i\, \sigma_j.$$

σ^2_p = portfolio variance

σ_p = Standard deviation of portfolio = σ^2_p

x_i = Proportion of portfolio invested in security i

x_J = proportion of portfolio invested in security J

r_{ij} = coefficient of correlation between i and J

σ_i standard deviation of i

σ_j standard deviation of J

N = number of securities.

Problem

Given the following example, find out the expected Risk of the portfolio.

Security	*Expected Return*	*Proportion % Invested (X)*	*SD σ*
D.C.M.	10	20	0.2
Escorts	15	20	0.3
TISCO	20	60	0.5

SD (Standard deviation) and coefficient of correlation is r.

r_{12} = 0.5 (r_1 with respect to r_2)

r_{13} = 0.1 (r_1 with respect to r_3)

r_{23} = –0.3 (r_2 with respect to r_3)

then

$$\sigma_p^2 = x_1^2\sigma_1^2 + x_2^2\sigma_2^2 + x_3^2\sigma_3^2 + 2x_1x_2r_{12}\sigma_1\sigma_2 + 2x_2x_3r_{23}\sigma_2\sigma_3 + 2x_1x_3r_{13}\sigma_1\sigma_3$$

Putting the above data into the formula

$$\sigma_p^2 = (0.20)^2(0.2)^2 + [(20)^2 \times (6 \times .3)^2 (.30)^2] + (.60)^2(0.5)^2 + [2(.2)(.2)(.5)(.2)(.3)] + [2(.2)(.6)(-0.3)(.3)(.5)] + [2(.2)(.6)(.1)(0.2)(0.5)]$$

$$= 0.0016 + .0036 + .09 + .0024 - .0108 + .0024$$

$$= 0.1 - .0108 = 0.0892$$

$$\sigma_p^2 = .0892$$

$$\sigma_p = \sqrt{.0892} = .299 = +.30 \text{ Portfolio Risk}$$

Parameters of Markowitz Diversification

Based on his research, Markowitz has set out guidelines for diversification on the basis of the attitude of investors towards risk and return and on a proper quantification of risk. The investments have different types of risk characteristics; some called systematic and market-related risks and the other called unsystematic or company-related risks. Markowitz diversification involves a proper number of securities, not too few or not too many which have no correlation or negative correlation. The proper choice of companies, securities, or assets whose return are not correlated and whose risks are mutually offsetting will reduce the overall risk.

For building up the efficient set of portfolio, as laid down by Markowitz, we need to look into these important parameters.

(1) Expected return.

(2) Variability of returns as measured by standard deviation from the mean.

(3) Covariance or variance of one asset return to other asset returns.

In general the higher the expected return, the lower is the standard deviation or variance and lower is the correlation the better will be the security for investor choice. Whatever is the risk of the individual securities in isolation, the total risk of the portfolio of all securities may be lower, if the covariance of their returns is negative or negligible.

Criteria of Dominance

Dominance refers to the superiority of one portfolio over the other. A set can dominate over the other, if with the same return, the risk is lower or with the same risk, the return is higher. Dominance principle involves the trade off between risk and return.

For two security portfolio, minimise the portfolio risk by the equation

$$\sigma_p = W_a \sigma_a^2 + W_b \sigma_b^2 + 2 (W_a W_b \sigma_a \sigma_b \sigma_{ab})$$

$$E(R_p) = W_a E(R_a) + W_b E(R_b)$$

R refers to returns and $E(R_p)$ is the expected returns. σ_p is the standard deviation, W refers to the proportion invested in each security σ_a σ_b are the standard deviations of a and b securities and σ_{ab} is the covariance or interrelations of the security returns.

$\sigma_p = \sqrt{\frac{\Sigma x^2}{n}}$, where Σx^2 is the sum of deviations from the mean squared.

σ^2 is square of standard deviation or called variance.

Covariance is

$$\text{Cov } x\,y = \frac{1}{N}\sum_{1}^{N} [(Rx - \overline{R}\overline{x})(Ry - \overline{R}\overline{y})]$$

The above concepts are used in the calculation of expected returns, mean, standard deviation as a measure of risk and covarience as a measure of inter-relations of one security return with another.

Markowitz Model

Risk is discussed here in terms of a portfolio of assets.

As referred to earlier, any investment risk is the variability of return on a stock, assets or a portfolio. It is measured by standard deviation of the return over the Mean for a number of observations.

Types of Risk (Summary)

I	II
Systematic	Unsystematic
(Market)	(Company Risk)
Examples	*Examples*
Interest Rate Risk	Labour Troubles
Market Risk	Liquidity Problems
Inflation Risk	Raw Materials Risks
Demand and Government Policy	Financial Risks
International Factors	Management Problems

Measurement of Risk (Example)

Standard deviation to be calculated: Average in Mean

Observations: 10% – 5% 20% 35% – 10% = 10% will be their Mean.

Deviation from the Mean	*Square of Deviation*
10 — 10 = 0	0
– 5 — 10 = –15	225
+ 20 — 10 = 10	100
+ 35 — 10 = 25	625
– 10 — 10 = –20	400
	Σd^2 = 1350

Standard Deviation (σ_p) $= \sqrt{\left(\frac{\Sigma d^2}{5}\right)} = \sqrt{\frac{1350}{5}} = \sqrt{270} = 16.43$

Scrip Deviation = 16.43

Let Market Deviation = 10.40

Total Risk $= \dfrac{16.43}{10.40} = 1.58$

Portfolio Risk

When two or more securities or assets are combined in a portfolio, their covariance or interactive risk is to be considered. Thus, if the returns on two assets move together, their covariance is positive and the risk is more on such portfolio. If on the other hand, the returns move independently or in opposite directions, the covariance is negative and the risk in total will be lower.

Mathematically, the covariance is defined as:

$$\text{Cov x Y} = \frac{1}{N}\sum_{1}^{N} [(Rx - R\bar{x})(Ry - R\bar{y})],$$

where, Rx is return on security x, Ry return security Y, and $R\bar{x}$ and $R\bar{y}$ are expected returns on them respectively and N is the number of observations.

The coefficient of correlation is another measure designed to indicate the similarity or dissimilarity in the behaviour of two variables. We define the coefficient of correlation of x and y as:

$$\gamma\ xy = \frac{\text{Cov xy}}{\sigma_x \times \sigma_y} \text{ where,}$$

Cov x y is the covariance between x and y and σ_x is the standard deviation of x and σ_y is the standard deviation of y.

Example:

	Return	Expected Return	Variance
I Stock x	7	9	−2
Stock y	13	9	+4
			Product −2 × +4 = −8
II Stock x	11	9	+2
Stock y	5	9	−4
			Product +2 × −4 = −8

Where, N = 2 The covariance equation is as follows:

$$\text{Cov} = \frac{1}{2}\ [(7-9)\ (13-9) + (11-9)\ (5-9)]$$

$$= \frac{1}{2}\ (-8) + (-8)] = \frac{-16}{2} = -8$$

The coefficient of correlation can be set out as follows:

$$\gamma\ x\ y = \frac{-8}{(2)\times(4)} = \frac{-8}{8} = -1.0$$

If the coefficient of correlation between two securities is –1.0, it is perfect negative correlation. If it is +1.0 it is perfect positive correlation. If the coefficient is '0' then the returns are said to be independent. To sum up, correlation between two securities depend (a) on covariance between them, and (b) the standard deviation of each.

In Markowitz Model, we need to have the inputs of *expected returns,* risk measured by *standard deviation of returns* and the *covariance between the returns* on assets considered.

Portfolio Management (Summary)

(Q) What is Portfolio Management?	(A) Management of large Investible Funds with a view to maximising return and minimising risk.
(Q) Investments are generally risky — the higher the risk, the higher the return. How to Manage this trade-off between Risk and Return?	(A) Efficient portfolios are those with minimum risk for a given expected return. For a planned return, risk can be minimised by using the concept of Beta for Systematic Risk and Diversification for Unsystematic Risk.

Two Models Compared

Markowitz Model *Utility Concept*	*Sharpe Model*
Utility of a portfolio is risk adjusted return. It is Equal to portfolio return minus risk penalty. Where Risk Penalty = $\frac{\text{Risk Squared}}{\text{Risk Tolerance}}$ It is portfolio risk, relative to the investor's risk tolerance. The optimal portfolio is one on the efficient frontier that maximises utility. To generate efficient portfolios the Markowitz Model requires — (a) expected return on each asset (b) Standard deviation of returns as a measure of risk of each asset, and (c) the covariance or correlation coefficients as a measure of inter-relationship between the returns on assets considered.	Optimal portfolio is set up by using the single index model of Sharpe. The desirability of any stock is directly related to its excess return to Beta ratio, namely Sharpe Index $= \frac{R_J - R_F}{\beta_J}$ Where, R_J is expected return on the stock, R_F is the risk free return, and β_J is the Beta relating the J stock to the market return. Then rank all the stocks in their order of the index value. In Sharpe Model, the return on any stock depends on some constant (α) called Alpha plus coefficient called β (Beta), times the value of a stock Index (I), plus a random component. The equation in $R_J = \alpha_J + \beta_J I + e_J$ in Sharpe Model.

SHARPE MODEL

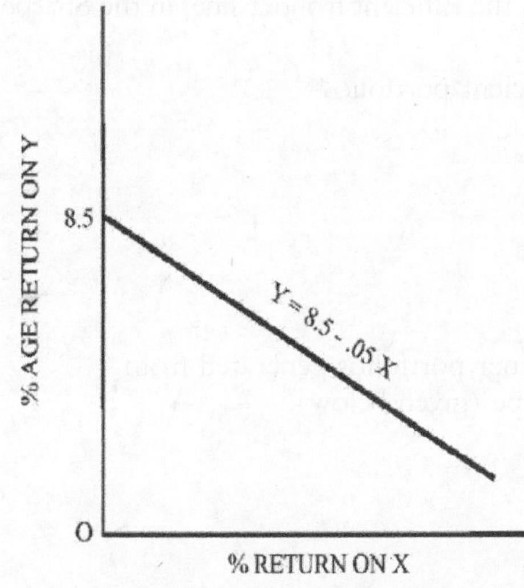

Sharpe Model Equation was set as, $R_J = \alpha_J + \beta_J I + e_J$, where,

R_J = Expected return on security J

α_J = Intercept of a straight line or alpha coefficient

β_J = Beta coefficient is the slope of straight line (Regression line)

I = Expected return on Index of the market

e_J = Error term with a mean of zero and standard deviation which is constant.

Alpha (α) is really the value of y in the equation when the value of x is zero. The return on the stock in relation to the return on the market Index, namely, β is a measure of the systematic risk of the market. The error term in the above equation explains the unsystematic risk.

a (α) is measured by making return on y as zero. In the following chart α is 8.5, which is the constant and Beta is .05, calculated for the data, used in the chart. If the return on the Index is say, at 25%, then R_J = 8.5 – .05 (25) = 7.25.

This means that if the market index gives a return of 25%, the security in question will give a return of 7.25% only. Systematic Risk only is used by Sharpe, and it is equal to $\beta^2 \times$ (variance of Index) $= \beta^2 \sigma^2$. Where σ^2 is variance of Index. Unsystematic Risk = Total variance – Systematic Risk plus the error term in his equation.

Sharpe Model (Contd.)

Practical Measurement of Return

Riskless Rate = 6% (Bank rate) or Bank Deposit rate (7.5%)

Risk Premium = 5 to 10% depending or the Risk or the Concept of Beta of the security.

$$\beta \text{ Beta} = \frac{\text{\% Price Change of a Scrip Return}}{\text{\% Price Change of the Market Index Return}}$$

Beta is thus a measure of Systematic Risk of the market only and does not represent the unsystematic risk. Market Risk is represented by BSE National Index, in the above formula. In the regression equation given below used by Sharpe, the Unsystematic Risk is represented by the error term, namely, (e), while a or α is the constant slope of the regression line, and Beta (b) is the measure of Systematic Risk.

Example for Regression Equation and calculation of Beta is given below:

$Y = \alpha + \beta X + e$ is the equation

$Y = 0.91 + 0.93X$, where,

$\beta = 0.93$ X = Market Return

Y = Scrip Return

α = Constant = 0.91

Examples of β, calculated

Reliance	—	1.955
ACC	—	0.931
Telco	—	1.153
Tisco	—	1.342
Colgate	—	0.946
Tata Tea	—	0.951

Source: Some Issues of Journal of Chartered Financial Analyst (ICFAI)

On the basis of the above estimates of the stocks Alpha, Beta and expected return and Residual variance (data derived from the above formulas), one can construct a series of efficient portfolios, by using a computer programmer. This will give out the series of corner portfolios and the line connecting them is the Efficient frontier line, in the Sharpe Model.

The chart below represents the corner portfolio sets, indicating the efficient portfolio.[@]

Efficient corner portfolios

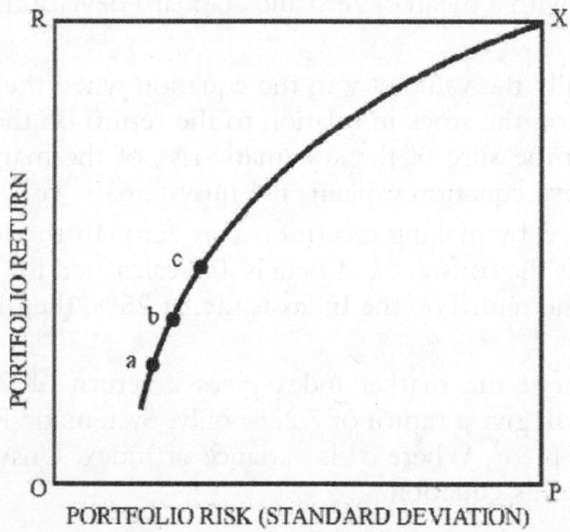

a, b, c... x are the corner portfolios generated from the equations of Sharpe (given below).

Equation for Portfolio Return

$$R_p = \sum_{i=1}^{N} X_i\,(\alpha_1 + \beta_i I) - 1$$

This is for calculating the expected return on portfolio where N = total number of stocks, X_i is the proportion devoted to stock i – β_i is the Beta on Stock i, I is market index return and is the same for all stocks estimated.

For Portfolio Variance

σ_p^2 = variation of portfolio return

σ_I^2 = expected variance of Index (Market)

e_i^2 = variation in security's return not caused by its relationship to the index.

@ Refer to Chapter 20, of D.E. Fischer & R.J. Gordon, *Security Analysis and Portfolio Management.*

Equation for Portfolio Variance

$$\sigma_p{}^2 = \left[\left(\sum_{i=1}^{N} X_i\beta_i\right)^2 \sigma_I^2\right] + \left[\sum_{i=1}^{N} X_1{}^2 e_i^2\right]$$

ARBITRAGE PRICING THEORY

Introduction

Like the Capital Assets Pricing Model (CAPM), Arbitrage Pricing Theory (APT) is an equilibrium model of asset pricing but assumes that the returns are generated by a factor Model. Its assumption *vis-a-vis* those of CAPM are set out first:

APT	*CAPM*
Investors do not look at expected returns and standard deviations. Based on the law of one price, if the price of an asset is different in different markets, arbitrage brings them to the same price.	Investors look at the expected returns and accompanying risks measured by standard deviation. Investors are risk averse and risk-return analysis is necessary.
Investors prefer higher wealth/returns to lower wealth. APT is based on the return generated by factor models.	Investors maximise wealth for a given level of risk.

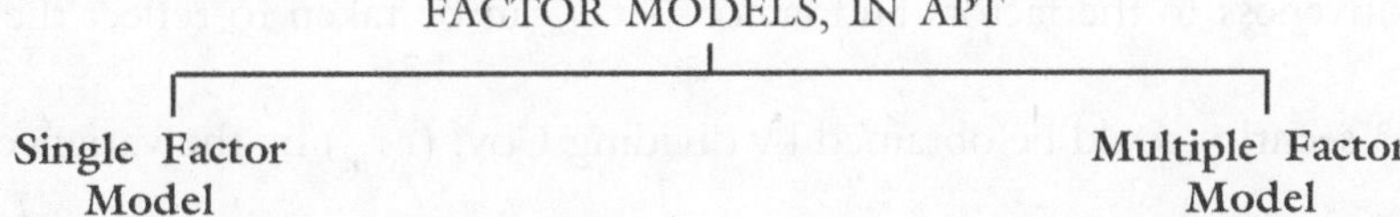

Single Factor Model	Multiple Factor Model
Asset price depends on a single factor, say GNP, or Industrial Production (IP) or interest rates, Money Supply, Inflation rates and so on.	A number of variables are taken into account for the Asset price model. This model takes more than one factor, referred to already into the equation say, F_i for interest rate and F_2 for I.P., etc.
Equation $\gamma_i = a_i + b_iF + e_i$;γ_i is expected return from asset i, a_i is the risk free return or constant, F is the value of one of the factors listed above, e_i is the error term (unexplained variables).	$\gamma_i = a_i + b_{i1}F_i + b_{i2}F_2 + e_i$ we can have F_1, F_2 F_3 etc. in the above equation, a_i is the expected value if all the factors are of zero values (a is constant).

Asset Selection in the Above Model

Investment strategies of many types can also be selected under this model. If there are many securities to be selected, and a fixed amount to be invested, the investor can choose in a manner that he can aim at a zero non-factor risk ($e_i = 0$). This is possible by combining securities to hedge out the sensitivity of a portfolio to all but one factor.

An example will explain this. Let there be three securities A, B and C with the following securities:

Security	*bi1*	*bi2*
A	–0.40	1.75
B	1.60	–0.75
C	0.67	–0.25

If he has ₹ 1,000, he invests ₹ 300 in Security A, ₹ 700 in Security B and nil in Security C, with proportions being 0.3 in A, 0.7 in B and 0 in C.

It will be seen from the equations below that the sensitivity to factors 1, and 2 will be 1.0 and 0 respectively.

$$bp_1 = (-0.40 \times 0.3) + (1.60 \times 0.7) + (0.67 \times 0)$$
$$= (-0.12) + (1.12) + (0) = +1.0$$

$$bp_2 = (1.75 \times 0.3) + (-0.75 \times 0.7) + (-0.25 \times 0)$$
$$= (0.525) + (-0.525) = 0$$

In the above fashion, it would be possible theoretically, although not in practice, to create *"pure factor"* portfolios that are sensitive to only one factor and have insignificant non-factor risk. But in practice, only impure factor portfolios can be created.

Components of Expected Returns

It is convenient to break up the expected return into two parts: (i) risk free rate of return, and (ii) the rest in the following equation; rf is the risk free return and λ_1 is the expected premium return per unit of sensitivity to the factor for Portfolio_i.

$$rp_1 = rf + \lambda_1$$

Similarly, the expected return on pure factor 2 portfolio

$$rp_2 = rf + \lambda_2$$

Thus, the investor by splitting his funds among risk free portfolios and pure factor portfolios, it is possible for him to form a portfolio with almost any sensitivity to each factor. Although theory claims that the non-factor risk can be reduced to zero, it is not possible in real life. Therefore, in practical investment or in portfolio operations, it is better to combine the Capital Asset pricing theory and the APT Model. Most investors prefer, no doubt higher levels of expected return and dislike higher levels of risk. The fact is that there is a trade off between them, which is not considered by the APT Model. Synthesis of CAPM and APT is therefore more realistic.

Beta coefficients can be used to reflect the risk factors and factor sensitivities can also be taken into account to arrive at the expected returns. Thus, if the returns are generated by two factor model, the Beta coefficient of a security will be related to its sensitiveness to the factors and factor Betas can be taken to reflect the different sensitivities of different factors.

Beta coefficient for a security could be obtained by dividing Cov. $(r_i r_m)$ by the variance of the Market Portfolio (σ_M^2)

Thus, $\beta_i = \dfrac{\text{Cov}(r_i r_m)}{\sigma_M^2}$

Security Betas can appear in factor Betas, if we ignore $\dfrac{\text{Cov}(r_i r_m)}{\sigma_M^2}$ in equation below.

$$\beta_i = \left[\frac{\text{Cov}(F_1 r_M)^1}{\sigma_M^2} \times b_{i1}\right] + \left[\frac{\text{Cov}(F_2 r_M)^1}{\sigma_M^2} \times b_{i2}\right] + \frac{\text{Cov}(r_i r_M)}{\sigma_M^2}$$

If the last term becomes zero, as referred to above, then,

$$\beta F_1 = \frac{\text{Cov}(F_i r_m)}{\sigma_M^2}$$

$$\beta F_2 = \frac{\text{Cov}(F_2 r_M)}{\sigma_M^2}$$

It will be seen that βF_1 and βF_2 are constants as they do not vary from one security to another, the Beta coefficient of a security is a function of its sensitiveness to the pervasive factors. Thus, by taking Betas of securities the question of sensitivity of security return to a factor is taken care of. By this, one can synthesize the APT Model and CAP Model in the empirical work.

Empirical Testing of APT Model

The CAPM as also the practical experience tells us that other things being equal, securities with large *ex-ante* betas will have relatively large expected returns. It does not mean that the actual *ex-post* returns will also be larger. But investment is made on expectation and hence the use of Betas, despite the fact that exact Betas may not really give an indication of actual returns in future.

Beta measurement is itself subject to limitations, as they change widely, with the number of years for which data are taken and the source of data, and the methods of compilation are subject to normal statistical limitations.

Using the actual data on Stock Price Index numbers and security prices of any Stock Exchange, one can compile Betas, the method of which has been explained earlier. Empirical studies done abroad on NYSE data (by Centre for Research in Security Prices (CRSP) at the University of Chicago) showed that the historical Beta values cannot be counted upon to predict the returns precisely. They are useful as some approximations and landmarks to go by.

In months, in which there were excess positive returns, the Beta factors were generally positive in the sense that stocks with historical Betas gave excess returns over the market. In periods when the excess returns were negative, the Beta factor was generally negative, in the sense that stocks with high historical betas, tended to under perform as compared to those with low-historical Betas.

In detailed tests of the original and Zero-beta CAPM, portfolio classes were used to examine the relationship between average returns and historical Betas. The graph below shows the actual relationship for the period 1938 to 1968. The vertical intercept, which corresponds to the zero beta Return, is 0.61% per month, while the average Treasury Bill rate, which corresponds to the risk free rate of interest, was only 0.13% per month. Assuming that Betas are measured relative to a Stock index, they are surrogates for true Betas, and they support the thesis of CAPM to a substantial degree.

Arbitrage Pricing Theory — Problem

Question

$\lambda_1 = 1.8$ Risk Free Rate $\lambda_0 = 7\%$

$\lambda_2 = 1.25$ $b_1 = 1.2$

$\lambda_3 = 0.50$ $b_2 = 1.5$

$b_3 = -0.75$

Answer:

Equation for APT Model

$$Eri = \lambda_o + \lambda_1 b_1 + \lambda_2 b_2 + \lambda_3 b_3 \dots$$

$$Eri = 7 + 1.8\ (1.2) + 1.25\ (1.5) + 0.50\ (-0.75)$$

$$= 7 + 2.16 + 1.875 - 0.375 = 10.66$$

The expected rate of return of the stock is 10.66%

Question

Calculate the equilibrium rate of return for the following three securities

Security	bi_1	bi_2
A	1.2	1
B	– 0.5	0.75
C	0.75	1.30

Answer:

Assume two factor Model as applicable which is → $E\ (r_1) = 4\% + 3\%\ bi_1 + 5\%\ bi_2$

$E\ (r_A) = 4\% + 3\%\ (1.2) + 5\%\ (+1.0) = 12.6\%$

$E\ (r_B) = 4\% + 3\%\ (-0.5) + 5\%\ (0.75) = 6.25\%$

$E\ (r_C) = 4\% + 3\%\ (0.75) + 5\%\ (1.30) = 12.75\%$

In the Graph below, OM is risk free return. Actual CAPM line is shown in the Graph to vary from the Zero Beta line to a substantial extent.

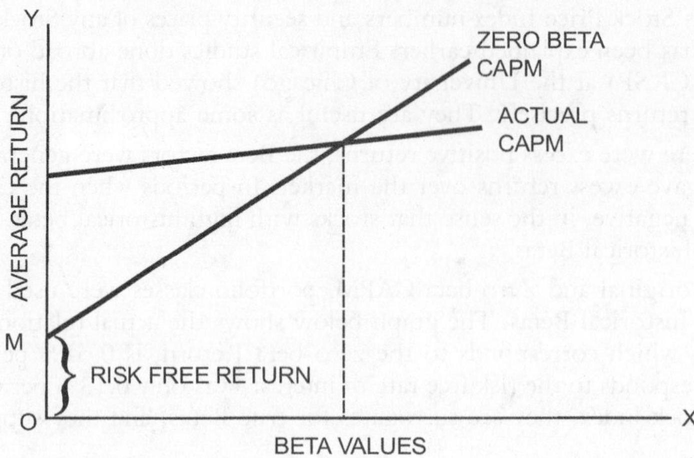

Source: William F. Sharpe
G.J. Alexander
Investment

Sharpe Model

Markowitz Model had serious practical limitations due the rigours involved in compiling the expected returns, standard deviation, variance, *covariance of each security to every other security in the portfolio. Sharpe model has simplified this process by relating the return in a security to a single Market index.* Firstly, this will theoretically reflect all well traded securities in the market. Secondly, it will reduce and simplify the work involved in compiling elaborate matrices of variances as between individual securities.

If thus the market index is used as a surrogate for other individual securities in the portfolio, the relation of any individual security with the Market index can be represented in a Regression line or characteristic line. This is drawn below, with the excess return on the security on the y-axis and excess return on the Market Portfolio on the x-axis.

The equation of the characteristic line is $R_i - R_f = a + \beta_i m\ (R_m - R_f) + r_i$

R_i is the holding period return on security i

R_f is the riskless rate of interest

Alpha is the vertical intercept on y-axis representing the return on the security when only unsystematic risk is considered and systematic risk is measured by Beta. ri is the residual component, not captured by the above variables.

$R_i - R_f =$	$\underbrace{\alpha p + rp}$	$\underbrace{+\ \beta pm\ (R_m - R_f)}$
Excess Return on Portfolio	Unsystematic Component of p's Excess Return	Market (Systematic) Component of p's Excess Return

S.M.L. GRAPH

Y

$\alpha + \beta M\ (R_m - R_f) + r$

$R_i - R_f$

βM

α

X

$R_m - R_f$

Optimal Portfolio of Sharpe

This optimal portfolio of Sharpe is called the Single Index Model. The optimal portfolio is directly related to the Beta. If R_i is expected return on stock i and R_f is Risk free Rate, then the excess return = $R_i - R_f$

This has to be adjusted to β_i, namely

$\frac{R_i - R_f}{\beta_1}$ which is the equation for ranking Stocks in the order of their return adjusted for risk.

The method involves selecting a cut-off rate for inclusion of securities in a portfolio. For this purpose, excess return to Beta ratio given above has to be calculated for each stock and rank them from highest to lowest. Then only those securities which have $\frac{R_i - R_f}{\beta_1}$, greater than cut-off point, fixed in advance can be selected. The basis for finding the cut-off Rate C_i is as follows:

Basis for Cut-off Rate

For a portfolio of i stocks, C_i is given by cut-off rate

$$\text{Cut-off Rate } C_i = \frac{\sigma_m^2 \sum_{t=1}^{J} \frac{(R_i - R_f)\beta_i}{\sigma e_i}}{1 + \sigma_m^2 \sum_{t=1}^{J} \frac{\beta_i^2}{\sigma e_i^2}}$$

σ_m^2 = variance in the market Index

σe_i^2 = variance in the Stock movement in Unsystematic Risk.

R_i, R_f, β_i have the same meanings as referred to above.

Take an example. $R_f = 10$, Beta = 1

Expected Return $R_i = 15$, σe_i^2 = unsystematic risk is given by 50, then

We have

$$\frac{(R_i - R_f)\beta_i}{\sigma e_i^2} = \frac{(15-10)1}{50} = \frac{5}{50} = \frac{1}{10}$$

Given σ_m^2 = market risk = 10.

Then

$$\sigma_m^2 \times \frac{\beta_i^2}{\sigma e_i^2} = \frac{(1)^2}{50} \times 10 = \frac{1}{5}$$

$$C_i = \frac{\sigma_m^2 \frac{(R_i - R_f)\beta_i}{\sigma e_i^2}}{1 + \sigma_m^2 \frac{\beta_i^2}{\sigma e_i^2}} = \frac{10 \times \frac{1}{10}}{1 + 10\frac{1}{5}}$$

$$C_i = \frac{10(1/10)}{1+(1/5)10} = \frac{1}{1.2} = 0.84$$

Example

We have to see that for the optimum C_i that is C^*, to be selected, the securities should have excess return to Betas above C_i. Excess return to Beta ratio should be above C_i to be included in the portfolio, to be precise. This C_i is that point which shows the cut-off point between those excess returns to Beta ratios above. The calculation of C requires data, which are shown below:

R_f = Risk free Return = 5%

Security Nos.	*Mean Return* R_i	*Excess Return* $R_i - R_f$	*Beta* β_i	*Unsystematic Risk* σe_i^2	*Excess Return to Beta Ratio* $(R_i - R_f)/\beta_i$
1	15.0	10.0	1.0	50	10.0
2	17.0	12.0	1.5	40	8.0
3	12.0	7.0	1.0	20	7.0
4	17.0	12.0	2.0	10	6.0
5	11.0	6.0	1.0	40	6.0

Based on the above data, we have to calculate the 'C' values for each security for inclusion in the optimum portfolio. The following Table gives the example:

Security	$\frac{(R_i - R_f)/\beta}{e_t^2}$ *Excess Return to Beta/Res Var*	$\frac{\beta_i^2}{\sigma e^2}$ *Beta Squared/ Res Var*	$\sum_{t=1}^{J} \frac{(R_i - R_f)}{\sigma e^2}$ *Excess Return to Beta Res var Cumulative*	$\Sigma \frac{\beta^2}{\sigma e^2}$ *Beta Squared/ Resi var Cumulative*	*C Value* *Cut-off Rate*
A	0.119	.01525	0.119	.01525	2.22
B	0.109	.01419	0.228	.02944	3.36
C	0.107	.01497	0.336	.04441	4.06

Calculation of Values

(A) In calculation of C; R_f = 7% R_m = 11% σ_m^2 = 26

$\frac{(R_i - R_f)\beta}{\sigma e^2}$ is 0.119, multiplied by σ_m^2

so 0.119 × 26, then divide it by σe^2

$$1 + \sigma_m^2 \frac{\beta_i^2}{\sigma e^2} = 1 + 26\ (.01525)$$

$$1 + \sigma_m^2 \Sigma \frac{(R_i - R_f)\beta}{\sigma e^2} = 0.119 \times 26$$

$$1 + \sigma_m^2 \Sigma \frac{\beta_i^2}{\sigma e^2} = 1 + 26\ (.01525)$$

$$\text{(A) } C_i = \frac{0.119 \times 26}{1 + 26(.01525)} = \frac{3.094}{1.3965} = 2.22$$

$$\text{(B) } C_i = \frac{.228 \times 26}{1 + 26(.02944)} = \frac{5.928}{1.7654} = 3.36$$

$$\text{(C) } C_i = \frac{.336 \times 26}{1 + 26(.04441)} = \frac{8.736}{2.1546} = 4.06$$

Res Var = Residual variance σe^2

σ_m^2 = market variance.

All securities with excess return to Beta ratio above the cut-off rate C*, say 3.0 in the above Table will be chosen in the portfolio. The calculation of cut-off point is also explained. In arriving at the optimal portfolio, the emphasis of Sharpe Model is on Beta and on the Market Index. Sharpe's optimal portfolio would thus consist of those securities only which have excess return to Beta ratio above a cut-off point.

By this method, selection of the portfolio has become easier due to the ranking of the securities in the order of their excess return and applying the yardstick of a required cut-off point for selection of securities. That cut-off point is related to the excess return to Beta rate on the one hand and variance of the market index σm^2 and variance of the stock's movement which is related to the unsystematic risk, namely σei^2.

It is thus seen that Sharpe's Portfolio takes into account both the systematic market related risk and unsystematic risk and residual risk.

Distribution of Investments

Once the choice of securities is made, then one has to decide the proportion of his funds to be invested in each security.

The percentage to be invested in each security is

$$X_i^0 = \frac{Z_i}{\sum_{J=1}^{N} Z_J}$$

Where,
$$Z_i = \frac{\beta_i}{\sigma e_i^2}\left(\frac{R_i - R_f}{\beta_i} - C^*\right)$$

The second expression in the bracket will determine the proportion of funds to be invested in each security. The first expression simply scales the weight on each security, so that the total is summing upto 1.

Suppose $\frac{\beta_i}{\sigma e_i^2} = \frac{2}{100}$

and $\frac{R_i - R_f}{\beta_1} = 10$ and $C^* = 5$

The value of $Z_i = \frac{2}{100}(10-5) = \frac{1}{10} = 0.1$

The proportion to be invested in $Z_1 = 0.1$

on similar lines $\frac{\beta_i}{\sigma e_i^2} = \frac{5.65}{100}$

and $\frac{R_i - R_f}{\beta_1} = 8$, then

the value of $Z_2 = \frac{5.65}{100}(8-5) = \frac{(5.65)\times(3)}{100} = \frac{16.95}{100} = 0.1695$

The proportion to be invested in Z_2 is 0.1695

$Z_1 Z_2$ ... etc., should total upto 1; so that whole fund is used.

Question 1

The return of Flex Stock is related to factors 1 and 2 as given below.

$(E)R_J = \lambda_0 + 0.6\lambda_1 + 1.3\lambda_2$

Where, 0.6 and 1.3 are sensitivity Coefficients, λ_1 risk premium is 6% and λ_2 is 3% and Risk free return (R_f) $\lambda_0 = 7\%$.

What is the stock's expected return?

Answer:

$$(E)\,\bar{R}_J = 0.07 + 0.6 \times (.06) + 1.3\,(0.03)$$
$$= 0.07 \times 0.036 + 0.039 = 0.145$$
$$= 14.5\%$$

Question 2

The reaction coefficients for two stocks and the market price λ are given below

Factor	λ	b_A	b_b
1	.09	.5	.7
2	–.03	.4	.8
3	.04	1.2	.2

Using APT model and risk free rate at 6% what is the expected return, if two stocks are equally weighted?

Answer:

$$(E)\ \bar{R}_A = 0.06 + .09(.5) - .03(.4) + .04(1.2)$$
$$= .06 + .045 - .012 + .048$$
$$= 0.141 = 14.1\%$$
$$(E)\ \bar{R}_B = .06 + .09(.7) - .03\ (.8) + .04(.2)$$
$$= .06 + .063 - .024 + .008$$
$$= 0.107 = 10.7\%.$$

If they are equally weighted (o.5 and 0.5), Then

$$(E)\ \bar{R}_p = 0.5(14.1) + 0.5\ (10.7)$$
$$= 7.05 + 5.35 = 12.4\%$$
$$= 12.4\%$$

There are two stock X and Y and three factors. Given the Risk free rate (R_f) at 6% λ_o corresponds to return on risk free asset or the λ in general reflects the market price of risk or expected excess return over the risk free return.

Given the earlier data on reaction coefficients

and if you are investing 1/3rd in X and 2/3rd in Y,

What would be the expected return?

Answer:

$$\Sigma\ R_x = \lambda + b_{1J}\ F_1 + b_{2J}\ F_2 + b_{3J}\ F_3$$

Using the above equations and ignoring the error term, we have

$$\bar{R}_x = 0.06 + 0.09\ (.5) - .03\ (.4) + .04\ (1.2)$$
$$= 0.06 + .045 - .012 + .048$$
$$= (0.153) - (.012) = 0.141$$
$$= 14.1\%$$
$$\bar{R}_y = 0.06 + 0.09(7) - .03\ (.8) + .04\ (.2)$$
$$= 0.06 + .063 - 0.024 + .008$$
$$= 0.131 - 024 = .107$$
$$= 10.7\%.$$

If we invest in the ratio of 1:2

$$\text{then } ER_p = 0.333\ (14.1) + 0.666\ (10.7)$$
$$= 4.695 + 7.126 = 11.82\%.$$

If we invest in the ratio 1:3 in the securities x and y

$$ER_p = 0.25\ (14.1) + 0.75\ (10.7)$$
$$= 3.525 + 8.025 = 11.55\%$$

Take Home Problems

Problem 1

Mr. 'X' owns a portfolio with the following characteristics:

Security	*Factor (1) Sensitivity*	*Factor (2) Sensitivity*	*Proportion*	*Expected Return*
A	2.50	1.40	0.30	13%
B	1.60	0.90	0.30	18%
C	0.80	1.00	0.20	10%
D	2.00	1.30	0.20	12%

Assume that the returns are generated by a two factor model. Mr. X decides to create an arbitrage Portfolio by increasing the holding of security 'B' by 0.05.

(*i*) What must be the weights of the other three securities in his portfolio?

(*ii*) What is the expected return on the arbitrage portfolio?

Answer: (1) Xa + Xb +Xc + Xd = 0

(2) Xa ba_1 + Xb bb_1 + Xc bc_1 + Xd bd_1 = 0

(3) Xa ba_2 + Xb bb_2 + Xc bc_2 + Xd bd_2 = 0

2.5xa + (1.6 × 0.05) + 0.8 × Xc+ 2 × d = 0

1.4 xa + (0.9 × 0.05) + 1 × xc + 1.3 × d = 0

Xa = –Xc – Xd – 0.05 from equation 1

when Xb = 0.05

Hint: Calculate Xa, Xb, Xc and Xd with Xb given as 0.05.

Problem 2

Gopal holds portfolio of two companies A and B with the following details.

C_i =	A	B
Security Return	10	5
Security Variance	0.0064	0.0016
Investment Proportion	0.5	0.5
Correlation	0.5	

Under the Markowitz Model what is the portfolio return and Portfolio Risk?

Problem 3

Following data relates to two securities in the market, i and j.

Security	R_p	σ	P_{ij}
i	9	7.56	
i	8	3.75	–0.5

Find out the minimum variance portfolio and compute its risk and return.

Problem 4

What is optimum portfolio in choosing among the following securities, assuming R_f = 5% and σ_m^2 = 10% and R_m = 11%?

Security	*Expected Return*	*Beta*	σ^2
A	15	1.0	30
B	12	1.5	20
C	11	2.0	40
D	8	0.8	10
E	9	1.0	20
F	14	1.5	10

28

MODERN PORTFOLIO THEORY

What is Modern Portfolio Theory (MPT)

MPT postulates that savers are generally risk averse and try to reduce risk by all possible methods. The markets are perfect and absorb all information perfectly and returns are the same whenever you enter the market. The principal of Dominance is applied to select a portfolio on the frontier line.

MPT depends on the concepts of diversification and use of Beta for reducing the risk and the concept of Dominance for selection of a Portfolio with least risk, with returns being given. These concepts are explained below:

Basis of Modern Portfolio Theory

The Tripod on which the MPT depends comprises the following concepts:

A. Diversification-Investment in more than one security, asset, industry etc. with a view to reduce risks

Diversification — An Example:

Expected Return of X = 20%

Expected Return of Y = 30%

Risk (σ) of Security X = 10%

Risk (σ) of Security Y = 16%

Coefficient of correlation, between X and Y can have three Scenarios –1, 0.5 or +1. Corresponding Graph looks as follows:

Investment in X 40% and in Y = 60%.

Return on Portfolio = 26% = (20 × 0.4 + 30 × 0.6)

Risk on Portfolio = 13.6%, which is normal average risk (10 × 0.4 + 16 × 0.6).

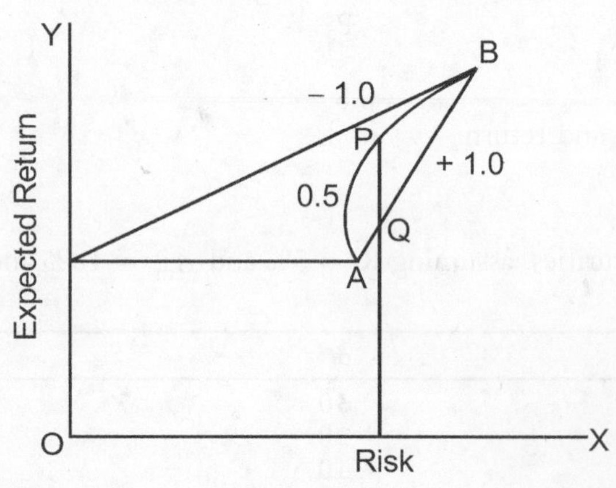

Fig. 28.1

If diversification has to give an advantage, the coefficient of correlation is to be considered. If the average risk of Portfolio has to be less than 13.6%, the Co-efficient of Correlation of these returns of X and Y has to be less than 1.0. If the Coefficient is + 1.0, the return moves along the straight line AB. Suppose it is – 1.0, then the risk can be reduced to zero, because the risk of the one can be perfectly offset by that on the other. If it is 0.5 (or anything between + 1.0 and –1.0) then the diversification can reduce the risk on the Portfolio and the return will move along the Curve. This is explained easily by graphical method rather than mathematical method. If you are on the Curve AB rather than straight line AB you can improve return without increasing the risk, at say point Q from Q to P at the same level of risk.

B. CAP Theory and Concept of Dominance (Capital assets pricing model)

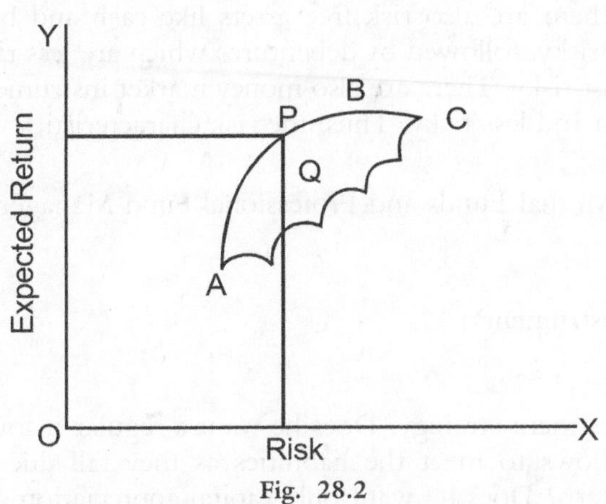

Fig. 28.2

Risk and return have a relationship. If you want to increase the return you should also be prepared to accept higher risk. You are entitled to various combinations of assets in your Portfolio. These combinations are called opportunity set — a set of all possible Portfolios given the constraint of money available for investment. The upper boundary of the opportunity set is called the efficient frontier because by so moving, you are improving the return for the same level of risk as shown below. You move from Point Q to Point P, both of which are within the opportunity set but by such move you improve the return and this proves to be more efficient. The Portfolio Manager has to do this by constantly analysing the company's performance/returns *vis-a-vis* the risk.

Dominance Concept

The Portfolio Manager has the opportunity to include risk-free assets in his Portfolio like a government bond or bank deposit. If he includes such risk free asset, he lowers the risk of the total Portfolio and moves from point V to point P by lowering the risk from 20% to 15% but by corresponding lowering of the expected return also (Fig. 28.3).

More importantly he will move on to a new efficient frontier point say from P to M. M will have the same risk as V but with a substantially higher return, say 35%. This shows that equities can be combined with bonds or other riskless assets and the concept of dominance will apply and he moves to an optimum point on the efficient frontier line (C – D).

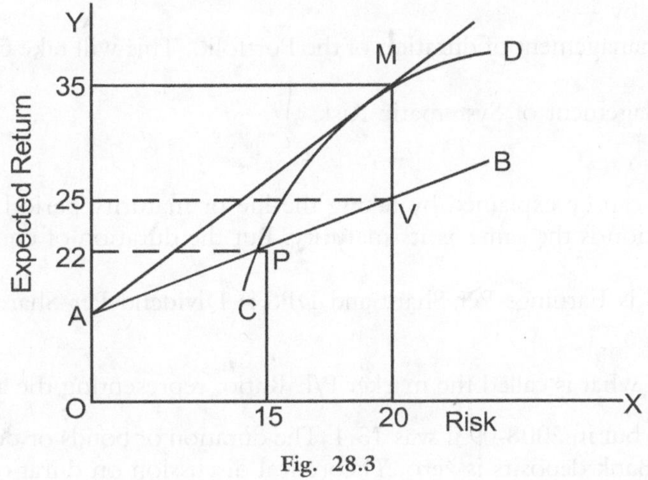

Fig. 28.3

C. Role of Beta

According to CAPM, the market related risk and not total risk is relevant. This systematic risk can be reduced by using Betas. It is a measure of sensitivity of the return of one asset to the market return.

Every asset will have a total return comprising two components.

(a) Risk free return — a return for mere waiting or loss of liquidity for the period of investment.

(b) Risk premium, which is return for risk taking and varies from asset to asset.

Modern Portfolio Theory postulates the following axioms:

(1) Diversification reduces the total risk but applicable only to company specific unsystematic risk.

(2) CAPM states that where shares are correctly priced every security is expected to earn returns commensurate with the risk it carries.

(3) The riskiness of a security is to be seen in the context of Portfolio or market related risk, but not in isolation.

(4) The importance of Beta is for managing non-diversifiable part of risk.

Portfolio Investment Strategy

Different assets have different risk characteristics; some of them are also risk free assets like cash and bank deposits. Among the Capital Market Instruments equities are most risky, followed by debentures which are less risky and then public sector bonds or government securities which are least risky. There are also money market instruments like commercial bills, treasury bills etc., which are of short duration and less risky. Thus, the risk characteristics vary from asset class to asset class.

The following major asset classes are used for Portfolios by Mutual Funds and Professional Fund Managers.

(a) Equities (variable income instruments)
(b) Debentures, Bonds etc. (Fixed income instruments)
(c) Cash and Money Market Instruments. (Short Duration Instruments)

Asset Allocation

Investor's data base is the starting point for designing an investment strategy. Does he want a regular income? How regular, monthly or yearly? Does he want regular cash inflows to meet the liabilities as they fall due for repayments? What is his asset-liabilities mix or inflow-outflow pattern? Does he want only capital appreciation or a mixture of both income and capital appreciation?

Broadly investor's objectives can be set out as income, growth and a mixture of both. Whatever is the objective, every investor of funds has some cash outflows, in the form of administrative expenses, salaries, wages, stationery and incidental expenses. As such some investment say from 5 to 10% is always kept in cash, bank deposits or money market instruments. The proportion in equity and debentures would depend upon the specific objective of the fund — income, growth or mixture of both.

Risk Management Strategy

Corresponding to two types of risks — diversifiable (unsystematic) and non-diversifiable risks (systematic) the portfolio risk can be managed by —

(a) Diversification and management of duration of the Portfolio. This will take care of the diversifiable risk and interest rate risk.
(b) Use of Beta for Management of Systematic Risk.

Duration

The concept of duration can be explained by taking the life or maturity period of the asset class. If the bond has zero coupon rate, its duration is the same as its maturity. But the duration of equity is infinity, but represented by $\frac{MP}{EPS}$ or $\frac{MP}{DPS}$ where EPS is Earnings Per Share and DPS is Dividend Per Share. The average Market price is P and EPS is related to MP by what is called the market P/E Ratio, representing the above equation, the market $\frac{P}{E}$ has its ratio at 21.6 in 2010-11 but in 2008-09 it was 13.4. The duration of bonds or debentures is the life to maturity and the duration of cash and Bank deposits is zero. Theoretical discussion on duration is left to a separate chapter.

EX: The duration can be made about 5 years by adopting the following investment pattern explained in a crude manner:

12% in Equity (25 years) 0.12 × 25	=	3.00
60% in Bonds/Debentures (5 year maturity and duration of 3 years) 0.6 × 3	=	1.80
25% in Money Market Instruments 0.25 × 1	=	0.25
3% in cash		– 0
Total Duration		5.05

For the elaboration of this concept, reference may be made to chapter on Bonds.

Beta

Management of Beta is done as follows:

Beta on equity shares varies from company to company. Calculate the Betas and take the average Beta, for selected Scrips in the Portfolio. If investor wants the market risk and market return, then the Beta of the Portfolio should be

1. If the actual shares in the Portfolio give a Beta of 1.2, then an investment of 80% in equities gives the Portfolio Beta as $1.2 \times 0.8 = 0.96$ and the rest of the 20% is invested in bonds and money market instruments.

If the investor is risk taking then the Portfolio should be aggressive with Beta of more than 1. If on the other hand he is risk averse, the Portfolio Beta should be less than 1 and it is a defensive Portfolio. Thus, the investment strategy should be decided after laying down first the allocation of funds to different asset classes in the form of proportions and then the selection of instruments and Scrips would be decided within each asset class, based on their fundamentals.

Table 28.1

Beta and Volatility (For the year 1993)

Names of the Company	*Betas*	*Price Volatility*	*EPS*	*Price/₹*
20th Century	1.519	12.6 Times	7.49	85
Appollo	1.6130	14.2 "	11.86	137
Essar Ship	1.448	8.4 "	2.82	41
Hotel Leela	1.525	6.1 "	0.62	34
I.T.C.	1.430	9.2 "	9.88	485
J.K. Synthetics	1.616	6.9 "	0.71	23
Nagarjuna Finance	1.430	23.3 "	6.04	19
Reliance	1.778	5.34 "	10.73	193
Thomas Cook	1.999	14.6 "	24.01	900
Hindustan Lever	0.859	3.8 "	7.03	375
Bajaj Auto	0.729	3.5 "	11.89	240
Boots Pharmaceuticals	0.604	4.8 "	6.79	217
Punjab Alkalies	0.502	6.6 "	10.14	99
Spartek Ceramics	0.243	4.4 "	5.67	87
Vindhya Tele Links	0.477	5.4 "	9.05	202

It will be seen from the above Table that Betas vary with the time periods of study; high Betas based on historical data do not reflect the price volatility and there is no guarantee that high Betas go with high return and low Betas go with low returns. Table 28.1 presents the data on selected companies with Betas, price volatility (High/low ratios) Earnings Per Share (EPS) and actual market price (data of 1993). It is seen from the Table that historical Betas are not correlated with either price volatility or earnings per share. As this is only for illustration, the period of the data may not be relevant. But the last six scrips have Betas less than one and their price volatility is also less. The Betas change with the time periods of data and the method of compilation. Betas are not exact replicas of volatility of the scrip, but only approximation and their relation with EPS is also not exact reflection of volatility.

Target Return

The basic principle in the market, is that the higher the risk taken, the higher is the return. An investor who wants only risk free return can have all his funds invested in Government bonds and bank deposits which will yield only risk free return of around 4 to 7% and sometimes more. But if the investor wants to have a higher return and takes risk accordingly, then risk premium will be available to him. Assuming the riskless return as 12% if he wants a return of 25%, then the risk premium should be 13%. The portfolio Manager has to invest the majority of his funds in equities with a Beta, of more than 1. If the market return is 20% then with a Beta of 1.3, he will get 26%, which is the target return.

Borrowing for Investment

Equities are most risky and have long duration and their Betas are high. Bonds have negligible Beta and moderate duration while Money Market instruments have negligible or zero duration. The range of Beta and duration can be widened by borrowing for investment. His debt-equity ratio becomes 2:1 and he gets a leverage of debt. If a fund manager with ₹ 1 lakh borrows another ₹ 1 lakh and invests ₹ 2 lakh, in equity Portfolio, even with a Beta of 1.00, his overall Portfolio Beta is actually 2.00 because his Portfolio is ₹ 1 lakh and his equity Portfolio is ₹ 2 lakh (which is 200% of his own Portfolio). This gives almost double the returns expected and even after paying the interest component on borrowed funds, he enjoys the leverage and improves his networth. This debt-equity ratio between:

Problems

Question 1

If the returns on stocks A and B are as follows:

Calculate the average rate of return for each stock during the given period.

If A and B are held in the 50:50 ratio in a portfolio, what is the portfolio return?

Year	*A's return*	*B's return*
1984	–12.24	–5.0
1985	23.67	19.55
1986	35.45	44.09
1987	5.82	1.20
1988	28.30	21.16
	81.0	81.0

Answer:

$$\overline{A} = \frac{81}{5} = 16.2; \overline{B} = \frac{81}{5} = 16.2$$

$$\sqrt{\sum_{1}^{n} \frac{Kt - KAve}{n-1}}$$

	Deviation		*Deviation Squared*		
1987	(–12.24–16.2)	=	$(-28.44)^2$	=	808.83
1985	(23.67–16.2)	=	$(7.47)^2$	=	55.80
1996	(35.45–16.2)	=	$(19.25)^2$	=	370.56
1997	(5.82– 16.2)	=	$(-10.38)^2$	=	107.74
1988	(28.30–16.2)	=	$(12.1)^2$	=	146.41
					$\frac{1489.34}{4} = 372.33$

$\sigma_A = \sqrt{372.33}$

$\sigma_A = 19.3\%$

Working in the case of σ_B is left to the reader.

For the portfolio, stock A and B are combined in the ratio of 50: 50

Portfolio Return Equation is

$$\begin{aligned}
rp &= (0.5)\ Ar + (0.5)\ Br.\\
&= (-12.24)\ 0.5 + (-5.0)\ (0.5) = -8.62\\
&\quad (+23.67)\ 0.5 + (19.55)\ 0.5 = 21.61\\
&\quad (+35.45)\ 0.5 + (44.09)\ 0.5 = 39.77\\
&\quad (5.82)\ 0.5 + (1.2)\ 0.5 = 3.51\\
&\quad (28.30)\ 0.5 + (21.16)\ 0.5 = 24.73\\
&\quad = \frac{81.0}{5} = 16.20
\end{aligned}$$

Portfolio Risk = Standard Deviation of Portfolio Calculation

$$\begin{aligned}
(-8.62 - 16.2)^2 &= (24.82)^2 = 616.03\\
(21.61 - 16.2) &= (5.41)^2 = 29.27\\
(39.77 - 16.2)^2 &= (23.57)^2 = 555.54\\
(3.51 - 16.2)^2 &= (-12.69)^2 = 161.04\\
(24.73 - 16.2) &= (8.53)^2 = 72.76
\end{aligned}$$

$$\sigma^2 = \frac{1,434.64}{4} = 358.66$$

$\sigma = \sqrt{358.66}$

$\sigma = 18.9\%$

The formula for covariance is as follows:

$\text{Covariance} = E(R_{1J} - \bar{R}_1)\ (R_{2J} - \bar{R}_2)$

Calculate the covariance between the A and B Stocks, given above.

Question 2

Stocks A and B showed the following returns for two years.

Year	Stock A	Stock B
1997	10%	12%
1998	16%	18%

(a) What is the expected return an a portfolio made up of 50% of A and 50% of B Stock and what is the portfolio risk?

(b) What is the standard deviation of each stock?

(c) What is the covariance of stock A and B?

(d) Determine the coefficient of correlation of stocks A and B.

29 PORTFOLIO MANAGEMENT: CONSTRUCTION, REVISION AND EVALUATION

The portfolio theory is the basis of portfolio management and relates to the efficient portfolio investment in financial and physical assets, including shares and debentures of companies. A portfolio of an individual or a corporate unit is the holding of securities and investment in financial assets. These holdings are the result of individual preferences and decisions of the holders regarding risk and return and a host of other considerations.

Fact Sheet — Clients' Database

The following preferences of the investor are to be noted first in investment decisions. These will constitute the database of the investor or client.

(1) Income and savings decisions — how much income can be saved for contingencies and the present position of wealth, income and savings of the investor.

(2) Asset preferences profile — preference for riskless assets like bank deposits or for risky stock market investment:

- (a) the degree of risk the investor is capable of taking and willing to take;
- (b) the risk aversion and preference for safety and certainty;
- (c) requirements of regular income;
- (d) objective of capital appreciation and growth;
- (e) objective of speculative gains; etc.

(3) Investor's objectives, constraints and financial commitments.

(4) Tax brackets into which the investor falls and his preference for planning the tax liability.

(5) Time horizon in which investment should fructify or results expected.

These and other factors constitute the "Fact Sheet" of the investor on the basis of which the individual portfolio is to be structured, constructed and managed.

The motives for saving are varied depending on the individuals. For example, provision for insurance, contingencies, contribution to PF, pension funds, etc., which are mostly contractual obligations, provision for future income, etc., are some of the motives. Some of the savers are influenced by interest return or stable income while others are by speculative gains or get-rich-quick motive. Some save autonomously as a matter of habit. Our researches have found that saving in bank deposits is sensitive to interest rates.

Objectives of Investors

The investors' objectives are to be specified in the first place. The objective may be income, capital appreciation or a future provision for contingencies such as marriage, death, birth, etc. Provision for retirement and accident could be covered by contractual obligations like insurance and contributions to PF and pension funds. A certain amount of savings has to be kept as cash with themselves or in deposit with banks or post offices to facilitate daily transactions for purchase and sale. While cash earns no interest, savings deposit with banks, co-operatives and POs would earn 4% on savings accounts. But when inflation is prevalent in the economy at the rate of 6 to 8%, this return of 4% will provide only a net negative real return to the savers. So the amounts kept in the form of cash and deposit with banks, etc., should normally be the bare minimum. The rest of the amount has to be spread in various investment avenues, earning higher returns than the normal inflation rate. These investment avenues are discussed in a separate chapter.

Motives for Investment

The investor has to set out his priorities of investment keeping the following motives in mind. All investors would like to have:

(1) Capital appreciation.

(2) Income.

(3) Liquidity or marketability.

(4) Safety or security.

(5) Hedge against inflation.

The investor gets his income from the dividend or yield or interest. There will be capital appreciation also in the case of equities. The liquidity and safety of an investment will depend upon the marketability and the credit rating of the borrower, namely, the company or the issuer of securities. These characteristics vary between assets and securities. An investor is also concerned in having a tax plan to reduce his tax commitments so as to maximise the take home income. For this purpose, investor should specify his income bracket, his liabilities and his preference for tax planning etc. The investment avenues have certain characteristics of risk and return and also of some tax concessions attached to them. These tax provisions as such can influence the investors in a very big way as these provisions will alter the risk return scenario of investment alternatives. It is, therefore, necessary that all these avenues should be assessed in terms of yields, capital appreciation, liquidity, safety and tax implications. The investment strategy should be based on the above objectives after a thorough study of the goals of the investor, in the background of characteristics of the investment avenues.

Tax Provisions

It is apt to start with the tax-exempt incomes of the securities in which investment can be made. The incomes by way of interest on PSU bonds, N.S. certificates, securities of the Central Government and those deposits specified by the Central Government are exempted from income tax subject to certain limits or conditions. The P.O. deposits, certificates and other claims operated by the P.O.s are exempted from income-tax up to a limit of ₹ 12,000. This exemption is, however, not applicable to Kisan Vikas Patra and NSC VIII Issue. Deposits in PPF and NSS are exempted from taxes in the year of deposit and subject to some limits in the year of withdrawal except in the case of NSS, which is, however, taxable in the year of withdrawal.

Under the category of insurance, in addition to LIC policies, the ULIP (of UTI) enjoys popularity due to the tax shelters: The invested amounts are exempted.

- Wealth tax exemption for all investments in shares and debentures along with other eligible investments.
- Income-tax exemption up to ₹ 12,000 aggregate income from bank deposits, shares, UTI units, P.O. deposits, Mutual Funds and other specified categories of investment.

All dividend incomes from companies in the hands of investors are free from income tax from 1997-98 onwards, but have become taxable in the hands of investors in 2002-03. As in 2006-07, investments upto ₹ one lakh are exempt from tax, if invested in approved securities like insurance, NSC, Five Year Term deposits with banks etc., under Section 80(C) of I.T.Act. Tax provisions as applicable have to be updated every year.

Capital Gains

Capital gains refer to profits earned on the transfer of capital assets, sale or exchange, etc. These gains are long-term gains, if they are held for more than 36 months for all assets except shares of a company for which this period is 12 months. Long-term capital gains are taxable at a lower rate of 20%. Under Sections 54E and 54F of the Income-tax Act, the long-term capital gains are exempt, if these funds are invested in Central Government securities, UTI and CGI Schemes and other specified bonds of semi-government bodies.

Income from interest on debentures and on company deposits is tax deductible at source, if it exceeds ₹ 2,500 p.a. Interest income beyond a limit in respect of bank deposits, royalty income, rental income, etc., are subject to tax deduction at source (TDS). The exemption available from income tax for NSS deposits up to ₹ 40,000 was since withdrawn in 1992-93. Tax exemption is also available in respect of income from government securities, semi-government bonds, bank deposits, income from mutual funds, etc., upto a limit. In the budget for 1990-91, a new scheme called Equity linked Saving Scheme was announced by the government under Section 88A of Income Tax Act to provide a tax rebate of 20% of the investment made in the eligible assets and new issues, or eligible M.F. Scheme.

This was extended upto a limit of total investment of ₹ 70,000 p.a. in 1996-97, in respect of investments in selected avenues such as Insurance, P.F., PPF, NSS and Infrastructure bonds, etc.

Details of tax provisions are discussed in a separate chapter.

Portfolio Construction[1]

Portfolio construction refers to the allocation of funds among a variety of financial assets open for investment. Portfolio theory concerns itself with the principles governing such allocation. The objective of the theory is to elaborate the principles by which the risk can be minimised, subject to a desired level of return on the portfolio or maximise the return, subject to the constraint of a tolerable level of risk.

Thus, the basic objective of portfolio management is to maximise yield and minimise risk. The other ancillary objectives are as per the needs of investors, namely:

(1) Regular income or stable return;
(2) Appreciation of capital;
(3) Marketability and liquidity;
(4) Safety of investment; and
(5) Minimising of tax liability.

In pursuit of these objectives, the portfolio manager has to set out all the various alternative investments along with their projected return and risk and choose investments which satisfy the requirements of the individual investor and cater to his preferences. The manager has to keep a list of such investment avenues along with the return-risk profile, tax implications, yields and other returns such as convertible options, bonus, rights, etc. A ready reckoner giving out the analysis of the risks involved in each investment and the corresponding returns should be kept.

Risk-return Analysis

All investments have some risks. Investment in shares of companies has larger risks or uncertainty. These risks arise out of variability of returns or yields and uncertainty of appreciation or depreciation of share prices, loss of liquidity etc. The risk over time can be represented by the variance of the returns, while the return over time is capital appreciation plus payout, divided by the purchase price of the share.

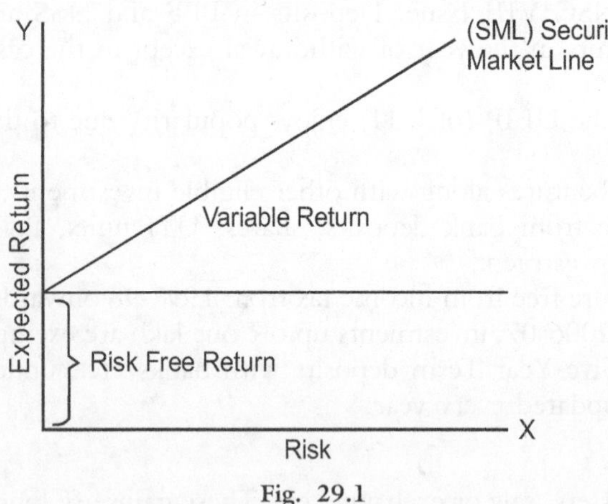

Fig. 29.1

Normally, the higher the risk that the investor takes, the higher is the return. There is, however, a riskless return on capital of about 6%, which is the bank rate charged by the RBI or long-term yield on Government securities at around 8% to 9%. This riskless return refers to lack of variability of return and no uncertainty in the repayment of capital. But other risks such as loss of liquidity due to parting with money etc., may, however, remain but are rewarded by the total return on the capital.

The risk-return relationship can be represented in a diagrammatic form as in Fig. 29.1.

Risk-return is subject to variation and the objective of the portfolio manager is to reduce that variability and thus reduce the risk by choosing an appropriate portfolio.

There are two types of risks, namely, (a) Market risk or systematic risk, and (b) Company specific risk or unsystematic risk.

The unsystematic risk can be reduced by diversifying the portfolio of scrips up to an optimum level of about 15 shares. These scrips should be so chosen that the risks on each of them are diverse and their variability of return is also different. By investing in such a diverse set of scrips, the total risk can be reduced as some of them may have positive and others negative covariance and they may vary in the degree of risk as well. The risk that can be reduced is called unsystematic risk and these risks are represented diagrammatically in Fig. 29.2.[2] The details are discussed in an earlier Chapter.

1. Refer to Graham and Dodd, *Security Analysis.*
2. Cohen, Zinbarg and Zeilkel, *Managing Investment Portfolios,* (Ed.) II. Maginn and D.L. Tuttle, *Investment Analysis and Portfolio Management.*

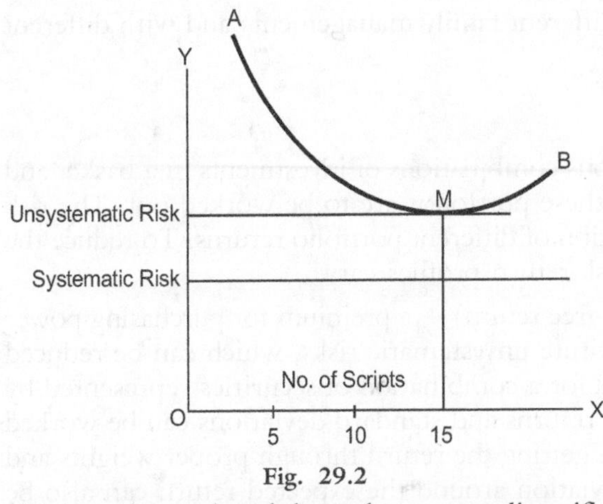

Fig. 29.2

The unsystematic risk can be lowered by diversifying into a basket of scrips. Thus, at the level of 15 scrips in the diagram, the lowest level of risk is obtained at the point M on the AB curve representing the unsystematic risk of the investor. Thus, a degree of diversification of investment is a necessary prerequisite of portfolio management and for reducing the risk. But beyond the point M, the portfolio becomes unmanageable and diseconomies operate as to increase risk rather than reduce it.

In the management of a portfolio, the problem of risk management is vital. Given the individual preference of portfolio holders, the portfolio is to be constructed in such a manner that it is exposed to the minimum risks which the owner can carry, subject to which the returns are to be maximised. Although the market-related risks cannot be reduced, the company-related risks can be eliminated or reduced through a proper diversification. As shown in the above diagram, a proper portfolio diversification into around 15 scrips of different groups of industries and companies would be able to reduce the company-related risks involved almost to a negligible proportion. But these companies and industries should not be unduly related or interdependent or under the same umbrella of industry groups or family of industrialists. An optimum degree of diversification can be secured which would minimise risk and optimise return, if the covariance of scrips included in the portfolio is less than 1 or negative. Interrelations of scrips included in the portfolio should be nil or zero.

Time Horizon of Strategy

Every investment strategy should have a time horizon from a short period of one year to a few years. Capital gains is considered long-term if capital market investment is for at least one year and other types of investment for at least three years. If investment is to be assessed every year, the past experience shows that the equity prices, reflected by the BSE Sensitive Index, may show varying degrees of rise or fall per annum, but over a period of 3 to 5 years, the market index invariably showed a rise of anything above the normal inflation rate of 8% per annum. So investment strategy should be for a medium time period of 3 to 5 years.

Portfolio management encompasses three major categories of activities:

1. Asset allocation — type of assets to be chosen among fixed income securities of the government or private corporate units, preferred stock debentures or equities, etc., of various groups of industries.
2. Review and shifts as between classes of assets to take advantage of risk-return characteristics, or changes in them, or in market conditions.
3. Security selection within each asset class such as choosing a higher growth type of companies (blue chips); or relocation of funds from low growth assets to high growth assets or securities.

Types of Risk

The risk is measured statistically by the degree of variance or standard deviation of returns. There is also a risk involved in time period of holding (the longer the period, the greater the risk) called liquidity premium. The holding of security is subject to the default risk in repayment of principal called default premium. The risks also arise due to interest rate variability, purchasing power changes, business default or financial failures. They can be named as interest rate risk, purchasing power risk, business risk, and financial risk, which are all part of systematic risks which lead to a risk premium. These are to be rewarded by a higher return in the market than can be secured on risk-free assets.

The above is the market-related risk. Besides, there is also group-related risk pertaining to a group of industries or firms. There is also a specific risk related to a company.

As per the Markowitz model,[3] the investors are generally risk-averse. To suit such investors, the portfolio has to be so designed as to maximise returns for a given level of risk. It is theoretically possible to identify an efficient portfolio, which satisfies the requirements of risk-return for an individual investor. This is possible through a detailed analysis of information on each security in each of the asset classes in terms of expected risk (variance of return) and expected return, and covariance of each of the security with every other security. In simple language, this efficient portfolio is a well-diversified portfolio comprising many securities with a low covariance so that the degree of risk is

3. H.M. Markowitz, *Portfolio Selection: Efficient Diversification of Investments* (John Wiley, 1959).

the lowest possible. Companies under different industry groups and different family managements and with different characteristics are to be chosen in that portfolio.

Efficient Portfolio

To construct an efficient portfolio, we have to conceptualise various combinations of investments in a basket and designate them as portfolios 1 to n. Then the expected returns from these portfolios are to be worked out. The risk on these portfolios is to be estimated by measuring the standard deviation of different portfolio returns. To reduce the risk, investors have to diversify into a number of securities whose risk-return profiles vary.

Thus, portfolios carry returns to compensate for interest risk (risk-free return) + a premium for purchasing power risk, market risk, business risk and financial risk. All these risks constitute unsystematic risks, which can be reduced or eliminated by diversification. Thus, for each individual security and for a combination of securities represented by the basket in the BSE Sensitive Index or National Index, the expected returns and standard deviations can be worked out. The expected return has to be weighted by the probable chance of getting the return through proper weights and the weighted average return should be worked out. The standard deviation around the expected return can also be worked out as shown below:

Return in Per Cent (1)	*Chance of Getting Return (2)*	*Expected Return in Per Cent (3) = 2 × 1*	*Standard Deviation of Expected Return in Per Cent (σ^2) (4)*
10	0.20	10 × 0.20 = (2.0)	$(10 - 13.4)^2 \times 0.20 = 2.31$ +
12	0.30	12 × 0.30 = (3.6)	$(12 - 13.4)^2 \times 0.30 = 0.59$ +
15	0.40	15 × 0.40 = (6.0)	$(15 - 13.4)^2 \times 0.40 = 2.56$ +
18	0.10	18 × 0.10 = (1.8)	$(18 - 13.4)^2 \times 0.10 = 2.12$
	1.00	(Wt. average 13.4)	$\sigma = 2.75$ $\sigma^2 = 7.58$

The standard deviation signifies that, on an average, each possible return is 2.7% away from the expected return of 13.4%. The deviation of 2.7% could be on either side of the expected return. This is the risk measure of a portfolio, which is already explained in an earlier chapter.

The efficient portfolio can be estimated by presenting the various portfolios in terms of expected return and standard deviations as shown in the following table:

Portfolio No.	*Expected Return in Per Cent*	*(Risk) Standard Deviation*
1	5	1
2	7	2
3	8	3
4	10	5
5	11	5
6	12	5
7	12	7
8	14	10
9	18	12

If we compare portfolio Nos. 4 and 5, we see that for the same standard deviation of 5, portfolio No. 5 gives an expected return of 11% higher than that on No. 4, thereby making it an efficient portfolio. If we compare portfolio Nos. 6 and 7, we see that with the same return of 12% in both the portfolios, standard deviation is lower in portfolio No. 6. Thus, portfolio No. 6 is an efficient portfolio.

These points can be depicted as in Fig. 29.3. The expected return is shown on the Y-axis and standard deviation measuring risk on the X-axis. The points connecting the expected return with its standard deviation can be shown as AB graph, constituting the feasible opportunity set. The outermost point on this graph is the most efficient portfolio, say, M on the AB graph while the AB graph is called the efficient frontier. M is the most efficient combination for the individual under consideration (Ref. *Investment Management* by Simha, Hemlata and Balakrishnan).

The individual investor is generally risk-averse according to the well-known author Markowitz. His objectives are influenced by the stage of life, his financial circumstances and psychological makeup. A young investor may have, for example, a higher level of tolerance of risk than a retired person or a middleaged person. The latter prefers a larger income with less risk. There is a trade-off between risk and return.

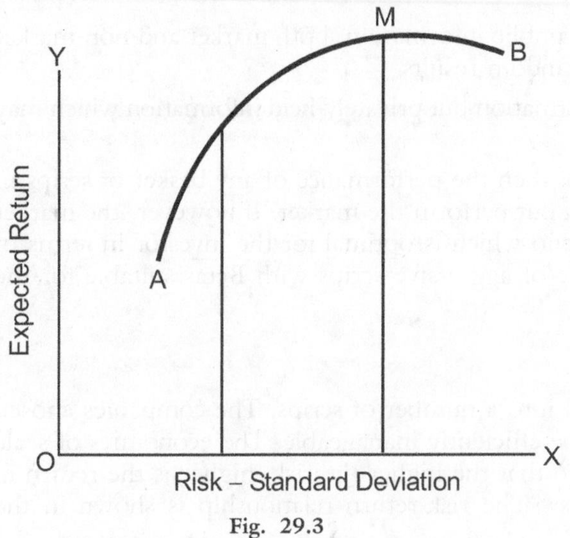

Fig. 29.3

According to the capital pricing model, efficient frontier is defined as a risk-return trade-off curve. It is efficient because it provides the maximum return at a given level of risk of the investor. The investor's capacity to take risk sets the point of optimum efficiency on this curve, which is the best for him. Diversification of securities and assets in the portfolio reduces the risk, provided their covariance is low and they are dissimilar in nature.

The total risk is measured by the standard deviation of the return, and market risk by the concept of Beta. Beta reflects that part of a portfolio's return and variation in returns which is attributable to the overall movement of the market rather than to any unique characteristic of the Company.

The efficient frontier of Markowitz and the use of Beta can be graphically represented as in Figs. 29.4 and 29.5. AB is the capital market line, representing the market possibilities of risk and return (given by the BSE Index). On the same graph, the efficient frontier curve is drawn as EF. At point M, for the given risk of OR, the return is maximised for the investor at OC.

In actual practice, β can be derived by the formula: Price of Scrip A (% age) divided by Prices of scrips included in BSE Index (% age) — the relation of the individual scrip to that of the basket of scrips as represented by the BSE Index. If Beta is 1 (slope is 45^0), then, on an average, one percentage return on the market basket will be associated with a one percentage return on the individual scrip. If Beta is greater than one it will give a larger return than the average market return. These high Beta scrips are very volatile and risk is also high. On the other hand, if Beta is less than 1 (called defensive scrips), the risk is low and the return is also lower than the market return. Depending on the investor's choice, the Beta is to be selected and scrips with such Beta should be held in the portfolio Fig. 29.5 depicts Beta as the angle made by the line of regression between market return and the individual scrip return.

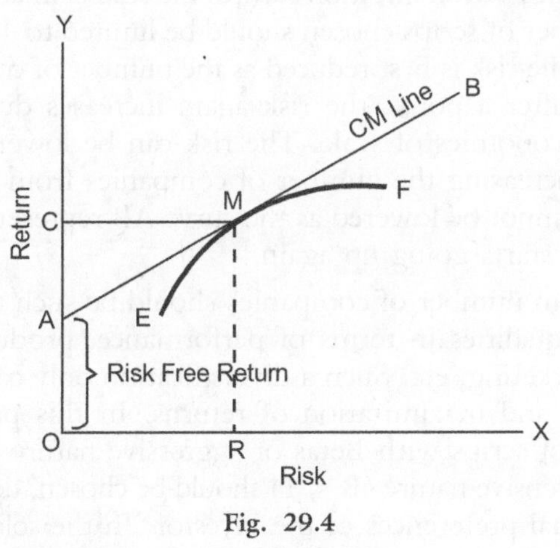

Fig. 29.4

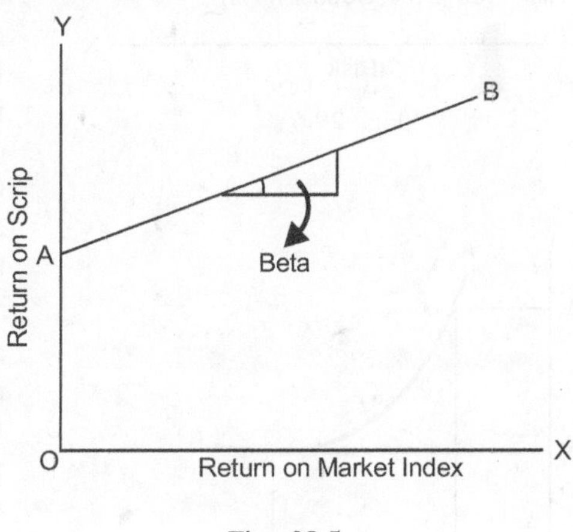

Fig. 29.5

Market Efficiency Theorem[4]

Since the behaviour of the market is outside the control of the investor, he can only reduce the specific component of risk by choosing the individual scrips with proper Betas to achieve the result of diversification and lower the risk. The comparative risks of alternative well-diversified portfolios can be measured by their Betas. If the markets are efficient, the performance of any portfolio would average out to that of the performance of the market and nobody can out perform the market.

4. D.C. Fischer & R.J. Jordan: *Security Analysis and Portfolio Management,* Chapter 1, 18 and 19.

In the real world, there are three different levels of efficiency of the stock market, namely, the weak form, the semi-strong form and the strong form. These concepts are useful in portfolio management for investors, and are discussed in details in an earlier chapter.

In the weak form, the successive changes in stock prices are independent of each other and the historical market data are already embodied in the existing price.

In the semi-strong form, stock prices adjust rapidly to all new public information, both market and non-market data, and action taken after the event will produce no more than random results.

In the strong form, stock prices fully reflect not only public information but privately-held information which may later become public.

If, in the real world, the market efficiency is of a strong form, then the performance of any basket of scrips in any portfolio is as good as any other and no individual investor can out perform the market. If however, the market efficiency is of a weak form, there is scope for selection of a portfolio which is optimal for the investor in terms of risk and return and yet out perform the market by a proper choice of aggressive scrips with Betas suitable for the purpose.

Diversification

Risk in a portfolio can be reduced by a proper diversification into a number of scrips. The companies chosen should not be too many or too few but of an optimum size as to be efficiently manageable. The economies of scale in management apply to this analysis. It will be seen from Fig. 29.6 that the higher the risk, higher is the return in the normal process. The risk-return relationship is shown in the graph.

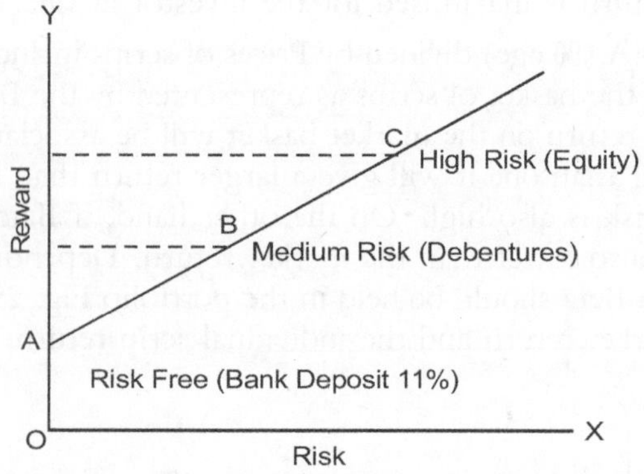

Y
C High Risk (Equity)
Reward
B Medium Risk (Debentures)
A
Risk Free (Bank Deposit 11%)
O X
Risk

Fig. 29.6

Depending upon the investor's preferences and his income requirements, the strategy of investment should be at A, B or C respectively. Assuming that he takes some risk at B or C, this risk can be reduced so far as it concerns the specific company risk, but the market risk is outside the control of the portfolio manager. The risk can be reduced by a proper diversification of scrips invested. It is also possible to have a combination of A, B and C positions in a portfolio so as to have a diversified risk-return pattern.

In order that this diversification secures the results in an optimal manner, the number of scrips chosen should be limited to 12-15. As Fig. 29.7 shows, the risk is first reduced as the number of companies is increased but after a point, the risk again increases due to the operation of diseconomies of scale. The risk can be lowered from OM to ON by increasing the number of companies from 5 to 15, after which risk cannot be lowered as the curve AB representing the unsystematic risk starts going up again.

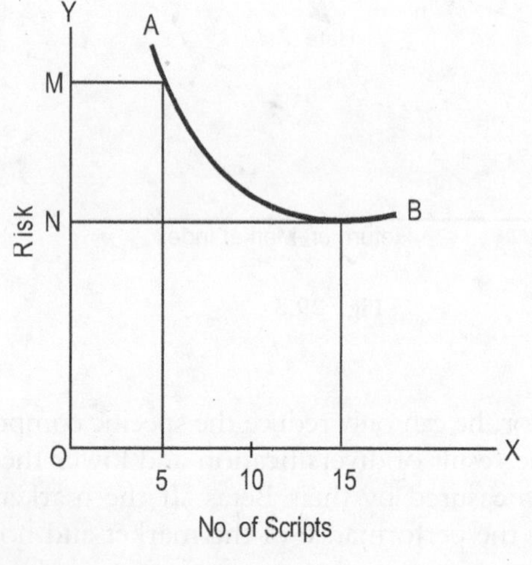

Fig. 29.7

The optimum number of companies should be such that they are of divergent qualities in terms of performance, product lines, management, marketing, etc. Such a diversification only can secure reduction of risk and maximisation of returns. In this process, a proper selection of scrips with Betas of aggressive nature (B > 1) and some with defensive nature (B < 1) should be chosen, depending upon the individual preferences of the investor. In the selection of these companies, all the processes explained above under portfolio management should be followed and after analysis and assessment, investment should be made.

Portfolio Management

Portfolio management is a process encompassing many activities of investment in assets and securities. It is a dynamic and flexible concept and involves continuous and systematic analysis, judgement and operations. The objective of this service is to help the novices and uninitiated investors with the expertise of professionals in portfolio management. Firstly, it involves construction of a portfolio based upon the fact sheet of the investor giving out his objectives, constraints, preferences for risk and return and his tax liability. Secondly, the portfolio is reviewed and adjusted from time-to-time in tune with the market conditions. The adjustment is done through changes in the weighting pattern of the securities and asset classes in the portfolio. The shifting of assets and securities will take advantage of changes in market conditions and in prices in the securities and assets in the portfolio. Thirdly, the evaluation of portfolio performance is to be done by the manager in terms of targets set for risk and return and changes in the portfolio are to be affected to meet the changing conditions.

Elements of Portfolio Management

Portfolio management is an on-going process involving the following basic tasks, and Schematic presentation of stages in portfolio management is given in Fig. 29.8.

(1) Identification of the investors' objectives, constraints and preferences, which will help formulate the investment policy.

(2) Strategies are to be developed and implemented in tune with the investment policy formulated. This will help the selection of asset classes and securities in each class depending upon their risk-return attributes.

(3) Review and monitoring of the performance of the portfolio by continuous overview of the market conditions, companies' performance and investors' circumstances.

(4) Finally, the evaluation of the portfolio for the results to compare with the targets and needed adjustments have to be made in the portfolio to the emerging conditions and to make up for any shortfalls in achievement *vis-a-vis* targets.

The collection of data on the investors' preferences, objectives, etc., is the foundation of portfolio management. This gives an idea of channels of investment in terms of asset classes to be selected and securities to be chosen based upon the liquidity requirements, time horizon, taxes, asset preferences of investors, etc. These are the building blocks for construction of a portfolio.

According to these objectives and constraints, the investment policy can be formulated. This policy will lay down the weights to be given to different asset classes of investment such as equity shares, preference shares, debentures, company deposits, etc., and the proportion of funds to be invested in each class and selection of assets and securities in each class are made on this basis. The next stage is to formulate the investment strategy for a time horizon for income and capital appreciation and for a level of risk tolerance. The investment strategies developed by the portfolio managers have to be correlated with their expectation of the capital market and the individual sectors of industry. Then a particular combination of assets is chosen on the basis of investment strategy and manager's expectations of the market.

Execution of Strategy

The next stage, namely, implementation and execution of this investment process, is the most critical process in the portfolio management. Here, the research, analysis and the judgement of the manager are very essential inputs in the process. His initiative, innovation and judgement would be the basis of his success in management. The performance of the portfolio is evaluated and adjustments are made in the portfolio composition from time-to-time. This is called monitoring and restructuring of portfolios for improving the performance to make it optimal and efficient. The changes in investor's conditions and in the market conditions and in industry performance are taken into account in the portfolio adjustments.

The porfolio thus constructed may relate to the needs of a given level of income, a provision for contingencies and a preference for fixed income, etc., of the investor. Some investors would prefer assets like real estate, gold, debentures or bonds giving a fixed income while a few would prefer riskless investments in PSU bonds — short-term or long-term government securities, etc. Certain risk-takers may prefer investment in high-yielding growth stocks and venture equities.

Monitoring

Monitoring of these portfolios is a continuous upgrading and changes in asset composition to take advantage of the market conditions and economic and industry performance. Portfolio monitoring is a continuous on-going assessment of the current portfolio to the goals, changes in investors' preferences, capital market conditions and expectations. The monitoring requires a periodic meeting with investors to know the changes in the conditions, continuous review of the investment policy relative to investors' preferences.

The current investment strategy reflects the capital market conditions and expectations and any changes in them will bring out the changes in optimal conditions in the portfolio. The portfolio is thus subjected to the ongoing review and assessment to change the composition of the portfolio in tune with the changing conditions in the market and of the investor.

To give specific examples, if market conditions change and the prospects of the cement industry are likely to be better in the coming year, as judged by the Government policy changes *vis-a-vis* the steel industry, then the investor preferences can be better satisfied by shifting from steel shares to cement shares. Besides, within the cement industry, a manager may shift from a poorly performing company like Orient Cement to a better performing company like India Cements or ACC. Similarly, changes can take place as between different asset classes such as moving from debentures to equities and *vice versa* or from income stocks to growth stocks, etc.

Thus, portfolio changes can be brought about by the changes in market expectations and from the quarterly or half-yearly results or yearly results of the companies, industry and economy. These adjustments of the portfolio may also be initiated due to changes in the managers' expectations of the company and market or asset classes. Certain changes in asset classes may have a time limit as a critical input. Thus, purchases and sales of equity shares on the stock market are to be well-timed based upon the assessment of the market technical position. This requires technical analysis in addition to fundamental analysis. In fact, any shift of the investment from one type of asset to another requires a careful analysis of time, risk-return and host of other factors.

An important characteristic of the portfolio is risk reduction, which can be achieved by a diversification of the portfolio into the various asset classes and securities within the asset class. Changes in security prices or market expectations of the manager may have necessitated changes in the asset composition. The efficient frontier in terms of modern portfolio theory may itself change the composition of the portfolio due to the change in the Beta value in the longer time horizon. The composition has to be changed to bring portfolio back to the optimal conditions and back to the efficient frontier line.

The investment alternatives for portfolio management are set out below:

1. Asset Classes:
   - (a) Equity — new issues
   - (b) Equity — old issues
   - (c) Preference shares
   - (d) Debentures — convertible and non-convertible — new and old issues
   - (e) PSU Bonds
   - (f) Government Securities
   - (g) Company deposits, etc.
2. Industry Groups:
   - (a) Textiles
   - (b) Cement
   - (c) Aluminium
   - (d) Petrochemicals
   - (e) Fertilizers
   - (f) Paper, etc.
3. High Income Yielding Securities; Blue chips and growth stock.

Regular dividend paying companies at a stable rate are income yielding shares. The blue chips are not only dividend paying regularly but their performance is above the average and the dividend distributions may increase over time. The growth stocks are shares with a large scope for capital appreciation in addition to good dividends.

4. Companies with export orientation and those with only domestic demand.
5. Companies based on location as those in the west, south, east and north of India.
6. Type of management, *viz.*, family type, professional type, etc.

Building of the Portfolio

The portfolio construction, as referred to earlier, is made on the basis of the investment strategy, set out for each investor. Through choice of asset classes, instruments of investments and the specific scrips, say of bonds or equities of different risks and return characteristics, the choice of tax characteristics, risk level and other features of investments, are decided upon. The construction of Portfolio and other elements in the portfolio management are here set out in Fig. 29.8.

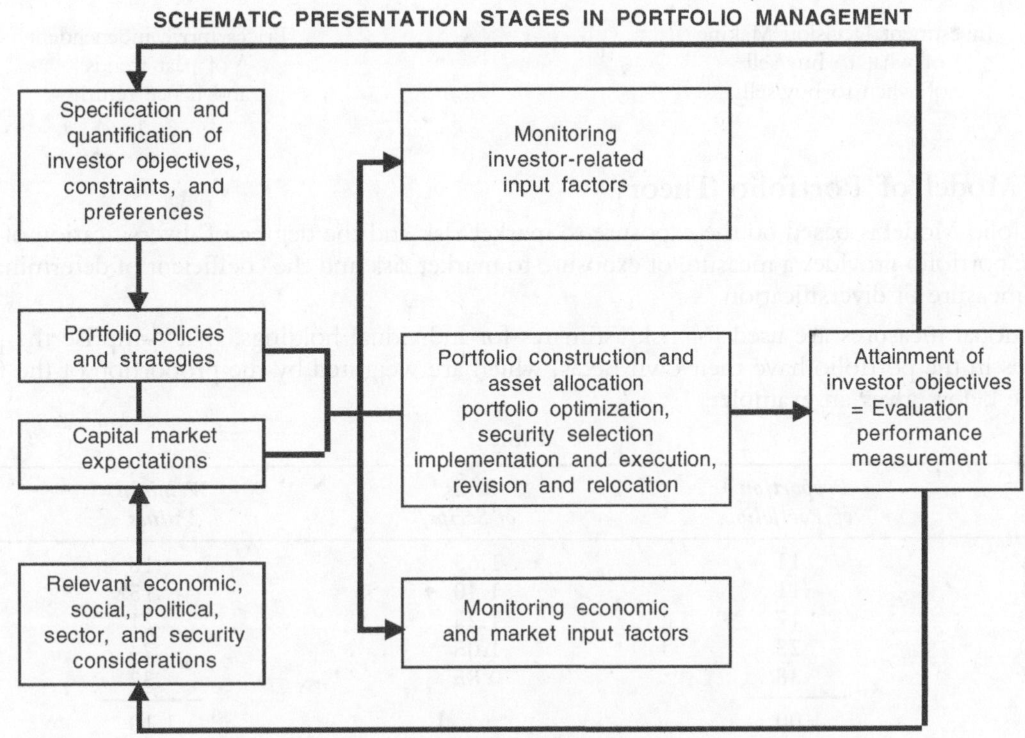

Fig. 29.8 Schematic Presentation of Stages in Portfolio Management

Source: J.L. Maginn and D.L. Tutte — *Managing Investment Portfolios.*

Portfolio Revision

After fixing the target Beta and duration of the portfolio, the investment activity starts with the selection of Scrips and Bonds, etc. But the portfolio once constructed undergoes changes due to changes in market prices and a reassessment of companies and the portfolio Beta and the proportion in each asset class will change to bring back the portfolio to the targetted level of Beta and duration. portfolio revision will take place and composition of portfolio will change. A change in interest rate will also affect the portfolio through change in duration. Constant market changes necessitate redjustment of portfolio leading to purchases and sales of equities, bonds etc., which in turn will result in change in Beta and duration.

Thus, any portfolio requires constant monitoring and revision. Operations on a portfolio will thus take place on a daily basis, keeping in mind, the targetted Beta, duration and return. Changes in investor's financial status, his preferences and market conditions, will also require changes in portfolio composition.

The next stage is performance evaluation which is referred to later. Before we discuss evaluation, it is necessary to set out some Theoretical tools like security analysis, Markowitz model, risk-return evaluation etc. These are referred to below, briefly, although they were set out in detail, in earlier Chapters.

SECURITY PRICING AND PORTFOLIO MANAGEMENT

Portfolio Management is based upon Security Analysis, which is an analysis of share prices.

(1) Analysis at Macro Level of Market and (2) Analysis at Micro Level of Company

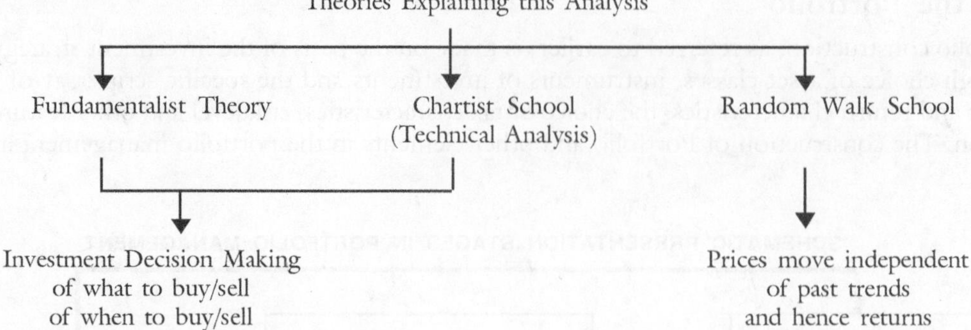

Markowitz Model of Portfolio Theory

This Portfolio Model is based on the exposure to market risk and the degree of diversification of the portfolio. The Beta of the portfolio provides a measure of exposure to market risk and the coefficient of determination, namely, R^2 provides a measure of diversification.

Cross sectional measures are used for risk estimates for individual holdings, that comprise the portfolio. The individual Scrips in the portfolio have their own Betas, which are weighted by the proportion of the funds invested in it. The Table below gives an example:

Table

Company	*Proportion of Portfolio*	*Betas of Scrips*	*Weighted Values*
Scrip A	.11	1.65	.18
Scrip B	.11	1.40	.15
Scrip C	.17	1.25	.21
Scrip D	.23	1.05	.24
Scrip E	.38	0.85	.32
	1.00		1.10

Depending on the risk preference of the investor, weights can be changed to get the desired portfolio Beta to less than 1.1 or more than 1.1 (got in the above Table).

In the same way, the portfolio R^2 or R can be calculated and compared with the market return and its R^2 or R. The standard deviation for the portfolio can be compared with that of the Market Index return and its R_1 to ensure that its R is suitable to the investor's risk preferences.

William Sharpe has suggested a new model. Instead of comparing the risk of each Scrip to every other Scrip, it can be compared with market risk, which leads to the comparison of market return to Scrip Return. He takes into account only the systematic Risk on the Portfolio (β).

$R_i = \alpha + \beta I + e$

α is the intercept of the straight line.

β is slope of the straight line or β co-efficeient.

I is expected return on Market Index, and e is the Random component.

The Sharpe Index method has given us two components of Risk.

Systematic Risk = $B^2 \times$ Variance of Index.

= $\beta^2 \sigma^2$

Unsystematic Risk = Total Variance of a Portfolio

Security Return – Systematic Risk = e^2

Total Risk = $\beta^2 \sigma^2 + e^2$

Total Risk of Market = Systematic Risk covered by Beta and Unsystematic Risk covered by diversification.

Risk Analysis

While the risks of fixed interest securities can be known as they are rated by agencies like ICRA and Crisil, the risk on equities cannot be assessed and has to be borne by the investor. The risk on equities is more than on bonds, debentures or fixed deposits and not amenable to scientific measurement as that is the residual risk of the firm. These risks may be due to inflation, interest rate changes, financial risk, business risk, market risk, liquidity risks, and other risks. Some of them relate to the market and economy and hence not controllable while the others are company specific in nature, which can be controlled and reduced by diversification. Thus, investment in more than one company and industry is necessary for reducing risks. Investment in too many companies, may not be desirable but investment in two companies in steel industry is not having the same risks as investment in one Steel Company and one drug company. Risk concepts and related aspects are dealt with already in another chapter.

EVALUATION OF PORTFOLIO PERFORMANCE

Investment analysts and Portfolio Managers continuously monitor and evaluate the results of their performance. The revision of portfolio investments is conducted on the basis of such monitoring and evaluation. The ability of Managers to out perform the market depends on their expertise and experience. The basic features of good Portfolio Managers are their ability to perceive the market trends correctly and make correct expectations and estimates regarding risk, returns, ability to make proper diversification, to reduce the company related risk and use proper Beta estimates for selection of securities to reduce the systematic risk. In such case, it is possible for an expert Portfolio Manager to show superior performance over the market. This performance also depends on the timing of investments and superior investment analysis through research and expertise in security selection. He has to have the acumen to select the under valued shares under each risk class, for which a high degree of equity research is needed.

The two major factors which influence his performance are the return achieved and the level of risk that the portfolio is exposed to. The Manager has to make proper diversification into different industries, asset classes and instruments so as to reduce the unsystematic risk to the minimum for a given level of return. The market related risk has to be managed by a proper selection of Beta for the securities.

Criteria for Evaluation of Portfolio

Portfolio managers and investors who manage their own portfolios continuously monitor and review the performance of the portfolio. The evaluation of each portfolio, followed by revision and reconstruction are all steps in the portfolio Management.

Managers and Analysts wish to know how well they performed in their investment strategies in terms of return *per unit of risk*, both in absolute terms and relative terms relative to overall market performance. They have to assess the extent to which the objectives aimed at are being achieved say in terms of income, capital appreciation, risk and returns, etc.

In this context, evaluation has to take into account whether the portfolio secured above average returns, average or below average, as compared to the market return. The ability to diversify with a view to reduce and even eliminate all unsystematic risk and expertise in managing the systematic risk related to the market by use of appropriate risk measures, namely, Betas, and selection of proper securities is thus the first requirement.

Superior timing and superior stock selection may result in above average return. Diversification in terms of Markowitz model or Sharpe's Single Index Model will reduce the market related risk and maximise the returns for a given level of risk. Market returns being related positively to risk, evaluation has to take into account:

(1) Rate of returns, or excess return over risk free rate.

(2) Level of Risk both Systematic (Beta) and Unsystematic and residual risks through proper diversification.

Under the Traditional theory, the evaluation is only in terms of the rate of return, particularly in comparison with other assets of the same risk class. The theory of Markowitz and Modern Portfolio Theory have opened up the avenue for selecting and evaluating the portfolios on the basis of risk adjusted return. Modern portfolio theory has postulated that the portfolio selection and evaluation should be on the basis of both Risk and Return and the objective should be to optimise the return for a given level of risk or to minimise the risk for a given level of return. Due to uneven fluctuations of returns and high degree of variability of returns, risk adjusted returns become the basis for evaluation. This is possible due to later developments involving the quantification of risk by the statistical measures of S.D., variance and covariance of returns of securities in a portfolio.

There was no composite index, which measures both return and risk under the Traditional Theory. In Modern Portfolio Theory it became necessary to develop some composite measures of both return and risk in portfolio performance, as the objective now is maximisation of return and minimisation of risk. Because of the trade-off between them, simple maximisation of returns or single goal of minimisation of risk will be defeating the objectives of Modern Portfolio Management.

It was in this context that later researches have tried to evolve a composite index to measure risk based returns taking into account the different components of risk, *viz.,* systematic, unsystematic and residual risk. The credit for evolving these criteria goes to Sharpe, Treynor and Jensen.

Example of Sharpe's Measure

Sharpe's measure is $ST = \frac{R_t - R_f}{\sigma_t}$

Where, ST is Sharpe index when, Rt is average return on portfolio, R_f is risk free return.

It measures total risk by standard deviation. Reward is in the numerator as risk premium. Total risk is in the denominator as standard deviation of its return. We get a measure of portfolio's total risk and variability of returns in relation to the risk premium which is the product of the portfolio Manager's expertise.

The method adopted by Sharpe is to rank all portfolios on the basis of evaluation measure ST. If one portfolio has more ST than another, the first one is better performer as per the Sharpe's measure. Take the following example:

Portfolio	*Average Return*	*S.D.*	*R_f (Risk Free Rate)*
A	20%	4%	10%
B	24%	8%	10%

By applying the above formula, we have

For A portfolio

$$St_A = \frac{0.20 - .10}{.04} = \frac{.10}{.04} = 2.50$$

For B portfolio

$$St_B = \frac{.24 - .10}{.08} = \frac{.14}{.08} = 1.75$$

As the first one is ranked higher at 2.5% more than the second 1.75, the first is a better performer. This is shown graphically as follows:

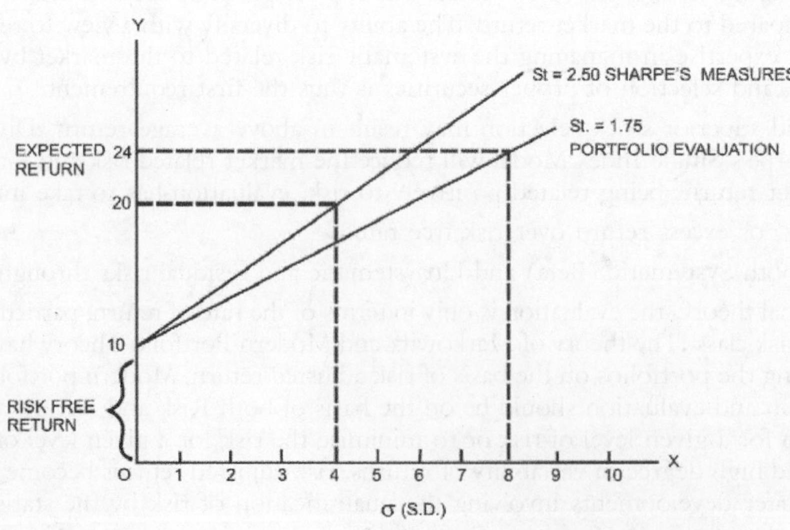

Fig. 29.9

Treynor's Measure

In Treynor's measure, the risk measure of standard deviation, namely, total risk of the portfolio is replaced by market risk, measured by Beta, which is not diversifiable. The equation can be set out as:

$$T_n = \frac{R_n - R_f}{\beta_n}$$

T_n = Treynor's measure of evaluation

R_n = Return on the portfolio, R_f = Risk free rate, B_n is Beta of the portfolio as a measure of systematic risk.

Treynor based his formula on the concept of characteristic line. This line is the least squares regression line relating the return to the risk and Beta is the slope of the line. The regression line takes the form of:

$R_p = \alpha + \beta x + e$

R_p is the return of portfolio,

α is the intercept reflecting the risk free return

β is the slope of the line and x is the market return and e is the error term.

Thus, concept can be graphically represented as follows:

Based on this characteristic line, Treynors formula is

$$T_n = \frac{R_n - R_f}{\beta_n}$$

which is explained above.

Beta is the slope of the line indicating the relationship between scrip return and Market Return.

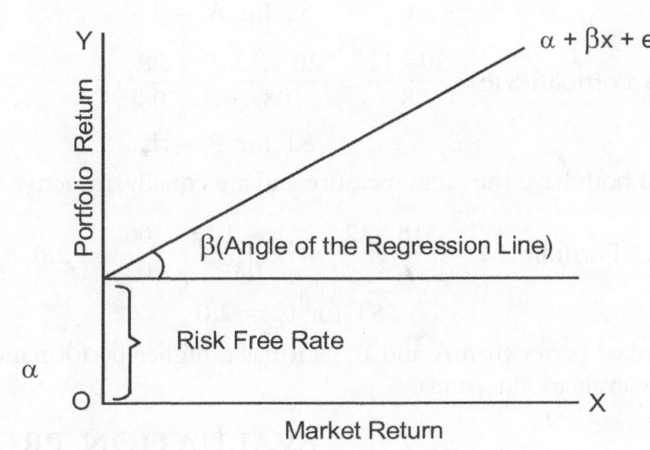

Fig. 29.10

Take a Problem as an example

Portfolio	*Return*	B_n	R_f
A	20	0.5	10
B	24	1.0	10

For A, $T_{nA} = \frac{.20 - .10}{0.5} = \frac{.10}{.5} = 0.2$

For B, $T_{nB} = \frac{24 - 10}{1.0} = = 0.14$

Portfolio 'A' performs better than Portfolio B as $T_{nA} > T_{nB}$.

The numerator in Treynor's formula is the reward, measured by risk premium or excess returns and denominator is volatility as measured by Beta coefficient.

The difference between Sharpe measure and Treynor measure is the following:

Sharpe takes the total risk of portfolio into account while Treynor considers only systematic risk as relevant to performance. Total risk consists of both systematic and unsystematic risk, while the latter is amenable to reduction by management of proper diversification, the former cannot be eliminated but borne by the investor. The higher this market risk one takes, the higher is the return. If diversification is perfect, and unsystematic risk is nil or negligible then the only elements of risk in both the portfolio measurements is the systematic variance. The ranking of portfolios on the basis of both the measures therefore should give identical results. But it is possible that these two measures in practice give varying results due to differences in the investment strategies and diversification techniques.

Problems

Example on Evaluation of Portfolio Performance

The Measure of Sharpe's performance evaluation may be calculated from the following data:

Three Portfolios of the Securities

Portfolios	*Return*	*Standard Deviation*	*Riskless Rate of Return*
A	16%	4%	12%
B	20%	8%	12%
C	18%	3%	12%

$$ST = \frac{R_i - R_f}{\sigma_i} \quad \text{Sharpe's Measure}$$

$$\text{For A Portfolio ST} = \frac{16-12}{4} = \frac{.16-.12}{.04} = \frac{.04}{.04}$$

ST for A = 1

$$\text{For B Portfolio ST} = \frac{20-12}{8} = \frac{.20-.12}{.08} = \frac{.08}{.08}$$

ST for B = 1

A & B both have the same measure and are equally attractive in performance. But take the case of portfolio 'C'.

$$\text{For 'C' Portfolio ST} = \frac{18-12}{3} = \frac{.18-.12}{.03} = \frac{.06}{.03} = 2.0$$

ST for C = 2.0

'C' ranked better than A and B, as it has a higher performance index according to the Sharpe's model and his performance evaluation formula.

EVALUATION PROBLEM

Comparison

Problem

Portfolio	*Return*	*Sd.*	*Riskless Rate*	*Beta*
A	6.00	15.24	3.0	1.00
B	3.30	4.92	3.0	2.85

Compare Treynor's Index with Sharpe's Index

Treynor's Index	Sharpe's Index
$T_n = \frac{r_n - r^0}{\beta_n}$	$S_t = \frac{rt - rf}{sd}$
For A	
$T_n = \frac{6-3.0}{1.00} = 3$	$S_t = \frac{6-3.0}{15.24} = \frac{3.0}{15.24}$
$T_n = 3.00$	$S_t = 0.19$

For B

$$T_n = \frac{3.30 - 3.0}{2.85} = \frac{0.30}{2.85} \qquad S_t = \frac{3.30 - 3.0}{4.92} = \frac{0.30}{4.92}$$

$$T_n = 0.1 \qquad S_t = 0.06$$

A comparison of the two measures, namely, Treynor's and Sharpe's performance Evaluation, is made in the above example.

Conclusion: By Treynor's measure the portfolio 'A' is better as it has a higher rank of 3.00 than that of B (0.1). By Sharpe index measure also, the same conclusion is arrived, namely, Portfolio A is better than 'B' as the former got a rank higher than the latter.

Jensen's Measure

Jensen's measure of the performance of portfolio is different from that of Sharpe and Treynor in that the latter provide a measure of ranking the relative performance of various portfolios on a risk adjusted basis while the former gives a measure of absolute performance on a risk adjusted basis. This standard, based on CAPM, measures the portfolio Manager's predictive ability to achieve higher return than expected for the given riskiness.

Jensen's Model

$R_{Jt} - R_{ft} = \alpha_J + \beta_J (R_{Mt} - R_{ft})$

R_{Jt} = Average return on portfolio J for period 't'

R_{ft} = Risk free rate of return for period 't'

α_J = Intercept of the Graph, measuring the forecasting ability of the Manager

β_J = Systematic risk measure

R_{Mt} = Average return on the Market Portfolio for period t.

It is possible that $\alpha_J = 0$, which is neutral performance or the same as that of market.

$\alpha_J > 0$, it is superior performance over the market

$\alpha_J < 0$, it is inferior performance

The Jensen's approach can be illustrated by an example.

The data on portfolio results, Beta of the portfolios and Market Index results are set out as follows:

Portfolio	*Return as Portfolio*	*Portfolio Beta*
1	18%	1.2
2	15%	0.8
3	21%	1.5
Market Index	16%	1.00

Market Beta 1.0 and Risk free Rate 10%

The return of 3 portfolios on the basis of CAPM are as follows:

$R_p = R_F + (R_{M1} - R_F)\ \beta$

(1) Portfolio I = 10 + (16 – 10) × 1.2 = 17.2%

(2) Portfolio II = 10 + (16 – 10) × 0.8 = 14.8%

(3) Portfolio III = 10 + (16 – 10) × 1.5 = 19.0%

Actual vs. Estimate Portfolio I = 18 – 17.2 = 0.8%

Portfolio II = 15 – 14.8 = 0.2%

Portfolio III = 21 – 19.0 = 2.0%

The above data show that the best managed Portfolio, as per Jensen's approach is that of Portfolio III, which has out performed the market and gave 2% return above that would have been got under CAPM for the given level of risk. While the actual return of portfolio 'P' is what is achieved, it may be above the vertical distance from the required return as judged by the market return.

The Jensen and Fama net selectivity measures may give opposite or different results. This is due to the use of total risk in one case and the systematic risk on the other. In both cases, the actual portfolio return is compared and evaluated as excess over the market return or required return for a given level of risk.

Evaluation Criteria for Portfolios

Treynor and Sharpe Index models provide measures for ranking the *relative* performances of various portfolios on a risk adjusted basis. But Jensen has constructed a measure of ***absolute*** performance on a risk adjusted basis.

A simplified version of his basic Model is given by:

$R_{Jt} - R_{Ft} = a_J + b_J\ (R_{mt} - R_{Ft})$

R_{Ji} = Average return on portfolio for period t

R_{Ft} = Riskless rate of return for period t

a_J = Intercept that measures the forecasting ability of the Manager

b_J = A measure of systematic risk

R_{Mt} = Average return on market for period t

Graphical Representation of Jensen's Measure is given below. For Sharpe and Treynor, the intercept of the line is at the origin but in the case of Jensen, it can be at any point, including the origin.

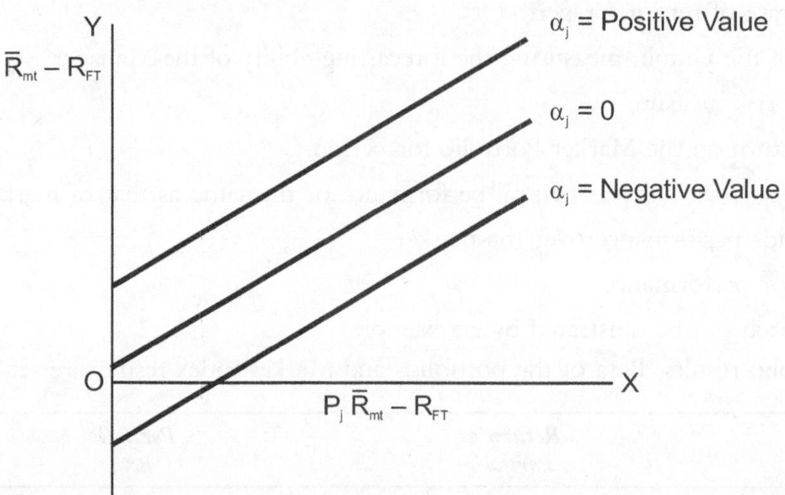

Fig. 29.11

If α, is positive it indicates superior performance, α, is negative it indicates inferior performance and α_0 is neutral performance — something similar to market average.

As compared to the normal evaluation of a portfolio as against the market portfolio in relative terms by Treynor and Sharpe, the Jensen's approach is more general and absolute in measure.

Thus, Sharpe's measure ST is set out as $ST = \dfrac{rt - r^0}{\sigma_t^{\ 2}}$, where rt is the average return on portfolio t and r^0 is the riskless return and $\sigma_t^{\ 2}$ is variance (risk measure) of the returns on portfolio. Here σ^2 takes the total risk while the same in formula of Treynor takes Beta, and Beta (β) is a measure of systematic risk and not total risk.

Treynor's measure is also set out as:

$T_n = \dfrac{r_n - r}{\beta_n}$, where r_n and r have the same meanings as under Sharpe's formula.

The graphical presentation of both is given below:

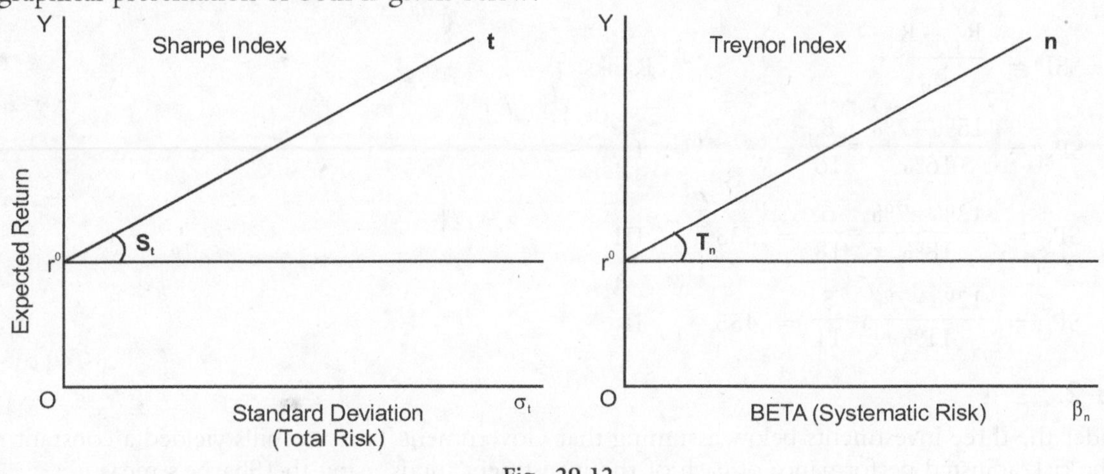

Fig. 29.12

The graphs are self-explanatory. While Sharpe Index used standard deviation (total risk), Treynor used Beta, the measure of systematic risk.

In the case of Sharpe model, the standard deviation measuring total risk (σ) is used. In Treyner model, only systematic risk (β) which is market related and can not be diversified is used. Their results will be different and need not be similar or identical.

PORTFOLIO PERFORMANCE EVALUATION

Problems

I Sharpe's Performance Measure

$$SP = \frac{\text{Risk npremium}}{\text{Totaln risk}} = \frac{R_p - R}{\sigma_p}$$

Where, SP = Sharpe's Index of portfolio performance for portfolio p

$\bar{R}_p$ = average return for portfolio p

σ_p = standard deviation of returns for portfolio

p = $\sqrt{\text{var (r)}}$

R = Riskless rate of interest, or $\sqrt{\text{Var (R)}} = 0$

Examples

Question 1

The rate of return and risk for three growth-oriented firms were calculated over the most recent 5 years and are listed below:

Growth Firm	*Return*	*Risk (σ)*
M	15%	16%
N	13	18
O	12	11

Rank each firm by Sharpe's index of portfolio performance if the risk free rate is 7 per cent.

Answer:

$$SP = \frac{R_p - R_f}{\sigma_p} \qquad \text{Ranks}$$

$$SP_M = \frac{15\% - 7\%}{16\%} = \frac{8}{16} = .5 \qquad \text{I}$$

$$SP_N = \frac{13\% - 7\%}{18\%} = \frac{6}{18} = .333 \qquad \text{III}$$

$$SP_O = \frac{12\% - 7\%}{11\%} = \frac{5}{11} = .455 \qquad \text{II}$$

Question 2

Consider the three investments below assuming that Government Treasury bills yielded a constant rate of 7%. Calculate the risk adjusted performance of each of the investment funds using the Sharpe's measures?

Year	*A*	*Deviation of A*	*B*	*Deviation of B*	*C*	*Deviation of C*
1993	+5	+2.4	+4	0.8	+6	+2
1994	+0	−2.6	+1	2.2	−1	−5
1995	−5	−7.6	−4	−7.2	−10	−14
1966	+8	+5.4	+10	+6.8	+18	+14
1997	+5	+2.4	+5	+1.8	+7	+3

Answer:

$$(\bar{R}) \quad \overset{(A)}{\frac{13}{5} = 2.6}; \quad \overset{(B)}{\frac{16}{5} = 3.2}; \quad \overset{(C)}{\frac{20}{5} = 4}$$

		(Deviation)^2 A	(Deviation)^2 B	(Deviation)^2 C
		5.76	0.64	4
		6.76	4.40	25
		57.76	51.84	196
		29.16	46.24	196
		5.76	3.24	9
σ_p^2	=	105.20	106.36	430
σ_p	=	10.25	10.31	20.74

Ranks

$$Sp_A = \frac{R - R_f}{\sigma p} = \frac{2.6 - 7}{10.2} = \frac{-4.4}{10.2} = -0.43 \qquad \text{III}$$

$$Sp_B = \frac{3.2 - 7}{10.31} = \frac{-3.8}{10.31} = -0.37 \qquad \text{II}$$

$$Sp_C = \frac{4 - 7}{20.7} = \frac{-3}{20.7} = -0.14 \qquad \text{I}$$

The ranks are as shown above.

Treynor's measure is as follows:

$$T_p = \frac{\text{Risk premium}}{\text{Portfolios beta coefficient}} = \frac{R_p - R_f}{\beta_p}$$

T_p = Treynor's index of performance for portfolio.
R_p = the average return for portfolio.
R_f = the risk free rate of interest. Var (R) = O
β_p = the beta for the portfolio.

Problem

(1) Rank the three Firms with the Treynor performance Index; given the following data

Growth Firm	*Return*	*Risk*	*Beta*	*Risk Free Rate*
M	15%	16%	1.15	7%
N	13%	18%	1.25	7%
O	12 %	11%	0.90	7%

Answer:

$$Tp = \frac{R_p - R_f}{\beta_p}$$

Ranks

$$Tp_M = \frac{15-7}{1.15} = \frac{8}{1.15} = 6.96 \quad \text{I}$$

$$Tp_N = \frac{13-7}{1.25} = \frac{6}{1.25} = 4.8 \quad \text{III}$$

$$Tp_O = \frac{12-7}{0.9} = \frac{5}{0.9} = 5.55 \quad \text{II}$$

(2) Three Mutual Funds have reported the following rates of return and risk over the last five years.

Growth Fund	*Return*	*St. Deviation (Risk)*	*Beta*
Shriram	15%	16%	1.15
Birla	13%	18%	1.25
ICICI	12%	11%	0.90

Rank each fund by Sharpe's and Treynor's performance evaluation criteria, given the Risk free Return (Rf) as 7%.

Answer:

Sharpe

$$\text{Sharp Index} = \frac{\overline{R}p - Rf}{\sigma p} \qquad \text{Ranks}$$

$$\text{Shriram} = \frac{15-7}{16} = \frac{8}{16} = 0.5 \quad \text{I}$$

$$\text{Birla} = \frac{13-7}{18} = \frac{6}{18} = 0.33 \quad \text{III}$$

$$\text{ICICI} = \frac{12-7}{11} = \frac{5}{11} = 0.45 \quad \text{II}$$

Treynor

$$\text{Treynor's Index} = \frac{R_p - R_f}{\beta_p}$$

$$\text{Shriram} = \frac{15-7}{1.15} = 6.96 \qquad \text{I}$$

$$\text{Birla} = \frac{13-7}{1.25} = 4.80 \qquad \text{III}$$

$$\text{ICICI} = \frac{12-7}{0.90} = 5.55 \qquad \text{II}$$

Both Sharpe's and Treynor's measures give the same results in ranking the portfolios.

Jensen's Performance Measure: (JP)

$$J_p = \frac{\text{Alpha}}{\text{Beta}}$$

Jensen's Alpha and the Beta Coefficients for four stocks are given below:

Stocks	*Alpha*	*Beta*
M	1.0	.9
N	1.25	1.25
O	1.07	1.15
P	1.15	0.85

Answer:

Rank

$$Jp_M = \frac{1}{.9} = 1.11 \qquad \text{II}$$

$$JP_n = \frac{1.25}{1.25} = 1 \qquad \text{III}$$

$$Jp_o = \frac{1.07}{1.15} = 0.93 \qquad \text{IV}$$

$$Jp_p = \frac{1.15}{.85} = 1.35 \qquad \text{I}$$

Questions

(1) Determine the Treynor's and Jensen's measures of portfolio performance from the following information.

Average rate of return on market portfolio = 18%

Average rate of return on this portfolio = 19%

Average risk free return = 12%

Standard deviation of this portfolio = 14%

Beta of portfolio, under consideration = 0.95.

(2) From the following data on returns and risks of portfolios A to E calculate Sharpe's measure and Treynors measure of portfolio performance, if R_f is 3%.

Portfolio	*Expost Return*	σ_t	*Beta*
A	7	3	0.4
B	10	8	1.0
C	13	6	1.1
D	15	13	1.2
E	18	15	1.4

(3) Given the following information on two Mutual funds Tatas, Birlas and the Market Index Portfolio, rank the performance of these from the available measures of Treynor and Sharpe?

	Tatas	*Birlas*	*Market*
R_p.	16	12	15.7
σ_p	13	9	13.0
β_p	0.83	0.66	1.0

and R_f (Risk free rate) = 6.2%.

Note: **For more Problems and Solutions in any chapter Refer to "Theory and Problems of Investments" — By J.C. Francis & R.W. Taylor.**

PORTFOLIO MANAGEMENT BY CORPORATES

Corporates are owned by investors, whose objective is maximisation of their wealth. Corporate ownership pattern in India shows that the bulk owners are the financial institutions and mutual funds, LIC, GIC and other corporates, leaving aside, the FFIs and FIIs OCBs and NRIs. The ownership of individual share holders, as an average, does not exceed an average of 20 to 30%. The interests of financial and non-financial institutions and corporates do not coincide with that of individual shareholders who are the true savers of the household sector while the former categories are only intermediaries.

Corporate Managers secure funds from banks, and FIs, next only to promoters and hence their interests stand prominent in the minds of portfolio Managers in the corporate business. The forgotten lot are the last category of individual investors, whose interests are different from those of others.

In the case of listed corporate securities, which are the concern of this book, there is no direct dialogue between corporate Managers and individual investors, except through the daily price quotation of the scrip on the exchanges or in General Body Meetings. The share price reflects the investor perception of that company, relative to others in the field.

The companies generally keep continuous contact and dialogue with financing bankers and financial institutions and not with other categories of investors, in matters of operations. The role of individual investors and remaining categories of investors can have their say only in the Annual general body meetings or other extraordinary general body meetings, called by the corporate management, as per law or requirements of Stock Exchanges or the Government.

The performance of corporates and their operations are also guided by the Government and SEBI Regulations, the Company law and the Listing Agreement with the Stock Exchange. The prudential norms for raising resources, allocation of funds and declaration of dividends, etc., are all governed by the Law and Government notifications from time-to-time.

Risk Return of Corporate Business

Leaving aside the above regulations and codes of conduct as laid down by law, government and by the Listing Agreement signed with the stock exchanges in respect of listed companies, the operations of companies, the risk and return aspects of their operations and the operational results show their impact on the share price quotations of that company on the stock exchange. A high risk company will have a low premium as against a low risk company in the share price quotations. A company which is a loan and investment type will be less preferred by investors, as compared with a manufacturing company and among manufacturing companies those well diversified in their activities like HLL, Reliance, L&T etc., are more preferred due to the less risk that the companies face in the market. The risk taken by the companies will get reflected through diversification of their product range, activities and lines of business, that they undertake or engage themselves. Usually a well diversified company is preferred to a company of uniproduct line of business. Among those diversified, those with larger return, high networth or larger profits will be preferred by investors.

Investment by corporate business may be in physical and financial assets. If it is investment in financial assets, the risk return analysis of Markowitz holds good. But of it is in physical assets, as part of business operations, we have to consider the project risk and revenue sensitivity which are, referred to later.

Kinds of Risk

Any company's business lead to different kinds of risk. These are briefly related to —

1. Business Risk: Related to type of activity.

2. Market Risk: Refers to demand and supply for the products and related factors.

3. Financial Risk: Relates to the method of financing the investment-debt component and leverage enjoyed by equity.

4. Purchasing Power Risk: Refers to the rise in prices which leads to rise in costs and squeeze on profits unless there is a corresponding rise in output prices, as well. Loss in the value of many due to inflation may lead to changes in business expectations and capital budgeting plans.

5. Interest Rate Risk: The financial structure and the relative costs of various components of capital and the average cost of capital will be affected by changes in interest rates. The net earnings and dividends and networth will be influenced by them.

The variability of returns which is risk by it self-depends upon many factors which are of two types, namely those related to market *(systematic risk)* and those related to company *(unsystematic risk)*. The examples of market related risks are given above. This type of risk cannot be reduced by diversification but can be measured and adjusted through the use of market Beta and the company Beta (as a measure of systematic risk). Market related risk is for the whole set of securities in the market represented generally by a well recognised index number.

Markowitz Diversification

Company related risks refer to the labour problems, input shortages, quality problems, management problems, changes in market conditions, financial structure and levaged debt, etc. These risks, called unsystematic risks, can be reduced by proper diversification. Markowitz diversification takes into account the relative variances of all the securities included in the portfolio but also their covariances, so that the sum of the risks of individual scrips is shortened or reduced by the relative inter-dependence of each of them on others or the negative or opposite effect of each of them in relation to others in the portfolio.

The share price of a company depends on how well the company diversifies so as to reduce its risk of unsystematic nature both the respect of their financial and physical investment. The company has various projects and the assessment of risk and return of project has to be related and assessed for finding its impact on its share price and investors' perception of that through an analysis of the company's cash flows — discounted cash flows — discounted by an appropriate discount rate to reduce the future cash flows to the present net asset value (NPV).

Beta provides a tool for the corporate managers to understand and determine the risk which they can take consistent with the expected return of investors, which is relative to market risk and return. Beta can be calculated by the following formula.

$$\beta = \frac{r_{Jm}\,\sigma_J\,\sigma_m}{\sigma_m^2}$$

where,

r_{JM} is the expected correlation between possible returns for the security and that of market portfolio.

σ_J is the standard deviation of security, "J" and σ_m is the standard deviation of market portfolio.

Beta as a Measure of Risk for the Company

The value of β is readily estimated for quoted securities which are well traded. The same for the market is taken as one and the Beta for a given security is estimated as greater than 1 or less than 1 (relative to market risk) as risk is relative and risk measures are also relative.

A Company's risk is partly related to market (calculated by the Beta measure) and partly to the company (calculated by its own standard deviation) which can be reduced by proper diversification into many securities, spread over a number of classes of securities, industries, asset classes and types of activities, undertaken by the company, etc.

The values of Beta are published by the Equity Research organisations of Economic Times, Dalal Street Journal and ICFAI. Journal, among others. The company Beta, as thus estimated has to be managed to meet the expected returns of industry group and the investors in that group. Basically, each company has to satisfy its investors, which is reflected in the share price quotations over a period, or at a point of time. The company management sees its operational results, reflected in its share/price quotation. Each company will be operating at a risk level and returns expected of that company should be comparable with those in the same level of risk. In corporate business its physical operations as also its financial operations should be at that level of risk, relative to return, which its investors prefer.

As per the latest Companies (Amendment) Bill of 2008, the investors are the owners and masters, who can question CEO and other management staff. Government intervention is expected to be replaced by investors' interference. The bill proposes to give more powers to investors.

Theoretical Framework

The CAPM provides an appropriate theoretical framework to the assessment of risk and return within the operating business of corporates. Investors are risk averse according to this theory and they expect a higher return from a more risky company and more risky project.

On the market portfolio, there is a market risk, which is the standard measure for comparison purposes. There is one risk namely market risk, which cannot be reduced by diversification and this is the only risk on which the investors need a premium. The other type of unsystematic risk can be reduced or eliminated by diversification and this may not give any premium return. By use of b, the required rate of return can be estimated on the investments that the corporate manager makes on behalf of investors.

By use of an appropriate discount rate on new projects, given their expected cash flows, the required rate on the division of business undertaking or the new projects can be worked out. At best, there are separate discount rates for each risk class, and the exercise of D.C. F Analysis has to be done.

Projects undertaken, are generally decided on the basis of business strategy but it must be also based on financial return estimates. These returns can be estimated on the basis of expected cash flows over the life period of the project and the use of a proper discount rate for estimating the present values of the expected cash flows. The risk associated with that return should also be calculated in terms of the variability of the return or use the industry β and compare it with the project b or the company b.

Investment decisions are made independent of financing decisions; but a Corporate Manager has to correlate them and at the time of taking investment decision the financing method or the mix of financial resources is also chosen so as to take advantage of any tax or other advantages or leverage in financing method. The project return is not independent of financing decision in practice although in theory they can be looked at as different decisions. As investor is sensitive to risk, a company with a higher b should also have a higher return. Here the equity b and the gearing to equity should be taken into account by the Corporate Manager, as that is the concern of equity holder of that company.

Dividend decision, the retention ratio and the profit allocation method adopted, have all a bearing on the risk-return perception of the investor and his expectation of the company. The corporate management decisions in this regard also influence the Equity Share price behaviour and corporate rating.

Revenue Sensitivity

From the industry β, as published from existing sources, remove the effect of financial gearing on equity risk. Then adjust the project β for relative operational gearing through cost structure effects. Then the revenue sensitivity of the project is explicitly studied. This is a measure of sensitivity of project revenue or sales to the company as a whole.

$$\text{Relative Risk of Project} = \frac{\text{Project } \beta}{\text{Company } \beta}$$

$$\text{Revenue Sensitivity (S)} = \frac{\text{Project revenue } \beta}{\text{Company revenue } \beta}$$

$$\text{Relative Operational Gearing (G)} = \frac{\text{Project gearing factor}}{\text{Company gearing factor}}$$

$$\text{Relative Risk} = \frac{\text{Project nnrevenuen } \beta}{\text{Company nnrevenuen } \beta} \times \frac{\text{Projectn gearing nfactor}}{\text{Companyn gearing nfactor}}$$

Company Revenue Sensitivity and Company gearing factor are also useful indicators of investor Perception of the Company

$\beta = S \times G$

According to Alan Bainbridge, @CAPM provides the appropriate theoretical framework to link the requirements of investors in terms of their risk return perception to that of the investment decisions of the Corporate Manager. The study and interpretation of share price moments is necessary for the Managers to manage the portfolio investment decision of the company. Firstly, the financing decision depends on the state of the primary market and secondary market and investor perception of the company's performance as judged by the movements in its share price. The company β and the industry β are relatively more stable and dependable parameters for integrating the risk with return (Premium on risk free return).

The corporate business has to focus their attention on measuring the market non-diversifiable risk, which requires a premium for investors. In assessing the viability of the project and its estimated return to equity holders, the effects of financial gearing are removed or ignored. Management has to consider the operational gearing in the sense of the revenues generated by the project and the costs involved through variable costs and fixed costs incurred in the project. The revenue sensitivity of the project is also to be examined by relating the projects contribution to the company income or net cash inflows or marginal profits created by the new project. The fundamental, strategic and market effects of a project on the company, undertaking it are taken into account and new risk return scenario emerging for the company is relevant to the investor for his assessment of the company's share price.

Agency Theory

Corporate management has to take the investor interests into account in making their financing, investment and dividend decision. As per the Agency Theory, the Corporate Managers are a group who are agents of the owner interests. The interests of company requires a reconciliation of the interests of the owners with the creditors and debtors of the company, among others which include the Government, consumers and the general public. Primarily the Management is an Agency of the investors or owner group and to promote their interest, the share market capitalisation has to be maximised which in turn depends in the net profits and profitability of the company, EPS, P/E multiple and Book value of the share. Maximisation of investor wealth is synonymous with maximisation of the company's networth or total assets. The capital efficiency, sales turnover and profit margin are the critical variables which reflect the impact of the investment and financing decisions of the management.

Agency theory postulates that management acts in the best interests of owners or investors and the objectives of both are the same. Thus, the operations of the company in portfolio management basically follow the principle of wealth maximisation at a given level of risk which is in tune with the interests and desires of investors.

Cash Flow Estimates

Assessing cash flows of project is the first step. These flows will depend on the outcome of specific events, such as capacity utilisation, probability of sales and cash sales etc., and the result of this exercise is the estimation of expected value of cash flows.

As a next step, a discount rate is to be chosen appropriate to the project risk. For knowing the project risk only the non-market risk need to be considered by the corporate Manager and expected return is to be ensured by him for maximisation of share valuation. But for choosing the discount rate, appropriate for the project, only market risk need to be considered. Project β can be estimated from the following equation.

$$\beta = \frac{r_{Jm}\ \sigma_J\ \sigma_m}{\sigma_m^2}$$

In the above equation, in addition to the risk of security (standard deviation), and risk of market, we consider the covariance between them r_{Jm} also. σ_m is also considered and is relatively more important.

Adjusting Company β for the Particular Project

The company β is first adjusted for financial gearing and then the estimate can be improved, by taking into account the operational gearing of the project compared to that of the company and the extent to which the revenues of the project are sensitive to general economic conditions affecting the company and industry. Financial gearing leaves its impact on the equity return because of its fixed costs. If a company has operational fixed cost, its return will also be sensitive to changes in revenue. Operational gearing affects the risk through the elements of cash flow, as seen in the following equation.

@ In the Book on Risk, *Portfolio Management and Capital Market,* by T.E. Cooke, J. Matatko and D.C. Stafford (Macmillan Co.).

Net cash flow = Revenue – variable cost – fixed costs

The above equation can be rearranged as shown below.

$$R = C - (V + F)$$

R is the present value of the revenue.

C is the present value of net cash flows.

V is the present value of variable costs.

F is the present value of fixed costs.

These terms are correlated to Stock Market share price and the beta values of the company and the market. The company has to bear these factors in mind in its portfolio management.

In sum, the Corporate Manager has to ensure that the financial structure of the project and operational gearing of the project are making the net cash in flows increase and thus ensure that the project improves the value of company worth in the eyes of investors and not reduce. In this process, the investment and financial decisions and dividend decisions are to be considered and the effect of financial gearing and operational gearing has to be isolated to arrive at the contribution of the new project to the total corporate image in the eyes of investor. The Corporate Manager has to ensure that the funds in his hands of the investors and shareholders are less productive than in the hands of the Corporate Investors and Finance Managers due to their better expertise and R&D efforts. A delicate balancing of the interests of company and of investors is necessary in this process. The corporate Manager operates his portfolio and undertakes the new projects keeping in view their contribution to the wealth of the company in which the investors are interested. The market capitalisation of the company's shares has thus to be kept in mind in the portfolio management of the company and its project selection, implementation and operations.

The relative wealth of the company is perceived in the context of the wealth of its competitors or the other companies in the industry. The investors weigh the wealth of the company in the context of his own relative wealth, to the extent of the shares that he holds in the company.

The corporate management has to bear in mind this aspect of the investor as the owner and master in whose interest portfolio management is operated.

Tax Planning by Corporates for Portfolio Management

Portfolio management aims at maximising the return given the level of risk and optimise the share values of the company. For this purpose proper tax planning is necessary so as to reduce the tax burden and increase the after tax profits of the company.

The present tax laws provide for a tax rate of 30% on the profit income of the domestic company and to foreign company with varied surcharges. There is also a minimum alternative tax (MAT) of 7.5 on the book profits of non-tax paying companies which take advantage of all tax incentives and rebates and show no taxable income. This rate was raised to 10% in 2006-07 in addition to giving them tax credits upto 7 years instead of 5 years hitherto. Besides, these companies have to include the long term capital gains arising out of the securities transactions as part of the income for the purpose of calculating the book profits. These provisions will plug some loopholes and raise the tax liability on the holding and investment companies which are taking the route of MAT for tax purposes.

The Banking cash transaction tax (BCTT) imposed 2004-05 is still applicable to companies having cash transactions to undertake. This constitutes a big headache for the companies and their accounts. All individuals and companies with huge transactions have to quote the PAN number henceforth. Besides the Fringe Benefits Tax (FBT) is also continued with some modifications in 2006-07. These concessions include tour and travel, and medical expenses and employer's contributions to the superannuation benefits to employees. The Fringe Benefits paid by companies to employees are taxable as income of the company, for the FBT. The Securities Transactions Tax (STT) continued to be imposed on transactions on stock markets with higher rates than before which again is a damper to trading on the stock market for companies and individuals alike.

As regards investment, the Govt. has provided for larger public investment on Agriculture, infrastructure and power sectors. The FDI inflows reached a high of $35 billion in the year 2008-09 and $22 billion in 2013-14 and the flow is likely to be maintained as many new sectors are kept open for private investment like power, Airport renovation, retail sector etc. The incentives for investment are restructured by deleting the Section 80L: and section 88 of the I.T. Act and replacing them by new Section 80C which provides for a lumpsum exemption of investment upto ₹ one lakh from 2005-06 for approved categories of investment which includes five year time deposits with scheduled banks, insurance, NSC and equity linked MF schemes, etc. Although these are more useful to individual investors, companies will also benefit from encouragement to equity market.

The MAT companies should continue to maintain their MAT status for tax planning purposes as the new rate of 10% is still lower than the usual corporate tax rate of 30% plus surcharge. The burden of FBT and BCTT can be lowered by proper tax planning and prudent investments on behalf of employees instead of showing them as expenditure. Thus the corporates can reduce their cash withdrawals and their fringe benefits to employees and increase those which are exempted from tax like the superannuation, insurance, medical and other permitted expenses for employees.

What is sought to be emphasized here is that corporates or individuals or MFs have an even chance for tax planning and increase their net after tax returns. The above account is a brief overview of the present tax system for the purpose of tax planning for portfolio management. The tax system may change from year to year but the principles of tax planning and the need for it cannot be over emphasized.

Indian corporate taxation at 33% including surcharge is at par with tax rates in other countries. It compares well with those in Brazil (34%), the USA (40%) Canada (36.5%) and Germany (38.29%). The rates in most Asian countries including China are in same range as in India.

In sum, corporate Portfolio Management involves all the major decisions of the companies like Investment, Financing and Dividend decisions. The objective being the wealth maximisation of the company, the portfolio manager has to take into account the project's cash flows to the company net of taxes and other hurdles. For long-term investments, i.e., the portfolio manager of the companies goes for the choice of projects, mergers, acquisitions and equity and bonds etc., on the basis of principles of risk weighted returns and diversification and dominance. Similarly, for short-term investment in money and capital market, considerations of liquidity, marketability and safety would be taken into account.

As against the limited avenues of investment for the individuals the corporate portfolio manager has additional avenues like new projects for diversification, takeover of potentially sick companies, mergers and acquisitions, expansion of capacities. These will change the risk-return characteristics of the company, if they also involve riskless assets like Govt. bonds, Treasury bills etc.

31

PORTFOLIO REVISION – FURTHER ASPECTS

Introduction

One most important factor is the Time value in Portfolio Revision. Time factor enters into portfolio in respect of bonds, government securities, equities and some other investments made by the portfolio manager.

Time has a value in money terms namely today's money is more valuable than that of tomorrow and a year hence. Portfolio is constructed at a time or over a period and the returns are also flowing at various times. Synchronisation of inflows and outflows is difficult, if not impossible and if achieved, it is called immunisation of the portfolio,

It is the general conception of the public not to evaluate values of money in terms of time factor. But a listed company in foreign stock exchanges are under an obligation to present financial data at both current prices and constant prices or in other words in constant dollars, which are derived by deflating the flows of money by inflation/deflation or changes in the value of money. Dollar is used as constant factor for its greater stability and general acceptance and companies foreign or domestic are now presenting the financial data both in rupees as well as dollars.

Any foreign company has to present the financial data, sources and uses and inflows and outflows in constant dollars for the benefit of the parent company. The tax factors and payment of royalty, charges, fees, etc., are all governed by this presentation in constant dollars. For dollar is parent company's currency in which they evaluate the performance, for the benefit of investors, global tax flows and global investment returns and portfolio management. But it is to be noted here that dollar itself is depreciating and non dollar companies prefer to present their data in terms of their own parent company's currency or in constant rupees or both.

An example of statement in foreign currency U.S.D. for the subsidiary, Essar Steel Trading, Free Zone Establishment Dubai (FZE) of the Essar Steel is given below:

As on March 31

	2009 U.S.D.	*2008 U.S.D.*
Gross Profit	14,245,605	4,925,991
Total Profit for the Year	9,316,080	1,851,197
Current Assets	7,949,058	50,360,856
Total Assets	90,702,484	159,791,607
Total Equity	12,824,068	3,509,988
Share Capital	1,634,877	816,727
Non-current Liabilities as Term Loans	–	15,000,000
Current Liabilities	177,876,416	141,281,619
Total Equity and Liabilities	190,702,484	159,791,607

Source: Essar Annual Report.

Cash flow and funds flow statements were also given in U.S. dollars for 2008 and 2009.

If the same data flow 2011-12, should be presented, they may be in current dollars or constant dollars. If the portfolio is to be revised, it depends on the data of the companies equity, instruments and other assets held in its portfolio of constant prices.

Portfolio Manager has to devise a formula for converting all data into constant rupees or dollars. Generally, profit booking trading and continuous revisions, buying and selling make it difficult to apply the formula whatever, it is on a continuous way. But Quarterly, half-yearly and yearly revisions for a constant currency is possible. But the investor generally does not insist on any mode of valuation. This should be made clear to public investors.

Formula Plan

In portfolio construction and revision, there can be many plans, each with its own characteristics. In brief, these plans are: Constant dollar value plan, constant rupee value plan, constant ratio plan, variable ratio plan, formulate plan, modifications of formula plan, Dollar Return Averaging and Dollar Cost Averaging etc. Some plans are chosen as per the requirements of investor client, some are imposed by the listing requirements of Stock Exchanges or by the guidelines of the SEBI. The companies having ADRS, GDRS, FCCBs, are quoted in Foreign Stock Exchanges including NYSE, NASDAQ. They have to present their data in current or constant dollars. Portfolio Manager may himself choose some plan, as in the case of formula plan. Reference was made earlier in the book on the nature and operations under the formula plan. This involves random investments at regular monthly or quarterly intervals. The instruments to be invested are already set in the order of their risk-return characteristics. Changes in market conditions or in the preferences, tasks and requirements of the investor are taken into account in the framing of the order of investments. This formula plan can be subject to modifications or alterations due to the factors, referred to above, there can be under performing assets, potentially non-viable units due to sudden changes in market conditions from bullishness to bearishness, leading to upsetting the whole set of preferred investments and result in the change of the order of investments. The formula plan has itself to be changed under these conditions.

The portfolio manager in his revision and monitoring of the investments funds that the actuals are not near the targets set. This will lead him to think of the modifications and changes in the formula plan. Basically, formula plan is based on the Principle of Random Walk Theory which states that prices may move in a random manner and entry and exit into the market may not be timed and entry into the market gives the same results any time you enter.

Some of the major steps in portfolio revision and evaluation are the basic ratio and Trend Analysis, use of charts and graphs, which are all relative to time, space and environment. Besides construction and revision of portfolio involves the cash flow/funds flow analysis marginal costs and average costs, *vis-à-vis* marginal and average return and profits and their allocation which are all relevant for analysing and understanding the share price valuation. The choice of scrips of companies depend upon the share price valuation and steps taken in their direction. Portfolio consists of varying assets, scrips, and instruments and securities. These components of the portfolio are all subject to constant changes due to time space and environment as referred to earlier. Among these factors, time is most important as we base our investments on the equated future flow of funds, cash, earnings and dividends/profits.

Unfortunately, funds of today are not the same in value as the funds of tomorrow or a year hence. Cash flows and funds flows and earnings and profits flows are not the same for all the years of investment horizon. They have to bring to equality for comparison by suitable adjustments for inflation or rise in prices, changes in exchange rates and interest rates. Even when we analyse the past data of 5 to 10 years, comparison is vitiated by the above factors. To forecast the expected future share price or earnings on the basis of analysis of the past incomparable data is a great mistake. There is need for plans for comparability.

In this case of some scrips which are quoted in different centres, countries or continents, a similar comparison is initiated by constant changes in inflation rates, exchange rates, interest rates. Space and environment go together and they vary with the location of the scrap, where it is quoted. Cross-sectional analysis of scrip price or time series analysis of the variables, used for the above analysis – fundamental or technical – suffer from the same defects.

Taking only time dimension, in the sense of the duration of the portfolio, the constituents of the portfolio will have to change, depending on the tastes, preferences, choice of risk and return of the investor. Firstly, formula plan adopted has to be changed depending upon the market conditions. This plan envisages investing regularly, every month a fixed sum of money on acquiring instruments and assets in a random fashion. This is expected to even out the variations in risk and return scenario of the total portfolio. The conditions may also dictate modifications in the formula plan, as there maybe continued bearishness or congestion in market conditions. Thus modifications should be part and parcel of the revision, which means, that formula plan adopted once, has to be subjected to reformulation and modifications to the needed extent.

Once targets are fixed they are subject to adjustments to make the actuals are in conformity with them to a large extent. The Portfolio Manager is not infallible and hence SEBI has made it mandatory to incorporate a clause in their contract with the customer that all risks are to be borne by the customer and whatever Portfolio Manager is doing in investment is only in advisory capacity to the best of his knowledge and results of his research in the money and capital markets.

In portfolio management various plans are agreed to be followed by the Manager of Customers funds, which are flexible and modifiable. Thus there can be constant dollar value plan, constant ratio plan, variable ratio plan and constant rupee value plan etc. Similarly in the area of net returns, there can be plans such as dollar cost averaging, and dollar return value averaging, so that costs and return are comparable and adher to the requirements of the customer in comparable and constant price value returns without any loss due to changes in prices or inflation, interest rate and exchange rate changes.

TIME VALUE OF MONEY AND SECURITIES

Time Preference for Money

For purposes of comparison of asset values or values of instruments in a portfolio, we have to have a common denominator such as net present values of all flows and principal of the instrument. For the NPVs time factor is an important component. We prefer today's money to that of tomorrow due to our pressing needs for consumption and cost of abstinence from the present consumption, fall in the value of money of tomorrow due to inflation and possible use of money when exchanged for tomorrow's money. Thus, when we lend money, we forego all the advantages of liquidity, ready usability, pressing needs, safety, etc. We abstain from present consumption when lent to somebody, or invested. All these will lead to what is called the time preference for money. To compensate for that, future money will have to be discounted to the present time, because both are not the same. Future money has to be more say 120, if the present money is ₹ 100, taking a discount factor of 20%, for one year.

Tomorrow's money or money a year hence has to be discounted to the present day by discount rate suitable as a reward for the above sacrifices. This is called discounting, used for cash flows or dividends to be received in future and to be calculated for the present values.

Similarly an investment of today, if it is to be returned after a year or so, today's money has to be compounded by a discount rate to equate to the future funds likely to be available in return. This is called compounding. Compounding and discounting are thus two major methods of analysing the time value of money.

Applications

In purchase or sale of share, bond or debenture, the price we pay has to be compared to the value of future flows in terms of dividends, or interest and future price realised. The principle of buy low and sell high has to be applied after an analysis of the present value of future flows of dividends, bonus, possible rights etc., as compared to the present price paid for it.

Future Value of a single Cash Flow

Year	*Principal at the beginning*	*Interest 10%*	*Principal at the end*
1	1000	100	1100
2	1100	110	1210
3	1210	121	1331

FC = $PV(1 + r)^n$; FV = Future value; PV = Present value; r = rate of interest; n = number of years.

Future Value of an Annuity @ 10%

1	*2*	*3*	*4*	*5*
1000	1100	1210	1331	1464 (1 + r)4
	1000	1100	1210	1331 (1 + r)3
		1000	1100	1210 (1 + r)2
			1000	1100 (1 + r)1
				1000 (1 + r)0
				6105

$$FV = A\,[(1 + r)^{n-1} + (1 + r)^{n-2}\ (1+r)^{n-3} + (1 + r)^{n-4} + \text{—} + (1 + r)^{n-n}]$$

$$= A\left[\frac{(1+r)^{n-1}}{r}\right]$$

Sinking Fund Factor

$$F = A\left[\frac{(1+r)^{n-1}}{r}\right]$$

$$A = F\left[\frac{r}{(1+r)^{n-1}}\right]$$

$$= F \times \frac{1}{\text{FVIFA}\,(r, n)}$$ (FVIFA means Future Value Interest Factor for Annuity)

Present Value of an Annuity @ 10%

0	*1*	*2*	*3*	
909.1	1000			$\frac{1000}{(1 + 0.1)^1}$
826.4	909.1	1000		$\frac{1000}{(1 + 0.1)^2}$
751.3	826.4	909.1	1000	$\frac{1000}{(1 + 0.1)^3}$
2478.8				

$$PVA = A\left[\frac{(1+r)^{n-1}}{r(1+r)^n}\right]$$

$$FVA = A\left[\frac{(1+r)^{n-1}}{r}\right]$$

$$PV = FV\frac{1}{(1+r)^n}$$

$$PVA = A$$

Equity Valuation

Dividend Capitalisation Approach

Present value of the dividends expected
\+ Present value of the resale price expected
= Value of an Equity share

Basic Assumptions

1. Dividends are paid annually.
2. The first dividend is paid one year after the equity share is bought.

Sinking Period Valuation Model

$$P_o = \frac{D_1}{(1+k)} + \frac{P_1}{(1+k)}$$

If the price is expected to grow at rate 'g'

$$P_1 = P_o(1 + g)$$

$$P_o = \frac{D_1}{(1+k)} + \frac{P_o(1+g)}{(1+k)}$$

$$P_o = \frac{D_1}{k - g}$$

where, K = Rate of interest

P_o = Present Price

Fundamentals of Valuation of Securities

If we need to estimate the present value of future flows, then the Discounting Method is used. If we want the future value of present investment, we have the Compounding Method. Both help the decision making process in investment in securities.

Discounting

If the final value of the present investment is ₹ 116 at the end of 3 years and if it is discounted to the present day at 5%, then it will be equal to ₹ 100 at present.

The formula for PV (present value)

$$PV = \sum_{t=1}^{T} \frac{C_t}{(1+r)^t}$$

C_1 represents the cash flows, t for period of years and r is the discount rate or is called internal rate of return in the exercises of capital budgeting.

Take an example: — r = 8%, payable once a year and t is 5 years and the factor value — summation of cash flows is ₹ 100.

$$\text{Then, } PV = \frac{100}{(1+0.08)^5} = ₹\ 68 \text{ (use Log Tables)}$$

This formula also applies to one period return of ₹ 100 at the end of 5 years, the present value of which is ₹ 68 at a rate of return of 8%.

Compounding

If the interest rate is 5% and PV is ₹ 100, the future value for one year will be ₹ 105, by using the formula of = $100(1 + 0.5)^1 = 105$.

In two years, it becomes $100(1 + 0.5)^2 = 110.25$

In three years, it becomes $100(1 + 0.5)^3 = 115.76$ and so on.

In the case of discounting, it is the reverse of the above formula namely.

$$PV = 100\left(\frac{1}{1+r}\right) + 100\left(\frac{1}{(1+r)^2}\right) + 100\left(\frac{1}{(1+r)^3}\right) \text{ etc.}$$

For the same three year period, at the end of 3 years, the future value should be ₹ 100 for investing ₹ 86.4 at present, when r = 0.5

These formulate are based on some critical assumptions of constant flow of cash every period, the same reinvestment rate and the period is fixed.

Bond Prices — Factors Influencing

Bond prices fluctuate with market interest rate *vis-a-vis* the coupon rate, inflation rate, tax factors, security provided maturity period, callable feature of the bond, credit rating of the company etc. Some bonds, are attached with call or put options. Call means that the company can repay before maturity, if interest rates have fallen. Put means that the investor can exercise the option for selling the low yielding bond to the high yielding bond of the same characteristics as before. Time and duration are the most important ingredients in Bond trading.

Formulae

Future value of a single cash flow formula is $FV_n = PV_n \times (1 + k)^n$

This is the same thing as compounding, referred to above:

$$14 + \frac{105-95}{6} = \frac{14+1.67}{100} = 15.67$$

Dividing both sides by $(1 + k)^n$ we get $PV_n = FV_n\left(\frac{1}{1+k)^n}\right)$ this formula $\left(\frac{1}{1+k)}\right)$ is called discounting factor or the present value interest factor (PVIF, kn)

There is also similarly a future value interest factor (FVIF, kn) for compounding.

Yield to maturity (Ytm)

Example (Short-cut Method)

$FV_n = 105$ k = 14% (I) Interest rate

PV = 95 N = number of years 6

$$Ytm = \frac{1+\left(\frac{F-P}{n}\right)}{\frac{F+P}{2}}$$; Putting the above values in the formula,

we have

$$Ytm = 14 + \frac{105-95}{6} = \frac{14+1.67}{100} = 15.67$$

15.67 becomes 15.67%

Ytm is thus 15.67% in the above example.

Net Present Value (NPV) is the most important factor for comparison of schemes, or plans for assets invested. The above discussion is only a corrollary of the presentation of Time value of money and importance of NPA. Projects or investments are to be compared after calculating their NPAs for selection of a project for implementation, any company compares the NPAs of the return flows of funds.

Constant Dollar Value Plan

In this plan all inflows and outflows are valued in dollars, whether received in rupees, yen, euro or dollars. Assume a Base date year 2005-06 and the corpus on that date will be in dollars only. If any amounts are received in any currency they will be converted into constant dollars using the deflator of the Base year 2005-06 = 100 and the deflator is arrived at after taking into account the degree of inflation in each year, with Base 2005-06 = 100 Amounts will be infused and amounts will be pumped out in any year since 2005-06, upto the present time 2011-12. An example will make the point clear.

Initial corpus 2005-06 Base year = 100.

I Receipts 2,00,000 rupees + 2,000 dollars

Conversion into constant dollars.

2,00,000 Rupees into dollars –	4,517 (Exchange rate 44.27)
dollars at 2005-06 prices	2,000
Principal Total	6,517
II Receipts in 2011	₹ 2,000 + 500 dollars
Rupees into dollars	44.27 (Exchange rate 45.17)
₹ to Dollar ₹ 45.17	500.00
Return/Yields	544.27

Total Quantum of corpus	$7061.27	6517
		544
		7061

Subsequent inflows are all taken in dollar values.

If there is inflation in U.S current dollars are converted into constant dollars by deflation.

The currencies in the portfolio are all converted into constant dollars. This exercise is done for every inflow and outflow. A time series of inflation rates or conversion factors are developed for regular updating the data into constant dollars. This is done by use of a formula plan. There is always provision for modification of the formulae plan, depending on the exchange rate and inflation rates in the respective countries. Conversion factors for constant rupees can also be in the same way.

Funds come in and go out, but revaluation is done once in a quarter when the results of the portfolio management are assessed. The need for conversion plan and formulation plan are obviated in the case of close ended fund. Some Trust Funds or Mutual Funds are operating the close ended funds. Initial subscription is invited in two to seven days and these subscribers are given certificates of their contribution. The Net Asset value of the fund and of each unit is required to be calculated and made public once in a quarter as per the Stock Exchange/SEBI Rules

Constant Dollar Cost Averaging

Portfolio revision needs a number of formulation formulae plans for achieving their targets. These are in the form of Index Series. Some of these is a formulation of real exchange rates and their relation to real economic variables. We have taken earlier the base year 2005-06 = 100. With this, we need to construct inflation index number for each of the years upto the present, nominal exchange rates and real exchange rates, cost of each scheme in constant dollars etc. Both costs and returns are to be in comparable dollars – current or constant dollars.

Every scheme involves, initial costs and running costs. These costs also include brokerage, management costs and other incidentals. The costs are first and met from initial contributions and later on from the returns from investments, in the form of yields, dividends, interest rates, appreciations etc. For every scheme, the Portfolio Manager maintains a cost series which include all costs, incurred by him in terms of dollars. Both costs and returns are set out in constant dollars as per the formula worked out by the manager. These costs are compared with returns for assessing the success of the schemes and portfolios. This involves dollar cost averaging in material terms and real terms and preparing a Table or of such series is made.

Correspondingly another Table of dollar return averaging is done and Table is prepared for each scheme. The returns and costs are both in constant dollars to maintain real comparability.

For compiling constant dollar values under any of its plans, first all inflows and outflows are accounted in terms of constant dollars.

For compiling the concerned Table, we need the following data in the form of Tables.

1. Inflation Index in inflows/India
2. Exchange rate of rupee versus dollar in each of the years
3. Real Exchange Rates of rupees for dollar
4. Returns and costs constant dollar terms.

Dollar cost averaging implies that the values of costs are denominated first in constant dollars. Next these dollar costs of all investments are averaged to arrive at an average dollar cost per unit. Then the return for unit is also calculated in a similar manner to arrive at dollar average return per unit of investment. Whether the investment is in equity, debt, gold or real estate, or government securities or private corporate debts. The same formulation is adopted. The formula plan is first set out, such as 80% equity plus 20% debt. This formulae can be modified due to the changed conditions in the market or in any investments, or changes in the financial position of the investor/public. The modifications of the formulae plan has to be put in the agreement or terms of the portfolio management. This will be useful for any needed changes in the plan, or modifications of the formulae plan.

Constant Ratio Plan

In investment and portfolio construction many fund managers offer investments under constant ratio plan. Under this plan, the ratio in which investments in equities and debt, Govt. debt and private corporate debts, etc., is kept constant at say 80% : 20% (Equity versus Debt). For the average risk averse investor, prefers more fixed income securities say Govt debt, etc. For them, the constant ratio may be fixed at 50% : 50%.

These ratios once fixed as constant they remain unchangeable and invariable until the scheme or fund ceases to exist. The investor or the saver has first the option to choose the ratio and pays yearly installments or contribution as ₹ One lakh or above. Such schemes are operated for 5 years to 20 years, after which the investor has the choice to exit at The NAV of the unit. He will get back the money at NAV multiplies by the number of units that he holds as on the date of exit. He has the option to keep a nominee to receive the funds in case of his death.

Such schemes are operated by the LIC, ICICI and some others for capital appreciation and growth of assets. Some offer insurance benefits also along with investment for growth. In case of the use of insurance benefit, a part of the contribution that the investor makes is gone for insurance as premium and the rest goes for investment to growth. In such event the growth funds will be valued lower than in the pure growth funds.

Constant Ratio plans go with the non-discretionary growth schemes or non-discretionary funds. These are mostly close ended funds and repurchase facility will be available as per the SEBI guidelines. Even in non-discretionary funds, the investor is generally given the choice to shift their funds from one growth fund to another, on the basis of the NAV of each of these schemes. Both schemes should be non-discretionary in nature so that the essential features of both will remain unchanged. They are therefore called Constant Ratio Plan or Fixed Ratio plan.

Variable Ratio Plan

These plans are invariably discretionary in nature, leaving the discretion to change the ratios, to the advantage of investor. The objective of all these funds is to maximise the wealth of the shareholder or the investor. With this objective, suppose the equity market is booming the portfolio manager may shift to equity of 50% from 60% of Blue Chip Companies. Similarly if yields of gilt-edged market are rising as compared with the yields of corporates, the manager, may shift some of the funds to gilt. The market for equity and debt are two major components for investments. The ratio in which funds are invested are variable under this plan of Variable Ratio. Suddenly some chips may go out of favour due to mismanagement. The manager has the discretion to shift the funds from this chip to other chips. Even in the case of gilt-edged market, some state govt bonds and semi-government bonds may became more attractive due to larger yields, due to RBI and Govt policy changes.

The portfolio consists of different asset classes – Equity of different types of companies, debt of govt and private sector, various instruments like preference equity, deferred equity, cumulative preference shares etc.

The portfolio may also consist of monetary gold, real estate, private unlisted shares of companies, Blue chips as well sick company shares. Some of them are there by chance, or due to change of conditions or mismanagement. The variable ratio plan is flexible and it can get rid of them at the earliest, as and when they realised that they are undesirable due to sickness, mismanagement or unlisted shares, whose transferability is negligible. They must have been first included for their high returns, despite transferability with a view to get them transferred at a later favourable time.

Variable ratio plan is most desirable plan for the small investor who has no investment expertise. But the portfolio manager who is shrewd intelligent and experienced takes benefit of these companies by buying at the right time and disposing them off at a convenient time. Operations in the daily market make possible under this plan. It can also take advantage of changes in the conditions in the market, changes in the mood and expectations etc. This will increase the value of the fund and the unit holders wealth (NAV).

For example, Gold Value in the Indian market has risen by $3\frac{1}{2}$ times over the decade of 2000-10. The inflation index as measured by W.P.I, rose by 67% during the same period (decade of 2000-10). Equity share prices as measured by BSE sensex shot up by 3.3 times over the same period which is comparable to the rise in gold prices. This indicates that investment in gold is also equally attractive as in the equity market. The manager under variable ratio plan has wide discretion to shift and changeover from one market to another, one asset to another and one instrument to another, so as to maximise the investors' wealth.

Conclusion

In portfolio revision, comparison of the performance of various portfolios is necessary. The comparison requires that values are at constant values and the NPV of all future flows are used for comparison. The NPVs calculation requires some knowledge of time value of money. Hence a brief account is first given of the time value of money discounting and compounding of values to make the flows of money comparable. Discounting of all future flows to the present is necessary to calculate the next present values of these flows. Exchanges of how to calculate the NPVs and how the projects are to be chosen based on these NPVs are given. The hire purchase projects to be chosen purchase, leasing etc. are all based on the use of NPVs.

Then discussion is centred on the constant dollar value plan, dollar cost averaging and dollar return averaging are used to derive the net constant returns on each of the plans and schemes. The concept of dollar cost averaging is explained in this context.

Formulae plan is any formula of combination of assets in a ratio like $(a_1 + a_2 + a_3) + (b_1 + b_2 + b_3)$ etc. and so on. a, b, c etc are the different asset classes like equity, debt, bonds, gilts, etc. The assets chosen and the formula to be set with can be modified to derive maximum wealth for the investor. Modifications of formula plan is as important element of the portfolio revision.

Lastly constant ratio plan, variable ratio plan and related advantages and disadvantages are set out. Whatever plan is used, it should the consistent, at constant prices and the comparable denominations. Investments are constantly and continuously reviewed, revised and changed through day to day operations in the market so as to maximise the returns and wealth of the investor.

32

LINEAR PROGRAMMING APPLICATION

Linear programming is a mathematical optimisation technique. This system requires solving the problem for a solution by having each one of the variables changed each time until the final solution is obtained. It is necessary to set out the mathematical formulation of a linear programming problem; the typical problem is one of optimising an objective function.

Problem Setting

Take the following objective function.

$Z = \sum_{i}^{n} C_J X_J$, subject to the following constraints.

$$\sum_{i}^{n} a_{ij} X_J \lesseqgtr b_i \ (i = 1, 2, 3....m)$$

and non-negative conditions

$X_J \geq 0$ (J = 1, 2, 3...n)

X_J = quantity of Jth variable of interest to the decision-maker, say the portfolio manager, where there are "n" variables considered.

C_J = per unit contribution to the objective function (Profit or Cost) of the Jth variable where there are "m" variables.

Z is the objective function such as maximisation of return or wealth.

a_{ij} is the coefficient of Jth variable in the ith constraint, where there are 'm' constraints and 'n' variables.

b_i is the ith requirement where there are 'm' requirements in all' for example, bi might represent quantity of a certain raw material or one asset or instrument of investment available to Portfolio Manager.

Linear programming assumes linear relation. Both the objective function and constraints are linear. It has the advantage of capability of handling inequality constraints. For example the Portfolio Manager may wish to maximise the return, subject to the constraint that no more than 100 scrips are kept in his portfolio. That is only a constraint and the number of scrips way be lower than that of maximum. Similarly, there can be a constraint of a given level of risk for the portfolio as a whole. There can be another constraint that the total investment should be equal to or less than a given level of wealth in the hands of Portfolio Manager.

Assumption for Linear Programming Model

(1) There is one objective function, say return maximisation which is linear.

(2) There is a constraint set by equations, which are also linear.

(3) The equations are defined with certainty.

(4) The equations and functions are continuous and homogeneous in a sense unidirectional.

Definition

A feasible solution to LPP is the set of values of variables, which satisfies the given set of constrains and the non-negative restrictions of the problem. There is always a best possible solution, which can be called optimal solution for any given set of conditions. A feasible solution is said to be optimal solution, if it also optimises the objective function 'Z' of the problem. The solution is thus the Best Feasible Solution (BFS).

Solutions of a LPP

Geometrical or Graphical Method

If the objective function 'Z' is a function of two variables, it can be solved by graphical method. If the problem is of three or more variables the graphical solution becomes complicated and difficult.

Simplex Method

This is the most powerful tool to solve the problem by L.P. Method. This requires the algebraic procedure which progressively approaches the optional solution. It takes time and patience and the solution has to be got manually by trial and error method.

The fundamental theorem of linear programming problem states that, if the linear programming has an optimal solution, then atleast one basic feasible solution must be optimal and forms the firm base for the solution of LP problem. According to this theorem, we can search for an optimal solution among the basic feasible solutions only, which are finite in number. Simplex method is a step by step procedure in which we proceed in systematic manner from an initial BF solution to other BF solution and finally in a finite number of steps to an optional BF solution, in such a way that the value of the objective function at each step is better than the preceding one. This is thus a trial and error method.

Finding a trial BFS of LPP and testing it whether it is the optimal solution or not and if not improving the first trial BFS by a set of rules and repeat the process until we arrive at the optimal solution, is the method used in this process.

Steps in Geometrical Method

(1) Consider all constraints and inequalities and equalities.

(2) Draw the lines in the plane corresponding to each equation in step one and non-negative restrictions.

(3) We find permissible region for the values of the variables, which is the region drawn by the lines shown in step 2.

(4) From the permissible region in step 3, find a point which gives the optimal value for the objective function 'Z'. We may get a corner point for the purpose.

Limitations of LPP are lack of simplicity except when it is a case of two variables, and unrealistic assumption of linear relationship and positive values of the variables. In portfolio management, an asset can give negative returns sometimes, due to capital depreciation or losses. The assumption of non-negative returns is thus unrealistic. Similarly, the assumption that returns will increase with every increase in investment or addition of assets is not always true in portfolio management. The linear relationship may not exist, in the real world in some cases.

Using linear equations, we can have (a) an unique solution, (b) an infinite number of solutions, and (c) no solution at all. When two lines are straight lines but parallel to each other without joining anywhere, there can be no solution to such a set of equations.

LPP Basic Solutions

Consider two equations given below, both of which are to be satisfied, namely

2 bonds + 8 equity = 10 (1) equation

or $2x_1 + 8x_2 = 10$

one bond + 2 equity = 5 (2) equation

or $1x_1 + 2x_2 = 5$

These equations are capable of graphical presentation. If we have to draw a graph for both equations, we have two lines as shown below:

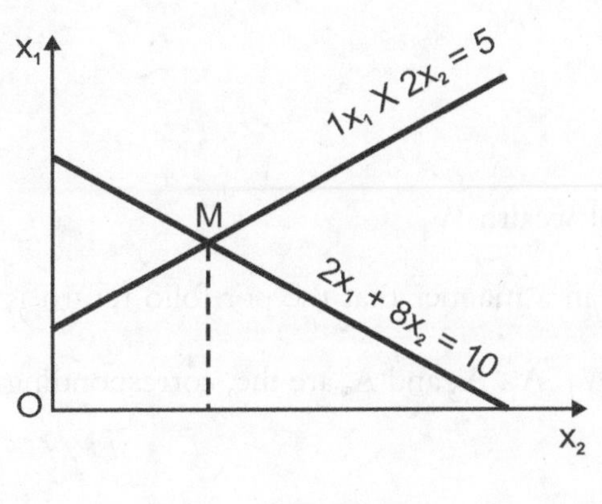

Fig. 32.1

The point of intersection of these two lines is "M", which gives the values of x_1 and x_2 which will satisfy both these equations. This is the case of a unique solution. On similar lines, there can be two equations with any number of solutions, when both lines join into a single straight line. When both lines are parallel without joining anywhere then there is no solution to such a problem.

Generally the number of variables 'm' is greater than 'n' the number of equations. As a rule we can have a basic solution by setting (n-m) variables equal to zero. Then we can solve for the resulting system of 'm' equations in 'n' variables provided they are independent and consistent.

Take an example of three equations and five variables, as given below:

Assume $Q_C \leq 50$

$$1.0\ Q_B + 1.6\ Q_C \leq 240$$

$$0.5\ Q_B + 2.0\ Q_C \leq 162$$

Now add to make

$Q_C + S_1 = 50$ (to convert inequalities into equalities)

Hence, S_1 is a slack variable and similar slack variables are added to others to derive the following three formulas or equations. These are three equations in five variables, obtained by converting inequalities into equalities.

$$OQ_B + 1Q_C + 1S_1 + OS_2 + OS_3 = 50 \quad \dots (1)$$

$$1Q_B + 1.6Q_C + OS_1 + 1S_2 + OS_3 = 240 \quad \dots (2)$$

$$O.5Q_B + 2.0Q_C + OS_1 + OS_2 + 1S_3 = 162 \quad \dots (3)$$

Where the restrictive provision is Q_B, Q_C , $S_1S_2S_3 > O$

For such a system, as any selection of an infinite variety of corporate equities, bonds and other assets in a portfolio, the set of feasible solutions are infinite. But these can be shown graphically as follows, (which is a very simplified example).

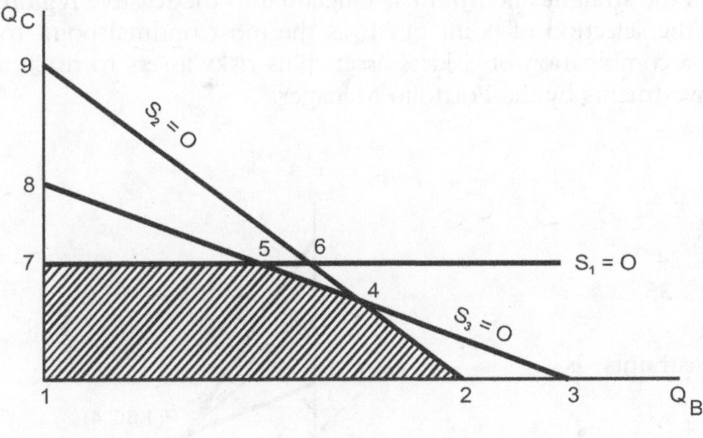

Fig. 32.2

The shaded part of the figure is reflecting the feasible solutions. Of these what are the basic solutions. There are 9 points of intersection and not all of them are basic feasible solutions. Only 1, 2, 4 and 5 and 7 are touching the corner points of the feasible solution portion of the region. It will be noted that optimum points are always the corner points and these lie on the frontier line and the optimum solutions are the basic solutions lying on the frontier line.

Linear programming can be applied when the portfolio manager has multiple investment avenues and constraints to the management of investment.

Assume the constraint is wealth w_1.

$$\sum_{i}^{n} I_i = A_1A_2A_3 - A_n \text{ (Portfolio Returns)}$$

Subject the constraints of $\sum_{i}^{n} I \geq W_1$, (Wealth for investment)

Maximise ΣI_1 = Return on the Portfolio

Where, A_1 A_2 A_3 etc., are all feasible assets in the portfolio.

and so on, where x_1 x_2 x_3 ... are the weights proportional to the total wealth W_1.

$\sum_{i}^{n} I_1 = x_1A_1 + x_2A_2 + x_3A_3$ — These $x_1x_2x_3$ values can be changed in a manner that the portfolio return is maximised subject to the constraint of $x_1 + x_2 + x_3$ etc., is 100% or less of W_1. A_1, A_2 and A_3 are the, corresponding assets.

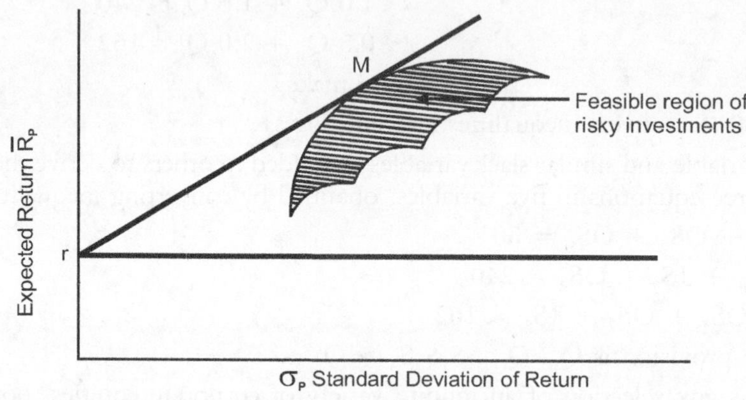

Fig. 32.3

In the above figure, a feasible region of risky assets is set out. The point 'r' is the risk free investment and 'M' represents the point at which the straight line from r is tangential to the feasible region of the risky investments. By a suitable mixture of r and the selection of point of M, as the most optimal point to the feasible region of risky investments, one can derive a combination of riskless assets plus risky assets to reach an optimal point of expected return on the portfolio of investments by the Portfolio Manager.

Example

Maximum Z, $= 5x_1 + 7x_2$

Subject to $x_1 + x_2 \leq 4$

$3x_1 + 8x_2 \leq 24$

$10x + 7x_2 \leq 35$

$x_1\ x_2 \geq O$

First we consider constraints as equalities.

$x_1 + x_2 = 4$

$3x_1 + 8x_2 = 24$

$10x_1 + 7x_2 = 35$

At point P in the figure, the data derived from the graphs,

$x_1 = 1.6$

$x_2 = 2.4$

$Z = 5(1.6) + 7\ (2.4)$

$Z = 8 + 16.8$

$Z = 24.8$

At point P, $x_1 = 1.6$

$x_2 = 2.4$

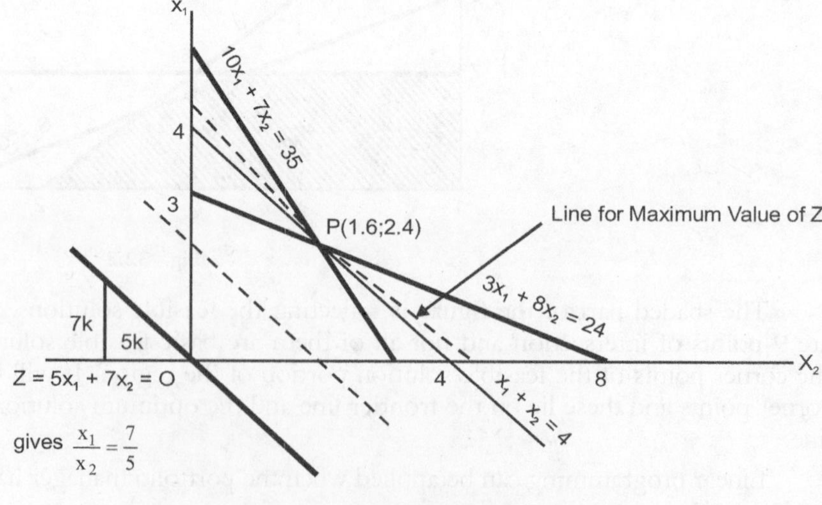

Fig. 32.4

Application of LP to Portfolio Management

W_1 and W_2: are wealth measures: $W_1 + W_2 \leq$ (Wealth)

r_1 and r_2 are the returns (fractions/%.....)

$r_1w_1+r_2w_2 \geq R$ (R= minimum return)

S_1 and S_2 are risks (These may be S.D's or C.V's (Coefficient of variations or *SD* Measure)

$s_1w_1 + s_2w_2 \leq S$

S: Maximum risk toleratable

Object/aim of the problem.

Objective function

Maximise $Z = c_1w_1 + c_2w_2$

Where, C_1 and C_2 are the utility coefficients

$$C_1 = \frac{r_1}{s_1}; \; C_2 = \frac{r_2}{s_2}, \text{ etc.}$$

Problem

Max: $Z = c_1w_1 + c_2w_2$

Subject to $r_1w_1 + r_2w_2 \geq, R$

$s_1w_1 + s_2w_2 \leq S$

$w_1 + w_2 \leq 1$

$w_1 \geq 0, w_2 \geq 0.$

Problem

w_1 and w_2 are the investments into two portfolios: I and II with returns $r_1 = 1.5$, $r_2 = 3.6$ and the risks $S_1 = 5/2$, $S_2 = 1/3$

and utilities $C_1 = \frac{r_1}{s_1} = \frac{3}{5}$ and $C_2 = \frac{r_2}{s_2} = 10.8$

Also minimum return anticipated = R = 1.8

and maximum risk that can be tolerated = 0.5.

LP Model

$w_1 + w_2 \leq 1$ (investment constraint)

$\frac{5}{2} w_1 + \frac{1}{3} w_2 \leq .5$ (risk constraint)

$1.5 w_1 + 3.6 w_2 \geq 1.8$ (return constraint)

$w_1 \geq 0$ (physical requirement)

$w_2 \geq 0$

To determine (w_1, w_2) that maximises the gross utility

$$Z = \frac{3}{5} w_1, + 10.8 w_2$$

Example

$w_1 + w_2 \le 1$ $\qquad$ $w_1 + w_2 \le 1$ $\qquad$ (1)

$\frac{5}{2} w_1 + \frac{1}{3} w_2 \le .5$ $\qquad$ $\frac{w_1}{.2} + \frac{w_2}{3/2} \le 1$ $\qquad$ (2)

Return $1.5\, w_1 + 3.6\, w_2 \ge 1.8$ $\qquad$ $\frac{w_1}{(6/5)} + \frac{w_2}{(1/2)} \ge 1$ $\qquad$ (3)

$Z = \frac{3}{5} w_1 + 10.8\, w_2$

Minimum return anticipated = 1.8

Maximum risk that can be tolerated =.5

Feasible region is ABCD. Of the feasible region, we have

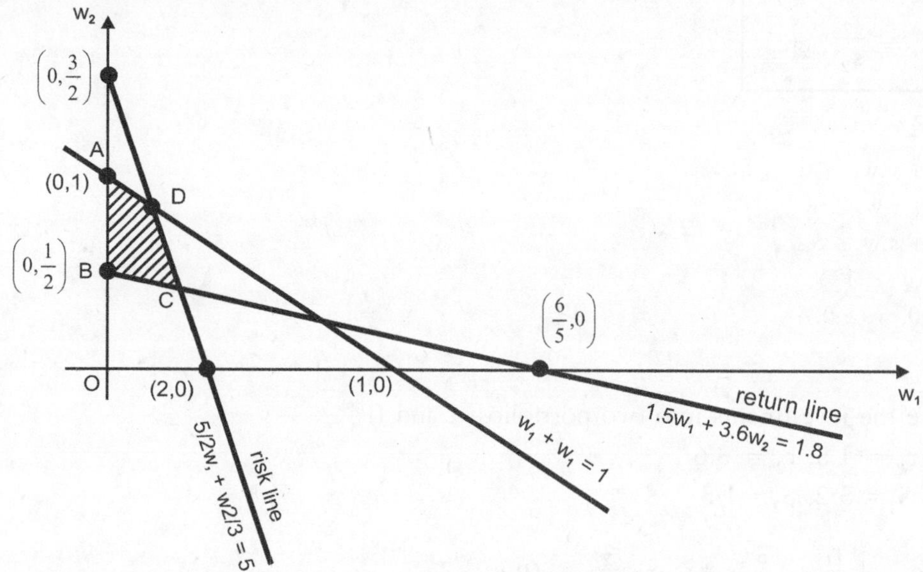

Fig. 32.5

$A = (0, 1)$ $\qquad$ $B = \left(0, \frac{1}{2}\right)$

$C = \left(\frac{12}{85}, \frac{15}{34}\right)$ $\qquad$ $D = \left(\frac{1}{13}, \frac{12}{13}\right)$

Z at A = 10.8

Z at B = 5.4 Utility is maximum at A when all amount is put in one asset only.

Z at C $= \frac{2061}{425} = 4.8.$

Z at D $= \frac{651}{65} = 10\frac{1}{65} = 10.02$

When the amount is distributed
Utility is maximum at D

Maximum utility is at D $= 10\frac{1}{65}$ and the distribution is

$$w_1 : w_2 = \frac{1}{13} : \frac{12}{13}$$

$= 1 : 12$ (The above figures are derived from the Graph)

Notes

$\frac{S}{s_1} = .2$ $\frac{R}{r_1} = 1.2$ $S = .5$

$\frac{R}{r_2} = .5$ $\frac{S}{s_2} = 1.5$ $R = 1.8$

$s_1 = \frac{S}{.2} = \frac{.5}{.2} = 2.5$ $= \frac{5}{2} = 2.5$	$s_2 = \frac{S}{1.5} = \frac{.5}{1.5} = \frac{1}{3}$
$r_1 = \frac{R}{r_1} = \frac{1.8}{1.2}$ $= \frac{18}{12}$ $= 1.5$	$r_2 = \frac{R}{.5} = \frac{18}{.5} = 3.6$
$C_1 = \frac{r_1}{s_1} = \frac{1.5}{2.5}$ $= \frac{15}{25} = \frac{3}{5}$	$C_2 = \frac{r_2}{s_2} = \frac{3.6}{1/3} = 10.8$

PORTFOLIO MANAGEMENT IN MUTUAL FUNDS

Introduction

As Mutual funds manage the portfolios of millions of investors, by using their funds, it is apt to set out an analysis of the mutual funds and their schemes in India; an attempt is made to do this in this chapter as it is a relevant subject for portfolio management.

In India, the only mutual fund operating for a long time since 1964 was the UTI. It is an open-ended mutual fund, whose units can be sold and repurchased at any time. It is in the public sector, enjoying a monopoly position and some unique tax benefits such as exemption from income-tax of its entire income. Although the UTI has operated a number of schemes linked to insurance and gifts, and some tax benefits, income declared by it to unit holders is not subject to any tax deduction at source and is exempt from income tax. Since 1995-96, there was a TDS, if the annual income is more than ₹ 10,000, which was removed in 1999-2000.

Mutual Funds have been set up since 1987 by the public sector banks following an Amendment to the Banking Regulation Act in 1983, which empowered the RBI to permit the banks to carry on non-banking business such as leasing, mutual funds, etc. under Section 6 of this Act. Since then, the SBI, Canara Bank, Punjab National Bank and some other nationalised banks have set up their own mutual funds. The business of mutual funds has caught the imagination of the financial community and has grown at a rapid pace in India. These funds cater mainly to individual investors and small savers. It was thrown open to private sector and foreign sector in 1992-93. During 1996 to 2002, this Mutual Fund business was in a bad shape due to depressed conditions in the capital market. There was a pick up in mutual fund business after 2003.

Definition

Mutual funds are associations or trusts of public members who wish to make investments in the financial instruments or assets of the business sector or corporate sector for the mutual benefit of its members. The fund collects the moneys of these members from their savings and invests them in a diversified portfolio of financial assets with a view to reduce risks and to maximise their income and capital appreciation for distribution to its members on a pro-rata basis. They enjoy collectively the benefits of expertise in investment by specialists in the trust, economies of scale which no single individual by himself could enjoy. Mutual fund is thus a concept of mutual help of subscribers for portfolio investment and management of these investments by experts in the field. These funds are set up under the Indian Trusts Act. UTI is governed by its own Act.

Types of Funds

These funds are of various types and set up for various purposes and objectives. Some are close-ended with contributions from members collected during a definite time-frame of a few days to a few months. Thus, the issue of CanGrowth was kept open for only a few days, while the LIC Mutual Fund (*viz.,* Dhanaraksha) was kept open for a few months. The life of the Fund, which is close-ended, may also be for a specific period of 3 to 7 years after which the income and profits in the form of capital appreciation etc. are all distributed back to the members after deduction of expenses of the Funds by its Trustees. Some of the mutual funds are open-ended like the UTI Scheme of 1964 under which units are purchased and sold throughout the year and a member can enter the scheme any time or walk out of it also any time. These are perpetual schemes without an end, each individual member enjoying the benefits of expert investment in the form of income and growth during the period of his stay with the UTI.

Further, the funds can be classified into three types by objectives, namely, those for income alone, for growth alone (capital appreciation) and for both. The income funds aim at the maximisation of income without pursuing the growth objectives, while the growth funds specialise in securing capital appreciation, irrespective of income. But Income and Growth Funds aim at both and in a judicious mix. These objectives decide the pattern of their investments.

These funds can also be classified into various types based on the pattern of their investments. Some funds may invest in debentures alone or fixed interest securities like the Government Bonds and Treasury Bills. Others may invest in variable dividend securities like equities and bonds of PSUs. There may be a few who invest only in government and semi-government bonds called gilt funds. In advanced countries, there are funds specialising in this manner and in fact some funds are set up only for investment in real estate. In countries like the USA and the UK, where the mutual fund business has grown vastly, there are thousands of such funds, some of them being quoted and traded on the stock exchanges as well. In these countries, mutual funds are well regulated but permitted to be set up in the private sector. In India, the funds business has just been initiated by breaking the monopoly of the UTI for the first time in 1987, but even so, the permission to set up mutual funds in India was confined only to public sector agencies until 1992. The policy has been liberalised since, to permit private sector also to set up Mutual Funds. There are at present 30 private sector funds operating in India along with foreign institutions and with 4 Public Sector Mutual Funds as in 2012.

Unit Trust of India

The UTI was created with the aim of tapping the savings of the small man and to deploy the funds for productive purposes, offering an attractive return and growth to the investors while minimising the risk element for individual investors.

Being the first of its kind and that too in the public sector, the UTI has been vested with both management and trusteeship functions in one body which is the Board of Trustees. The Unit Trust of India Act, 1963, under which UTI was constituted, did not initially permit it to take up activities other than dealing in "units" defined under the Act, investment and dealing in securities and other business arising out of the formulation of any unit scheme. These restrictions have now been removed and the UTI has been permitted to take up such other activities as direct lending of funds, bill rediscounting, leasing, financing of housing projects, and hire-purchase financing and to set up subsidiaries for many financial services and banking.

The growth in the business of UTI, especially during the eighties, has been spectacular. The gross sales of units (under all schemes) which has amounted to ₹ 10 crores in the first year, *i.e.,* in 1964-65, recorded a rapid growth, especially since 1982-83 and rose to ₹ 3,701 crores in 1988-89, and further to ₹ 4,122 crores in 1990-91. UTI along with all its funds have a total investible funds of about ₹ 60,000 crores, as at end March 2002 with more than 60 schemes after which UTI was split into two units effective February 2003.

UTI Schemes for Resident Indians

The UTI offered a variety of investment schemes (funds) to the investing public. It had in all, six open-ended investment schemes, viz., Unit Scheme 1964, Unit Scheme 1971 (Unit-Linked Insurance Plan), Unit Scheme for Charitable and Religious Trusts and Registered Societies 1981, Capital Gains Unit Scheme 1983, Children's Gift Growth Fund Unit Scheme 1986 and Parents' Gift and Growth Fund Unit Scheme 1987, catering to the various sections of society. A special mention needs to be made here of the more popular amongst the open-ended schemes, *viz.,* those of 1964, 1971 and 1983.

Of the close-ended schemes, a majority are Monthly Income Schemes, specifically aimed at the retired and aged investors, giving the latter an assured level of income with a total safety of capital. Among the close-ended ones, the Monthly Income Schemes with Extra Bonus and Growth benefits seem to be more popular with the investors. Unit Scheme 1964 became involved in a scam due to mismanagement in 2000-2001. This scheme was temporarily suspended and then replaced by special bonds.

For domestic investors, the UTI introduced a growth-oriented mutual fund known as "Master-shares" in September 1986. The scheme was very popular, attracting funds of ₹ 1.58 billion against the original target of ₹ 500 million. The NAV of master-shares has moved up and down many times since then, and quoted at less than par value of ₹ 10 for sometime before 2003, when UTI was restructed.

Offshore Funds

The Unit Trust of India took the initiative of entering the international arena by launching the close-ended 'India Fund', in 1986, providing an opportunity for non-resident Indians and other foreign individuals and institutions to make portfolio investments in the Indian capital market. The fund is quoted on the London Stock Exchange.

This was followed in July 1988 by the 'India Growth Fund', also close-ended, and quoted on the New York Exchange. The issue price for the fund is $10 and the NAV and the current quotations are substantially higher. The initial subscriptions to the two funds were limited to £128 million $60 million, respectively. There are presently more than six off-shore funds set up since 1984, by the UTI whose market value has crossed $1 billion by end January 2000. There are of course many other off-shore funds, set up by SBI, IDBI and other public sector units.

SBI Mutual Fund

The SBI Markets Limited, SBI's merchant banking and leasing arm, floated the SBI Mutual Fund (SBIMF) as manager and trustee in 1987. The SBIMF has so far developed many schemes for the benefit of the domestic investing public: Magnum Regular Income Scheme (MRIS), 1987, Magnum Tax Saving Scheme (MTSS) 1988-89, Magnum Regular Income Scheme (MRIS) 1989 and Magnum Monthly Income Scheme (MMIS) 1989 (MTSS) 1990, (MRIS) 1990 etc. The last mentioned scheme was kept open for more than a month. All the four schemes are basically income-oriented in nature, although an element of capital appreciation is built into them. As the name itself suggests, MTSS 1988-89 provided for a tax rebate of 50% of the amount invested therein under Section 80 CC of the Income Tax Act, 1961, subject to a maximum of ₹ 20,000, inclusive of other investments eligible under this Section.[@] Similarly, the two MRIS conferred on investors a rebate on income up to ₹ 12,000 under Section 80L of the Income-tax Act, 1961. The first three close-ended funds launched by SBIMF in the span of a year and a quarter enabled it to mobilise funds to the tune of ₹ 2.47 billion and created investible resources of about ₹ 2.60 billion by March 1989. There are a number of other Schemes floated by the SBI cap later on.

India Magnum Fund N.V.

Although a relatively new entrant in the mutual fund industry, the SBI Mutual Fund has made remarkable strides in a short span of time. The government has approved the State Bank of India's proposal to launch an off-shore Mutual Fund named "Indian Magnum Fund N.V." This close-ended fund, constituted in Netherlands Antilles, is managed by the SBI Capital Markets Limited, in association with Morgan Stanley Asset Management, New York, a well-known international investment management institution. The targeted amount of mobilisation is US$ 100 million and the duration of the fund is 25 years. It garnered $157 million by end-October, 1989, when it was closed.

Other Funds

Another public sector bank to enter the mutual fund field is Canara Bank who, through its subsidiary Canbank Financial Services Limited, has created the Canbank Mutual Fund (CMF). The Canbank Mutual Fund has launched many schemes so far, viz., "Canshare", a growth-oriented fund with no guaranteed fixed return and "Canstock", a purely income-oriented fund on the lines of SBIMF's Magnum 1. Both these close-ended funds have fared well in the market and have declared handsome return to the investors. To cater to the demands of the corporate sector, the CMF floated two other pure money market funds — Cancigo and Cangilt — which are purely liquid funds created to attract the surplus funds of the corporate sector. Other funds called "CanGrowth" and "CanStar" were floated in 1989, for the public investors and a host of other schemes were floated later on.

Close on the heels of these mutual fund companies, the Life Insurance Corporation of India (LIC) has also constituted its own mutual fund named "LIC Mutual Fund" (LICMF). The fund was launched, on June 19, 1989, and many products have been offered for investment. The three schemes opened first for investment are: *(i)* "Dhanashree" close-ended income and growth-oriented scheme, open till October 31, 1989, of units with a face value of ₹ 10 each and a minimum number of units 100, with a guaranteed rate of return of 11% p.a.; *(ii)* "Dhanaraksha" — open-ended recurring investment scheme, the maximum amount of investment under which is ₹ 60,000 (spread over a period of 10 or 15 years), and which offers life and accident cover; *(iii)* "Dhanavriddhi" — an open-ended fixed investment scheme with investment spread over 7 years to 10 years, the starting insurance cover being equal to the amount invested, subject to a maximum of ₹ 40,000. All these schemes of the LICMF are similar to the schemes offered by other mutual funds, with the additional benefit of life and accident insurance cover in the case of "Dhanraksha" and "Dhanavriddhi."

While several mutual funds as above are already in operation other commercial banks like the Indian Bank, Central Bank of India, Punjab National Bank of Baroda and Bank of India and financial institutions like the General Insurance Corporation of India, have either singly or jointly, taken steps to set up their own mutual funds and their

@ All the tax exemptions for mutual funds are replaced by one, *viz.*, 20% rebate for an investment of ₹ 10,000 in equity linked schemes, which was also scrapped in 2005 tax reforms.

schemes are also in operation. Early in 1992, the Government Policy was changed to allow private sector mutual funds also to operate on equal terms with public sector mutual funds.

Overall Progress in India

The Mutual Fund movement gained momentum in India only since 1987, UTI being the only institution in the field till then. Its performance as well as the response received by the schemes floated SBIMF and CMF — the two initial entrants — in recent years should certainly make one optimistic about the future of this movement. GIC and LIC Mutual Funds are also reportedly evoking good response from the investing public. These developments and the entry of other commercial banks and private corporate sector have shown good potentiality for their growth in India. The Mutual Fund Schemes now numbering about 755 as in March 2007 have become more transparent and data on their investments and NAV of the schemes are published regularly, as per SEBI guidelines. Net resources mobilised by MFs since 1987-88 when public sector banks and FIs were allowed to operate for the first time rose from ₹ 2,300 crores to ₹ 52,482 crores by 2005-06 and to ₹ 94,062 crores by 2006-07, and to ₹ 78,545 crores in 2009-10. There was recession in the economies of DCs adn LDCs, including India, during 2009-10, when there was a net repayment in 2008-09 and 2010-11. As of end 2014, amount of ₹ 54,607 crores was outstanding with mutual funds.

Investment Policy

The investment policy of the fund would depend on the objectives of the fund, namely, income, growth or both. Normally, one-third of the funds is used for investment in the money market and government bond market where the liquidity is good. Of the rest, the bulk of the amount would be invested in fixed interest securities like debentures (CD or NCD etc.) or fixed deposits with companies, if the objective of the fund is income. If, on the other hand, the objective is growth, the bulk of the investment would be in equities and new issues. The relative proportions would depend on the importance of the objectives of income and growth. Only a small proportion of the funds would be kept as bank deposits or Treasury Bills or in money market for conversion into ready cash.

The MFs manage the investible funds of the public with their expertise in portfolio management in all permitted markets.

For All MFs - Common Rules

While the RBI guidelines for mutual funds set up by banks are welcome, banks which have floated mutual funds want that the regulatory framework for operating such funds should be common for all agencies wishing to float such funds and that there should be no discrimination between the different government agencies. SEBI has also started regulating mutual funds registered with RBI. The guidelines are issued by SEBI in 1992 while those of RBI are for Money Market Funds and for FIIs and FFIs in addition to OCBs, NRIs and Foreigners.

The banks are given permission for their mutual funds, set up by them to underwrite public issues just as the Unit Trust or insurance companies. They also are permitted to participate in the inter-bank call money market since 1990.

Since bank mutual funds are to be constituted as trusts, it was felt that these funds should be treated as trustee securities and entitled to all the tax benefits available to such securities. In such case, the income on such funds are totally tax-free as in the case of UTI.[@]

All incomes of Mutual funds have now been exempt from taxation as in the case of UTI. Recently, mutual funds have been permitted to operate in the money market and the RBI has announced its willingness to permit banks to set up money market mutual funds, in 1995.

Advantages of Mutual Funds

Mutual funds increase the mobilisation of investible funds of the community by pooling the resources of a large number of small savers for corporate investment. Mutual Funds reduce the risk of shareholding for the holder, by evolving schemes, suitable to the preferences of the saver looking for either income or capital gains. The mutual funds develop the expertise by setting up a professionally-managed structure which would look after the needs of the investing public for gainful and low-risk investment.

Some mutual funds are also area specific or purpose specific, *e.g.*, Japan Fund, India Fund etc., which necessarily provide access to foreign investors into domestic securities of particular economies.

More recently, instrument specific funds were started as for example Reality (Real Estate) Funds, Infrastructure Funds etc.

@ A mutual fund is exempted from tax payment under Section 10 (23D), provided it distributes 90% of its profits.

The mutual funds can promote the investment habit of the rural and semi-urban areas and increase the proportion of investing public and of the shareholding population in India. This purpose could not be achieved to any significant extent in India.

Progress in Nineties and After

In the developing countries like India, mutual funds have a very important role to play in channelising savings into the capital market. By building up expertise to assess financial viability of projects and prospects for individual scrips, these institutions help cushion the risks for individual investor. There is considerable wisdom in encouraging commercial banks to float mutual funds in view of their very large clientele. The decade of the nineties was a decade of mutual funds. Together with industrial liberalisation, a number of new instruments and institutions heralding a new era of financial liberalisation have come up. Mutual funds will be the wave of the future as they represent an excellent instrument for the mobilisation of savings of the rising middle class in India.There were 4 public sector MFs and 30 Private Sector MFs at one time, by end March 2012.

Regulation of Mutual Funds

Leaving aside UTI, which has been existing since 1964, two Financial Institutions, namely, LIC and GIC has set up their Mutual Funds in 1989 and 1990 respectively. Since 1987, starting with SBI, a number of Public Sector banks have set up Mutual Funds, which have been regulated by the RBI. The Mutual Funds of LIC and GIC were regulated by the Investment Division of Ministry of Finance.

After SEBI got legal status in 1992, all Mutual Funds have been brought under its supervision, except the Money Market Mutual Funds and offshore Mutual Funds, which are also bound by the guidelines of RBI, and Ministry of Finance. Nearly ₹ 60,000 crores were collected by UTI and an estimated ₹ 417,300 crores by various Mutual Funds set up since 1987, as contributions of savings from investors at end March 2009. The Mutual Fund movement has got a startling momentum by 1990-91 but there was a setback to this in 1992, following the securities scam in which a number of banks and Mutual funds were involved in Financial irregularities. Since then, the SEBI has tightened its regulations. By end March 2009, Mutual Funds had investments in Debt bonds at ₹ 81,803 crores and in corporate equity at ₹ 6,985 crores — a total of ₹ 88,788 crores. Assets under Mutual Funds Management and at end March 2014 were ₹ 3,25,200 crores.

The new guidelines were laid down in respect of Mutual Funds for authorisation and licensing of all Mutual Funds and each of their individual Schemes. As visualised by the Government Policy, not only public sector, but private sector and joint sector mutual funds are now permitted and licensed by the SEBI. All Mutual Funds including bank sponsored MMMFs, and many schemes of UTI are brought under the supervision of SEBI.

The legal structure and organisation of Mutual Funds as laid down by SEBI guidelines is as follows:

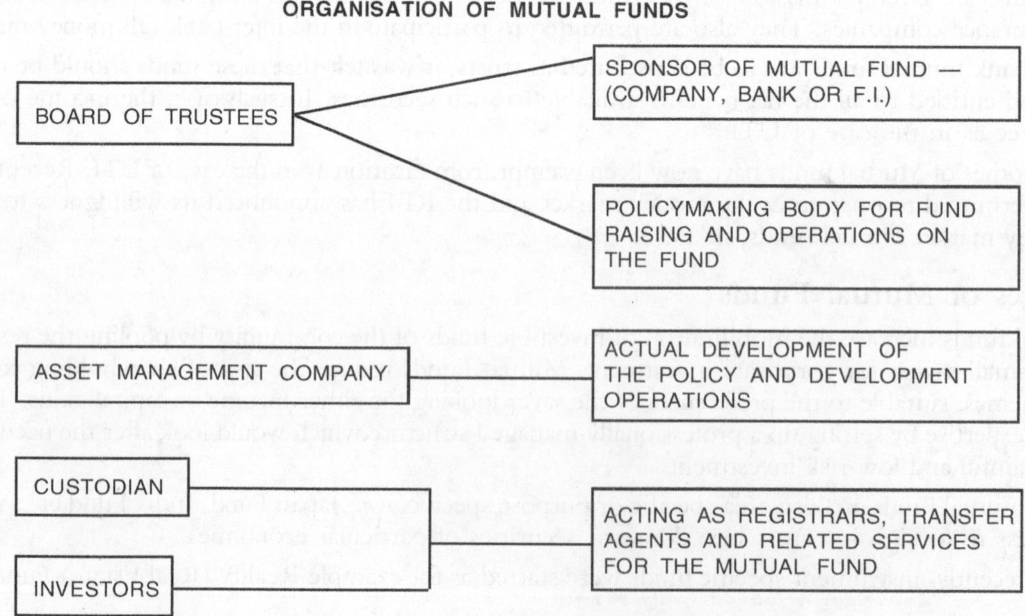

Licensing and authorisation of existing mutual funds was initiated by the SEBI, along with the licensing of Merchant Bankers, even before the SEBI has got legal status in April 1992. As mutual funds were set up by public sector banks, they were authorised by the RBI and each of their schemes were to be approved by the latter. But gradually SEBI took over the responsibility of authorising and supervising them except in the case of pure Money Market Mutual Funds or the off-shore Mutual Funds which are governed by the regulations of RBI and Ministry of Finance.

Money Market Mutual Funds (MMFs)

The MMFs can be set up by scheduled Commercial Banks and FIs, or companies as defined under Section 4A of Companies Act. The limit for these Funds set up by banks is at 2% of the sponsoring bank's fortnightly average aggregate deposits. They are intended to operate only in money market instruments like commercial paper and as they should encourage individual participation in these funds, only individuals and NRIs can subscribe to the Schemes of MMFs. It was extended to companies also later. The minimum locking period was 30 days but was reduced to 15 days in 1998 and no minimum return should be guaranteed. The bank's reserve requirements will not apply to these funds, as per the Guidelines. During 2000, these funds were brought under the sole supervision of SEBI. They are to be separate entities as Trusts. They are given some further concessions like cheque writing facility under the Monetary Policy Statement for 1999-2000 for Gilt Funds and Liquid Income Schemes. Later on, the RBI has also allowed the Private Sector to set up MMFs. RBI guidelines for MMMFs are given separately.

MMMF's Regulation

It was decided in October 1999 that RBI will cease to regulate the Money Market Mutual Funds and that SEBI will take over the regulation of them like other Capital Market Mutual Funds. MMMFs, registered with RBI will have to seek SEBI registration from October 1999. The banks and Public Financial institutions, which floated MMMFs were asked not to offer Money Market deposit accounts. If the banks want to operate MMMFs, they have to set up asset Management Company with an investment of ₹ 10 crores. Besides they have to follow the Trust Structure, necessary for setting up of Mutual Funds, as per the SEBI guidelines.

This change was necessitated to bring all the MMMFs on par with Liquid Funds, floated by regular Mutual Funds. They will no longer be required to observe a lock in period of 15 days, as hitherto, under the RBI guidelines; uniformly all Mutual Funds are brought under a single window control of the SEBI. The deposits of banks are insulated from the deposit accounts of MMMFs which separates banking business from the Mutual Fund business.

The banks will have to set up separate outfits of a Mutual Fund and observe all the SEBI guidelines, if they want to operate any schemes of Money Market Mutual Funds. They have also to take prior permission of RBI before approaching SEBI. This is a healthy development in many ways, as the SEBI can now regulate on an even level all the Mutual Funds, whether they are operating in the Money Market or capital market. Secondly, banks will have to separate their money market mutual fund business and follow the regular mutual fund route to operate any schemes of deposit accounts for money market operations. Control will also be strengthened and the growth of MMMF business will be on healthier grounds.

It has been decided to allow cheque writing facility to gilt funds and to those liquid funds' Income schemes of Mutual Funds, which predominantly invest in Money Market instruments upto not less than 80% of their corpus, subject to the same safeguards, as prescribed for MMMFs. The RBI has issued operating guidelines in this regard.

The MMMFs might have been set up in the Private Sector or public sector, by banks, F.I.s, foreign institutional agencies or Foreign Security Firms with an Indian partner. But all of them were regulated by the RBI before October 1999. But after that, the regulation of these has come within the fold of SEBI. Besides, they have to conform to all SEBI guidelines with regard to Mutual Funds and Asset Management Companies.

The SEBI and RBI has come to an agreement in January 2000, with regard to the regulation of the Debt Market Segment in the capital market. The RBI and the Government designed that the sole agency of regulation of all segments of the Capital Market should be SEBI only. In this background, the control of Money Market Funds has come to be vested in the SEBI.

Authorisation of New Mutual Funds

All Mutual Funds which are not exclusively dealing in Money Market instruments require authorisation from the SEBI. This authorisation is granted by the SEBI as per government guidelines since in March 1992.

Sponsor of Mutual Fund should be eligible for which it should be Registered Company, scheduled Bank or all India or State level Financial Institutions of good track record, positive networth, good management, fair dealings etc., sponsoring registered company should have a 40% stake in the paid-up equity of the Asset Management Company to be set up by the sponsor.

The AMC should be a private or public limited company either listed or not. The AMC may be a new or an existing company, carrying on the business of merchant banking, venture capital, leasing or any other financial services. If the sponsoring company is having a stake of 40% of its net worth as required, the rest can be brought in by public issue, NRIs or foreign equity participation as permitted by the RBI. The AMC should not invest funds in any company under any of its schemes managed by it for which it has provided any financial service. The SEBI should approve the Memorandum and Articles of Association of the AMC. The AMC itself will be approved by the SEBI based on the MAA (Memorandum and Articles of Association), its business lines and subject to the restrictions on its business imposed under the guidelines.

The guidelines lay down the authorisation process subject to the following conditions:

(A) Sponsors to be eligible should be a Private or Public Limited Company, bank or F.I. The sponsoring agency should set up a Trustee.

(B) Trustee should be eligible and the Trust Deed should have the approval of SEBI. Eligibility of trustee depends on the composition of the Board of Trustees, their earlier experience and expertise, professional qualifications, etc., of each of the members of the Board, their past track record and organisation and management of Trustee Company. This appointment is subject to the SEBI's approval. The Trust Board would lay down the policy.

The SEBI while granting the authorisation for the setting up of a Mutual Fund, would also approve the AMC and Custodian as part of the package. The Custodian should be different from the AMC which would manage the Fund. The Sponsor and Trustee Companies cannot act as Custodian. If the sponsor has a custodian division, it can act for other Mutual Funds not set up by the sponsor. There should be no areas of conflict between the interest of Custodian and the Mutual Funds, for which a custodian is rendering services. The investment criteria, expenses and income distribution etc. are all controlled by SEBI, through their guidelines.

The approval of any agency as Custodian would depend upon its track record, experience, quality of service transparency and computerisation and other infrastructual facilities. The SEBI, may stipulate any conditions for the Custodian to act for the mutual fund in question or for one or more Mutual Funds.

Every scheme of Mutual Fund as much as the Mutual Fund should be approved by the SEBI. Every Mutual Fund should have designated a compliance officer who would deal with SEBI and is responsible for compliance with SEBI guidelines and conditions.

All applications for such approvals should be in specified forms either for authorisation of Mutual Fund or any of its schemes. It will thus be seen that the authorisation of Mutual Fund would involve approval of the sponsor, the trustee, AMC and the Custodian all together, who are responsible for the management of Public Funds.

STRUCTURE AND GROWTH OF M.F INDUSTRY

The MF industry in India started in 1964 with the Unit Trust of India (UTI). It has mobilized savings of the public for investment in the stock and capital markets. The resources mobilized by it in 1970-71 was only ₹ 18 crores which grew to ₹ 4,548 crores by 1999-2000. After that, there were more repayments than inflows due to investment mismanagement by UTI, as a result of which the UTI was split into two units — one in the public sector taken over by the GOVT. and the other in the private sector regulated by the SEBI.

This industry was thrown open to the public sector banks and the Financial institutions by an amendment to the BR Act, in 1983. Early in the nineties, there were nine such public sector mutual funds, run by banks and LIC, GIC and IDBI. They also ran into difficulties and by March end 2009 there were only 4 such MFs excluding the UTI. When they started operations in 1987-88, they raised ₹ 250 crores which increased to ₹ 7,477 crores by 2005-06 and ₹ 14,726 crores in 2009-10. The reasons for such fatalities are the bearish market conditions and lack of the needed expertise among the public sector human resources. There were repayments on 2010-11.

This industry was thrown open later in 1992-93 to private and foreign sectors and a number of companies jointly or singly with the foreign counterparts have started operations and they proved their efficiency much more than the other agencies existing in the industry. At one time, there were 45 such agencies doing business as MFs which came down to 30 private sector agencies by 2012. They started operations in 1993 when they mobilized the resources from the public of about ₹ 1,560 crores which went up to ₹ 41,581 crores by 2005-06 and ₹ 47,968 crores in 2009-10 and ₹ 48,790 crores in 2013-14. The performance of the private sector was far superior in terms of raising resources and in management of the investment funds. Their share in the total mobilization of resources was raised from nil in 1992-93 to about 80 to 88% of the total mobilization. In 2008-09, however, there were repayments (net) of 28,685 crores of rupees due to economic recession.

In 2006, the MF industry in India was ranked as the 24th in the world with $ 88 billion assets. This was an improvement due to the booming economy, and shining financial markets in India in the recent past with a growth rate of 7% to 9% in GDP. The U.S stands first in the world MF industry followed by Luxembourg and Fance. India's performance is not rated well despite all bullish factors in the economy due to Govt. policies, tax structure and risk aversion of the average Indian. There is large potential for growth of this industry in India, which may hopefully be realized by the entry of Pension funds into the capital markets by the passage of the pending bill called the Pension Bill.

Mutual Funds Present Status

Many private sector mutual funds have entered the fray but the performance was initially far from satisfactory with the market price of many schemes quoting below the NAV which is calculated by dividing the market value of all investments + Accrued income and Receivables + other assets minus liabilities and accrued expenses except unit capital and Reserves by the number of units outstanding. Valuation norms for calculation of NAV are laid down by SEBI. Mutual funds have to deduct tax at source, if they pay a dividend above ₹ 10,000 p.a. at a rate of 15% for individuals and 20% for companies. These tax provisions change from year to year.

Mutual funds can incur initial expenses of 6% of total funds raised and 3% every year. They have to pay 90% of their net income as dividend to unit holders.

Mutual funds are now permitted to invest upto 100% of mobilised funds in money market instruments for six months from their subscription and again revert back to 100% in these instruments six months before redemption. The details of these investment and accounting guidelines are prescribed by the SEBI.

There are always fresh funds coming in and some funds closed due to redemption while there are some under repurchase facilities, as in the case of open ended funds. Close ended funds should normally be listed on stock exchanges, except when there is a repurchase provision.

The face value of mutual fund units is normally ₹ 10, but sometimes ₹ 100. For those listed and traded, there is a market price, which is different from Net Asset value. As the return for the long-term investors is more, than the total return on investment by the total funds' investment performance, since launch, the investor's annual return on such schemes may not be higher than 13-15%. But some schemes have done relatively well such as Master Share and some relatively poor such as Master Gain. Master share was also quoted below par and US 64 scheme was also in a bad shape since July 2001, and was dismantled. The UTI has to be rescued by the Govt. in 2003 and restructed into UTI-I and UTI-II. The latter has come to be privately managed and regulated by SEBI.

The SEBI has set up a committee on Mutual funds late in 1995 and its recommendations were available in 1996. These relate to standardisation of N A V, calculation, exemption from listing for some schemes, management remuneration to AMCs, accounting practices, fixation of a band of 7% between purchase and repurchase prices and standardisation of such practices, etc. These aim at healthy growth of mutual fund business in India. Early in 1998, the AMCs have been asked by SEBI to double their Networth from ₹ 5 crores to ₹ 10 crores. SEBI (Mutual Fund) Regulations were amended to permit MFs to trade in derivatives and trading/investments in Foreign Markets for portfolio balancing.

Taxation and M.Fs

So far as the MF is concerned, under section 10 (23D) of the Act, any income received by the MF is exempt from tax. Under Section 115 R, income distributed to a unitholder or investor of the Mutual Fund shall be charged to tax at a flat rate of 10% plus surcharge if any, payable by the MF. But for funds, investing more than 50% in equity or equity related instruments the dividend distributed by MF is exempted from the above (10% plus surcharge) for three years from April 1, 1999.

The steep increase in tax rate on the income distribution by Mutual Funds from 11 to 22% in respect of debt oriented schemes and the withdrawal of the benefits under Sections 54 EA, and EB to Mutual Funds had a negative impact on mutual fund industry from 2000-01. From 2002-03 the income distribtued by MFs is taxable in the hands of investors.

SEBI has been notifying from time to time regulations governing the Mutual Funds, their operations, their advertisement, meeting of Trustees etc. with a view to better disclosure, investor protection and better services. For example, it is notified that any delay in repayment of moneys under schemes, which have matured by Mutual Funds is subject to penal interest rate.

So far as the unitholders are concerned, no tax is deducted at source and under Section 10 (33) of the I.T. Act, any income received by them will be exempt from income tax in their hands. Any capital gain of a long-term nature (if the same is held by investor for more than 12 months) will be subject to the following rates of tax.

As in 2005-06, dividends declared by Debt Funds are taxable. Equity oriented funds are exmpt from capital gains tax net; only open ended and close ended funds are exempt from dividend distribution tax.

For residents, there is no tax deduction at source, as per the Act and the Regulations under the Act. For Non-residents, the TDS on capital gains of short-term nature is 30% and of long-term nature at 10%. For Foreign Companies, the TDS on Capital gains of short-term nature is at 30% and of long-term nature at 20%. The only exemption from TDS or taxation of capital gains is in respect of Tax saving equity linked schemes of M.Fs. As in 2005-06 there was no tax on long-term capital gains, but short-term gains are taxable at 10% only in respect of securities transactions.

Wealth Tax

The units of M.Fs. are not treated as wealth and hence no wealth tax is payable.

Gift Tax

The units of any value can be gifted without attracting gift tax by both the donor and the donee. The Gift Tax Act 1958 was repeated in October 1998, whereby no gift tax is payable. But now the gift becomes part of the income of the donee and is taxable in his hands.

Tax Benefits

Before the Union Budget for 1999-2000 Mutual Funds and Venture Capital Funds were given tax treatment on par. If they declare 90% of their income of investors, their income is free from any taxation. In the Budget of 1999-2000, exemption was given from income tax for all income received in the hands of investors from the UTI and other Mutual Funds which was withdrawn in 2002-03. Exemption was also given from dividend tax for 3 years for US 64 scheme and all open ended equity oriented schemes (with more than 50% investment in equity) of UTI and other MFs.

Saga of Fortunes of MFs

Since 1964 and upto 1987-88 UTI strode the scene like a colossus, alone in the field as a single public sector Mutual Fund. By 1990-91, there were 5 public sector mutual funds already set up, controlling a market share of mutual fund business of 10% in the country. By 1993-94, the private and foreign sector mutual funds started their foray into this business. The International names, Morgan Stanley, Tanners, Jardine Fleming, Merril Lynch, Prudential etc. have appeared on the scene of Mutual Funds.

There was a large scale erosion in the market values of investments by UTI due to their mismanagement and scams. Net resources mobilised by UTI fell from a peak of ₹ 11,057 crores in 1992-93 to a net out flow of ₹ 6,314 crores in 1995-96. The net amount mobilised from public picked up from a low of ₹ 170 crores in 1998-99 to ₹ 1,999 crores in 2000-01, ₹ 15,653 crores in 2009-10 and ₹ 401 crores in 2013-14. The Table below gives a picture of resource mobilisation by Mutual Funds over the last decade and a half since 1990-91. Mutual Funds control and manage ₹ 5.92 lakh crores of assets as at end March 2011.

Table
Net Resource Mobilisation by MFs

(in ₹ crore)

Year	*UTI*	*Public Sector MFs*	*Private Sector MFs*	*Total*
2008-09	– 3659	1,10,443	– 31,425	– 24,641
2009-10	15,653	14,726	48,166	78,545
2010-11	– 16,635	– 15,683	– 16,281	– 48,600
2011-12	– 3,179	– 1,127	– 39,525	45,413
2012-13	3,938	8,544	62,457	74,938
2013-14	4,461	7,416	46,798	54,607

@ Private Sector Mutual Funds were permitted from 1993 only.
Note: Figures in parenthesis are percentages to total.
Source: RBI.Handbook of Statistics.

The share of UTI fell from a high of 82. 7% in 1993-94 to a low of 7.8% in 2006-07, while the share of private sector mutual funds rose from 13.9% in 1993-94 to 84.5% in 2006-07. The best performance of MFs was in 2007-08 when they raised ₹ 1.8 lakh crores in total but there was net repayments in 2008-09. There was a net outflow of funds from UTI which led to lower mobilisation of funds in 2001 to 2003. The Association of Mutual Funds (AMFI) publishes data on Mutual Funds regularly.

UTI whose share was 95% of the market in 1995-96, declined to 60% in 1998-99. There are about 29 AMCs with an asset base of ₹ 3.26 lakh crores of which the share of the private sector was 80%, as in 2006-07.

The trend in the industry, as in general, was towards financial strengthening, mergers, takeovers etc. The weaker ones are either closed or taken over the years 1995-2000. Equity Funds started looking up and showed better performance in 1999, while debt funds were popular between 1996 to 1998. That was the worst period for equity funds as stock and primary markets were in doldrums. The years 1999 and 2000 and 2003 to 2006 saw again the revival of equity Cult and hey days for Mutual Funds to thrive, as Stock and Capital markets turned bullish and economy turned into a recovery phase.

The minimum paid-up capital of AMC was raised to ₹ 10 crores, but many foreign AMCs were set up more recently with 5 to 10 times the minimum required. An asset base of ₹ 500-700 crores was felt necessary for an AMC to break even. Many public sector mutual funds like those of Bank of India, Bank of Baroda, Canbank GIC etc., have had difficult times. The process of mergers and restructuring helped some to revive. But the private and foreign mutual funds, barring a few exceptions have fared better than public sector mutual funds. The tax slabs in 1999-2000 Budget have helped the mutual funds. The revival of stock markets and low interest rates and economic recovery have boosted the equity sentiment. But it was temporary and equity markets were depressed in 2001 and 2002 but the boom period ruled from 2003 onwards. The boom continued upto 2007-08, but later their fortunes were revesed due to adverse market conditions and global economic recession and economic slowdown in India.

The asset base of Mutual Funds has increased by 5 times over the decade. The annual growth rate is about 30%. The trend to merger and takeover has helped the private sector mutual funds, while restructuring and financial strengthening has aided the public sector mutual funds. The competition to the public sector from the private sector was a healthy trend to boost the industry. The year 1999 saw the turning point in the mutual fund industry and the new millennium was ready for a take off in this industry. Investor education, change in the stock market sentiment and new distribution channels like banking and internet, Demat form of shareholding have all helped the industry.

Stock Lending by Mutual Funds

The Mutual Funds have approached the SEBI approved intermediaries to enter into agreements to operate stock lending scheme. The Mutual Funds which showed interest in equity lending are the Canbank, Reliance, Kothari and Alliance Capital. They want to earn additional income by activising their idle core investments in their custody for badla lending of securities. This type of lending has risks associate with it namely reinvestment risk and potential asset-liability mismatch. The Stock Lending Scheme was approved by the SEBI, subject to some guidelines.

Lending increases portfolio returns on the stocks lent. But potential losses may be there due to over exposure to low credit quality clients. Lending securities to such clients is a real risk. When the MF lends securities, they are transferred into the name of the intermediary or the borrowing broker, while all corporate benefits continue to accrue to the MF. Thus, the MF benefits from two streams of income — one received for lending securities and another for reinvesting the cash proceeds so received. As against these benefits, the MF will have to face liquidity risk, reinvestment risk and expose the funds to the credit and interest rate risks arising out of stock lending and consequential inflow of cash. There are cases when lending institutions have lost their funds, as in the case of Harris Trust & Savings Bank, and Mellon Bank in the U.S.A.

EVALUATION OF THE PERFORMANCE OF THE MFs

The evaluation of the performance of the MFs can be graded in two respects — one in respect of the funds mobilization from the public and second in respect of the portfolio performance of the MFs to the growth of the economy through the deployment of funds in financial markets.

The resource mobilization as seen in the data given above in the chapter is no doubt good but if it is due to large funds contributed by the corporates and not direct from the individual savers, it is no achievement. In the absence of the data of details and breakdowns, it is difficult to arrive at any worthwhile conclusion in this respect. During the end of 2009, it was reported that nearly one lakh crores, of bank funds are were deposited with MFs and that the RBI has asked banks to withdraw these funds from MFs. The born continued up to 2007-08, but later their futures were reversed due to adverse market conditions and global economic recession and economic slowdown in India. Besides, there is no consistent growth of funds mobilized by the MFs, as there are variations from year to year and in some years, the net resource mobilized was also poor or negative due to depressed market conditions and poor performance of the MFs themselves. If there is good mobilization during 2005 to 2008, it was due to private sector MFs and booming market conditions. In the year of 2006-07, of the total net mobilization of ₹ 94,062 crores, about ₹ 79,000 crores was due to private sector MFs. During 2008-09, there was a large net outflow from MFs mainly on account of UTI and private sector MFs.The first conclusion is therefore that funds mobilization *prima facie* was poor but for the private sector MFs.

The MF contribution to the growth of the stock and capital markets is however very substantial, next only to the FFIs and FIIs. About ₹ 4.17 lakh crores of funds were the assets of the MFs which were deployed in the markets as assets as at end March 2009. These funds are used for the portfolio management for and on behalf of the public, which leads to the growth of the corporate sector and through them of the economy. The BSE Market capitalization has grown by 17%, while the growth of the economy in 2006-07 was by 9%. But the returns given by the MFs to the public was much less than this. This shows that the MFs in India could not out perform the market return, as expected in theory. If some of the funds could do it, they are only the foreign controlled and managed MFs in India.

Following from the above analysis, it was also clear that the portfolio management by MFs was far from satisfactory except for a few foreign controlled and managed MFs. The reason for this state of affairs is that the expertise and experience in this line by the personnel handling in the AMCs has been far from satisfactory. This conclusion is buttressed by the fact that the weak were weeded out during the last few years. In the public sector, UTI has the distinction of mismanagement of funds under the US 64 during 1999-2001, necessitating the Government interference in the UTI affairs and splitting the UTI into two units — one taken over by the Govt. and other privatized to be controlled by the professionals in the FIs. Of the nine public sector MFs originally set up, five were wound up or merged with others. Of the 45 private sector MFs functioning at one time, there are only 24 functioning as in March 2009 and 30 at end March 2011, showing the woefully high mortality rate among the MFs. The reason was the their poor performance leading to lack of viability and inadequate public support to them. The above facts clearly evidences the truth of lack of expertise among the AMCs doing the portfolio management for MFs. But the MFs have good potential.

Latest Trends

The performance of mutual funds and the investor confidence in them have received a setback since 1996, particularly due to poor performance of UTI and many scams involving UTI and banks. The nexus between banks and brokers has struck a blow to the Stock and Capital Markets and led to a negative resource mobilisation during 1995-97 by all mutual Funds; mainly due to UTI. Since then the performance of all Public Sector Mutual Funds showed a marked deterioration, while the performance of Private Sector Mutual Funds revealed a relatively better performance. The main depressing factor was the poor stock market conditions, following scams and poor asset management in UTI and public sector mutual funds, particularly during 1997-2001.

The U.S.1964 of UTI, which was the pioneering scheme of UTI was in deep trouble and recorded a massive loss of market values of assets in 2000-01. Three Committees, namely those of Deepak Parekh, Malegam and Tarapore have made drastic recommendations for privatisation and restructuring of UTI during 1998-2001. A scheme of protecting investor interests and of bringing the UTI under the surveillance of SEBI like other mutual funds by change of UTI Act has been announced early in 2002, and become effective in June 2003.

The SEBI regulations of mutul funds were liberalised and streamlined from time to time. Mutual Funds were allowed to invest in mortgage backed securities of investment grade and above, which would help housing finance since April 2000. Open-ended funds can now invest upto 5% of their net asset value in equity instruments of unlisted companies. Investment limit in such equities was kept unchanged at 10% for close-ended schemes. The maximum limit for investment in respect of open-ended funds was raised from 5% to 10% of NAV in listed companies, in June 2000. SEBI has also banned mutual Funds from making assurance of returns or make any claims on the basis of past performance.

The norms relating to code of conduct of MFs, criteria for classification of NPAs and their disclosures, treatment of income accrued on NPAs and provisions to be made, disclosures of NPAs in the half-yearly portfolio reports were streamlined. The period of initial offer of a scheme and despatch of certificates, standardisation of format, treatment of unclaimed deposits and the standards of trading by the employees were tightened. Disclosure and transparency standards relating to the Asset Management Companies (AMCs) were also made stricter.

As referred to earlier structural reorganisation of UTI took place in 2003, with its splitting into two entities UTI-I and UTI-II. UTI-I has taken over all fixed income schemes like US 64. UTI-II have got all NAV based schemes and has come to be regulated by SEBI and managed by private sector agencies on professional likes.

U.S. 64 scheme of UTI was wound up in its original form in May 2003, with the govt. taking over all its assets and liabilities. UTI-II continued since then with its schemes run on professional lines and in the private sector.

As regards the other public sector mutual funds, their performance also fell short of market expectations. Only the private sector mutual funds out performed the public sector MFs during the years 2001 to 2007, in terms of their resource mobilisation and assets base. The MFs were permitted to trade in derivatives and invest in foreign listed companies upto 10% of their funds, if such foreign listed companies have corresponding investments in Indian companies. The MFs are now permitted to invest abroad upto US million 200 dollars limit for each fund and a total US $4 billion for all MFs. Debt market was given a boost by govt. raising the limits for FII investment in it and MFs are mostly interested in this market.

During 2004 to 2009, MFs have expanded their activity to boom in the equity market by shifting to equity linked schemes but this was mostly confined to private sector MFs. The major weakness of the MF movement was that it could not penetrate much into rural and semi-rural areas so far.

Inequities in Taxation of Mutual Funds

As taxation stands in 2009-10, there are a number of steps taken for encourging the mutual fund industry. The investor in mutual fund will not have to pay tax on his income on hand. The mutual funds have to pay taxes on income distribution under certain conditions. If their investments in equity is less than 65%, they have to pay income distribution tax as in 2006, as against the earlier criteria of 50% in equity.

Open ended equity oriented funds will now be treated on par with close ended equity funds for exemption from dividend distribution tax. But the Debt oriented funds continue to pay the dividend distribution tax at 12.5% and also to pay the long-term capital gains tax at 10% without indexation and tax 12.5% with the indexation. But equity oriented funds are exempt from long-term capital gains tax.

The inequity as between Debt markets and equity markets continue to plague the MF industry. While investors prefer Debt oriented funds, taxation benefits the equity oriented schemes. The securities transactions tax (STT) continued from 2004 onwards, it was raised by 25% in the year 2005-06, which again discourages the genuine investors. MF investment in Debt was far larger than in equity for the last few years, despite the Government incentives for investment in equity. During the year 2008-09, for example, the MF investment in equity was 8% of the total.

The liberalisation of overseas investments by MFs from $1 billion to $2 billion and the removal of requirement of 10% reciprocal share holding in corporates invested in will not benefit the investor much due to insufficient opportunities abroad for such investments. Similarly, the raising of limit on investments in Govt. debt and in Corporate debt by the FIIs will not benefit the investor or the MFs. The Govt. efforts to develop the Debt market particularly of the secondary market in corporate debt has not fructified so far due to ad hoc measures taken.

The measures taken to constitute an Investor Protection Fund with the SEBI will not help, as such Protection funds exist with the major stock exchanges already. The taxation system prevailing in MF industry is thus a mixed bag, containing only a few measures which will benefit the industry.

TRADING IN PORTFOLIO MANAGEMENT

Introduction

Investment and Disinvestment are two sides of the same coin and they are part of the portfolio management as trading involves both investment and disinvestment. When we deal with investment management, it automatically encompasses, disinvestment also, as what is investment for one is disinvestment for another, particularly in the secondary market. In portfolio management, investment and disinvestment go together as the portfolio is changed form time-to-time depending on the changes in the needs and preferences of the investor and following the changes in market conditions and information flows. If an investment decision is made based on some criteria, it follows that decision can be reversed leading to disinvestment, if the criteria is not satisfied. If thus investment and disinvestment go together, why do we need a separate treatment for disinvestment?

If investment is an art and science, the more so is the Disinvestment Process. In certain conditions of Prolonged bearishness in the stock market, depressed conditions in the primary market or disturbed crisis situations due to excess liquidity or liquidity crunch in money market and call money segment, etc., disinvestment becomes a major problem leading to liquidity crisis and insolvency and even defaults. If investment is an important activity, the disinvestment is more so as trading in any market involves both investment and disinvestment. Days were there, when banks and financial institutions used to make only investments in money market instruments and Gilt-edged securities and rarely did they make any disinvestment. The majority of individual investors are reported to have been holding their investments for life time or twenty to thirty years, as per some surverys. The Indian investors, banks, financial institutions etc., have been used to make only investments and the art of disinvestment and trading for booking profits and gains or to take any advantage of any changes in yields, interest rates and price appreciation etc., has not developed well in India and it needs some expertise and experience.

What is Disinvestment?

Investment refers to conversion of money or cash into securities, stocks, debentures, bonds or any other claims on money. On the same lines, disinvestment involves the conversion of money claims or securities into money or cash. Here money is used in the sense of coins, currency and credit instruments like cheques, MT, TT, DD etc., which are payable to drawee or holder in due course and on demand. If these instruments have a usance period and a fixed maturity date, they are credit instruments like Bills of Exchange, Treasury bills, Commercial and trade bills which are all short-term claims on money. Disinvestment relates to those instruments as well. If the claims are of long-term nature, like shares, bonds and debentures etc., they are part of the capital market and investment and disinvestment criteria are slightly different in terms of risks and return in addition to differences in duration and maturity, from investments in other markets. Disinvestment may also refer to sale, transfer and disposition of any investments. As investments are risky, so also the disinvestments. In that sense, disinvestment management is also an art and science in operations. In fact, trading in securities and money market instruments involves both, Investment and Disinvestment. As in the case of investment decisions in portfolio management, the disinvestments are to be based on rational and scientific grounds. The need for money, changes in information flows and many other factors influence the disinvestment decisions.

Risks and return are to be weighed and the costs of information and transaction costs, etc., are to be considered and alternative opportunities lost due to disinvestment are to be assessed and a decision to disinvest has thus to be taken on many rational grounds, which are part of this management science.

Why Disinvestment?

Some of the reasons why disinvestment takes place are listed below:

(1) Mergers and acquisitions of companies by which shareholders are sometimes adversely affected due to dilution of equity.

(2) Government Policy Changes affecting the economy in general, fiscal and monetary policies influencing the company or industry in question.

(3) Tax changes or tax rate adjustments, which adversely affect the company.

(4) Dividends and Earnings data and deteriorating fundamentals of the company.

(5) Timing as determined by the technical analysis and chartist method of locating trend reversals and sell signals for the purpose of disinvestment.

(6) Disinvestment is part of the investment process and as investment is a part of the portfolio management, so is the disinvestment process. They are two blades of the same Scissors.

(7) Due to changing market conditions, some companies become potentially sick or show symptoms of maturity and stagnancy which are to be disinvested as early as possible.

(8) Disinvestment is also needed for good companies for profit-making and booking capital gains or capital losses. In the case of banks and financial institutions dealing in Gilt-edged securities, P.S.U. bonds and semi-Government, and trustee securities, the process of investment and disinvestment is a regular feature for adjustment in SLR or CRR position and for responding to changes in yields and duration.

(9) Disinvestment is needed to take advantage of changes in interest rates, yields, capital appreciation or depreciation or avoidance of capital losses, changes in duration of the portfolio and a host of other reasons, in the Bond management strategies.

(10) In many cases as in the case of individuals and mutual funds, disinvestment takes place to meet the transaction or repurchase needs or to adhere to any guidelines of SEBI or the RBI.

Role of Disinvestment

Disinvestment is equally important as investment in Portfolio Management for many reasons. In some situations, disinvestment becomes unavoidable due to unexpected changes in the market conditions, fall in share prices, likely changes in Government policies or problems of the company leading to its sickness, fall in sales and profits etc. Disinvestment may also be needed due to change in the conditions and preferences of portfolio investors.

Disinvestment will also become necessary for fundamental factors and technical factors. On the basis of the study of fundamentals, a number of companies in one's own portfolio are likely to show stagnant growth or no growth, reduced profits, lower P/E ratio, losses resulting in wiping out $1/4^{th}$ to ½ of the networth of the company. If the investor perceives such impending developments he has to disinvest in such securities. If for example even bigwigs like ITC and Shaw Wallace were involved in abnoxious scams involving millions of foreign exchange drain from the country, many investors sold off their shares of these companies. When Sandoz and Hind Ciba agreed to merge the Sandoz shareholders were unhappy with the terms of conversion of shares of Hind Ciba, many were prepared to dispose off their shares. Yet another reason could be Government Policy changes. Due to continued drift in infrastructure industries, of particularly electricity and crude, the fear of rise in oil prices had led to a crash in Auto and cement shares in December 1996. The impending slow down in the economic activity has led to continued bearish phase in the market, when disinvestment could be planned by some investors particularly in industries depending on the infrastructural facilities.

Even in B_1 Group of cash shares on BSE, many companies were quoting below par many times due to poor fundamentals. In 1999, the BSE has created a separate category of 'Z' group to comprise of such companies which are violating the listing requirements and ignoring investor complaints and their interests. Since June 1996 the BSE sensex fell to a three year low of 2713 on December 3, 1996 from a three year high of 4643 reached an Sep. 12, 1994. On June 17, 1996 the sensex was 4131 and fell to close at 2795 on Dec. 3, 1996 — a fall of 33% in five months. In such a scenario of continued bearishness, disinvestment becomes a problem and investor loses heavily on any such disinvestment. In all these situations disinvestment requires more expertise than investment itself. It stood at a high 28,225 at end July 2015.

Disinvestment Under Adverse Conditions

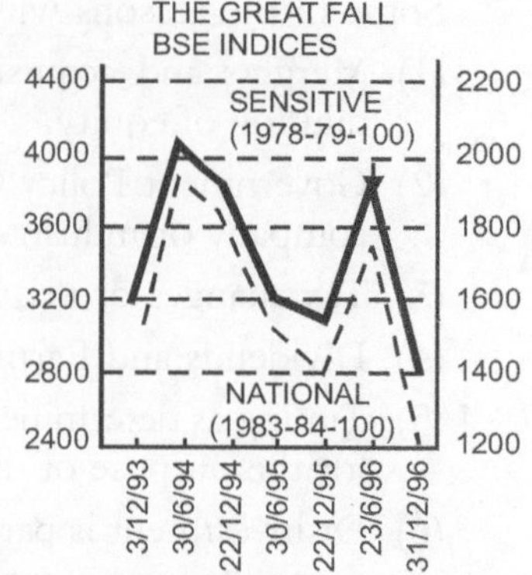

Disinvestment becomes impossible when the security prices are quoting well below the purchase prices. This is true of the majority of the newly listed companies also. It is understood that out of 2601 new issues listed between January 1, 1994 and July 12, 1996, 2505 issues (96% of new issues) were quoted below issue prices leading to erosion in the value of investment. Some 75 companies in B_1 Group on BSE have reached new lows with 14 of them quoting below par value of ₹ 10.

Out of 55 listed schemes of Mutual Funds on BSE as many as 43 were quoting at prices lesser than the NAV. Most of the investors of mutual funds would thus find it difficult to make any disinvestment, as they would lose heavily on any sales. Money is tied down in such apparently illiquid investments. In effect the liquidity is not possible, although in theory, the liquidity is provided by a quotation. In such a scenario also, disinvestment is a critical problem.

BSE Sensex has reached peak of 4643 in Sept. 1994 and then fell into a continued bearish phase to reach a low of around 3038 in December 1995 — a fall of 35% or so, but went up again to around 3367 at end March 1996 before falling to a three year low of 2713 by mid December 1996 — a fall of 20% (see accompanying table). These ups and downs are seen in the attached chart for the period 1993 to 1996. With the fall in prices values have also fallen. Thus, the annual turnover was ₹ 84,536 crores in 1993-94 fell to ₹ 50,064 crores in 1995-96 but rose again to ₹ 124,284 crores in 1996-97. During the month of December 1996, when the sensex reached a three year low, the daily turnover was only ₹ 400 crores a day; as against an earlier peak of ₹ 2,000 crores a day on BSE. The low of 1998 was 2,951 on June 22 as against a high of 4,605 on August 6, 1997. The volatility rate was 11% in 2004-05 and rose to 16.7% in 2005-06, on the BSE. It however fell to 9% in 2006-07.

The three year low of B.S.E. Sensex was 2741 reached on October 23,1998. At end March 1999, the sensex reached 3739, as compared to 3893 at end March 1998 a fall of 3.9% over the year 1998-99. There was a recovery from October 1999 and zoomed to reach a new all time peak of 6150 on Feb. 14, 2000. As compared with the low of 2742 reached on Nov. 30, 1999, the Sensex showed a rise of 124%, as on Feb. 14, 2000. There was unprecedented volitility in the market with prices moving violently on either way such that the SEBI has intervened in the market by imposing special volitility margins on selected scrips from January 2000 onwards.

The value of trade and price increase both on NSE and OTCEI have similarly declined for prolonged periods. Such depressed state of the markets create problems for disinvestment. In the OTCEI for example volume of trade fell from ₹ 365 crores in 1994-95 to ₹ 107 crores in 1996-97, bulk of the fall being in listed equity shares. On NSE, the number of listed companies stood at 793 and permitted securities at 320 as at end March 2002, with an annual turnover of ₹ 5.13 lakh crores in 2001-02 which was one and half times that of the BSE.

The long-term trends in BSE share price indices are seen in the following Table:

End March data	*1990*	*1991*	*1995*	*1996*	*1999*	*2001*	*2005*	*2006*	*2007*	*2008*	*2009*	*2010*	*2011*	*2012*	*2012-13*	*2013-14*
BSE Sensex	781	1168	3261	3367	3740	3604	6493	11280	13,072	15,644	8,996	17302	18,605	17,482	20,120	18,202
% age Change over the year	+15.4%	+49.5%	(–13.8%)	+3.2%	–3.9%	–27.9%	+16.1%	73.7%	16.0%	19.6%	–57.5%	92%	10.8%	-9.4%	11.6%	10.5%

After reaching a low of 2904 in April 2003, the sensex moved up with occssional reactions to reach 5612 in March 2004 and 6493 at end March 2005 and a high above 12,000 by April 2006, and 13,308 in March 2007. There has been a general uptrend from 2002-03 (average of 3206) to 12,277 in 2006-07 a rise of 3.8 times. Between June 2006 and June 2007, these was a rise of 44%, with occasional reactions. As at end January 2010, it was at around 16,000. In 2010, there was a sharp rise 92% as against a drop of 57.5% in 2009.

As against three year low of 2902 in April 2003, it has reached on all time peaks of 11,986 on April 19, 2006. The boom period continued from 2003 to 2007. This was also reflected in the amounts of new issues in the primary market as well as in FII inflows. Net FII investments in the capital market rose from a net outflow of ₹ 182 crores in June 2002 to net inflow of ₹ 292 crores in March 2003 and a peak inflow of ₹ 8,811 crores in March 2004, and ₹ 7,886 crores in March 2005. An all time high of 21,207 in Sensex index was seen in January 2008 and it stood at 28,225 at end July 2015. Taking the period of 2007 to 2010 when there was a high volatility, there was a high of 17,790 in the index in January 2009 and a low of 8,047 in March, 2009.

New Issue Trends

(₹ *Crores*)

Year	*1992-93*	*1994-95*	*1995-96*	*1998-99*	*2000-01*	*2003-04*	*2004-05*	*2005-06*	*2006-07*	*2008-09*	*2010-11*	*2011-12*	*2012-13*	*2013-14*
Public Issue	6,059	19,699	10,529	2,602	5,391	1,470	9867	16,938	27,175	2,674	22,203	13,305	7,157	7,105
Rights Issue	12,627	6,741	5,843	2,411	528	853	3,615	4,216	3,428	11,997	5,152	2,375	8,945	4,576
Total	18,686,	26,440	16,372	5,013	5,919	2,323	13,482	21,154	30,603	14,671	24,830	15,680	16,102	11,681

Source: RBI Annual Reports

The depressed primary market conditions are clearly seen during 1995-96 to 2002-03, and these have repercussions on the secondary market as well. The Granger's causality tests showed that in India there are inter connections between the primary markets and secondary markets and causality runs both ways. If an investor wants to disinvest in primary market there is no way for him except for the shares to be listed on the secondary market. If the secondary market is depressed, funds are tied down in the market and creates illiquidity among investors, which in turn makes the primary market stagnant and depressed. Thus, both the wings of the capital market and the institutional agencies in the capital market find it difficult to disinvest and get out of the markets, in such situations. There was however a pick up in secondary market in 2003-04 and public offers of many PSUs were over sub-scribed in the primary market and this uptrend continued during 2003 to 2007.

Disinvestment Motivated by Market Condition

The primary market conditions are depicted over a period of five years both in respect of public issues and rights issues. At the boom times of the market, namely, 1993-94 and 1994-95 either public issues or rights are both received well by the investors, when the stock market conditions were also good, but not so in 1995 to 2002.

The principles of disinvestment in any market are the basic tenets which are set at below:

Trading/Investment

(a) Buy low and sell high. Buy lower and sell only when the purchase price plus some gain is available; when the market is declining, buy at the lowest and sell atleast to cover the purchase price.

(b) When trading, a margin of 10% gain or loss or stop loss order can be set at 10% to get into disinvestment.

(c) In a Portfolio of shares, sell only overpriced shares whose fundamentals have weakened and bottomlines are expected to decline.

(d) Sell, to start with, Cats and dogs of companies in the Portfolio even when no profit can be booked. Short-term losses can be booked to show against short-term gains for tax purposes.

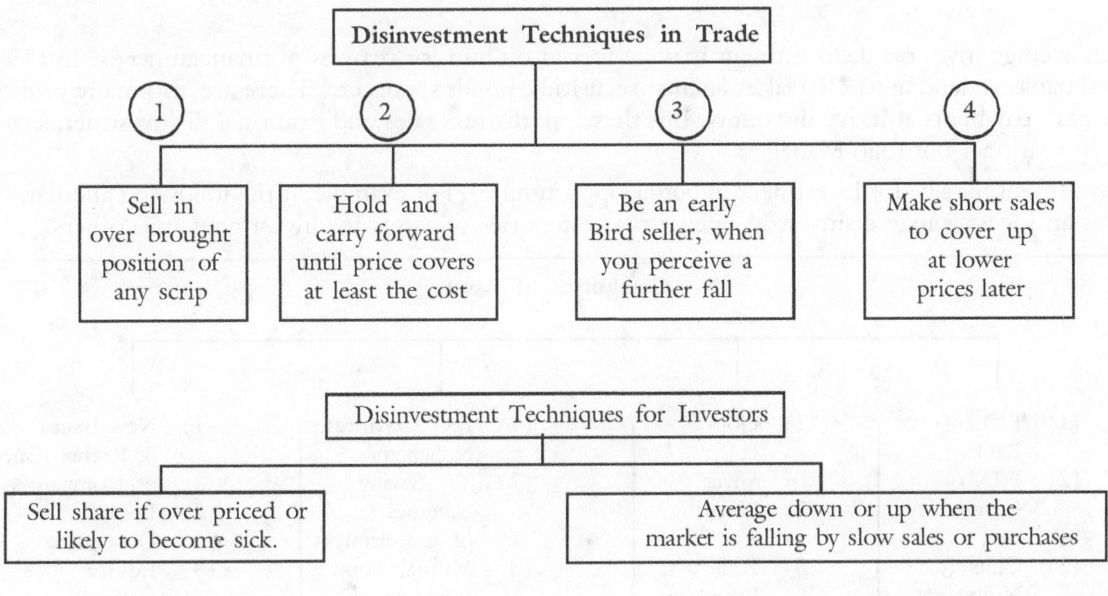

Normal Principles of Disinvestment are:

Buy	: Underpriced shares, Growth shares, new product and promising Companies.
Sell	: Overpriced shares, stagnant and decadent Companies or those expected to show declining bottom lines.
Hold	: When Companies are good, and promising, but market conditions are bad or the Company's share price is moving in a narrow grove.
Average up	: When the market is going up, sell in small quantities to average up the sale price.
Average down	: When the market is going down, buy in Small quantities, and sell when there is technical recovery or when there is buying support at around the settlement time.

Follow the Contrary Position: When there are over bought conditions in some scrips, then follow the principle of short sale and when there are many sellers in a scrip buy and carry forward without taking delivery.

Taking delivery and giving delivery are necessary for mutual funds and some Trust funds, LIC, GIC, etc., but for the companies, individuals and institutional agencies, taking and giving delivery can be avoided in trading for disinvestment.

Types of Disinvestment

Disinvestment, as referred to earlier, is as necessary as investment. In review and revision of portfolio management, *disinvestment* is an accepted method of adjustment of the portfolio to the preferences of investors, changes in market conditions and fresh information flows forthcoming from time-to-time. In the equity market, some scrips lose their charm due to poor financial performance and changes in market demand, financial mismanagement, when disinvestment in those shares become necessary. In the bond market, any needed changes in duration of the Portfolio, changes in interest rates and expectations of yield changes and monetary and credit policy changes will influence disinvestment decisions. Government bonds of low yields are switched for high yields. In times of expected rise in interest rates or yields, Portfolio Manager may switch from short-term bonds to long-term bonds and *vice versa.* The risk of change in interest rates is higher, the higher the maturity period and lower the Coupon Rate. The long maturity bonds suffer capital losses for rise in yields and in times of rising interest rates and yields, the capital losses on long bonds have to be offset by reinvestment of interest at higher yields. The adjustments of maturities, duration, swifts as between different bonds, with varying coupon rates are all part of the bond management strategies, which requires active trading.

Similarly, in times of depressed equity markets, the Treasury Manager may shift investments from equity to bond market, particularly when interest rates are rising as in 1996. When both bonds and equity markets are bearish, as in 1997-98 the investor may shift from capital market to other markets like commodities, futures, gold, silver and real estate, etc.

For an average investor, disinvestment may be forced on him for reasons of financial needs. In Dec. 1996, the RBI allowed banks to lend upto ₹ 10 lakhs against securities, bonds shares etc. There are also many brokers who buy on spot for cash payments at heavy discounts. But these are distress sales and irrational disinvestments to be avoided by trained and rational Portfolio Managers.

Disinvestment may be for investment in better opportunities. For example, if the following alternatives are taken into account an investor may disinvest in one or two categories of assets for investment into others.

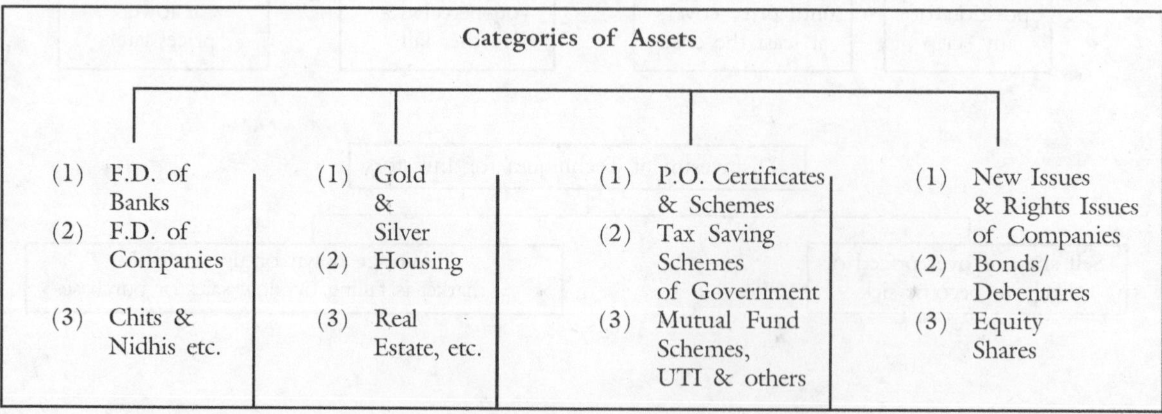

Assume that the investor has 13% coupon bonds of Government and 16.5% Bonds of ICICI. Suddenly the Gold prices fell to a new low and he is bullish on gold in 1997. He will disinvest in bonds and prefer to buy gold at lower prices of \$ 360 per fine once as against a peak of \$ 384, two months ago. See the accompanying Chart. In March 1999, monthly average gold price was \$286 per fine ounce, which was a very steeper fall than in equities during the same period (Oct. 97 to March 99).

Factors Influencing Disinvestment

Disinvestment takes place as an offshoot of the following financial activity in the markets.

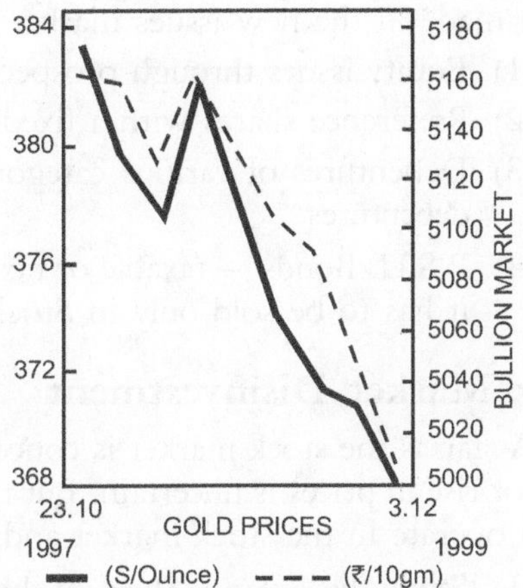

(1) Trading and speculative gains by short-term investors lead to disinvestment in the stock market.

(2) Booking Profits, both short-term and long-term due to capital appreciation in the markets.

(3) Avoiding possible losses by disinvestment in potentially non-viable and sick units, through research based fundamental Analysis.

(4) Taking advantage of interest rate changes or changes in expected yields.

(5) Adjustment of the portfolio of investments through continuous investment and disinvestment activity and shifting from low yielding to high yielding instruments and from low priority activity to high priority activity and from less profitable activity to more profitable activity.

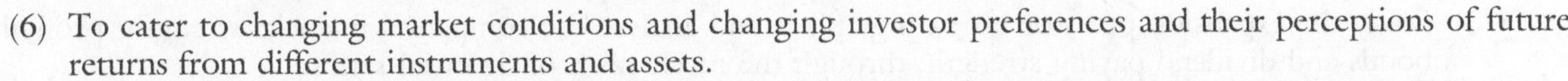

(6) To cater to changing market conditions and changing investor preferences and their perceptions of future returns from different instruments and assets.

(7) To take advantage of potential gains from various sub-markets such as from equities to bonds and *vice versa*, or from money market to capital market or from one sub-market like ICD to Bill discounting or from one market to another like shifting from capital market to gold market or commodities markets etc.

(8) Disinvestment for reasons of financial hardships and urgent need for cash leading to distress sales.

ROLE OF FUNDAMENTAL FACTORS

How to make Disinvestment Decision?

Disinvestment decision of a person depends on his preferences, income, wealth and his likes and dislikes. For example, a retired person requires regular income, safety of his funds, much more than the speculative gains or appreciation. On the other hand, a young working Executive who has regular monthly income invests for capital appreciation. A businessman may invest for tax planning purposes. Thus, the objectives of investors would be different for different persons and one has to be clear of his objective before one makes a decision for disinvestment.

Objectives

Normally the objectives of an average investor are: income, safety of funds, liquidity or marketability and capital appreciation. Disinvestment may aim at liquidity or safety or for just booking profits.

Investment Avenues

The alternative investment avenues for the investor are to be considered first, so as to satisfy the above objectives of investors. The following categories of investments are open to investors as avenues for investment and disinvestment.

(a) Investment in Bank Deposits — Savings and Fixed Deposits: This is the most common form of investment for an average Indian and nearly 40% of funds in financial saving are used in this form. These are least risky but the return is also low. One may shift funds from here to bonds or Company deposits for higher return.

(b) Investment in P.O. Deposits, National Savings Certificates and other Postal Savings Schemes: Many people in villages and semi-urban areas are investors in these schemes due to lower risk of loss of money and greater security of funds. But returns are also lower than in Stocks and Shares, which may lead to disinvestment. Some may shift to chit funds or Nidhis. Interest rates on savings media were reduced during 2000 to 2003.

(c) Investment in Mutual Fund Schemes or UTI Schemes: These are less risky than direct investment in stocks and shares as these enjoy the expert management by the Portfolio Manager or Professional experts. They also have the advantage of a diversified portfolio involving the reduction of risk and economies of scale reducing the cost of investment. But at times when mutual funds show poor returns, one may disinvest in them for better return elsewhere, as in the case of years 1997 to 1999.

(d) Investment in New Issues Market: A new entrant in the Stock Market should preferably invest in New Issues of existing and well reputed companies either in equity or debentures. Incidentally the instruments in which investment can be made in the new issues market are:

(1) Equity issues through prospectus or rights renounced by existing shareholders.

(2) Preference shares with a fixed dividend either convertible, into equity or not.

(3) Debentures of various categories — convertible fully, convertible partly, convertible and non-convertible debentures.

(4) P.S.U. Bonds — taxable or tax-free bonds with fixed interest rates. If investment is made in Primary market, it has to be sold only in Stock Market.

Stock Market Disinvestment

As far as the stock market is concerned, investment and disinvestment in shares is most risky as the likelihood of fall or rise in prices is uncertain. But the returns may also be high commensurate with risk. A host of imponderable factors operate in the stock market and a genuine investor has to do the following things:

(1) Study the Balance Sheet of the company and analyse the prospects of rise in Gross block, sales and profits.

(2) Analyse the Market Price in terms of book value and profit earning capacity (or P/E ratio) and examine whether the share is overvalued or undervalued.

(3) Study the expansion plans or tax savings plans and analyse the company's financial strength, profitability, bonus and dividend paying strength, through the mechanism of financial ratios.

(4) Study whether the management is professional and good and whether other accounting practices are dependable and consistent. The company becomes attractive to buy if the financial ratios support the view that the fundamentals are strong and the shares are worth buying.

(5) Lastly, if the price of the share is overvalued on the basis of the projected earnings for the coming half year or one year and its P/E ratio is higher than the industry average, then it is worth selling. For assessing the undervaluation and overvaluation, analyst and his analytical power count.

Fundamental Analysis

What ratios one should look into for Balance Sheet Analysis of a company for making a disinvestment decision? Any decision in this regard is to be based on a study of fundamental factors of the company and the intrinsic worth of the shares.

There is no single ratio which will explain the share price performance of a company. The whole Balance Sheet has to be analysed including the footnotes for knowing the strength of a company and its share price performance. For a casual investor who has no professional background and no time for analysing the whole Balance Sheet, he should however look into the Balance Sheet of the company and analyse the data for five or more years in respect of the following variables:

1. Efficiency in the Use of Capital: Examine the ratio of equity to Gross block or to capital employed (equity+preference capital+reserves+long-term debt capital). This will indicate how efficient the company is in capital use, and if inefficiency is apparent, it is a fit case for disinvestment.

2. Leverage Ratio: Examine how equity holders benefit by borrowed capital through the debt-equity ratio. The leverage is provided by debt capital to the equity- holders. If debt is very large and earnings potential is declining, it is a high risk company to be disinvested.

3. Turnover Ratio: This is the ratio of sales to the equity capital explaining how equity capital is used for improving sales. If sales are not rising and unutilised capacity is growing, it may grow sick anytime.

4. Profitability Ratio: Examine how sales would improve the profits through a study of the ratio of Gross Profits to Sales — G.P. Morgan relates the G.P. divided by sales turnover or net profits and profitability of operations.

5. Shareholders' Return: The ratio of net profits to equity will indicate the return to shareholder. But as all earnings either paid as dividend or ploughed back into reserves as depreciation or any other reserves, are belonging to the shareholders only PBDT Profits Before Depreciation and Taxes (Gross profits-minus interest) are the total earnings for equityholders, of which a part is paid as taxes, a part as dividends to shareholders and the rest is ploughed into reserves for use by the company. All earnings should therefore be considered for profitability.

6. Dividend Policy: As the shareholders are interested in a regular dividend distributed to them dividend paid divided by the total net profit will indicate the dividend policy of the company. A company which is not earning good profits or dividend is skipped for two or more years, it is a Company likely to be sick and can be disinvested.

7. Book Value: As the share price is an indication of the company's networth and its intrinsic value, the book value is one of the measures of share price and is calculated as the networth divided by number of equity shares. If the book value is eroded by 50% due to losses over years, that Company should be disinvested immediately.

8. Earnings Per Share (EPS): The net profits divided by the number of equity shares of the company give the earnings per share (PBDT divided by the number of equity shares). This will represent company's earning capacity for equityholders. If EPS is declining over a couple of years, it is a fit case for disinvestment.

9. P/E Ratio: Market price divided by the Earnings Per Share (EPS) would indicate the multiple by which the price discounts the earnings per share of the company; a low P/E ratio relative to other companies in the same industry would indicate that price is attractive for a buy provided other financial parameters of the company are also good. But if the company is not earning good profits every year, has no expansion plans and is skipping dividends then that company has to be disinvested.

10. Expansion Plans: If the company has no expansion plans, it will not grow and so is the sales. The company will have no potential to realise higher sales. and higher profits in the coming years. If on the other hand the growth of gross block and growth of sales are both high and profit margins are low, then the efficiency is poor and profit margins would not improve if efficiency is low and then the company is likely to be in red. Such company's share will be low priced at present and hence it is better to get out of such companies.

More details are set out in the chapter of Fundamental Analysis.

FIIs and the Art of Contrariness

Most institutional investors and traders do not have long-term view of gains. Investment bankers and FIIs have started taking a short-term view of the market. Their purchases and sales have a major impact on the price trends in India. Studies made by CMIE, RBI and other Research bodies have shown that FII investment is the major cause of instability in the market prices. So one of the principles of disinvestment is to follow contrary view to that of FIIs. If there is a net selling by FIIs, keep off the market, if you cannot buy. When FIIs have turned buyers, sell the investments that you would like to disinvest. Besides, it is necessary for all traders and institutional investors to keep a tap on what FIIs feel and write about various companies in their portfolios. As FIIs have turned out to be major players in the Indian markets, their views and statements expressed orally or in press have found to have some influence on the market which the traders and operators in the market have to keep a pulse on.

Disinvestment Through study of Indicators is recommended. Although the markets may be depressed and caught in a bear hug, there are times when there will be technical corrections rallies and short upward movements. The traders in need of disinvestment have to keep a continuous watch on the price chart, moving Average chart and ROC chart. The price and rate of price changes indicate the deceleration and acceleration of the price trends and volumes and rates of change of volumes support the trends or indicate to likely reversals albeit short, even for a day, may be taken advantage by the traders for disinvestment. These technical factors are discussed in detail earlier.

FII Investments in India

According to a study of SEBI, released late in December 1996, FII investments have not slowed down and that they are not the cause of the present depressed conditions in the market. The fact which that study missed is that the reasons for bearishness are domestic factors of sluggish economic growth and industrial progress, slow down in the pace of infrastructural production, and unfriendly policy measures of the Government etc.

The cumulative FII investment from November 1992, when they were first permitted to enter into Indian capital market upto end 2001, was a total of about ₹ 55,000 crores. The study revealed that the months in which there were large net investments were also the months when the markets were buoyant (Nov. 1993 to June 1994, June 1995 to September 1995 and January 1996 to July 1996). These upswings in investments were followed by very low net investments, thereafter, presumably due to many depressing factors. It was found that their net investment was negative in 1998-99. What happened was that their net investments were bunched in a few months in a year when the markets were also bullish. Months with large net investments were followed by very low investments in other months. Being large holders of funds, their entry and exit in the market had a significant effect on the ups and downs in the market sentiment and in price fluctuations, which any investor has to watch out for disinvestment. The Role FIIs in the market is to be watched for disinvestment. The accompajying graph shows a brief period of ups and downs in the FDI inflows.

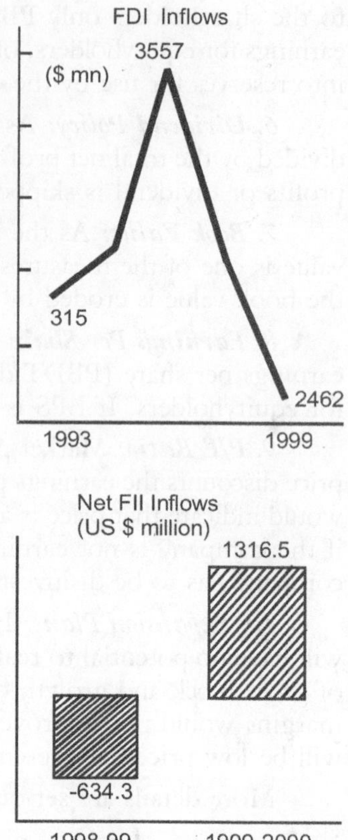

The Table below on the Data on Net FII Investment shows that there was decline in the amounts during 1997 to March 1999 and thereafter particularly from Nov. 1999, there was a pick up in their net investments. From October 1999, the secondary market also started picking up due to improved sentiment following the news of improved fundamentals of the economy, establishment of a stable Government at the centre after the general elections in October 1999 and change in Government policies.

Table

Net FII Investment (Portfolio)

	(₹ in crores)
1998-1999	-257
1999-2000	13,112
2000-2001	12,809
2003-2004	52,279
2004-2005	41,854
2005-2006	55,307
2006-2007	31,713
2007-2008	1,09,741
2008-2009	– 63,618
2009-2010	13,518
2010-2011	13,838
2011-2012	1,46,487
2012-2013	85,571
2013-2014	29,680

Source: RBI Handbook of Statistics.

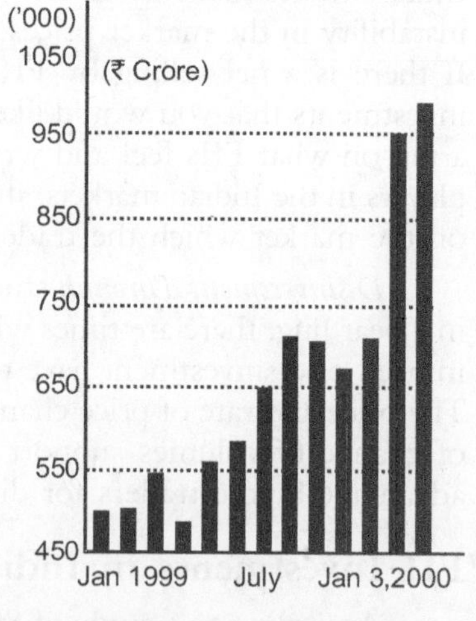

FII investments peaked off in 1996-97 and after declining for the next two years picked up again 1999 and 2000 and reached a new peak of ₹ 13,112 crores in 2001. The above charts also indicate the same story for the years 1994 to 1998 and the chart on market capitalisation on BSE during 1999 shows the trends, similar to those of FII investments on a monthly basis (not shown in this chart). Since 2003, there was a sharp uptrend in FII inflows, when the capital market was booming. This establishes the strong correlation between FII inflows and the stock prices in India and the influence of foreign markets have on the Indian markets.

Role of Technical Factors

Technical analysis of the market is the best way to keep informed of the likely trend reversals. If Advance-Decline lines are showing a trend and also a possible reversal, all the other market indicators have to be watched, namely, price indices, FII purchases and sales, volume turnover in A group and B_1 and B_2 together for reflecting the speculative and investment trends, daily high-low positions for the shares to be disinvested, spread or volatility of price movements and scrupulously follow the daily price charts, moving average price lines and look out for single point and double point sale signals for confirmed price reversal indicators to make disinvestments. The chart given here depicts the price and volume relationship of a scrip for illustration.

The chart gives the price and volume lines for a close study. The chart provides an example for giving buy and sell signals through the moving average price charts. These signals can be checked up by a number of other indicators like ROC or oscillators, RSI and MACD etc. The example of a company scrip studied is Rasi Cement, whose daily price chart and moving average price trends are studied to give signals for disinvestment also.

Although there are standard methods of disinvestment by study of fundamentals and weeding out those potentially sick and those with declining bottom lines and deteriorating fundamentals, those are to be accepted as a first step. Once companies to be disinvested are located, it may not be possible to disinvest due to market conditions. Here comes the second step of study of technicals for locating the proper timing.

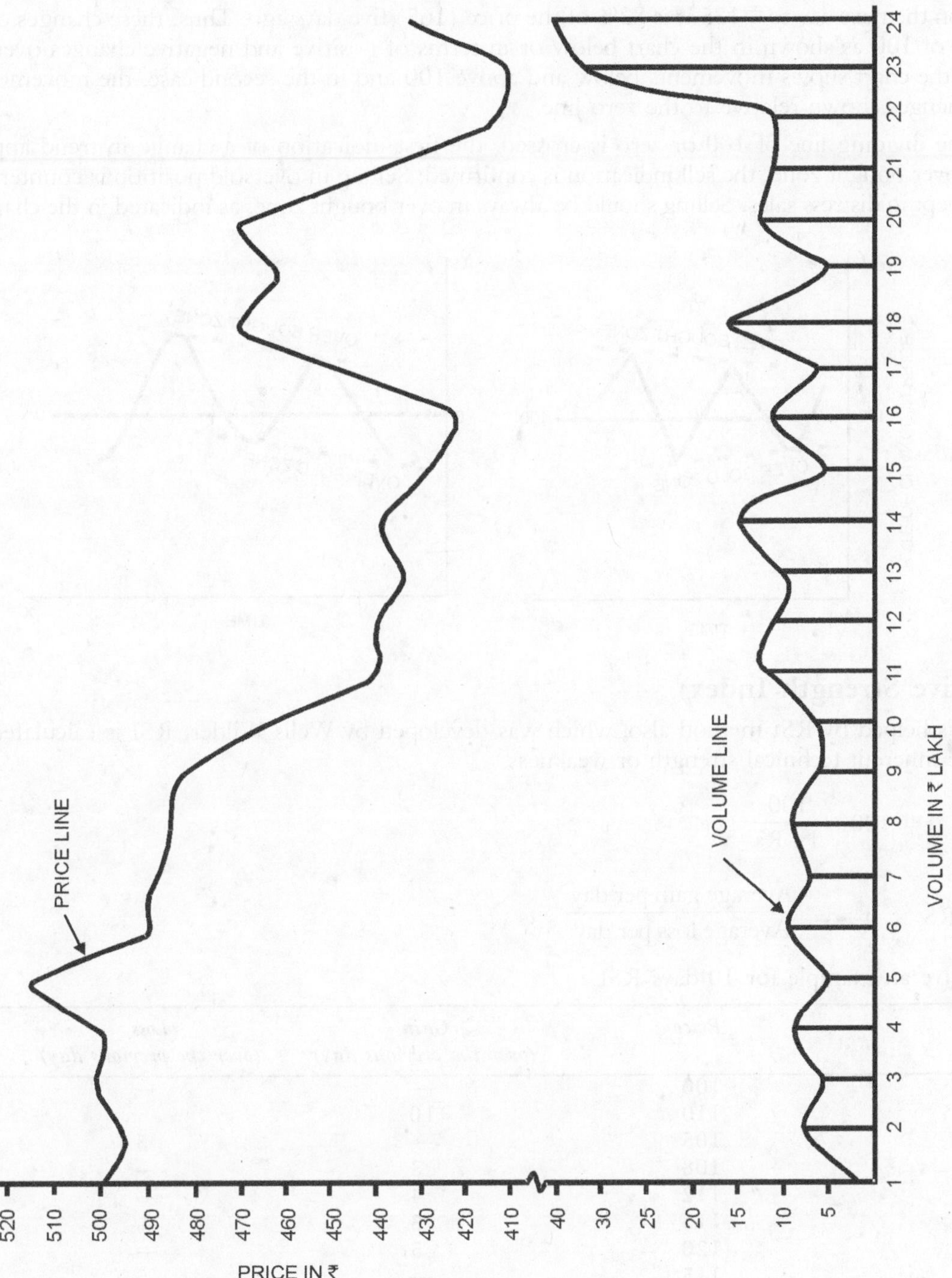

Timing of Disinvestment (Through Technical Analysis)

Unless the disinvestment is a distress sale, it has to be well timed to reap the optimum gain. Such timing can be sought from research analysis of the market Trends called the Technical Analysis. Reference was made earlier to the Chartist method, moving average method and diagnosis of reversal trends for getting the sell signals. Some more important tools are referred to below:

ROC or oscillators. It is an important indicator for identifying the trend reversal and knowing the overbought position or oversold position in a scrip.

Rates of change in prices or oscillators can be calculated for daily closing prices or weekly or monthly or any period of days. Suppose we have chosen 5 days oscillators to coincide with the trading period. The first day closing quotation is say ₹ 150 and after 5 days the closing quotation is ₹ 165 which is 110% of the price five days ago. Suppose the price fell on the next day to ₹ 135 it is 82% of the price (165) five days ago. Thus, these changes can be expressed on either side of 100 as shown in the chart below or in terms of positive and negative changes over the period. In the first case, the chart shows movements below and above 100 and in the second case, the movements are positive or negative changes shown relative to the zero line.

When the dividing line of 100 or zero is crossed, the first indication of a change in trend appears and when it crosses the over bought zone, the sell indication is confirmed. Selling in oversold position is counter productive and inadvisable except in distress sales. Selling should be always in over bought zone, as indicated in the chart shown below.

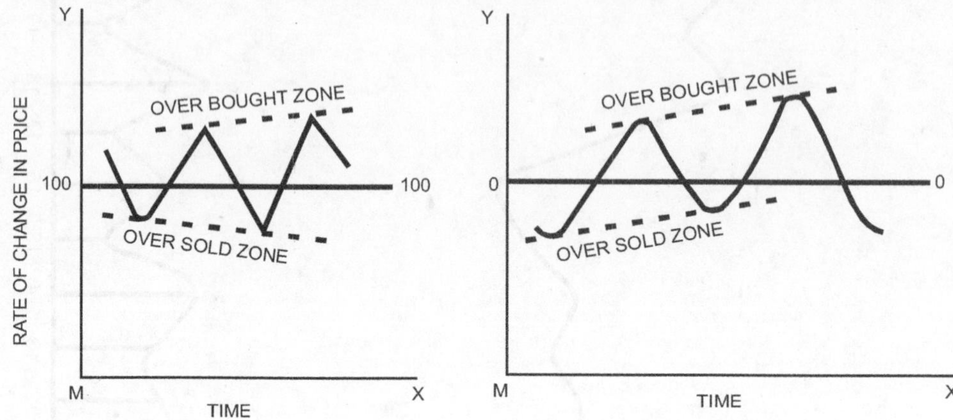

RSI (Relative Strength Index)

Timing is helped by RSI method also, which was developed by Wells Wilder. RSI is calculated for each scrip to identify the inherent technical strength or weakness.

$$RSI = 100 - \frac{100}{1 + Rs}$$

$$\text{Where, RS} = \frac{\text{Average gain per day}}{\text{Average loss per day}}$$

Let us give an example for 10 days RSI

Days	*Price*	*Gain (over the previous day)*	*Loss (over the previous day)*
1	100	—	—
2	110	10	
3	105	—	5
4	108	3	—
5	112	4	—
6	115	3	—
7	120	5	—
8	115	—	5
9	110	—	5
10	95	—	5
10 days' average		$\frac{25}{10}$	$\frac{20}{10}$
Gain/Loss		2.5	2.0

$$RS = \frac{2.5}{2.0} = 1.25$$

$$RSI = 100 - \left(\frac{100}{1+1.25}\right) = 100 - 44.4 = 55.6$$

The subsequent observations should be used to compile a series of RSI data.

After calculating such data for a number of days, a graph as shown below can be drawn representing the data on RSI. The Graph foretells a rise or a fall and time for disinvestment. One can develop his own skill in tracing turning signals, for both purchases and sales based on the reversal trend.

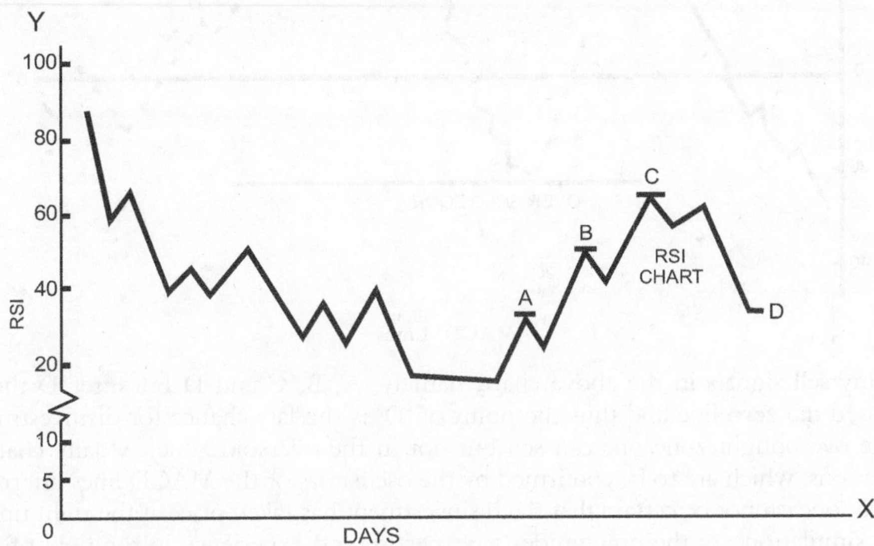

In daily movement of prices, there will be both rise and fall. If we take closing prices and compare them, sometimes each successive top will be higher than the previous top and at a point when next peak is lower than the previous one, the first sign of change of trend or sell signal is registered. In the above chart, for example there are three peaks each rising above the previous one (A, B, and C) and afterwards if the peak is lower than C and even B, we have sell signals for disinvestment. One should always sell in scrips which are in overbought zones and even selling short will pay-off on some occasions.

The disinvestment decisions have to be taken with extreme care to make the optimum profit. As it is not possible for many to capture the exact peak, the prudent investor will sell around 5 to 10% on either side of the peak, as a rule of the Thumb. On continuous study of these charts, one can develop the needed expertise for correct timing of investment and disinvestment decisions.

On a study of RSI chart with that of the daily price chart, one can see either divergence or convergence of their trends. If the share price is moving up when RSI is falling and *vice versa* they are examples of divergence, which indicate the likely turning points in the trend of share prices for the purpose of disinvestment; if divergence occurs in the over bought zone, then sell signal may be indicated. The Resistance and support lines are easily discernible by a study of these charts over a long period of time, in the RSI lines as in the daily price charts. Break outs, and reversals should be noticed in the overbought zone when disinvestment can be made.

Moving Average Convergence and Divergence (MACD)

MACD is another indicator used for disinvestment and investment process. It measures the convergence and divergence between two exponential or simple moving averages. Two series of closing price data-one for short-term moving average of say 12 day and the other for 26 days of long-term moving average. The MACD should reflect the absolute differences between these two moving averages. With differences shown on the Y-axis and days represented on the X-axis the chart can be drawn with a MACD line oscillating across the zero line.

As long as the MACD line moves above the zero line but likely to cross it, we have to select a point for disinvestment. Care has to be taken to see that some false signals are not pursued, but disinvestment may be based on some confirmation of likely trend to cross the zero line from above. This means that the short-term moving average is above the longer one, and the MACD is positive and in the opposite case, it is negative and falls below the zero line. This is seen from the above chart of MACD.

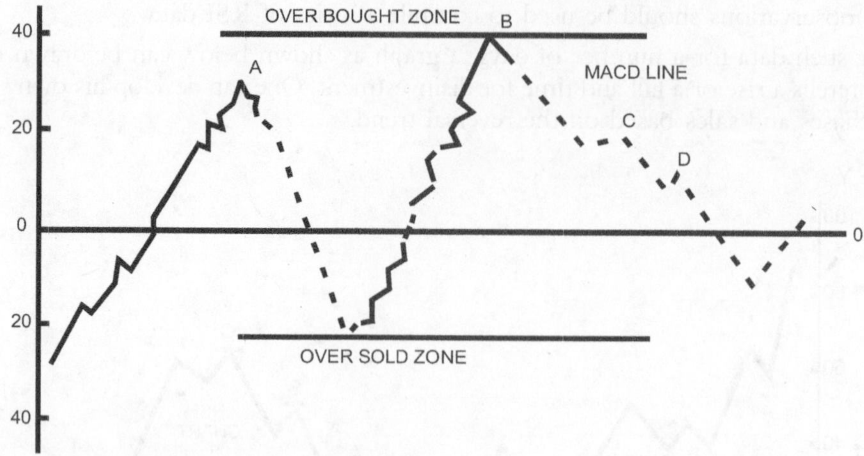

MACD Lines

One can see many sell signals in the above chart, namely, A, B, C and D but after D the line started falling continuously and crossed the zero line and thus the point of 'D' is the last chance for disinvestment with advantage. If the market is in the overbought zone one can sell but not in the oversold zone. A daily chart of prices will first give preliminary indications, which are to be confirmed by the oscillators or the MACD lines referred to in this chapter. Even with confirmation, one cannot be certain that the disinvestment has taken place at the right time. Experimentation, and research through simulation are the only guides to expertise and experience in the field of technical analysis to act as an aid for disinvestment management.

More details are set out in the Chapter on Technical Analysis.

Disinvestment by Government Sector

So far, we have dealt with disinvestment as a science and art of management by individuals, Portfolio Managers, Mutual Funds, companies and financial institutions etc. For these units and agencies, investment and disinvestment go together and are part of their trading and funds management.

For Government which has considerable investments in industrial ventures, both in manufacturing, trading and services sectors, disinvestment is a different issue. In India, the Policy of Socialistic Pattern of development pursued by the Government since the fifties has resulted in considerable investments by the Government in public enterprises. Nearly ₹ 2.3 lakh crores of public funds are invested in these PSUs

Since 1985, the PSUs were allowed to borrow from the market directly and this has resulted in raising large sums of money from the capital market by the PSUs also. This has no doubt reduced their dependence on the government budgetary support, but many PSUs could not resort to public borrowing due to their non-viable nature and poor state of their financial position. Since 1991, the policy changed in the direction of privatisation and deregulation.

The Public borrowing by PSUs continued through issue of taxable and tax free bonds. Total borrowing of this type stood at ₹ 16,632 crores in 2000-01, and ₹ 13,404 crores in 2007-08 and ₹ 53,608 crores in 20010-11.

In 1993-94, the net disinvestment was a negative figure of ₹ 48 crores and the disinvestment figures since 1994 have substantially improved, until 1996, when again the disinvestment fell to a disappointing low of only ₹ 1,397 crores as against the Budget provision of ₹ 7,000 crores, for 1995-96.

The disinvestment process by the government was started in 1991-92 after the economic reforms were initiated in July 1991. During 1992, 1993 and 1994, there was a moderate disinvestment by the PSUs. But there was a setback to this process later due to poor investment climate in the economy and the continued bearish conditions in the market during 1995-96.

The process initiated in 1991-92 met with massive criticism about the mechanics of disinvestment on the one hand, that is through the route of mutual funds and public financial institutions, and secondly, on the ground of higher premiums charged on these disinvested shares. Thus, after they were listed as in the case of SAIL, BHEL, IPCL, etc., the prices fell in the market reflecting the higher premiums charged by the FIs and Mutual Funds, when they were disinvested. There must be some miscalculations of the intrinsic worth of the disinvested shares and of the investors perception of their worth. There was also utter disregard of market perceptions. Thirdly, some of these PSUs have under-performed as compared with the expectations of the investors and the rating given to the management efficiency and financial fundamentals came for serious doubts and criticism.

Subsequent disinvestment process met with some resistance from the investors as a result. But the disinvestment process picked up again in 2000-2001.

Problems of PSU Disinvestment

As referred to earlier, disinvestment became a problem to the government due to poor or non-viable financial position and fundamentals of many PSUs. Besides, PSU disinvestment has met with some difficulties during 1995-96 due to highly depressed market conditions and investor resistance to equity. The Budget for 1996-97 has provided for disinvestment of ₹ 5,000 crores by the PSUs as against which only ₹ 382 crores were actually raised in 1995-96. Yearwise details of disinvestment by government in equity holdings of PSUs are as follows:

		Disinvestment@ (₹ in Crores)
1994-95	Accounts	5,078
1995-96	"	1,397
1996-97	"	380
1997-98	"	912
2000-01	"	2,125
2002-03	"	3,151
2003-04	"	16,953
2004-05	"	4,424
2005-06		1,581
2006-07		534
2007-08		38,795
2008-09		566
2009-10		24,581
2010-11		22,845
2011-12 RE		18,688
2012-13 RE		25,890
2013-14 RE		25,841
2014-15 RE		63,425

Source: RBI Handbook of Statistics.

During 1994-95, the disinvestment process was fairly successful, having raised ₹ 5,078 crores mostly due to sales to FIs, MFs, etc., but in 1995-96, as against the Budget provision of ₹ 7,000 crores, only ₹ 382 crores were raised excluding Bonus Shares, for reasons explained earlier. The Budget for 1996-97 has again provided for a larger amount of ₹ 5,000 crores, which did not materialise due to continued bearish phase, in both the primary and secondary markets during the whole year 1996, particularly since July 1996. In 1999-2000, the actual realisation of disinvestment proceeds worked out to only ₹ 1,724 crores. In Union Budget 2001-02, the target for disinvestment was put at ₹ 12,000 crores, against which the actuals were ₹ 3,646 crores (not shown in the above table).

A disinvestment commission was set up in 1996 to lay down guidelines for disinvestment of PSUs, under the chairmanship of Mr. G.V. Ramakrishna. It was reported that this commission has engaged the services of three Indian Credit Rating agencies to study 40 PSUs referred to them for possible disinvestment. The allotted PSUs were studied by the respective credit rating agencies for their future profitability, technology levels, share value and other relevant details. Their reports were released to the commission. A separate Dept. of Disinvestment was created by the Govt. to establish a systemic policy approach and hasten the process of disinvestment in 1999.

NAVARATNAS

Among this list of companies, there are a good number of profitable giant PSUs like BHEL, IPCL, SAIL, ONGC, OIL, BSNL, Air India, ITI, BEML etc., for disinvestment. Of these nine were identified as Navaratnas to be eligible for a quick pace of disinvestment. Although there was some proposal that the World Bank would fund through a grant, the Commission on disinvestment to help its process of privatisation and for undertaking disinvestment successfully, there has been no receipt of such funds so far.

The immediate cause of anxiety for the government is the continued bearish phase of the market upto 2003, which made it impossible for the government to disinvest the PSUs successfully. There has been criticism in the past on the disinvestment process by the government followed earlier to which a reference was made already. Bids were

@ From 2005-06, Disinvestment Receipts are not part of Central Receipt, but credited to Separate Investment Fund Account.

called from FIs, MFS and UTI etc., for contribution to the proposed amounts of equity issue to be disinvested. Reportedly, merchant bankers were also not involved and no underwriting was resorted to. The public offer was also made in some cases for parts of the amount disinvested. As the experience has shown, many such PSU shares were quoted below the issue price, after they were listed, with the result that public investors were scared of investing in PSU shares, even when they are profit-making. The premium charged by them may be high or the expectations of investors were too high and they were disappointed. The normal process of such disinvestment in foreign countries is to entrust such jobs to well established security firms and merchant banks to buy wholesale and retail them later to public at very realistic prices in good market conditions. That seems to be one of the ways to be followed in India too. Right pricing and right timing are equally important. For right pricing, credit rating and a study of the strength of fundamentals is necessary. Evaluation of the NAV and auditor's reports on the possible price range, in which one should sell are also necessary. These and other aspects were dealt with in the Reports of the Disinvestment Commission and their recommendations are under active consideration and implementation by the government. But disinvestment by the Government of PSUs has come to stay, but some policy changes were made after 2004 due to the influence of the Left parties on the government.

Central Public Sector Undertakings

As at end 2009, there were 236 operating PSEs, of which 134 were profit making and 102 were non-profit making. At the end 2003 there were 62 PSUs, considered for disinvestment; only 49 are being taken up now. Out of 419 State PSUs only 221 units are being taken up for disinvestment or reconstruction. The gross profit as a percentage of capital employed was 16% in 1997-98. This gross profit does not tell the net return to the government, which is 7.7 per cent for all PSEs, on the capital invested by the Government. Their borrowing cost on an average was higher at 12 per cent. The gap is met from the Budget revenues which is a drain on the public exchequer.

The divestment process was slow due to delays in administrative decision making red tape, and difficulties in implementation due to market conditions. Towards the end of 1999, the Government have set up a separate Department of Disinvestment and Disinvestment Commission was reconstituted in July 2001.

DIVESTMENT METHODS OF GOVERNMENT

For 1999-2000, a target of divestment amount was set at ₹ 10,000 crores. To achieve this target, the Government have decided on three possible methods, namely the SPV or special purpose vehicle, the Trust Route and the Warehousing method.

The SPV method and Trust methods involves the setting up of a separate body to which the Government would pass on its holding and which in turn arranges for divestment. The main difference between SPV and Trust methods is that the Trust method provides for a mechanism of checks in the absence of parliamentary audit, while the SPV method lacks this mechanism.

Under the warehousing method, there are some ways like a buy back arrangement with the Government on outright sale to FIs and a Trust, market making by the FIs for the Government holdings. In all these cases, FIs and mainly public FIs will have to bear the burden. The Government have to negotiate with the FIs, in respect of the most suitable method for each of these models.

The buy back arrangement is flexible in that the FI can buy the stock from the Government to ultimately pass them on to the public. If there is any fall in prices, the government would buy back at the original sale price. This flexibility is not there in the other methods of warehousing. In the case of out right sale to FIs, it is good for the government to close the deal leaving the FIs to book profits or losses in their sale to public. But it would appear as if the FIs are forced by the government.

OPEN BIDDING PROCESS OF DIVESTMENT

The objective of open bidding process in its transparency in resources raised by the Government by selling its stake. This is not the same as the adoption of strategic partner route as recommended by the Nitesh Sengupta Committee. The Finance Ministry under pressure to raise resources is attempting to sell a singificant stake in Bharat Petroleum Corporation and IBP on the lines of the sale of the stake in IPCL, which attracted bids from major players in oil sector like SOROS Group, Mitsubishi and Reliance Industries.

A Proposal on Mutual Fund Route

In December 1999, the FIs and banks have planned to set up an Asset Management Company and Mutual Fund owned by them by putting in their own funds to the extent of ₹ 4,000 crores. All major Public Sector FIs, LIC, GIC,

UTI, SBI and a few other public sector banks will put in funds. The AMC will buy at the market going rates the offered stock held by the Government in the major oil, Telecom and I.T. Public Sector undertakings. There will be about a dozen companies which are profit making.

The AMC will hold them and disinvest as and when the market can absorb. It is estimated that the capacity to absorb by the market may be limited, and any public issue route may not absorb all the divestment planned by the Government.

The planned Mutual Fund is likely to be managed by the UTI, as it has got enough experience in this line. The mutual fund route is preferred, as warehousing route may not really transfer risk from the Government. Direct issue at home or abroad may not fetch the required money. But this proposal was not pursued by the govt.

Banks' Divestment Scheme

The Government have planned to divest some 5 public sector banks in 1999-2000. It would sell its equity stake in the following profit making banks, namely PNB, Allahabad Bank, Andhra Bank, I.O.B. and Punjab and Sind Bank. Under the existing policy, they will issue Initial Public Offers (IPOs) to the public for subscription. This policy continued to be operative at present. Banks are making IPOs to augment their capital base.

The respective amounts of equity held in major banks are as follows: as in March 2011.

As in March 2011

Govt. Holding in PSU Banks

	Govt. stake (%)	Equity base (₹ cr)
Oriental Bank of Commerce	58	250.98
Dena Bank	58	286.82
Andhra Bank	58	485.5
IDBI Bank	65	723.79
Bank of Baroda	57	367
Vijaya Bank	57.7	433.52
Allahabad Bank	58	446.7
Union Bank of India	57.1	505
Corporation Bank	58.5	143.44
Punjab National Bank	58	315.3
Indian Overseas Bank	65.9	544.8

Source: RBI, Trend and Progress of Banking in India. 20010-11.

The buoyant response to the Syndicate Bank issue in 1999 has prompted the Government to clear the public issues of these banks. Besides there was over subscription many times in respect of IPOs by Syndicate Bank. Bank offerings have in general done well as in the case of Corporation Bank, even when the market conditions were bad. Denationalisation and privatisation is part of the agenda of banking reforms, which the government wants to pursue.

The bank privatisation is planned to bring down in stages in the Government holdings near to the level of 33% of total equity. Bank shares were in good demand in the equity market during recent years of 2004 to 2007 when the capital markets were in boom conditions. During the year 2005-06, in particular, many public sector banks like Andhra Bank, Canara Bank, UCO Bank, etc. went for public issue to raise fresh capital which was used to repay the Central Government their equity capital in part to bring their holdings down. These issues were over subscribed to reflect the mood of the market for disinvestment by the Govt. and the ephoria for banking stocks in the market, after 2006.

Disinvestment Policy

A Disinvestment Commission was set up in 1996 which recommended a shift from public offerings to trade/strategic sales with transfer of management in respect of many PSUs. A Department of disinvestment was constituted in 1999 as a nodal department to speed up the process of disinvestment and to formulate policy lines for this purpose. Since 2000-01 major policy decisions include the closing down of PSUs, which could not be revived, disinvestment of all non-strategic PSUs upto 74% and protection of workers interests through safety nets. During 2002-03, Disinvestment process was announced through strategic sales of blocks of shares to strategic partners. Modernisation and upgradation of PSUs, creation of new assets and generation of employment and setting up of a Disinvestment Proceeds Fund during

2002-03, were aimed at. But actual realisation of these plans fell far short of targets. Realisation through disinvestment during 1991 to 2003 stood at ₹ 28,208 crores for the centre as against a target of ₹ 78,300 crores. During 2003-04, the disinvestment has exceeded the target of ₹ 14,500 crores, mainly through open public offers. The Government at the centre has changed in 2004, the policy due to the position of left parties to disinvestment. Even so, dis investment continued at a slower pace. In April 2007, Maruti disinvestment was reported to have brought in a fund of ₹ 2,360 crores.

Recent Government Disinvestment Process

During 2003-04, Government disinvested in many public sector undertakings. There was good public response to public issues of ONGC, IPCL, IBP, CMC, Dredging Corporation of India and GAIL. Even the nascent PSUs like Power Trading Corporation and Petronet LNG Ltd. received good response from the FIs and public in their public offers. There are 36 listed PSUs, whose prices on the Stock Exchange have recorded new highs early in 2004. More specific examples of leading Government undertakings are BPCL, HPCL and IOC. The disinvesment process has progressed well even by state governments with Gujarat, Andhra Pradesh, etc, leading in this regard. The stakes of state government in some profit making undertaking were brought down during 2003-04. The listed public sector banks, including SBI were the major gainers on the Stock Exchanges, as their productivity per employee has gone up. The banks' stocks represented by the bank stock Index of BSE showed a substantial rise and bank stocks were in good demand in boom conditions of recent years.

ICICI Bank was in good demand at a price of ₹ 314 per share, Axis Banks at ₹ 580, SBI at ₹ 288 as at early August 2015.

35 SECURITIES MARKET REPORT (BSE)

Relevance of the BSE Market Reports

This book deals with the Securities Analysis and these securities are traded on the stock exchange and hence their reports and their anlaysis is relevant here. Secondly, in the portfolio management, the security return is compared with the market return in the context of the risk free return. Similarly, the security risk is weighed against the market risk and the covariance of the returns of the securities in a portfolio is checked for auto correlation with the market risk instead of with each individual security risk in the portfolio. The portfolio risk is not sum total or the arithmetical average of the individual risks in the portfolio, but it can be more or less than the sum total of risks of all securities in the portfolio because of the covariance as between the returns of the securities in the portfolio. It is in this context that the Market risk and market return are highly relevant for our treatment of the subject. These are closely related to the market reports which are discussed in this chapter.

Through the study of the BSE prices in the form of the index namely sensex, the whole market is supposed to be covered instead of those of about 2000 actively traded scrips on a daily basis. The trade volume or turnover in the market in addition to the price index are the major indicators of the market behaviour. These two indicators are set out juxtaposed with the independent variables which are supposed to influence the market price behaviour in the Table below. These are the money supply or liquidity available for trading and GDP or output of the economy as reflectors of the economic performance and the stock market is supposed to be window of the economy. In addition to the domestic money flowing into the market, there are foreign flows coming from the FIIs and FFIs, OCB for portfolio management. The money supply has other claimants for their analysis namely output as reflected in the GDP growth rate and the inflation, which is expected to be reflected in the WPI index and its growth rate, and these are also included in the table below.

The other factors which may influence the stock market prices are commodity prices and the gold prices, gold being a money metal, is an alternative to the investment in the stocks. The index of commodities is already reflected in the WPI and Gold prices are also presented here in the Table. The Gold investment is a major competitor to the stock market investment.

It will be seen from the Table that BSE index and volume turnover are closely related with money supply growth, vindicating the Monetarist theory of asset and commodity prices. Besides, the GDP growth as well inflation as reflected in the WPI index are also positively related with the BSE sensex and its turnover, which upholds the logical conclusion of modern monetarist theory. Both Gold prices and stock prices moved up jointly during the boom condition of 2004 to 2008. This period is also characterized by higher rate of inflation, and higher rates of GDP growth. These are all attributable to the larger inflows of Foreign funds for portfolio management and the larger liquidity in the economy. During the period of 2009 and 2010, however, the markets were more volatile and trend was uncertain. There was therefore a lower index of BSE prices, as well as a lower turnover. This was attributed to lower growth of money supply and lower GDP growth rate during this period. The Gold prices continued to rise as well as commodity prices as reflected in the WPI index. There was a diversion of funds from the stock market to commodity markets and Gold market, during the period 2009-10. The years 2009 and 2010 were exceptional in the sense that market were bearish or in congestion with fluctuation on either side. The same can be said of the period 2001 to 2003, when there was a downslide in BSE sensex, and in volume of turnover, which are caused by slower growth of M3 and lower Foreign investment in India. The WPI numbers were also lower, as much as the GDP growth rate.

The table below presents these data and their major drawback is that some figures are in absolute numbers like BSE turnover, Foreign inflows, and gold prices. These have some particular relevance to the objective of our study. The others are rates of growth or incremental rates. The reason for keeping these data, as such, is that our objective is not to conduct a regression analysis and fit in a regression line to know the extent of their inter-relations or calculate the regression coefficient. Our object is to vindicate some conceptual relations between these variables and to bring out in particular the role of the studies including those of the IMF have vindicated the role of Foreign inflows into developing countries on their stock prices and the volume of their turnover. Our objective being modest to test the truth of these claims and to butterss the role of liquidity, both domestic and foreign, on the BSE sensex, the data in the Table was kept in the simple form to pave the way for the students to conduct more scientific analysis on topics like this.

During the period, 2003 to 2008, BSE sensex rose sharply by about 5 times, and so also in the BSE turnover. The rise in M3 was from 12% to 22% during this period. Taking the absolute figures, money supply rose by two times. These trends are accompanied by similar uptrends in the case of the Gold Prices, by two times, and foreign inflows by 23 times, during the period 2003 to 2008. In 2008-09, however there was a steep fall in foreign inflows. In fact, there was a negative growth which means there was an outflow of funds. Money supply growth was also lower. BSE sensex was lower as also the volume of turnover. This was supported by a fall in growth rate of GDP and a rise in inflation leading to stagflation in the economy.

Table

	1	2	3	4	5	6
Years	*BSE Sensex 1978-79 =100 Averages*	*BSE Turnover Cash Segment (₹ lakh crores)*	*Broad Money M3 Growth (Money Sypply) Growth Rate*	*Foreign inflows (₹ in Crores)*	*GDP Annual Growth Rate*	*WPI Inflation Index*
2000-01	4,270	10.01	16.8	12,609	4.4	7.2
2001-02	3,332	3.07	14.1	9,639	5.8	3.6
2002-03	3,206	3.14	14.7	4,738	3.8	3.4
2003-04	4,492	5.02	16.7	52,279	8.5	5.5
2004-05	5,741	5.18	12.0	41,854	7.5	6.5
2005-06	8,278	8.16	16.9	55,307	9.5	4.4
2006-07	12,277	9.56	21.7	31,713	9.7	5.4
2007-08	16,569	15.78	21.4	1,09,741	9.0	4.7
2008-09	12,366	11.0	19.3	−63,618	6.7	8.1
2009-10	15,565	13.7	16.8	1,53,516	8.0	3.8
2010-11	18,605	11.0	16.0	1,92,432	9.6	9.6
2011-12	1,742	6.1	6.6	84,101	18.7	8.02
2012-13	1,802	5.4	7.5	1,03,107	15.8	7.42
2013-14	2,120	5.2	5.4	1,05,786	11.9	8.90
2014-15	2,750	7.5	9.4	1,29,989	11.5	5%-6%

Note: Broad Money (M3), GDP growth rate, WPI index are not absolute figures but growth rates. BSE turnover and foreign inflows are in absolute figures (₹ Crores). So is the case with Gold prices as so many rupees per 10 gms. Both the dependent variables as BSE Sensex and BSE Turnover are the actual numbers, as published by BSE.

Source: RBI, Handbook of Statistics. Website: rbi.org.in.

Objectives

The object of this chapter is to familiarise the reader with the Jargon used in the Daily Stock Market Reports. An analysis of the daily reports and interpretation of these data and information in the Reports is a necessary kit of the Security Market Analyst. It is, therefore, relevant for all Finance students to know the technique of analysis of the Daily Market Reports.

In India there are 24 Stock Exchanges including the Interconnected Stock Exchange which started operating in 1999. Of these, only two BSE ad NSE, account for about 80% of the total volume of trade in India. Of these two, only BSE has the hoary antiquity, width and depth of the market for equities with the largest number of scrips and a wide range of companies listed on it. Besides as the daily reports of BSE are more detailed and varied, an attempt is made to analyse the BSE Reports supplementing it with NSE Reports, wherever necessary. Infact, the BSE Reports for equity trading are more elaborate, while NSE Reports for Wholesale Debt segment encompassing gilt-edged market and Money market are more relevant. BSE Reports are thus taken for indepth analysis in this chapter and these Reports as published in Economic Times are taken as the basis for our analysis.

Global Comparison

With the operation of FIIs in India and given the role of FFIs in the capital market operations in India and with Indian Companies getting listed NASDAQ and other foreign stock Exchanges, in addition to the already existing trading abroad of our GDRs and ADRs, Indian markets are getting increasingly globalised. Many I.T. companies like INFOSYS are traded Nasdaq in the U.S. and the sentiment of trade there is getting reflected on Dalal street as well. This trend to globalisation of Indian stock markets is evident particularly since the New Economy Stock got prominance in the new millennium after the year 2000. The BSE Reporting is thus getting increasing attention the world over and has thus become necessary to attempt here an analysis of its coverage and sophistication.

Overview of BSE Market Report

The Stock Exchange, Mumbai has the largest number of listed companies of nearly 5000 on its trading list. But the number of traded scrips on any day varies from 2000 to 3000. These scrips have been put under four categories, namely 'A', B_1, B_2, and "others". These include 'T', 'S' and 'Z' groups, whose prices are quoted and reported daily. 'T' is Trade to trade category and 'S' group are those traded on Indonet of BSE while 'TS' is trade to trade group, traded in 'S' category.

There are about 200 companies in 'A' group as in 2009, which have rolling settlement system These scrips in the forward list are having the carry forward facility. B_1 and B_2 groups including the T, S, Ts and 'Z' groups cover the rest of the scrips, which are traded roughly on any day. 'Z' group shares are quoted separately and are not included in B_1 and B_2 groups. Besides, scrips kept in depository form are quoted separately as those of Depository stocks. Similarly those in compulsory Rolling settlement system are quoted in a separate format. 'Z' category includes those which are not giving good investor services and not having good fundamentals. As in earyly 2010, only two categories of scrips are quoted namely "A" Group and others. The item "Others" include B_1, B_2 and Z groups referred to above. These include T, S and TS groups under daily quotations in E.T.

The debt trading was minimal on BSE and it is mostly concentrated on NSE. About a handful of private sector bonds and 5 Debentures and sometime less are quoted on any day on average in recent times by the BSE. Besides BSE also puts out daily a list of stocks with high volumes of trade and low prices, used mostly for speculation. At the other end, a list of high fliers in speculation involving a rise or fall in prices between 8% to 12%, hitting the circuit band at bottom or top is also published daily. The net long purchase positions and net short sale positions in all the scrips available for carry forward can be got daily in the published data. There is a list of first 25 toppers in turnover on the BSE. There is also a Table of scrips with rising prices and falling prices over the last five trading days under the Head of Gainers and Losers.

Globalisation Trend

The episodes of activity during any recent period bear evidence of good correlation between BSE and Nasdaq sentiment and volatility trends. The fears of U.S. Economy and Fed have been felt on Nasdaq as much as on BSE. The opening up of the economy and of its markets has its impact on the Indian financial markets, whether it is capital market, Money market or Forex market.

The Table below presents the data on correlation between the volatility on Nasdaq and that on the Asian markets. The normal daily performance of volatility since 1993 was generally having lower correlation in India relative to other Asian markets like China, Hong Kong, Singapore, Taiwan etc. But this correlation increased after episodes of wild swings such as those with 3 to 5% daily rise or fall on the Nasdaq. This would mean that even Indian markets can have tailspins, based on the volatility of world markets. The Nasdaq of U.S.A. is now collaborating with London and Tokyo markets of similar nature and common Listing and trading for 24 hours in a day in many scrips will be the order of the day in the coming years.

In the above context, the BSE Report should be analysed first for any global links or reflection of global trends. The chart below should be the basis of evidence of interlinkages between Indian markets and foreign markets. In particular, NASDAQ of U.S.A. Dow Jones of New York Stock Exchange, FTSE index of London Stock Exchange, NIKKEI of Tokyo Stock Exchange and Hang Seng Index of Hong Kong Stock Exchange should be examined after Juxtaposing them with BSE and NSE Indices of India. The adjacent Table on Stock Market Price Indices for one day (May 8th 2000) bears out the trends on the BSE in comparison with Skindia GDR Index (reflecting the performance of our companies Abroad) and Dow Jones, of New York, FTSE of London etc. Thus the BSE Sensex fell on that day by 230 points and Nikkei average by 239 points and Hang Seng by 367 points.

Volatility and Correlation

Correlation with Nasdaq	*Normal daily performance Since' 93*	*Only for the days when Nasdaq rose/fell by over* 1%	2%	3%	4%	5%
China	23.1	31.9	39.3	52.2	60.1	63.5
Hong Kong	33.2	46.1	54.8	63.2	63.1	70.3
India	10.5	16.5	27.6	33.8	38.8	45.1
Indonesia	21.5	30.4	41.3	48.4	63.2	68.4
Korea	21.5	29.6	37.4	50.2	66.7	64.9
Malaysia	22.7	31.7	41.7	53.6	61.8	70.4
Philippines	23.6	36.3	48.5	55.8	59.0	52.0
Singapore	26.7	39.0	48.2	54.4	59.4	68.1
Taiwan	13.4	21.1	28.3	29.1	39.2	40.3
Thailand	17.2	26.4	32.8	36.8	50.1	62.4

During normal times correlation between Nasdaq and Asian markets, including India, was quite low. However correlation rises significantly after episodes of wild swings.

Note: For Asian markets, performance is taken for the day following the Nasdaq performance day. Performance is based on local currency indices. E.T., May 9, 2000. In more recent times, on February 5, 2010, pressure from Europe led to a steep fall of 434 points (2.7%). On the same day, the U.S. and European markets were lower and emerging market index was down by 2.5%. This was due to reports of balooning European deficits, rising U.S. unemployment figures, and crash in world commodity and energy prices. Nikkeri of Tokyo fell by 2.9% and Hong Sang fell by 3.3%.

Source: CLSA.

More Recent Episodes

On July 27, 2007, sensex nose-dived by 542 points to 15,234 on a single trading day showing a fall of 3.4%. On Aug. 1, 2007, there was another plunge of 615 points — (5.4%) due to global tremors. This was a reflection of global picture of a fall in Wall Street and Asian markets, due to fears of a slow down in U.S. economy following the credit market turmoil in U.S. globalisation of all Asian markets has been evidenced from the data or the Indices of the major markets in the world.

Table – World Indices

Index	*Index No.*	*Fall of Basic Points % age*
Sensex (BSE)	15,234	542 (–3.5)
FTSE (London)	6,219	32 (–0.05)
NIKKEI (Japan)	17,284	418 (–2.36%)
Taiwan (TWSE)	9,162	–4.22%
Hong Sang (HSI)	22,570	–2.70%
Malaysia (JCI)	2298	–2.83
Australia (AS30)	6127	–2.76

Source: E.T. July 28, 2007@.

It is seen from the Table that the fall in stock market prices in India is a reflection of the general trend of the Asian markets, which in turn emerged from the developments in the global markets of London, New York etc, This is a clear example of the globalisation of the Indian markets. Similar was the case with upswings on the BSE sensex.

Market Trends (10-10-2012)

STOCK INDICES			
Sensex	18793.36	↑	0.45%
Nifty	5704.60	↑	0.50%
Nikkei	8769.59	↓	1.06%
Hang Seng	20937.28	↑	0.54%
Strait Times	3065.91	↓	0.35%

CURRENCIES			Absolute Change
US Dollar	52.74	↓	0.09
Euro	68.24	↓	0.09
OIL			
Dubai Crude $	108.71	↑	1.10

The fall was almost universal, despite strong fundamentals of our companies the sentiment was bearish on that day. The Skindia GDR however showed a mild upswing indicating that the underlying investor interest abroad in our companies may be different from that of Indian Investors and Foreign investors in India. But Nasdaq sentiment was weak due to fears of the outcome of the forthcoming U.S. Federal Reserve meeting (slated for the third week of May). The BSE as also Nasdaq was hit by rumours and the strong currents of FII operations. The Press reports from time-to-time the quotations of Nasdaq 100 share prices, FTSE 100 equity stocks and Dow Jones 30 stock prices, under the head of International Stocks. The Stock Prices of Popular Indexes are also given separately.

Now ET publishes every Saturday, selected global Indices as for example German DAX, US, NASDAQ, UKS FTAE and others like those at Asian markets, China, Japan, Hong Kong, Singapore, Israel etc.

Stock Markets – Price Indices – Example

THE ET SHARE INDICES	***As on May 8, 2000***	***Absolute Change***
Mindex	4187.29	(–333.04)
Lifex	1358.78	(–16)
Brandex	1076.56	(–56.13)
OTHER INDICES		
BSE Sensitive	4463.40	(–230.48)
BSE 100	2265.84	(–123.29)
BSE 200	483.76	(–25.65)
S&P CNX Nifty	1365.05	(–57.35)
CNX Nifty Jr.	2681.45	(–98.40)
S&P CNX 500	1018.75	(–47.27)
Skindia GDR	1004.89	(+13.70)
Dow Jones	10523.38*	(–54.48)
Nasdaq	3727.23*	(–89.59)
FTSE	6195.60	(–43.20)
Nikkei	18199.96	(–239.40)
Hang Seng	14901	(–367.64)

Note: Figures in brackets are absolute changes over previous day.
Source: E.T., May 9, 2000.

It will be of interest to note that on the previous trading day namely May 5 (Friday) speculative buying by FII led the upswing by 3% from 4554 to 4694 showing a net gain of 140 points. On Monday May 8, 2000 speculative profit taking led to sales by FIIs which resulted in a fall in sensex by 5% from 4694 to 4464 — a loss of 230 points on one day. On both these days, some share prices have hit the circuit breakers. The present level of circuit breaking is 8% to 12% in both directions. This means that if the price of any scrip rises or falls by 12%, trading in that scrip is stopped for some time as per the prevailing SEBI guidelines. This is in the nature of trading restriction, comparable to high margins. In fact, the SEBI has already imposed volatility margins on highly speculative scrips. On top of volatility margins, the circuit breakers act as a check on undue speculative upswing or downswing on the scrip price. Thus, the off loading of Infosys and Wipro shares by FIIs led to their prices hitting the circuit break limit of 12% floor, on May 8th. On the other hand a number of I.T. scrips such as Digital, Global Tele. Satyam, HCL, Infosys have hit the ceiling limit of circuit breakers at 12% on the upswing, on May 5th (the previous trading day).

Market Trends ET (24-9-2012)

As on 24th Sept. 2012

STOCK INDICES			
Sensex	18694.41	↑	0.11%
Nifty	5673.90	↑	0.08%
Nikkei	9091.54	↑	0.25%

Hang Seng	20698.68	↑	0.02%
Strait Times	3067.13		0.03%
CURRENCIES			Absolute Change
US Dollar	53.38	↑	0.10
Euro	69.03	↑	0.02
OIL			
Dubai Crude $	108.35	↑	1.05
GOLD (₹/10GM)			
Gold Spot: Mumbai	31510	↑	110
Gold Spot: Delhi	31975	↑	250
BOND YIELDS			
10-Y Goi	8.16	↓	0.01

Source: E.T., 24-9-2012.

Daily Report Analysis

The Text of the Report for one day namely May 8th is used to explain the analysis. The fall of 5% in sensex on that day was due to FII selling, as seen earlier. Secondly, most of the speculative attacks were on the I.T. stocks and New Economy stocks, like HLL, Zee etc.

Daily reports in the press contain the details of prices, volumes of trade, highs, lows etc. These details are given under various heads like Technology Stocks, Compulsory Rolling Stocks, etc., and under various groups like A Group, B_1, B_2, "Others", etc. BSE also publishes daily the data on corporate news on book closures, record dates etc.

The graphs on next page, provide a bird's eye view of trading from 10 AM to 4 PM on one day in the form of Graphs (1) and (2) on BSE sensex and NSE Index (S&P CNX Nifty). Sensex fell from 4744 to 4463 during the trading day, on May 8, 2000, while the NSE Nifty dropped from 1423 to 1365. The next two graphs (3) and (4) give an overview of a fortnight trading from April 20 to May 8th, both on the BSE and NSE. These two charts clearly bring out the sea-saw movements and volatile upswings and down swings in the Index. The next two graphs (5) and (6) give the volumes of trade in value terms (₹ crores). The volumes an BSE include both A' and B group separately while the volumes on the NSE are generally higher. There were similar trends in the episode of July 27, 2007.

The NSE although started trading only in 1994, picked up volumes very fast and is now leading even the B.S.E in this respect. The reasons are not far to seek, as its members are high networth companies, FFIs, FIIs, Indian FIs, banks and mutual funds and listed companies traded are again the top rated and well traded high net worth companies. The listed companies on the NSE are only about one-third of the listed companies on the BSE but market capitalisation on BSE is about the same as the NSE market capitalisation. But the trade turnover on NSE is higher than on the BSE and both NSE and BSE together account for about 70 to 80% of all India trade turnover. Nearly more than 9,000 companies are listed as various stock Exchanges in India, of which about 5,000 companies are listed on BSE. Almost all companies of good networth of more than ₹ 10 crores are now listed on the BSE (about 4,829 on BSE and 1,432 on NSE as on Feb., 1, 2010).

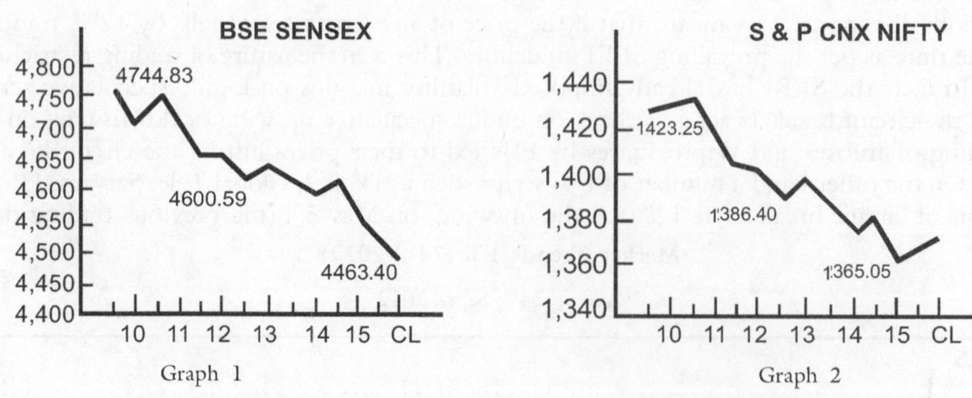

Graph 1

Graph 2

OVERA FORTNIGHT

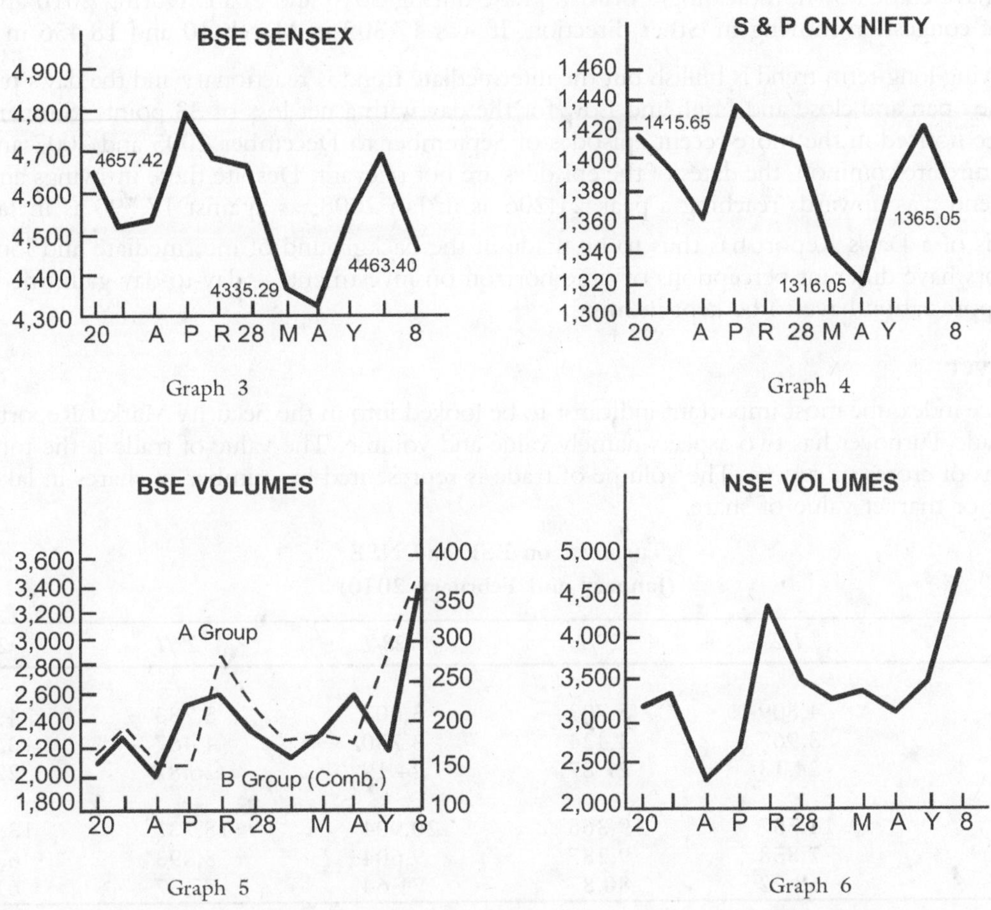

PRICE INDEX SNAPSHOTS OF THE MARKET

The data on BSE Sensex and NSE Nifty are presented in the accompanying table to give a micro picture of a day's performance in the background of broad time frame of three year High and Low. If the data are to be reframed, the day's high and low are to be seen in the background of one year High and Low and three year High and Low. As the Table below shows the extent of the range is narrowing down over period.

Market Snapshot

	Sensex	*Nifty*
Thursday, October 18, 2012		
Open	18667.72	5681.10
High	18705.19	5684.35
Low	18535.37	5633.90
Close	18610.77	5660.25
Change (Abs)	33.07	12.25
52-Wk High	(Oct. 5) 19137.29	(Oct. 5) 5815.35
52-Wk Low	(Dec. 20) 15135.86	(Dec. 20) 4531.15
3-Yr High	(Nov. 5, 10) 2108.64	(Nov. 5, 10) 6338.50
3-Yr Low	(Dec. 20, 11) 15135.86	(Dec. 20, 11) 4531.15

— Three year Range – 1.4 times

— One year Range – 1.2 times

— Day's Range – 0.3 times

This is indicative of the role of time but the highest in the recent past is 21,206 reached in Jan. 2005. After this the heights have come down, indicating a bearish phase during 2010 and 2011. During 2010 and 2011 market was in a stage of congestion moving in either direction. It was 17,302 in March 10 and 18,456 in March 2011.

The underlying long-term trend is bullish but the intermediate trend is reactionary and the day's picture is bearish by comparing the open and close and High and Low for the day with a net loss of 33 points. Similar upswings and downswings were noticed in the more recent episodes of September to December 2005 ánd 2007 and 2009-10. As swings of this nature are common, the dates of the episodes are not relevant. Despite these upswings and downswings, the long-term trend was upwards reaching a peak 21,206 as in Jan 2008, as against 17,790 as in Jan 2009.

The analysis of a Day's Report has thus to be made in the background of intermediate and long term trends. Different investors have different perceptions of time horizon on investment — day-to-day gain, medium term gain and long-term appreciation have to be kept in mind.

Trade Turnover

Next to price index, the most important indicator to be looked into in the Security Market Reports is the volume of trade. The Trade Turnover has two aspects namely value and volume. The value of trade is the total of purchases and sales in terms of crores of rupees. The volume of trade is represented by number of shares in lakhs, irrespective of the face value or market value of share.

Turnover on BSE and NSE
(January and February 2010)

	1/2	*29/1*	*28/1*	*27/1*	*25/1*
BSE					
Turnover (₹ Cr.)	4,809	5,703	5,007	5,783	4,844
Share Trd. (Lakh)	3,967	4,424	3,750	4,467	3,826
Trades (Lakh)	24.13	27.87	24.19	26.87	22.72
NSE					
Turnover (₹ Cr.)	14,757	19,366	20,904	18,733	13,349
Shares Trd. (Lakh)	7,858	9,287	9,604	8,893	6,636
Trades (Lakh)	68.22	80.87	71.64	75.37	61.70

On both the counts, the data on BSE and NSE are presented in the above Table from 25/1/2010 to 1/2/2010 for a period of 5 days of trading. This will give an idea whether the volume is increasing, or decreasing or fluctuating in a range of limits. The Table presented shows that broadly the value of turnover has increased upto 28/1 and then declined, while the volume in terms of number of shares is fluctuating with in a narrow range. This would mean that although sentiment is weak, an undercurrent of firmness is visible, in that the economic fundamentals of the corporate sector are continuing to be strong. Advances are definitely more than declines indicating the bullish trend or continuation of bull phase.

Up and Down on BSE
(on Feb. 2, 2010)

Daily No. of traded Scrips

	'A'	*'B_1'*	*'B_2'*	*Others*	*Total*
Advances	153	1227	313	474	2167
Declines	46	351	72	236	705
Unchanged	--	21	5	19	45
Total	199	1599	390	729	2917

Note: As NSE data show similar trends as on BSE, the data on NSE are not shown here.

Advance/Decline Line

The underlying trend can also be seen by the accompanying Table on "Up and Down on BSE". The number of Advancing and Declining Scrips and those unchanged are presented in the Table on the basis of category-wise scrips namely 'A' group, B_1, B_2 groups and others. The fact that advances are more in the "A" group indicates that larger number of investment scrips are being bought and buying pressure is more. But the fact that there are larger number of Speculative in 'B' group — investment type — reflects the firm sentiment underlying in the market. Out of 2917 scrips quoted and traded on that day (Feb. 1, 2010), leaving aside 45 scrips which have not recorded any change in prices, 2167 scrips recorded upward movement while only 705 scrips recorded declines. Similar exercise can be done for any period by the reader.

Table on
FII Activity (₹ *in crores)*

Date	Equity			Debt		
	Buy	*Sell*	*Net*	*Buy*	*Sales*	*Net*
29/1/2010	3,940	3,743	197	625	316	309
28/1/2010	3,496	5,660	–2,164	1,144	1,365	–221
27/1/2010	2,957	4,877	–1,920	531	447	84
25/1/2010	1,629	2,529	–900	1,393	191	1,202
22/1/2010	3,247	5,307	–2,060	835	2,154	–1,319
Total for Jan	59,368	60,505	–1,137	20,220	11,415	8,805

MF Activity (₹ *in crores)*

Date	Equity			Debt		
	Buy	*Sales*	*Net*	*Buy*	*Sales*	*Net*
29/1/2010	1,330	696	633	2,753	2,977	–224
28/1/2010	1,937	825	1,113	3,625	4,438	-814
27/1/2010	1,029	1,205	–176	2,553	1,981	572
25/1/2010	727	884	–157	4,009	2,137	1,872
22/1/2010	1,163	1,004	–159	4,419	1,714	2,705
Total for Jan	16,562	17,880	–1,312	72,527	44,127	28,399

Note: As the last totals are for the whole month of January, the total of weeks' trading will not tally, under each of the rows.

Source: E.T. dated February 2, 2010. These data are shown to indicate the volume of their total purchases and sales influencing the market.

Role of Institutional Agencies (FII and MF Activity)

In Daily reports, as much as in the longer time horizons, both investment and speculative activity have to be captured in Daily Reports as they leave their own impact on the market. This impact is seen both in price and volume of trade and they are inter-linked. The price and volume trends and their interpretation were discussed in the chapter on Technical Analysis. So far as the daily reports are concerned, technicals, plays a greater role than fundamentals as the temporary demand and supply factors are tossed from pillar to post by sentiment, expectations and psychological factors. (See the tables in above).

It was already noted that trading on May 5th 2000 was Teji (bullish) while trading on the next trading day May 8th, was Mandi (bearish) both involving wide swings of 140 to 230 points in a day and both swayed by market rumours and sentiment. These days are classical examples of the role of sentiment on the market. The fundamentals of the economy are good. The intrinsic factors in the I.T. sector, which is subject to speculative onslaughts are sound or the rumours. Regarding Infosys and Wipro were found to be unbased, and these scrips alongwith some other New Economy scrips were found to touch the circuit breakers both at the ceiling and floor (12% on either side which was in fact wider than the 8% limit which was fixed earlier). This limit was further raised to 16% in June 2000, and stood at 12% as in February 2010.

The above sentimental factors which play havoc on the market are aided by the institutional players in the market who have the muscles of money power. These major institutional players on the BSE are the FIIs, FIs and Mutual Funds. The data on their daily purchases and sales are published by the SEBI on a daily basis. It is obligatory as per the SEBI guidelines, that these agencies report their trade details to SEBI and Stock Exchanges. Accordingly, these data can be had from the daily Reports in the financial press. But these data come with a time lag of one or two days. Some data of FII and MF operations for a week are given in the prepage.

As the above Tables show, bulk of the funds are pumped in and out by FIIs, involving a total of purchases and sales of about ₹ 4,000 to 6,000 crores on a day. If their purchases are more than sales involving a net long position, the market may turn out to be bullish and if net sales are more involving a short position, the market may turn bearish.

The fact that short position is more risky and more speculative is known and that is one of the reasons why SEBI has prohibited payment of Badla to naked short sellers from May 2000. They have no owned or borrowed shares in those scrips, but yet they sell the shares meant for carry forward, in the hope of covering them later when the prices fall. They are typical bears and if they are lucky and if prices fall, they gain by differences in prices. But SEBI does not want to encourage them with the Badla incentive also and hence prohibited the payment of Badla to them, irrespective of whether they gain or lose.

The activity of Mutual Funds and their purchases and sales involving ₹ 400 to 600 crores is another major factor, influencing the market sentiment. Their total volume of trade and their net position indicate whether there is in market over bought or over sold position. In fact, as per SEBI guidelines Mutual Funds can not speculate but give delivery and take delivery and cannot participate in the badla activity. Even so, their sheer volume of trade has some influence on the market. FIIs are more interested in equity while M7 are active in Debt market.

As judged by their trading activity over the trading cycle of 5 days, the mood of the market can be explained. This type of swings of bullish and bearish nature accentuate the volatility of the market and the FII activity and Mutual Fund purchases and sales reflect these moods and infact accentuated or attenuated by their activities. They are also therefore considered as one of the main indicators of the market as reported in the press.

Trading Cycle

BSE also publishes its settlement programme, for all groups of scrips namely A, B_1, B_2, and "others", The settlement is after 5 days of trading with a trading cycle of Monday to Friday week. The attached extract gives the illustration in this regard.

The settlement numbers based on a fixed pattern of weekly settlements of Monday to Friday are published in advance for three settlements at a time. Their pay-in and pay-out dates are also indicated in this print out.

BSE Settlement Programme

Sett. No.	*Particulars*	*Settlement Period*		*Proposed Settlement*	
		First Day	*Last Day*	*Pay-in Day*	*Pay-Out Day*
6	A, B_1, B_2 & "Others"	02/05	05/05	11/05	13/05
7	A, B_1, B_2 & "Others"	08/05	12/05	19/05	22/05
8	A, B_1, B_2 & "Others"	15/05	19/05	25/05	27/05

The BSE Settlement Programme was changed due to Rolling Settlement system later on. For the month of February 2010 an example of the method of presentation of this data is given below:

Settlement No.	*Trading Day*	*Pay in/Pay out Day*
DR 205	29/1	2/2/2010
DR 206	1/2	3/2/2010
DR 207	2/2	4/2/2010
DR 208	3/2	5/2/2010
DR 209	4/2	8/2/2010
DR 210	5/2	9/2/2010
— etc.	— etc.	— etc.

Note: No Delivery period is also given for each of the settlement numbers separately for Demat form and physical form of Deliveries.

Source: E.T. February, 2, 2010.

The investor with this information of pay-in and pay-out will know in advance when he is expected to give shares for sale or receive shares on purchase and when he has to give a cheque or receive a cheque.

Dates of the data taken for illustration vary widely but this does not make much difference for the development of analytical skills and interpretation of the data, which this chapter aims at.

Record Dates and Book Closure

Another information that one should have when trading on a Stock Exchange is the Record dates or Book closure dates of listed companies. On and around these dates — one week on either side or a fortnight as the case may be — the scrips in this regard enter into no delivery period and the buyer cannot get delivery of shares nor give delivery of shares, as the books of Register of members are closed for declaring a dividend or for entitlement of Bonus or Rights shares. Such scrips on "No-Delivery" periods, have to be avoided.

The attached Table gives the details of companies with their book closure or Record dates and the purpose of closing the books. All the details of companies coming out with the respective announcements in a period of a fortnight to two months are generally provided in this Table. As per the Companies Act, every company has to give notice of these record and book closure dates to the investors. The Listing Agreement also calls for these data from the companies to the Stock Exchange atleast 42 days in advance.

The Table shows the companies coming out with these dates during forthcoming one or two months in advance. This Table given in May 2000, lists the companies coming out in the months of May to July 2000. The letters "B.C." stands for Book Closure and "RD" stands for Record Date and the date or dates during which the books are closed are also indicated here. A fortnight before and after these dates, the investors have to take care for the "No-delivery" period for those scrips. The quotations will be Ex-dividend, Ex-nights or Ex-Bonus, etc. This table is given only for illustration and its role in trading.

Book Closures and Record Dates

Company Name	*B.C. R.D.*	*Book-Closure Record-Date*	*Purpose*
Aarti Inds.	RD	04/02/2010	36% Interim Dividend
Anuh Pharma	RD	23/02/2010	200% Interim Div.
Bharat Elect.	RD	04/02/2010	60% Interim Dividend
CHL	RD	19/02/2010	15% Interim Dividend
Dalmia Cemen	RD	15/02/2010	50% Interim Dividend
Deccan Chron	RD	05/02/2010	50% Third Int. Div.
EID Parry	RD	05/02/2010	300% Interim Div.
Educomp Solu.	RD	06/02/2010	50% Interim Dividend
Ganesh Poly.	RD	11/02/2010	5% Interim Dividend
Geaves Cott	RD	10/02/2010	15% IInd Interim Div.
KRBL	RD	12/02/2010	Stock Split/₹ 0.15 per share Interim Div.
Oriental Car	RD	10/02/2010	10% IInd Interim Div.
Page Inds.	RD	04/02/2010	60% Interim Dividend
Precision Wr.	RD	05/02/2010	24% Interim Dividend
Reliance Cap.	RD	27/01/2010	Redemption of NCDs
STC India	RD	18/02/2010	25% Interim Dividend
Super Tanner	RD	09/02/2010	Bonus Issue
VST Tillers	RD	09/02/2010	Bonus Issue
Vital Comm.	BC	29/09-30/09	AGM

Source: E.T. 30/01/2010.

Circuit Band Hitters

The Scrips which have hit the circuit breakers or the band of price limits of 8 to 12% on either side are also published both by the BSE and NSE. The price data of today's close, previous close and percentage change involved in each of the selected scrips and their volumes are also presented in their daily Reports. The scrips which break the circuits are of two categories namely the Day's Best and Day's worst at BSE, indicating upswing and downswing scrips respectively. The investors will come to know from the data, the scrips in which speculation is more or less concentrated on that day. These data are published in ET daily, under the caption "BSE at Best" and the "WORST BSE".

Alongwith this data, the first 10 top turnover toppers in group A_1 B_1 and B_2 and NSE are listed along with the number of shares traded, gross value of trades and number of trades. From these data, one can know how many toppers have hit the circuit breakers, what is the average value of the trade and the proportion of shares traded to the outstanding shares of each of these companies.

Speculative Positions

Badla and carry forward was allowed in about 150 scrips falling in A group on the B.S.E. The data on their daily net *short* position and *long* positions and the volume (number of shares) and value (₹ Crores) in respect of each other these scrips used to be published. The short positions are net sales made without the intention of giving delivery of shares and long positions are net purchases made without the intention of taking delivery of shares. Each broker's net short sales and net long purchases are added to arrive at the total net short positions and net long positions held by all members in each of the scrips, allowed to be carried forward. The data of total net short sales and net long purchases both in terms of number of shares and their values in rupees, are available with the Exchanges and not published now.

The interpretation of these data is easy once the reader knows the mechanics of badla trading, speculative trade and investment trade and the role of volumes and price etc., which are set out in earlier chapters of this book. One can identify the scrips subject to high speculation, whether the net sales position is more than the net purchase position, leading to backwardation charges and what is the technical position in each of the scrips and in the total market as a whole etc. A shrewd analyst can also know the likely trend in each of the scrips during the settlement period, based on the net accumulated purchases or sales outstanding which have to be squared up or unwind the position or carry forward by the last day of the trading cycle for each settlement.

Short sales positions are those of bears while long purchase positions are those of Bulls and the relative strengths of bulls and bears are known from these data. If any of the bulls or bears are weak and the market is going against them, they may turn out to be defaulters and the Trade settlement Guarantee fund has to be used to salvage the market at that time. As Badla trading was helped by rolling settlement system and ALBS for shares these data are not published. The data on Automatic Lending and Borrowing System are not available on a daily basis in published data.

Surveillance System

The Stock Exchange Surveillance system and their trading control system aim at imposing margins, operate the circuit breakers, impose limits on brokers in respect of any scrips or total for all scrips and convert trade in any scrip to a Rolling settlement basis or for spot trading and cash delivery etc would all be based on the analysis of the above data on trade turnover and price movements during the trading time of 10 A.M. to 4 P.M. on any day, now replaced by 9 A.M. to 4 P.M. or any day. These data are also used by SEBI and Research groups and Investment Analysts.

Index Details

BSE also gives out daily the sensex data along with prices, performance of each of the scrips included in the Index (30 in number), their market capitalisation and the Day's weightage of each of these scrips in the total Index. Market capitalisation is derived by multiplying the number of outstanding shares in each of the companies by their day's closing price. The proforma used is as follows:

Company's name, Day's closing price; previous trading day close' percentage change in price for the day, Market capitalisation of that scrip, Day's weightage of each of these scrips in the Index; and the percentage change in weightage.

Similar data with respect to ET. Mindex which includes 36 actively traded scrips on the BSE and NSE, are also presented in a similar fashion giving out their market capitalisation and changes in it. The NSE scrip prices are also similarly presented for S&P CNX Nifty giving out the price and market capitalisation data in respect of the 50 most actively traded scrips included in the Nifty. Barring the minor details of small changes, the trends arrived at in respect of price, market capitalisation and its weightage in the total index etc., are almost similar in all these Indices.

Economic Times used to publish daily data on three of its Indices namely ET 100, ET Mindex (regular for its 36 scrips used to) ET Lifex, ET Brandex and ET Textiles (all with 1999 = 100) and INSTANEX SKINDIA in U.S. dollars for GDR and ADRs quoted in foreign markets, but issued by Indian companies. In addition, a few financial Journals, CRISIL and a few Stock Exchanges have their own price Indexes. Their Base date, as also the composition and weightage may vary from Index to Index but the trends derived are almost similar. ET publishes weekly once the sectors that rose and those that fell. MF funds data, Top 10 Low P/E and High P/E, Price to BV dividend yield etc.

Note: ALBS is automatic lending and borrowing system.

BSE Stock Tables

The Table in ET on BSE/NSE scrips gives the Market Trade Quotes on each day.

The first figure in brackets given is the BSE Stock code. This is followed the company's stock name like ACC or ABB Ltd. etc., then followed by previous day's closing price in brackets. The next four figures are today's opening, High, Low and closing.

The prices of today are followed in brackets by the volume of traded shares and Net traded value.

The next line gives in italics the corresponding price on NSE for the same scrip. Then there is separate row for P/E Ratio, followed by the last row with the 52 week High and Low of the scrip. In between, M cap is shown in ₹ crores in the case of Sensex based scrips. The M Cap is Market Capitalisation which is the closing price multiplied by the outstanding number of shares, P/E is the ratio of the stock closing price divided by the Earnings per share (EPS). Here EPS is defined as the company's net profits in the last two half years, or 12 months or the last four quarters, (depending upon the availability of data) divided by the total number of outstanding shares. In case any company's name is underlined, that means that its closing price falls below the last offer price which is the price that the company has last offered its shares to the new or existing shareholders through public offer, rights issue or private placement.

In the event a scrip is quoting at a new high or new low, the entire line is shown in bold type with 'H' or 'L' next to the price. A significant change in price (3% rise or fall of 'A' group scrips or 15% change in the case of cash shares) is shown in BSE scrips with a Bold Type + or – after the figures depending upon whether it is rise or fall.

The BSE Quotations are given in various categories namely A, B_1, B_2 and "others". The "others" include 'T', 'TS', 'S' and 'Z' categories. 'T' is trade to trade or spot delivery. 'S' is scrips traded in BSE Indonet, which provides a nation-wide platform for trading. These symbols of T,S, etc., are shown at the end of the line.

'TS' refers to those of trade to trade segment in 'S' group. 'Z' refers to companies listed not complying with listing requirements and not attending to investor grievances as required by law and rules.

Main Indicators

Economic times gives regularly the data on major Indices and other Indices as shown in the attached sheet. The Tables provide the data on Index of today's prices (closing) as against the closings of the previous trading day and the percentage change over the day. These data relate to previous day and published in E.T. on the next day.

Among the major Indices, the three Indices of ET and BSE sensex BSE 100 BSE 200 and BSE #500 are given alongwith S&P CNX Nifty, S&P CNX 500, Skindia GDR, DSE, CSE and MSE Indices. The last three namely DSE, CSE and MSE Indices belong to the three major stock Exchanges of Delhi, Kolkata and Chennai. The Instanex Skindia GDR traces out the prices of Indian Companies' GDRs traded and quoted abroad.

There are tables on New Highs and Lows, both on BSE and NSE. They give 52 week High and Lows and all time Highs and Lows. They are of special significance for the extent of speculation on the Exchanges.

The main Index series available are shown in the table below. In the daily quotations by the E.T. gives scrip name, close % age change, open, daily H/L, volumes while the last columns date is rotated as follows, Tuesdays – P/E, Wednesday – Market Cap, Thursday – Institutional Holding, Friday – 52 days H/L, Saturday – Dividend in a year P/BV Beta etc.

(May 9, 2000)

Major Indices				Other Indices			
Index	*Today's*	*Previous*	*Chg.*	*Index*	*Today's*	*Previous*	*Chg.*
ET Mindex	4371.39	4187.29	184.10	BSE-500	1502.37	1468.05	34.32
ET Lifex	1354.43	1358.78	-4.35	BSE-100	2321.61	2265.84	55.77
ET Brandex	1103.06	1076.56	26.50	BSE-200	495.53	486.76	8.57
				Skindia GDR	956.30	1004.89	-48.59
BSE Sensex	4578.49	4463.40	115.09	DSE	916.89	905.61	11.28
S&P CNX Nifty	1378.55	1365.05	13.50	CSE	1979.63	1969.96	9.67
S&P CNX 500	1040.31	1018.75	21.56	MSE	5167.59	5074.11	93.48

E.T. May 10th, 2000. There are other indices for all the other sectors, Published once in a week by ET.

The above indicators are published once on Saturday now. The fall in Skindia GDR Index only shows that the foreign investors are guided by a separate set of factors. Infact this index showed a rise on May 8 when all other Indices showed a steep fall. On May 9, 2000, the declines were lower at 638 while the number of advances was higher at 688. The value of turnover was however lower in May 9, as compared to May 8. The uptrend in prices was around 2.6% — (a gain of 115 points in the Sensex) on May 9, as against a fall of nearly 5% on May 8, 2000. More recently, on Jan. 27, 2006, the Sensex spurted by 185 points to touch 9870, as against a three year law of 2904, reached in April 2003.

Face Value

The face value of scrips varied from ₹ one to ten and SEBI has allowed listed companies to have any face value dropping the fixed face value system in 1999. Some companies have shares of ₹ 1, ₹ 2, ₹ 4, ₹ 5, ₹ 20, ₹ 50 and ₹ 100, while a vast majority continued to have ₹ 10 as face value. Such changes in face value are indicated by suitable asterix with the face value being shown in brackets, at that place itself. Scrips having quotes below the face value are not shown and included in New Highs and New Lows. An Astertix against P/E ratio indicates, that the Earnings data relate to the last four quarters.

Market Macro Indicators

The BSE also gives the P/E ratio jointly for all the sensex companies on a daily basis as also for the National Index (100). On similar lines, the ratio of market price to book value for all sensex companies together is also provided in the BSE. These aggregate P/E ratios and price to book value ratios in respect of BSE sensitive series (30) and BSE National Series (100) are useful as bench marks indicative of the market performance relative to the corporate fundamentals, as reflected in EPS and Book value etc.

As important Indicators of BSE, the RBI published the following data in its Annual Reports for 2009, in respect of BSE activity.

	1998-99	*2000-01*	*2004-05*	*2006-07*	*2008-09*	*2009-10*	*2010-11*	*2011-12*	*2012-13*
(1) BSE Sensex (Average)	3294.78	4269.69	5741	12277	12366	15,585	18,605	1,742	1,709
(2) Price Earnings Ratio (relating to Sensex)	12.86	23.9	16.6	20.3	13.7	20.08	21.20	18.56	3.52
(3) Price-Book value Ratio (relating to Sensex)	2.26	3.6	3.3	5.1	2.7	3.75	3.59	3.40	2.90
(4) Yield per cent per annum	1.82	1.3	2.0	1.3	1.8	–	1.8	3.42	5.44
(5) Turnover (₹ crores)	3,11,999	10,00,031	5,18,717	9,56,185	11,00,074	35,774	11.035	7,404	62,149
(6) Market capitalisation (₹ crores) at end March	5,42,942	5,71,653	16,98,428	35,45,041	30,86,076	61,64,157	68,36,878	18,83,360	63,879

Source: RBI — Annual report 2008-09.

Badla Statistics

Reference was made earlier to carry forward business permitted in about 150 scrips in 'A' group on a weekly basis on the BSE. Net outstanding short sales and net long purchases are permitted to be carried forward on the settlement day once in a week on the last trading day. For the purpose of carry forward, the stock Exchange fixes the clearing rate which is almost the same as the closing rate on the last trading day for each of the scrips. The BSE has the closing price on the last trading day which is generally the clearing rate fixed for carry forward for badla trading. Net outstanding position, scripwise is known by the BSE authorities, as also overall position. The larger the net outstandings, the better is supposed to be interest in a given scrip. Badla rate will depend partly on the cost of funds borrowed from the money market. More importantly it also depends on the net technical position of the scrip in the market. If funds are available cheaply, there will be lower badla rates and larger carry forward and better sentiment. Liquidity flow is the basis for this.

Generally, as it is easy to borrow funds than borrowing scrips, net outstanding purchases will be more than net outstanding sales in any scrip. If in any scrip, the net outstanding positions are small as in the case of ABB Ltd, Arvind Mills and Asian paints, it must be due to lack of interest in the scrip and badla rates for these scrips will be high if few badla financiers are interested in them. The supply will be less relative to demand for them for badla finance. But in respect of popular scrips like ACC Appollo Tyres etc. the badla rates will be relatively low; long positions are high relatively both the volume and value as the companies are fundamentally good to hold. (The Tables for Badla Statistics were not published after 2000).

It will thus be seen that there are a wide variety of factors which influence Badla rates and that these are not expressed in percentage per annum, but in terms of Rupees and paise per share for a fortnight or three weeks, after which the positions will be reversed again. Badla if borrowed in money terms for long positions or borrowed in terms of shares for short position are for periods of 15 to 20 days for each settlement. Borrowing shares for carry forward business is part of Badla business, which NSE arranges under what is called Automatic lending and borrowing scheme (ALBS).

Some questions which an insider only can understand and the Stock Exchange authorities will know relate to the number of short sellers, the quantity of short sales in each scrip and whether they are naked short sales or covered etc. Similarly, what are the net long purchase positions, whether they are cumulatively growing or declining for each of the members involved and any set of members, who are cornering these positions or acting in collusion to manipulate the prices and what is the level of long purchases that each member has got and for how many days that position is carried forward etc., are the other relevant questions known only to the Authorities.

If the market has to be sound, there should be both long purchases and short sales and no member or a group of members should accumulate any position, so as to adversely affect the net balance in the market. Besides and more importantly the concerned members involved in carry over position should be financially sound and viable. There should be no undue accumulation or liquidation of position all of a sudden. Generally, market players know the other players in the market and their financial soundness. Financially weak members have to be avoided in this game so as to avoid defaults and difficulties in payments. Shrewd players play safe here, in Badla trading.

All the above information will be available with the Stock Exchange authorities and the major players in the Badla trade may know the answers to many of the above questions. But the general reader or ordinary investor will not be able to understand the inside position from the published data. For a shrewd analyst who has been on the Job for long, the likely trends in the performance of scrip prices and the technical position in the market etc., can be understood and forecasted through charts and moving Average methods in technical analysis. The technical position reflecting the daily demand and supply factors, prices and volume etc. depend on the prevailing long and short positions in each of the scrips and net outstanding position and floating stocks in the scrip and the members' position in the scrip and their financial backing etc. The Analyst should have a grasp of all these factors. Badla trading was replaced by Compulsory Rolling Settlement System in most of the Stocks during June-December 2001, whereby settlement and payments have to be done on the 5th day from the trade date under T + 5 Settlement System. T + 1 Settlement System is now operating. Badla lost its relevance with the introduction of derivatives trading in 2000. Since then, the badla statistics and reports were stopped due to lack of relevance.

Derivatives Trading

In the month of June 2000, both BSE and NSE started trading in Index Derivatives with three types of contracts, namely one month, two months and three months. The trade data in this Section are published on a daily basis with information on Open, High, Low, Close, number of contracts, number of trades, value in ₹ and outstanding position in the market.

Under futures head, the data on Sensex futures, Nifty futures, equity futures on BSE and NSE, which are traded currently are given separately in the Daily press. Similarly, under the head of options, Sensex options, Nifty options equity options on BSE and NSE with call options and put options separately are also reported, on a daily basis. The data presented include previous close, present prices, traded quantity, value, number of contracts, etc., in respect of futures. Similarly, in the case of options, price, premium, traded quantity national value in ₹ lakhs, number of contracts, alongwith open interest, expiry dates of contracts etc., are furnished in the daily press.

During 2001, trading in options and futures on individual stocks was started, and future growth potential is great in this segment. Total turnover for the Derivative Sector had crossed the ₹ 10,000 crore mark on the NSE even in December 2001. By March 2009, it reached about ₹ 110 lakh crores on NSE, but BSE was lagging far behind in this segment.

Index futures were introduced in June 2000 and index options in June 2001, stock options in July 2001 and stock futures in November 2001 both in BSE and NSE, while interest rate futures were introduced on NSE only in June 2003.

Monthly turnover in derivatives on NSE was almost three times the turnover in the cash market.

Trading Pattern in the Markets

The trading turnover in the NSE is more than in the BSE, because of larger volume of trade in higher networth companies listed and the larger volume of trade by FIIs, FIs and MFs and other investors on the NSE. The Market capitalisation on the other hand is higher on the BSE due to a larger number of companies listed and their higher networth.

The market capitalisation as a percentage of GDP at current prices was almost one hundred percent as in March 2008 when the sensex was at 16,569 level. The MC should have gone to about one and half times of GDP at current prices at one time. This reflects the growth in importance of the equity markets in the economy. But as at end March 2012, it was near to about 69 per cent of GDP Strong fundamentals of the corporate sector and of the stock market as an index of the state of the economy, were evinced clearly.

The trading value was about ₹ 16 lakh crores in 2005 in the cash market on the NSE which has gone up to three times or more on the Futures and options markets although it was started only recently in 2000 and 2001. Futures are more popular than the options in F&O segment. Besides the interest rate futures although permitted by the RBI has not taken off on the NSE. During 2005-06 the turnover in the cash segment was about ₹ 16 lakh crores on the NSE. while the same in the F&O segment it was ₹ 48 lakh crores — about three times that in the cash segment — which indicates the growth in importance of the F&O segment in stock market due to the operations of foreign institutions and foreign investors. In 2011-12 when the turnover in the cash market was ₹ 28 lakh crores, that in the derivative segment had gone up to ₹ 313 lakh crores about Eleven times that in the cash market.

There are two inferences from the above discussion. One is that the NSE is more prominent in the derivative market than the BSE. Second, the derivative markets have by themselves become more significant in trading than in the cash market in the Indian Stock markets.

In 2010-11, market capitalisation at current prices constituted 93% of GDP. The annual turnover on NSE cash section was ₹ 35.77 lakh crores in 2010-11. The turnover of the derivative market in the same year was ₹ 292 lakh crores, which is almost 8 times the volume in the cash segment. NSE far surpassed the BSE in both the cash turnover and derivative turnover. The volume of corporate debt, traded on the NSE which has a responsibility to develop this market was ₹ 50,150 crores in 2011-12 as against ₹ 45,060 crores in 2010-11.

SELECTED BIBLIOGRAPHY

1. Graham, Dodd and Cottle: *Security Analysis,* McGraw-Hill Book Co. Ltd.
2. William Sharpe: *Portfolio Theory and Capital Markets,* McGraw-Hill.
3. William Sharpe and Gordon, J. Alexander: *Investments,* Prentice Hall, India.
4. Donald E. Fischer and Ronald J. Jordan: *Security Analysis and Portfolio Management,* Prentice Hall of India Ltd.
5. Jack Clark Francis: *Investments, Analysis and Management,* McGraw-Hill.
6. Russel J. Fuller and James L. Farrel J. R.: *Modern Investment and Security Analysis,* McGraw-Hill International Editions.
7. William Edward and Findlay M. Chapman: *Investment Analysis,* Prentice Hall of India Ltd.
8. Cohen, Zinberg and Ziekel: *Investment Analysis and Portfolio Management,* Dow Jones Irwin Co. Private Ltd.
9. V.A. Avadhani: *Investment and Securities Markets in India,* Himalaya Publishing House.
10. V.A. Avadhani: *Capital Market Management,* Himalaya Publishing House.
11. V.A. Avadhani: *Investment for Beginners,* Himalaya Publishing House.
12. V.A. Avadhani: *A Manual on Stock Broking,* Himalaya Publishing House.
13. Robert A. Strong: *Portfolio Management Handbook,* Jaico Publishing House.
14. E.J. Elton and M.J. Gruber: *Modern Portfolio Theory and Investment Analysis,* John Wiley & Songs.
15. Frank K. Reilly: *Investment Analysis and Portfolio Management,* The Dryden Press.
16. G.J. Alexander and J.C. Francis: *Portfolio Analysis*, Prentice Hall.

REFERENCES

1. Dougall, Herbert E., *Investments,* Prentice Hall, Eaglewood Cliffs, N.T.
2. Badgar and Kaffman, *The Complete Guide to Investment Analysis,* McGraw-Hill Book Co.
3. Badger, Eastman and Others, *Investment Principles and Practice,* McGraw-Hill.
4. L.M. Bhole, *Financial Institution and Cohen Zenburs and Sental Investment Markets* — L.M. Bhole Tata McGraw-Hill.
5. *Financial Analysists' Handbook,* eds. S.N. Leirne, D.J. Irwin, Homewood, Illinois.
6. J. Peter Willionson, *Investment — New Analytical Techniques,* Praeger Publishers, New York.
7. Elton and Gruber, *Modern Portfolio Theory and Investment Analysis,* John Wiley & Sons.
8. Hampton John J., *Modern Financial Theory Perfect and Imperfect Markets,* Roston Publishing Company, New York.
9. Sharpe W.F., *Portfolio Theory and Capital Markets,* McGraw-Hill Book Co.
10. Frank K. Reilly., *Investment Analysis and Portfolio Management.*
11. G.J. Alexander and W.F. Sharpe, *Fundamentals of Investments,* Prentice Hall, New York.
12. D.J. Siegel and D.F. Diegel., *Future Markets,* The Dryden Press.
13. Benton E. Glup., *The Basis of Investing,* John Wiley & Sons.
14. Engine, F. Brigham, *Fundamentals of Financial Management*, The Dryden Press.

JOURNALS FOR REFERENCE

1. Journal of Finance
2. Journal of Financial Economics
3. Journal of Business
4. Journal of Financial and Quantitative Analysis
5. Journal of Portfolio Management
6. Harvard Business Review
7. Financial Analysts Journal
8. Journal of Banking and Finance
9. Journal of Business Finance
10. Journal of Business and Financial Statistics
11. Economic and Political Weekly
12. Capital Market

13. Dalal Street
14. Business India
15. Indian Economic Journal
16. Indian Economic Review
17. Indian Journal of Economics
18. RBI Publications
19. CMIE Publications
20. ICFA Publications
21. Financial Dailies like E.T., F.E. etc.

INDEX

E

F

J

K

N

O

T

U

V

W

Y